THE EVANGELICALS

THE STRUGGLE TO SHAPE AMERICA

FRANCES FITZGERALD

SIMON & SCHUSTER

New York London Toronto Sydney New Delhi

Simon & Schuster
1230 Avenue of the Americas
New York, NY 10020

Portions of this book were initially reported and published in *The New Yorker* in the
following articles: Reporter at Large—"A Disciplined, Charging Army" (5/18/1981);
Reflections—"The Bakkers" (4/23/1990); "Holy Toledo" (7/31/2006);
"The New Evangelicals" (6/30/2008).

Photo research by Alexandra Truitt & Jerry Marshall www.pictureresearching.com

First Simon & Schuster hardcover edition April 2017

SIMON & SCHUSTER and colophon are
registered trademarks of Simon & Schuster, Inc.

For information about special discounts for bulk purchases,
please contact Simon & Schuster Special Sales at
1-866-506-1949 or business@simonandschuster.com.

The Simon & Schuster Speakers Bureau can bring authors to your live event.
For more information or to book an event contact the Simon & Schuster Speakers
Bureau at 1-866-248-3049 or visit our website at www.simonspeakers.com.

Manufactured in the United States of America

3 5 7 9 10 8 6 4 2

Library of Congress Cataloging-in-Publication Data

Names: FitzGerald, Frances, 1940– author.
Title: The Evangelicals : the struggle to shape America / Frances FitzGerald.
Description: New York, NY : Simon & Schuster, 2017. |
Includes bibliographical references and index.
Identifiers: LCCN 2016025851 (print) | LCCN 2016027703 (ebook) |
ISBN 9781439131336 (hardcover : alk. paper) | ISBN 9781439131343
(pbk. : alk. paper) | ISBN 9781439143155 (ebook)
Subjects: LCSH: Evangelicalism--United States—History. | Fundamentalism—
United States—History. | Christianity and politics—United States—History. |
United States—Church history.
Classification: LCC BR1642.U5 F565 2017 (print) | LCC BR1642.U5 (ebook) |
DDC 277.3/08—dc23
LC record available at https://lccn.loc.gov/2016025851

ISBN 978-1-4391-3133-6
ISBN 978-1-4391-4315-5 (ebook)

For Jim as always

CONTENTS

THE
EVANGELICALS

INTRODUCTION

WHEN JIMMY CARTER, a liberal Southern Baptist, ran for president in 1976, the pollster George Gallup estimated that fifty million Americans were "born-again" Christians, and *Newsweek* magazine ran a cover story, "Born Again! The Evangelicals," explaining who these millions of people were.[1]

Four years later the Christian right emerged in force, declaring holy war against "secular humanism" and vowing to mobilize evangelicals to arrest the moral decay of the country. Jerry Falwell, a fundamentalist pastor, Pat Robertson, a televangelist, and conservative Southern Baptists led the charge against the gay rights movement, abortion, and the banning of school prayer. At an enormous rally in Dallas Ronald Reagan became their standard-bearer, and won the presidential election with the help of evangelical votes.

The sudden appearance of the Christian right shocked most political observers. Who were these people, and where did the crusade against "secular humanism" come from? Journalists wrote furiously about these questions until the mid-1980s, when the movement seemed to die away. The Christian right was forgotten for several years, as were evangelicals generally, until the telescandals of Jim and Tammy Bakker and Jimmy Swaggart. Then evangelicals were forgotten again. The pattern continued. As the veteran journalist Joe Conason wrote, the political coverage of evangelicals was "a cycle of neglect followed by sensationalism and then more neglect." Rick Warren, the best-known of evangelical preachers, told journalists in 2005, "It's a funny thing to me that every five years American journalism reintroduces evangelicals to America. It's like starting with Carter—you know there's a headline, 'Who are Evangelicals?' Well, it's not like they're a fringe group."[2]

Even the well informed tend to have very short attention spans when it comes to evangelicals. Many equate evangelicals with fundamentalists or the Christian right when only a minority belong to either group. Others dismiss them as a marginal group doomed to extinction with the process of modernization. In fact evangelicals compose nearly a quarter of the population. They are also the most American of religious groups, and during the nineteenth century they exerted a dominant influence on American culture, morals, and politics. By the mid-twentieth century the United States was becoming a more secular nation, but since 1980 many evangelicals, led by the Christian right, have struggled to reverse the trend, and while they have not entirely succeeded, they have reintroduced religion into public discourse, polarized the nation, and profoundly changed American politics.

The category "evangelical" is, of course, not a political but a religious one. The word "evangelical" comes from the Greek "evangel," meaning the "good news," or "the Gospel." While the word could be claimed by all Christians, evangelical became the common name for the revivals that swept the English-speaking world in the late eighteenth and early nineteenth centuries. In America the series of revivals, known as the First and the Second Great Awakenings, with their emphasis on simple Bible preaching and immediate conversion, touched virtually all Protestant denominations. For most of the nineteenth century almost all Protestants would have called themselves evangelicals in the sense that they believed they had been born again in Christ and had a duty to evangelize, or spread the good news of the Gospels in America and abroad.

Today white evangelicals are a very diverse group that includes, among others, Southern Baptists, Mennonites, Holiness groups, Pentecostals, Dutch Reformed groups, and a number who belong to nondenominational churches. Many have little in common except for the essentials of their faith. As the religious historian George Marsden writes, "Evangelicalism today includes any Christians traditional enough to affirm the basic beliefs of the old nineteenth-century evangelical consensus: the Reformation doctrine of the final authority of the Bible, the real historical character of God's saving work recorded in Scripture, salvation to eternal life based on the redemptive work of Christ, the importance of evangelism and missions, and the importance of a spiritually transformed life." [3]

This book is not a taxonomy or attempt to describe the entirety of evangelical life, but rather a history of the white evangelical movements necessary to understand the Christian right and its evangelical opponents that have emerged in recent years. It purposely omits the history of African American churches because theirs is a different story, mainly one of resistance to slavery and segregation, but also of the creation of centers for self-help and community in a hostile world. Some African American denominations identify as evangelical, but because of their history, their religious traditions are not the same as those of white evangelicals. Only long after the success of the civil rights movement did some black churchmen begin to enter the story of the white evangelicals and their internal conflicts. What is important to stress is that the white evangelical world has always been changing, though it has retained many of the characteristics acquired during its history. In any case, no movement, including the Christian right, has ever been static or completely coherent. Evangelicals have had some influential leaders, but in essence their world is decentralized and difficult to lead, much less to control.

The book begins with the two Great Awakenings, the first in the late eighteenth century with the end of Puritan society, and the second in the decades after the American Revolution. The first, led by Jonathan Edwards and the English revivalist George Whitefield, helped make a nation out of the disparate colonies by crossing the colonial boundaries and spreading the evangelical faith from north to south. The separation of church and state in the Constitution, though only a federal law, permitted evangelical denominations, such as the Methodists and the Baptists, to evangelize freely in spite of the established churches in states such as Connecticut and Virginia. It created a marketplace of religion, giving all denominations and sects an incentive to increase their flocks, and beginning a process that made America the most religious country in the developed world. The Second Great Awakening, which began a decade or more afterward, was in essence a revolt against the Calvinist establishment that led to the disestablishment of the last state-subsidized churches, and made the United States a more egalitarian society.

Many of the revivalists of the Second Awakening were lay preachers, who, working on the frontiers, created a populist religion focused on conversions that introduced an anti-intellectual strain into evangelicalism. The more established preachers began reform movements in areas such as education, health, temperance, and criminal justice. In the North some, such as Charles Finney, were abolitionists, whose campaigns against slavery led indirectly to the first feminist movement.

The Second Great Awakening inaugurated a period of evangelical hegemony, or what the religious historian Martin Marty calls the Evangelical Empire. For most of the nineteenth century, in spite of increasing Catholic immigration, evangelical Protestants dominated all cultural institutions, including the public schools and the universities. In this period there was no real distinction between religion and politics. Still, it was not the Golden Age the Christian right looks back to with nostalgia. For one thing, a series of divisions rent Protestant society. In the first part of the century northern and southern evangelicals parted company over slavery. The southern defense of slavery extinguished the reformist zeal, affected evangelical theology, and made the South a closed society. Meanwhile many new intellectual currents flowed through the North. After the Civil War, Darwinian evolution and other aspects of modernist thought, such as German biblical criticism and a new epistemology, divided northern evangelicals between liberals, who embraced modernist thought, and conservatives, who rejected it. At the same time industrialization and urbanization elicited different reactions from the two: the modernists sought structural reform to help labor in its conflict with capital while the traditionalists continued to believe that the conversion of individuals and prayer would heal the rift between the two. Evangelicals today debate these issues, but many of those Protestants who identify with modernist thought and social reform no longer call themselves evangelicals.

Toward the end of the century conservative ministers associated with the great evangelist Dwight Moody formed Bible societies to defend the traditional religion against what they saw as the apostasy of the mod-

ernists. Taking from the Princeton seminary the idea that every word of
the Bible was "inerrant," or absolutely and literally true, and from John
Nelson Darby, the English sectarian, the prophecy that civilization was in
an inevitable decline and was heading toward the great battle of Armageddon in which Christ would return to restore His kingdom in Jerusalem,
they fashioned an essentially new religious amalgam that eventually became known as fundamentalism.

The fundamentalist-modernist conflict that erupted after World War
I took place among the Baptists and Presbyterians but affected all Protestant denominations and profoundly marked the fundamentalists, who lost
and had to leave their denominations. After the Scopes trial in which the
great lawyer Clarence Darrow defeated William Jennings Bryan in a rhetorical battle over evolution, most informed people thought fundamentalism dead. To the contrary, it grew mightily in the North, through the work
of separatist pastors, radio preachers, and tent revivalists, who preached
to rural Americans and to those who migrated to the fast-industrializing
cities in the 1920s, '30s, and '40s.

After World War II, when Americans poured into churches and syna-
gogues, Billy Graham, then a fundamentalist, attracted enormous crowds
to his revivals. In the 1950s he became a celebrity, well known in Washington, and a confidant of important men such as the oil baron Sid Richardson and Richard Nixon. His preaching evolved, and in the hope of
bringing all Protestants into his big tent, he broke with the fundamentalists, and called himself an "evangelical." The term, which had gone out
of use, he and fellow moderates defined as a conservative Protestant who
had been "born again." For many years not all conservative Protestants
used it, but eventually the term stuck in part because pollsters, journalists,
and academics used it in order to describe the confusing set of conservative denominations and independent churches. Fundamentalists then
became a subset of evangelicals, and most of them were separatists who
had left their denominations.

Graham and his mentor, Harold Ockenga, the Presbyterian pastor of
the Park Street Church in Boston, knew the importance of creating institutions. Ockenga, who had helped found the Fuller Theological Seminary
in Pasadena, California, formed the National Association of Evangelicals

to gather conservative Protestants and create an alternative to the liberal National Council of Churches. Graham started a magazine, *Christianity Today*, as a rival to the liberal *Christian Century*. Both flourished, but soon developments within other sectors of conservative Protestantism changed the balance of power in the evangelical world. One was the explosive growth of Pentecostalism, and the spread of Pentecostal beliefs to the liberal Protestant denominations and the Catholic Church. The second was the integration of white southern evangelicals into the life of the nation for the first time since the Civil War. Of the two, the first was more surprising, but the second was more politically significant.

Pentecostalism had begun among the poor, black and white, in a Los Angeles mission in 1906. The movement had spread quickly across the South and Southwest, and segregated denominations formed, but in the 1920s and '30s white Pentecostals, like their black counterparts, remained largely poor farmers, or people working in marginal jobs in the cities. Their distinctive belief was that all the gifts of the Holy Spirit, like speaking in tongues, prophesying, and healing, were available to believers today as they were to the apostles at Pentecost. Before World War II most Protestants looked down on Pentecostals, calling them "snake-handlers" or "Holy Rollers." In the 1950s, however, many Pentecostals became middle-class, and one of the tent revivalists, Oral Roberts, left his tent to preach on radio and television, to build a university, and to make Pentecostals respectable. In the 1960s, a time of spiritual experimentation, some of the Pentecostal beliefs caught on with liberal Protestants and Catholics, who integrated them into their own church doctrines and practices. The so-called charismatic renewal movement took on a life of its own, spreading even to conservative Protestants.

In the same period white southerners, including evangelicals, emerged from the isolation they had proudly suffered since the Civil War. By then the dominant religious force in the South was the Southern Baptist Convention. Its theology had been untouched by modernism, and Southern Baptists thought it to be the pure Gospel of the New Testament. Until the Second World War the SBC had stood as a bastion against social change, championing states' rights, white supremacy, and the existing economic order. In the villages the church reigned supreme as the arbiter of morals, the social order, and the truth of the Gospel. The arrival of northern industry, highways, and federal regulations therefore came a as shock to the system. The growth of cities, improvements in education, and involvement with the rest of the country created a cosmopolitan elite. Some of the heads of the SBC belonged to it and became more theologically and politically moderate. In 1954 the SBC's Christian Life Commission persuaded the Convention to accept the Supreme Court decision on *Brown v. Board of Education*, and three years later its chairman acted as mediator between President Dwight Eisenhower and Governor Orval Faubus in the conflict over admitting black students to Little Rock Central High School. What did not change was the commitment of SBC leaders to evangelism. When southerners moved out of the South, many to Southern California and the cities of the Midwest, where industry was booming, they formed their own congregations, and the SBC followed, building churches at an astonishing rate and moving out across the country until there were Southern Baptist churches in every state. The SBC's office in Washington thus became a power to reckon with.

The 1960s and early 1970s—the so-called Long Sixties—saw the election of the first Catholic president, the Supreme Court decision banning prayer and Bible reading in the schools, the civil rights movement, the protests against the Vietnam War, and the *Roe v. Wade* decision. Surprisingly, only the fundamentalists objected to all of them. Other evangelicals took moderate stances on many of them, and the period passed quietly. It even saw the growth of a small evangelical left in the colleges.

The reaction came later, first with the upsurge of fundamentalism in the South, and then with the appearance of new leaders. Billy Graham, who had associated himself with Nixon even during Watergate, lost his influence; separatist Baptists grew in number, and fundamentalist Southern Baptists successfully challenged the moderate leaders for control of the Convention. Jerry Falwell and a host of pastors and televangelists took to national politics, forming the Moral Majority, the Christian Voice, and the Religious Roundtable. A talented preacher, Falwell picked up on the grassroots rebellions against "the sixties" in all its forms, from sex education to homosexuality, to the federal government's insistence on the integration of Christian schools. He also voiced the southern sense that Washington was encroaching on states' rights, and that Jimmy Carter was weak on national defense and was destroying the economy with deficit spending. Out of all this, he constructed a jeremiad that conservative Christians had to get into politics or see the destruction of the nation. With a few changes the Christian right has used the same jeremiad ever since. Falwell and Reagan created a bond that was more rhetorical than real, but the South moved gradually into the Republican Party from the presidential level on down.

The Christian right was a populist movement, and it had only two systematic thinkers, R. J. Rushdoony and Francis Schaeffer. Of the two Rushdoony was by far the more radical. He proposed that Christians should reconstruct the society based on biblical law, a theonomy that would lead directly to the coming of Christ. Reconstructionism, his school of thought, was too outlandish to be adopted fully by more than a few people, but his ideas circulated anonymously in a watered-down form. Schaeffer, by contrast, was a major intellectual celebrity, who lectured in evangelical colleges, wrote best-selling books, and made two influential documentary series, one released in 1979, condemning abortion in such vivid terms it changed the minds of thousands of evangelicals. In the book he published two years later he wrote that humanism was "a total world view" standing in complete antithesis to the "Christian world view," and that humanists used the concept of "pluralism" to mean there was no right and no wrong. Schaeffer died in 1984, but ever since many Christian right leaders have testified to the profound influence he had on their thinking.

Jerry Falwell had to shut down the Moral Majority in the late 1980s, but he was soon succeeded by Pat Robertson, the son of a U.S. senator from Virginia who had built a successful television network. A contradictory figure, he had political ambitions, yet to the embarrassment of his father, he hosted a television program in which he claimed to heal the sick and to avert hurricanes. In 1988 he ran for the Republican nomination for president, and when he lost, he supported the establishment candidate, Vice President George H. W. Bush. Shortly afterward he formed the Christian Coalition to change Republican politics with the boyish-looking Ralph Reed as his executive director. A brilliant political organizer, Reed trained

Christian right activists to run in local races, figured out new tactics to attract "pro-family" voters to the Republican Party, and distributed millions of voter guides favorable to socially conservative Republicans. By the 1992 election the Coalition had not only become indispensable to the Republican politicians, but also was integrated into Republican ranks and in control of the GOP apparatus in eighteen states.

During the first two years of Clinton's administration the Coalition, along with other Christian right organizations, experienced an explosive growth in membership and financing. In the midterm elections the GOP gained a major victory that put Republicans in control of the House for the first time in forty years. White evangelicals moved decisively into the Republican camp, giving the party 75 percent of its vote. The Coalition by its account mobilized four million voters and helped the Republicans sweep the South. It seemed unstoppable until the House leadership decided to impeach Clinton. The effort ended in disaster for the GOP, and the Coalition broke apart, beset by financial difficulties.

By 2000 even many Christian right stalwarts almost gave up on the movement. George W. Bush, however, had been born again; he spoke their language, and he knew how much Republicans depended on the Christian right with its influence on evangelical voters. His first administration saw a growing alliance between the two because he gave them access to the White House and supported some of their favorite programs, but most of all because of what they perceived as his strong leadership after 9/11 and in waging the Iraq War. The major Christian right figures in this period were James Dobson, the founder of Focus on the Family, and Richard Land, the head of the policy arm of the conservative SBC. Like Falwell and Robertson, they believed that America had been a Christian country and would be one day again. Between them they revived the moribund movement by making a concerted effort to ban gay marriage in the states. The 2004 election was close, particularly in the key state of Ohio, and when they succeeded in passing referenda against same-sex marriage, they could take credit for Bush's victory.

In the second Bush administration the Christian right had its greatest triumphs and became more radical than before. Its alliance with the increasingly unpopular Bush administration, however, created a backlash in

Congress, in the general public, and even among evangelicals, who feared they had become identified merely as a part of the Republican Party. Around 2005 many leading evangelicals, such as Rick Warren, began to distance themselves from the Christian right, and some began to voice dissent publicly for the first time. Known as the "new evangelicals," many of them took up social justice issues, such as poverty and climate change.

The decline of the Christian right had begun. Jerry Falwell and other Christian right leaders, now in their seventies, died or retired, and no one took their place. The baby boomers and the subsequent generations had absorbed the social changes that had taken place since the 1960s, and many of the older concerns had receded. According to polls, the young were more inclined to worry about the environment than their elders and were more in favor of an active government at home. Abortion was an important issue for them, but homosexuality was not, and in 2007 one in three favored same-sex marriage. Most took the equality of women for granted, and on the whole they were more tolerant of the views of others and believed the U.S. a pluralistic country.

After Obama won the 2008 election, policy-oriented new evangelical leaders faced off over the president's health care bill against the Catholic bishops and the remaining Christian right leaders, who believed its mandates on contraception and abortion would violate their religious freedom. The bill passed, but Obama's victory coincided with an economic crisis that began on Wall Street and spread to Main Street, causing the worst recession since the Great Depression. The reaction this time came from the right in the form of the Tea Party, a movement financed by libertarian corporate barons, such as Charles and David Koch. At the grassroots level Tea Party members supported programs, such as Social Security, they perceived as going to productive members of society, such as themselves, but opposed government "handouts" to undeserving "freeloaders," a category that seemed to be made up of the young, undocumented immigrants, and people of color. These people, the Tea Party members seemed to feel, were destroying the fabric of American culture. Christian right activists, who shared much the same sentiments, melded into the Tea Party, the larger and more powerful group.

The "new," or progressive, evangelical leaders fought for the cap and trade bill to reduce greenhouse gases in the atmosphere, for the protection of the poor against budget cuts, and for immigration reform with a path to citizenship for undocumented immigrants. On immigration reform they were joined by groups such as the National Association of Evangelicals and the Southern Baptist Convention because the Bible spoke of welcoming strangers, but also because they already had Latinos and Asians in their churches, and they saw that their prospects for growth lay in evangelizing these and other immigrants.

Growth had become an important issue because in the first decade of the new century the evangelical population had plateaued. Some denominations, such as the Pentecostal Assemblies of God, were growing with Latino converts, but the enormous Southern Baptist Convention was losing members every year. What was more, the number of Americans who had no affiliation to any church was growing fast. One solution, the evangelical leaders knew, was to bring more immigrants into their churches.

The trouble was that many people in the pews of white evangelical churches did not want immigrants, whom they felt were destroying American culture. They also knew that most Latinos, both Catholics and evangelicals, voted Democratic and that many supported legal abortion and same-sex marriage.

By the time of the 2016 election, the evangelical world had become a complex place. The Christian right no longer dominated evangelical discourse. Further, it had taken up a more secular language—there was little talk of Christianizing America. In Washington many thought the Christian right dead, but Republican legislators in the red states passed scores of laws restricting abortion and LGBT rights. That Donald Trump, the thrice-married libertine, won the Republican nomination for president with many evangelical votes confounded most evangelical leaders. Clearly something was happening that would change American politics, and the Christian right would not be what it had been before.

I

THE GREAT AWAKENINGS
and the EVANGELICAL EMPIRE

THE ORIGINS of evangelicalism as a distinct form of Protestantism lie in the revivals that swept back and forth across the English-speaking world and Northern Europe in the eighteenth and nineteenth centuries. In the American case, the revivals came in two waves. The earlier, known as the First Great Awakening, peaked in the 1740s but set off reverberations that continued to the time of the American Revolution. The later one, the Second Great Awakening, began just after the end of the War of Independence and continued intermittently in various parts of the country through the 1850s. Everywhere, the revivals involved a rebellion against the formalism of the established churches and an effort to recover an authentic spiritual experience: a religion of the heart, as opposed to the head. And everywhere, they introduced a new idea of conversion as a sudden, overwhelming experience of God's grace. In Europe the established churches survived and incorporated the pietistic strain within their own traditions. But in America the revivals transformed Protestantism. They undermined the established churches, led to the separation of church and state, and created a marketplace of religious ideas in which new sects and denominations flourished. At the same time, they made evangelical Protestantism the dominant religious force in the country for most of the nineteenth century.

In America the periods were, not incidentally, ones of rapid demographic growth, and social, as well as political, change. The expansion of settlement and commerce opened space for initiative and innovation, and small, integrated communities dissolved into an expansive, mobile society. The itinerant revivalists themselves embodied this mobility and this reach. In offering individuals the possibility of a direct relationship with God they helped adjust the society to its new circumstances and to transform the hierarchical colonial order into the more egalitarian society of the nineteenth century. After the Revolution many of them explicitly preached individual freedom, the separation of church and state, voluntary association as a primary means of social organization, and republicanism as the best form of government. Awakenings, as the scholar William McLoughlin tells us, "are periods of cultural revitalization . . . that extend over a period of a generation or so, during which time a profound reorientation of beliefs and values takes place." [1]

The two Great Awakenings are not just a matter of historical interest. Some of the attitudes formed at the time, such as the spirit of voluntarism, have become a part of our common heritage. Others have had a particular and lasting effect on American Protestantism. Indeed, to ask what is religiously or culturally distinctive about either mainline or evangelical Protestants today is to find that most explanatory roads lead back to their particular inheritance from the Great Awakenings. On the evangelical side, for example, the revivalists of the eighteenth and nineteenth centuries pioneered mass evangelism and introduced new communications techniques that, with additions and modifications, have been used by evangelical preachers ever since. In their eagerness to save souls, the revivalists introduced vernacular preaching styles, de-emphasized religious instruction, and brought a populist, anti-intellectual strain into American Protestantism. Then, as most of them saw it, America was a Christian— read Protestant—nation.

The First Great Awakening

The First Great Awakening began among the Congregationalists, the direct heirs to the Puritans of New England, in the midst of what William McLoughlin and other historians have described as a crisis of religious authority. The Puritans had established close-knit communities, bound by covenant, where church and state cooperated in an effort to build a Holy

Commonwealth. Calvinists, they believed that God, unreachable and unknowable, determined everything that went on in His creation and that human nature was totally corrupt ("utterly depraved") and had been since Adam's fall. Life, therefore, was a constant struggle with Satan. God, in their view, had reason to condemn all mankind to hell, but because of Christ's atoning sacrifice on the cross, He had arbitrarily decided to save an elect few "saints." Through piety and soul-searching, men might come to hope they were among the elect and might experience an infusion of His grace. But whatever God willed, all men had a duty to help each other, to respect the clergy and the magistrates, and to obey the law. As reformers, the Puritans believed that God might work among them to create a New Jerusalem, "a city upon a hill," if only men kept their covenant with God and submitted themselves to the will of the community. Ultimately, they believed, Christ would return, either to establish a millennial reign of peace on earth, or, as the emissary of a wrathful God, to destroy it.[2]

The Puritans were dissenters from the Church of England and from medieval aristocratic traditions, but their society, like most of those in Europe at the time, was stratified and patriarchal. In the preface to the covenant signed aboard the *Arabella*, John Winthrop wrote: "God Almighty in his most holy and wise providence hath so disposed of the conditions of mankind, as in all times some must be rich and some poor, some high and eminent in power and dignity, others mean and in subjection." After the early days of the settlement, clergymen and the civil governors, who came from the propertied elite, assumed authority for regulating the affairs of the community in much the same way that Puritan fathers regulated the affairs of their households. These Puritan rulers valued order above all other social virtues and saw themselves as responsible only to God. Family discipline, as well as the theology preached from the pulpit, taught that man's duty was submit to authority and to accept his station within the God-given hierarchy.[3]

By the eighteenth century, this Puritan order faced both social and ideological challenges. Congregationalism remained the established religion, its churches subsidized by taxpayers in all but one of the New England colonies. (Rhode Island, settled by Baptists, was the exception.) Yet the immigration of other Christians and nonbelievers had eroded the Puritan control of the polity. Then, too, the westward movement of the settlers and the growing wealth of landowners and merchants bred a new spirit of individualism. Economic controversies erupted, pitting settlers against the gentry who ran the colonial governments, and political factions emerged. At the same time, Enlightenment ideas about free will and the power of reason circulated among educated people, causing some to doubt fundamental Calvinist doctrines, such as predestination and human depravity. Congregationalist clergymen preached obedience to the God-given order, but many people could not fit their lives into the old patterns—though they were haunted by guilt for their apostasy. In the first two decades of the century, Increase Mather and other clergymen concluded from their reading of the biblical prophecies that human society was descending into such a state of sin and chaos that God would intervene cataclysmically and Christ would return to deliver His judgment on mankind. Such was their sense of crisis.[4]

The revivals in New England began in 1734 in a citadel of orthodox Calvinism: the church of Jonathan Edwards in Northampton, Massachusetts. The son and grandson of Congregationalist ministers, Edwards had studied science, or natural philosophy, as it was then called, at Yale and had read the works of Isaac Newton and John Locke. In college, he had struggled with the idea of God's total sovereignty, but one day, walking in his father's pasture, he had a conversion experience. Looking up at the sky and the clouds, he had, he later wrote, a sense of the glorious majesty and grace of God, and as he looked around, this divinity appeared to him in everything, the trees, the grass, and the water. Later in his theological works, he used the methods of the Enlightenment thinkers to revitalize Calvinist theology and to defend it from the clergy swayed by Enlightenment humanism. In 1729, at the age of twenty-six, he assumed the pulpit of his grandfather's church in Northampton. Finding that many in the parish, in particular the young, had fallen away from the moral standards of the church—there was "tippling," "carousing," and "chambering"—he went to work, holding meetings and prayer sessions around the parish. Five years later, while he was giving a series of sermons on justification by faith, an outbreak of religious fervor occurred in his parish. People laughed and wept, some saw visions, and many were filled with hope and joy. In the space of six months three hundred people were converted, bringing the total membership of his church to six hundred—nearly the whole adult population of the town. Visitors came to his church, and the revivals spread to towns up and down the Connecticut River and from thence to other parts of New England. In his account of these events, Edwards attributed the revival to a sudden, surprising descent of the Holy Spirit.[5]

Edwards was not a highly dramatic or emotional preacher—he read his sermons from a manuscript or detailed notes—but he nonetheless had a powerful effect on his listeners.

In his revivalist sermons, he began by telling people what they already believed: that as sinners they deserved everlasting punishment. In case they had forgotten what this meant—or had put it to the back of their minds—he used vivid language to describe God's wrath. In his most quoted sermon, "Sinners in the Hands of an Angry God" (1741), he used particularly vivid rhetoric. "The God," he said, "that holds you over the Pit of Hell, much as one holds a Spider, or some loathsome Insect, over the Fire, abhors you, and is dreadfully provoked." Sinners, he said, could look forward to "Millions of Millions of Ages, in wrestling and conflicting with this almighty merciless Vengeance; and then when you have so done . . . you will know that all is but a Point to what remains." In concluding, however, he delivered, as always, a message of hope: "And now you have an extraordinary Opportunity, a Day wherein Christ has flung the Door of Mercy wide open, and stands in the Door calling and crying with a loud Voice to poor Sinners; a Day wherein many are flocking to him, and pressing into the Kingdom of God."[6]

Revivals had occurred before among the Puritans and their descendants, but the call of the preachers had been to covenant renewal—or obedience to the God-given order of ministers and magistrates. Edwards, however, was preaching the evangelical message that individuals could have a direct relationship with Christ—and that Christ would save not just the apparently worthy, but all those who would receive His grace. Previous revivals had been local and short-lived. This one, however, kept going on, and not just among the Congregationalists, but also among the Presbyterians, the descendants of the Scots-Irish Puritans who had settled in the Middle Colonies, and the Dutch Reformed of New York. With the arrival of the English evangelist George Whitefield in 1739, the revivals spread through all of the colonies.

Unlike Edwards, who was a theologian and pastor, Whitefield (1714–70) was an itinerant evangelist and by far the most popular preacher of his day. An Oxford graduate and an Anglican minister, he had a powerful voice, a dramatic preaching style, and an ability to simplify church doctrines for a mass audience. (He had studied acting and David Garrick, the greatest actor of the day, said that he could seize the attention of any crowd just by pronouncing the word "Mesopotamia.") At Oxford, he had met John and Charles Wesley, the founders of a pietistic movement within the Anglican Church known as Methodism. A Calvinist, he had theological differences with the Wesleys, who had adopted Arminian, or free will, doctrines, but in college, he, like John, had a profound religious experience that banished all doubts he had about his salvation. This experience, which he called a "new birth," became his criterion for conversion, and with the Wesleys he established it as a staple of revivalist preaching.

In 1738, Whitefield made the first of seven voyages to the American colonies, and two years later, at the age of twenty-six, he traveled up and down the Eastern Seaboard, preaching in the major cities and towns. His sermons had already caused a sensation in London, and in America he drew crowds of thousands to open-air meetings. Even the skeptical Benjamin Franklin was impressed by his voice and delivery. With the help of the media of the day—the newspaper reporters who heralded his meetings and the printers who published his sermons and journals—Whitefield became the first intercolonial celebrity and an inspiration to local revivalists across the country. By the end of his year in America, evangelicalism had turned into a countrywide movement with a radical wing fomenting religious rebellion.

Gilbert Tennent, a Presbyterian whom Whitefield met not long after his arrival in Philadelphia, was one of the leaders of the rebellion. The minister of a parish in New Brunswick, New Jersey, and a formidable preacher (Whitefield called him "a son of thunder"), he had come to America with his family from Ulster in 1718, during a period when many Scots-Irish were immigrating, and a year after the founding of the first Presbyterian Synod in the colonies. His father, William, a Presbyterian pastor, had established a small academy, known as the Log College, in rural Pennsylvania to train local ministers. Gilbert had gone to Yale, but he and his four brothers had grown up in the pietistic and intellectually informal atmosphere of the Log College. All had become converts to evangelicalism, and during the 1730s he, his brothers, and several of the Log College graduates had held revivals in Presbyterian churches in the region, preaching salvation through a sudden experience of God's grace.[7]

These revivals filled the pews of many rural churches, but a number of the more orthodox Calvinist ministers of the Philadelphia Synod objected. Some questioned the spiritual validity of the "crisis conversions" and complained of the methods used to obtain them. (One Log College minister was accused of giving "whining and roaring harangues" that "terrified to distraction" some of the "deluded Creatures" who followed him.)[8] Others suspected that the theological education of the Log College graduates did not meet Presbyterian standards, and many felt that the itinerant revivalists were intruding on settled parishes and attempting to turn people against their own pastors. In 1738 the Synod in Philadelphia created a New Brunswick Presbytery for Tennent and his colleagues, but voted that other presbyteries could refuse itinerant preachers and promised that the Synod would evaluate the credentials of all ministerial candidates who had not graduated from well-known universities.[9]

In 1740, Gilbert Tennent took the occasion of Whitefield's arrival in Philadelphia to make the case for his evangelical convictions and to mount an incendiary attack against the anti-revivalist party. In "The Danger of an Unconverted Ministry," a sermon he gave to a congregation about to choose a new pastor, he held that no minister, no matter how learned, who had not undergone a conversion experience, or been called to preach by the Holy Spirit, had the power to save souls. He went on to call the "unconverted" anti-revivalists "hypocritical Varlets," "dead dogs that can't bark," and "a swarm of locusts." Comparing the "unconverted" to the Pharisees who opposed the itinerant ministry of Jesus, he accused them of being greedy for money and social status, and so conceited about their learning "they look'd upon others that differed from them, and the common People, with an Air of Disdain." In conclusion, he urged the congregation to find another minister if the one sent to them did not preach the Gospel.[10]

A year later, the Philadelphia Synod, quite understandably, expelled the New Brunswick Presbytery, but Tennent and his colleagues persevered. In 1745, the Log College men, joined by other ministers, created a new synod with presbyteries in four states and founded the College of New Jersey (later, Princeton University). The "New Side" Presbyterians—as they were now called—sent itinerant evangelists into every hamlet that asked for them, and, following the Scots-Irish diaspora, carried the revivals into Virginia and North Carolina. Their success was such that when Presbyterians reunited in 1758, the New Side ministers outnumbered Old Side clergy by three to one.[11]

Whitefield also traveled through New England in 1740, gathering huge crowds, and the following year Gilbert Tennent, at his request, continued his work in the region. Encouraging evangelical preachers, converting others to the cause, and inspiring some to great heights of fervor, the two created a wave of revivals that, Jonathan Edwards wrote, were "vastly beyond any former outpouring of the Spirit that ever was known in New England."[12] By the end of two years, Edwards began to feel that something momentous might be happening. "It is not unlikely," he told his parishioners in 1742, "that this work of God's Spirit, that is so extraordinary and wonderful, is the dawning, or a least, a prelude of that glorious work of God, so often foretold in Scripture, which in the progress and issue of it shall renew the world of mankind . . . And there are many things that make it probable that this work will begin in America."[13]

Increase Mather had preached that Christ's millennial reign would come only after cataclysm caused by the declension of human society, but Edwards rejected this premillennial eschatology for its opposite. He saw revivals as evidence of God's favor and His determination to redeem mankind without an Armageddon or a personal Second Coming. This optimistic, postmillennial view echoed the Puritan view that God might begin His work in America. Edwards's vision was not of a dramatic interference by God in the course of history but rather of human spiritual progress that would gradually bring a reign of peace and harmony into the souls of men.[14]

For all of Edwards's optimism, the revivals inspired by Whitefield and Tennent created as much of a reaction in New England as they did in Pennsylvania. Until then, most of the Congregationalist clergy had seen the revivals as yet another season of renewed piety and welcomed the increased attendance in their churches. But the huge crowds Whitefield and Tennent drew, the revivalists' appeal to individuals over the heads of the clergy, and Tennent's denunciations of "unconverted" ministers seemed uncomfortable novelties. Further, the two itinerants encouraged less decorous revivalists, whose preaching caused extreme reactions like screaming, fainting, and convulsions. Even worse, some of these radicals, such as James Davenport, preached in settled parishes without permission, fired up lay exhorters, and urged the "saved" to separate themselves from the impure churches of their "unconverted" and "Christ-despising" ministers. To local clergymen, this new phase of the revivals seemed an attack not just on the established church but on the whole social order—which to an extent it was.[15]

Moderate revivalists, such as Edwards, distanced themselves from the radicals, and conceded that "errors" and "disorders" had occurred. But even the moderates were challenging the established authorities of church and state by denying them sanctifying power and relocating religious authority to an experience in the hearts of individuals. What was more, even they used vivid language to waken people from their lethargy, to make them feel their own sense of guilt so that they could rid themselves of it through the ecstatic experience of being born again in Christ.[16] An anti-revivalist party therefore grew up, and while some of its members concerned themselves mainly with the encroachments on their parishes and the unseemly emotions evoked by the radicals, others attacked the revivalist New Lights on theological grounds.[17]

Between 1741 and 1743 Charles Chauncy of the First Church of Boston carried on a debate with Edwards via printed sermons and treatises that began with a dispute over the emotions raised in the revivals and ended with an argument about the nature of religion itself. A minister much influenced by Enlightenment thinking, Chauncy at first merely inveighed against what he saw as the excesses of the radical preachers, but from there he went on to question whether the anguish and joy the revival-

ists evoked were works of the Holy Spirit, or simply psychological disturbances. Edwards, who had spent much time pondering that very issue,
replied that while not all emotional manifestations signified conversion,
conversion had to begin with a lifting of "pious affections." True religion,
he argued toward the end of the exchange, was essentially emotional—a
"sense of the heart" about the glory of God.

Chauncy for his part insisted that sinners required knowledge of the
Gospels before they could achieve grace. It had not escaped him that the
revivalists aggressively reasserted the doctrines of God's sovereignty and
human depravity, and he came to believe that revivals produced contempt
for reason and for human ability. "An enlightened Mind, not raised Affections," he wrote, "ought always to be the Guide of those who call themselves Men."[18]

By 1743, debates over the revivals, many of them carried on in far less tem-
perate language, rent convocations of Congregationalist ministers. These
public conflicts shook the confidence of laymen in the ecclesiastical establishment. The irony was that the New Light revivalists had undermined
the authority of the clergy by preaching the harshest version of traditional
Calvinist doctrines, while some of their opponents defended the status quo
by emphasizing themes more in tune with Enlightenment thought, such
as the importance of reason, education, and good works. In any case, the
public conflicts gave the radicals the opening they were looking for.[19]

Just a year after Whitefield's visit to Boston, groups of people in Connecticut and other parts of New England began to withdraw from the
Congregationalist churches to form prayer groups and churches of their
own. Calling for a return to the purity of the early church, these Sepa-
rates took laymen they believed graced by the Holy Spirit as ministers
and attempted to strip away the accretions of history from their ecclesiastical practices. Those who rejected the practice of baptizing "unsaved"
infants largely left the Congregationalist fold to become Separate Baptists.
Inspired by the radical revivalists, these Separate groups proved as trou-
blesome to the civil authorities as to the orthodox clergy. With liberty of
conscience as their rallying cry, they struggled to attain exemption from
the taxes that supported the established churches. When the request was
turned down as "schismatic," many refused to pay. Fined and sometimes

jailed as tax dodgers, they practiced civil disobedience and published tracts denouncing the magistrates and clergy as a tyrannical upper class.[20]

Subsequently, they called for an end to all tax support for religion and for the right of religious dissent. Their petitions went largely unanswered, but after the Revolution, they became leaders in the movement for the disestablishment of the church from the state. In the meantime, many Separate Baptists set out for the Middle Colonies and then for North Carolina and Virginia.[21]

The South proved fertile ground for the evangelicals. The Anglican Church had been the established church in Virginia, Maryland, the Carolinas, and Georgia since the settlement of the colonies, but it had neither independence nor power. The local landed gentry, who dominated the church vestries, opposed the creation of a diocese, preferring to keep the clergy and the ecclesiastical taxes under their own control. As a result, the church had no bishop, no ecclesiastical machinery, and little leverage with the Church of England. The task of an established church was to hold society together under the rule of religion, but because London sent few ordained priests, and the parishes were immense and sparsely populated, this could hardly be done. By the mid-eighteenth century, the expansion of settlements into the frontier districts left many in the South outside the sphere of organized religion. Those churches that flourished were essentially fiefdoms of local gentry and identified with a class system that sharply distinguished the aristocrats from common people and slaves. The wealthy sat in private pews, and from the pulpits came messages that the lower classes should be obedient and defer to their betters. Further, the scholastic theology taught by the ministers had driven many of the less educated out of the churches and some of the best educated, like Thomas Jefferson and James Madison, beyond Christianity into Deism.[22]

In 1744, evangelical missionaries began to move into the southern colonies to fill the institutional vacuum. The first to arrive were New Side Presbyterians, who at the request of a group of pious laymen came to minister to a congregation in Hanover County, Virginia. The governor of Virginia had no liking for dissenters, but Rev. Samuel Davies, a graduate of the Log College and a learned man, somehow convinced him that the New Sides were orthodox Presbyterians with as much a right to preach in Virginia as they had in England. In the 1750s Separate Baptists from Connecticut established churches in Sandy Creek, North Carolina, and gradually pushed on to the coast and into Virginia and South Carolina. They were not as politic as the Presbyterians. Fresh from their battles in New England, they maintained that civil authorities had no right to interfere with religion and refused to ask for licenses to preach or to abide by the laws against itinerancy. Many were fined or jailed for breaking the law, and others were attacked by mobs in midst of their enthusiastic meetings. Then, in the late 1760s, some of the first Wesleyan missionaries came to America and journeyed south. Methodism was still a movement within the Anglican Church, and the itinerants were welcomed by a few local ministers—until they began to entice their congregants into schism.[23]

The New Side Presbyterians, the Separate Baptists, and the Methodists had theological and other differences, but they were alike in preaching a radical break with a society dominated by the values of the landed aristocracy. As in the North, the evangelicals called for a dramatic conversion—a profound psychological change—that would separate the individual from a sinful past. In the South, they put equal stress on growing to grace within a religious community separate from "the world." Southern aristocrats engaged in foxhunting, horse racing, dueling, and dancing; they dressed in fine clothes, gambled at cards, and cultivated witty conversation. But the evangelicals condemned all of these markers of social prestige as the trifling activities of the godless. (The Separate Baptists went so far as to call learning one of the frivolities of the unsaved.) They dressed plainly, lived abstemiously, and preached that the true worth of a man depended simply on his piety and moral discipline. As the historian Donald G. Mathews has shown, the converts to evangelicalism were not by and large the aristocrats or the very poor; rather they were hardworking farmers and tradesmen battling a class system and the lawless, socially chaotic world at its margins. To such people, the evangelical churches offered fellowship and help in achieving orderly, disciplined lives. Within the church, individuals would be separated from the unregenerate, instructed in Christian behavior, and held to it under the "watchful care" of the community. Then, too, the churches offered social status. As Mathews tells us, the word "respectable" lost its connotation of social rank and came to mean "pious" or "moral." This program clearly had great appeal, for by 1776 there were almost twice the number of evangelicals in the South as there were Anglicans.[24]

The revivals of the First Great Awakening continued through the 1760s and trailed off thereafter, though the evangelical sects continued to proselytize. By the time of the American Revolution, evangelicalism had penetrated all three sections of the country; it had created divisions in two of the major Protestant denominations, inspired an evangelical Baptist movement, and shaken the rule of the established churches.

The Second Great Awakening

The Second Great Awakening was even more explosive than the first. The revivals, which began not long after the War of Independence and continued intermittently until the Civil War, coursed through the whole country and through all the major Protestant denominations, sweeping away the stricter aspect of Calvinism and creating a simpler, more democratic faith that accorded with the spirit of the new country. With the passage of the First Amendment and the gradual disestablishment of the churches in the South and New England, the revivalists gained complete freedom of action. The revivals threw up new denominations and sects and made the country more religiously diverse while at the same time turning the vast majority of American Protestants into evangelicals.

Shortly after the War of Independence, revivalist preachers, most of them Methodists, Baptists, and Presbyterians, set out to church the unchurched on the frontiers of the expanding country, moving west through Kentucky and Tennessee, then into the South and the Middle West. In 1790, according to the first U.S. government census, 94 percent of the American settlers lived in the original thirteen colonies. By 1850, more than half lived outside of them in the states and the territories to the west. Meanwhile, even without much immigration, the population grew at an astonishing rate, rising from two and a half million to twenty million in the seventy years following the Revolution. In this burgeoning country, the social and political arrangements left over from the colonial period, and the Federalist vision of a country ruled by an educated minority of merchants and landowners, soon became obsolete. As the historian Nathan O. Hatch has shown, the frontier revivalists participated in the social and political upheavals of the postrevolutionary period and in the struggle to create a more egalitarian society. To reach their audience in a world without churches, they created new methods of proselytism and a simplified form of evangelicalism: a folk religion characterized by disdain for authority and tradition.[25]

The Second Great Awakening broke out in camp meetings in Kentucky and Tennessee at the turn of the nineteenth century. In 1801, a meeting in Cane Ridge, Kentucky, drew some twenty thousand people—a vast number in those sparsely populated territories—and it lasted almost a week. Multiple speakers preached from platforms around the encampment all day long, and emotions ran high. According to Barton Stone, a Presbyterian minister and the main organizer of the meeting, many people were affected by "bodily agitations," some laughing uncontrollably, others dancing, singing, running, or falling down in a faint. Evangelicals had seen such phenomena before, but never on such a scale. When news of the meeting spread, revivals broke out around the region with crowds of thousands gathering to listen to preachers in the hopes of experiencing similar religious ecstasies. The Methodists, Baptists, and Presbyterians had resumed evangelizing in the South after the end of the Revolutionary War and had seen a modest rise in their church memberships, but the revivals produced a sudden surge of conversions on both sides of the Appalachians and laid the foundation for growth of a new order of magnitude in the succeeding years.[26]

During the Second Great Awakening, no denomination worked as hard, or made as many converts, as the Methodists. Previously a small group within the Anglican Church, the American Methodists established their own independent Episcopal church in 1784 and immediately prepared themselves for work on the frontiers. Under the leadership of Francis Asbury, an itinerant preacher who had come to America in 1771, they divided the country into districts and directed resources away from the settled areas and toward the peripheries. Asbury, who later took the title of bishop, made camp meetings a regular part of church activities and assembled a small army of circuit riders—some seven hundred of them by the time of his death in 1816—who traveled hundreds of miles a year on horseback to preach to the unconverted and to tend to their flocks in scattered settlements. Asbury, who himself rode an annual circuit of five thousand miles, established an orderly hierarchy under his command. Every district had an elder in charge, who reported to the bishop; the circuit riders had assigned routes; the congregations, or the "societies," gathered by them were divided into cell groups, or "classes," of twelve to fifteen people that enforced discipline and nurtured the religious life of their members. But the Methodists combined a central control with an egalitarian style and a democratic inclusiveness. Where there were no ordained clergymen, laymen were recruited to perform pastoral functions, and lay participation was always encouraged. The circuit riders, though full-time professionals, were characteristically young and poor. Many of them started out as lay leaders of "classes" on the frontier and, like the people they served, few had more than a grade-school education.[27]

The Baptists grew almost as rapidly, though their ecclesiastical structure was almost the opposite of the Methodists'. A group of independent churches, they banded together in regional and national associations, which—being voluntary and democratic—sometimes split apart over doctrinal issues and sometimes joined with others to create more powerful organizations. The large associations had missionary societies, and some assigned itinerants to preach the Gospel in areas where there were no Baptist churches. But most of their evangelists were independent preachers. John Leland, a prominent Baptist, best known for his support for Jefferson's bill establishing religious freedom in Virginia, traveled, by his own account, the equivalent of three times around the globe between the Revolution and 1824, and preached eight thousand sermons. The typical Baptist evangelist, however, was a farmer licensed to preach by his church who moved into a new area and gathered a congregation. These farmer-preachers were self-supporting, and like the Methodist ministers, they rarely had any more education than their congregants.[28]

By 1800 the Presbyterians were well organized in the South with two synods and seven presbyteries, and in 1801, they established a Plan of Union with the Congregationalists to evangelize New York state and the territories to the west. But their gains were mainly in the settled areas, for their intellectually weighty Calvinism was not well suited to frontier evangelism. For one thing, it required a well-educated clergy, and that limited the number of ministers they could deploy. It also required sustained preaching and teaching—and therefore a more conservative approach to evangelism. Many Presbyterians were horrified by what they heard about the Cane Ridge meeting. Their General Assembly banned camp meetings and gradually withdrew from the practice of revivalism. Presbyterians on the frontiers, however, refused to abide by the Assembly's restrictions. Some modified their message, while others rejected the doctrinal and educational requirements of the denomination. These defections led to schisms and the formation of new sects: the Cumberland Presbyterian Church and a "Christian" movement that thirty years later joined with a group formed by Alexander Campbell, another dissident Presbyterian, to create a new denomination, the Disciples of Christ.[29]

The frontier evangelists gained authority not from ecclesiastical credentials, but from their ability to appeal to audiences. Unlike the settled clergy, they preached without notes in colloquial language and used earthy humor and commonsense reasoning. Storytellers rather than didactic moralists, they dramatized biblical stories and vividly described the torments of hell. Of Lorenzo Dow, an independent Methodist and one of the most popular preachers in the first two decades of the revivals, a contemporary wrote:

> His weapons against Beelzebub were providential interpositions, wondrous disasters, touching sentiments, miraculous escapes . . . a raging storm might be the forerunner of God's immediate wrath; a change of element might betoken Paradise restored, or a new Jerusalem . . . He might be farcical or funereal. He had genius at all times to construct a catastrophe.[30]

In the early years of the century, learned Congregationalists and Presbyterians, such as Timothy Dwight, grandson of Jonathan Edwards and the president of Yale, and his student Lyman Beecher, denounced these new methods as barbarous and opined that unlettered preachers could not arrest human depravity or stand as pillars of civilization and moral influence. These eminent men were not only Calvinists but Federalists, and the revivalists were more subversive than they initially understood. As Hatch has shown, many revivalists championed popular sovereignty and the cause of the backwoods people against the merchants and land specu-lators. Some of the most popular preachers were not just religious enthusi-asts but radical Jeffersonians who spoke of the rights of man and of liberty of conscience. Lorenzo Dow, for one, condemned the distinction made between "gentlemen" and "peasants," and called upon people to throw off the shackles of deference and to think for themselves. John Leland, a con-troversial figure among Baptists, not only promoted disestablishment, but opposed all forms of clerical organization, including mission societies in his own denomination. For Leland, religious freedom meant not just that the state should not interfere in religious affairs but that each individual had a right to liberty of conscience, and that nothing, neither churches nor families, should interfere with it. "Religion is a matter between God and individuals," he wrote, "and the individual conscience should be free from human control."[31]

In those parts of the country where the established denominations held sway, revivalists inveighed against the wealth and pretensions of the genteel clergy and called them oppressors of the poor. In particular, they attacked the orthodox Calvinists for their assumption of cultural authority, their efforts to legislate morality, and their preoccupation with arcane phil-osophical systems. The leaders of some of the evangelical sects—Francis Asbury, Alexander Campbell, and Barton Stone among them—went so far as to contend that the Protestant Reformation had not done its job well enough and that the entire Christian tradition had been a sordid history of corruption in which the priesthood had wielded theologies and rituals to enslave the minds of the people. Thus lumping Puritan Calvinism with Catholicism, they called for the restoration of the primitive church of the apostles. *Sola scriptura*—no creed but the Bible—had been a tenet of Protestantism since Luther, but some frontier revivalists took this to mean that there was literally no authority in matters of faith except for the Bible. Leland, for one, maintained that each individual had right to his own in-terpretation of the Scriptures; Campbell, whose anticlericalism was just as thoroughgoing, urged that the traditional distinction between the clergy and the laity be abolished—along with all prescriptive theology—so that people could read the "plain facts" of the Bible for themselves.[32]

To many orthodox clergymen, religious freedom seemed to be leading to a situation in which, as one wrote, "Every theological vagabond and peddler may drive here his bungling trade, without passport or license, and sell his false ware at pleasure."[33] Heresies, the orthodox feared, would multiply, and dissident sects would turn the country into a religious anarchy. In upstate New York during the 1830s and 1840s, their fears appeared to be justified, for in counties between Lake Ontario and the Adirondacks, a region so often lit by the fires of revival it became known as "the burned-over district," self-made evangelists preached original ideas, and new religious movements flourished. In 1831, William Miller, a farmer and a lay Baptist, declared that his study of the Bible showed that Christ would come again in 1844 to save believers from a doomed, sinful world. Licensed as a Baptist preacher, he delivered hundreds of lectures and sermons about the coming Advent and built a movement of preachers and layman. By 1844, some fifty thousand people were convinced that the Day was coming, and in the excitement some gave up their worldly occupations, sold their property, and went up to the tops of hills to await the Savior. When the day passed without event, not all were wholly disillusioned. Some thought Miller had merely made an error of reckoning, others that Christ had come but not in the flesh. Later, those whose faith survived were gathered into the Seventh-day Adventist Church.

Then, just a year before Miller announced his prophecy, Joseph Smith, the son of farming family that had settled near Palmyra, New York, published a book he said had been inscribed on ancient gold plates he unearthed near his village. His treasure, the Book of Mormon, revealed that Israelite tribes had come to the American continent long before the Indians, and that Christ had come to America after his death and resurrection in Jerusalem. In the next decade he gathered disciples, made converts in England and across the northern United States, and founded the Church of Jesus Christ of Latter-day Saints. Meanwhile, spiritualism, Swedenborgianism, and other imported spiritual practices proliferated in upstate New York. In addition, numerous religious communes sprang up, among them the Oneida Community, an extraordinary social experiment led by a Yale-educated Presbyterian, John Humphrey Noyes, where property was shared and free love practiced in the name of absolute Christian fellowship.

Still, the religious inventiveness of upstate New Yorkers in those years was exceptional, and after the explosions that followed the Cane Ridge camp meeting, no new schisms or sects appeared in the South. Instead of anarchy, the revivals produced something more like uniformity in the newly settled areas and the South. The Methodists, Baptists, and Presbyterians dominated the preaching circuits, and while maintaining their denominational distinctions, they developed a common form of evangelicalism: a simplified religious system well adapted to frontier communities.

Calvinism formed the backdrop to this system, but key doctrines, such as irresistible grace, limited atonement, and unconditional election, played no part in it. Predestination, as Hatch points out, never had much appeal to those at the bottom of the social scale because of the implication that God had ordained, and took pleasure in, human suffering. The Methodists, who had worked among the poor in an industrializing England, had rejected this doctrine from the start, along with the doctrine that God would save only a small elect and condemn everyone else to hell. In a further breach with Calvinism, the Methodists also proposed that Christians could forfeit their salvation by sliding back into sin and, on the other hand, that they could seek a "second blessing" and achieve perfect holiness. The Baptists and Presbyterians tried to uphold Calvinist doctrines, but as Enlightenment thinking about human nature became a part of the American atmosphere, these doctrines seemed more and more to defy common sense. Further, they proved poor tools for evangelism in the egalitarian world of the frontier, and not long after 1800 the revivalists resolved these issues in favor of free will and salvation for all who chose it.[34]

Brought down to earth and stripped of theological complexity, the evangelical message was clear and urgent.

As the historian Samuel S. Hill writes, there was good news and bad news, all of a piece. The bad news was that all are sinners, lost without God and condemned to hell; the good news was that those who repented and opened their heart to His saving grace would live in a sweet, close relationship with God and would gain everlasting life. Other doctrines were taught,

such as Jesus' sacrifice for mankind on the cross, but all of them were simple
and functional tenets undergirding this message. As Hill puts it, "Christianity thus interpreted is a problem-solution system." At revival meetings, the
emphasis was on the experience of a new birth, rather than on any exercise
of reason or knowledge of doctrine. Afterward, it was on participation in
a church community that taught moral discipline and preachers gave small
attention to examining the theology on which it was based.[35]

This folk religion proved extraordinarily successful in the South. Between 1801 and 1807 the number of white Methodists in the South grew
from 46,000 to 80,000, and the Baptists made similar gains. The pace of
conversions continued at much the same enormous rate for the next several decades. With small competition from the Anglican Church, even
after its reorganization into the Protestant Episcopal Church of the United
States, and almost none from other denominations, Methodists and Baptists, followed by regular Presbyterians, evangelized the Atlantic states and
the regions beyond the Appalachians. By 1850, they dominated the entire
South from Virginia to Florida and west to Texas and Missouri.[36]

The evangelicals made huge strides in the rest of the country as well.
By 1850, more than a third of all religious adherents in the country were
Methodists, over 20 percent were Baptists, and 11.6 percent were Presbyterians.[37] Even in New England, the Methodists became the second largest
denomination. All the same, the New England Congregationalists with
their strong intellectual tradition and their sense of public responsibility
gave the Second Great Awakening a different character in the North than
it had in the South.

When Francis Asbury and his circuit riders brought Methodism back
from the frontiers to the rural parishes of New England after the turn of
the nineteenth century, Calvinism was already under siege by dissident
Congregationalists. More than a half a century before, Charles Chauncy
and a few other Boston clergymen had, in addition to opposing the revivals, rejected the doctrine of total depravity, insisting that human beings had
a spark of divinity that could be cultivated. Championing human ability
and reason, they fostered a school of thought within Congregationalism
that by 1815 created a breach within the denomination. The movement
was called Unitarianism by the orthodox, but the name was in some ways

misleading, for the liberal Congregationalists who established themselves at Harvard and in the Boston churches in early nineteenth century had nothing to do with the Deist English movement of the same name and no real interest in the scholastic debates about whether God was One or Three. Their object was to refashion a biblical Christianity free of external creeds, and what concerned them most deeply were the ethical implications of Calvinist doctrines.

In 1819, Rev. William Ellery Channing, the spiritual and intellectual leader of the movement in the 1820s and '30s, gave a sermon, a manifesto for the movement, in which he decried, among other things, the doctrine of substitionary atonement. The idea that Christ was sacrificed to appease the wrath of God for the sin of Adam was horrible, he preached: it turned God into a monster and the mission of Christ on its head. Christ came not to change God's mind but "to effect a moral or spiritual deliverance of mankind" by his example and teaching as well as by his death and resurrection. The way of Christ, he declared, was marked by "the spirit of love, charity, meekness, forgiveness, liberality and beneficence."[38] For Unitarians, God was not the capricious, wrathful figure of the Calvinists but a God of moral perfection. He was, Channing said, like a good father who cares for his children, takes joy in their progress, hands out punishments for their misdeeds, and readily accepts their penitence. "We look upon this world as a place of education," he preached, in which God "is training men by prosperity and adversity, by aids and obstructions . . . by a various discipline suited to free and moral beings, for union with Himself, and for a sublime, ever-growing virtue in heaven."[39]

To Timothy Dwight, these liberal Christians were no better than pagans and potentially even more disruptive of the Christian order than the backwoods preachers. Yet realizing that predestination and other church doctrines were proving obstacles even to Yale students, Dwight tried to make his Christianity sound reasonable. More important, he encouraged two of his former students, the theologian Nathaniel W. Taylor and the activist minister Lyman Beecher, to mount an intellectual defense of Calvinism and to renew the church through revivals.[40]

Between 1813 and 1823, Taylor revisited the issues that Jonathan Edwards had tackled and came up with conclusions more in keeping with

Enlightenment humanism. In the first place, he denied the imputation of Adam's sin to all mankind. Morality, he reasoned, implied a moral agency, which in turn implied the power of choice. So, while man was disposed to sin, he could choose otherwise with the help of the Holy Spirit. Edwards had believed that man had the freedom to act only in his own selfish interest, but Taylor, following the lead of the Edwardsian theologian Samuel Hopkins, proposed that man also had a disposition to benevolence, and could act for the common good. It followed that salvation would come to all who chose it. Christ, Taylor further maintained, did not die on the cross as atonement to God for the sin of Adam; rather He chose to sacrifice himself to bring men into harmony with God's moral law and to allow them to receive salvation.[41]

Channing argued that the revision of Calvinism was incoherent and unsustainable, and he was right in the sense that it was supplanted within a couple of decades. Still, "Taylorism," or New School theology, immediately caught on among New England Congregationalists and Presbyterians and permitted Lyman Beecher to reinvigorate the Congregationalist churches after disestablishment and to prepare them to compete with the Unitarians on one hand and the Methodists and Baptists on the other.[42]

Like his mentor, President Timothy Dwight, Beecher had no liking for the tendencies of Jeffersonian democracy, and he had fiercely resisted disestablishment. But, a pragmatist and a man of formidable energies, he adapted quickly when the Connecticut government severed its links with the churches in 1818. Taking up Taylor's theology, and calling it, as Taylor did, true, orthodox Calvinism, he enlisted fellow preachers and mounted revivals of a restrained sort in Connecticut, and then in the rest of New England. In 1826, he took a pulpit in Boston and conducted revivals aimed at the Unitarians. As new converts were made, he and his allies organized them into voluntary associations for mission work and moral reform. Some of these groups led local crusades against dueling and for the enforcement of the Sabbath laws. Others, such as the Home and Foreign Mission Society, the American Bible Society, the American Tract Society, and the American Society for the Promotion of Temperance, developed into powerful organizations with chapters throughout the northern states. All were in theory interdenominational but in practice dominated by Congregationalists and Presbyterians. Beecher infused them with his evangelical zeal and with his growing interest in taming the barbarous West. His ambition, he sometimes suggested, was to make the nation over in the image of New England, where educated ministers played a leading role in shaping the society. The project was an essentially conservative one, and he succeeded in the sense that states adopted the blue laws and maintained the traditional patriarchal laws regulating family affairs. Still, the benevolent associations proliferated and grew socially progressive as they became infected by the millennialism and perfectionism of Charles Grandison Finney.[43]

Of all the revivalists of the period, Charles Finney was by far the most influential. His career was unusual, and his rise to stardom swift. In 1821, when he had a profound conversion experience, he was twenty-nine years old and a lawyer in a small town in upstate New York. Leaving his practice, he studied theology with his pastor and was ordained as a Presbyterian minister two and a half years later. With no interest in taking a settled ministry, he traveled the backwoods of the north country on horseback, making home visits and preaching for a female missionary society. In 1826 he moved south to Oneida County, and at the invitation of local ministers he preached revivals in Rome, Utica, and other burgeoning towns along the Erie Canal, attracting throngs and making some three thousand converts in Oneida County alone. From there, he took his revivals to the major cities of the East Coast, and by 1832 he had become the most sought-after preacher in the country and the best-known evangelist since George Whitefield.

A tall, handsome man with a clear voice and blazing eyes, Finney preached directly and dramatically in what he called "the language of common life." Speaking extemporaneously, or from a bare outline, he looked at people in the audience straight in the eye and addressed them as "you." His sentences were short and cogent, and his expressions colloquial. "When men are entirely earnest about a thing," he wrote, "their language is direct, simple."[44] Instead of using literary allusions, as most Presbyterian ministers did, he illustrated his points with examples taken from the "common affairs of men." He had learned much from the Methodists of the north country, and much from his former profession. Like a lawyer making a case to a jury, he made structured arguments, anticipated objections, and seemed to address each person directly. "It did not sound like preaching," the journalist Henry B. Stanton wrote of one sermon. "The discourse was a chain of logic, brightened by felicity of illustration and enforced by urgent appeals from a voice of great compass and melody." [45]

Like most Presbyterians in western New York, Finney preached Taylor's New School theology, but, unfettered by academic training and New England orthodoxies, he preached free will and human ability in a much blunter fashion than did Taylor or Beecher. Original sin, he declared, is not a "constitutional depravity" but rather a deep-seated "selfishness" that people could overcome if they made themselves "a new heart." "Sin and holiness," he declared, "are voluntary acts of mind." He was just as clear about the role of the preacher in bringing people to salvation. "A revival," he wrote in 1835, "is not a miracle, or dependent on a miracle, in any sense. It is a purely philosophical result of the right use of the constituted means." In his view, God had established no particular system for promoting revivals, and "new measures" were from time to time necessary. In the early days in Rome and Utica Finney cajoled and browbeat his audiences, addressed sinners by name, and encouraged women to pray and exhort with the men. His preaching produced powerful emotional reactions, even among merchants and lawyers who had attended church for years and sat unmoved through other revivals. People groaned, sobbed, and laughed, and one man fainted dead away. [46]

When rumors of his revivals reached Boston, Lyman Beecher wrote a colleague that Finney's new measures were violations of "civilized decorum and Christian courtesy" and that their general adoption "would be the greatest calamity that could befall this young empire." He conjured up the barbarianism that succeeded the fall of the Rome, the rule of mobs during the French Revolution, and, somewhat closer to home, the Cane Ridge revivals. We are, he declared, "on the confines of universal misrule and moral desolation [wherein] the mass shall be put in motion by fierce winds before which nothing can stand." He went on to deplore Finney's view that "all men, because sinners, are therefore to be treated alike by ministers of the Gospel without respect to age or station in society." This, he warned, would lead to "a leveling of distinctions in society" that would be "the sure presage of anarchy and absolute destruction." The Presbyterian ministers of Oneida County, however, defended their colleague, and Beecher had to make his peace with the upstart.[47]

Finney later modified his measures and found the voice that Stanton described, but the contrast between his vision and Beecher's was as great as the New Englander supposed. Born in 1792 and brought up in a pioneering farm family in western New York, he was a nineteenth-century man, fully in tune with the spirit of Jacksonian democracy: its expansive individualism, its faith in progress, and its egalitarianism. In his preaching the emphasis was always on the ability of men—and women—to choose their own salvation, to work for the general welfare, and to build a new society. At the start of his career he, like most frontier preachers, concentrated on the need for conversion, but by 1830 he had broadened his focus to the responsibilities of Christians. Converts, he preached, did not escape life. Rather, they had a duty to begin new lives dedicated to "disinterested benevolence" and work for the attainment of God's kingdom on earth. Finney was not talking about Armageddon, as William Miller was, but rather of the prophecy embraced by Jonathan Edwards: that increasing righteousness would usher in a thousand-year reign of true Christianity that would culminate with Christ's return to earth. Finney's version of this optimistic, postmillennial eschatology was, however, less pietistic and less supernaturalist than Edwards's. Christians, he preached, might bring in the millennium if, with God's grace, they could rid the world of its "great and sore evils." In the revivalist excitement of the mid-1830s, he even preached that the millennium might come in just a few years if the churches did their duty.[48]

Finney published few sermons before 1835, and the accounts of his early revivals were based largely on rumor. But his Rochester revival of 1830–31, which attracted the religious press and clergymen from all over the region, was well enough documented to permit historians to reconstruct not just what he said and did but how he affected his audience. According to the historians Paul E. Johnson and Mary P. Ryan, he changed not just the spiritual life but also the politics and the social structure of the region.[49]

Built on the falls of the Genesee, just south of Lake Ontario, Rochester

had until 1823 been no more than a small market town. But with the arrival
of the Erie Canal linking the region with New York City, the Genesee Valley become almost overnight one of the greatest grain-growing regions
in the world, and Rochester the first inland boomtown. Rochester milled
and exported Genesee wheat and became a center of manufacturing, producing everything from guns to furniture.

The established merchants and manufacturers had run their shops as
extensions of their own patriarchal households, but by 1830 their small
businesses had become commercial operations with a workforce of un-
attached young men who lived in boardinghouses and drank, caroused,
and brawled as they pleased. Alarmed by the disorder among their workers, the manufacturers pressed for temperance legislation, but with the
extension of the franchise to men without property, the city fathers no
longer controlled the town government. At the same time conflicts over
issues such as whether Sabbath observance should extend to prohibiting
the Sunday mail rent the churches, setting clergymen against each other
and wealthy laymen against their own ministers. To many it seemed that
that the town had become ungovernable.[50]

At the invitation of local ministers Finney arrived in September 1830,
and for the next six months he preached at a Presbyterian church almost
every night and three times on Sunday. On weekdays, he and other ministers held prayer meetings, while his wife, Lydia, and other evangelical
women counseled families and prayed with women in their homes. According to Johnson, the revival began among church members and spread
to their family members and friends. People of all denominations came
to hear Finney, and soon the church services were so crowded that people prayed out in the snow. By the spring, the churches had gathered in
hundreds of converts—six hundred for the three Presbyterian churches
alone—and sympathetic revivals were breaking out across New York and
New England. A temperance crusade led by Finney's protégé, Theodore
Weld, had merchants smashing their barrels of whiskey and letting thousands of gallons flow down the streets and into the Erie Canal. Sectarian
divisions were forgotten, as were the old conflicts. Lawyers, merchants,
manufacturers, master craftsmen, and their wives were welded into an
evangelical community that subsequently converted most of the working-

men of the town. Then, as Ryan tells us, in the wake of such revivals, men and women formed voluntary associations to discourage vice, to care for the poor, and to help women bring up their children. Temperance was largely observed, and eighteenth-century patriarchal households turned into nineteenth-century middle-class homes.[51]

According to Johnson, the transformation owed much to Finney's "new measures." The revival was quieter than those in Rome and Utica, but as always with Finney, it involved emotional group prayer. In church services and daytime meetings, ministers prayed out loud, others joined in, and often people broke into tears, confessed their sins, and blessed the Lord. Instituting one new measure, Finney put those on the verge of conversion on an "anxious bench" in the front of the church, where the whole congregation could see them when they felt the spirit and stepped forward. Prayer and conversion thus became public, intensely social events, where men and women expressed their deepest feelings before a crowd. After people had humbly asked for mercy and watched many others do the same, they found a new sense of trust in one another. Family ties were strengthened, enemies made up, and strangers found a sense of community.[52]

It was Finney's message that showed the direction of change. In the context of a society in which traditional patriarchal rule was disintegrating, his insistence that every person had "the power and liberty of choice" was doubly liberating. It pointed to a spiritual democracy in which all people—employers and workers—were equally capable of controlling their own lives. It also pointed to a spiritual equality between the sexes. Women of the period had no legal rights in a marriage, but Finney gave them the same moral authority as men. Then, too, his concept of original sin meant that children were not depraved beings whose will had to be broken, but innocents to be nurtured and educated. Further, Finney preached that everyone, not just the ministers and magistrates, bore responsibility for the society. Piety and personal morality were not enough: Christians had to prove "useful in the highest degree possible" in advancing God's kingdom.[53]

By the time of the Rochester revival Finney had already begun to preach in the major cities of the East Coast. In the space of four years,

1828–32, he held protracted revivals in Wilmington, Philadelphia, New York, Providence, and Boston, as well as in towns of western New York. In all those cities, his message of a democratic Christianity and the building of God's kingdom resonated with laymen and the less conservative clergy, but in New York he found partners, men with the power to effect social reform at a national level. His hosts in the city were not clergymen but rather a group of businessmen who were prospering in the rapidly expanding economy. Transplanted New Englanders, ambivalent about their new wealth, these men contributed generously to the benevolent associations Beecher had helped establish, and under the leadership of two silk merchants, Arthur and Lewis Tappan, they were in the process of building a veritable empire of benevolence in New York. Finney urged them on to greater efforts of philanthropy. "The world is full of poverty, desolation, and death; hundreds of millions are perishing, body and soul," he preached. "God calls on you to exert yourself as his steward, for their salvation; to use all the property in your possession, so as to promote the greatest possible amount of happiness among your fellow-creatures."[54] Inspired, the Tappans and their friends formally engaged to give away all their profits, putting aside only what they needed to support their families. In the early 1830s they took up a series of new causes, among them the establishment of manual labor colleges in the West, and the abolition of slavery.[55]

Finney had spoken out against slavery since he first arrived in New York. Northern evangelicals commonly regarded slaveholding as a sin, but by 1830 the importance of the cotton trade to the northern port cities made many established preachers reluctant to condemn it. In New York alone, some seven thousand southern merchants, most of them slave owners, had taken up residence, and were generally welcomed by northern merchants and bankers with growing markets in the South. But Finney preached against slavery in vivid terms, calling for an end to "this great national sin," and refused to give communion to slaveholders. The Tappans, for their part, took up the cause with a passion. In 1833, just after the British Parliament outlawed slavery in the West Indies, they founded the New York Society for the Abolition of Slavery at the tabernacle they had built for Finney, while mobs gathered outside and threatened to burn the church down. Two months later the American Anti-Slavery Society was formed with Arthur Tappan as its president and its headquarters in New York.[56]

The national society included groups in other cities, notably William Lloyd Garrison's New England Anti-Slavery Society in Boston, but the New York society contributed most of the funds and, almost on its own, created a mass base for abolitionism. Garrison, a crusading young journalist, published a newspaper, *The Liberator*, which stirred up the South with harsh denunciations of slaveholders and calls for immediate emancipation. But his influence in the North was limited. He never dealt with the problems "immediate emancipation" would create for black or white southerners, and, as time went on, he diluted his message—and infuriated the New England clergy—with an equally passionate advocacy of feminism, pacifism, and anarchism. The New Yorkers were more practical. They called for the immediate beginning of a gradual emancipation process, and they focused on swaying public opinion. They, too, distributed a newspaper, *The Emancipator*, and antislavery tracts, but they soon realized that working directly with church communities was far more effective, and through Finney they found a cadre of field-workers and a leader in Theodore Weld.[57]

A convert of Finney's and a ministerial student, Weld had a keen intelligence and a gift for persuasive oratory. He had become a passionate opponent of slavery after traveling across the South. The Tappans had enlisted him to find a site for a seminary in the West, and in 1832 they chose Lane, a fledgling college in Cincinnati. Weld enrolled along with Henry Stanton and forty other students, most of them Finney converts from western New York. He soon persuaded his fellow students to form an antislavery society and to teach literacy to the impoverished freedmen of the city, but the Lane trustees, most of them local businessmen, refused to allow such activities. Weld and his classmates quit the seminary in protest, and he and Stanton signed on as traveling agents for the American Anti-Slavery Society. In the fall of 1835, he lectured on abolition at Oberlin, a struggling manual labor college, taken up by the Tappan brothers, where most of the Lane rebels had repaired. Some thirty students joined the cause and for two years constituted most of the field staff of the national society. Weld later recruited forty more agents, most of them ministers or ministerial students.[58]

In the next two years Weld campaigned for abolition across Ohio, Vermont, western Pennsylvania, and western New York, while Stanton labored in Rhode Island and Connecticut. Regarding abolition as a moral issue, Weld used Finney's evangelical language and many of his revival measures. In the towns he visited, he stayed for weeks, lecturing for two to five hours each night and persuading local converts to visit their friends in the daytime. Often mobs greeted him with a barrage of eggs, snowballs, or stones, but generally after a couple of days the disturbances stopped and his audiences grew. At the last meeting, he would ask all those who had made a decision for abolition to stand up, and often the entire audience stood. As in the case of Finney's revivals, the enthusiasm spread to neighboring towns. In 1837, Weld's voice gave out, but that year the national antislavery society in New York counted a thousand local societies in the North, most of them in the regions where Weld and Stanton had worked. Abolitionism had become a self-propagating mass movement, one that every year sent wagonloads of petitions to Congress.[59]

Finney, for his part, looked askance at the movement he had inspired. Slavery, he believed, was the national evil that cried out the loudest for reform, yet the abolitionists, he felt, were making a serious mistake by focusing exclusively on antislavery agitation. Slaveholding was, after all, a sin, and, like other sins, it should be addressed in a religious context. In Finney's view, the churches were abetting slavery by their silence, but if Christians of all denominations came forward and "meekly but firmly" branded slavery evil, "a public sentiment would be formed that would carry all before it." Otherwise, he predicted, the nation would be caught up in ideological strife. In July 1836, he wrote Weld asking if he did not fear that "we are in our present course going fast into a civil war." Abolition, he argued, should be made "an appendage of a general revival of religion . . . just as we made temperance an appendage of the Rochester revival." He feared, he wrote, "that no other form of carrying this question will save our country or the liberty or the soul of the slave." But he could not convince Weld or the Tappan brothers.[60]

Finney was sorry to see Weld and his classmates quit their ministerial training, in particular because in 1835 he accepted a professorship at Oberlin. One of his ambitions was to train "a new race of ministers—" the college needed his help, and he needed a less taxing schedule. He had contracted cholera in New York during the epidemic of 1832 and had still not recovered from the effects of the cure. The arrangement was that he would also preach in New York for several months of the year, but his health was not up to the task. In later years, after he had regained his strength, he spent long periods away from the college preaching revivals in the East and in England and Scotland, but for the time being he settled in at Oberlin to teach theology, to write, and to pastor its church.[61]

Thanks to Finney's celebrity, Oberlin grew apace, and under his influence it became a center of progressive evangelical Christianity. To ensure that the Lane disaster was not repeated, Finney had made two conditions for his employment: that the trustees should not interfere with the internal regulation of the school and that black students should be accepted on the same basis as whites. In practice, not many black students applied, but the school became a force in the Ohio antislavery movement and hub on the Underground Railroad. Then, too, in 1834, Oberlin had opened its doors to women and became the first coeducational college in the country. The school naturally attracted idealistic students and teachers. In its 1839 statement of principles, the faculty declared that its commitments included "a recognition of equal human rights as belonging to all . . . deep sympathy with the oppressed of every color," and "a consecration of life to the well-being of suffering humanity."[62] Academic freedom was another commitment. Students and faculty debated all the public issues of the day, and in classes students were encouraged to think for themselves, to challenge received wisdom and defend their views in oral arguments. Finney believed the Socratic method of teaching valuable, and not just for students. He himself, he wrote, not infrequently got "useful instruction" from the "learning and sagacity and talent" of his students. But then to Finney theology was not a study of fixed ideas but a process of discovery.[63]

Oberlin was primarily a religious college, and almost every year waves of revival passed through it, during which the whole community observed days of fasting, prayer, and introspection about how to live a more Christian life. After a particularly intense revival in 1836, Oberlin's president

Asa Mahan, Finney, and a few other faculty members came to the view that the converted could attain a higher level of sanctification. Through complete faith in Christ, believers could receive a second blessing of the Holy Spirit and attain Christian perfection. The doctrine, known as perfectionism, had originated with John Wesley, but Finney thought Wesley too much concerned with sensibility, or states of feeling, and not enough with moral responsibility. To him, sanctification meant "a higher and more stable form of the Christian life" in which Christians lived in perfect obedience to God's law and devoted themselves completely to loving God and their neighbors. His version of perfectionism had nothing to do with that of the antinomian John Humphrey Noyes, who had declared himself without sin. In Finney's view all Christians, even sanctified ones, were subject to temptation, to backsliding, and even to losing their salvation. All he was really proposing was that Christians could grow in their faith and act more as Christ would have them. Still, the doctrine scandalized many Congregationalist and Presbyterian ministers, for Finney and his colleagues were taking yet another step away from Calvinist teachings on human depravity. Even some of Finney's friends in New York state denounced sanctification as a dangerous error, and the Ohio Synod shunned the college.[64]

Yet, as always, Finney was speaking to the needs of many believers. During the revivals of the 1840s, perfectionism spread through many evangelical denominations and to New York, the Middle West, and eventually to England and Scotland. In their work on the frontiers, the Methodist circuit riders had largely neglected the doctrine, but now groups of Methodists in cities and towns preached the second blessing, along with Oberlin preachers. To some disciples, sanctification involved an intense inner struggle for an experience of union with God and a withdrawal from worldly affairs. But to many evangelicals, like those at Oberlin, it meant a call to further ethical seriousness and a belief in God's immanence and His readiness to transform the present world through the Holy Spirit. According to Timothy L. Smith and other historians, the fervor for Christian perfection brought enthusiasm for social reform to a new height.[65]

From the 1830s until the Civil War, northern evangelical Protestants—Methodists and Baptists as well as Congregationalists and New School

Presbyterians—undertook a large array of social reform efforts. They built asylums, schools for the deaf and dumb, hospitals for the tubercular; they reformed the penal system and the prisons. In the 1840s and '50s city churches and interdenominational organizations turned their attentions from simple evangelism to serving the needs of new immigrants and the native poor. Chapters of the Home Missionary and Tract Societies built mission churches and Sunday schools, offered help with job placement, and distributed food, clothing, and money. In Philadelphia, five thousand volunteers from churches and charitable societies divided the city into sections for systematic visitation and the relief of every indigent home. In New York, a Methodist minister with help from low church, or more evangelical Episcopalians, built an early type of a settlement house with schoolrooms, shops, living quarters, and a chapel.[66]

Temperance was a major evangelical concern, and as the movement grew it branched out into dietary and other health reform movements. Early-nineteenth-century Americans drank prodigiously—perhaps four times as much as Americans do today—and those who could afford it ate vast quantities of meat, often five or six types of flesh in a sitting. City people rarely exercised, and the bathtub was not yet an American fixture. Many distinguished doctors recommended changes in personal habits, but it took evangelical preachers—among them, Dr. Sylvester Graham, the promoter of an unappetizing diet of unseasoned vegetables, cereals, and bread made out of unbolted whole wheat flour—to rouse general interest in a healthy eating, exercise, and bathing.[67]

Educational reform was another evangelical priority. In the 1830s, Finnyite ministers in upstate New York began a campaign to improve the common schools with better-trained teachers, better equipment, and a more extensive curriculum. They and others, principally Horace Mann and Lyman's daughter, Catherine Beecher, called for the abandonment of rote learning and of corporal punishment to instill discipline. Later, Mann, a legislator and head of the Massachusetts Board of Education, brought European educational methods to the United States and designed what became the American public school system. The content of instruction quite naturally became evangelical Protestant.

At Oberlin, and in other quarters, millennial and perfectionist zeal extended to international affairs. In 1828, evangelicals formed the American Peace Society, a movement that included pacifists and those who believed that war could be justified only if the cause and the methods employed accorded with a higher moral law. During the 1840s, the American Society and its English counterpart convened international conferences on the Continent, attracting such eminent figures as Victor Hugo to discuss ways of reducing international tensions. These conferences were mostly talk—and war between the United States and Europe was not a threat at the time—but the Americans at least were entirely serious about state-sponsored violence. In 1838, Baptist missionaries and Finnyite evangelicals had protested the forcible expulsion of the Cherokee from Georgia. In 1846, the peace groups condemned the war with Mexico as an unjustifiable war of aggression.[68]

The women's rights movement that came to life in the late 1840s was not an evangelical enterprise. Few ministers supported the movement, and even the Oberlin faculty did not advocate legal rights for women. Still, the feminist movement owed much to the evangelical revivals. Finney had, after all, insisted on the liberty and power of every individual. He and his fellow preachers had encouraged women to speak in public and to take an active role in their communities. In many of the benevolent societies that emerged from the revivals women outnumbered men. Then, too, abolitionism led logically to the idea of equal rights for women. Most of the leading feminists—Elizabeth Cady Stanton, Susan B. Anthony, Lucretia Mott, the Grimké sisters, Lucy Stone, and Antoinette Brown Blackwell—started out as antislavery activists. Some, like Anthony and Mott, had worked with Garrison; others had close ties to Finney and his converts. Elizabeth Cady married Henry Stanton and Angelina Grimké married Theodore Weld; Stone and Blackwell were Oberlin graduates. As Robert Fletcher, a twentieth-century president of Oberlin, wrote of the antebellum faculty, "They seemed to have failed entirely to realize that education would open to women the way to all the other privileges hitherto the property of the male."[69]

By 1840, the antislavery movement had grown to include Methodists, Baptists, and Unitarians, but it was divided. Under the influence of John Humphrey Noyes, Garrison called upon Christians to come out of churches that permitted the existence of slavery and to renounce their allegiance to the violent and coercive government of the United States. Evangelical ministers in the movement were united in their opposition to Garrison's "come-outism," and most of them thought it proper to engage in the political process. Still, they differed on tactics. Should they create an abolitionist party, or make common cause with politicians who simply opposed the extension of slavery to the West? Could violence be justified to free the slaves, and was the Union to be sacrificed for the cause of emancipation? The antislavery preachers did not agree on all issues, but together they provided a powerful force for emancipation as a moral imperative. In 1846 Finney spoke to the argument that slavery was a lesser evil than the division of the Union. "A nation," he wrote, "who have drawn the sword and bathed it in blood in defence of the principle that all men have an inalienable right to liberty; that they are born free and equal. Such a nation . . . standing with its proud foot on the neck of three millions of crushed and prostrate slaves! O horrible! This less an evil to the world than emancipation or even than the dismemberment of our hypocritical union! O shame, where is thy blush!"[70] Finney, needless to say, supported the war when it came.

2

EVANGELICALS NORTH *and* SOUTH

THESE DAYS it has become common for evangelical leaders attempting to move the agenda beyond opposition to abortion and gay rights to urge evangelicals to reclaim their nineteenth-century heritage of social reform. Their effort to create a usable past for their own reformist projects rests on the commonly held idea—one found in history textbooks as well as in the works of many eminent historians—that the Second Great Awakening not only made evangelical Protestantism the dominant religion in the country but that it created a Protestant consensus that set the cultural and social agenda for the rest of the century.

Only at the beginning of the twentieth century—so this history goes—did the Protestant consensus fall apart over modernist thinking and the Social Gospel, dividing evangelicals from liberal Protestants.

There is some truth to this account, but the nineteenth-century consensus went only so far. The Union troops marching to war singing "The Battle Hymn of the Republic" could have testified to its limits. The issue of slavery split the three major evangelical denominations, and in 1845 the Methodists and the Baptists formally divided along regional lines because of it. Clearly, not all evangelicals were followers of Beecher and Finney. But that was not the end of their differences. As Donald G. Mathews, Samuel S. Hill, and other historians of the South have shown, evangelicalism developed so differently in the two regions of the country that even by the 1830s northern and southern evangelicals did not agree on such fundamental issues as the role of the church in society. Further, their religious beliefs and practices had diverged to the point where the southern clergy could claim that the South was the only Christian part of the country. Many, but not all, of these differences arose because of the division over slavery.

In the two decades after the American Revolution, the Methodists, Baptists, and Presbyterians opposed slavery. The Methodists, who made the most vigorous and successful efforts to convert enslaved Africans, were the most adamant in their opposition.[1] The Wesleyans had always preached to the poor and the oppressed; both John Wesley and Francis Asbury were influenced by the Quakers, who since the mid-eighteenth century had given emancipation a prominent place their moral agenda and had succeeded in persuading their members to manumit their slaves. Then, too, in the wake of the American Revolution, Methodists seemed infected by the spirit of liberty. In 1780 the Methodist General Conference of preachers determined—in language reminiscent of the Declaration of Independence—that slavery was "contrary to the laws of God, man and nature, and hurtful to society," as well as "contrary to the dictates of conscience and pure religion."[2] The preachers ordered their circuit riders to free their slaves and urged all Methodists to do the same. In 1784, they went further and promised to excommunicate all Methodists who did not free their slaves within two years. This, as it turned out, was going too far. The order created such dissension among the southern laity that it threatened to destroy the nascent church, and six months later it was rescinded. Still, the circuit riders continued to preach against slavery and to exhort slaveholding Methodists to do their Christian duty and free their fellow human beings.[3]

Yet exhort as they might, the circuit riders, and those southern Baptist and Presbyterian preachers who joined them in the effort, failed to convince their flocks that slavery was an evil that had to be extirpated. Instead of decreasing, as was generally expected, the number of slaves in the South increased rapidly with the expansion of cotton cultivation. In 1812, the Methodist General Conference gave in to political expediency and allowed the local conferences to make their own regulations on slavery.[4] Four years later, it admitted, "Little can be done to abolish the practice so contrary to the principles of moral justice."[5] Rather than fight a losing battle, the younger generation of southern preachers turned their efforts to persuading slaveholders to improve conditions for their slaves—thus in effect sanctioning slavery. As Mathews points out, the evangelicals, unlike the Quakers, were intent on converting as many people as possible, and unwilling to make opposition to slavery a condition for salvation, they ended by embracing the slaveholding system. Then, and as their membership grew, they effectively became southern society.[6]

In the North, the antislavery movement grew rapidly after 1830, and southern evangelicals soon felt themselves under assault. Garrison and Finney associates flooded the South with pamphlets and used the language of evangelicalism to condemn slaveholding and to preach the duty of emancipation. Some northern ministers called upon their denominational agencies to censure and excommunicate slaveholders; others, concerned about a rift in the church, tried to defend their southern brethren but could never go as far as the southerners wanted by absolving slaveholders of a grievous sin. Forced to defend their own moral standards, the southern clergy came up with new arguments. Slavery, they claimed, was a civil institution outside the scope of the church. Slavery was biblical: the God of the Old Testament sanctioned it for the Hebrews, and the apostle Paul recognized its existence in Roman society and did not denounce it. Slavery was necessary to the economy of the South. It was a burden to the white man but necessary to prevent insurrection and anarchy. As the abolitionists noted, every new argument brought them closer to the position that slavery was a positive good.[7]

The controversy within the denominations went on for more than a decade. It came to a head in 1844, when the Methodist General Conference excommunicated a southern bishop who held slaves, and when the Baptist General Convention declared it would not instate any missionary not pledged to emancipation. The following year, the southern Baptists and Methodists—with a combined total of three million members—broke away from their denominations, the Methodists to form the Methodist Episcopal Church, South, and the Baptists to form the Southern Baptist Convention. Now freed from the need to conciliate their confreres, southern evangelicals mounted a comprehensive defense of slavery based squarely on the idea of racial inequality.[8]

The southern evangelical shift from emancipationism to a defense of slavery had consequences beyond the matter at hand. In the first two decades of the nineteenth century, southern evangelicals had launched a variety of reform movements, among them the abolition of imprisonment for debt, the amelioration of prison conditions, and the expansion of suffrage. But the reform movements all lost momentum before reaching their goals. In defending slavery against hostile northern opinion, southerners began to regard the advocacy of any kind of reform as potentially threatening. As they saw it, to open any facet of the social order to challenge might bring slavery into question. Their reasoning, as the historian Carl Degler noted, was not wholly paranoid. After all, if they looked north, they could plainly see that those active on behalf of women's rights, or any of the other reform movements of the day, also had antislavery opinions.[9]

Then, as the rejection of emancipation led to the rejection of all social reform, the claim that slavery was a civil institution outside the scope of the church led to a comprehensive doctrine known as "the spirituality of the Church." Advanced by Presbyterian thinkers, but generally accepted by southern evangelicals, the doctrine held that "the Church, as an order of grace, was permitted no official involvement in the social reform of the state, an order merely of justice." This doctrine of ecclesiastical separation from social and political affairs was certainly a defensive reaction to the slavery controversy, but it was also a reversion to type. Before the Revolution, the Presbyterians, Baptists, and Methodists, then small beleaguered sects in colonies ruled by Anglicans, had called upon their converts to withdraw themselves from "the world" to live within their own pure, separated Christian communities. In the early years of the nineteenth century, when evangelicals were gaining ascendance in the South and a part of a national movement was fired by reformist enthusiasms, they changed their approach. But the northern assaults on slavery in the 1830s seemed to revive their old sense of isolation and alienation. The South, as they figured it, was "the sacred community" and the North, "the world." Yet in the context of the South, the refusal of the evangelical churches to take any part in the "social reform of the state" was not, as it was in the eighteenth century, a defensive measure to protect a pure, saving remnant, but rather an abandonment of the prophetic role of the church and a means of preserving the social order they had helped to create.[10]

The doctrine of the "spirituality of the church" reigned in the South for the next 150 years. In practice, the churches never completely abstained from social involvement or even social reform—they agitated for temperance and for blue laws—but the doctrine was invoked whenever the churches did not wish to deal with "mere" issues of justice, such indeed as issues of racial justice.

In the antebellum period, the divergence between evangelicals in the two regions was not just in their attitude toward social reform, but in the way they defined the Christian life. In the North, perfectionism was widely taught; conversion propelled evangelicals into the work of building the Kingdom of God on earth, and optimism reigned.[11] Ironically, perhaps, the perfectionism of the great evangelist Finney diminished the importance of the conversion experience. As Samuel Hill tells us, the struggle with self gave way to a commitment to struggle for social reform and, as it did, even the experience seemed to change from a life-altering drama to a sense of renewal, more gradual in its operation. In Hill's view, there was nothing surprising about this. In Calvinist theology, God was always about the business of bringing the whole world—the individual, society, and nature—under His governance. The New England Puritans had never separated personal holiness from the work of building the Holy City. Thus, after years of intense focus on inner experience, the evangelical Congregationalists and Presbyterians were restoring the balance. Along with many Methodists and Baptists, they were also restoring what Hill calls "the standard three-dimensional approach" to religion, in which the ongoing life in the church was as basic as the entrance to it, and in which the Christian was always in the process of becoming a Christian. In sum, Hill writes, evangelicalism in the North was becoming less evangelical.[12]

In the South, the opposite occurred. Around 1830, many of the religious patterns established during the earlier frontier revivals solidified into orthodoxy. Evangelism—or the saving of individual souls—remained the overriding concern and was understood to be the main contribution of the church to society. Camp meeting revivals continued but as a predictable and orderly part of denominational activities. The conversion process, too, became more uniform and more controlled: voices, visions, and physical struggles with the Devil were rarely reported. Yet, stylized as it was, the conversion process remained an anguished private struggle with sin and guilt, and the experience the crux of an individual's religious life. In church meetings, it became common practice for members, even years after the fact, to give personal testimonies about how they came to convert, what the experience was like, and how it changed them. Conversion was a social act in that it entailed joining a church, abiding by its standards, and becoming a role model for others, but the society thus conceived was a small one. Morality, as the clergy preached it, had mainly to do with the individual's behavior in the context of family and church.

In matters of personal conduct, southern evangelicals held to the same puritanical standards as their northern counterparts, but they lacked their social ethic. As a theological matter, religion was seen primarily as a matter of the individual's relationship to God and to Christ as a personal savior.[13]

Paradoxically, this intensely individualistic, asocial religion created an extraordinary degree of social cohesion among white southerners. It helped, of course, that the South was in many ways a homogeneous region—largely rural, largely agricultural, and largely composed of small communities, where relationships were face-to-face. With its limited economy, it attracted few new northerner settlers and few immigrants from abroad. Its white inhabitants were almost uniformly of English, or Scots-Irish, descent, and by the 1830s it had no independent intellectual class. The Methodists, Baptists, and Presbyterians had built the schools and most of the colleges. They had also evangelized the region with such success that they had turned the South into a country where virtually everyone believed in the Bible and in personal salvation from sin—whether they were church members or not. The denominations had their differences, as over the issue of baptism, but on most matters of doctrine and religious practice, an evangelical consensus prevailed.[14] With the clergy focused on the task of evangelism, their doctrines received so little scrutiny that laypeople took them for granted: the Bible was an infallible guide in every situation, and the church taught what was written in it. Coming into contact with people who read the Bible differently, southerners, unconscious of their own scrim of interpretation, concluded that those others were not Christians. This popular evangelicalism, combined with a growing uniformity in attitudes toward slavery, helped create a strong sense of regional identity. By 1840, there was a South. There was also a southern religion—one that, in the relative isolation of the region, survived well into the twentieth century.[15]

Evangelicals never dominated the North in quite the same way. The North was, after all, not a region, as the South was, but simply the rest of the country, and in the decades before the Civil War it was beginning to industrialize, its cities were growing apace, and manufacturing and market towns were springing up across the Middle West. Immigration—mainly from Germany and Ireland but from other Northern European countries as well—was changing its ethnic composition. Evangelical Protestants made up the vast majority of the churchgoing population, but they had to share the space with a variety of new religious groups, some of them indigenous, like the Mormons and Adventists, some of them immigrants, like the Lutherans and the Roman Catholics. Not all of these were welcome—in particular not the Irish Catholics. There had been a few Catholics in America since the first settlements, but the Irish were not only Catholics but poor, and by the 1850s there were more than a million of them in the northern cities. The historic Protestant phobia about the Church of Rome reasserted itself in a virulent and paranoid form: the Catholics were spreading disease, crime, and corruption, and the pope—identified as the Whore of Babylon—was going to take over the country and destroy republicanism. A nativist movement, for some years embodied in the Know-Nothing Party, engaged in mob violence and desperately but unsuccessfully tried to restrict immigration. Yet northern Protestants had eventually to recognize that, whether they liked it or not, the Catholics, too, were a part of American society.

Then, too, the Second Great Awakening had a liberating effect on northern intellectuals and made the North even more religiously diverse. At Yale, Taylor and the others continued to work out their New School or New Light theology; traditional Calvinist theologians established themselves at Princeton; and from among the Unitarians in and around Harvard came Transcendentalism and the literary renaissance of Emerson, Thoreau, Hawthorne, Melville, and Whitman. The intellectual environment was open enough to admit even the most uncomfortable ideas from Europe. Beginning in the 1820s, northern religious scholars took up the historical and textual analysis of the Bible that German scholars had practiced since the mid-eighteenth century. By the 1840s, Theodore Parker, a Unitarian radical and an abolitionist, and Moses Stuart, a conservative Congregationalist who had studied with Timothy Dwight at Yale, had made this critical approach to the Scriptures so well known that even southern evangelicals had to react to it. (Realizing full well that such an approach undermined their defense of slavery, they denounced it and hardened their own literalist interpretation of the Scriptures.) Then, in the 1850s, Asa Briggs, a distinguished Harvard botanist, corresponded with Charles Darwin in England and provided him with information for his forthcoming work, *On the Origin of Species*. A devout Presbyterian, Briggs understood perfectly well what a challenge the theory of evolution would present to the Protestant clergy, and in later years he wrote extensively on how evolution might be reconciled with Christianity. In sum, most of the elements of what was later called "modernism" were already in place in the North before the Civil War.[16]

3

LIBERALS *and* CONSERVATIVES
in the POST-CIVIL WAR NORTH

The New Theology and the Social Gospel

The standard account of how liberal and conservative Protestants came to a parting of the ways goes in brief something like this: In the 1880s Darwinian evolution, modern Bible scholarship, and the problems of an industrializing society posed enormous challenges to traditional evangelical beliefs. Liberal clergymen adapted their theology to modern scientific thinking and proposed that Christians must concern themselves with structural reform of society. Conservatives, for their part, deplored what they saw as accommodation to secular culture and reasserted traditional evangelical beliefs in the authority of the Bible and in reform through the regeneration of individuals. The conflict between the two culminated in the fundamentalist-modernist controversies of the 1920s that split the northern Protestant denominations.

This account has its variations. Secular and mainline Protestant authors have stressed the failure of the conservatives to adapt to modernity, while evangelical authors have maintained that the liberals in their accommodation to the culture and their adoption of foreign ideas left true Christianity behind. Yet the difference between these two versions is not as great as the difference between both of them and the best scholarship on the subject by liberal and evangelical historians. To read, for example, Gary Dorrien's comprehensive history of the liberal Protestantism in the nineteenth century or George Marsden's groundbreaking book on the origins of fundamentalism is to see that the standard account is badly in need of revision.

Certainly liberals and conservatives came to different conclusions about biblical scholarship, Darwinian evolution, and social reform, but these issues were hardly the only ones that divided them. As Dorrien and Marsden have shown, the both sides had a much wider range of commitments, and on some of them their differences ran so deep as to make the two sides incomprehensible to each other. These differences evolved slowly over the second half of the nineteenth century, and, as Marsden has shown, it was not just the liberals who changed. The conservatives, though essentially traditionalist, also struggled with the issues of the period and came up with novel ideas, some of them also imported from abroad.

How could it have been otherwise? In the period between 1860 and 1920 the United States went through an economic and demographic upheaval. A largely agricultural nation when the Civil War broke out, it had by 1910 become the leading industrial and manufacturing power in the world, with 200,000 miles of railroads and steel production greater than that of Great Britain and Germany combined. In this period the population tripled, growing from 31.5 million in 1860 to 106 million in 1920, and the cities grew at an explosive rate. New York, Philadelphia, and other large East Coast cities more than doubled in size, while the population of Chicago and the newer midwestern cities multiplied many times over. The railroad terminals in the states to the west—such as Minneapolis, Kansas City, Omaha, Portland, and Seattle—went from villages to major metropolitan cities in the thirty years after the Civil War. By 1920 fifty percent of the American population lived in cities or towns, and the cities had become considerably more cosmopolitan. Between 1865 and 1920 over 28 million immigrants arrived in the United States. After 1890 most of the new arrivals came from Eastern and Southern Europe, and whereas their predecessors had largely been Protestants, they were for the most part Catholics, Greek Orthodox, or Jews. By 1910 the proportion of the foreign-born remained roughly what it had been a half a century earlier, but like the Irish before them, the new arrivals settled largely in the big cities; in the twelve largest cities the foreign-born made up some 40 percent of the population.[1]

In this period the American industrial revolution went into its second stage. In the 1870s most industrial firms were small enterprises manufacturing for local markets, but the railroads created a national market, and by the end of the century large corporations had established themselves in almost every industry, and the main industries—railroads, steel, and oil—were dominated by a few huge enterprises. Characterized by centralized, bureaucratic control of most phases of production and distribution, the corporations brought a new pace to technological innovation, mightily increased productivity, enhanced the national wealth, and brought prosperity to many Americans. But as they created, they also destroyed. Family farmers lost control of their produce to the railroads and the other middlemen, and small businesses were wiped out. Financial panics and depressions were now devastating because of their scale. Then, too, while vast fortunes were made by the small group of men who built the large corporations, few of the corporate gains were passed along to the industrial workers. In the years 1880–1910 unskilled laborers commonly earned less than $10 a week, and in 1900 some 70 percent of all industrial laborers worked ten hours or more a day, and many of them worked a six- or seven-day week. From the 1870s to the First World War labor and business waged an almost uninterrupted series of conflicts, many of which broke out into violence and some of them into pitched battles between workingmen and militias.[2]

What was happening to the country was hard for many Americans to grasp. Writing in 1905, Henry Adams said of his own education, "The American boy of 1854 stood nearer to the year 1 than the year 1900."[3]

In this period American Protestants built more churches than ever before and the percentage of churchgoers in the population increased substantially.[4] All the same, modernization meant that many Americans spent their workday lives in secular domains. The new industries, relentlessly rationalized to increase production, left no place for the myth, miracles, tradition, or even the ethics that came with face-to-face contacts between employers and employees. Adams's "virgin" steadily gave place to "the dynamo"—or to what religious historians have called "the disenchantment of the world." The production of knowledge was similarly disenchanted by an intellectual revolution that went far beyond Darwinian evolution. In 1850 most American colleges were evangelical schools where religion permeated all branches of knowledge, where Protestant ethics were explicitly taught, and where for scientists the chief reason to study nature was to glory in the marvels of God's design. By the end of the century, however, the best colleges had become universities based on a German model, where knowledge was divided into separate, specialized disciplines and where new standards of objectivity gradually squeezed the supernatural out of them, relegating religion to the divinity schools.[5]

American Protestants understandably came up with different responses to these enormous changes. The liberals strove to understand the new realities and to incorporate the new ways of thinking into their Christianity, hoping to create a third way between secular disbelief and what they saw as an intellectually and morally incredible orthodoxy. The conservatives, appalled by what they saw as liberal apostasy, gave their efforts to bolstering orthodox doctrines and in their way attempting to explain what was happening in this strange new world. The two parties evolved along separate tracks and did not come into direct conflict until the early twentieth century, but the evolution of fundamentalism cannot be understood apart from the development of liberal theology.

The Liberals

The liberal theology of the 1880s—known then as the New Theology—had no single author but was rather the work of several religious thinkers, Newton Smyth, Theodore Munger, and Washington Gladden the most important among them. All three were Congregationalists brought up on the New School theology. Munger had studied with Taylor at Yale in the 1850s; Gladden, who came from the district burned over by Finneyite revivals, attended Williams College in the 1850s; and Smyth, a decade younger, went to the conservative Andover seminary after serving in the Union army during the Civil War. All were pastors, as opposed to academic theologians: men in touch with the laity and less concerned with constructing a comprehensive theology than with inspiring their educated congregations to a renewal of faith.

According to the religious historian Gary Dorrien, their move toward a new theology began with their sense of frustration with what they felt was the sheer unreality of orthodox dogmatism, even in its Taylorite form. As mature men, they simply cast the old orthodoxies aside. In separate manifestos for a new theology, they rejected the central Calvinist doctrines, such as predestination, eternal punishment, and Christ's death as the atonement to God for the sin of Adam. God, they insisted, was perfectly just, moral, and loving—a good father to His children who had sent Christ to earth to serve as an example of ethical perfection. Humans, they preached, were not innately depraved but had the God-given power of reason and the ability to model themselves on Christ. What made a Christian, they taught, was the development of moral character. The heart of religion, Gladden maintained, is not its ritual forms, or dogmas, or the feelings it evoked, but its effects on personal character. "You become a Christian by choosing the Christian life and beginning immediately to do the duties which belong to it," he wrote.[6]

Such ideas, while hardly orthodox, had been preached by William Ellery Channing in the 1830s. The proponents of the New Theology did not go as far as the Unitarians in reorienting the philosophical tradition. Still, they rejected the epistemological basis of American Protestantism to that point. In this and in other matters, their guide was not a German philosopher but Horace Bushnell, a Congregationalist theologian of the previous generation.

A student of Nathaniel Taylor's and contemporary of Charles Finney's, Bushnell spent most of his career as pastor of a Congregationalist church in Hartford, Connecticut. A series of profound spiritual experiences led him to believe that "the very beauty and spirit of Christ himself" was available to all. In the 1840s he took the position that the clergy placed far too much emphasis on revivals—which in his view were too individualistic, episodic, and reductionist—and far too little on the nurturing of Christians within the institutional church. He was in many ways a conservative. His social views accorded with those of his genteel congregation, and as a believer in the superiority of Anglo-Saxon culture, he preached against slaveholding but not for equal rights for black Americans. He lived until 1876, but he refused to accept Darwinian evolution because of his belief that the supernatural was an active force in the world, and he never read the German higher criticism of the Bible. Yet his book *God in Christ*, published in 1849, challenged the way the American clergy of his day read the Bible and opened the door for them to the world of modern thought.[7]

In the 1830s, virtually all American theologians—Congregationalists, Presbyterians, and Unitarians alike—assumed theology to be a science whose aim was to produce exact formulations based on evidence. This way of thinking came from scholastic modes of argumentation and the methodology of the natural sciences in the seventeenth century. Generally, the Bible was thought to be a storehouse of facts and propositions and the task of theologians was to systematize these facts and to ascertain the general principles to be found in them. Theologians differed on how the authors of the Scriptures had received their revelations, but all, including the Unitarians, assumed that every passage in the Bible had only one meaning, and that all readers through history could understand it.

Bushnell's challenge to this whole way of thinking rested on the new science of philology and on Samuel Taylor Coleridge's ideas about the indeterminacy of language. Words are not thoughts, Bushnell proposed, but merely the signs by which thought is expressed. Even factual terms— like "dog" or "house"—are merely names of genera, not exact representations of particular things as they are observed. As for the words of "thought and spirit," such as "love," "sin," "salvation," and "justice," they are hopelessly fluid, endlessly various in their signification. Words don't translate thought from one mind to another, Bushnell wrote, but merely give hints or images of the thought. Further, language consists of symbols agreed upon by social groups, so the historical context of words are crucial to understanding them, and changing times require new definitions. Dogma-based theologians, he argued, ignore the instability of the abstractions they use and work out Christian systems that are consistent but false simply because of their consistency. As for the Bible, it is, he wrote, a cryptic text, necessarily so, because inspiration is just that and not the literal word of God. The authors of the Scriptures, the inspired witnesses to spiritual truths, could not convey these truths directly. Rather, like all good writers, they did their best by multiplying forms or figures, and by creating paradoxes and contradictions to give as many hints as they could to their inspiration. The Bible, he wrote, is "a vast literary work of the imagination," some of it poetry, most of it narrative, and all of it is best approached in the way that sensitive literary critics approach the rest of literature. Congregationalists and Unitarians alike, he charged, reduced its rich polyphony to singular propositions, but it offended piety and intelligence to claim that the meaning of God's self-expression in Christ could be captured in "a few dull propositions."[8]

Delivered first as a series of lectures at Harvard, Yale, and Andover, *God in Christ* outraged the clergy, left to right. Unitarians called Bushnell a Transcendentalist, Congregationalists charged him with leading a Unitarian attack on creeds, and Old School Presbyterians accused him of Socinianism, Sabellianism, Pelagianism, and every other heresy then on the books. His literal-minded clerical audiences found the work incomprehensible; he barely escaped a trial for heresy, and few read his later books. But Munger, Gladden, and other pastors of the next generation read Bushnell with new eyes. "He was a theologian as Copernicus was an astronomer," Munger wrote. "He changed the point of view, and thus . . . changed everything." His theory of language allowed them to accept the modern German scholarship of the Bible while continuing to read the Scriptures as revelation.[9]

Since the late eighteenth century German scholars had been analyzing the books of the Bible in the same way they examined other ancient texts. Using the new disciplines of philology, archaeology, anthropology, and literary analysis, they had attempted to answer such questions as when and where each book was written, who wrote it, how it compared to other books, and how it related to the other literature available at the time. (Julius Wellhausen, for example, found that the Pentateuch, the first five books of the Bible, was not written by Moses, as had been thought, but was edited versions of texts written by many different people over a long period of time.) This textual and source analysis, known as the higher criticism, had led to a whole new school of theology, whose founder, Fredrick

Daniel Ernst Schleiermacher, proposed that the proper subject of theology was human experience of the divine.[10]*

Before the Civil War, German theology and scholarship had come to the United States only indirectly, and even by the 1880s, the higher criticism had only a handful of American practitioners, and few in the clergy even knew what it was. As devotees of Bushnell, the proponents of the New Theology believed it was leading to a better understanding of the Bible, but as nonspecialists they made virtually no use of its findings in their works. The main lesson they took from it was that the Bible was best understood historically, as a record of God's continually unfolding revelation to living men, who interpreted it according to "the temper and habit of the age." Similarly, Christian doctrines developed over time reflecting the changing experience of men through the centuries. With Schleiermacher, they believed that the question of how to follow Christ was always somewhat new. What most called orthodoxy, Newton Smyth wrote, was "orthodoxism," a dogmatic stagnation, whereas true orthodoxy was "the continuous historical development of the doctrine of Jesus and His apostles" or "fidelity to the teachings of the Spirit of Truth throughout Christian history." Theology, Munger wrote, should not create an alien structure of abstractions but should immerse itself in the rich complexity of actual life. For Munger, Smyth, and Gladden this dynamic view of history and theology found confirmation in the modern natural sciences.[11]

In the 1870s and '80s many educated clergymen, including some of the younger Princeton conservatives, accepted Darwinian evolution, along with modern geology, as legitimate science. Calvinists had always believed that science revealed God's laws for the universe and that science and religion would always be compatible since the Truth was one. Following the lead of Asa Gray, many argued that accepting evolution did not entail accepting the atheistic naturalism that some interpreters of the theory, among them Thomas Huxley and Herbert Spencer, attributed to it. God, they argued, was involved in the whole process of creation, and the creation story in Genesis was the way the ancients had of conveying the truth

---

*Lower criticism was the study of extant Biblical texts, querying their dates, their settings, and their relationship to each other to determine which were the most reliable.

of a science they did not know. Further, they argued, evolutionary theory had its limits. The fact that humans evolved from lower creatures did not negate the fact of human uniqueness because it could not explain free will, the moral sense, religious feeling, or the mystery of personal identity.

Munger, Smyth, and Gladden made all of these arguments, but, unlike those who were simply attempting to reconcile the new science with Christian beliefs, they maintained that evolution served the interests of the living Christian faith. Evolution, Munger wrote, confirmed the Christian idea of the unity of creation. It also showed creation not as a single act of God in the distant past but an ongoing work in which God is always present. God, he wrote, "is immanent in all created things—immanent yet personal—the life of all lives, the power of all powers, the soul of the universe." If we shrink at linking humans with the material and animal worlds, he argued, "it is because we have as yet no proper conception of the close and interior relation of God to all his works." [12] There was, in other words, no dichotomy between the sacred and the secular realms. On the other hand, he made the Victorian distinction between nature and spirit, between the natural world, governed by instinct and necessity, and the human spirit, which in its relation to the spirit of God was free. Humans, he wrote, cannot be totally free because they must carry along some of their evolutionary inheritance, but they can move toward spiritual freedom and a closer relationship to God. To Munger evolution seemed to confirm the optimistic postmillennial vision of continuing moral progress, the triumph of the spirit over sinful nature, and the spread of righteousness. To Gladden it also seemed to show that human society was moving toward the Kingdom of God on earth in spite of its present-day ills. [13]

The Social Gospel

Politicians were slow to realize that the growth of industry after the Civil War had brought structural change to the economy and to much of American society. In his autobiography Theodore Roosevelt wrote of the period, "The power of the mighty industrial overlords . . . had increased with giant strides, while the methods of controlling them . . . through the Government, remained archaic and therefore practically impotent."[14] The clergy were just as slow to recognize the structural transformation. Washington Gladden did not in 1882, when he arrived in Columbus, Ohio, to pastor the First Congregational Church. But after a coal miners' strike that was crushed by the company whose top executives belonged to his congregation, he began to preach that the church had much to say about wealth, inequality, and labor. "We must," he said, "make men believe that Christianity has a right to rule this kingdom of industry, as well as all the other kingdoms of this world." His philosophy was that, just as individuals practiced the Golden Rule, so employers and their employees should practice cooperation and disagreements should be negotiated in a spirit of fellowship.

In an effort to mediate a strike in Cleveland in 1886 he endorsed trade unionism while condemning the warlike tactics of both sides. "Are you not all children of one Father?" he asked. His first strategy was to appeal to the moral feelings of the owners and business executives, but eventually realizing that altruism was possible only in small groups, he preached a decentralized economic democracy where profit sharing would substitute for wage labor. In the mid-1890s the deepening conflict between capital and labor drove him to a more realistic view of the economy and to an explicitly pro-union stance. He opposed socialism—or state ownership of most businesses—on the grounds that it would stifle creativity, but more important because it seemed to him far too grandiose a project for this enormous continent and one that would require an unimaginable degree of human wisdom to work. Still, he believed that the monopolies—in those days the railroads, the telephone services, the electrical and water supply companies that effectively taxed the public as opposed to responding to the laws of supply and demand—should eventually be state-controlled. And he came to believe that if the dream of a cooperative economy could be realized, it would be as a form of industrial democracy gained through union-organized collective bargaining.[15]

Gladden's views about the means of achieving a just society changed over time, but Gladden never had any doubt that social reform was an integral part of the Christian mission. "The vital and necessary relation of the individual to society lies at the basis of the Christian conception of life," he wrote. "Christianity would create a perfect society, and to this end it must produce perfect men; it would bring forth perfect men, and to this end it must construct a perfect society." Christ had prayed, "Thy Kingdom come, Thy will be done, on earth as it is in heaven."[16] With Christ's coming, Gladden preached, the Kingdom of God had broken through into nature and history. Enlarging its dominion had always been the work of Christianity, and because of Christ's ongoing presence in the world, much had been accomplished, but much remained to be done. The task of the church was, now as always, the regeneration of the social order as well as the regeneration of man, and that meant suffusing the institutions of society with the Christian spirit of truth and love.[17]

That in essence was the Social Gospel. Though later attacked by conservatives as something new and alien to Christianity, it grew out of Charles Finney's postmillennial vision of regenerate Christians building the Kingdom of God on earth. The connection was direct, for brought up in the burned-over district, Gladden had begun his career by preaching crude imitations of Finney's revivalist and abolitionist sermons.[18] Still, the Social Gospel was something new. Finney and his contemporaries had decried the extremes of wealth and poverty but failed to imagine that the cause could be anything but sin—like intemperance, or the lack of altruism. The antebellum reformers had made efforts to help the poor, but Gladden had come to see that the problem of poverty was systemic and that social injustice was inherent in the new structures of power that developed with industrialization and laissez-faire capitalism. Then, too, he came to the view that society—with all its institutions, laws, doctrines, customs, and sentiments—had power of its own. The Gospels, he acknowledged, were directed toward individuals, but society was the medium through which the individuals understood them. Thus, personal and social regeneration were inextricably linked and had to proceed in tandem.[19]

Many, but not all, theological liberals adopted the Social Gospel in the 1890s, and some of its proponents were theological conservatives, but their politics were those of the Progressive movement. While not all Progressives subscribed to it, the Social Gospel gave the movement its crusading evangelical spirit. Some of its leaders, such as Josiah Strong, also supported Theodore Roosevelt's imperial ventures on the grounds that the American mission was to spread democracy and Christianity to the ends of the world. Others did not. Walter Rauschenbusch, the movement's major theologian after the turn of the century, was of the peace party, as Gladden was. He called himself a socialist but, like Gladden, he believed in a decentralized market economy. His vision was of American liberal democracy extended into the economic sphere, but he had no blueprint for it, and he applauded Roosevelt's reforms. His stature in the movement came less from his policy prescriptions than from his evangelical piety and his use of modern scholarship on the New Testament to articulate the Social Gospel. Well aware of the growing fundamentalist movement, he maintained that Jesus in the course of His life abandoned the apocalyptic prophecies of the Jews under Roman tyranny for a faith that the Kingdom of God would come through growth and development, starting with something as small as a mustard seed.[20]

When Munger published his manifesto for the new theology in 1883, he claimed to be writing for a movement that was already in existence. That wasn't exactly the case, but in a sense he was right. Certainly Henry Ward Beecher, Lyman's son and the most popular minister of his day, had been preaching elements of the New Theology since the 1870s, and many Congregationalists of Munger's generation were reading Bushnell and some of the European modernists. Then, in the years that followed, the New Theology spread so rapidly as to suggest that the new views had been gathering for some time and the hold of the old orthodoxy was not as strong as it seemed. In the 1890s it gained adherents in the major Congregationalist and New School Presbyterian seminaries like Andover, Yale, Oberlin, and the Union Theological Seminary in New York City. In that decade, some two thousand Americans went off to German universities to acquire the tools of modern historical criticism. At the same time, the New Theology crossed into other denominations, and by the end of the century its leading practitioners included a Methodist at Boston University and Baptists at the University of Chicago's Divinity School.[21]

The result was a considerable diversity of views. Some theologians were more gospel centered, some more oriented to experience and more optimistic about human endeavors, but they had a general agreement on certain broad principles: God manifests Himself in history and therefore

Christianity had to be open to modern knowledge. Christianity was a quest, a life-religion, not an ironclad set of doctrines, and central to that quest was the eternal question of how best to follow the ethical example of Jesus. By the end of the century, liberal theologians had not resolved such theological issues as whether God had ever intervened directly in human affairs, as the biblical authors said He did. Nor had they resolved the more practical issue of Christianity's relationship to other religions, but in speaking of "the fatherhood of God and the brotherhood of man," they certainly meant that Christians should rise above sectarian differences to work for the good of the whole society.

The Conservative Reaction

"The Bible is absolutely infallible, without error in all matters pertaining to faith and practice, as well as in areas such as geography, science and history."

—Jerry Falwell, *Listen, America!*, 1980

"We believe that the world will not be converted during the present dispensation, but is fast ripening for judgment, while there will be a fearful apostasy in the professing Christian body; and hence that the Lord Jesus will come in person to introduce the millennial age, when Israel shall be restored to their own land, and the earth shall be full of the knowledge of the Lord; and that this personal and premillennial advent is the blessed hope set before us in the Gospel for which we should be constantly looking."

—Niagara Bible Conference creed, 1878[22]

The last quarter of the nineteenth century was a period of considerable theological creativity—and not just on the liberal side. From the conservatives came new defense of biblical authority, a new premillennial eschatology, and new Holiness doctrines. These innovations appeared in different groups and denominations, but as Dwight Moody, the great revivalist of the period, demonstrated, they had affinities with each other and with traditional Calvinist doctrines. Taken together, they formed a mirror image of the New Theology, their common attributes being an intense supernaturalism, a focus on individual salvation, and pessimism about the future of civilization. As much as the New Theology, they created a break between nineteenth- and twentieth-century American Protestantism. What was more, their doctrines proved more durable, for while liberal theology developed and changed over time, losing its millennialism and its Victorian character, these strains of antimodernist thinking remained largely intact in the twentieth century.

Among these doctrines, new and old, lie the roots of the major antimodernist movements of the early twentieth century. Fundamentalism was one of them, but not the only one.

In the decades after the Civil War, Methodist preachers set off a Holiness revival movement across the nation. At camp meetings its evangelists preached a version of the Wesleyan doctrine that regenerate Christians could with sufficient piety receive a second blessing from the Holy Spirit and become sanctified, or free from sin. Most of antebellum Holiness preachers had—with the Oberlin perfectionists—taught sanctification as a gradual process and put the stress on Christian growth and social reform. The camp meeting revivalists, however, took what had been a minority position: that the second blessing was a sudden descent of the Holy Spirit that gave believers the power to conquer sin. The national organizers hoped to channel converts into the Methodist churches, just as the early-nineteenth-century revivalists had done. But as time went on, local interdenominational Holiness associations sprang up, and so did independent Holiness evangelists who preached divine healing and encouraged ecstatic worship practices the Methodists found unseemly. The organizers could not control these preachers, and gradually it became clear that what they were facing was a populist reaction against institutionalized, middle-class Methodism: the churches with their pipe organs, their well-dressed church-on-Sunday congregations, and their seminary-educated clergy. Taking their gospel to the poor, the Holiness preachers gathered independent congregations in the South, the border states, and the West.

During the 1890s, many of these congregations seceded, or were expelled, from the Methodist Church, and in the next decade a number coalesced into denominations, among them the Pilgrim Holiness Church and the Church of the Nazarene.[23]

In the meantime the movement developed a more radical wing, known as Pentecostalism for its distinctive doctrine that all the gifts of the Holy Spirit are as available to believers today as they were to the apostles at the time of Pentecost. For Pentecostals, glossolalia, or speaking in tongues, is a sign that the Holy Spirit has entered the life of a believer and that other gifts, like divine healing and prophesying, may follow. The first mass outbreak of tongue-speaking occurred in Los Angeles in 1906 at the Azusa Street Mission, a poor inner-city church with black and white congregants. Word of this phenomenon circulated in Holiness circles, and before long Pentecostalism was spreading across the country into black and white churches, making converts out of Baptists as well as Methodists. Holiness and Pentecostal ministers differed over glossolalia, but both demanded an extreme asceticism and the separation of Christians from the politics and culture of the ungodly world. Christ, they taught, would soon come to destroy the earth and establish His righteous kingdom.[24]

Still, as the standard histories indicate, fundamentalism was by far the most significant antimodernist movement of the period. Its ministers were the only ones to take on liberal theology directly, and in the 1920s they and influential laymen, such as William Jennings Bryan, made a concerted effort to purge the churches of what they saw as modernist apostasies. The conflict was local—fought out mainly within the northern Presbyterian and Baptist denominations—but it affected all of American Protestantism, creating the breach that exists today between liberal, or mainline, churches and conservative, or evangelical, churches. It was also the watershed of twentieth-century evangelicalism.

The term "fundamentalist" was coined in 1920 by Curtis Lee Laws, the editor of a conservative Baptist paper who was calling for the formation of a "General Conference on the Fundamentals" within his denomination to protest the incursions of liberal theology. But the fundamentalist movement took shape in the nineteenth century and emerged in the early years of the twentieth. In *The Roots of Fundamentalism*, the historian

Ernest R. Sandeen located its origins in the millenarian movement that flourished at Bible and prophecy conferences of the last quarter of the nineteenth century. Later George Marsden in his masterful study *Fundamentalism and American Culture* showed that the fundamentalism of the 1920s was a broader movement with antecedents in traditional Calvinism and in conservative revivalism, as well as in millenarianism. The trait, he wrote, that distinguished fundamentalists from other conservatives was the militancy of their antimodernism.[25]

The architects of fundamentalism were not, as often imagined, rural southerners but, to the contrary, well-educated northern ministers, most of whom preached in high-steepled urban churches. The photographs of ministers such as A. J. Gordon and Reuben A. Torrey show men in three-piece black suits and wing collars with neatly trimmed beards and mustaches in the fashion of the day. Like the early liberal theologians, virtually all were Congregationalists, Presbyterians, or Baptists—heirs to the intellectual Calvinist tradition. And, like the liberals, they drew upon European ideas to construct a new theological amalgam in the intellectual crucible of the North.

The makers of fundamentalism were not simply conservatives. All the same, they were immersed in ideas and ways of thinking that the liberals had put behind them. As Marsden has shown, their differences with the liberals were not just doctrinal but deeply philosophical. The two stood on opposite sides of an intellectual revolution—or in the terminology of Thomas Kuhn, a paradigm shift. That is, the two had different ways of understanding science, history, and, most profoundly, the nature of the truth. These older ways of thinking are clearly not just a matter of historical interest, for perhaps half of evangelicals continue to reject Darwinian evolution and to claim, as Falwell did, that the Bible is infallible in matters of geography, science, and history as well as in those of faith and practice. Many Americans today consider these beliefs irrational, and perhaps understandably, for over time the rational philosophical structure that lay beneath them has been forgotten, leaving only a superstructure of beliefs and attitudes. The architects of fundamentalism were, however, well-educated clergymen who articulated their theology and its underlying philosophy precisely. Among the most influential of them were the scholars at the Princeton Theological Seminary.

Princeton Theological Seminary

In 1820 William Channing, noting the defection of Yale, had declared the old Calvinist orthodoxy dead, but the verdict was premature, for the old orthodoxy remained a living tradition within the Presbyterian Church. New England Presbyterians adopted Taylor's New School theology, along with the Congregationalists, but most of the Scots and Scots-Irish Presbyterians of the Middle States and the South remained faithful to the Westminster Confession of 1647 and the elaborate catechisms associated with it. New School versus Old School disputes rent the church for years, and even after the Civil War began, split the church into northern and southern denominations, Old and New School disputes continued within the northern denomination. The intellectual center for these Old School Presbyterians was the Princeton Theological Seminary, founded by the General Assembly in 1812. Charles Hodge, its reigning theologian for over half a century, made it the seminary's mission to defend the historic faith against all error. In the *Biblical Repertory and Princeton Review*, a journal he edited for over forty years, he and his colleagues dissected the deviations of other theologians and condemned the heresies that seemed to spring up like dragons' teeth in other seminaries. In the 1830s and '40s, they denounced the New School Presbyterians both for their free will doctrines and for their promotion of revivals and interdenominational reform societies that in their view undermined the institutional church. Later they and their successors denounced Bushnell's theology, Oberlin perfectionism, and the higher criticism of the Bible. While they did not claim to have stemmed the tide of error, they did claim that the Calvinism of the Reformation had been preserved without flaw at Princeton. "I am not afraid to say that a new idea never originated in this Seminary," Hodge declared toward the end of his career.[26] At the centennial of the seminary in 1912 its president, Francis L. Patton, declared that Princeton "simply taught the old Calvinistic Theology without modification; and she made obstinate resistance to the modifications proposed elsewhere . . . Princeton's boast, if she had reason to boast at all, is her unswerving fidelity to the theology of the Reformation."[27]

In practice, Princeton theology came only indirectly from the Reformation, and the seminary produced at least one significant new idea. All the same, what the seminary taught in 1912—or 1920—was not that different from what it had taught a century before. The intellectual consistency owed in large part to Hodge's long career and to the dynasty he established. Born in Philadelphia in 1797, Hodge was just three years younger than Finney and five years older than Bushnell. A professor of theology at the seminary from 1822 to his death in 1878, and its principal for a quarter of a century, he educated three generations of students and developed a systematic theology for the school. His oldest son, A. A. Hodge, succeeded him in his prestigious chair in Didactic and Polemic Theology, and on his death in 1887 he was in turn succeeded by Charles's faithful student, B. B. Warfield, who held the chair until 1920. All three were prolific writers, the editors of prestigious journals, and influential figures in the Presbyterian Church. Together they brought seventeenth- and eighteenth-century thinking into the twentieth century.

In the early nineteenth century, both Old and New School seminaries were influenced by post-Reformation doctrines and ways of thinking, but Hodge and his Princeton colleagues drew their theology directly from the seventeenth-century scholastic Francis Turretin, whose three-volume *Institutes* was the textbook used at Princeton until Hodge's own *Systematic Theology* was published in 1871–72. Turretin had systematized Calvinism in the period of the Counter-Reformation, and, like many other Protestant scholars of the period, he had adopted the rationalistic approach of his Catholic critics, the better to defend the new faith. In the previous century Luther and Calvin had in the tradition of Augustine given priority to faith over reason. They looked to the Bible for its divine wisdom, but believed, as Calvin asserted, that the witness of the Holy Spirit was the ultimate ground of faith. But the seventeenth-century scholastics, in the tradition of Aquinas, required external evidence for the truth of Christianity— evidence that for Protestants existed in the Bible alone. Theology was for them the highest of the sciences, and dialectics the method of reaching the truth.[28]

Hodge and his colleagues grounded their theology in a strand of post-Enlightenment thinking known as Common Sense Realism. A Scottish school of philosophy developed by the eighteenth-century scholar Thomas Reid, Common Sense Realism dominated American philosophical thinking in the early nineteenth century, but the Princeton seminary's allegiance to it was particularly strong. It was brought to Princeton directly by John Witherspoon, the Scots clergyman who served as the president of the college just before the Revolution. James McCosh, the Scotsman who became the president of the college in 1868, was the last important American exponent of the Scottish Realism.[29]

As formulated by Reid and his colleagues, Common Sense Realism was an effort to provide an alternative to the idealism of Immanuel Kant and the skepticism of the Scottish philosopher David Hume. In answer to those who questioned the basis for human knowledge of self and the world, the Scottish Realists took in essence the approach of Samuel Johnson when he kicked a rock to refute Bishop Berkeley's theory that humans perceive only their own mental constructs. They held that the external world exists independent of consciousness; that humans have an innate capacity to apprehend it directly; and that this faculty, which Reid called "common sense," is the surest guide to the truth. For Reid, "common sense" was not an acquired competence, but a faculty that existed prior to, and independent of, reason and experience. It is, he explained, "a part of the furniture which nature hath given to human understanding" and "an inspiration of the Almighty." In his view, this faculty—this God-given mind-furnishing—permitted humans to apprehend the first principles of morality just as certainly as other aspects of reality. A disciple of Francis Bacon, Reid also believed there were laws of morality and of human behavior, just as there were laws of physics, and that these could be discovered by Bacon's inductive method of arranging and systematizing the facts as they were observed.[30]

Scottish Realism with its optimistic, democratic view that anyone could discover the truth appealed to many Americans, and it had particular appeal to the Protestant clergy because it posited the spiritual nature of consciousness and it involved no skepticism about religious truth. Archibald Alexander, the first president of the seminary, said it was the only philosophy compatible with Christianity. Of course, as most Americans understood it, Common Sense Realism was simply commonsensical, but in the hands of the Princeton theologians it led to conclusions that Bushnell, at least, found absurd. As Marsden points out, Old School Presbyterians, raised on the Westminster catechisms, tended to view the truth as a stable entity that, when expressed in precisely stated propositions, would be understood by everyone at all times in exactly the same way. The Scottish Realists' assertion that basic truths are much the same for all persons at all times and places reinforced this assumption and lent it the prestige of Enlightenment science. Differences in the personal or historical perspectives of the biblical authors—and of the readers of the Bible—could then be ignored. Further, if moral laws could be adduced in the same way as the laws of physics, then theology was a science, too.[31]

In his *Systematic Theology*, Hodge wrote:

> If natural science be concerned with the facts and laws of nature, theology is concerned with the facts and the principles of the Bible. If the object of the one be to arrange and systematize the facts of the external world, and to ascertain the laws by which they are determined; the object of the other is to systematize the facts of the Bible, and ascertain the principles or general truths which those facts involve.[32]

The Bible would therefore have to be read literally with no allowance for myths, metaphors, or different levels of meaning. If "the beautiful solo of Dr. Bushnell" should "seduce us from cleaving to the letter of the Scriptures, by telling us the Bible was but a picture or a poem," Hodge wrote, the cause of Christianity would be lost.[33]

Hodge had a warm piety, but he believed—with Turretin—that only external evidence could support religious truth claims. The Westminster Confession held—with Luther and Calvin—that the "infallible truth and divine authority" of Scripture must ultimately derive "from the inward work of the Holy Spirit, bearing witness by and with the truth in our hearts." But to Hodge, this inward experience could not carry the burden of proof in the way that the words of the Scriptures did. "The Bible is to the theologian what nature is to the man of science," he wrote. "It is his store-house of facts." To Hodge it seemed obvious that God would provide nothing but accurate facts. Bushnell's notion that inspiration applied to the thoughts, not the words, of the biblical authors seemed sheer nonsense to Hodge. How could there be such a thing as a wordless thought? Writing in 1857, he contended that God's purpose was to communicate a "record of truth," and for such a record "accuracy of statement" was essential. The Bible, he asserted, "is infallible, and of divine authority in all things pertaining to faith and practice, and consequently free from all error whether of doctrine, fact or precept."[34]

American Protestants had great reverence for the Bible, and most would have said it was "true." But in declaring the Scriptures "free from all error," Hodge was taking a theologically eccentric stance. For all his claim of fidelity to the Reformation, his position was not that of Luther or Calvin. Luther had freely acknowledged that the Bible contained various contradictions and errors of historical fact. He judged that the prophets had often erred in their predictions, and he taught that the Gospel message, which was oral in character, should not be equated with the scriptural text. Calvin, though more cautious, had judged that the biblical writers were not overly concerned with factual accuracy and that some of their ideas about natural phenomena (that the moon was larger than Saturn) came from the worldview of the ancients. For both the truth of the Bible lay not in such details but in the deeper wisdom and its capacity to bring faithful readers to the saving knowledge of Christ through the illumination provided to them by the Holy Spirit. True, many post-Reformation dogmatists had, in an effort to shore up Protestant truth claims, contended that the Bible was verbally inspired and error-free. Turretin had been adamant on the subject. "The prophets did not make mistakes in even the smallest particulars," he wrote. "To say they did would render doubtful the whole of Scripture." But this position did not become canonical. For one thing, it was well known that the successive transcriptions and translations of the Bible did not perfectly accord with each other. For another,

Turretin had explained that the Bible was errorless because God had dictated the words to the biblical authors, and the idea that the apostles were nothing more than scribes was unacceptable to many theologians. The seventeenth-century Westminster Confession made no mention of inerrancy but simply stated that the Scriptures were "given by the inspiration of God to be the rule of faith and life."[35] Two centuries later Turretin's position was the creed for the Old School Presbyterians.

Pressed to explain how biblical authors got every word right, Hodge and his successors said they didn't believe in mechanical dictation and, though they had certainly read Turretin thoroughly, they claimed no one had ever believed in such a thing. "The Church has never held what has been stigmatized as the mechanical theory of inspiration," Hodge wrote. "The sacred writers were not machines." What, then, was the explanation? Their answer was that the method by which the Holy Spirit had inspired the writers to select the right words was inscrutable.[36]

Hodge, for his part, acknowledged that some small errors might have crept into the Bible, as flecks of dust into the marble of the Parthenon. But in the 1880s, when German biblical scholarship was taking hold in most other seminaries, his successors, A. A. Hodge and B. B. Warfield took a firmer stand. In a jointly written article in the *Presbyterian Review* of 1881 Hodge declared that "all the affirmations of the Scripture of all kinds . . . are without any error," and Warfield went so far as to say, "A proved error in Scripture contradicts not only our doctrine, but the Scripture claims and, therefore, its inspiration in making those claims." In other words, if even the tiniest error were found in the Bible, all truth claims for the Christian faith would collapse.[37]

Wagering all of Christianity on the accuracy of every single "and" or "but" in the Scriptures would seem a foolhardy thing to do. However, the Princeton scholars had a few years earlier added a qualification: the doctrine of inerrancy applied only to the "original autographs" of the Bible. The surviving copies of the Scriptures, they conceded, had been corrupted by scribal errors; it was the manuscripts that came from the hands of the prophets that were infallible. The qualification was a retreat, but a strategic one. The "original autographs" did not, of course, exist, so no "proved error" could be found in them, and the Princeton doctrine was safe from biblical scholarship. Yet the fact that Hodge and Warfield were positing an imaginary Bible was a subtlety lost on most nonscholars. For many Presbyterians, the Bible they held in their hands was on the authority of Princeton inerrant, and every sentence was to be taken for fact.[38]

The Princeton scholars made biblical inerrancy their bulwark against the higher criticism of the Bible, and such was their influence on the Presbyterian General Assembly that it became the major test of orthodoxy for the church as a whole. In the 1880s Hodge and Warfield fiercely debated the issue with Charles Briggs, an Old Testament scholar from Union Theological Seminary with whom they shared the editorship of the *Presbyterian Review.* Briggs maintained that the higher criticism, as he interpreted it, was entirely compatible with the Westminster Confession, but in 1892 the General Assembly convicted Briggs of heresy and resolved, "That the Bible . . . when freed from all errors and mistakes of translators, copyists, and printers, is the very Word of God, and consequently wholly without error."[39] On the basis of this new doctrine, heresy charges were subsequently brought against two other progressive seminary scholars. One was convicted, the other quit the church, and Union Theological Seminary broke its ties with the denomination.[40]

In the meantime, however, other conservative ministers adopted biblical inerrancy as the basis for an apocalyptic end times prophecy involving the approach of Armageddon and the return of Christ to rapture His saints into the air.

The appearance of a new premillennial movement surprised the Princeton scholars and the liberals alike. The idea that the world would end because of increasing human wickedness was, of course, well known to American Protestants, but after the failure of William Miller's prediction that the world would end in 1844, millenarianism had fallen into disrepute. Then, too, at least since the 1830s, optimistic postmillennialism had been far and away the dominant worldview of American Protestants. Even the devastations of the Civil War had not seemed to dim the faith that with sufficient vigor Christians could bring in the Kingdom of God. By the 1880s faith was the strongest among progressives, but even conservatives, who generally took the position that only God knew the why and wherefore of the Second Coming, also tended to think that Christ would return after righteousness was spread throughout the world.[41]

The movement had begun almost invisibly in the 1860s, when small groups of American clergymen began discussing the apocalyptic prophecies that had been circulating in Britain since the French Revolution. In the English tradition of interpretation the focus was on the prophecies in the books of Daniel, Isaiah, and Revelation, and there was general agreement that the world was rushing toward an imminent judgment, that Christ would literally return to earth, that there would be terrible Tribulations, and that the Jews would return to Palestine before the commencement of the millennial age. There were important disagreements as well. Were the events prophesied in Revelation already under way, or would they begin sometime in the future? Was a biblical "day" to be reckoned as a year? And how were the chronologies of future events in Daniel and Revelation to be harmonized? In their journal, the *Prophetic Times*, the American clergymen debated these and other issues, such as whether the pope or Napoleon III might prove to be the Antichrist. Daniel 9 clearly said that the Messiah would establish his kingdom on earth "seventy weeks" after the Jews began to rebuild Jerusalem. However, the fall of Napoleon III in 1870—on top of the failure of Miller's prediction—made them uncomfortable with putting an exact date on the Second Coming.[42] Solutions to these problems lay in John Nelson Darby's interpretative scheme that put the Advent in a future outside of human history.

A dissenter from the Church of Ireland, Darby traveled widely in the northern United States in the 1860s and '70s decrying the apostasy of the established churches and proselytizing for his separatist group, the Plymouth Brethren. Just how and when the American millenarians took up his interpretation is not entirely clear because, content within their denominations, they wanted nothing to do with the Brethren and rarely gave Darby credit for solving the puzzles they had faced in cracking the biblical code. Yet certainly by the mid-1870s some of them took his ideas for their own and began to elaborate and systematize them.[43]

Darby's interpretation of the prophecies involved the idea that there were dispensations, or successive periods of human history, marked off in the Scriptures by some change in God's method of dealing with mankind, from the Abrahamic covenant to the foundation of the Christian church. Each involved tests that mankind had failed. Dispensationalism became the name for Darby's interpretation, though the idea of dividing scriptural history into periods was not new. The originality of his scheme lay in his idea that the current dispensation, the age of the church, was not included in the prophecies vouchsafed to the Jews. According to Darby and his disciples, God had two different plans operating in history, one for Israel, or earthly humans, and another for true Christians, the heavenly people. His plans for earthly people had been revealed in the covenants He made with Israel, but the current dispensation had nothing to do with them. Daniel 9, as the dispensationalists read it, meant that the Messiah would establish his kingdom 490 years (or seventy times seven weeks) after the rebuilding of Jerusalem began, but according to their calculations, Christ had died on the cross exactly 483 years (or sixty-nine weeks) afterward. God had then turned His attentions to the gentiles—an eventuality unforeseen by the Old Testament prophets—and halted the prophetic clock for Israel with "a week," or seven years, to go. How long this parenthesis—the age of the church—would last, the Scriptures did not reveal, but it could end at any time. At the end of it, Christ would come for His saints—true Christians—and secretly rapture them up into the air. Then God would return to dealing with Israel, the prophetic clock would start again, and in the following week, or seven years, all the rest of the prophecies for the earthly people would be fulfilled.[44]

According to the dispensationalists, the Tribulations would be cataclysmic for all who were left behind. An Antichrist, a false prophet, would appear, backed by the united apostate churches; at the same time the Beast, a political leader, would unite ten nations, forming a new Roman Empire; the Jews would return to Palestine, some would be converted, and these would be terribly persecuted by political leaders until, at the end of seven years, Christ returned with an army of His saints to defeat the combined forces of the Antichrist and the Beast at the battle of Armageddon.[45]

Dispensationalism with its ingenious solution to the issue of timing and its promise that true Christians would escape the Tribulations had obvious attractions, and from the mid-1870s on many millenarians proselytized for it at Bible and prophetic conferences with increasing success.

The Princeton scholars thought this new doctrine unbiblical and could not understand how otherwise faithful Christians could embrace it, but accounts of the Bible conferences show how readily it emerged from the intellectual environment that Princeton had helped to create.

A popular post–Civil War innovation, the Bible conference brought conservative clergymen of various denominations together at summer resorts for a week or two of lectures and Bible reading. The earliest and most influential of them, the Niagara Bible Conference, was an annual retreat for ministers from well-to-do urban churches. Its guiding spirit was James Hall Brookes, a Presbyterian minister with a church in St. Louis, Missouri, who had spent a year at the Princeton seminary before his ordination. One of the leading expositors of Darbyism, Brookes brought dispensationalist speakers to the conference every year. The coming apocalypse, however, was not the only concern of the clergymen. Indeed, the main purpose of the meetings was to put up a defense of the faith. The fourteen-point creed Brookes wrote for the 1878 conference (officially adopted in the 1890s) began with the lament: "So many in these latter times have departed from the faith; . . . so many have turned away their ears from the truth, and turned unto fables; so many are busily engaged in scattering broadcast the seeds of fatal error [that] . . . we are constrained by fidelity to Him to make the following declaration of our doctrinal belief." Of the fourteen articles in the creed, only the last concerned the premillennial Advent. Most of the rest were restatements of evangelical Calvinist doctrines such as the sinfulness of man and the necessity of a rebirth in Christ through the agency of the Holy Spirit. All these doctrines put God firmly in charge of history, but the first of the articles showed that His ways were not entirely inscrutable. "The Holy Ghost," it read, "gave the very words of the sacred writings to the holy men of old; and . . . His Divine inspiration . . . extends equally and fully to all parts of these writings, historical, poetical, doctrinal, and prophetical, and to the smallest word, and inflection of a word, provided such word is found in the original manuscripts." [46]

With the Princeton scholars, Brookes and colleagues believed that theology was a Baconian science of arranging and systematizing facts in the Bible, and the doctrine of biblical inerrancy gave them confidence that, say, their calculations of weeks (or years) were absolutely accurate. According to one dispensationalist, these figures were "established, firm as the ordinances of the heavens" and "science, the boast of modern times, has nothing more fixed, nothing more exact." Their method of classifying the "facts" was, however, somewhat different from Princeton's. In their Bible readings—which substituted for sermons—they would take a word or a proposition and, with the help of a concordance, find some, or all, of the references to it in the Bible, and read them off one after another with hardly a comment. As Marsden writes, this practice, known as proof-texting, turned the Bible into an encyclopedia, or a dictionary, where words or concepts appeared shorn of their textual and historical contexts. Quite simply, it turned ideas into things that could be piled up in any order.[47]

Dispensationalism and the intellectual predispositions that lay behind it were, Marsden writes, basic to fundamentalist thinking, and yet the fundamentalism of the 1920s was a heterodox religious movement that included other elements, some of them apparently contradictory. But then its progenitor, and in a sense its creator, was not a theologian but a lay preacher, Dwight L. Moody.

The major revivalist of the second half of the nineteenth century, Moody himself was no fundamentalist. Far from it. His goal was quite simply to bring as many people as possible to Christ, and in his preaching career, which spanned three decades, he navigated among the various conservative religious movements of his day, and, with small regard for Calvinist orthodoxy, or even consistency, picked out the themes that seemed to win him the most souls. "It doesn't matter how you get a man to God as long as you get him there," he said.[48] Like his contemporary Henry Ward Beecher, Moody was irenic and undogmatic: a bricoleur who created his own message out of disparate elements. That the fundamentalism of the 1920s combined conservative Calvinism with revivalism, and dispensationalism with a strand of holiness teaching can best be explained by Moody's own personal inclinations and his decisions about what worked best. That fundamentalism became a movement was also indirectly his doing, for, a formidable organizer, he built a series of institutions, among them a summer conference where conservative clergymen from different camps found common cause in the struggle against liberalism, plus a Bible institute that became the premier training school for fundamentalists and the model for the rest.

Doubtless few preachers today consciously model themselves on Moody, yet Moody's influence on twentieth-century evangelicalism goes far beyond his role in the development of fundamentalism. The professional way he organized his revivals informed all subsequent revivalists from Billy Sunday to Billy Graham, and his businesslike approach to evangelism continues in the practices of modern megachurches. Modern versions of the music he used can be heard in many such churches, and the echoes of his preaching are far stronger in evangelical churches today than those of the militant fundamentalists who succeeded him. Moody was a Victorian figure, his sentimentality and hardheaded practicality perfectly in tune with the popular culture of his day. As Marsden writes, "Perhaps as much as Henry Ward Beecher, though in quite a different way, he helped to fuse the spirit of middle-class Victorian America with evangelical Christianity." [49] Beecher's blend of Romanticism and faith in the progress of science and morality seems long out-of-date to liberal Christians today, but many evangelicals still hold to Victorian standards of morality, and when they invoke the lost world they want to restore, it is the storied world of Moody's America.

Moody's youthful travails seem to come straight from a Victorian novel written for the edification of Protestant children. Born in Northfield, Massachusetts, in 1837, the son of a ne'er-do-well mason who died when he was four, Moody spent his childhood helping his widowed mother support a family of nine children on a small farm. He never got past seventh grade. At seventeen he went to Boston to work in his uncle's shoestore, but his uncle paid him so little he struck out for Chicago two years later. There he found better jobs with boot and shoe companies, and through hard work, thrift, and financial shrewdness he prospered. Joining a conservative Congregationalist church and the newly formed Young Men's Christian Association, he made his way up in Chicago society. At the same time, he threw himself into the work of evangelizing in the poor sections of the city, handing out tracts and rounding up children for Sunday school. Moody never went through a dramatic conversion experience, but the prayer meetings of the national urban revival of 1857–58, known as the Businessmen's Revival, deepened his faith. In 1860 he quit the shoe business to devote himself to religious activities.

For the next twelve years Moody worked indefatigably on a variety of endeavors in and around the city. He built a Sunday school for slum children and an interdenominational church with money raised from Cyrus McCormick and other wealthy businessmen. During the Civil War, he became an agent for the City Relief Society and worked in army camps for the United States Christian Commission. Afterward, he became president of the Chicago YMCA and the lead organizer for the national Sunday school movement. All the while, he evangelized on street corners, distributing tracts and calling out after passersby, "Are you a Christian?" His enthusiasm was such that some in Chicago called him "Crazy Moody," but his practicality and the organizational skills he brought to every task won him the respect of the city's evangelical establishment and of church leaders across the country.[50]

Moody's career as a revivalist took off abruptly. In connection with his Sunday school and YMCA work, Moody had made a few trips to Britain and met some of its leading evangelical preachers. When asked to conduct a few modestly conceived revival meetings, he succeeded beyond anyone's expectations and returned in June 1873 with a song leader, Ira Sankey. In Scotland, where the Presbyterian Church had split into three warring factions, he brought the clergy together and touched off what the religious press described as a national revival. Suddenly famous, he spent the next year holding mass revivals in major British cities from Belfast to Birmingham. In London, where he ended his triumphal tour, he spent five months preaching in huge halls in working-class neighborhoods and at the Royal Opera House, where dignitaries from the Princess of Wales to the Duke of Marlborough came to hear him. When he and Sankey arrived back in New York, they were greeted as heroes. The American press reported that these two humble Americans had taken Britain by storm and stirred the heart and soul of the Empire. Prominent clergymen from across the country pleaded with Moody to hold revivals in their cities, and wealthy laymen, such as John Wanamaker and William E. Dodge, promised to raise the funds. Praise for Moody came both from liberals, such as Henry

Ward Beecher and Phillips Brooks, and from anti-revivalist conservatives, such as Charles Hodge and his Princeton colleagues.[51]

In the United States, as in Britain, the enthusiasm for Moody came in part from the churchmen's sense of crisis about the rapid growth of an impoverished urban working class. The Earl of Shaftesbury, an evangelical Tory and one of Moody's most important English backers, warned that to deprive "the masses" of "the checks and restraints of religion" would be to invite Communism, anarchy, and mob rule.[52] In the United States, where "the masses" included millions of immigrants from Eastern and Southern Europe, the danger of class warfare seemed compounded by the inrush of papism and revolutionary ideas. Whereas Gladden and a few other clergymen were beginning to look at the structural causes of poverty, most felt that the solution lay in evangelizing the poor and instilling the Protestant virtues of sobriety, thrift, and industry. Reaching "the masses" was, however, beyond the capability of most seminary-educated ministers, so, like Shaftesbury, many clergymen and captains of industry thought Moody the right man for the job.[53]

In America, as in Britain, Moody spoke in enormous halls with platforms big enough to hold hundreds of choir singers, local ministers, and local businessmen, such as George Armour in Chicago and Cornelius Vanderbilt II and J. P. Morgan in New York. Well financed, the revivals were also well organized with committees for publicity, home visitation, temperance, Bible study, and the training of ushers set up in advance. The halls were always packed, and in the big cities, such as New York and Philadelphia, the revivals were attended by more than a million—though many people came night after night. Still, Moody's revivals never had quite the results that the clergy and his wealthy backers hoped. Observers often reported that his meetings were filled with well-dressed, respectable-looking people, and clearly many of them were church members already, for church membership in the cities he visited showed small gains after his revivals. Moody himself sometimes complained that there were too many Christians crowding his meetings and taking up all the best seats. In fact, the idea that Moody could convert the huddled masses was a fantasy. Revivalists, as their name implies, can give life only to a dormant religiosity, and most of the immigrants came from other religious traditions. The new working class did include Protestants, but ten-hour shifts in primitive factories hardly permitted them the leisure to attend church services, even if they were so inclined. In any case, Moody's appeal was not to the wretched factory laborers but to people much like his younger self: rural-born Americans with Protestant backgrounds who were making their way in the cities in white-collar jobs. And by these people he was greatly admired.[54]

In his book *Modern Revivalism: Charles Grandison Finney to Billy Graham*, William G. McLoughlin Jr. gives a vivid account of Moody's revivals. Stout and full-bearded, Moody dressed like a businessman and preached with a blunt forthrightness. His sentences were short, and he often used colloquial idioms, homely illustrations, and earthy anecdotes. According to observers, he had "a remarkable naturalness, a want of all approach to affectation or sanctimoniousness," and a "straight-forward, slap-dash style" that "gives a fascinating air of reality to all he says." His preaching never elicited ecstatic groans or shouts, but he often told sentimental stories that brought tears to the eyes of his listeners: stories of prodigal sons and praying mothers, dying children and long-suffering wives. One of his favorites involved a wounded Civil War soldier who, because of the pleas of his mother, came to Christ and died a happy man. Ira Sankey, suave and graceful, sang his sacred solos in a sweet lyrical baritone, and his songs told often similarly sentimental, or bathetic, stories about redeemed profligates or pure little children who were cruelly treated, died, and went to heaven. But Moody also had a lively sense of humor and an ability to move his audience straight from tears to laughter.[55]

Moody often said that he preached "the fundamentals" or "the good old doctrines of our fathers," but what he meant by that was not the panoply of Calvinist doctrines but simply, "Man is fallen; Christ comes to seek, redeem and save him." Like Finney—and like all subsequent revivalists—he preached that conversion entailed simply a change of mind. Appealing to an interdenominational audience, he avoided discussions of creeds and doctrines and focused on what to him seemed to be the essential message: sinners could achieve eternal life by believing that Christ died for their sins. In practice, he often reduced conversion to the simple act of confessing belief in "the fundamentals," and promising to give up wine,

tobacco, dancing, theatergoing, and novel reading: in short by living up to
the code of personal morality that rural Protestants believed to be Christian. "If we want any thing we want right living," Moody said. "God wants
downright uprightness." In this respect, his message was that of the early-
nineteenth-century frontier evangelists transferred to the new frontiers
of the city.[56]

Where Moody differed most from the Calvinists was in his depiction of
God as a loving "person." He had, he once said, preached Calvinism until
1868, when he heard Henry Moorhouse, a Plymouth Brethren evangelist,
preach seven sermons on the text, "For God so loved the world . . ."[57]
The transcendent deity who governed the world inscrutably, or according
to moral law, was in any case too much of an abstraction for him. In his
sermons, God was brought down to earth and humanized in the figure of
Jesus. According to Moody, Jesus had not died just to save mankind, He
had come to be a loving friend and helper to all who believed in Him. "The
gospel is this," Moody preached in one sermon: "that Christ has Come to
meet your need. There is not a need you feel in your heart to-day but that
Christ can meet if you let Him. God sent Him here to meet man's need."
He continued, "I have known him now for upwards of twenty years a
shepherd. He has carried my burdens for me. Oh, it is so sweet to know
that you have one to whom you can go and tell all your sorrows! You
can roll your burdens at his feet . . . Think of Christ as a burden-bearer!"
Christianity, as Moody described it, seemed to be a matter of establishing
a close personal relationship with this sentimentalized Savior.[58]

Moody, according to Marsden, felt as much uneasiness about eternal
punishment as Henry Ward Beecher. In any case, he never described the
torments of hell, but led his listeners to repentance by picturing scenes
of suffering on earth. The martyrdom of Stephen, the whipping of Paul,
his own tale of a drowning man trying to board a crowded lifeboat—
these were stories he told in dramatic detail. In one famous sermon, he
described Christ's last hours—the crown of thorns, the scourging, the
nailing of his body to the cross—in a manner that one auditor said was
"so life-like as to be absolutely painful." Hell, along with the almighty,
unapproachable God, had disappeared into the distance: the focus was on
the trials of individual human beings. Heaven, on the other hand, was no

abstraction for Moody. When he spoke of it, he painted a peaceful urban scene of people walking its streets with their departed loved ones, the saints and the apostles.[59]

On the controversial issues of the day, Moody took conservative positions, but in the most general of terms. He preached biblical infallibility, though he didn't use the word, much less the Princeton formulation of inerrancy. Rather, he spoke of the truthfulness of the Bible, and pointed to the fulfillment of prophecies in both the Old and New Testaments, dwelling on those that foretold the coming of the Savior. "If there was one portion of the Scripture untrue," he said, "the whole of it went for nothing."[60] He rejected Darwinian evolution and the higher criticism of the Bible, but never denounced their advocates and preferred to ignore their existence. In addition, he preached premillennialism. He had, it seemed, heard the dispensationalist version of it from the Plymouth Brethren—from Moorhouse, or even from Darby himself—but he never went into detail. His message was simply that the world was growing more and more wicked, and that one day, and possibly within the hour, the trumpet would sound and that Christ would return to separate true Christians from the rest. Darby's pessimism about human history seemed at odds with Moody's own practical and activist nature, but then he believed the doctrine a powerful spur to conversion. "I don't know of anything that will take the men of this world out of their stocks and bonds quicker than [the thought] that our Lord is coming again," he said. In any case, his own role was clear to him. "I look upon the world as a wrecked vessel," he famously declared. "God has given me a lifeboat and said to me, 'Moody, save all you can.'"[61]

Consistent with this position, Moody said nothing of social reform or of the obligation of Christians to the welfare of the society at large. While he spoke of doing all for the glory of God, there was no Puritan command to responsibility for the community, no call to disinterested benevolence, or to building the Kingdom of God on earth. The highest duty of Christians, he said, was "to visit the homes of the poor and wicked and tell them how the Son of God came into the world to seek the fallen and those who were lost."[62] His focus was on the individual, and the sins he generally decried, like intemperance and laziness, had no victims beyond

the individual and his family. Possibly, as Marsden writes, Moody believed
that if every American embraced Christ and the good old Protestant virtues, all social problems would disappear.[63] However, because he never
preached social salvation, the proposition came only in its negative form.
Speaking at a meeting in New York City in 1876, when fifty thousand men
were out of work because of the latest financial crash, he declared that
the cause of the suffering was that "the sufferers have become lost from
the Shepherd's care." As he explained it, the poor were responsible for
their poverty. "I do not believe we would have had these hard times if
it had not been for sin and iniquity. Look at the money that is drank up!
The money that is spent for tobacco! That is ruining men—ruining their
constitutions." In Moody's view there could be no other explanation. "We
live in a land flowing with milk and honey," he said. "God has blessed this
nation; yet men complain of hard times." He was not against charity, but
charity for him was always secondary to soul winning. And too much
charity in his view did "a great deal of mischief" by encouraging people
to expect handouts when they should be working for a living.[64]

In the 1870s it was hardly uncommon for Protestant clergymen to
preach that the Puritan virtues of thrift and industry would help a man
succeed in life. But Moody went a step farther. He preached that conversion itself would bring prosperity. "It's a wonderful fact that men and
women saved by the blood of Jesus rarely remain subjects of charity, but
rise at once to comfort and respectability," he declared. As evidence, he
sometimes pointed to the wealthy men on the dais with him and sometimes to his own Horatio Alger story. "The whole of my early life was one
long struggle with poverty," he said, "but I have no doubt that it was God's
way of bringing me to himself. And since I began to seek first the kingdom of God, I have never wanted for anything." Explained in this way,
prosperity seemed a supernatural gift to those who converted. "I don't see
how a man can follow Christ and not be successful," he said. Thus, while
many preachers, conservatives, and liberals decried the materialism of the
Gilded Age, Moody made his peace with it.[65]

In the 1880s, while continuing to conduct revivals, Moody increasingly
turned his attention to training ministers and laymen to carry on his work
of evangelizing the country and world. In his hometown of Northfield,

Massachusetts, where he built a house and came to reside, he started a seminary for girls and later a school for boys to provide a Christian education to young people "in the humbler walks of life." In 1886 he convened a month-long meeting of students from college YMCAs to encourage them to take up mission work abroad. Out of it came the Student Volunteer Movement, which by the turn of the century had recruited several thousand college students in the United States and Britain for the task of "the evangelization of the world in this generation." The same year, he began to raise money from Chicago magnates, among them Cyrus McCormick, J. V. Farwell, and Marshall Field, for a Bible institute in Chicago to give laymen a one- or two-year Christian education so that they could work as missionaries among workingmen in a way the clergy could not. "One great purpose we have," Moody said, "is to raise up men and women who will be willing to lay their lives alongside of the laboring class and the poor and bring the gospel to bear upon their lives." Then, too, in 1880 he inaugurated a summer Bible conference at Northfield that continued until his death in 1899.[66]

To the Northfield Bible Conference Moody brought British and American ministers of his wide acquaintance. Most were conservatives alarmed by the growth of liberalism in their denominations, and most of the Americans, including his closest associates, were premillennialists. For many summers, the main subject was dispensationalism, but the conference was more pietistic and more oriented to evangelism than the Niagara Conference. Often the meetings focused on Holiness teaching. Moody had heard Holiness preachers in his Chicago days, and in 1871 he had an intense experience of infilling by the Holy Spirit. In England some years later he picked up, and preached, a strand of Holiness teaching developed by Anglican ministers and known as Keswick for the Lake District town where they held conferences. In a curious transatlantic exchange, the doctrine had been brought to England by Asa Mahan of Oberlin and other American Presbyterians, who, unlike Finney, taught the second blessing as a dramatic experience of sanctification. Fearful of any association with perfectionism or the recent brands of Wesleyan Holiness teachings, the Anglicans specifically rejected the idea that man's sinful nature could be eradicated for the view, much more acceptable to Calvinists, that the tendency to sin could be counterbalanced if the believer surrendered himself wholly to Christ. The central idea was that an infilling of the Holy Spirit could lead the believer to a "victorious life" of righteousness and endue him with the power for service. Evangelism and witnessing were seen as the principal manifestations of this service, and in England the movement was closely connected with mission work. When Moody brought Keswick preachers to Northfield, it was this emphasis on power and action that most appealed to his friends and colleagues. In particular the dispensation-alists, who as Calvinists had been deeply skeptical of Holiness doctrines, found Keswick a complement to their own teachings. According to Mars-den, it provided them with a subjective confirmation of the faith to stand alongside objective arguments from the Bible and it offered a personal "victory" to individuals in a civilization that was beyond repair.[67]

By the 1890s, Moody's circle of close friends and lieutenants included a number of powerful younger ministers who preached biblical inerrancy, dispensationalism, and Keswick Holiness. Among them were Reuben A. Torrey, A. C. Dixon, William J. Erdman, A. J. Gordon, C. I. Scofield, and James M. Gray.[68] Some were evangelists, others pastors of urban churches, but all were activists who promoted Bible conferences, Bible institutes, and societies for mission work and urban evangelism. In the early years of the twentieth century these men took the lead in creating the fundamen-talist movement.

The trait that distinguished these men from Moody was clearly etched in the answers that Moody and Torrey gave to a question put to them by a Moody publication in 1899: What was the teaching of Christ in regard to error? Moody's answer was, "Christ's teaching was always constructive . . . His method of dealing with error was largely to ignore it, letting it melt away in the warm glow of the full intensity of truth expressed in love." Torrey's response was quite the opposite. "Christ and His immediate disci-ples immediately attacked, exposed and denounced error," he wrote. "We are constantly told in our day that we ought not to attack error but simply teach the truth. This is the method of the coward and trimmer; it was not the method of Christ."[69]

Reuben Torrey (1856–1923), Moody's closest associate in 1890s and his presumptive heir, was an exemplar of the new generation. The son of a

New York banker and a graduate of Yale and Yale Divinity School, Torrey had studied in Germany for a year, where he had conceived a passionate hatred for the higher criticism. Afterward, he went to Minneapolis, where he pastored a Congregationalist church and headed the city's missionary society. In 1889 Moody appointed him the first superintendent of his Bible institute and five years later the pastor of his Chicago church. Along the way, Torrey became a master of Niagara-style Bible reading, a premillennialist, and one of the leading teachers of Keswick Holiness. He aspired to being a popular revivalist, and after Moody's death he conducted a series of large-scale revivals in the United States and abroad.[70]

Revivalism, however, was not Torrey's calling. For one thing, he had a high view of his own opinions and no sense of humor. As McLoughlin put it, "On the street he usually wore a high hat, and he always talked as if he had one on." On the dais, as off it, he lectured, exhorted, and argued with grim determination, often seeming more intent on saving his own version of the truth than upon saving souls.[71] For another, he spent much of his time in theological pursuits. He wrote or edited some forty books, and like most dispensationalists he figured himself as a kind of a scientist, engaged in what he said was a "careful, unbiased, systematic through-going, *inductive* study and statement of Bible truth." One of his major works, *What the Bible Teaches*, was a five-hundred-page compilation of biblical "propositions" supported by proof texts in the style of an encyclopedia.[72]

One of Torrey's major contributions to the fundamentalist movement was in building the Moody Bible Institute. Moody had seen the institute as an adjunct to revivals: a school that would give laymen some Bible knowledge and some training in the "aggressive methods" of Christian work so they could become pastor's assistants, Sunday school teachers, Bible readers, urban evangelists, and foreign missionaries. As the first superintendent, Torrey fashioned the curriculum in his own theological image and proved an effective administrator. By 1900 the institute had graduated over a thousand students from its two-year course and was referring to itself as "the West Point of Christian Service." His success demonstrated that Bible institutes could train huge numbers of Christian workers—without exposing them to the liberal apostates at the denominational seminaries. By 1915 a score of such institutes had sprung up in major cities around the country, among them A. J. Gordon's institute in Boston; the Northwestern Bible Training School founded by William Bell Riley; C. I. Scofield's Philadelphia School of the Bible; and the Bible Institute of Los Angeles, where Torrey spent the latter part of his career. These schools, all headed by dispensationalists, became centers of militant antimodernism and the training grounds for the evangelists of fundamentalism.[73]

4

THE FUNDAMENTALIST-MODERNIST
CONFLICT

The Split in the Northern Denominations

Building the Fundamentalist Movement, 1900–1915

In the 1890s and the early years of the twentieth century liberal theology took hold in most of the major seminaries and divinity schools—Harvard, Yale, Andover, Union Theological, Boston University, Oberlin, and the University of Chicago. By 1914 a whole generation of graduates from these seminaries was preaching the New Theology, transforming some denominations, such as the Congregationalists and Methodists, and making deep inroads into others, like the Presbyterian and Baptist churches. The shift in Protestant thinking had progressed to the point that that biblical infallibility and the immutability of church doctrines were no longer common understandings among educated people in the North.

In the first decade of the new century, liberal clergymen had reason to think that a peaceful change was under way. Tranquillity reigned within the denominations, and in 1908 thirty-three northern denominations combined to form the Federal Council of Churches, an organization designed to spur ecumenical efforts in evangelization and social reform. Dominated by Social Gospelers such as Washington Gladden, Walter Rauschenbusch, and Shailer Mathews, the dean of the University of Chicago's Divinity School, the FCC adopted a social creed on behalf of industrial workers. First promulgated by the Methodists, the creed called for such measures as the abolition of child labor, a reduction in working hours, old age and disability insurance, a living wage for workers, and "the most equitable division of the products of industry that can ultimately be devised." One of the FCC's first acts was to investigate a steel strike in Bethlehem, Pennsylvania, and to champion the workers' cause.[1]

Conservative evangelicals believed, as always, that the salvation of souls should be the first concern of Christians, and for most of them social reform meant closing saloons and gambling dens and supporting Sabbath laws. Still, a few were social progressives, and others went along with the FCC program in the interests of promoting evangelism, charity, and the prohibition of alcohol. The Moody Bible Institute, dedicated to proselytizing workers, even called the social creed "a most righteous and reasonable appeal on behalf of laboring man which we should like to forward to the utmost of our ability." Such was the power of progressivism that in the succeeding years all the major northern denominations followed the FCC's lead and created social service agencies to work for the poor in the burgeoning cities.[2]

The fundamentalist movement was, however, taking shape in this period among Bible school men and conservatives within some of the northern denominations. In 1910, the Presbyterian General Assembly, still dominated by Princeton seminary professors and other Old School Presbyterians, adopted a five-point declaration of "essential doctrines": the inerrancy of Scripture, the virgin birth of Christ, His bodily resurrection, substitutionary atonement, and the authenticity of Jesus' miracles. To many Presbyterians, the reduction of the rich theology of the church to just five "essentials" seemed a departure from tradition, and the choice of doctrines arbitrary. But then the declaration came in response to questions raised about the orthodoxy of certain Union Theological Seminary graduates, and the five points were those the liberals were least likely to accept.[3]

Three years later conservative Presbyterians drove Charles Stelzle, a highly respected advocate for workingmen, to resign from his post as head of the Presbyterian Bureau of Social Service. Charles R. Erdman, the son of William J. Erdman and a Princeton seminary professor who chaired the standing committee on the Board of Home Missions from which the bureau depended, later wrote that the church had been arrogating functions not its own. "The supreme function" of the church, he wrote, "is to secure, on the part of individuals, wholehearted devotion and allegiance to Christ" and "to increase its membership as rapidly as possible." A gospel of good works, he conceded, came with a gospel of grace, but that did not mean "the adoption of a so-called 'social gospel' which discards the fundamental doctrines of Christianity and substitutes a religion of good works." He went on to attack the view that the Kingdom of God could be introduced by the church and to maintain that only the personal return of Christ would rid the world of its injustices and social sins. Erdman was a premillennialist, but a reaction to the Social Gospel was building among conservatives generally.[4] Billy Sunday, the most popular revivalist since Moody, registered the reaction. A former baseball player who to the dismay of Torrey and others at the Moody Bible Institute preached in his shirtsleeves and engaged in what they considered vulgar theatrics, Sunday had a good ear for what his aspiring middle-class audiences wanted to hear. In the early years of the century he had supported Theodore Roosevelt and civic reform, but around 1912 he began attacking the Social Gospel. "Some people are trying to make a religion out of social service with Jesus Christ left out," he declared. "We've had enough of this godless social service nonsense."[5]

The years 1910–15 saw the publication of a twelve-volume series of essays titled *The Fundamentals: A Testimony to the Truth*. The series was conceived and financed by Lyman Stewart, an oil wildcatter, who with his brother Milton had made a great fortune in the Union Oil Company in California. A Presbyterian who found the church too lax in its doctrinal standards, Lyman had visited both the Niagara and the Northfield conferences and had become a premillennialist. In 1908 he contributed to the foundation of the Bible Institute of Los Angeles and started publishing religious books. His major project was to enlist "the best and most loyal Bible teachers in the world" to write a comprehensive "testimony" to Christian doctrines that he would distribute free to every "pastor, evangelist, minister, theological professor, theological student, Sunday school superintendent, YMCA and YWCA secretary in the English-speaking world." The series of essays, as he envisioned it, would stem the tide of modernist infidelity and "count for both time and eternity."[6]

The first editor Stewart found for this ambitious undertaking was A. C. Dixon, a fiery premillennialist Baptist who, when Stewart met him, was serving as pastor of Moody's church in Chicago. Later Stewart recalled that at their first meeting Dixon was "replying to something one of those infidel professors at Chicago University had published." Dixon compiled the first five volumes, and when he left Chicago for a church in England, he was succeeded by members of the editorial board he had established: first Louis Meyer, a Chicago Presbyterian with a ministry to Jews, and then Reuben Torrey. Published in paperback format, each volume was sent out when finished, and by the time the twelfth volume appeared, a total of three million booklets had been distributed.[7]

When completed, *The Fundamentals* comprised ninety essays by sixty-four British and American authors, some of them seminary professors such as B. B. Warfield and Charles R. Erdman of Princeton, and others by Bible school men, such as James M. Gray, Torrey's successor at the Moody Bible Institute. Taken together, the essays testified to the concerns and the ambitions of the emerging fundamentalist movement.

The series, Ernest Sandeen wrote, seemed constructed like a wheel. On the outer rim were a miscellany of thirty pieces that included personal testimonies, appeals for missions, and attacks on "heretical" faiths like Roman Catholicism, Mormonism, and Christian Science. Three essays dealt with Darwinism, one of them calling it the work of the devil, the others arguing that evolution could not explain the origin of life or the uniqueness of human beings, but allowing that the "days" of creation might have been very long and admitting the possibility of some limited form of evolution in God's plan. The spokes of the wheel—another third of the essays—were apologetics for doctrines such as the virgin birth of Christ and personhood of the Holy Spirit. At the hub were twenty-nine essays on the authority of the Bible. Fifteen were attacks on the higher criticism, or on what the authors called "unscientific" criticism based on "hypothesis-weaving" and prejudice against the supernatural and the miraculous. Five of them made the case for biblical inerrancy, some going further than Princeton by suggesting the Bible had been dictated by God.[8]

Surprisingly, given the aggressive temper of Stewart and his editors, the polemics were couched in fairly moderate language. Then, although half of the American contributors were millenarians, only two essays proclaimed the Second Advent, and none promoted dispensationalism. Clearly Stewart and his editors had decided to restrain themselves in the interests of creating a united front of conservative evangelicals against the common enemy. Apparently, however, the editors were more alarmed about the liberal threat than most conservatives, for the theological journals and the popular religious press virtually ignored the whole enterprise. Later, however, fundamentalists looked upon these widely known—if little read—volumes as a landmark in the development of their movement.[9]

In the first decade of the century the millenarian movement had been in crisis. Many of American founders, including A. J. Gordon and James H. Brookes, who had dominated the Bible and prophecy conferences for two decades, had passed from the scene. With their passing a controversy had broken out among the younger leaders over whether the Rapture would come before or after the Tribulations. Sides were taken, and the two groups, each with its own periodical, attacked each other's positions. In a movement that depended on absolute certainty about biblical dates and the identity of such figures as Gog and Magog, there could be no compromise and, as with the Byzantine disputes of old, the quarrel turned ugly. One side charged that its opponents' doctrines came from the fanatical utterances of British heretics; the other side accused the first of being in the grip of a demonic delusion. The pre-Tribulationist party eventually gained the upper hand for reasons that, according to Sandeen, had less to do with their superior skill at exegesis than with the attractiveness of their position that Christians would be raptured before the Tribulations. Still, in 1901 the schism put an end to Niagara and the British-American prophecy conferences. Then, too, with the higher biblical criticism established in the seminaries, millenarianism no longer attracted ministers as educated and as respected in their denominations as Gordon and Brookes. A 1919 survey of 236 professors at twenty-eight seminaries of eight major denominations found that only seven professed premillennial beliefs.[10]

Millenarianism nonetheless flourished in Bible schools, missionary societies, revivalist tents, and even in some urban middle-class churches. In general, the younger leaders were more entrepreneurial than their predecessors. A. C. Gaebelein, for example, a German immigrant with

a ministry to the Jews of New York, put on dozens of prophecy conferences across the country and published a journal, *Our Hope.* The heads of
Bible schools, among them James M. Gray of the Moody Bible Institute,
Reuben Torrey at the Bible Institute of Los Angeles, and William Bell
Riley, who had founded a school in Minneapolis, also published journals,
held conferences, and filled missionary societies and local pulpits with premillennialist preachers.[11] Most important, the younger leaders published
the texts that consolidated the movement and have provided the foundations for American premillennialism ever since.

In 1908, Lyman Stewart republished a primer for the Darbyite prophetic system written by William E. Blackstone in 1878. A successful Illinois businessman and an associate of Moody's, Blackstone had been one
of the first American Zionists. In 1891 he had sponsored a memorial to
President Benjamin Harrison, signed by 413 prominent Americans, among
them Cyrus McCormick, John D. Rockefeller, and J. P. Morgan, urging
that Palestine be given back to the Jews.[12] His book, studiously footnoted
with Bible verses, proclaimed that the end of the world was coming and
that developments from the spread of Communism, nihilism, and apostasy to the expansion of travel and knowledge were sure signs of the end
times. Stewart rescued the book from obscurity and distributed it free
to an enormous list of theology professors, students, and missionaries—
many of whom would later receive *The Fundamentals.* He also gave Blackstone a $5 million fund to promote other dispensationist literature.[13]

The same year Stewart contributed funds toward the publication of
the most influential of all premillennial texts and, according to one fundamentalist historian, the single most influential publication in the history
of fundamentalism: the Scofield Reference Bible.[14]

The editor of the bible, C. I. Scofield (1843–1921), had no formal education and came to religion only after incidents generally omitted from
his biography. Raised in Tennessee, he went to war at age seventeen and
served with distinction in the Confederate army. Afterward he practiced
law in Kansas and was elected to the state legislature. At some point he
began drinking heavily, and in 1877 he fled the state amid accusations that
he had stolen political campaign funds from a former partner. Abandoning a wife and two children, he went to St. Louis, where after two years

he landed in jail on forgery charges. But he made a complete conversion in jail and soon afterward began working in Moody's revival campaign in the city. Licensed to preach in 1883, he moved to Dallas, where in the course of a decade he built large Congregational church, a Bible school, and a mission to Central America. In St. Louis he had become a disciple of James Brookes, and by 1890 he was writing on dispensationalism, offering his own Bible correspondence course, and speaking at the major prophecy conferences. Later he moved to Northfield to pastor Moody's church and to head the Northfield Bible Training School. In 1902 he took a sabbatical and went to work annotating the Bible with support from backers Gaebelein had found for him.[15]

Published by Oxford University Press in 1909, the Scofield Reference Bible had an attractive format with copious notes on the pages that identified biblical characters and permitted readers to follow themes from one book to the next through a system of cross-references. His commentary included material found in other reference Bibles of the period, but it imparted much new information as well. From it many Americans learned for the first time of the calculation made by the seventeenth-century Anglican bishop James Ussher that the creation occurred in 4004 BC after a catastrophe destroyed "the primitive order," killing all the animals and leaving their traces as fossils. The Scofield Bible taught Keswick Holiness doctrines, but mainly it canonized dispensationalism. Its introduction proclaimed that the Bible was a document written by God and that its successive revelations prefigured Jesus' death on the cross and the establishment of His Kingdom after the present dispensation of the church. Throughout the text the commentary explained the meaning of cryptic prophecies—revealing, for example, that the "little horn" in Daniel 8:9 referred to a Syrian king of the pre-Christian era, whereas the "little horn" of Daniel 7:7–8 referred to the Beast of the Tribulations to come. Like Darby, he assigned Jesus' life to the older Jewish "dispensation of the law," rather than to the Christian "dispensation of grace"—thus relegating the Sermon on the Mount and the Lord's Prayer to a pre-Christian era. In line with the dispensationalist consensus of the period, he predicted the return of the Jews to Palestine in the last days and identified Russia as the Magog of Ezekiel 38.[16] The Scofield Reference Bible proved so successful that it was republished in 1917. By the 1940s, it had sold two million copies, and by the 1960s, five or ten million more. Not only did it reach a mass audience, but it also proved far more persuasive than any dispensationalist tract. Interpolated within the text of the King James Bible, the notes seemed the authoritative interpretation—if not a part of the Bible itself. According to students of the subject, readers often could not remember whether a particular idea they encountered came from the notes or text, and some memorized the notes along with biblical verses.[17]

In part because of Scofield's Bible, dispensationalism spread not just among Presbyterians and Baptists but to the Holiness groups and the Pentecostals, who had little or no contact with its Calvinist advocates. These separatists from the Methodist tradition had always preached a premillennial Second Coming, but in the pre–World War I period, as they developed from sects into churches and denominations, they adopted the elaborate Darbyite prophetic system.[18]

World War I—The Conflict Begins

The outbreak of World War I came as a terrible blow to liberal Protestants and Social Gospel advocates. The years 1907–14 had been the high point of the Progressive era.

The nation had been at peace, and reformers under Presidents Theodore Roosevelt, William Howard Taft, and Woodrow Wilson had done much to regulate industry and the nation's financial system, to promote clean and efficient government, to conserve natural resources, and to improve the lot of workers and the poor.

Progressive reformers had a sense of limitless possibilities. There was, the historian Samuel Eliot Morison remembered, "a euphoria in the air, peace among the nations, and a feeling that justice and prosperity for all was attainable through good will and progressive legislation."[19] Many religious progressives believed that the Kingdom of God might be realized in modern history. In his 1912 book *Christianizing the Social Order*, Walter Raushenbusch wrote that the transformation of society on the Christian principles of democracy and justice had already begun. Washington Gladden wrote that the eventual victory of those who believed in the justice of a square deal was assured. The Lord, he preached, was closer to that age than to any other. Men like Rauschenbusch and Gladden were well aware of the military buildup going on in Europe, but they nonetheless assumed that the progress of civilization was ushering in a reign of peace among Christian nations, and that future wars would be limited to underdeveloped countries. Shailer Mathews, the dean of the divinity school at the University of Chicago and the president of the Federal Council of Churches, was caught up in the euphoria. "We were engaged in making a new world," he wrote. "It was a thrilling hope." [20]

The conflagration that suddenly overwhelmed Europe on a scale never seen before, involving all its great powers, put an end to these millennial hopes. It "shattered all optimism," Mathews wrote. "It argued a breakdown of forces which we believed were shaping up a new world order . . . the power of Christianity to prevent violence was seen to be negligible. The Kingdom of God disappeared in the smoke and the poison gas and the treaties of a civilization that was anything but swayed by the principles of Jesus." Human nature "was still untamed." [21]

Conservative Protestants had no more anticipated the coming of war than the liberals. According to Samuel Eliot Morison, "Almost every shade of American opinion had assumed that a general European war was unthinkable." Still, as believers in the depravity of human nature, they did not share the liberals' sense of disillusionment. Indeed, the premillennialists among them felt their beliefs reinforced, for here was proof of their dire predictions about the decline of the age. "It is a great thing to know that everything is going on according to God's schedule," said William Pettingill of the Philadelphia School of the Bible. "We are not surprised at the present collapse of civilization; the Word of God told us all about it." Far from causing despair, the outbreak of hostilities inspired hope for the Second Advent. "WAR! WAR!! WAR!!!" exclaimed one Pentecostal journal. "The Nations of Europe Battle and Unconsciously Prepare the Way for the Return of the Lord Jesus to Establish His Kingdom Upon Earth." [22]

To the dismay of the liberals, World War I did much to stimulate interest in premillennialism. Unfamiliar with the intricacies of European politics, many Americans felt that a catastrophe of such proportions must have biblical significance, and the dispensationalists claimed to know what it was. Old prophecy books—among them the Scofield Bible—were updated and republished, and premillennial journals ran articles speculating on the import of each new military offensive and each new peace overture. The millenarian leaders did not agree on every point, and a few made rash predictions about the date the Tribulations would begin. Still, as the war progressed, events seemed increasingly to be matching up with their prophecies. Dispensationalists had long believed that that the end times would see a revived Roman Empire composed of ten nations and a northern confederacy headed by Russia rising to meet each other in battle at Armageddon. In 1914 the geopolitical map of Europe bore no relationship to this north–south division, but with the breakup of the Austro-Hungarian Empire and Russia's withdrawal from the alliance against Germany, the map conformed more closely to the predicted alignment. That Russia would lead the northern confederacy seemed to Gaebelein and others to be confirmed by the 1917 revolution, which brought an atheistic, Communist government to power. Then came the disintegration of the Ottoman Empire and in December 1917 the thrilling of news of General Edmund Allenby's capture of Jerusalem. With the British favoring the establishment of a national home for the Jews in Palestine, the restoration of Israel seemed a distinct possibility. Scofield, normally cautious about assigning significance to current events, wrote a friend, "Now for the first time, we have a real prophetic sign." [23]

From 1914 to 1917 most Protestant leaders opposed intervention in the conflict, as did Americans generally. The exceptions were a few liberals, such as Lyman Abbott, a Boston Episcopalian, and Harry Emerson Fosdick, a New York Baptist, who represented an interventionist constituency of college-educated East Coast Anglophiles who argued the cultural and economic importance of Britain to the United States. Otherwise, both liberals and conservatives supported neutrality for the reasons that most other Americans did: the United States should stay out of Europe's quarrels as it had since the Revolution. Oddly enough, the most passionate anti-interventionists came from the left and the right of the theological spectrum: from among Social Gospelers and premillennialists. Gladden, for one, attributed the war to the corruption of Europe's ruling classes and argued that there was no moral justification for going to war. Shailer

Mathews saw the war as a threat to progressive reforms in the United States, and as president of the Federal Council of Churches he campaigned vigorously for neutrality and against military preparedness.

The premillennialists, on the other hand, argued that no government was especially blessed, that any effort to solve the world's problems was useless, and that war, though inevitable, was terribly wrong. In 1914 Reuben Torrey preached, "We should love our country but not at the expense of other countries. . . . The law of love should be the law of nations as well as of individuals." Afterward, he spoke out against the draft, counseled against "war madness" that would lead to a massive military buildup, and in early 1917 sadly concluded, "No real Christian can relish the suffering that will come to real Christians on both sides." The de facto alliance was not generally acknowledged, but the convergence of views was such that in 1916 *The King's Business*, the leading premillennial journal, published by the Bible Institute of Los Angeles, quoted the pacifist Bertrand Russell at length and reprinted a peace sermon by the well-known liberal preacher Henry Sloane Coffin.[24]

Still, when President Wilson committed American troops to war in April 1917, Protestant leaders across the spectrum fell into line behind him, as most Americans did. Initially, many supported the war only dutifully. Some liberals, like Coffin, spoke of it as an unfortunate necessity, and premillennialists took the line that intervention was America's duty and Christians should obey their government even though nothing much good could come of the war.[25] By the end of 1917, however, the national mobilization for war and a major campaign by the government's Committee on Public Information to mobilize public opinion had created a war fever in the country. Protestant ministers who had previously urged peace turned into militants. Many, including liberals in some of New York's grand churches, denounced the German militarism, equated "Kaiser Bill Hohenzollern" with "Kaiser John Barleycorn," and told stories of German atrocities. Randolph H. McKim, from his pulpit in Washington, D.C., reported, "It is God who has summoned us to this war . . . This conflict is indeed a Crusade. The greatest in history—the holiest. It is in the profoundest and truest sense a Holy War."[26] Billy Sunday, who had taken no interest in the war until then, took to calling himself "God's recruiting officer" and fanned the growing anti-German furor with talk of "a great pack of wolfish Huns whose fangs drip with blood and gore." Zeal for war and zeal for the Gospel, he preached, were much the same thing. "Christianity and Patriotism are synonymous terms," he declared, "and hell and traitors are synonymous."[27]

On the other hand, many Social Gospel leaders were carried away by Wilson's soaring rhetoric about fighting a war to end all wars and his call for a League of Nations. Gladden quoted Wilson's claims repeatedly. Other nations had gone to war for the sake of their material self-interest, but America had no selfish ends to serve. It was entering the war for the sake of democracy, justice, world peace, and human rights. "To make the world safe for democracy, to defeat a monstrous aggression, [and] to create a new organization of mankind"—that, Gladden wrote, "defines our destiny." For him, Wilson's war aims were the Social Gospel writ large. Shailer Mathews, who in 1916 had helped found the League to Enforce Peace, an organization that called for a league of nations to prevent war, also viewed the American war as a moral crusade. He dropped his classes to become executive secretary for war savings for the state of Illinois and gave scores of speeches across the country portraying the war as a struggle for democracy and for Christian ideals. The experience exhilarated him, and the wartime solidarity of the country seemed to him to reveal that America was not just a collection of individuals but "a glorious super-person, possessed of virtues, powers, ideals, daring and sacrifice." In his book *Patriotism and Religion*, published in 1918, he urged—in the vein of Billy Sunday—that there was a deep kinship among the spirit of democracy, true religion, and patriotism. "For an American to refuse to share in the present war . . . is not Christian," he declared.[28]

For all of Wilson's idealistic vision of America bringing peace, justice, and democracy to the world, the government's campaign to mobilize patriotic sentiments led to witch-hunting in the United States. From the start, many Americans suspected the loyalty of the German Americans and Irish Americans in their midst, and saw the socialists, who opposed the war, as a potential fifth column. The Espionage Act of 1917 and the Sedition Act passed the following year mandated heavy fines and imprisonment for anyone encouraging disloyalty or obstructing the war efforts.

Government officials, aided by self-styled patriots, discovered pro-German conspirators and Bolsheviks wherever they looked. Altogether fifteen hundred people were prosecuted under the Espionage and Sedition Acts, among them the pacifist minister of a church in Vermont and Eugene V. Debs, the four-time Socialist candidate for the presidency, who was sentenced to twenty-five years in jail.[29]

In this fraught atmosphere the fundamentalist-modernist conflict erupted. What had been in the main a theological dispute took on cultural, political, and even national security dimensions. Given the propensity of liberals to advocate tolerance and inclusion, it was one of the ironies of the period that the first strike came from the liberal side.

In 1917 Shailer Mathews delivered a broadside against premillennialist doctrines in a widely distributed pamphlet, "Will Jesus Come Again?" For the next two years he, along with his divinity school colleague Shirley Jackson Case and other liberal Bible scholars, engaged in unrelenting polemics against premillennialism in books, pamphlets, and articles. Liberal theologians had always seen dispensationalism as a falsification of Scripture and biblical history, but with its wartime popularity they came to see it as a political threat to all they stood for. In the introduction to his book *The Millennial Hope: A Phase of War-Time Thinking*, published in January 1918, Case wrote that the current upsurge of millennial thinking "strikes at the heart of all democratic ideals" by denying human responsibility for the reform and betterment of society. That year, Mathews's scholarly journal, *Biblical World*, published a series of essays attacking the movement on biblical and political grounds. In a particularly overwrought piece of invective, "The Premillennial Menace," published in July, Case suggested that its advocates preferred a German victory because it would bring us "nearer to the end of the present world." A few months before, he had told the *Chicago Daily News* that $2,000 a week was being spent to spread the premillennialist doctrines. "Where the money comes from is unknown, but there is a strong suspicion that it emanates from German sources. In my belief the fund would be a profitable field for governmental investigation." In his article Case repeated his call for an investigation. "The American nation," he wrote, "is engaged in a gigantic effort to make the world safe for democracy." Hence it would be "almost

traitorous negligence to ignore the detrimental character of premillennialist propaganda."[30]

Case's accusations of disloyalty were scurrilous and his call for government action a descent into the paranoia of the day. Further, his charge
that the premillennialists lacked enthusiasm for the war was outdated, for
by early 1918 the millenarians had succumbed to the war propaganda and
had become as rabidly anti-German as anyone in the county. That spring
James Gray of the Moody Bible Institute across town wrote that he had
come to see the defeat of the Germans as a godly cause. "Hitherto we have
felt it to be the Christian's duty to serve his government in this conflict,"
he wrote, "but now this secondary obligation, strong as it is, fades out of
sight in the thought of our responsibility to God as executioners of His
avenging justice." Possibly the attacks from the Chicago Divinity School
had helped prompt his change of heart, but the pressure of public opinion
was ubiquitous, and at much the same time premillennialists across the
country abandoned their doctrinal stance against involvement in earthly
conflicts to urge a holy war against Germany. In January 1918, *The King's
Business*, once a pacifist magazine, began to equate the kaiser with the
predecessors of the Antichrist to suggest that he might be in league with
the pope and the Mohammedans. A May editorial called Germany "Satan
personified" and declared, "Never did Crusader lift battle-ax in holier war
against the Saracen than is waged by our soldiers of the Cross against the
German." From this position the premillennialists turned on the liberals,
pointing out that biblical criticism had its roots in German *Kultur*—or the
same soil that nourished German militarism. "The new theology has led
Germany into barbarism, and it will lead any nation into the same demor-
alization," Gaebelein wrote.[31]

Still, it was true, as Case pointed out, that the premillennialists did not
support the war to make the world safe for democracy. Some of them held
a theory that spreading democracy would only give power to more and
more sinful people, that anarchy would ensue, and the world would turn
to authoritarian leaders, who usher in the end of the age. Others believed
that well-meaning efforts to improve the world were Satan's way of lulling
Christians into complacency. Still others simply thought Wilson's whole
enterprise hopeless.[32] In 1918 millenarian leaders convened two prophecy

conferences, one in May that brought three thousand people to Philadelphia to celebrate Allenby's occupation of Jerusalem, and another in November, just after the armistice, that overflowed New York's Carnegie Hall. At the second meeting Reuben Torrey declared that those many people on both sides of the Atlantic who were "filled with all kinds of fantastic hopes and anticipations" were "doomed to disappointments." Peace in the world, he said, "is a delusive hope; the League of Nations can never achieve more than temporary cessation of hostilities." But, he said, "my heart is not heavy, not a bit. . . . The Lord is coming." [33]

The controversy over the League of Nations marked a historic turning point. In the past evangelical Protestants had often disagreed about foreign policy, but never along theological lines. In the late nineteenth century some conservatives and some Social Gospel ministers had promoted American imperial adventures in the Pacific as a part of the American Christian mission, while others on both sides had objected to the use of military force. Then, during World War I the majority of liberals and conservatives had swung in tandem from fervent opposition to fervent advocacy of the war. The issue of the League however pitted liberals against hard-line conservatives, and in the following years it became clear that the two parties had come to a deep ideological divide on the role of the United States in the world.

By 1919 virtually all religious liberals, including the most anti-German of them, supported American participation in the League of Nations and the Interchurch World Movement, an ambitious and short-lived effort to raise enormous sums of money and coordinate all the mission and benevolent agencies of American Protestantism. [34] Harry Emerson Fosdick, who had preached to the American troops in Europe, underwent a dramatic conversion. The mass slaughter of troops and civilian populations had so appalled him that he publicly repented of his "atrocious" pro-war sermons, embraced Gandhian nonviolence, and for the rest of his life preached that nationalism was the breeding ground of chauvinism and militarism. Proposing that nations had to give up some of their sovereignty to avert future wars, he urged American participation in international organizations such as the World Court and dreamed of an effective world federalist system that would bring total disarmament. Shailer Mathews for his part never recanted his wartime positions and never became a pacifist, but from then on he gave a considerable amount of his energies to organizations that promoted peace through collective security.[35] The Bible school men, on the other hand, turned to nationalism and isolationism, parting company not just with the liberals but with their own prewar pacifism and Torrey's "law of love" among nations.

In 1919 James Gray called the pressure to join the League of Nations "the third greatest crisis" in American history. By then most premillennialists had decided the League would be the precursor to a revived Roman Empire and that nonparticipation would make it easier on the United States when Christ returned to judge the gentile nations. But Gray's objections were not entirely on theological grounds. In an issue of the Moody Bible Institute's *Christian Workers Magazine* he wrote that for America to join the League would be "national suicide" and referred readers to the tracts of the secular lobby, which portrayed the League as incompatible with the "fundamentals of American independence." Then, rather than counsel prayer that God's will be done, Gray and his fellow premillennialsts called upon Christians to oppose American participation in the League and, because war was inevitable, to resist the disarmament of the United States.[36]

The premillennialists' call to unilateralism seemed to fly the face of their doctrinal fatalism, but, as Marsden explains, the premillennialists were also heirs to the Puritan assumption of responsibility for the country, and the tension between their two commitments remained an ever-present paradox in their thinking.[37] The tension, however, often seemed to resolve itself on more or less pragmatic grounds and in terms of the dominant sentiment in their constituencies. For example, premillennial revivalists, such as Sunday, actively opposed drinking and gambling, whereas the stay-at-home theoreticians tended to be fatalistic about the decline of American morals. During World War I premillennialists oscillated between fatalistic withdrawal and activism, along with the rest of the country, and in opposing the League they were hardly alone. When Wilson failed to persuade European leaders to accept his views of a just peace, an isolationist reaction to foreign entanglements set in, and in March 1920 the U.S. Senate refused to ratify the Treaty of Versailles and the League of

Nations. In any case, from that time on, militant nationalism and hostility toward international organizations became the approach of millenarian fundamentalists in their activist mode.

The Postwar Period and the Battle Royal

World War I was hardly the disaster for the United States that it was for Europe. All the same, more than 53,000 American soldiers had died, and the national mobilization for war had so dislocated the American economy that in the immediate postwar period there was widespread unemployment and bitter industrial strife. In 1919 and 1920 a wave of strikes and lockouts, involving over four million workers, shut down almost every industry from steel to textiles to the railroads. Employers charged that anarchy was taking over and launched a national union-busting campaign. Most of the major strikes were called by the conservative American Federation of Labor, but radicals were involved in some of them, and fired up by wartime propaganda, the press and much of the public attributed all of them to anarchists and Bolsheviks. After May Day riots in several large cities and a spate of anarchist bombings, many Americans believed that an organized attack against the government and capitalism was under way. The wartime fears about Bolshevism erupted into a "Red Scare" and a hunt for left-wingers and foreigners with radical ideas. A number of states passed anti-sedition laws, and in December 1919 the U.S. attorney general, A. Mitchell Palmer, launched a series of lawless raids arresting several thousand resident aliens and jailing or deporting many of them. Such was the hysteria that when a distinguished Methodist bishop led a Commission of Inquiry into a steel strike, he was harassed and called a Bolshevik even by members of his own church.[38] In November 1920 an almost unknown Republican senator, Warren G. Harding of Ohio, was elected president with 61 percent of the vote—the largest landslide in American history to that date.

The Red Scare ended, but a nativist reaction took its place. In 1921 the Congress passed a law limiting the number of aliens admitted annually to 3 percent of the foreign-born in the United States, based on the 1910 census; three years later a still more stringent law virtually ended immigration from anywhere except Northern Europe. Meanwhile, the Ku Klux Klan, revived by an erstwhile Protestant preacher, broadened its targets from African Americans to Catholics and Jews. Recruiting in the small towns of the North and the South, the Klan at its peak in 1923 had three million members and political power in half a dozen states. What was left of the reforming instincts of American Protestantism went into the passage of two constitutional amendments, the Eighteenth banning the sale of alcoholic beverages, and the Nineteenth giving women the right to vote. Prohibition was seen as a reform by most Protestant denominations, but it was also a part of the reaction against Catholics, immigrants, and labor unions. Billy Sunday, who always knew what his conservative (and increasingly small-town) audiences wanted to hear, cheered on the Palmer raids, boosted the anti-immigration laws, and worked for Prohibition, all with equal enthusiasm, and all in the name of restoring "pure Americanism."[39]

In this period, Bible school and denominational fundamentalists abandoned the defensive and essentially conservative position represented in *The Fundamentals* for the militant antimodernism that characterized the fundamentalist movement from then on. Beginning in 1918, they went from more or less peaceful coexistence with the liberals in their denominations to organized efforts to drive modernism out of the churches and schools. The war had turned them into activists, and the political alarms of its aftermath persuaded them that a crisis was at hand. In 1919 A. C. Gaebelein, who had seen the Bolshevik Revolution as the rise of the Beast in Russia, concluded that the Beast was lifting its head in America and that the world was going through a period that might end *"by giving birth to a World Communist Internationale, in which our civilization and religion will be totally destroyed!!!"*[40] According to Marsden, this perception of a nation in crisis gave such conservatives a new sense of urgency about the liberal apostasy in the churches and the decline of Christianity in the culture at large. Marsden is surely right, but it also seems the case that in the period of reaction that followed the war many fundamentalists believed that they could win.

The fundamentalist offensive included three separate endeavors. One was to build a nationwide interdenominational fundamentalist movement; another was to take control of major northern denominations; and the third was a campaign to drive Darwinian evolution out of the public schools. These projects came from different quarters and were never co-ordinated, but the offensive on all three fronts took place more or less simultaneously, and at the beginning it took most liberals by surprise. Even in 1919 few liberals understood the extent of the fundamentalists' anger or appreciated that the stakes for them were nothing less than survival of Christian civilization in America.

In the succeeding years William Jennings Bryan became known as "Mr. Fundamentalist," but the title should really have gone to William B. Riley (1861–1947) an activist minister who played a major role in all three of the fundamentalists' campaigns. In 1917–19 he almost single-handedly launched the fundamentalist movement, but the idea of waging a holy war against modernism had occurred to him long before World War I.

The son of a poor Kentucky farmer, Riley had trained for the ministry at the Southern Baptist Theological Seminary in Louisville. There he had met Dwight Moody, and, after assisting at some of his revivals, he had become one of the great man's most ardent disciples. In 1893 he took a pulpit in Chicago, and four years later moved on to Minneapolis to pastor the First Baptist Church. A tall, handsome man with a resonant voice and considerable oratorical powers, he was ambitious, aggressive, and unafraid of conflict. In the space of five years he turned First Baptist from the private preserve of the Minneapolis Baptist elite into a huge fundamentalist church filled with working people and headed by a board he controlled. In the early years of the century he conducted revivals across the region and, like Billy Sunday, made a name for himself crusading against prostitution, gambling, alcohol, and the corrupt city bosses who profited from the dens of iniquity. Unlike Sunday, however, he dressed like a banker and spoke from a position of high ecclesiastical authority. "We need," he said on one crusade, "a federation of these forces that shall bring down the whole hand of better public opinion upon the lawless and criminal classes to teach those who have no regard for moral truth a sense of obedience to the law, and who their masters are." [41]

During his four years in Chicago Riley had often debated University of Chicago Divinity School professors at meetings of the city's Baptist

Association. In 1909, in response to a book by one of Shailer Mathews's colleagues, he wrote a book-length attack on the kind of theology practiced at the Divinity School. Professors at Chicago and seminaries like it, he charged, denied "every fundamental of our holy faith," including biblical infallibility and the premillennial Second Coming. The result was "an awful harvest of skepticism" that endangered the very life of the church. "Is it not," he asked, "high time the conservative and constructive ministers of our country united forces for the successful defense of the faith once delivered?" When the University of Chicago was picked as the site for the 1910 Northern Baptist Convention, he wrote friends proposing that conservatives should gather in a Chicago church a few days before the convention to protest the "creeping modernism" in the denomination. His proposal, however, was not taken up, and Riley, otherwise occupied, dropped the matter until the crisis of World War I.[42]

By 1917 Riley was not only running a very large church and a Bible school but he was editing religious journals and speaking at conferences across the country. That year he published *The Menace of Modernism*, a book with a more alarming message than the first. Numerous Antichrists, he reported, had invaded not just the seminaries but also most of the institutions of American higher education, including the state universities and many of the colleges founded as Christian schools. Within these hallowed halls of learning, professors were teaching Darwinism and contempt for biblical truth. In alliance with modernist ministers they were attacking the nation's Christian heritage and undermining the moral foundations of the society. The book was pervaded by a sense of alarm about the danger to American culture, but, as Riley's biographer, William Vance Trollinger, noticed, it also contained a note of personal animus. Arrogant college professors, Riley complained, pretend to be the only "men who really think." They talk as if only uneducated people disagree with them and ignore all the highly educated ministers who believe the Bible inerrant and Darwinism unscientific. Modernist ministers, even those who could not fill a church with four hundred people, he wrote, are welcomed by them as speakers, but conservatives have "about as good a chance to be heard in a Turkish harem as to be invited to speak within the precincts of a modern State University."[43]

In his own fashion Riley was alluding to an important development. Just two generations before, clergymen had headed most of the colleges and universities in the country, and pastors were regarded as intellectual leaders in their constituencies. But during the academic revolution of the 1890s the universities had adopted standards of objectivity that relegated religion to the divinity schools. "The secular elite" was not a phrase in Riley's vocabulary, but he was perfectly right that college educators were undermining the cultural authority of the clergy and driving ministers, such as himself, out of the centers of American intellectual life. His anger at this alienation echoed through fundamentalist polemics for the rest of the century.

Riley's book concluded with another call for a "confederacy" of "true and evangelical conservatives" to resist the onslaught of infidelism—and this time his fellows responded.[44]

A regular on the premillennial conference circuit, Riley spoke at the Philadelphia prophecy conference in May 1918. That August he met with other leaders at Reuben Torrey's summer home in Montrose, Pennsylvania, to lay plans for another conference in Philadelphia the following May. Impatient with the passivity of prophetic speculation, he persuaded the group to broaden the agenda of the forthcoming conference to the fundamentals of the faith and to commit to the formation of an interdenominational association of conservatives. When matters drifted, he used the November prophecy conference in New York to make preparations for a "world conference on the fundamentals" in the spring.[45]

The May 1919 conference, advertised as the first meeting of the World Christian Fundamentals Association, attracted six thousand people and extensive coverage in the regional newspapers. Riley and his fellow organizers spoke of a country in crisis where "thousands of false teachers, many of them occupying high ecclesiastical positions, are bringing in damnable heresies" and where a "Great Apostasy" was "spreading like a plague." Still, they held out hope for a national revival. The deans of all the major Bible schools spoke on points of doctrine, and a nine-point creed was adopted. Riley pronounced the event "of more historic moment than the nailing up, at Wittenberg, of Martin Luther's ninety-five Theses." After the convocation he took a group of singers and fourteen speakers on a cross-country tour, holding three- to six-day conferences in the major cities along their path. The most extensive religious endeavor the country had seen for many years, the tour gave the nascent movement national publicity and encouraged pastors across the country to join the cause.[46]

Chosen president of the association, Riley set up five standing committees headed by prestigious ministers, and announced a series of ambitious goals, among them the standardization and accreditation of Bible schools, the creation of a fundamentalist seminary, and the establishment of a foundation to rival Rockefeller's. The Committee on Conferences, headed by Riley himself, proved extremely successful. By 1921 Riley claimed that he and associates had held over two hundred conferences in cities and towns across North America. The rest of its committees, however, did very little, and as an organization the World Christian Fundamentals Association never cohered. The problem, Riley's wife tactfully put it, was "some personal incompatibilities and a constant tendency towards independent leadership."[47] Fundamentalist ministers were, after all, men of strong egos. Those who had built up their own churches or Bible schools were rulers of their own fiefdoms, and, as believers in absolute standards of right and wrong, they tended to be authoritarian of temperament. Riley claimed that running the WCFA was a cooperative effort, but, a prime example of the type, he took the lead and simply expected others to follow him. In 1924 he found to his surprise that a bewildering array of new organizations had cropped up: the Anti-Evolution League, the Fundamentalist League of the Pacific Coast, the American Bible League, the Defenders of Science and the Scriptures, and many more. "In our judgment," he wrote, "[most] of these movements ought to be simply a state organization of the World's Christian Fundamentals Association."[48] Predictably, however, his attempt to bring these groups under WCFA control met with obdurate resistance, and by 1926 it became clear that his effort to create an overarching interdenominational fundamentalist organization had failed. Where he succeeded, in spite of himself, was in spurring the formation of dozens of independent fundamentalist groups across the country.

Crises Within the Denominations

The major battles in the fundamentalist-modernist conflict were fought within the northern denominations, and principally within the Northern Baptist Convention and northern Presbyterian Church, both of which had strong modernist and antimodernist parties. The southern denominations were almost unaffected because modernist thinking had never penetrated the deeply conservative evangelicalism of the South. The Congregationalist Church was untouched for the opposite reason: by 1920 it had become a thoroughly liberal church. Then, because fundamentalism was an outgrowth of Calvinism, denominations such as the Methodists and the Disciples of Christ had few fundamentalists in the strict sense of the term. Still, the successes of the Baptist and Presbyterian militants in the early 1920s galvanized conservatives across the denominations, creating a strife that roiled most of the northern churches for years.

Baptists

The fundamentalist struggle within the Northern Baptist Convention began during the annual meeting of 1919, a gathering otherwise not very different from those of years past. Formed in 1907, the Northern Baptist Convention was a loose association of churches and a successor to another such a body. The Baptist tradition gave emphasis to liberty of conscience and the independence of congregations with the result that the churches ranged over a wide theological spectrum. Sects had emerged from time to time, and even among the General Baptists who constituted the majority, there had been a continuing tension between the more and the less Calvinist churches. Formed to support foreign missions and other agreed-upon enterprises, the Northern Baptist Convention had no confession of faith and no ecclesiastical authority over its constituent churches and seminaries. The liberals had been instrumental in putting it together, and they had always played a part in its leadership. Shailer Mathews, for one, had served as its president in 1915 and 1916.[49] It was therefore not out of the ordinary that at the 1919 convention Harry Emerson Fosdick was chosen to give the main address, that the leadership proposed certain centralizing measures—such as the creation of a unified budget—or that the Convention voted to join the Interchurch World Movement.

This time, however, conservatives reacted. They railed against Fosdick, decried the centralizing measures as a liberal plot to take over the denominational machinery, and denounced the Interchurch World Movement as the religious equivalent of the League of Nations. Then, too, they decided to organize just as William B. Riley had suggested they should ten years before.

A month before the Northern Baptist Convention of 1920, Curtis Lee Laws, the editor of a conservative Baptist periodical, *The Watchman-Examiner*, and 154 other conservatives issued a call for a pre-convention gathering on "Fundamentals of Our Baptist Faith." Three thousand ministers and laymen turned out for the meeting: some of them, like Riley, premillennialists; others, like Laws, doctrinal conservatives. Laws described the participants as "fundamentalists," thereby coining a term, and he defined the group as those "who mean to do battle royal for the fundamentals."[50] At the meeting the conservatives founded the National Federation of Fundamentalists of the Northern Baptists and chose a well-known premillennialist preacher, J. C. Massee, as president. Most speakers at the meeting condemned the spread of modernist theology within the church, but Massee and Riley set the agenda for the forthcoming convention with impassioned speeches about the dangers of false teachings in the Baptist seminaries, colleges, and secondary schools.[51]

The new organization, known as the Fundamentalist Fellowship, scored two immediate victories. The NBC withdrew from the Interchurch World Movement—though in part because some liberals thought it too ambitious. In addition, the NBC appointed a committee of nine, most of them fundamentalists, to investigate the doctrinal soundness of the denominational schools. When the committee reported back to the 1921 convention, however, one of the difficulties the fundamentalists faced in purging the denomination became obvious. The report criticized teachers in various institutions and urged that "Baptist communities throughout the country . . . displace from the schools men who impugn the authority of the Scriptures as the Word of God and who deny the deity of our Lord," but it pointed out that the Convention itself could do nothing about such cases. The NBC, after all, had no official doctrinal position and hadn't the power to act as a court.[52]

In anticipation of such an outcome, the fundamentalist leaders had decided to press the Convention to adopt a statement of faith to set theological boundaries around the denomination, as the Baptist leadership had sometimes done in the past. Drawing upon several historic Baptist confessions, Laws, Massee, and others had written a brief seven-part statement of faith. The creed made no mention of biblical inerrancy or the premillennial Advent, but at the pre-convention meeting of the Fellowship Riley and other militants endorsed the statement, thinking that such a minimalist creed might be adopted. At the last moment, however, Massee and other Fellowship leaders decided to put off proposing it to the Convention, apparently because they feared it would fail without more careful preparation.[53]

Riley was furious, and the more so the following year when the Fellowship leaders decided on another postponement. In the midst of the 1922 convention he forced the issue by introducing a resolution that the NBC adopt the New Hampshire Confession of 1833. The liberals, however, had anticipated such a move, and Cornelius Woelfkin, a New York pastor, immediately offered a substitute: "That the New Testament is the all-sufficient ground of our faith and practice, and we need no other statement." The tactic was ingenious. The resolution appealed to the Baptist tradition of liberty of conscience, and it presented those who supported a creed with the unpleasant prospect of voting against the New Testament. After a heated three-hour debate on the convention floor, Woelfkin's motion passed by a vote of 1,264 to 637.[54]

The defeat split the Baptist fundamentalists irreparably.

Instead of persuading Riley that Fellowship leaders had been right to put off the issue of the creed, passage of the resolution convinced him that the Fellowship leaders "had softened under the persuasive voice of their opponents" and the result was indecisiveness and lack of a coherent strategy. Declaring that victory could not be achieved "by compromise, connivance or even by conciliation," he left the Fellowship with a company of hard-liners and in early 1923 formed a new group, the Baptist Bible Union.[55]

Like Riley's WCFA, the Union was made up largely of premillennialists. Its leaders included A. C. Dixon, the first editor of *The Fundamentals*, T. T. Shields, the best-known Canadian fundamentalist, J. Frank Norris, a firebrand with churches in Detroit and Fort Worth, Texas, and John Roach Straton, a New York City preacher famous for thunderous preaching against gluttony, gaming, drink, and indecency in "the modern Babylon." Their goal was to unite sympathetic northern, southern, and Canadian Baptists, but their main accomplishment was to undermine support for fundamentalism in the NBC. Instead of trying to enlist wavering conservatives, Riley denounced "soft souls" who would repudiate the deity of Christ for the sake of peace. The "vocabulary of Christianity does not contain the word 'compromise'!" he declared. Certainly his vocabulary did not. Undaunted by his previous failure, he came to the 1924 convention with an ultraconservative statement of faith and made a scene on the floor. The same year Straton brought up a sensational charge of heresy against an NBC missionary and called for a full investigation of disloyalty in the mission field.[56]

By then, Massee, Laws, and the other Fellowship leaders realized that a successful attempt to impose doctrinal conformity might well split the Convention and imperil its foreign missions. Forced to choose, they found, Marsden writes, that "their doctrinal militancy was simply not as strong as their zeal for spreading the gospel."[57] They refused to support Riley's statement of faith, and, making common cause with the liberals, J. C. Massee offered an alternative to Straton's proposal: the Convention would send out a committee to look into the state of Northern Baptist missions generally. The following year the committee reported back that most of the NBC's missionaries were loyal to the faith and that spreading rumors to the contrary did severe harm to the denomination's efforts. When the BBU pressed for a doctrinal test of orthodoxy for missionaries, Massee supported an "inclusive policy" that recognized liberal and conservative points of view. At the 1926 Convention, the militant forces were greatly reduced in number. After another Riley motion was overwhelmingly defeated, Fellowship leaders called for an end to the controversy, and the BBU campaign came to a close.[58]

Presbyterians

The struggle among northern Presbyterians was even more dramatic than that among the Baptists, and for several years it seemed that the fundamentalists would win. The denomination was, after all, highly articulated, and an alliance of doctrinal conservatives and premillennialists had controlled the powerful General Assembly for some thirty years. In the 1890s the Assembly had brought heresy charges against three of the most famous liberal seminary professors and compelled them to leave the denomination. It also had declared certain doctrines essential to the church. This practice had begun in 1892 with the Portland Deliverance on the inerrancy of the Scriptures, and culminated with the five-point confession that was adopted in 1910 and reaffirmed in 1916. The conservative leaders of the postwar period were, like their forebears, denominational loyalists skilled in Presbyterian politics—not wild cards like Riley. In the previous century Old School Presbyterians had ejected the New School from the denomination. The conservatives held enough votes in the General Assembly that the fundamentalist militants thought they could do likewise with the modernists, and by the early 1920s some were simply waiting for an occasion.[59]

In May 1922, Harry Emerson Fosdick gave them all the provocation they needed with a sermon titled "Shall the Fundamentalists Win?" Though a Baptist, he was by special arrangement the associate pastor of the First Presbyterian Church of New York, and his sermon, directed at both denominations, made the liberal case so effectively that it was reprinted in three journals and widely distributed in pamphlet form. Liberal Christians, Fosdick argued, were trying to see the new knowledge about the physical universe and human history in terms of the Christian faith and their faith in terms of the new knowledge, as Christians had often done in the past. Fundamentalists, however, were trying to shut the doors of Christian fellowship to them by driving stakes of doctrine around the church. Fundamentalists, he observed, insist we must believe in certain special miracles, such as the virgin birth of Jesus; they insist we believe that the Bible was dictated by God; that the blood of Christ, shed in substitutionary atonement, placates an alienated deity; they insist we believe in the Second Coming of our Lord in clouds of heaven to set up a millennium. Fundamentalists, he said, have a right to their views, but not to their intolerance. Can we, he asked, imagine Jesus claiming as his own those who hold one view of, say, biblical inspiration and throwing into outer darkness those who hold another? What is needed, he said, is first, "an intellectually hospitable, tolerant, liberty-loving church" fit for a generation brought up on scientific inquiry and, second, a sense of penitent shame that Christians are bickering over minor matters of doctrine when they should be attending to a world that was staggering under colossal problems and crying out for justice, mercy, and faith.[60]

The sermon created a furor among conservatives and unleashed a pamphlet war. Conservative Presbyterians found it a clear case of heresy, and Clarence E. Macartney, a prominent Philadelphia pastor, initiated the counterattack with a sermon, "Shall Unbelief Win?" Liberal preaching, he charged, was "slowly secularizing the Church" and if evangelicals continued to allow the minority of modernists and rationalists to spread their message, the result would be "a Christianity of opinions and principles and good purposes, but a Christianity without worship, without God and without Jesus Christ."[61] Under his guidance the conservative Philadelphia Presbytery petitioned the General Assembly to condemn Fosdick's sermon and to instruct the Presbytery of New York to see that further preaching in the First Church conformed to orthodox Presbyterian doctrines. Because New York was the most liberal of the presbyteries, the proposal, slated to go to the 1923 General Assembly meeting, was a challenge to liberals generally.[62]

The fundamentalists' case was greatly strengthened when J. Gresham Machen turned his full attention to the controversy with the publication of *Christianity and Liberalism* in 1923. A protégé of Francis Patton and B. B. Warfield, Machen, then age forty-two, was the anointed heir to the whole tradition of the Princeton seminary. A classicist and New Testament scholar, educated at Johns Hopkins and the Princeton seminary, he had spent a year in Germany studying with leading Bible scholars, only to reject modernist thinking and to return to the fold of Old School Calvinism. At a time when Princeton under the leadership of a new president, J. Ross Stevenson, was hiring professors for the practical task of training evangelical pastors, Machen carried on the intellectual work of Charles Hodge and his successors in biblical exegesis and apologetics—or the defense of doctrine. Ideas were to him the most important terrain in the battle against what he and many other conservatives saw as the increasing secularization of the culture. In an address at Princeton in 1912, Machen maintained that the church faced a desperate emergency. Evangelism had its place but it was not the answer because it could only pick up a straggler here and there. The heart of the problem lay in the secularization of intellectual life, and it was in the universities where the cultural apostasy had to be fought. "What is today a matter of academic speculation," he said, "begins tomorrow to move armies and pull down empires." What the church needed, more than anything else, he argued, were intellectual warriors willing to battle secular culture and "to mould the thought of the world in such a way as to make the acceptance of Christianity something more than a logical absurdity." [63]

Where Machen differed from his Princeton predecessors was in his radical libertarianism. Born in Baltimore, the son of aristocratic southerners, he had grown up with the mythology of the Lost Cause and the vision of a society based on agrarian and spiritual values. Living in the industrializing North, he perceived the whole development of modern society as tending toward centralization, standardization, and the destruction of individual liberty. The loss of individual freedom was to him the worst part of secularization, and for it he blamed not the corporations but the increasing power of government. While many of his conservative colleagues called for laws against saloons, gambling, and Sabbath breaking, he fought all legislation that might infringe on individual freedom. Among other things, he opposed the compulsory draft, child labor laws, the national park system, and even a Philadelphia anti-jaywalking ordinance. Consistent to a fault, he, almost alone among Presbyterian leaders, opposed Prohibition. [64]

In the introduction to *Christianity and Liberalism* Machen decried the tendency of the modern world toward "a drab utilitarianism in which all higher aspirations are to be lost."

He then proposed that liberalism in its attempt to reconcile Christianity with modern science has become "a religion so entirely different from Christianity as to belong in a distinct category." In his first chapter he addressed what had been the main point of contention since the days of Horace Bushnell. Liberals, he charged, deny the very basis of Christian religion. They maintain that Christianity is an evolving tradition based in human experience and that doctrines are merely the expressions of that changing experience. But this is absurd. Christianity is based on the actual facts of history, as recounted in the New Testament, and doctrines are the setting forth of those facts. Without those two elements "joined in absolutely indissoluble union," there was no Christianity but merely "some indefinite type of religious aspiration," such as existed before Christianity appeared. Doctrines, he wrote, lie at the heart of New Testament, and an attack on Calvin, Turretin, or the Westminster divines is ultimately an attack not on the seventeenth century but on the Bible and against Jesus Himself.[65]

Machen proceeded to contrast the teachings of liberalism with that of his Old School Calvinist faith. Liberals, he charged, have lost sight of "the great presumptions of Christianity," such as the sinfulness of man, the awful transcendence of God, and the truth of the Bible. When they speak of "God," they do not mean the same thing that Christians do. The root of liberalism, he maintained, lies in naturalism, or denial of God's direct intervention in the origins of Christianity, and its logic must eventually drive out the supernatural from Christian belief. Liberalism was therefore "no mere 'heresy'—no mere divergence at isolated points from Christian teaching"—but, in spite of its use of traditional terminology, not Christianity at all. Machen's conclusion followed inexorably: liberalism was not Christianity, and therefore liberal ministers, if they were to pursue "the path of honesty," should separate themselves "from those confessional churches, whose confessions they do not, in the plain historical sense, accept." A separation between the two parties in the Church, he declared, "is the crying need of the hour."

Christianity and Liberalism was widely read, and not just by religious conservatives. Indeed, several influential secular commentators wrote that Machen had made a convincing case. Walter Lippmann called the book "the best popular argument produced by either side in the current controversy." *The Nation* and *The New Republic* published essays arguing that the fundamentalists had logic on their side when they invited the modernists to leave their denominations, for if the modernists contradicted the traditional creeds, then it would be only gentlemanly for them to withdraw and found churches of their own. "Fundamentalism," the editor of *The Nation* wrote, "is undoubtedly in the main stream of Christian tradition while modernism represents a religious revolution as far-reaching as the Protestant Reformation." These secular intellectuals had, it seemed, become so detached from religion that they imagined seventeenth-century reasoning normative for the church. Yet such was their prestige that many liberal Protestants feared that the logic of the fundamentalist position had prevailed.[66]

By the time of the 1923 General Assembly, the fundamentalists had gained another powerful champion in William Jennings Bryan. After three presidential campaigns and two years as secretary of state, Bryan, then age sixty-three, had a national following among Democrats. He was also the most popular speaker at Chautauqua meetings and on many evangelical Bible circuits, where he had lectured tirelessly for two decades. A Presbyterian elder long involved with denominational affairs, he was, as the liberal journal *The Christian Century* put it, "the most widely influential layman in the church."[67]

For the past few years Bryan had made common cause with the fundamentalists, but in many respects he was not one of them. His Christianity was a throwback to the antebellum evangelicalism of Charles Finney, where revivalism combined with dedication to social reform, and where adherence to basic Calvinist doctrines went together with belief in the progress toward the establishment of the Kingdom of God. A theological conservative, he averred faith in biblical infallibility, the virgin birth of Christ, and the other "essential" doctrines of Presbyterian fundamentalism. Still, he hadn't much interest in the fine points of theology. When asked if he could explain everything in the Bible, his answer was always, "If we will try to live up to that which we can understand, we will be kept so busy doing good that we will not have time to worry about the things we do not understand." He once admitted he had never had time to study the differences among Baptists, Methodists, and Presbyterians.[68] Bryan had, after all, a wide evangelical audience, and his emphasis was always on the ethical aspects of Christianity. "Religion," he said, "is the foundation of morality in the individual and in the group of individuals." Bryan assumed the truth of Christianity, but his defense of it was essentially pragmatic. Rather than arguing for its factuality, as Machen did, he argued the good it did for humankind. "There has not been a great reform in a thousand years that was not built about [Christ's] teachings," he proclaimed, and "there will not be in all the ages to come." [69]

At a time when religious conservatives and reformers were pulling apart, Bryan refused to leave either camp. Within his denomination he had long advocated political and social activism, or what he called "applied Christianity." His postwar agenda for the Presbyterians was much the same as what he urged upon the Democrats: taxation, trust regulation, the improvement of labor conditions, peace and disarmament, Prohibition, and women's suffrage. [70] A believer in ecumenical efforts, he had served on committees of the Federal Council of Churches and of the Interchurch World Movement, and he had worked closely with liberal Social Gospelers, such as Gladden and Steltze. Yet in the postwar years he became caught up in the sense of crisis that prevailed in fundamentalist circles about the growing secularization of the culture. While Machen identified the enemy as liberal theology, Bryan saw the principal threat to Christianity as the teaching of Darwinism in the colleges and schools.

Bryan came to this idea in stages. He had never believed that man was descended from the apes, and he had always considered evolution unscientific "theory"—meaning to him "a guess," as opposed to a Baconian truth drawn from the classification of facts. But he had never objected to those who thought otherwise until World War I. To Bryan, as to other Social Gospelers, the war came as a shocking disconfirmation of the belief in the continuing progress of Christian civilization. Seeking an explanation, he found it in books that argued that German militarism stemmed in a straight intellectual line from the idea of natural selection and the survival of the fittest through Nietzsche's philosophy. [71] Not only Bryan but W. B. Riley and other fundamentalist Baptists accepted this explanation, and after the war they came to the conclusion that the spread of Darwinism was undermining the moral foundations of the United States. [72]

In 1921 Bryan published a lecture, "The Menace of Darwinism," and a book, *In His Image*, arguing that the theory of evolution was destroying belief in God by contradicting the word of the Scriptures and by substituting the idea of the brute survival of the fittest for the Christian conception of man. His real enemy was Social Darwinism, but as he saw it, natural selection inspired hatred and struggle at every level, eliminated sympathy and the spirit of brotherhood, and halted the impetus to moral and social reform. "The great need of the world today is to get back to God—back to a real belief in a living God," Bryan wrote. No progeny of the brute, man was made in the Father's image; God beckoned man upward, and the Bible pointed the way.[73]

The book sold over a hundred thousand copies, and, buoyed by its success, Bryan took up a crusade against Darwinism (or what he imagined it to be). With Riley and others of the World Christian Fundamentals Association he campaigned in states across the country for laws banning the teaching of evolution in the public schools. "A scientific soviet," he warned in one lecture, "is attempting to dictate what shall be taught in our schools, and in doing so, is attempting to mold the religion of the nation. It is the smallest, the most impudent, and the most tyrannical oligarchy that ever attempted to exercise arbitrary power." Along with Bryan's populism came a distrust of experts and bureaucrats, and the view that democracy meant popular sovereignty and the absolute right of the majority to rule. Teachers, he told the West Virginia legislature, have the liberty to say what they please as individuals, but "they have no right to demand pay for teaching that which parents and the taxpayers do not want taught. The hand that writes the paycheck runs the school."[74]

In February 1922 Bryan debated Fosdick on evolution in the pages of *The New York Times* and proffered a new proposal: ministers who do not accept the biblical witness "should be honest enough to separate themselves from the ministry," and the majority of believers should take control of their churches. There is not room in one church, he held, for those who believe in evolution and those who do not.[75] The following year he took the fight to his own denomination.

For the newspapers the headline event of the 1923 Presbyterian General Assembly was the last-minute decision of Bryan to run for moderator of the Assembly. He was one of four candidates in the race, and on the first

two ballots he came close to getting the 439 votes he needed to win. Two
of the other candidates withdrew before the third ballot, leaving Bryan to
face Rev. Charles F. Wishart, the president of the College of Wooster, a
Presbyterian school that taught evolution in its science curriculum. Bryan
was confident of victory, but Presbyterian conservatives were divided on
the issue of Darwinism. Some of these highly educated ministers were
theistic evolutionists. Gresham Machen, for one, privately held the view
that although evolution could not explain the origins of the world, or the
creative acts of God that men called miracles, evolution was ordinarily
God's way of working His will in nature.[76] On the third round of voting
Wishart won by a narrow margin. Apparently he had picked up support
from those unwilling to see evolution divide the Assembly, for when, two
days later, Bryan introduced a resolution designed to cut off funding for
all Presbyterian schools that taught evolution, the Assembly responded by
passing a substitute resolution withholding support only from any school
that teaches "a materialistic evolutionary philosophy of life, or which dis-
regards or attempts to discredit the Christian faith."[77]

But Bryan was not finished. The main business of the meeting was
Macartney's complaint about Fosdick's sermons in the First Church of
New York, and Bryan weighed in on the fundamentalist side. First, he
helped persuade the Assembly to reaffirm the five fundamentals of the
faith adopted in 1910, and then in the midst of a heated debate, he joined
the faction that supported a resolution condemning Fosdick's sermon and
directing the New York Presbytery to require that preaching in the First
Church conform to Presbyterian doctrines. The proposal passed by a substantial margin, and in a letter to his daughter Bryan counted it as "a great
victory for orthodox Christianity—other churches will follow." It means
"a new awakening for the church."[78]

The liberals realized the seriousness of their situation, and inspired by
Henry Sloane Coffin, a New York minister who taught at Union Theological Seminary, they decided to fight back. On the closing day of the
meeting eighty-five delegates filed an official protest against the Assembly's action. A few weeks later a group of ministers began working on a
formal response to the Assembly's resolution. The paper, which became
known as the Auburn Affirmation, had, when released six months later,

150 signatories, most of them liberals or moderates but a few of them well-known conservatives.[79]

The Affirmation opened with a statement declaring the orthodoxy of its signatories and affirming the Westminster Confession. It went on to give a brief history of the Presbyterian Church in America, stressing the freedom it historically gave its ministers to interpret the Scriptures and the Confession. Under its constitution, the Affirmation asserted, doctrinal changes could be made only by the concurrent action of the General Assembly and the presbyteries. The five-point declaration was thus unconstitutional. It was also, the signers maintained, extra-biblical, and it committed the church to certain "theories" concerning church doctrines that the Westminster Confession did not. Surely, they said, the fellowship of the church should be broad enough to include all those who hold to the church's "great facts and doctrines," regardless of the theories they employ to explain them. In conclusion, the signers maintained that they were obliged to defend the liberty of thought and teaching in order to preach the Gospel effectively, and they called for denominational peace "in the face of a world so desperately in need of a united testimony to the gospel of Christ."[80]

Seeing a battle ahead in the next Assembly, the fundamentalists also marshaled their forces. In series of large-scale meetings in several cities Macartney, Machen, and others described the perilous condition of the church, where ministers were refusing to acknowledge the true meaning of church doctrines. The issue, Macartney said, was not just whether ministers had the right to interpret the Confession of Faith to suit themselves, but something far more serious: whether they had the right to deny the carefully recorded facts of the Bible. Machen, for his part, published numerous articles insisting that modernists were not Christians because, no matter how much of the Christian doctrine they affirmed, they affirmed it as a matter of inner experience and not as a fact. In a December meeting the fundamentalists raised the stakes by accusing the modernists of imperiling the "the very foundations of the moral order among men and nations" by rejecting "the great facts upon which the Christian revelation rests."[81] Such was the crisis caused by epistemological differences.

At the opening of the 1924 General Assembly the fundamentalists turned to Macartney to lead them, and Bryan placed the pastor's name in nomination for moderator. The liberals, realizing that one of their own could never be elected, reluctantly backed Charles Erdman, a fundamentalist but one who, having served on the denomination's home and foreign mission boards, favored a united church. Erdman, however, lost to Macartney by eighteen votes, and once in office, Macartney made Bryan vice moderator and appointed conservatives to all the important committees. Coffin, for one, despaired, writing his wife that a split in the church appeared all but inevitable. Yet the Assembly seemed curiously paralyzed. Fundamentalists brought the Auburn Affirmation to the attention of the body, but no action was taken on it. A resolution that all those on Presbyterian boards and agencies be required to affirm the five points was turned down. The Assembly settled the problem of Fosdick by inviting him to become a Presbyterian. The move insured his resignation from the First Church, but a discussion of his theological views and a challenge to the New York Presbytery were avoided. Machen wrote his allies that they had suffered a great defeat and that "if we regard the battle as over, we are traitors to our cause." [82]

In the months that followed Machen took on a more activist role. In early 1925 he and seven of his allies sent a letter to over a thousand supporters claiming the church was in crisis and urging them to hold mass meetings and elect fundamentalist delegates to the May convention. In a sermon he published himself, he wrote that if the church resorted to paganism, true Christians ought to withdraw from it, as Protestants had from the Catholic Church in the sixteenth century. [83] In addition, he launched an attack on his colleague Charles Erdman, who had decided to run again for moderator, making public a dispute that had been simmering quietly at the Princeton seminary for several years.

To outsiders the Princeton dispute seemed one of those debates over trivial issues that come from the clash of outsized personalities in a small faculty. A premillennialist, a social conservative, and a contributor to *The Fundamentals*, Erdman referred to himself as fundamentalist. Still, because he was one of the Princeton faculty hired to train pastors, and much influenced by Dwight Moody, he put the emphasis on evangelism and righteous living—as opposed to the defense of the truth. His previous career as a pastor and his involvement in the denominational mission boards had accustomed him to the give-and-take of denominational politics and reinforced his proclivity to subordinate theoretical issues to practical concerns. Machen, by contrast, had spent his entire career in the seminary, and having never married, he had no experience of the need to make compromises even in his domestic life. In a sense the conflict was personal—the two cordially disliked each other—but, more important, it was ideological. When Erdman wrote at one juncture that the only division in the seminary concerned "spirit, methods or policies," not doctrine, Machen retorted, "There is between Dr. Erdman and myself a very serious doctrinal difference indeed. It concerns the question not of this doctrine or that, but of the importance which is to be attributed to doctrine as such."[84] The difference reflected the division among Presbyterian conservatives generally and marked the line between the exclusivists, who demanded doctrinal purity, and the inclusivists, who, like Erdman, did not want theological issues to destroy the unity and the evangelical outreach of the church.[85]

As the 1925 General Assembly approached and Erdman staked his claim for moderator on strict adherence to the church constitution, Machen, along with eight of his allies, distributed a statement charging that Erdman was the candidate of the modernists. In a subsequent article, he wrote, "Dr. Erdman, despite his personal orthodoxy, had the plaudits of the enemies of the gospel," thus differing from those who had "laid aside all personal considerations and stood for the defense of the Christian faith." Erdman, he wrote, did not appreciate the crisis that faced the church or understand that "a policy of palliation and of compromise will in a few years lead to the control of our church . . . by agnostic Modernism."[86]

The personal attack on Erdman was impolitic, for even though the exclusivists seemed to have a slight working majority in the Assembly, Erdman, a jovial and well-liked man, was elected moderator. The key issue that year was a report from the Judicial Commission that allowed the Assembly to review the New York Presbytery's ordination of ministerial candidates who refused to affirm the five-point creed. This was precisely the ruling that the exclusivists needed to begin uprooting liberalism from the church. Coffin and his allies were, however, prepared for it. When the Assembly passed the measure, Coffin leaped to his feet and read a prepared statement declaring that the ruling was unconstitutional and that the New York Presbytery would not comply with it. Clearly the liberals were ready to leave the church if the ruling stood. Coffin hoped that would not be necessary. Over the course of the year he had developed a cordial relationship with Erdman, and during the tense moments that followed his statement, Erdman, in another carefully prepared move, left the moderator's chair and proposed that a special Commission of Fifteen be appointed to study the spiritual condition of the church "to the end that the purity, peace, unity, and progress of the Church may be assured." The motion, seconded by Coffin and William Jennings Bryan, passed by a wide majority that included fundamentalists, who, like Bryan, recoiled in the face of an imminent schism in the church.[87]

Composed largely of conservatives, the Commission of Fifteen might have produced a murky document with compromises just sufficient to keep the liberals in the church, but to the surprise of many it went much further than that. In reports to the 1926 and the 1927 Assemblies, it echoed the Auburn Affirmation in stressing the church's history of toleration and the limits on the power of the General Assembly. Contrary to the claims of Machen, it stated, "Presbyterianism is a great body of belief, but it is more than a belief; it is also a tradition, a controlling sentiment. The ties which bind us to it are not of the mind only; they are ties of the heart as well."[88] In unambiguous language the Commission affirmed the authority of the presbyteries in licensing and ordaining ministers; it also rejected the right of the General Assembly to make statements concerning the necessary articles of faith that were not direct quotations from the Westminster Confession. It thus overturned the 1925 Judicial Commission ruling and rendered void the Assembly's often reiterated declaration of the five fundamental doctrines.[89] In sum, it gave the liberals exactly what they wanted and reversed every gain the fundamentalists had made since the Portland Deliverance of 1892 on biblical inerrancy.

There was another important development as well.

Within a few months of the committee's report in 1926, the Assembly decided to delay the Princeton seminary's appointment of Machen to the important chair of ethics and apologetics and to name a committee to investigate the controversies at the seminary. The investigation led to a reorganization of the seminary's governing boards to ensure a broader representation of theological positions on the faculty. In 1929 Machen and three other faculty members quit in protest and founded a seminary of their own. Princeton remained relatively conservative, but the school turned away from its doctrinal rigidity, and the hundred-year reign of Charles Hodge and his successors came to an end.[90]

The Scopes Trial and the Defeat of the Fundamentalists

The setback of the fundamentalist effort to drive the modernists from the northern Baptist and Presbyterian churches owed to the unwillingness of many conservatives to break up their denominations. Still, the collapse of the fundamentalist position in 1926–27 and the victory of the liberals were far more sudden and dramatic than was warranted by the relative strength of the various parties. It would in fact be hard to explain except for the trial of a young science teacher, John Scopes, for teaching evolution in a Tennessee school.

In March 1925 Tennessee became the third southern state to adopt a law against the teaching of evolution in the public schools. Bryan had much to do with this legislation. For the past three years he had been crusading against evolution across the country with William B. Riley, J. Frank Norris, and other members of the World Christian Fundamentals Association. In a number of southern states they had found support among local politicians and waged major campaigns. Riley held mass meetings—twenty-two of them in Kentucky alone—while Bryan went on speaking tours and addressed joint sessions of state legislatures.[91] The Tennessee bill was introduced after Bryan gave a lecture in Nashville, and passed after copies were sent to members of the legislature. By far the strongest of the laws, it cast evolution as denying the Genesis account of the creation of man, and it actually criminalized the teaching of it in state-funded schools.

The American Civil Liberties Union, eager to challenge the constitutionality of the law, offered to defend anyone prosecuted under it. John Scopes, a young biology teacher working in the small town of Dayton, was persuaded by two local businessmen to make himself the test case. He was arrested in May and the trial was set for July. Had Roger Baldwin and the other ACLU leaders had their way, the trial would have been a quiet one, and when Scopes lost, as he was sure to do on the facts, they could have taken the case to the higher courts to challenge the law. However, Bryan, spurred on by Riley at a WCFA convention in Memphis, decided to join the prosecution and was named counsel to the attorney general of Tennessee. Clarence Darrow immediately volunteered his services to the defense. With that Baldwin concluded that the issue of civil liberties versus states rights would fade into the background, and the trial would be a contest of "the Good Book against Darwin, bigotry against science, or, as popularly put, God against monkeys."[92]

The trial in which Bryan and Darrow faced off over modern science and the literal truth of the Bible in Dayton, Tennessee, was the most famous court case of the period. The contest between the golden-tongued populist at home in his constituency of the rural South, and the urbane skeptic, the most celebrated courtroom lawyer of his day, riveted the national attention for weeks. It later became the stuff of legend, high school history courses, and numerous scholarly histories, yet few accounts describe the consequences it had for fundamentalists.

Even before the trial began, both participants and observers proclaimed the contest would be the decisive battle between fundamentalists and modernists. Remarkably, it was. By all accounts, regardless of their point of view, the trial ended with a humiliating defeat for Bryan and for the cause of literalist Bible believers. In the northern Baptist and Presbyterian denominations, many conservatives dropped their support for the fundamentalist positions, and the militants, so close to victory just a year before, beat a bitter retreat. The trial had turned fundamentalists into outsiders within a dominant liberal Protestant and secular culture. No longer, Marsden writes, could fundamentalists "raise the level of discourse to the plane where any of their arguments would be taken seriously. Whatever they said would be overshadowed by the pejorative associations attached to the movement by the seemingly victorious secular establishment."[93] How the trial could have effected such a transformation is on the face of it mysterious, but, as the anthropologist Susan F. Harding has explained, it was a matter of how the trial was depicted, first by the national newspapers and then by fundamentalists themselves.[94]

The promise of an epic battle between Bryan and Darrow over evolution and religion turned the Scopes trial into a media spectacular and a major tourist attraction. For two weeks in July that year Dayton, a hill town of 1,700 people northeast of Chattanooga, became the news capital of the nation. A radio station affiliated with the *Chicago Tribune* created a national radio hookup and broadcast the news from Dayton live across the country. Over a hundred journalists from big-city newspapers descended on the town and sent out almost 150,000 words a day via telephone and telegraph. As visitors poured in from around the region, the town took on a carnival atmosphere, its streets filling up with vendors of hot dogs and lemonade, circus performers with chimpanzees, and innumerable Bible-shouting, psalm-singing preachers. The journalists made much of the local color, describing Holy Roller meetings, preachers with banners urging people to read their Bibles and avoid damnation, and the fundamentalist judge from Gizzard Cove who was to rule over the proceedings. H. L. Mencken, reporting daily to the *Baltimore Evening Sun*, exulted, "The thing is genuinely fabulous. I have stored up enough material to last me 20 years."[95]

Bryan came to town a few days ahead of time and immediately declared that the trial would be a "duel to the death" between evolution and Christianity. Followed around by admiring throngs, he seemed to reporters to be in his element. One night, *The New York Times* reported, he went up into the hills and preached to two hundred people about a great religious revival that would start in the South and sweep the nation. The mountaineers, said the *Times*, listened to him with rapt countenances, and his final words were met with "a reverential hush." To these plain folks, the reporter concluded, "Bryan is more than a great politician, more than a lawyer on trial, more even than one of our greatest orators, he is a symbol of their simple religious faith." Mencken naturally took a more jaundiced view. Describing Bryan's admirers as "gaping primates," "yokels," "hillbillies," and "morons," he wrote, "There were many . . . who believed that Bryan was no longer merely human, but had lifted himself up to some level or other of the celestial angels. . . . It would have surprised no one if he had suddenly begun to perform miracles." As for Darrow, "All the local sorcerers predict that a bolt from heaven will fetch him in the end." [96]

Legally speaking, the trial was hardly a contest. The prosecution called four witnesses who testified that Scopes had taught evolution and rested its case. The defense based its entire case on the testimony of fifteen scientists and clergymen it had brought to Dayton to argue that Darwinism was good science and compatible with Christianity, but the judge refused to admit their testimony into evidence. The jury thus quite understandably found Scopes guilty after a deliberation of eight minutes. Later Scopes's conviction was overturned on a technicality, so that the ACLU could not pursue the case. Still, the duel that Bryan had promised took place in a dramatic fashion.

Dayton residents and visitors had come to hear the eloquent lawyers argue, and they were not disappointed. By the time the last defense witness was dismissed and the final arguments seemed to be at hand, the crowd had grown so large that the judge moved the court outside lest the courthouse collapse. When the proceedings resumed on the lawn of the building, Darrow and his team did something completely unexpected. Instead of resting their case, they asked Bryan to take the stand as an expert witness on the Bible. The attorney general objected, but Bryan could not refuse the challenge. The two men mounted a platform built for visiting revivalists, and for the next two hours Darrow grilled Bryan relentlessly. [97]

Darrow began by questioning Bryan on his interpretation of well-known Bible stories. Did he believe that the whale swallowed Jonah, that Joshua made the sun stand still, that the Flood actually took place, and that Adam and Eve were the first people? Bryan answered in the affirmative to all these questions, stating at one point that he would believe that Jonah swallowed "the big fish" if the Bible said so, since "one miracle is just as easy to believe as another." Bryan, however, did not know that "the big fish" that swallowed Jonah in the Old Testament was called a whale in the New Testament. He did not know how Eve could be created from Adam's rib, where Cain got his wife, or what would happen if the earth stood still. When Darrow pointed out that Bryan's personal Bible put the creation of the earth at 4004 BC, Bryan responded that the date was the calculation of some man, and he thought that the earth was older than that, but he didn't know how old it was. Darrow then made him admit to a lack of knowledge about geology, philology, other religions, and ancient civilizations. In one of their most notorious exchanges, Darrow led Bryan to say he believed the earth revolved around the sun, not the sun around earth, as the book of Joshua had it. In another, he led Bryan to say that the six "days" of creation were not necessarily twenty-four-hour periods. Apparently Bryan did not read the Bible literally at all times.[98]

The interrogation came to an end with the two men on their feet shaking their fists at each other. "The only purpose Mr. Darrow has is to slur the Bible," Bryan exclaimed. "I object to your statement," Darrow retorted. "I am examining you on your fool ideas that no intelligent Christian on earth believes."[99]

The judge abruptly dismissed the court until the next morning, and many spectators, including townspeople who had come to cheer Bryan, gathered around Darrow to congratulate him on his performance. Bryan's testimony was later expunged from the record, but his words had already been wired around the nation along with stories reporting that he had suffered a devastating defeat. Bryan had hoped to put Darrow on the stand the following day, but the attorney general, who had enough of such pyrotechnics, refused to allow it, and the defense lawyers declined to sum up their case, thereby depriving Bryan of the opportunity to deliver a closing speech. Five days later Bryan died during an afternoon nap.[100]

As might be expected, the impression of the interrogation conveyed by the big-city reporters was that Darrow had revealed Bryan's ignorance and the absurdity of his biblical literalism, and that he had clearly demonstrated the superiority of science and modernist thinking. In the North Bryan became the object of ridicule and derision in newspapers, in coffee shops, and even in a Broadway play. His death quieted the mockery, but it seemed to be evidence that even he understood the depth of his defeat and the hopelessness of his cause. The reportage on the trial had situated fundamentalism in the rural South, amid Bible-thumping "cranks and fanatics," "plain folk," and "hillbillies." Fundamentalism was, it seemed, an old-fashioned backwoods religion of uneducated people, who held on to their "simple beliefs" and belonged to a culture that would soon be over-run by the juggernaut of the modern world.

There were a few things wrong with this picture. In the days just following the trial, Bryan, the eternal optimist, never gave the impression of a beaten man. He spent the time polishing his unread speech for publication and preparing to continue his crusade against evolution.[101] In the second place, there were no fundamentalists in Dayton. By definition—their own as well as Harry Emerson Fosdick's—fundamentalists were militant antimodernists, and virtually all of them were northerners. What reporters saw in Dayton were traditional southern evangelicals, or preachers of local folk religions, but not fundamentalists. Indeed, one of the curiosities of the trial was the absence of Bryan's fundamentalist allies. William B. Riley, J. Frank Norris, and J. C. Massee had been invited by Bryan, but all three had decided to go instead to the National Baptist Convention in Seattle, where a crucial fight was expected. The Presbyterians, Macartney and Machen, had also declined Bryan's request for assistance. Apparently Bryan had not realized that the two did not completely reject evolutionary biology, and that Machen opposed state control over education. Then, too, and perhaps for similar reasons, none of the dozens of conservative Protestant journals with national circulations sent observers to Dayton.[102]

Why, then, was the trial so devastating to the northern fundamentalists? In the absence of the religious press it was, of course, entirely constituted for Americans by the skeptical big-city newspapers. Still, as Susan Harding points out, these journalists could not have rendered a generally acceptable verdict on their own. The fundamentalists had to acquiesce to the judgment, and they did.

The climactic encounter between Darrow and Bryan was interpreted as a crushing defeat for Bryan, but, Harding writes, it could have been represented as his victory: the drama of a man standing up for God and the Bible and taking upon himself the ridicule and scorn of unbelievers, and further, a demonstration that evolutionary thought was an attack on true Christianity. Darrow could have been cast as a cynic who "hated" the Bible, a bigot who mocked the common man, a villain that Bryan exposed. Toward the end of the interrogation, Bryan himself suggested this story line by speaking of "a giant conspiracy of atheists and agnostics against the Christian religion." But fundamentalists, including those who read the trial transcript, never took up this line.[103]

Conservative Protestants naturally construed the dramatic encounter differently than did the reporters. Most of them passed over the details and attacked Darrow's line of questioning and the harsh treatment of Bryan by the press. In his memorial address for Bryan, Riley assailed "the blood-sucking journalists" and called Darrow's questions "captious and conscienceless." "Imagine," he said, "converting the opposing attorney into a witness for the defense by putting snap judgment questions concerning the exact years when a number of heathen religions were born, and then trying to make it appear as if the failure to answer them offhand was a lack of knowledge, if not intelligence."[104]

A conservative Presbyterian minister writing in a denominational journal decried "a great noise of ridicule" from the news reporters and described Darrow's questions as "repulsive, abusive, ignorant, tiresome twaddle about Bible questions that no true student of God's Holy Word would ever think fit to answer." Such accounts did not, however, claim that Bryan won the contest.[105]

The fact was that fundamentalists also thought Bryan had failed, but for reasons that they could not admit. It wasn't that they thought he had fallen into heretical error in maintaining that the six "days" of creation were probably "ages," for such was the consensus among northern conservatives at the time. That and other metaphorical readings of the Bible were deemed perfectly acceptable in fundamentalist circles. The idea that biblical literalism meant that every word in the Bible was to be understood in only its narrowest and most literal sense was merely a modernist caricature. The problem, Harding explains, was essentially rhetorical. For fundamentalists, she writes, a proper defense of the Bible required "active, aggressive Bible quoting, an ability to parry 'infidel objections' and 'standard village atheist questions,' and a willingness to assert that every claim, every word, every jot and tittle in the Bible was literally true." In their own internal contests, they gave higher ground to the preacher who through rhetorical ingenuity could produce a more "literal" interpretation than the next. Darrow in his questions about Bible passages used the techniques of fundamentalist rhetorical combat, but Bryan, who came from a wider evangelical background, failed to respond in kind. The fundamentalists, Harding writes, were trapped. They could not contest the outcome of the duel because Darrow played it by their own rules.[106]

The convergence of the fundamentalists' interpretation with that of the big-city journalists gave the impression that the modernist version of events was true. Fundamentalists, Harding writes, got caught up in the modernist narrative. They saw themselves, as they were seen, "acting out, in the body of William Jennings Bryan, modernist preconceptions and scenarios." The authorial voice of the country now seemed to belong to secularists and liberal Christians, and by its terms fundamentalists were cultural outsiders—people without a legitimate voice.[107]

Had Bryan lived, the story might have had many more chapters, but his death put a theatrical end to it. To fundamentalists as to others, it seemed that Bryan had been killed by Darrow and the superior forces of modernist thinking.[108]

In mid-1926 *The Christian Century*, the leading voice of liberal Protestantism, reported that "so decisive a rout of fundamentalism was unexpected." Yet, in retrospect, the editors wrote, "anybody should be able to see that the whole fundamentalist movement was . . . wholly lacking in the qualities of constructive achievement or survival." It will henceforth, they predicted, "be a disappearing quantity in American religious life." Where the northern denominations were concerned, the editors were more or less right, for in the years after the Scopes trial, many fundamentalists quit their denominations, and most of those who remained dropped into silence and attended to the needs of their own congregations. Mencken, however, thought the movement far from dead. "Heave an egg out of a Pullman window," he famously wrote, "and you will hit a Fundamentalist almost anywhere in the United States today." Fundamentalists, he continued, "are thick on the mean streets behind the gas works. They are everywhere where learning is too heavy for mortal minds to carry."[109]

In the years that followed, fundamentalists seemed to be acting out the roles that the modernists had assigned to them. In 1926, two of their nationally known leaders were caught up in perfectly Menckenesque scandals. J. Frank Norris, who was feuding with the Catholic mayor of Fort

Worth, shot one of the mayor's supporters dead. His plea of self-defense convinced the jury, but the fact remained that the pastor had fired four shots at an unarmed man who had come into his office. The same year T. T. Shields took over a failing Baptist college in Iowa on behalf of the Baptist Bible Union, and in an effort to turn it into a fundamentalist institution created turmoil on campus by dismissing many of the professors and sending spies to look for dissenters in the student body. When it was rumored that he was having an affair with a college secretary, the students rioted and the college collapsed.[110]

Then, too, after Dayton the militant Baptists pressed on with their anti-evolution campaign. In a whirlwind of uncoordinated activity, Riley, Straton, Norris, and dozens of newly formed groups, such as the Bible Crusaders of America and Gerald B. Winrod's Defenders of the Faith, held hundreds of rallies around the country and in the space of three years introduced thirty-seven anti-evolution bills into some twenty state legislatures.[111] Their rhetoric was extreme and sometimes conspiratorial. Riley, for example, connected evolution with atheism and "Sovietism" and suggested that support for evolution was the work of "some great organization with a sinister purpose." As a result of their efforts, Mississippi and Arkansas passed laws similar to that of Tennessee, and the governor of Texas, Miriam "Ma" Ferguson, personally saw to it that evolution was eliminated from the Texas school textbooks. Still, most of their bills failed to pass, and their campaigns engendered a reaction in the North, where the opposition included conservatives who believed in the Genesis account of creation but wished to maintain a line of separation between church and state.[112]

By the time the crusade to change state laws fizzled out, it had reinforced the notion that fundamentalism was the religion of uneducated rural southern folk and obscurantists who wished to purge modern knowledge from the public schools. In 1929 Walter Lippmann, who just a few years before had hailed Machen's *Christianity and Liberalism*, wrote that fundamentalist ideas no longer appealed to "the best brains and the good sense of the modern community." Like Lippmann, most in the new centers of cultural power, principally the press and the universities, believed that fundamentalism had become irrelevant and would eventually fade away. The fundamentalists themselves added to this impression, for many spoke as though theirs was a lost cause and adopted a rhetoric of martyrdom. The Northern Baptist separatist Oliver W. Van Osdel, for example, urged his colleagues not to seek the world's acceptance but to emulate "the rejected Son of God in these days of declension and compromise."[113] By general agreement the fundamentalists had become outsiders—strangers in a strange land.

5

THE SEPARATISTS

I N THE fall of 1949, not twenty-five years after the Scopes trial, a young fundamentalist began preaching revivals in major American cities, attracting enormous crowds. In Los Angeles he drew 350,000 people to his eight-week tent crusade. In Boston two months later he preached to 105,000 people in eighteen days, packing the Opera House, Symphony Hall, and the Boston Garden. And on he went to Columbia, South Carolina; Portland, Oregon; Minneapolis; Atlanta; and back to New England, the throngs overflowing the largest halls.[1]

Billy Graham, a lanky figure in sherbet-colored suits with wide lapels and polychrome hand-painted ties, preached with passionate intensity. His voice raw, his arms windmilling, he sounded all the old revivalist chords: "The Bible says, ye must be born again! The sinfulness of man's heart is the source of all this world's woes" . . . "Today the message has not changed from Isaiah's time. It is the same. *Repent ye! Repent ye!*" . . . "There is no alternative! If Sodom and Gomorrah could not get away with sin, if Pompeii and Rome could not escape, neither can Los Angeles!" . . . "If we don't have a revival . . . in the next month or next year, we might not have any more time. Like Israel in the time of Isaiah, America is drifting away from God."[2]

Billy Graham, the newspapers reported, was a powerful preacher, who could hold an audience rapt with an intake of breath. To those who met him he seemed a nice young man, friendly, open, and sincere. But where his crowds came from puzzled many a Protestant minister.

For most of the past twenty-five years the country *had* seemed to be drifting away from religion. Prohibition, backed by most of the Protestant denominations, had been a disastrous failure. Even Protestants who went to church on Sundays were apparently drinking moonshine or bootlegged liquor on Saturday nights, for the sale of alcohol decreased by only a third. Organized crime flourished; otherwise law-abiding citizens were treated as criminals; and the inability of federal and state agencies to enforce the law made a mockery of the American justice system. In 1933 more than three quarters of the states voted for the Twenty-first Amendment that repealed the Eighteenth Amendment. Then, too, the Great Depression, instead of drawing people to the consolation of religion, drove many away. Church attendance dropped off sharply in the major northern denominations, and the tent revivalists lost their congregations. Billy Sunday held his last crusade in 1930, and those who hoped to succeed him were largely ignored. Aimee Semple McPherson, a Pentecostal preacher who in the 1920s had thrilled crowds across the country, found herself a dimming star, preaching in cities like Wichita.[3] In fact, the only national revivalist of the period was not a religious figure at all, but President Franklin Delano Roosevelt, and he, unlike Woodrow Wilson, made his appeals to the country in completely secular terms.

After the Scopes trial fundamentalists had been relegated to the margins of Americans society, and later some of their most prominent leaders made the liberals' case by drifting off into bigotry and political extremism. Throughout the 1920s J. Frank Norris maintained that the Catholics were attempting to take over the government and overturn the Constitution. If that happened, he wrote, "They would behead every Protestant preacher and disembowel every Protestant mother. They would burn to ashes every Protestant Church and dynamite every Protestant school. They would destroy the public schools and annihilate every one of our institutions." He described the slaughter of Protestants on St. Bartholomew's Day, 1572, and declared, "This same bloody beast now undertakes to control the politics of this country."[4] In the early 1930s a number of other leaders, among them Arno Gaebelein, James M. Gray, William B. Riley, and Gerald Winrod, embraced the notorious forgery *The Protocols of the Elders of Zion* and integrated it into their end times scenarios—uncomfortably, as it sat with their prophetic Zionism. According to Riley, a Jewish-Communist cabal was secretly plotting to establish a single world government and to impose a uniform atheistic religion on the enslaved populations of the world. Riley and Winrod, who led the Defenders of the Christian Faith, maintained that apostate Jews were already taking over American finances, courts, and newspapers and, as Riley put it, making ready to "filch the land of all its gold, take over its cattle and its farms and possess themselves of all its factories, arts and industries." In addition they and other fundamentalist leaders charged that the New Deal was preparing the way for the Antichrist and pointed to blue eagle insignia of the National Recovery Administration as the mark of the Beast.[5] The Roosevelt administration, Riley wrote, was clearly "a Jewish-controlled regime"—the evidence being that Eleanor was "pink," some of the brain trusters were secret Stalinists, and the president himself had Communist sympathies. Like the notorious Father Charles Coughlin and his Protestant associate, Gerald L. K. Smith, some of these fundamentalist leaders became Nazi sympathizers. Hitler, Riley wrote, has snatched his country "from the very jaws of atheistic Communism" with "help from on high." Traveling in Germany in 1937, Gaebelein wrote, "A new Germany has arisen. . . . There is no question in my mind that Hitler was an instrument of God to save Germany and Europe from the Red Beast." Winrod, who also visited Germany in the 1930s, became a public apologist for the Nazi regime and during the "Brown Scare" of the 1940s was indicted by the U.S. Justice Department for sedition.[6]

Yet just a decade later, Billy Graham, this good-hearted, somewhat bland, all-American figure, was preaching crusades in one major metropolis after another, from Dallas, Texas, to Syracuse, New York, conducting services under the klieg lights of some of the largest football and baseball stadiums in the country with the support of prominent businessmen and politicians.[7]

Graham's timing was, as it turned out, serendipitous. Beginning in the latter years of World War II a religious upwelling took place across the country. After the soldiers came home, had families, and the economy took off, Americans started going to church in record numbers. By the evidence of one survey, church membership in the decade 1945–55 rose from seventy to a hundred million people. The money put into church construction went from $409 million in 1950 to more than a billion dollars by the end of the decade. According to all surveys, not just the number but also the percentage of Americans who attended church increased dramatically. By one estimate the percentage of the population with a church affiliation rose from 43 percent before the war to 55 percent in 1950 to 69 percent in 1960.[8] Protestants, Catholics, and Jews poured into churches and synagogues in more or less equal proportions. Every major Protestant denomination gained large numbers of new adherents, and membership in some of the small denominations multiplied several times over. This upsurge in churchgoing took place without the creativity, the enthusiasms, and the chaos of previous periods of national revival. If it was a revival at all, it was a sedate, orderly, and respectable affair.[9]

The Protestants who swarmed into the churches and the revival tents in this period included a great many fundamentalists and other evangelical conservatives. That fact was not well understood at the time. The outcome of the fundamentalist-modernist controversy had, after all, been interpreted as a victory for modernism, and since then the liberals, in control of the seminaries, had taken the leadership roles in the major northern denominations, and some had become a part of the intellectual establishment. In the 1950s the theologians Reinhold Niebuhr and Paul Tillich riveted the attention of liberal American intellectuals generally. Forgotten was the fact that in the fundamentalist-modernist conflict the liberals had narrowly won their right to exist in the northern Baptist and Presbyterian denominations. The fundamentalists had lost, but the winners had been the inclusivist conservatives, and they represented those many in the pews who paid no attention to the doctrinal disputes of their leadership.

Then, too, conservatives continued to dominate the South and to make up a significant percentage of other large northern denominations, such as the Disciples of Christ. A number of the smaller denominations were entirely conservative. These included the Holiness and Pentecostal churches, much influenced by fundamentalism, and some Anabaptist groups, such as the Mennonites. They also included denominations established by mid- to late-nineteenth-century immigrants from rural Northern Europe, among them the Christian Reformed Church from the

Netherlands, the Lutheran Church—Missouri Synod from Germany, and the Swedish Baptists. These had taken on fundamentalist characteristics as their congregants became English-speaking and integrated themselves into American society. These various conservative groups had been a part of the landscape for many years, but uncontroversial and separated from each other by region and denominational boundaries, they were hidden in plain sight.[10]

What was more, the militant fundamentalists never fit the role the liberals had assigned to them or accepted their designated fate. They had lost the battle for prestige, but they did not lose their sizable constituencies, and as before, fundamentalism flourished with new groups springing up, as one historian put it, like dandelions. Their leaders, contentious and authoritarian, never created a national organization that reflected fundamentalist numbers. Still, many of them, such as Reuben Torrey, James M. Gray, William B. Riley, and J. Frank Norris, were spiritual entrepreneurs, who during the 1930s and '40s built networks of local churches and an array of institutions to train young preachers and to propagate the faith. In the "religious drought" experienced by mainline denominations, their flocks increased—as did those of many conservative groups, like the Southern Baptist Convention. On the whole, cultural exile suited the fundamentalist leaders. Indeed, some stepped deliberately into outsider roles, portraying themselves as martyrs and the faithful as a beleaguered remnant fighting the Devil incarnate in all the forces of the secular and the apostate world. This stance inspired conspiracy theories of the vilest sort, but it also fostered group solidarity and attracted Bible-believing Protestants alienated in the strange new world of global depression and global war. From their wanderings in the wilderness, the fundamentalists emerged stronger than before.

During the 1950s fundamentalists divided into two camps, corresponding to the two conflicting impulses present in fundamentalism since its inception: one to guard doctrinal purity without compromise; the other to reclaim America and to gain the world for Christ through revivals. Virtually all fundamentalists believed in both courses of action, but in the 1940s many felt they had to make choices, and the two impulses materialized in the form of two parties: one separatist, militant, and often politically extremist; the other inclusivist, bent on regaining respectability and cultural influence, preferring to be called "evangelical" as opposed to "fundamentalist." The two parties were, however, not completely distinct, for both came out of the crucible of the fundamentalist-modernist controversy. Indeed, to trace the intellectual lineage of the leaders of both parties in the 1950s—and well after that—is to discover as it were a family tree linking them, personally or institutionally, with men like Torrey, Riley, Norris, and Machen.

How the fundamentalists survived and extended their reach during the Great Depression and World War II was ignored by religious historians at the time. Liberal churchmen, certain that liberal theology, or secularization, was the trend of the twentieth century, were in denial. Only in the 1980s when such trained evangelical historians as George Marsden and Joel Carpenter came on the scene was the subject explored. By the account of Carpenter and younger evangelical scholars, a large but unknown number of fundamentalists left the major denominations in the 1930s to join, or found, independent local Bible churches—or they left liberal denominations for more conservative ones. More, however, remained in the mainline denominations, sheltered within conservative churches and in some cases regional bodies like presbyteries and state conventions. Both groups, however, gave increasing support to the building of a network of transdenominational agencies, some of which had been founded many years earlier.[11]

Of these agencies, the most important were the Bible institutes, and in the 1930s and '40s their number grew at an impressive rate. According to Carpenter, there were 50 of them in 1930 and 144 in 1950. Some were no more than evening classes held in a local church, but others developed into comprehensive centers of religious activity, training pastors as well as laymen and exercising many of the functions of a denomination. By the early '30s these included the Bible Institute of Los Angeles (BIOLA), Gordon College of Theology and Missions in Boston, the Philadelphia School of the Bible, the National Bible Institute in New York City, and Northwestern Bible and Missionary Training School in Minneapolis. The largest of them and the pacesetter for the rest, the Moody Bible Institute, drew students from all over the country, put on conferences in hundreds of churches a year, and published a magazine that by 1940 had forty thousand subscribers.[12]

Fundamentalists also founded seminaries and liberal arts colleges, though few with any academic standing. The Baptist seminaries for the most part offered only pastoral training for students without a college degree. The handful of seminaries that served Presbyterians had postbaccalaureate programs but the most influential was the Dallas Theological Seminary, founded by a colleague of C. I. Scofield, which specialized in the teaching of dispensationalism. As for the colleges, most of them developed out of the Bible schools, and all emphasized training for mission work and church activities. Bob Jones University, named for the Alabama evangelist who founded it in 1927, became well known among northern and southern fundamentalists, but it had no accreditation of any kind. By far the most prestigious was Wheaton College in Illinois. Established by Methodists before the Civil War, Wheaton, unlike most of its peers, had retained its conservative evangelical character, and under the presidency of fundamentalist J. Oliver Buswell Jr. (1926–40) it became academically respectable and the largest liberal arts college in the state, with over a thousand students.[13]

Fundamentalists were scattered all over the country, but summer Bible conferences brought huge numbers of people together each year, and enthusiasm for missions fostered cooperation among far-flung congregations. At a time when the mainline denominations were retrenching on overseas evangelism, fundamentalist Bible schools and colleges turned out hundreds of missionaries a year. During the mid-1930s fundamentalists contributed one out of every seven North American Protestant missionaries, and by the early 1950s the proportion had doubled. Fundamentalist publications increased in numbers and circulation, and when commercial radio became available, fundamentalist evangelists took to it, as to a revival tent with unlimited space. They bought airtime on local stations or networks and paid for it through appeals to their audiences—something mainline ministers were loath to do. Fundamentalist centers, such as Moody, BIOLA, and John Roach Straton's New York church, developed Bible study and children's programs, and a number of preachers attracted regional followings on the air.[14]

Fundamentalism was also spread by charismatic preachers who built their own religious empires in various regions of the country. In a world with few established institutions, they created their own, and pioneering the way for others, they made personal (and family) empires a permanent feature of the fundamentalist world. William B. Riley was one of the most successful of these preachers, and in his book *God's Empire* the historian William Trollinger describes how Riley made his Bible school an agency for the fundamentalist colonization of the upper Midwest.

Not long after taking over the First Baptist Church in Minneapolis, Riley discovered that the rural churches in the upper Midwest (Minnesota, Iowa, Nebraska, Wisconsin, and the Dakotas) were chronically under-staffed, and some had had to close down for lack of a pastor. Inspired by the Moody school, he founded a nondenominational institute, the North-western Bible and Missionary Training School, to train ministers and lay workers to bring these churches back to life. His school began modestly in 1902 with seven students in a church classroom, but Riley, who excelled at fund-raising and administration, gradually built it up. By 1917 the school had eighty-one students, and afterward, as halls and dormitories were con-structed, the enrollment mounted, reaching 388 by 1935—with many more students attending evening classes. By then Riley had determined his stu-dents should replace the apostate ministers in the urban churches as well. That year he founded a seminary, and later a college of liberal arts, but these remained adjuncts of the Bible school until the time of his death in 1947.

As Trollinger tells us, most of the students at Northwestern came from working- and lower-middle-class families; few had any formal education beyond high school, and many were older people looking for a new start in life. Tuition cost almost nothing, but most students had to work long hours at outside jobs to pay for their board and books. At Northwestern students learned no Greek or Hebrew. In their two- or three-year pro-grams they studied the English Bible, learned Riley's way of interpret-ing it, and had practical training in evangelism—or how to propagate the doctrines that Riley said were "forever settled in heaven." Every semester students had to perform Christian service work, and while their service included mission work in jails, hospitals, logging camps, and Native American reservations, much of their time was spent in the poor rural churches of the region. In these churches they taught Sunday school classes, spoke at youth meetings, gave musical performances, and even preached on Sundays to congregations without a pastor. Every summer they fanned out across the region to run vacation Bible schools for children.[15]

In time, Northwestern became well known around the upper Midwest, and an increasing number of churches, grateful for its assistance, looked to the school for pastors. Most of these were Baptist, for Baptist congregations could hire their own ministers, and unlike some other denominations, the Northern Baptist Convention did not have educational qualifications that would prevent Bible school graduates from being ordained. By 1935, 155 Northwestern graduates were serving as pastors or evangelists in the region, and by 1940 the number had reached 224. These Northwestern pastors were willing to work for much lower wages than seminary-trained ministers, and because many of the rural churches were too poor to pay a supporting salary, many pastors served two or more congregations. Trained to evangelize, a number built congregations for churches that had shut down, or were on the verge of having to close. The result, Trollinger writes, was the appearance of explicitly fundamentalist churches where moderate, liberal, or folk evangelical churches had been before.[16]

Northwestern-trained pastors tended to maintain a close relationship with their alma mater, receiving the same services they themselves had once performed. In return their congregations sent funds and students to the institute. Then, as Northwestern grew, it gained the resources to give the pastors further support: a monthly magazine that provided sermon outlines, biblical exegesis, and practical advice; and an extension service for their churches to create what one administrator called "an indoctrinized" and a "trained and efficient laity." It also held a summer Bible conference for fellowship and study, and in the 1930s the conference attracted some thirty thousand people a year. Then, too, Riley himself maintained personal connections with his graduates. After his defeat in the National Baptist Convention in 1926, he served as a one-man placement office, recommending new graduates to churches that asked for them, and sometimes moving an older graduate from one church to the next. Often he made tours of the region to encourage his "boys"—and to see that they stayed true to the faith and loyal to their alma mater.[17] In this way he created a denomination within a denomination.

By 1930 Northwestern graduates made up at least 35 percent of Northern Baptist ministers in Minnesota. The percentage increased in the next two decades, as did their numbers throughout the upper Midwest. National Northern Baptist Convention leaders almost yearly sought to mandate stricter educational requirements for their ministers such as seminary training or at least the completion of an NBC-prescribed reading course, but the Depression was not the time to raise educational standards, and Riley and other fundamentalist leaders put up a successful resistance. By 1935 Northwestern graduates controlled three out of six local Baptist associations in Minnesota, and at the 1936 state convention they took on the liberal leadership with their own slate of candidates and won. The election made Riley the de facto head of the Minnesota Baptist Convention, and he maintained control of it for the next ten years.[18]

As leader of the state delegation to the NBC, Riley fought running battles with the national leadership. At the same time he fought to keep his graduates within the Convention. At Northwestern, prospective ministers were constantly told that anti-Christian modernism had infected the NBC, and understandably many concluded that they should lead their congregations out of the denomination. NBC officials had foreseen such an exodus. In a 1935 report—one of the many urging a change in educational requirements—an NBC committee noted that "too many men are coming out of certain institutions who can be anything else as well as Baptists, but they turn to the Baptist ministry because our democratic form of government offers easy access to the Baptist church." In other words, Bible schools like Riley's were installing nondenominational fundamentalists in Baptist churches. Three years later the NBC's Board of Education declared that the situation had reached a point of crisis. In the central and western states, it observed, "The ministry of our churches is rapidly filling up with the graduates of Bible schools and other short-course institutions." As the board saw it, the most serious problem was that "Bible school graduates have been trained away from loyalty to our denomination . . . and they are constantly leading away from . . . our churches that heretofore have been loyal members of our fellowship. . . . Unless this strong tendency be checked," it warned, "nothing but disaster faces our denomination." Riley, however, hoped that fundamentalists might one day prevail in the NBC, and it was a measure of his power over his graduates that he held most of them within the denomination until he decided to leave it himself.[19]

In 1943 the NBC's Foreign Mission Society appointed an outspoken social activist as its executive secretary. Riley and other fundamentalists objected vehemently, and when the Society refused to rescind the appointment, they established their own agency, the Conservative Baptist Foreign Mission Society. NBC officials refused to recognize this new body, and in retaliation Riley persuaded the Minnesota state convention to withhold 50 percent of its funding to the NBC. The ensuing controversy came to a head at the national convention in 1946, when Riley and other fundamentalists offered a series of resolutions almost identical to those he and his colleagues had proposed in the early 1920s. Apparently they had decided the moment had finally come to take over the convention, but as before, all their resolutions were soundly defeated, and an amendment making representation of churches in the NBC a function of the percentage of funds they contributed to the convention passed overwhelmingly. Separation now seemed the only course open to them, and shortly after the convention they, with Riley's support, founded the Conservative Baptist Association. In May 1947 Riley personally tendered his resignation to the NBC. He died in December that year at age eighty-six, and a few months later, the Minnesota Baptist Convention, along with fundamentalist churches in other states, followed their leader and quit the denomination for the Conservative Baptist Association.[20]

Riley's rebellion was the most serious schism the Northern Baptist Convention endured, but it was hardly the only breakaway of its kind. From the late 1920s through the 1940s, hundreds of fundamentalist congregations cut themselves loose from the major northern denominations and formed new associations, for instance the Independent Fundamentalist Fellowship, founded in 1930 by former Congregationalists.

Most of these separatist churches and associations were Baptist—for exactly the reasons NBC officials had pointed to—and some of them, like the CBA and the General Association of Regular Baptists, a group formed in 1932 by a rump party of the old Baptist Bible Union, took root in particular regions of the West and Midwest and survived into the twenty-first century with a thousand or more churches.[21] In one of the most important developments of the period, fundamentalists made inroads into the South and Southwest, creating networks of separatist Baptist churches that by the 1970s had moved the fundamentalist center of gravity below the Mason-Dixon line.

The man most responsible for bringing fundamentalism to the South was J. Frank Norris, the Fort Worth preacher who had fought the fundamentalist wars of the 1920s with Riley, Shields, and Straton. Norris is not remembered fondly in Texas. His name is generally associated with disgraceful attacks on fellow ministers, extremist politics, and scandals of the most lurid sort. His direct theological heirs tend to bowdlerize his life story. Yet Norris managed the impressive feat of importing militant antimodernism into a region where there were no modernists.

Norris began his career as highly successful Southern Baptist minister. Though brought up by an alcoholic father on a small farm in the hill country of West Texas, he went to Baylor University and from there to Southern Baptist Theological Seminary in Louisville, where he graduated first in his class. He pastored a church in Dallas, then edited the leading Texas Baptist newspaper, and in 1909 took the pulpit of the First Baptist Church in Fort Worth, known as "the church of the cattle kings." Respectability, however, did not suit him. True to his country roots (which he shared with Lyndon Johnson) he had what an acolyte called "a barnyard vernacular," a coruscating wit, and a need to dominate every other man in the room. He called making converts "hanging hides on a barn door." [22] Not long after taking over First Baptist, he deliberately drove the well-to-do out of his church with sensational sermons and attacks on the Fort Worth establishment. Like Riley, he created a huge, adoring congregation of working-class people, but he made enemies as well. When in 1912 he accused the mayor of corruption and the city fathers of encouraging vice and iniquity, his church was destroyed by fire, and he was indicted and nearly convicted of arson. Fourteen years later he was indicted again, this time for shooting and killing a friend of the current mayor. He pleaded self-defense—the man had barged into his office after threatening him on the telephone—and he was acquitted of murder. The facts in both cases remain murky.[23]

Around 1917 Norris began to develop relationships with such northern fundamentalists as Riley, Gray, and Dixon. By 1922 he was a premillennialist, a biblical inerrantist, and a charter member of both the BBU and WCFA. In Texas Norris called southerners to a holy war against the infidel modernist doctrines spreading into the South. For lack of a Shailer Mathews or a Harry Emerson Fosdick to attack, he discovered "modernists" disguised as respectable Southern Baptists. Professors at Baylor, he charged, were teaching evolution; the pastor of an influential Texas church had reviewed a modernist book and therefore was a modernist; an Old Testament scholar at the Southern Baptist Theological Seminary was teaching the higher biblical criticism—though his students thought he was doing the opposite. These charges did not sit well with his SBC colleagues. In 1922 thirty-three prominent Texas Baptists signed a statement calling Norris "divisive, self-centered, autocratic, hypercritical and non-cooperative." The following year the Baptist General Convention of Texas ejected him.[24]

Expulsion from the SBC put Norris just where he wanted to be. He solidified his ties with the northern fundamentalists, exchanging pulpits with Reuben Torrey and campaigning with Riley's WCFA against the teaching of evolution in the Texas schools. He conducted revivals across the country and started a Bible school in Fort Worth that later evolved into a seminary. "My work has prospered more by my being 'out,' more people have turned in sympathy toward my work than if I were in," he wrote a colleague sometime later.[25]

When not otherwise occupied, Norris battled the forces of evil in politics. In the 1970s he railed against Texas judges he deemed lax in enforcing Prohibition. He urged Fort Worth citizens to oust all Catholics from the city government, and before the 1928 presidential election he campaigned tirelessly against Al Smith, the first Catholic to run for president. Thereafter his politics became less than consistent. At first he supported the New Deal on the grounds that it would avert revolution, then he turned against it on the grounds that it was the Communist revolution. He never engaged in anti-Semitism, but he praised the Nazi regime for saving Germany from Communism until 1938, when, remembering his premillennial Zionism, he condemned Hitler for persecuting the Jews. He opposed U.S. involvement in Europe until 1940, then, in another about-face, he preached revivals to rally support for intervention and praised President Roosevelt. In a postwar crusade against Communism, he allied himself with his former enemy, the Catholic hierarchy, and discovered Red fifth columnists in the leadership of the Southern Baptist Convention.[26]

All the while his celebrity grew, and his empire expanded. A part of his charm, it seems, was that he was always raising Cain, and no one knew what he might do next. In 1935 he took on a second church, Temple Baptist, in Detroit, and detaching it from the Northern Baptist Convention, he created a huge congregation of rural white Southerners who had come to work in the auto factories. In Detroit and Fort Worth he broadcast his sermons on the radio, and by 1946 his two churches had a combined membership of 25,000—the largest congregation, he boasted, under the leadership of a single pastor. In addition he created satellite churches by gathering converts from his revivals and sending them his Bible school graduates as pastors. By the time the war broke out, he had led these newly formed churches and a number of others into an organization called the Premillennial Baptist Missionary Fellowship (later the World Baptist Fellowship).[27]

In the 1940s Norris consorted with many powerful people, among them Detroit automobile executives and leading Texas politicians such as Tom Connolly and Sam Rayburn. The Texas state legislature invited him to speak on several occasions and once honored him for his work in rooting out Communists. Just before the war, he traveled to England with the blessings of Roosevelt administration officials, and met with Winston Churchill; later he gained an audience with Pope Pius XII. Political power clearly appealed to him, for during the 1948 campaign he corresponded with both Harry Truman and Thomas Dewey, assuring both of them that they would win.[28]

The only people Norris seemed unable to deal with were his fellow Protestant ministers. The SBC leaders were his natural enemies, and throughout his life he continued to accuse them of everything short of Satanism. But he also broke with allies, such as William B. Riley, and he attacked his own protégés, often in ways calculated to cause them public humiliation. Unable to tolerate even a hint of independence, or the possibility of competition, he reserved the worst punishments for those he chose to succeed him in one or another of his ministries. He'd appoint loyal pastors, then rescind the offers, or he'd countermand their decisions, or he'd play a practical joke. (He cut one of them off in the midst of a radio broadcast and laughed while the minister preached to himself in the glass booth of the sound studio.)[29] Not everyone understood his humor, but all of them had fair warning. Asked by an acolyte late in his life what he would do differently if he had the chance, he said, "I would never have a Sunday School . . . I would have a pigtight organization. I would build it all around J. Frank Norris."[30] Naturally there were defections, among them that of his unfortunate son, who had followed him into the ministry. In 1950, two years before his death, one of his oldest and most trusted lieutenants, G. Beauchamp Vick, righteously decamped with a number of followers and created a schism in the World Baptist Fellowship.[31]

Norris's empire split apart, but after his death his brand of fundamentalism continued to spread through the South and Southwest at a greater pace than before. He had left two strong institutions, his Fort Worth church and his seminary, and under new leaders his World Baptist Fellowship grew apace. Then, two of the protégés he had alienated proved even more successful institution builders than he. John R. Rice (1895–1980), an evangelist who had started half a dozen fundamentalist Baptist churches in the Dallas area before he broke with Norris, founded a newspaper, *The Sword of the Lord*, that by 1956 had a circulation of over a hundred thousand and had become an important fundamentalist periodical. His books sold millions of copies, and his conferences attracted thousands of pastors each year. He also helped organize the Southwide Baptist Fellowship, an organization that by the early 1970s had a membership of two thousand pastors.[32] Beauchamp Vick, for his part, took over the Temple Baptist Church in Detroit and with his supporters established the Baptist Bible Fellowship and College in Springfield, Missouri. The Baptist Bible Fellowship, which in the 1950s and '60s focused on church planting, became the most successful of all the separatist networks. By the 1970s the college was the largest Bible school in the country, and by the early 1980s the Fellowship had nearly three thousand churches and well over a million members—one of whom was Jerry Falwell.[33]

Presbyterian fundamentalists, unlike their Baptist counterparts, tended to stay within their denomination, but in the 1930s there was one significant defection: that of J. Gresham Machen. The group he led out of the church was small, but it proved important to both wings of the fundamentalist movement in the 1950s.

Machen, who had quit the Princeton Theological Seminary with a group of faculty and students in 1929, had established a new seminary, Westminster, in Philadelphia. His ambition was to make Westminster what Princeton had been: an internationally recognized center for orthodox scholarship and the most influential seminary in the Presbyterian Church. Machen, however, could not put up with what he saw as the increasingly lax doctrinal standards in his denomination, and particularly in its Board of Foreign Missions. At the 1933 General Assembly he launched a full-scale attack on the Board; when rebuffed, he and colleagues announced the formation of an independent board of foreign missions, explicitly designed to deflect funds from the denominational board. The Assembly reacted just as the National Baptist Convention had in a similar circumstance. It declared the new board unconstitutional and directed all Presbyterians to sever their connections with it or face disciplinary action. Machen refused to recognize the Assembly's decision and declared his denomination, the Presbyterian Church USA, "an apostate church." The 1936 Assembly expelled him and eight of his colleagues, and a few months later he and others formed a new denomination, the Orthodox Presbyterian Church.[34]

The new church was not a success. In the first place, few Presbyterians followed him out of the denomination to join it. Even his friend Clarence Macartney, who had led the fundamentalist rebellion with him, thought better of splitting the denomination and resigned from the board of the Westminster seminary with twelve other trustees. Then, the tiny new church divided into two factions: on one hand the Old School Calvinists, led by Machen, and on the other hand the evangelical fundamentalists, led by Oliver Buswell, the president of Wheaton College, and Carl McIntire, the young pastor of a large New Jersey church. The dispute between the two factions began when McIntire criticized the Westminster seminary for not requiring its students and faculty to forswear the use of alcohol. McIntire, who had been a student at Princeton and had followed Machen to Westminster, knew full well that the strict Calvinists regarded the prohibition of alcohol as extra-biblical and an infringement on their "Christian liberty." However, he and Buswell hoped to build a separatist movement on a broader base than that of confessional Calvinism, and McIntire meant to lead it. He had been a founding member of the independent board of foreign missions (and one of those defrocked with Machen), and earlier that year he had established a new fundamentalist weekly, the *Christian Beacon*. The conflict soon expanded to a dispute over dispensationalism, and a power struggle ensued. McIntire and his allies wrested control of the independent missions board from Machen, but finding themselves in the minority in the new church, they left it and founded their own church and seminary. In the midst of this conflict Machen, then only fifty-five, died suddenly on New Year's Day 1937, engaged in what he must have seen as the dispiriting task of fund-raising in North Dakota.[35]

In the 1930s and '40s most liberal intellectuals continued to cling to the notion conceived during the Scopes trial that fundamentalism was a largely rural phenomenon. In fact by then it had developed a rural component, thanks to men like Riley and Norris. Still, the major fundamentalist institutions—the big churches, the Bible schools and seminaries—were in the cities. Fundamentalism attracted a great variety of people, but by all evidence its main constituency was small-town Protestants who had come to the cities to work in the factories and mills.[36] Noticeably, there were high concentrations of fundamentalist churches, or gospel tabernacles, in the fastest-growing cities, like Detroit, where the auto industry took off in the 1920s, and Los Angeles, where military bases, oil refineries, and defense industries proliferated during and after World War II. There was a logic to this. As Nancy Ammerman, a scholar of the movement, puts it, "Fundamentalism is most likely to be found at the points where tradition is meeting modernity rather than where modernity is most remote." In the late nineteenth century fundamentalism had developed along similar points of conflict—Dwight Moody's audiences had been largely made up of recent migrants from the countryside—yet making the transition from rural to city life was, generally speaking, a great deal more wrenching in the second quarter of the twentieth century than it had been in Moody's day. After World War I the cities lost much of the Victorian Protestant culture that had grown up in small-town America and that survived in many regions of the country. Educated people often made the transition from country to city without much stress, but for the less educated, Marsden writes, the journey often entailed a traumatic cultural upheaval analogous to that experienced by immigrants from abroad. Those who retained the worldview of Victorian Protestantism found themselves in a pluralistic society where their beliefs were considered outdated or even bizarre. Fundamentalism appealed to uprooted rural Americans, as it did to Protestants who had fairly recently immigrated from the countryside of Northern Europe.[37]

In reaction to the strange new environment of the cities, fundamentalists formed the equivalent of urban ghettos: church communities in which they could separate themselves from what they considered the corruptions of "the world." They couldn't of course separate themselves entirely, but they typically spent many of their nonworking hours in church, or church-related activities, and held to such traditional evangelical behavioral standards as abstinence from alcohol, card playing, social dancing, and theatergoing. Bible studies were stressed, and the zealous interpolated their conversation with biblical phrases and etched Bible verses onto jackknife handles, automobile spare-tire covers, and plaques for the walls of their homes. Such practices served as boundary markers between the Lord's people and the apostate others. A moviegoer, for example, was "not a consecrated Christian," no matter what other Christian virtues he seemed to possess.[38]

Fundamentalist churches offered shelter from modernist ideas and "worldliness," but fundamentalists, unlike Amish farmers, were not separatists who simply wanted to preserve their own ways, but the Lord's army contending for the "the faith once delivered." They were, as they saw it, the saving remnant and the rightful heirs to American civilization. Whether they figured themselves as martyrs or as potential conquerors, militancy became important to their sense of identity. Their preachers kept up their diatribes against modernism long after the liberals had stopped listening to them and fought each other over tiny doctrinal differences. As the historian Joel Carpenter writes, rhetorical aggressiveness and machismo became a part of their mystique, and military metaphors abounded. Sunday sermons denouncing theological errors or the sins of the flesh raised the barriers around their flocks, and—as Norris clearly understood—served as a form of entertainment for the righteous. In any case, the fundamentalist warlords kept discovering new enemies, and whether they picked up on such commonly held prejudices as anti-Catholicism or anti-Semitism, or attacked the New Deal, the new enemy was always the worst threat to Christianity ever known. For fundamentalists, the world was always in a state of crisis, with Satan ever appearing in new guises. It was, a former believer wrote, "virtually impossible to grow up in a fundamentalist church in the second quarter of the twentieth century (or to be a member of such a church whatever one's age) without seeing not only the church but all of life in Manichean terms." [39]

Whether they stayed in their denominations or not, fundamentalists became increasingly isolated from their fellow Protestants and the rest of the country. Some found this a secure and happy state, and fighting the good fight a fulfilling task. Others, however, began to feel uncomfortable with the endless controversies and painfully aware of their second-class status in the Protestant world. The solution they envisioned was not compromise but a national revival that would restore conservative Protestantism to its former preeminence—or, as they saw it, to bring America back to Christianity. The division between the two groups manifested itself in the early 1940s with the formation of two new organizations, both of them led by former students of J. Gresham Machen.

In 1941, just three years after splitting from Machen's church, McIntire made his bid for the leadership of the fundamentalist movement. Bringing together two tiny Presbyterian groups—his own and another—he founded what he grandly called the American Council of Christian Churches. Declaring war on the Federal Council of Churches, he invited all those churches that had left their apostate denominations to join in creating a "twentieth-century Reformation." [40]

At the same time an old friend of his, Harold Ockenga, was in the process of mounting an organization to unite conservative Protestants, and McIntire's announcement caused him some concern. Ockenga was another member of the close-knit group of students who had left Princeton for Westminster with Machen, but his career had taken a different turn. On graduating he had served as an assistant pastor in Clarence Macartney's church, and when the conflict erupted over the independent mission board, he had sided with Macartney and remained within the denomination. In 1936, after earning a doctorate in philosophy, he took the pulpit of one of the cathedrals of fundamentalism, the Park Street Church on the Boston Common, and became widely known for the eloquence of his preaching and the vigor of his leadership. A lay evangelist who belonged to his church, J. Elwin Wright, had several years earlier created the New England Fellowship, an association of churches that put on evangelistic campaigns, conferences, summer camps, and Bible study programs across the region. Wright's organization was unique in the country in that it included a variety of conservative churches: separatist, fundamentalist, Pentecostal, ethnic, and mainline. In 1939 he had begun to explore the possibility of creating a national association of a similar kind. The project appealed to Ockenga, and by 1941 the two had talked with ministers across the country and were planning to call an inaugural meeting the following year. But McIntire had upstaged them.[41]

Initially Wright and Ockenga hoped the two groups might cooperate, but they soon realized that cooperation was the last thing McIntire had in mind. A grandstander who never spoke of his projects in less than cosmic terms, McIntire envisioned "a revolutionary realignment of American Protestantism," but he would allow only separatists to join his American Council of Christian Churches and he vilified those fundamentalists—such as Ockenga—who stayed within their denominations. Clearly he would never join an organization that he didn't control, and he was far more concerned with attacking the Federal Council of Churches than with promoting a national revival. Wright and Ockenga therefore decided to go ahead with their own plans.[42]

In 1942 Wright and Ockenga convened a conference in St. Louis and launched the National Association of Evangelicals. For them and their fellow organizers the purpose of the association was to bring together a wide range of evangelical groups into a united front that could represent evangelical issues to the government, act as a national clearinghouse for evangelical programs, and foster the cooperation among churches that would permit community-wide revivals. Their fervent hope was to stir a Great Awakening across the land. In their view the NAE would have to steer a course between the shoals of modernism and the rocks of the negative, contentious fundamentalism that had led to the fragmenting of the church. At the conference, Ockenga, a tall, imperious figure, delivered a spirited address. America, he said, was in peril because Christianity was disintegrating. Evangelicals had "suffered nothing but a series of defeats for decades" because of the "terrible octopus of liberalism," the "poison of materialism," and "floods of iniquity." Yet when things looked the darkest, God would use his faithful remnant to bring a revival. Evangelicals, he said, were scattered and needed to organize for "a new era in evangelical Christianity." [43]

The following year six hundred people from nearly fifty denominations turned up at a constitutional convention in Chicago and formally inaugurated the NAE. Still, the sizable coalition the founders had hoped for did not emerge. The largest denominations, such as the Southern Baptist Convention and Missouri Synod Lutheran, decided that their own organizations were quite sufficient. A number of other important groups backed off because of McIntire. The New Jersey pastor, who had caused a commotion at the first meeting, attacked the NAE for failing to take a "definite stand" against the Federal Council of Churches, and when the NAE leaders were goaded into a counterattack, he accused them of battling true Christians rather than the FCC and "the enemies of the Lord." With that, the heads of some of the major fundamentalist institutions, such as the Moody Bible Institute and Wheaton College, sidled away from the NAE for fear of alienating their separatist constituencies—though Bob Jones Sr. and John Rice became members for a time. Wright, now on the defensive, began attacking the Federal Council, and in 1944 the NAE changed its bylaws so as to bar denominations that were members of the FCC. Wright, however, soon realized that McIntire, no stranger to what Ockenga called "a back-alley scrap," had outmaneuvered him. The several denominations that belonged to the FCC quit the fledgling NAE, and the fundamentalist chiefs did not return. [44]

By 1948 the NAE comprised eighteen small denominations—most of them Pentecostal—and its constituency, which included individual churches and individual members, amounted to just 750,000. Its founders had intended to create an organization with a positive, constructive approach, but after their attacks on the Federal Council, liberal Protestants came to see the NAE as just another sectarian enterprise, hardly distinguishable from McIntire's group. Wright and Ockenga were disappointed. Still, the NAE gradually made a place for itself on the national scene. Whereas the American Council remained a tiny organization, little more than a platform for McIntire's tirades against the FCC, the NAE doubled in size during the 1950s and spun off a number of special-purpose groups, such as the National Religious Broadcasters, mission societies, and an organization of conservative theologians. With an office in Washington it worked on practical issues like promoting military chaplaincies, thus demonstrating that conservative Protestant churches could work together for certain specific ends. By 1960 it was still a small organization, almost invisible to mainline Protestants, but by its very existence it opened up a fault line between militant separatists and the evangelical fundamentalists who led it.[45]

The National Association of Evangelicals was so-called because it included Pentecostal and other conservative denominations, but the term "evangelical" didn't mean very much because liberals also regarded themselves as evangelicals. Fundamentalists used the terms "fundamentalist" and "evangelical" interchangeably. However, during the skirmishes with McIntire in 1943 the editor of the NAE magazine wrote of a "growing chasm" between militant fundamentalists on one side and on the other a group that he said "we will designate as evangelicals for the sake of distinction." The difference was then more like a hairline fracture than a "chasm," but in the following years it widened, and Ockenga and other NAE leaders took to calling themselves "evangelicals" in order to escape the associations of bigotry and narrowness attached to militants such as McIntire.[46]

As a small bureaucracy atop independent denominations and churches, the NAE proved incapable of creating the revivals that Wright and

Ockenga longed for. Still, around the time the NAE came into being, fundamentalist broadcasters had begun to attract large audiences from across the spectrum of conservative Protestantism. The most important of these was Charles E. Fuller, a Californian, who in the mid-1930s had developed a Sunday evening program, *The Old Fashioned Revival Hour.* The program, which featured folksy preaching, gospel singing, and interaction with the audience through letters read and discussed on the air, proved so popular it was taken up by a national radio network, the Mutual Broadcasting System. By 1942 the program was carried on more than 450 stations, and though the secular media ignored it, it had the largest audience on radio, surpassing even the Bob Hope show.[47]

Fuller had an unlikely background for a popular evangelist. Born in 1887, the son of a prosperous orange grower, he graduated from Pomona College, married the college-educated daughter of a physician, and had a successful career dealing in citrus fruits and Southern California real estate. At age twenty-nine he was converted by a fundamentalist radio evangelist, and from 1919 to 1921 he studied at the Bible Institute of Los Angeles under the tutelage of its president, Reuben Torrey. Finding his calling as a preacher, he taught a Bible class at the Presbyterian church near his home, and in 1925 led it out of the Church and reorganized it as an independent fundamentalist congregation. Ordained by the Baptist Bible Union, he served as pastor of this breakaway church for the next eight years. He became a member of the BIOLA board, and when Torrey's successor was deemed insufficiently militant, he took a leading role in replacing him. In sum, he had become an archetypical separatist.[48]

Still, Fuller deeply believed in a national revival, and after taking up a radio ministry in the early 1930s, he realized that if he was to build a sizable audience, he had to avoid the fights that wracked and divided fundamentalists. Accordingly, he began to downplay doctrinal differences and to make a warm, positive presentation of the Gospel. He remained a premillennialist and sometimes preached dispensationalist readings of the Bible in detail, but his main message, repeated every Sunday evening, was simply that Jesus loves you and Jesus saves. The program, Marsden writes, "was frankly 'old fashioned,' designed to evoke nostalgia for the revival

style of one's youth." Fuller, in other words, had found his audience—
largely composed of older people—by recovering the evangelical style
that prevailed before the emergence of militant fundamentalism.[49]

Meanwhile other evangelists were taking the opposite tack and
organizing revivals for young people with modern, and distinctly postfundamentalist, measures. The revivalists were not established figures
but young men in tune with the emerging teen culture, who borrowed
unashamedly from popular entertainers, Hollywood pictures, and secular
radio shows. Their model was Percy Crawford, a radio evangelist famous
in the 1930s for his love of sporty clothes, fast cars, and practical jokes. His
program, *Young People's Church of the Air*, featured trumpet trios playing
jazzed-up gospel tunes and sermons delivered in the rapid-fire manner
of radio news reporters. During the war years a protégé, Jack Wyrtzen,
held youth rallies throughout New York City, where he preached and performed with a band. His blend of religion and entertainment proved so
popular with teens and young servicemen that by 1944 he was holding
rallies at Carnegie Hall and Madison Square Garden. Toward the end of
the war, ministers in other cities—Washington, Detroit, Minneapolis,
St. Louis, Indianapolis, and Chicago—took up the Wyrtzen format and
put on youth rallies, bringing in whatever talent was available, such as
sleight-of-hand artists, ventriloquists, and close harmony groups. At the
time "juvenile delinquency"—an elastic category that stretched from gang
members to bobby-soxers—preoccupied respectable people across the
country, and these "Youth for Christ" rallies, held on Saturday nights, attracted the support of churches and civic clubs, such as Rotary and Lions.[50]

Under the leadership of Torrey Johnson, a thirty-four-year-old Illinois
pastor, Chicagoland Youth for Christ became the hub of the movement,
and in 1945 Johnson incorporated it as an international organization. Well
connected in Chicago and a natural impresario, Johnson put together a network of "Christian businessmen" and conservative churches to produce
rallies with dance bands or zippy gospel singers and fiery young preachers in gaudy suits. The apotheosis of his work was a patriotic-religious
pageant with a choir of five thousand and a three-hundred-piece band
at Soldier Field on Memorial Day 1945. During the rally war heroes and
famous athletes attested to their faith, high school cadets performed the

flag ceremony with four hundred marching nurses, evangelists spoke of a national revival, and missionaries dressed in the costumes of foreign lands dramatized their call for "the complete evangelization of the world in our generation." [51]

The Youth for Christ rallies peaked in 1946 with an estimated nine hundred events across the nation. Their numbers declined after the servicemen went home, but in many communities they had brought diverse conservative Protestants together. They had also created a bench of young revivalists eager to show their mettle and to reach the world for Christ. One of them was Billy Graham.

6

BILLY GRAHAM *and* MODERN
EVANGELICALISM

N O AMERICAN revivalist before or since achieved the success that Billy Graham did in the middle years of the twentieth century. Indefatigable and constantly in motion, he evangelized on five continents and with the advantages of radio, television, and airplanes spoke to more people than any other preacher before in history. In the United States he was the first truly national revivalist since George Whitefield. His Viking features appeared on the cover of every national magazine, and from 1955 on he ranked high on Gallup's list of the most admired men in America. In the 1950s fundamentalists remained a small minority, but in tune with the times and the major politicians of the day, Graham struck a chord that resonated throughout the country. With President Eisenhower he helped forge a connection between religion and patriotism designed to unite Americans against Communism. At the same time he changed the shape of American Protestantism. In the late 1950s it seemed that he had brought both liberals and conservatives together, but the consensus—more apparent than real—shattered in the 1960s over civil rights and the Vietnam War. His lasting achievement was to bring the great variety of conservative white Protestants, North and South, into his capacious revival tent under the name "evangelicals."

Graham continued to preach revivals until 2005, when age overtook him, but the considerable influence he had wielded had long since gone. By 1980 he had become an icon encrusted in celebrity to whom presidents and foreign heads of state paid ritual homage. In the intervening years his revivals continued to attract enormous crowds, and his craggy profile remained as well known as those on Mount Rushmore. Still, as distinct as his features remained, his views had become so indistinct that he seemed to stand for only the vaguest idea of American righteousness. His politics had changed considerably since the 1950s, but few journalists asked him his opinions, and few historians of religion examined his legacy. In consequence, evangelicals and others have largely forgotten the role he played in propagating fundamentalist thinking and in creating a conservative coalition that included an array of Protestant groups that had never been brought together before. Though the least contentious of men, he contributed to the creation of conservative-liberal divide that went right through American Protestantism.

In the early days of his preaching Graham told the story of the young prophet Amos, the simple shepherd, "the hillbilly," delivering a message from God to the King of Israel. "And let me tell you something!" he said, wet with exertion. "When God gets ready to shake America, he might not take the Ph.D. and the D.D. and the Th.D. God may choose a country boy! God may choose a man no one knows . . . a hillbilly, a country boy! who will sound forth in a mighty voice to America, 'Thus saith the Lord!'" Striding back and forth across the stage, his forefinger slashing the air, he repeated, "Thus saith the Lord! Thus saith the Lord! Thus saith the Lord!"[1]

Graham was a country boy. Born in 1918, he grew up on his father's two-hundred-acre farm near Charlotte, North Carolina, and as a kid he milked cows, plowed the cornfields, and picked turnip greens. But he was no hillbilly. The farm, well managed by his father, supported the family of six in a redbrick house with indoor plumbing. His parents were people of standing in the community and good Presbyterians. The church the Grahams belonged to, the Associate Reformed Presbyterian, was part of a conservative synod established in 1822 that held to a strict interpretation of the Westminster Confession. Every evening the family read the Bible and prayed together; on Sundays they went to church and otherwise read religious tracts and listened to radio programs such as Fuller's *Old Fashioned Revival Hour*. According to Marshall Frady, the liveliest of his biographers, Billy, a rambunctious kid, liked these Sunday confinements no better than he liked farm chores or school, but then the families of all the kids he knew practiced the same diligent pieties. Baptists, Methodists, or Presbyterians, the respectable people in town made up a solid phalanx of born-again Bible believers who didn't smoke or drink, and whose main entertainments were community picnics, church suppers, Bible retreats, and revival meetings.[2]

When Billy was sixteen, Mordecai Ham, an itinerant evangelist and an associate of J. Frank Norris known for theories involving *The Protocols of the Elders of Zion*, pitched his tent in Charlotte and delivered a series of hellfire-and-brimstone sermons. Billy, along with many others in the town, went to see this new attraction, and one evening, nudged by a friend of the family, he walked down the sawdust trail to the platform and was "born again." The problem, a friend later told Frady, was that Ham had preached on the "the Devil's Big Three"—dances, card parties, and booze—and while Billy wanted to give up these things, he couldn't because he didn't do any of them. Instead, he became for a while uncharacteristically priggish.[3]

Preachers were prestigious in the Grahams' community, but in his youth Billy seemed one of the least likely to take a pulpit. An exuberant, gregarious lad, who dressed spiffily, drag-raced his father's car, and liked kissing girls, he had no vision of his future. He didn't want to stay on the farm, and while he dreamed of becoming a major league baseball player, he was no athlete. After high school his mother sent him to Bob Jones College because she had heard it was a good Christian school. He lasted just one semester. The grim barracks of the fundamentalist academy, the harsh discipline, and the innumerable picayune rules drove him out by Christmas. Then, because of a friend, he went to the Florida Bible Institute, a small school near Tampa that had taken over a luxurious resort that had failed in the crash of 1929. A member of Riley's World Christian Fundamentals Association, the school was designed to train evangelists, but initially its principal attractions for Graham were its less stringent rules, its orange groves, and a nearby golf course. Still, when a girlfriend left him for being insufficiently focused, he had a serious spiritual crisis and surrendered himself to Christ one night on the eighteenth green.[4]

After that, he took to preaching on street corners, in derelict missions, trailer courts, and rural churches with hounds in the sandy yards outside.

"He'd preach to a stump if there was nothing else," a friend recalled, "anything that'd just stand still for a minute." Coming under the tutelage of one of his deans, he was rebaptized and ordained as a Southern Baptist. He also worked as caddie on the golf course, and thanks to two piously inclined businessmen, who liked their caddie's energetic preaching style, he went on to Wheaton College with all expenses paid for a year.[5]

Graham was no scholar, but he graduated from Wheaton and married a classmate, Ruth Bell, who had grown up in China, where her father, Nelson, a conservative southern Presbyterian, had been a medical missionary. He took over a small Illinois church, but he preferred evangelistic preaching to pastoral work, and when, eighteen months later, Torrey Johnson asked him to join Youth for Christ, he accepted with alacrity. As a field representative in charge of organizing local YFC units in 1945, Graham embarked upon an evangelistic marathon, forging through forty-seven states and most of the provinces of Canada in just three years. He also made six visits to war-torn Europe with Johnson and teams of young pulpiteers. In those years he adopted the flamboyant dress of the swashbuckling YFC preachers and used the events of the day as a lead-in to his message, modeling his delivery on the clipped rhythms of Walter Winchell. From Johnson he learned how to organize large-scale rallies, how to appeal to business and civic groups, and how to attract the press. He also met many of the leading figures in the fundamentalist world, one of whom created an odd diversion in his career.[6]

In February 1945 Graham preached at homecoming rally for the Northwestern schools in Minneapolis, and William B. Riley, who was seated on the dais, later asked the local YFC director, "Where did you get that young man? He's a comer!" Soon afterward Riley began pursuing Graham to take over the presidency of his schools. By that time Riley needed a successor, and, characteristically, he preferred a rising young evangelist he had hardly met to one of his obedient, long-serving lieutenants. Graham demurred. His evangelistic career was just taking off; he knew nothing of administration; and Riley, old and cantankerous, was engaged in his final furious struggle with the Northern Baptist Convention. Still, Graham did not give Riley a definite no.[7]

In August 1947, Riley, then bedridden, called Graham to his side, pointed an emaciated finger at him, and, according to Graham, said, "You are the man to succeed me, Billy. I've known it for some time. You will be disobeying God if you refuse this. I'm leaving this school to you as Elijah gave his mantle to Elisha—as Saul appointed David king of Israel, so I appoint you head of these schools, and I'm going to meet you at the Judgment seat of Christ with them."[8] Put this way, the offer was impossible to refuse, and when Riley died six months later, Graham found himself in charge of Riley's kingdom.

Uncomfortable in his new position and unable to resist the call of the revival road, Graham spent little time at Northwestern. By arrangement with the board he raised money but delegated the management of the school to aides, while he beat back and forth across the country ten months a year. The job was nonetheless taxing, for even before Riley's death, the faculty of the schools and others in the Northwestern community had become engaged in a typical fundamentalist struggle: the militant separatists against the more militant separatists. When Graham took the side of the first, the other faction attacked his administration of the school. Unable to resolve the conflict, Graham resigned in February 1952. He was well out, for the struggle went on until 1956, when the militant separatists separated from the separatists, and forming a seminary and a denomination of their own, pulled down Riley's kingdom.[9]

By 1947 Youth for Christ was so well established across the country that Graham could accept invitations from ministers to conduct revivals of a more general sort. For the next two years he and a small team of musicians and organizers conducted two- and three-week campaigns in cities from Grand Rapids to Miami to Baltimore. His revivals, conducted in tents or rented halls without much advance publicity, were hardly distinguishable from those of a dozen other freelance evangelists traveling the country in those days of religious resurgence. Graham was, as he himself said, still a country boy. Tall and awkward, he had a rough-hewn voice and was given to flailing his arms and stabbing the air with a raised finger. When he told Bible stories, he used slangy vernacular and acted out the parts—preening and strutting in the role of Belshazzar, or prancing around like an uppity pig in the story of the Prodigal Son. Calling for revival, he would stalk the platform, assaulting the audience with vivid descriptions of the horrors that came from man's rebellion against God. According to his Youth for Christ peers, Graham had a kind of incandescence on the platform that came from his passionate sincerity. Yet even his most fervent preaching did not always meet with success. After a particularly disastrous ten days in Altoona, Pennsylvania, in the summer of 1949, where the local ministers proved uncooperative and a deranged woman could not be pacified, some of Graham's team members worried that they had come to the end of the road. Still, they picked up and went on to Los Angeles in September.[10]

In Los Angeles local fundamentalists had done some advance work and had pitched what they called the "Canvas Cathedral" on a vacant lot downtown with a banner announcing, "Something's Happening Inside 6,000 Free Seats   Dynamic Preaching   Glorious Music." Just two days before the campaign began, President Harry Truman announced that the Soviet Union had successfully tested an atomic bomb. Graham used the shocking news as the headline for his first Sunday afternoon sermon.

> This nation now knows that Russia has the atomic bomb! Today Moscow announced that Russia has been piling up bombs for over two years. . . . Do you know the area that is marked out for the enemy's first atomic bomb? New York! Secondly, Chicago! And thirdly, the city of Los Angeles! Do you know the Fifth Columnists, called Communists, are more rampant in Los Angeles than any other city in America? God is giving us a desperate choice, a choice of either revival or judgment. There is no alternative! . . . Judgment is coming just as sure as I am standing here!

From there Graham went on to speak of a world divided into two irreconcilable camps: on one hand Bible-based Western culture and on the other Communism, "a religion that is inspired, directed and motivated by the Devil himself who has declared war against Almighty God."[11] On other evenings Graham declaimed on the paganism and immorality of modern America—the growth of crime, divorce, and juvenile delinquency—and the need to return to the old-time religion. In closing he would pounce to the edge of the stage and confront the audience directly. "If we're not guilty of one thing, we're guilty of another . . . 'Thou shalt not murder'—

so you say you haven't. Well, there are hundreds of husbands in this city *who are killing their wives by neglect.* There are boys and girls out there who are *killing their mother and father* with the wild life you are leading. *You are guilty of murder!*" Then the music would swell up behind him, and he would call for those who wanted to be sure of their salvation to make a decision for Christ.[12]

The crusade went on with moderate success, and the three-week engagement was extended to four. Then two things happened: Stuart Hamblen, a former rodeo star with a popular radio show, declared he had been saved by Graham, and William Randolph Hearst sent a telegram to his newspaper editors saying, "Puff Graham." A swarm of reporters and photographers appeared in the tent, and Graham's revival became front-page news. His audiences burgeoned; Hollywood stars showed up; the wires and the news magazines ran stories; and by the end of another four weeks of preaching Graham had become a national celebrity.[13]

Swept along in a gale of publicity Graham arrived in Boston six weeks later to preach in Harold Ockenga's Park Street Church. The National Association of Evangelicals magazine had given Graham favorable coverage in his Youth for Christ days, but Ockenga had had his doubts about this slangy young evangelist who had never seen the inside of a theological school.[14] Still, Ockenga longed for a revival, and the more conventional evangelists he had invited had failed to raise the temperature. Graham, however, packed the Park Street Church, Mechanics Hall, the Opera, and finally Boston Garden—leaving thousands of people on the streets outside. At the invitation of numerous ministers, he returned in the spring and preached in all the major New England cities, ending his tour with a rally on the Boston Common, where George Whitefield had preached in 1740. Ockenga was beside himself with enthusiasm. At the annual NAE convention in April he told the crowd, "You do not have to wait till next year. You don't have to wait ten years. You don't have to pray any more, 'Lord, send a revival.' The revival is here!"[15]

By background and education Billy Graham was well positioned to preach the national revival of conservative Protestantism that Ockenga and his fellow NAE leaders dreamed about. He was a fundamentalist; his views on such matters as biblical infallibility, the virgin birth, and the Second Coming were perfectly orthodox. On the other hand, he had been brought up in a world innocent of modernism and far from the din of the fundamentalist battle with apostasy. As a result, he had none of the scars that most fundamentalists bore from the defeat. He had no sense of alienation, no martyrdom complex, no need to look for enemies, and none of the resentment that fundamentalists, even those as sophisticated as Ockenga, felt about their second-class status in the Protestant world. As a revivalist, he knew that people didn't want to hear about doctrinal disputes, and having been a Presbyterian and a Southern Baptist, he had little interest in denominational differences. He stood, as he told the NAE convention in 1952, for "a spiritual ecumenical movement" of all "born-again believers." [16] At the time he was often compared to Dwight Moody. But Moody's audiences were entirely northern, and Graham, who came from a border state—in a different period—could speak to southerners and northerners alike. Where he resembled Moody was in his confidence that he spoke for the essential American religion.

After the New England revival, Graham continued his triumphal procession across the country—Fort Worth, Shreveport, Memphis, Seattle—his city-wide campaigns, or crusades, as he called them, lasting for four or five weeks at a time and drawing audiences of 300,000 to 500,000 people. Along the way he built a highly efficient organization, the Billy Graham Evangelistic Association, which elaborated upon the techniques of mass evangelism developed by Moody and Billy Sunday. The prodigious advance work included the mobilization of churches, the formation of a local committee to raise money, extensive advertising in the local media, and the training of thousands of volunteers. Businessmen's luncheons, prayer groups, and work committees would be set up weeks before the crusade, and often Graham himself would come to speak to civic groups or the state legislature. To assure a reasonable turnout, organizers would obtain commitments from local churches to fill half the seats at the nightly services. During the crusade, interest would be heightened by spectacular open-air rallies and the appearance of politicians and Christian celebrities—sometimes Graham's friends Dale Evans and Roy Rogers with his horse, Trigger. When the campaign was over, the organizers would announce how many people had attended and how many "inquirers" had come forward and signed decision cards for referral to local churches. They would also present an audited account of the financial intake and expenses so there could be no doubt about the fiscal rectitude of the Billy Graham Evangelistic Association or any of its local partners.[17]

By 1954 Graham had held crusades in twenty-five major American cities and had spoken directly to some eight million souls. His column, "My Answer," appeared in seventy-three newspapers, and his weekly radio program, *Hour of Decision*, had an audience of fifteen million in the United States and abroad. He had changed somewhat in the course of four years. The advertisements for his crusades no longer read "Dazzling Array of Gospel Talent" or "Sixth Great Sin-Smacking Week." He had given up his colorful clothes for conservative ties and subtly textured gray or brown suits tailored in London. He spoke deliberately, and his voice had acquired a deep bronze resonance, as some imagined the voice of God. He had stopped telling jokes about kicking mules and saying that people saw Noah before the Flood as "a crazy old fellow" with "a screw loose somewhere." He quoted eminent thinkers, and his readings of the Bible were less literalist than they had been just two years before when he had specified the dimensions of heaven and hell in cubic miles. In later sermons he said it didn't matter whether heaven literally had streets of gold or hell had lakes of fire, for heaven "represents reconciliation and fellowship with God and Christ," and "Hell essentially and basically is a banishment from the presence of God."[18]

By then Graham was moving in exalted circles. As he said during his 1952 crusade in Washington, D.C., "I'm appealing to a higher-type social strata."[19] He had gained the backing of some of the most powerful businessmen in the country, among them Henry Luce, the investor Russell Maguire, and the oil baron Sid Richardson. Politicians of both parties flocked about him. He gave his first devotional in Congress in April 1950 and caught the eye of House speaker Sam Rayburn, who declared, "This country needs a revival, and I believe Billy Graham is bringing it to us." After that he was often invited to prayer meetings, ceremonies, and luncheons hosted by senators as ill assorted as Lyndon Johnson and Everett Dirksen. During his Washington crusade, he gave a sermon on the steps of the Capitol and addressed one hundred legislators on the subject of

"Christ and Communism." That year he met Eisenhower and spent a few days with him on the campaign trail. After the election he often visited the president in the White House, and once at his Gettysburg farm, and the two corresponded with some regularity. He also had frequent meetings with Vice President Richard Nixon and the pious Presbyterian secretary of state, John Foster Dulles.[20]

In 1952 he went to see President Truman, but made the gaffe of repeating his conversation with the president to reporters and re-creating the pose they had struck in prayer. Truman refused to see him again.[21]

Graham liked the company of powerful men, and throughout his career many politicians courted him because of the large constituency he represented, or in the hope that his blindingly righteous presence might envelop them. Eisenhower, however, didn't need Graham for electoral purposes, or as a scandal deflector. He appreciated what Graham was doing for the country, though he wasn't a fundamentalist, and Graham wasn't an Eisenhower Republican. The affinity between the two of them owed to the particular connection that they and many other Americans made between religion and the security of the country in the 1950s.

In his Youth for Christ days Graham had learned that speaking of current events attracted attention, and while in his revivals he confined himself to generalities, he often spoke on his weekly radio program about specific issues in world affairs. One of the primary purposes of *Hour of Decision*, he told his listeners, "is to keep you abreast of fast-moving world events and try to interpret them for you in the light of Scripture." As a Christian news analyst, he paid particular attention to developments in East Asia—long the primary mission field for American Protestants. After the Communist victory in China and the outbreak of the Korean War in 1950, he charged that Roosevelt and Truman had betrayed Chiang Kai-shek and Syngman Rhee by playing into the hands of the Russians at Tehran, Yalta, and Potsdam. In 1952 he told an audience that the Korean War was being fought because "Alger Hiss shaped our foreign policy and some of the men who formulate it [now] have never been to the East." He complained that Truman had gone to war without consulting the American people, and later that Truman had been "cowardly" in refusing to follow General Douglas MacArthur's advice to pursue the war to victory, even if it meant bombing military bases in Communist China. When the Eisenhower administration ended the war by negotiation in 1953, he told his radio listeners, "This is the first war in American history we have not won . . . we have shown our moral weakness. We have shown that when pressed we could betray our friends and compromise with the enemy." There can, he preached, "be no parleying or compromise with evil." He admired Syngman Rhee's intransigence, but his real hero was Chiang Kai-shek, and as late as 1956 he was calling for Chiang to invade the Chinese mainland and claiming that he had been told if Chiang could stay one month, "whole armies would desert to his cause and there would be a general uprising."[22]

Europe seemed to concern Graham less. In the fall of 1951 he predicted "an economic downfall" for America if the "give-away" program of foreign aid to Western Europe continued. In a sermon he maintained that "one CARE package did more good than all the Marshall Plan aid." However, he occasionally urged the United States to encourage armed revolts in Eastern Europe, and after the Soviets crushed the Hungarian rebellion in 1956, he condemned Western leaders for not daring to stand up to the Russians.[23]

Graham never spoke ill of Eisenhower, but his foreign policy prescriptions were those of the president's Republican opponents: Robert Taft and the other midwesterners who denounced containment and called for "unleashing Chiang" and to "roll back" in Europe—policies that Eisenhower believed might lead to World War III. Then, like many right-wing Republicans, Graham raised fears that "Communists and left-wingers" were infiltrating America's schools, colleges, churches, and national security agencies. In 1953, at the height of the investigations into subversion in government by the Jenner, Velde, and McCarthy committees, he said in a radio sermon: "While nobody likes a watchdog, and for that reason many investigation committees are unpopular, I thank God for men who, in the face of public denouncement and ridicule, go loyally on in their work of exposing the pinks, the lavenders and the reds who have sought refuge beneath the wings of the American eagle." When Joseph McCarthy was censured by the Senate, Graham complained that the Senate was fiddling "over trifles" and was "bringing disgrace to the dignity of American statesmanship."[24]

In his revivals Graham rarely failed to bring up the threat of Communism, atomic weapons, and World War III. Indeed, these secular dangers often seemed to substitute for the fear of hell, or the coming of Armageddon, that previous revivalists had used as a spur to conversion. However, he often described men and nations as the instruments of higher powers. "My own theory about Communism," he said in September 1957, "is that it is master-minded by Satan. . . . I think there is no other explanation for the tremendous gains of Communism in which they seem to outwit us at every turn, unless they have supernatural power and wisdom and intelligence given to them."[25] Compromise with the Communists was therefore impossible. "Either Communism must die or Christianity must die," he said, "because it's actually a battle between Christ and anti-Christ." Like most dispensationalists, Graham maintained that the Antichrist had arisen in Russia, and each new Middle Eastern crisis, from the rise of Gamal Abdel Nasser in Egypt to the nationalization of Iranian oil, to the deployment of American troops to Lebanon in 1958, provided him with an occasion to predict that Armageddon would take place when "the armies of the north" moved on the Middle East.[26]

Dispensationalists believed human history was on the road to destruction, and Armageddon could not be averted. Like them, Graham sometimes proposed that all that humans could do was to convert, evangelize, and await the Second Coming. "We may have another year, maybe two years, to work for Jesus Christ, and [then] . . . it's all going to be over," he said in 1951. Two years later he said, "I sincerely believe, if I can study the Scriptures aright and read current events and keep with my current reading, that we are living in the latter days. I sincerely believe that the coming of the Lord draweth nigh." Still, having figured Armageddon as a battle between Christian America and Communist Russia, he often held out hope for the future of the country. Once, when asked how the conversion of all Americans would stop the Soviets, he said, "I sincerely believe that if Americans turned to God at this moment, we would have divine intervention on our side." On another occasion he said more specifically that if the nation would repent of its sins, "God himself would intervene and frustrate and blind the Russians as he did the armies of old." At other times he struck a more Arminian note: "Only as millions of Americans turn to Jesus Christ in this hour and accept him as Savior, can this nation possibly be spared the onslaught of demon-possessed communism." "You say, 'But Billy, I am only one person.' Ah yes, but when you make your decision, it is America through you making its decision." In other words, Graham sometimes invoked Communism as a part of an end times prophecy and at other times as a part of a jeremiad in which Americans had a choice to make.[27]

Eisenhower, the pragmatic statesman, would not, it might be imagined, have found Graham's apocalyptic scenarios any more congenial than his policy prescriptions. At the beginning of the Cold War, however, he and other members of the internationalist foreign policy establishment took to using similarly apocalyptic rhetoric to promote another kind of American revival.

In his memoir, *Present at the Creation*, Dean Acheson describes the famous meeting of February 27, 1947, in which President Truman, Secretary of State George Marshall, and he, then under secretary of state, asked the congressional leadership to make the first Cold War commitment: a grant of $400 million to the governments of Greece and Turkey. Acheson and his superiors believed that if these governments did not hold firm, the Soviet Union would extend its influence into the Mediterranean and undermine the fragile non-Communist consensus in countries of Western Europe. The problem lay in convincing the midwestern Republican leaders, historically promoters of the American mission in Asia and isolationists with regard to Europe, that the United States had vital interests in the region.[28]

"I knew we were met at Armageddon," Acheson later wrote of the meeting. "These congressmen had no conception of what challenged them." After Marshall tried and failed to convince them with a geopolitical argument, Acheson took the floor and launched into a highly charged impromptu speech, calling Greece and Turkey the key to the worldwide ideological struggle between good and evil, freedom and dictatorship. "Like apples in a barrel infected by one rotten one," he said, "the corruption of Greece would infect Iran and all to the east. It would also carry infection to Africa through Asia Minor and Egypt, and to Europe through Italy and France . . . and if this happened, America itself could not be secure."

The son of an Episcopal bishop, Acheson knew the language of his opponents. His jeremiad carried the day, and three weeks later the president announced what become known as the Truman Doctrine, promising to support "free peoples" everywhere in their struggle against Communist subversion.

Acheson apparently learned from this success. As secretary of state in 1950, he authorized a wide-ranging analysis of the U.S.-Soviet conflict that concluded with a call for an unprecedented peacetime U.S. military buildup. The interagency document, known as NSC-68, characterized the Soviet Union as "inescapably militant," "animated by a fanatic faith, antithetical to our own," and seeking to "impose its absolute authority over the rest of the world." According to NSC-68, the Soviets were developing the capability to fulfill their grand design while the relative strength of the free world was declining. Already they had the capacity to overrun Western Europe and by 1954 ("the year of maximum danger"), when they would have an estimated two hundred atomic bombs and the bombers to deliver them, they could, by "striking swiftly and with stealth," deliver a devastating blow to "the vital centers of the United States."

Acheson later admitted that the purpose of the document was to "bludgeon the mass mind of 'top government,'" and that when he went around the country that year "preaching" a military buildup, he made points that were "clearer than truth." [29]

Throughout the 1950s national security officials—and the foreign policy establishment generally—constantly worried that the American people, used to thinking the country invulnerable between two oceans, might not choose to make the economic sacrifices needed to sustain the Cold War effort. Eisenhower, who believed that no victory was possible and that the containment of Communism would have to continue indefinitely, became the chief worrier. In the first few months of 1953 he and his advisors developed a campaign, known as Operation Candor, to teach Americans about the threats they faced in "an age of peril"—an operation that Eisenhower's chief of staff, Sherman Adams, described as "a fiber-toughening exercise." As a part of the campaign, Eisenhower from time to time talked frankly about the power of nuclear weapons: the effects of radioactive fallout, the possibility that the H-bomb might even blow "a hole through the entire atmosphere" and destroy all civilization. He argued that the vastly increased defense expenditures had been forced on the United States because the Communists had rejected every offer of peace. Eisenhower himself described the Soviet military threat without hyperbole, but under his administration national security agencies and blue-ribbon commissions often issued studies much like NSC-68, whose conclusions, selectively leaked, indicated that the Soviets were developing the capability to disarm and defeat the United States. Indeed, in national security circles apocalyptic scenarios became a more or less ordinary means of communicating a sense of urgency about military preparedness.[30]

Eisenhower's worries about the American people, however, went deeper than whether or not they would pay for his military budgets. In a wartime letter to his wife he wrote:

Just as the [First] World War brought in an era of almost hysterical change and restlessness, so will this one bring about revolutions in our customs, laws and economic processes. If we could hope for a greater mass discipline—self-imposed—there would be cause for rejoicing; the danger is that special economic, industrial or social groups will apply pressures that will either be disruptive or might force, for a time at least, the adoption of some form of dictatorship in our democracies. Either outcome would be tragic. . . . It looks as if we must face a long struggle.[31]

A few months after taking office he wrote in his diary: "The principal contradiction of the whole [American] system comes about because of the inability of men to forgo immediate gain for a long term goal."[32]

In Eisenhower's view men were innately selfish, and if they could not voluntarily restrain their natural impulses and get along together, the result would be chaos or tyranny. He had some hope that education and rationality would help men make the right choices, but believing that selfishness and cupidity will never be wholly eradicated from within us," he assumed that reason had its limits. Only religious faith, he thought, had the power to restrain selfishness and enable people to get along together in a democracy. In a speech addressing American fears after the first successful H-bomb test he declared, "If there is no religious faith whatsoever, then there is little defense you can make of a free system." On the other hand, "So long as we seek favor in the sight of the Almighty, there is no end to America's forward road." He asked Americans to take to heart the biblical dictum that with faith all things are possible and said, "America is great and is powerful, and it can do anything when we are united among ourselves." Then, like Woodrow Wilson before him, Eisenhower described America as the spiritual hope of the world. "In our own endurance and vision rests the future of civilization and of all moral and spiritual values." [33]

As the sociologist Robert Wuthnow tells us, Eisenhower was hardly alone in making the connection between personal faith and the health of the nation. Talcott Parsons, and other well-known sociologists of the period, described American culture mainly in terms of its "values." According to Parsons, social cohesion was contingent on a clear hierarchy of values with religion providing the capstone of this hierarchy, its ultimate values organizing all the rest. Clergymen and secular thinkers argued that a good society depended upon individuals acting responsibility to uphold moral and democratic values, and the sense of responsibility was best supported if individuals felt themselves accountable to a sacred authority. "Democracy without God is an empty word and morality without religion is an idle dream," declared Hugh Lamb, the Catholic bishop of Philadelphia. Lewis Mumford, the cultural critic, likened the relationship between religion and society to that between Greenwich Mean Time and local time: religion provided an absolute standard against which to measure social policies and correct the course of the state. Religious values were, in other words, seen by many as universally valid and applicable to the whole society. [34]

In his speeches Eisenhower used religious rhetoric more than most other presidents and repeatedly called for a spiritual revival. He instituted national prayer breakfasts, and during his presidency the Congress added the words "under God" to the Pledge of Allegiance and had "In God We Trust" engraved on the currency and adopted as the national motto over "E Pluribus Unum." In 1954 he and his Presbyterian pastor created the Foundation for Religious Action in the Social and Civil Order to "unite all believers in God in the struggle between the free world and atheistic Communism." The Foundation, whose board members included Billy Graham and Norman Vincent Peale Jr., held conferences in which Protestant, Catholic, and Jewish clergymen, along with pious national security officials such as Leo Strauss, chairman of the Atomic Energy Commission, gave speeches on the spiritual factors in the anti-Communist struggle. At the first of these conferences Eisenhower proclaimed that the Foundation would show how to "take the Bible in one hand and the Flag in the other, and march ahead." In 1955 the Republican National Committee resolved that President Eisenhower "in every sense of the word is not only the political leader but the spiritual leader of our times."[35]

Eisenhower, who had no denominational affiliation until after his election, when he joined the Presbyterian Church, espoused no particular religion for democracies. "Our form of government has no sense unless it is founded in a deeply religious faith, and I don't care what it is," he famously said shortly before taking office. He added, "With us of course it is the [Judeo]-Christian concept, but it must be a religion that all men are created equal."[36] In his view all religions taught the same essential truth: the need to restrain selfishness for the greater good. Whatever he himself believed about the Almighty, he invariably described religion as a public utility: "a national resource," an "advantage," a "strength," a "weapon." "Spiritual strength," he said, is "the real source of America's power and greatness." Religion and patriotism thus became inextricably linked. In 1955 he told the American Legion, "Recognition of the Supreme Being is the first and most basic expression of Americanism. Without God, there could be no American form of government nor an American way of life." It followed that the Almighty approved of Americanism, as Eisenhower defined it, and of the struggle his administration was waging for the future of civilization.[37]

Eisenhower and Graham did not agree on theology or foreign policy, but they agreed on the place of religion in what both considered perilous times. They agreed that America was fighting atheistic Communism and that national survival rested on the belief of Americans in God. "A spiritual awakening," Graham said, "will restore our spiritual heritage, create moral stamina and consciousness, bring back the sanctity of the home . . . strengthen the bulwarks of freedom and bring integrity back to the people of the world." They agreed that patriotism and religious belief were synonymous and that America had a moral and spiritual mission to redeem the world. "If you would be a loyal American, then become a loyal Christian," Graham said in one sermon, and in another, "We are created for a spiritual mission among the nations." Graham, of course, did not believe that just any religion would do. In a sermon titled "Satan's Religion" he offered five ways Americans could "most effectively combat Communism." The first was "by old-fashioned Americanism"; the second "by conservative and Evangelical Christianity"; the third by prayer; the fourth by spiritual revival; and the fifth "by personal Christian experience." "The greatest and most effective weapon against Communism today is to be a born-again Christian," he said.[38]

Despite his sectarian perspective, Graham's position was closer to Eisenhower's than to that of liberal Protestant leaders, all of whom objected to the conflation of Christianity with Americanism, and some of whom had a disconcerting tendency to call for nuclear disarmament and talks with the Communist Chinese. It was also closer to the majority position of the day. In 1949 Graham had styled himself as Amos, the prophet crying in the wilderness, but in four years he had become a pastor of the national civil religion.

*   *   *

Graham had always sought to attract mainline Protestants. An irenic preacher, he had by 1954 brought numbers of them to his revivals, but not as many as he had hoped. The problem lay with the clergy. Outside of the South, the sponsors of his crusades had been mainly fundamentalist ministers, and, intentionally or not, they had driven most of the mainline clergy away. In 1951 and 1953 Graham turned down invitations to hold a crusade in New York because his fundamentalist sponsors represented only a small percentage of the city's clergy, and no other ministers joined them. However, in a crusade in London in the spring of 1954 Graham—after an initial flap over his attacks on British socialism—had found a welcome from a wider spectrum of Protestant clergy than he had had in the United States. The English churches had never been split by a militant fundamentalist movement, and conservative evangelicals had their place in most of them. Even the Archbishop of Canterbury, when persuaded that Graham was not some American fanatic, had attended one of his revivals. The experience made Graham even more confident that he could make inroads into the major northern American denominations, if only he and his NAE allies could shed the fundamentalists' reputation for anti-intellectualism and belligerence.[39]

One of Graham's hopes lay with the Fuller Theological Seminary, a nondenominational institution in Pasadena founded by the radio evangelist Charles Fuller in 1947. Fuller had originally thought to build a missionary training college, but Harold Ockenga had persuaded him that what was needed was a scholarly center with the intellectual weight of the old Princeton seminary. At Fuller's request Ockenga had recruited the first faculty members, and while unwilling to leave his Boston church, he had served as president in absentia and then as an important member of the board. The project of the seminary, as he saw it, was to reform fundamentalism by bringing it back to its Reformed and evangelical roots and making its theology intellectually respectable. By 1954 the seminary had under his guidance rejected separatism. Its younger professors were moving the school away from the intricacies of dispensationalism and urging a positive engagement with the culture. Ockenga called this "the new evangelicalism." Still, the faculty was divided between those who believed the preeminent cause was defending the fundamental truths against all error and those who believed that students should be exposed to competing views and taught a spirit of free inquiry. It was a matter of attitude, not doctrine.[40]

Graham, who was close to Ockenga and a number of the faculty members, believed in the work of the seminary, but worried that its impact would be too long in coming. The answer, he began to think, was a serious periodical that would represent the neo-evangelical perspective. The idea for a journal with scholarly articles, news, and reviews for the use of ministers had been proposed to him in 1951 by Fuller professor Wilbur Smith, but Graham had put the idea aside for a couple of years. Toward the end of 1953, he later recalled, he had awakened in the middle of the night, gone to his desk, and written down ideas for "a magazine similar to the *Christian Century*, one that would give theological respectability to evangelicals" and "appeal especially to men who were open to the biblical faith in the mainline denominations." He had decided to call the magazine *Christianity Today*, and he had even drawn up a tentative budget. His father-in-law, Nelson Bell, who had founded *The Presbyterian Journal*, had proved enthusiastic about the idea and had gone about making inquiries among ministers. Still, because of Graham's hectic schedule, it was another year and half before the project got under way.[41]

By the spring of 1955 Graham had interested several businessmen of his acquaintance in the magazine, but it was J. Howard Pew of the Sun Oil Company who gave the critical support, pledging $150,000 for each of the first two years and promising to provide major funding for several additional years. A northern Presbyterian and self-proclaimed expert in the theology of John Calvin, Pew was an ardent political conservative who believed the Scriptures endorsed his own version of laissez-faire capitalism and thought the church shouldn't concern itself with social reform. He had previously chaired a layman's committee of the National Council of Churches (the successor to Federal Council of Churches) designed to restrain the political liberalism of the organization. The committee, he felt, had been a failure. In a letter to a businessman friend, he lamented that 30 percent of the American clergy were "ideological Communists . . . Socialists . . . [or] various shades of pink," and that this minority controlled "the machinery of our denominations." A new voice, he wrote, was needed to represent the view of the majority, and *Christianity Today* might be the answer. Graham worried that Pew might try to change the focus of the magazine from theology to politics, but in Pew's favor was the fact that he had no interest in fundamentalist doctrinal conflicts.[42]

With the Pew money secured, Bell gave up his surgical practice to become executive editor of *Christianity Today*, and Ockenga agreed to become chairman of the board. Realizing that it might take years to build a subscription base, Graham decided to send the magazine out free of charge for two years to every Protestant minister in the United States and the other English-speaking countries. He also decided to locate it in Washington, D.C., because, as he later explained, "I was a friend of Eisenhower's . . . I also had many friends in the House and Senate. I felt a magazine coming from Washington would carry with it an unusual authority. We also wanted our editor to mingle with congressmen, senators and government leaders so he could speak with first hand knowledge of the issues of the day." [43]

The magazine still needed an editor. Graham's first choice, Wilbur Smith, had, after a long period of indecision, declined the position on account of his age. Another Fuller professor, Harold Lindsell, then suggested a younger colleague, Carl F. H. Henry, a brilliant scholar and the first acting dean of the seminary. A theologian with two doctorates, one of them from Boston University, and a background in journalism, Henry had obvious qualifications for the job, but Graham worried that he was too much of a fundamentalist. In a reply to Lindsell, he asked whether Henry would be ready to take criticism from typical fundamentalist leaders and, "Would he be willing to recognize that fundamentalism is in need of an entirely new approach and that this magazine would be useless if it had the old fundamentalist stamp on it?" The new periodical, he wrote, would "plant the evangelical flag in the middle of the road, taking a conservative theological position but a definite liberal approach to social problems." Its "view of Inspiration," he wrote, "would be somewhat along the line of the recent book by Bernard Ramm, which in my view does not take away from Inspiration but rather gives strong support to our faith in the Inspiration of the Scriptures." [44]

The letter showed how far along Graham's thinking had come. The book he referred to, *The Christian View of Science and Scripture*, was then causing a major stir in fundamentalist circles because Ramm had challenged the assumption that the Bible was a reliable source of scientific data and proposed that Christians might properly believe in a divinely guided evolution of the species. [45] Graham had never made such a daring proposal in his sermons, but clearly he thought it should be discussed.

Carl Henry wanted the job, but when formally asked to take it, he had reservations about the direction the new journal seemed to be taking and thought his own firm beliefs might disqualify him. On one hand he was a theological conservative who took a strong stand on biblical inerrancy. His convictions, he wrote Graham, were that "the authoritative Scripture is the watershed of modern theological controversy" and that "Liberalism and Evangelicalism do not have equal rights and dignity in the true church." [46] On the other hand he believed social reform a part of the Christian message. In 1947, while still at Boston University, he had written a short book, *The Uneasy Conscience of Modern Fundamentalism*, charging that, as a result of their war with modernism, fundamentalists had abandoned their social responsibilities and had failed to contest even such "admitted social evils as aggressive warfare, racial hatred and intolerance, the liquor traffic, and exploitation of labor or management, whichever it may be." To Graham he wrote, "capitalism is not beyond Christian criticism," and, clearly thinking of Pew, he referred the evangelist to a speech he had recently given to the NAE rebuking conservative Protestants who "implied that capitalism was the ideal economic form of the Kingdom of God." [47]

The board of *Christianity Today* eventually decided that neither Henry's theological nor his social views disqualified him for the editorship and appointed him. Graham continued to worry that Henry might alienate the mainline ministers, and Pew fretted that he might be some kind of a socialist, but Henry had decided to run essays with a range of opinions, and the three proved able to work together. The first issue of *Christianity Today* appeared in October 1956, and by the following spring the magazine had begun to attract paid subscribers and notice in the secular press. [48]

In the meantime Graham himself moved decisively away from the fundamentalist right. In 1955 he accepted an invitation from the Protestant Council of the City of New York to hold a crusade in Madison Square Garden in the spring of 1957. The Council, which represented a large percentage of the ministers in the metropolitan area, had ties to the National Council of Churches, and many of its members were liberals. Jack Wyrtzen and the fundamentalists who had repeatedly invited Graham to come to New York under their auspices were naturally infuriated, and the more so when Graham accepted invitations to speak at liberal seminaries. In London the previous year Graham had invited a prominent American liberal minister to sit on the stage with him and had told reporters, "The ecumenical movement has broadened my viewpoint, and I recognize now that God has his people in all churches." At Union Theological Seminary—the historic bastion of liberalism—he again spoke favorably about the mainline ecumenical movement and said kind words about the liberal ministers he knew. Carl McIntire, who had never supported Graham because of his ties with Ockenga and the National Association of Evangelicals, took the occasion to attack him directly, as did Bob Jones Sr. who had initially supported him. They and a number of lesser-known figures denounced Graham for consorting with apostates at Union Theological Seminary, praising ungodly men, and selling out to the modernist Protestant Council.[49] Graham, however, continued to provoke them. In a February 1956 article in *Look* magazine he wrote, "There are so many shades of fundamentalism and so many shades of liberalism, it is increasingly difficult to point to a man and say he is a 'liberal' or he is a 'fundamentalist' without qualifying explanations." He was, he said, a fundamentalist if that meant someone who accepted the fundamental doctrines, but "if by fundamentalist you mean 'narrow,' 'bigoted,' 'prejudiced,' 'extremist,' 'emotional,' 'snake-handler,' 'without social conscience'—then I am definitely not a fundamentalist."[50]

In this period Graham had a powerful champion in John R. Rice, the former Norris protégé whose newspaper, *The Sword of the Lord*, had become the most influential fundamentalist periodical in the country. One of the guardians at the gates of orthodoxy, Rice was always on the lookout for the slightest sign of error, but he had seen Graham as the hope for a national revival and had made the evangelist a member of his board. When Graham went to Union Theological Seminary, Rice merely chided him for unwisely fellowshipping with liberals. Graham, he declared, could never become a modernist; he was "God's anointed man, being used tremendously in great revivals." But doubts began to form in his mind. New York fundamentalists pointed out that cooperation with the Protestant Council in the crusade meant that Graham would have to send at least some of his converts to liberal churches. Might he not, they asked, dilute his gospel message to accommodate his new friends? Then in March 1956 *Christian Life*, a popular conservative monthly, ran an article titled "Is Evangelical

Theology Changing?" Its conclusion was yes. "Fundamentalism has become *evangelicalism*," the editors wrote, the difference between the two being that fundamentalists stressed, "Ye should earnestly contend for the faith," whereas evangelicals emphasized, "Ye must be born again." Along with this major shift in tone, the editors wrote, younger theologians, such as Ramm and Henry, were moving away from dispensationalism and taking more positive views of science, scholarship, and social reform. Rice called the article "sophomoric."[51]

In June Graham made matters worse by charging that the real reason revival had not come to America was "the name-calling and mud-slinging" among evangelicals. What difference did it make, he asked, who sponsored a meeting as long as there were no strings attached? Rice by then had had enough. Privately he asked Graham to reaffirm in writing the *Sword of the Lord*'s statement of faith. Graham bluntly told him to drop his name from the board. In November, after the first issue of *Christianity Today* appeared, Rice made the break public, writing that Graham no longer considered himself a fundamentalist. He later attacked Graham's motives, charging that the evangelist wanted "the prestige, the financial backing and the worldly influence" of the Protestant Council. Graham, however, had clearly decided he did not need the likes of Rice. At an NAE meeting in early 1957 he called his critics "extremists," and decried the tendency to "think a person is not a Christian unless he pronounces our shibboleths and clichés exactly as we do." As if that were not enough, he uttered what to strict fundamentalists were fighting words: "The one badge of Christian discipleship is not orthodoxy but love." When his remarks appeared in *Christianity Today*, Rice erupted in a fury of mixed metaphors: "Dr. Graham is one of the spokesmen and perhaps the principal spark plug of a great drift away from strict Bible fundamentalism and strict defense of the faith." Graham was in other words anathema.[52]

By the time the crusade began in May 1957, fundamentalists had split irrevocably into two camps: neo-evangelicals versus militant separatists— or those who admired Graham versus those who thought he had left the fold. In the wake of the schism "fundamentalist" came to be a term used almost exclusively by the separatists.[53]

*   *   *

By May Graham and his neo-evangelical allies had many reasons for optimism about success in the coming crusade. By the count of his organization he had the support of 1,500 New York churches. Even some Episcopalian ministers had been won over when he met with them personally. At Union Theological Seminary, he had received a standing ovation from students and faculty, and the president of the seminary, Henry Pitney Van Dusen, had volunteered to serve on the local crusade committee. Neo-evangelicals credited this achievement not just to Graham's break with the militant fundamentalists—plus his personal charm—but to the shift they saw occurring in liberal theology.[54]

A month after *Christian Life* published "Is Evangelical Theology Changing?" it ran a companion piece, "Is Liberal Theology Changing?" Its answer again was yes. The article reflected the considerable optimism among neo-evangelicals that in recent years liberalism had been chastened by global disasters and by the devastating critique of Karl Barth and other neo-orthodox theologians. "Repentant liberals," the magazine reported, "were scattering like dust raised by a housewife's broom to a dozen different positions—many of them not far from what evangelicals believed to be orthodox Christianity." In general, the article maintained, liberals were taking a more respectful attitude toward the Bible, returning to belief in the sovereignty of God, acknowledging the supernatural in Christianity, and putting a renewed emphasis on the conversion experience. Yes, liberals still clung to certain erroneous doctrines and to the higher criticism of the Bible, but, the piece concluded, a general return to orthodoxy was not out of the question. In an interview in the June issue of the magazine Graham sounded the same optimistic note, maintaining that "extreme liberalism within the church" was in full retreat and the church was putting "a new and wonderful emphasis on personal evangelism and a conversion experience." Carl Henry was only a bit more skeptical. Neo-evangelicals, he wrote in the summer of 1957, were too prone to assume that liberalism had been curbed and stripped of its defenses; still, it was true that the old centers of liberal thought had long been engaged in making adjustments and were "eager to get beyond the fundamentalist-modernist controversy."[55]

The neo-evangelicals had some reason for taking this view. Certainly liberal theologians held a number of different positions. They always had, but Social Gospel liberalism with its optimism about human progress was far from dead. It flourished in many of the elite seminaries, such as Union, Yale, and Boston University, as well as at *The Christian Century*. Important churchmen, such as Henry Sloane Coffin and Henry Van Dusen, preached it throughout their entire careers. In spite of the Great Depression and two world wars, they continued to believe that human endeavors for world peace, social justice, and ecumenism would help bring in the Kingdom of God. True, Karl Barth and others had attacked that view. The editors of *Christian Life* were right about that. They were also right about the renewed emphasis on soul winning within the mainline denominations.

Fundamentalists had caricatured liberals as merely social reformers, but evangelism had always been a part of the liberal tradition, and even some of their favorite enemies like Rauschenbusch, Fosdick, and Coffin had perfectly evangelical beliefs in the conversion of individuals to faith in Christ and in redemption from sin through the power of grace. Coffin, who became the president of Union Theological Seminary in 1926, characterized himself as an evangelical liberal and maintained that liberalism and evangelicalism were both vital to the American religion.[56] In the 1930s the mainline clergy were struggling to maintain their congregations, but they continued to believe in conversion as well as in Christian nurture, and when the religious upsurge began in the latter years of World War II, a conversionist excitement took hold of them. By May 1947 at least thirty major denominations had launched evangelistic programs. In community after community mainline clergymen conducted "visitation evangelism" campaigns to find the unchurched and to add their names to the membership roles. "By general agreement," a Federal Council of Churches official reported in 1946, "evangelism is of the essence of the Christian task as Protestants conceive it." When the FCC was reorganized in 1950, its successor, the National Council of Churches, made evangelism one of its priorities. Like many Catholics and Jews, most mainline Protestants believed religion a support for a healthy democratic society. Bromley Oxnam, a

Methodist bishop so politically liberal he was hauled before the House Un-American Activities Committee to testify that he wasn't a Communist, wrote in 1946: "A revival of religion . . . by which the individual heart is changed . . . is the most certain way . . . to preserve freedom."[57]

In such an atmosphere not only the neo-evangelicals but also many mainline clergymen believed that evangelicalism was bringing Protestants together. In 1950 John Mackay, the liberal president of the Princeton seminary, called for an end to the "horseplay" of labeling people as fundamentalists or modernists and urged that all churches place the emphasis on the biblical idea of "evangelicalism."[58]

The enthusiasm for evangelism plus the political and social conservatism of the period largely accounted for Graham's success in finding mainline backing for his New York crusade. Mass revivalism was controversial in mainline circles, and none of their ministers practiced it, but such was the enthusiasm for soul winning that 40 percent of the Protestant Council members actively supported the crusade. That was enough because another 40 percent didn't oppose it.[59] A group of influential laymen, among them George Champion, the president of Chase Manhattan, who chaired the Council's Department of Evangelism, strongly backed the proposal. The executive committee of the crusade, once assembled, constituted, as Marshall Frady wrote, "a high commission of national respectability." Chaired by Roger Hull, president of Mutual Life of New York, it included Howard Isham, vice president of U.S. Steel, Henry Luce, William Randolph Hearst Jr., Ogden Reid of the *Herald Tribune*, Robert Kintner of ABC, Norman Vincent Peale Jr., and Henry Van Dusen. It was, in other words, as establishmentarian as the committees that had supported the major nineteenth-century revivalists. Indeed, the lay sponsors eventually included members of the same families—Vanderbilts, Goulds, and Whitneys—that had backed the Moody and Sunday crusades, and members of the Phelps and Dodge families, which had backed mass revivals since they brought Finney to New York in 1830. Many of Graham's sponsors belonged to liberal churches, but much like Moody's nineteenth-century backers, they believed that religion was a good thing for the country, and they believed that Graham could bring the masses into the church. Henry Van Dusen, for example, agreed with his UTS colleagues that Graham delivered "simple answers to simple questions," but he argued that mass audiences required "a more readily digestible form" of the gospel than "'the strong meat' of a sophisticated interpretation." Billy Graham, the refrain went, got results.[60]

Graham's New York crusade opened in Madison Square Garden on May 15. That night he took his text from Isaiah and preached, as he often did, on the threat of Communism and the H-bomb, on God's judgment on Sodom and Ninevah, and on the need for a city-wide revival. During the crusade he touched on social issues, such as poverty and race relations, but as usual he skirted politics and divisive theological issues.[61] On some evenings he spoke about the problems of the modern condition—emptiness, loneliness, guilt, nervous tension, and the fear of death—offering a decision for Christ as cure for every benighted soul. On other evenings he decried immorality, proposing that if only church people would quit drinking, gambling, and lying, and live a Christian life, a revival would surely come. The Christian life, as he described it, often seemed to be a matter of seemly domestic behavior. "A Commandment says, 'Thou shalt not commit adultery.' A woman commits this sin when she deliberately dresses in such a way as to entice a man. . . . Bad temper. You explode when things don't go to suit you and kick up your heels." The Christian wife "should keep herself attractive and give the husband a big kiss when he comes home from the office instead of yelling at him from the kitchen. Don't gossip. Don't nag. . . . And you husbands, how long has it been since you sent her some flowers? They like little things." In general, Graham counseled, Christians should live a disciplined life and obey parents, teachers, and all those in authority. It did not, he said, take a great sinner to make a great saint. "You don't have to go to the Devil first to find Christ! The gospel can prevent you from getting scarred by sin. You can come to Christ now and save all that!" In his concluding invitations to repentance he insisted that the decision wasn't an emotional one. "It's primarily a commitment you make with your will, not your mind, not your emotions." To Frady, a line of Scripture Graham quoted, "Let all things be done decently, and in order," seemed the essential text of the crusade.[62]

Before the crusade began Graham said that he faced the city "with fear and trembling," for if the critics "crucified" him, "every engagement we have in the world might be canceled." His crusade machinery was, however, in good order. On opening night eighteen thousand people came to the Garden—the largest turnout for the first night of any American crusade. The media coverage was extensive. Even *The New York Times* devoted two full pages to the service and included a transcript of Graham's sermon. A decision was made to broadcast the Saturday night services live on national television, and some six million viewers outside the New York area tuned in the first Saturday. The local attendance kept up, and the crusade, originally scheduled to run for six weeks, went on into July. On the 20th, the day planned for the closing service, a hundred thousand people turned out for a rally at Yankee Stadium—a record crowd for the stadium—and Vice President Nixon made an appearance, bringing greetings from the president. After several more extensions and more outdoor gatherings, the crusade culminated and came to an end with a Labor Day rally in Times Square. Facing a crowd that filled the square and stretched for blocks up Broadway, Graham thundered, "Let us tell the whole world tonight that we Americans believe in God . . . that we are morally and spiritually strong as well as militarily and economically. . . . Let us tell the world that we are united and ready to march under the banner of Almighty God, taking as our slogan that which is stamped on our coins: 'In God We Trust.' " [63] In effect the speech was a proclamation of victory for the civil religion of the Eisenhower years.

In its postcrusade assessment the Graham organization reported impressive statistics. The crusade had been the longest-running, most heavily attended event in the history of Madison Square Garden, with an average attendance of eighteen thousand a night for three months. Counting the crowds at the outdoor rallies, the total attendance had topped two million, and over 55,000 had signed cards making decisions for Christ. In terms of these numbers, the New York crusade had clearly been the most successful revival in American history. Yet the numbers were elliptical. The attendance figure, for example, did not reveal how many people came to hear Graham, for—with his encouragement—many people came more than once; nor did it show how many were New Yorkers. Before the crusade began, Graham had asked his radio listeners across the country to take their summer vacations in New York to attend the services. Before the Yankee Stadium rally he sent a letter to his prayer partners entreating them to come to the event. "Whatever the effort and sacrifice, I hope you will be there. We need you . . . we would not want to have empty seats," he wrote. For the nightly services his organization reserved 7,500 of the Garden's 19,000 seats for delegations coming by bus and train from places as far away as Houston and Louisville. Another 3,700 seats were reserved for the crusade's supporting cast of ushers, counselors, choir members, and guests, leaving only 7,800 seats for the general citizenry of New York. A few weeks into the crusade, Graham exclaimed, "This is not the so-phisticated city that I first thought it was. They're just plain people here! They respond to the Gospel just as the people in Miami or Omaha or Charlotte." But then a great many in the audience were from places like Omaha and Charlotte.[64]

Local ministers hoped the revival would produce a flood of new churchgoers. The Garden, however, seemed to be filled with neatly dressed people who knew the hymns and carried Bibles. As later surveys indicated, most of those who came forward to make a decision for Christ were church members already. When *The New York Times* queried partic-ipating ministers in the metropolitan area four months after the event, the ministers reported that 64 percent of the decision cards they received came from their own church members, and most of the rest came from people who never joined up. The Protestant Council of New York after-ward estimated that six to ten thousand people were added to the rolls of its 1,700 churches.[65] The Council did not complain, but this was a pretty poor showing for the greatest single evangelistic effort in the history of the country.

To students of revivals like William McLoughlin, the results were not surprising. In other cities Graham's crusades had produced much the same phenomena: huge crowds and relatively few new church members. Graham himself admitted his own statistics showed that a high percent-age of those who signed decision cards were church members already.[66] What was more, mass revivalism had followed much the same pattern since the Civil War. Dwight Moody had also turned out huge crowds of middle-class churchgoers and had also failed to reach the poor and the lost. But then both Graham and Moody had chosen to preach, as it were, to the choir of those who already believed in decency and order. Graham's sponsors, however, didn't seem to notice the paucity of converts any more than Moody's had. A year later Graham held a crusade in San Francisco with the endorsement of the Oakland and San Francisco Councils of Churches, the Episcopal Diocese of California, the Presbytery of San Francisco, and numerous Methodist churches—and with much the same results.[67] In this period of evangelical enthusiasm the enormous crowds seemed to be enough.

The crowds Graham drew were certainly impressive, and with people from so many different churches involved, they helped convince clergymen and commentators that—the fundamentalist fringe aside—Protestants had put their disputes behind them and were coming together over basic values and basic religious tenets. That was the conventional wisdom of the period, and it has survived in histories written decades later.[68] But people can be wrong about each other, and in this case both the neo-evangelicals and Graham's mainline supporters were engaging in wishful thinking. Beyond Graham's "simple message" the conservative-liberal divide remained as deep as before.

Carl Henry and other neo-evangelicals spoke confidently about a conservative swing in the mainline denominations under the influence of the neo-orthodox theology of Karl Barth. *Christianity Today* gave many pages to examining the similarities between Barth's theology and fundamentalist orthodoxy, but in their fond hope for a renaissance of conservatism, they were looking in the wrong direction. Mainline seminarians certainly read Barth, but his influence in America was short-lived and never profound. It was Reinhold Niebuhr who dominated mainline theology and who transformed the liberal Protestant consciousness.[69]

In the 1930s Niebuhr, the professor of social ethics at UTS, had leveled withering criticism at the faith of Social Gospelers in the perfectibility of man and the certain progress of society toward the Kingdom of God. The liberals, he charged, had equated God with history, reduced politics to moral striving and reduced religion to moral striving and personal faith. In *Moral Man and Immoral Society* (1932) he argued that human groups and institutions could never overcome the self-interest, or the collective egotism, that sustained their existence, no matter how many moral men they contained. Politics was inevitably about the struggle for power, and liberal Christianity had to give up its sentimental idealism for the sake of justice and peace. For this reason he abandoned the pacifism espoused by many mainline denominational leaders in the 1930s. In subsequent books he argued that the Social Gospel's "moral man" was an illusion, too, for no act, no matter how altruistic, is devoid of egotism, and evil is always constitutive in the good. Liberal Christians, he wrote, needed to regain the Christian sense of the tragedy of life and the concept of original sin. In his later, more theological works he invoked the classical Reformed themes of divine transcendence, providence, judgment, redemption, and grace.[70]

Because of his devastating attacks on liberal theology, Niebuhr was often called a "neo-orthodox" theologian, but as the religious historian and ethicist Gary Dorrien writes, he took for granted the basic assumptions of liberal theology: the authority it gave to individual reason and experience, its openness to new knowledge, and its emphasis on Christianity as the spiritual and ethical life of the individual rather than on the doctrines and life of the church. He had a profound respect for the Bible—the Old Testament and the New—and to him one of the central defects of liberal theology was its failure to take such scriptural stories, such as the Genesis account of creation, seriously. To dismiss them as merely prescientific explanations of events was in his view to ignore their profound religious meaning. The story of Adam and Eve bringing sin into the world when they ate from the tree of knowledge was for him the revelation of the tragic existential reality: precisely because humans had the capacity for self-transcendence they would inevitably commit the sin of pretending to be more than the finite beings they knew they were. For Niebuhr, however, these stories were myths and to read them literally, as traditional orthodoxy did, was to turn them into absurdities. With his UTS colleague Paul Tillich he developed the theory that all religion had a mythic nature. Myths, they proposed, were the essential mode of encounter with the sacred: the means of expressing the dimension of depth in life that transcends history and points to "the ultimate ground of existence."[71]

Under the rubric of "neo-orthodoxy" Niebuhr was often lumped with Barth, but he was one of Barth's harshest American critics. He considered a theology that based its claims on revelation and faith alone as "positivism that stands above reason," a dogmatic and abstruse form of otherworldliness that amounted to "a new kind of fundamentalism or an old kind of orthodoxy."[72] He admired Barth's resistance to the German church after Hitler took power, but he deplored the ethical quietism of his theology and his contention that Christians should trust in God and abandon their pretensions to reforming society. Niebuhr had charged American liberals with naive moralism, but like them, he believed that Christians had a mission to work for a just world. He himself was deeply involved with public policy. In 1939 he had advocated American intervention in the war against Nazi Germany, and in the immediate postwar period he had helped shape the ideological framework for the containment of the Soviet Union. Communism, he wrote, was a perverted religion that had created a totalitarian movement bent on world domination. Like his friend George Kennan, he believed the movement would eventually self-destruct because of its internal contradictions, but that in the meantime it had to be contained. Occasionally he differed with National Council of Churches colleagues over their calls for nuclear disarmament because in his view the relaxation of international tensions led to disarmament and not vice versa. But he was no political conservative. A Socialist in the 1930s, he was by 1947 actively involved in Democratic Party politics through the liberal organization Americans for Democratic Action. Niebuhr had indeed chastened liberal Protestant idealism, politically as well as theologically, but if anything, he had made liberalism more liberal by dethroning what he called the reverse fundamentalism of the modernist approach to the Bible and by insisting on the contingency of political solutions and the need for a sense of humility.[73]

As for the liberal clergy who thought that Graham and his theological allies were putting fundamentalism behind them and joining mainstream Protestantism, they were also badly mistaken. Ockenga, Henry, and the other neo-evangelicals had rejected the contentiousness and anti-intellectualism of the fundamentalists, and Graham had almost single-handedly created a break with the militant separatists. Theologically, however, they had hardly moved at all. True, the Fuller scholars had abandoned the dispensationalist practice of searching current events for signs of the end times, but they remained generally premillennialist, and given the seductions of Barthian neo-orthodoxy, biblical inerrancy had become, if anything, more important to them than before. Rather than modifying their view of inspiration, as Bernard Ramm proposed, they held firmly to the Hodge-Warfield doctrine that the Bible was inerrant in its original autographs. In efforts to create an intellectually respectable defense of orthodoxy the leading Fuller theologian, E. J. Carnell, tried to find a way to accommodate evolutionary biology and to account for the obvious discrepancies in the Bible, but inerrancy proved just too high a barrier for him. Fundamentalism, Marsden writes, was deeply internalized at Fuller. It was also in a sense enforced because the scholars feared alienating the fundamentalist and conservative evangelical groups that made up Fuller's constituency.[74]

In this period Henry, Graham, Ockenga, and other neo-evangelicals often spoke of the need to address social problems, but in the Eisenhower years they did not seem able to find any to tackle. Most of them were, after all, Taft Republicans, who espoused the economic philosophy of Moody and their other nineteenth-century forebears. Graham spoke for most of them when he insisted that the nation continue to be devoted to "the individualism that made America great," or, alternatively, to "the rugged individualism that Christ brought." Graham didn't ignore the existence of corporations—he often spoke of "the dangers that face capitalism"— but he seemed to ignore their institutional nature. Industrial conflicts, he promised, could be settled in a trice if only labor and management would bow on their knees to God. He urged employers to treat their workers fairly, but he deplored unionism—at least in the South. In Greensboro, North Carolina, he spoke of the Garden of Eden as a place where "there were no union dues, no labor leaders, no snakes and no disease."[75] Carl Henry, who did understand the corporate nature of the modern economy, and who had insisted that capitalism was not above Christian reproach, never wrote or published any criticism of corporate behavior in the pages of *Christianity Today*. Possibly he wanted to, but according to his memoir, Nelson Bell and J. Howard Pew kept him on a tight rein. He published articles by J. Edgar Hoover, and on international issues *CT* took the Taft-Goldwater Republican line.[76]

In 1947 Henry had berated fundamentalists for failing to take action against the "evil" of "racial hatred and intolerance," but in the decade that followed most neo-evangelicals seemed to ignore the growing movement to end segregation. Billy Graham could not, and the issue posed a terrible dilemma for him. He wasn't a racist—he had moved well beyond his North Carolina upbringing—and in 1950 he stated flatly, "All men are created equal under God. Any denial of that is a contradiction of holy law."[77] Nonetheless, white southerners made up a considerable part of his audience, and in the early 1950s he held segregated meetings in the South. When northern reporters grilled him about this practice, he explained that he followed local customs in whatever part of the country he was in. Increasingly, however, he came under pressure from northerners and southern black ministers to take a stand against segregation. For a couple of years he went back and forth on the issue, sometimes contradicting himself about what the Scriptures did or didn't say about segregation. In 1953 he refused to permit segregated seating in his Chattanooga crusade— he removed the rope barriers around the black section himself—but in Dallas a few months later he accepted the sponsoring committee's designation of separate areas for blacks and whites, explaining that in Dallas segregation was the law. The following year, after the Supreme Court ruled against public school segregation in *Brown v. Board of Education of Topeka, Kansas*, he determined never to hold a segregated meeting again.[78]

Still, his difficulties were hardly over. In 1955 his fellow Baptist minister Martin Luther King Jr. began a bus boycott in Montgomery, Alabama, the first in series of nonviolent protests against the Jim Crow laws. In the South racial tensions ran high. In 1956 Eisenhower, whose chances for re-election could have been harmed by racial strife, wrote Graham and asked him to help promote "both tolerance and progress in our race relations problem." Graham agreed. In a series of meetings with a range of black and white southern religious leaders, he counseled gradualism. "I believe the Lord is helping us," he said, "and if the Supreme Court will go slowly and the extremists on both sides will quiet down, we can have a peaceful social readjustment over the next ten-year period." Attacked by both segregationists and northern liberals, he continued to seek a middle ground. During his New York crusade in 1957 he invited King to give the invocation at an evening service, but refused King's request that he not appear on a platform in Texas with the ardently segregationist governor of the state. On one occasion that summer he tentatively came out for civil rights legislation, but in an article in *Life* magazine he confined himself to pleading for an end to racial intolerance through an exercise of neighborly love. In a sermon he proclaimed, "The one great answer to our racial problem in America is for men and women to be converted to Christ"—as if the South were not peopled with born-again Christians.[79]

Graham also did not respond to King's plea that he hold crusades in the Deep South. He shied away from the term "integration," and when speaking of racial intolerance he often suggested that blacks and white northerners were equally culpable—even when the violence against the civil rights marchers was at its height.[80]

In the months before the New York crusade and during it, Niebuhr was Graham's most persistent critic. The evangelist, he wrote, is "a personable, modest and appealing young man" whose approach is "free of the vulgarities which characterized the message of Billy Sunday"—and that, he said, was progress. Still, he wrote, "It would be interesting to know how many of those attracted by his evangelistic Christianity are attracted by the obvious fact that his new evangelism is much blander than the old. For it promises a new life, not through painful religious experience but merely by signing a decision card. Thus a miracle of regeneration is promised at a painless price by an obviously sincere evangelist. It is a bargain."[81] Mainly, though, Niebuhr attacked the evangelist's approach to social problems. Graham, he charged, had the "perfectionist illusion" that conversion at a revival not only offered a man forgiveness from sin but freed him from all future temptation to sin. In his "pietistic fundamentalism," Niebuhr wrote, he "reduces faith to "a simple panacea for all the ills of the world" and proposes to solve "all the problems of life by asking bad people to become good and to prove it by loving one another." Coming around to the issue of civil rights, Niebuhr noted that racism flourished along with revivalism in the South and called upon Graham to follow the example of Charles Finney, who had made the abolition of slavery central to the experience of repentance and conversion. Graham, he wrote, should make his converts feel that their Christian duty entailed actively working toward the end of segregation and racial discrimination.[82] But this Graham would never do.

In desegregating his crusades and speaking out against racism, Graham was far ahead of his southern constituency and ahead of most northern conservatives, including those that normally followed his lead. The NAE did not make an official statement against segregation until 1956 and then dropped the issue for the next seven years. For a time King thought Graham might make a further contribution to the struggle, but the evangelist disappointed him. During the sit-ins of 1960 Graham urged southerners to obey the law, but said, "I am convinced that some extreme Negro leaders are going too far and too fast. I am also concerned about some clergymen of both races that have made the race issue their gospel. This is not the gospel!" While King languished in the Birmingham jail in the spring of 1963, Graham told *The New York Times* that his "good personal friend" would be well advised "to put on the brakes a bit." [83] In general he opposed the confrontational tactics of the civil rights movement and "forced integration," prescribing instead Christian neighborly love. Accordingly, he refused to endorse the Civil Rights Act of 1964 or the Voting Rights Act of 1965. (The NAE and *Christianity Today* also had nothing to say about them.) Only when the laws were passed did he support them to the extent of saying that they must be obeyed. Yet even in the summer of 1965 he equated the "extremists" in the civil rights movement with the Ku Klux Klan, saying that Alabama would be an exemplar to the nation if only both quieted down.[84]

In his reflections on Graham in 1956–57, Niebuhr had pointed to the irreducible differences between liberals and neo-evangelicals; he had also brought up the issue that in the 1960s created a clear-cut divide in the northern white Protestant churches.

By the 1950s the leaders of the northern mainline denominations and their Council of Churches had a long record of opposing the Jim Crow laws in the South, and in the postwar period they had worked to promote government policies that aimed at creating greater racial equality. Still, in line with the prevailing notion that religion instilled good values, and values led to right behavior, they had largely confined themselves to preaching, teaching, and making institutional pronouncements. With his campaigns of civil disobedience Martin Luther King showed them the gap between the country's vaunted democratic and religious values and the realities of racial oppression. In 1961 a few Protestant ministers joined the Freedom Riders, and a year or so later many northern church leaders found they could no longer stand by while their black counterparts were beaten and jailed for engaging in peaceful demonstrations and boycotts. Along with Catholic and Jewish leaders, prominent Episcopalian and Presbyterian clergymen joined the civil rights demonstrations, and around the time of the 1963 March on Washington they gained endorsements from their denominations and from the National Council of Churches. After that, the mainline clergy joined the protests in increasing numbers. A 1968 study of the Protestant clergy in California showed that nearly a quarter had taken part in some kind of civil rights demonstration.[85]

Theologically conservative Protestants did not join the civil rights marches or work for civil rights legislation, and some within the large northern denominations submitted resolutions contesting the actions of their leadership. Few openly opposed the aims of the civil rights movement. Instead some argued the denominations should not be involved as organizations, while others took the line that that the clergy should confine themselves to religious instruction and saving souls.[86] A half century earlier theological conservatives had been out in the streets demonstrating for Prohibition, but many of them now insisted on the separation of the church from the political arena. The liberals took the opposite tack. Inspired by King's passionate Christian witness, the activists increasingly came to view the fight for social justice as the preeminent mission of the church. The enthusiasm for evangelism that had gripped them in the 1950s faded into the background.

By the early 1960s Protestants were clearly dividing into two camps: those who espoused direct action for social reform and those who espoused conversion as the remedy for all ills. The division between the social justice party and the evangelical party in the 1960s made a much wider swath through the churches than the fundamentalist-modernist controversy had, but in part because it ran along existing theological lines it involved no dramatic conflict.[87] Rather the two sides simply drifted away from each other. The liberals, who dominated the major northern denominations, made common cause with the other religious groups involved in the civil rights movement, and deeming the nonparticipants irrelevant to the problems of the country, all but forgot about the conservatives in their midst. As in the 1930s, they noticed only the politically intrusive figures, in this case Carl McIntire and Billy James Hargis, who attributed the civil rights movement to a Communist conspiracy.

The extent of the conservative party was in one sense easy to miss, for as in the past the conservatives were institutionally and theologically scattered. The neo-evangelicals had assumed a leadership role, but the NAE had failed to bring the dozens of conservative denominations and the thousands of other conservative churches under one roof. Further, the neo-evangelicals paid small attention to theologies outside their Reformed tradition, and the separation between the northern and southern denominations remained as wide as before. Still, Billy Graham continued to attract enormous crowds all over the country. He called himself an "evangelical Christian," and used the term to denote all the "born-again" believers who attended his revivals. Most in his audiences continued to identify themselves as members of their respective denominations— Conservative Baptists, Lutherans of the Missouri Synod, Swedish Baptists, members of the Assemblies of God, Southern Baptists, and so on—but for journalists the term "evangelicals" proved useful as a way to refer to conservative Protestants in all their puzzling variety. The liberals did not contest this use of the word as they would have at an earlier time, and by the 1970s many conservatives were allying with those of other conservative Protestant traditions by calling themselves "evangelicals."

7

PENTECOSTALS *and*
SOUTHERN BAPTISTS

B ILLY GRAHAM and his neo-evangelical allies were not just bent on evangelism. They aimed to create a coherent social and intellectual framework and to forge an interdenominational coalition of evangelicals around it. To men like Carl Henry, a theologian, these projects appeared ambitious but hardly impossible. The success of *Christianity Today* and the enormous popularity of Graham seemed to show they had the intellectual heft and the drawing power to lead a diverse group of theological conservatives in the direction they chose. What they didn't count on was that developments within other sectors of conservative Protestantism shifted the whole balance of power within the evangelical world.

One of these was an explosive growth of the Pentecostal denominations and of independent ministries, such as that of Oral Roberts, and the spread of Pentecostal beliefs to most of the Protestant denominational families and to the Catholic Church. The second was the integration of southern evangelicals into the religious and political life of the nation for the first time since the Civil War. Of the two developments the most surprising was the first.

Pentecostalism had, after all, begun among the poor and outcast in a Los Angeles mission revival in 1906. The movement had spread quickly across the South and Southwest and segregated denominations had formed. But in the 1920s and '30s white Pentecostals—like their black counterparts—remained largely poor farmers or people working at marginal jobs in cities. Oral Roberts, the son of a Pentecostal Holiness preacher, had a not untypical childhood. Growing up in southeastern Oklahoma, he and his brothers followed their father to revival meetings in tiny towns; the boys, with one pair of overalls each, picked cotton and sometimes went hungry at night. Most Pentecostal preachers then had no religious education, and some, like Oral's father, were self-appointed evangelists with no formal education at all. What they had was a sense of desperate urgency because the Tribulations were already at hand. To them the world was a wicked place, corrupt, and hopelessly lost. Vinson Synan, the son of a Pentecostal Holiness bishop and a historian of the movement, remembered, "There was hardly any institution, pleasure, business, vice, or social group that escaped the scorn and opposition of Pentecostal preachers." Their catalogue of "social sins," he wrote, included tobacco, liquor, Coca-Cola, movies, medicine, life insurance, public swimming, professional sports, jewelry, and makeup. Many Pentecostals couldn't afford such worldly things, but in denouncing them their preachers effectively separated their congregations from much of the rest of society. In addition they separated themselves from each other, their associations splitting over and over again into tiny sects because of minute doctrinal differences or personal rivalries. However, what they all had was the spiritual ecstasy that came when the Holy Spirit descended on their meetings. People then spoke in tongues, danced, burst into holy laughter, or, "slain in the spirit," fell to the floor as if in a faint. At such times the preacher might prophesy, or cast out demons, and heal the sick. Even in everyday life the supernatural could break through at any minute, and it was as real as anything in the natural world.[1]

In her 2011 book, *Holy Ghost Girl*, Donna M. Johnson, the daughter of a tent revival organist, wrote:

My Pentecostal grandparents and their children existed in a reality that was an extension of biblical times. They believed the temporal world lay like a fine curtain over the realm of the eternal. At any moment the archangel Michael might reach through the veil and tap them on the shoulder with a heavenly message. Or the devil might slip through and tempt with some cheap bit of finery. It could be hard to tell one from the other at times, . . . but no one questioned the veracity of the experiences.[2]

Oral Roberts's parents prayed to Christ in such a conversational manner that, Oral remembered, "I actually thought that Christ lived in our house, was a member of the family."[3]

Before World War II most other Protestants paid small attention to the Pentecostals. They called them "Holy Rollers," and sometimes "snake-handlers" because a few small sects in Appalachia believed in testing their faith by picking up poisonous serpents. Only the Holiness groups, from which the movement had come, and the fundamentalists, from whom they had taken much of their theology, paid them serious attention—and these were their fiercest critics. The Holiness groups also engaged in ecstatic worship but drew the line at speaking in tongues and Holy Spirit baptism. The fundamentalists for their part maintained that the charismata, the gifts of the Holy Spirit granted the apostles at Pentecost, had come to an end in the first century, and the Lord had performed no miracles since the days of Peter and Paul. More essentially, fundamentalists were the people of the written Word and rationalistic proofs of the faith, whereas the Pentecostals put spiritual experience higher than doctrine and dogma. For these reasons, but doubtless also because of the competition for souls, both Holiness and fundamentalist ministers routinely denounced Pentecostals as superstitious, fanatical, demon-possessed, and apostates. At the same time psychologists who studied the movement concluded that those who spoke in tongues must be victims of mental illness or personality disorders. Pentecostals thus remained isolated from the rest of American Christianity until World War II.[4]

The Pentecostal movement nonetheless continued to grow, and in the religious surge of the postwar period its denominations grew proportionately faster than most of the rest. The Assemblies of God, by far the largest of the white denominations, went from 150,000 members in 1930 to 400,000 in 1955. With the expansion of industry, many Pentecostals left the rural South for the emerging cities of the Sun Belt, and while most joined the working class, some went into business and prospered. Substantial new churches appeared in cities from Charlotte, North Carolina, to Los Angeles, and—as was the pattern with the Methodists in the mid-nineteenth century—their congregations called for educated preachers. Accordingly, the denominations that had once embraced every self-appointed evangelist built Bible colleges, adopted stricter doctrinal standards, and weeded out the preachers who did not adhere to them. In the congregations bent on middle-class respectability the taboos on such "social sins" as sports, movies, television, and makeup melted away. In such churches—many of them Assemblies of God—worship services became more predictable and orderly with ministers using their authority to call down spontaneous eruptions of speaking in tongues. Then, too, the larger denominations took steps to gain acceptance among other evangelicals. After Wright and Ockenga brought them into the National Association of Evangelicals, they joined other evangelical organizations, and their leaders took up basic neo-evangelical politics: anti-Communism, anti-Catholicism, and anti-liberal church ecumenicism.[5]

The Assemblies of God held to the Keswickian view that sanctification was a gradual process and not, as those descended from Wesleyan Holiness groups would have it, a crisis experience after conversion that eradicated the individual's sinful nature. In this respect its theology was close to that of other evangelicals.[6] The churches that remained far on the outside were the tiny "Oneness" or "Jesus Only" groups, whose view of God was unitarian, as opposed to trinitarian.

Still, for many the attractions of Pentecostalism had nothing to do with an orderly Sunday service led by a well-schooled minister. What many wanted was the ecstatic experience of the Holy Spirit baptism and the miracles of prophecy and healing that could descend upon anyone, or a whole crowd, at a meeting. Holy Spirit revivals therefore broke out here and there beyond the control of the denominations, including some that introduced radical new doctrines.

In 1948 a powerful outburst of Pentecostal charismata occurred at a small Bible school in Saskatchewan, Canada, recently founded by four independent preachers. Faculty and students reported many of the signs and wonders that had occurred at Azusa Street, but this revival—which went on for months—involved distinctive practices like extended fasting and the transmission of Holy Spirit gifts by the laying on of hands. The preachers who led it emphasized exorcism and spiritual warfare. More provocatively, they rejected denominational authority and proclaimed a theocratic chain of command through the fivefold ministry of apostles, prophets, evangelists, pastors, and teachers that, they said, was coming into being as the last days approached. Like the early Pentecostals, they described their revival as "the latter rain," mentioned in Joel 2:23, that came just before the harvest in Palestine, and which in the dispensationalist scheme marked the prelude to the Rapture. Yet they broke with dispensationalism in prophesying the victory of the church. According to later written texts, they believed that the saints who appeared in the last days would be "overcomers" with all the attributes of Jesus, and that these "Manifest Sons of God" would themselves usher in the millennial reign of Christ and restore man to his rightful state before the Fall.

Known as the New Order of the Latter Rain, this intensely millenarian movement spread rapidly through North America via camp meetings, conferences, and emissaries from the Bible school. In 1949 the General Council of the Assemblies of God pronounced its eschatology unscriptural, and many Pentecostal ministers warned of the authoritarian character of its teachings about submission to the new apostolic order. The movement eventually lost momentum but its teachings caught on in some Pentecostal circles, and in various permutations survived into the twenty-first century.[7]

Far more important in the postwar period was the wave of healing revivals that swept through the Pentecostal world. Just at the time Billy Graham and his fellows were crossing the country with their Youth for Christ rallies, Pentecostal evangelists began to itinerate, putting up tents in town after town, and offering deliverance from sin, sickness, and Satan. By the early 1950s their numbers had multiplied, and scores of them were drawing crowds into their traveling tents with a blend of old-fashioned revivalism and the exorcism of physical ills. Each faith healer had his own style, and the competition was fierce. One boasted of holding the secret to immortality; another produced a "Jesus fragrance" that eliminated body odor and killed bugs. The tent services generally went on for many hours with singing, praying, preaching, and exhorting, but the climax was always the moment when the preacher stepped forth to work his miracles. The sick were healed, demons cast out, and later the floor of the tent would be covered by discarded crutches, braces, bandages, and wheelchairs.[8]

Several of these evangelists were gifted orators, and at least three of them, William Branham, A. A. Allen, and Oral Roberts, had a lasting influence on the Pentecostal world.

Branham, often credited with starting the movement, was a Baptist preacher, born dirt poor, who took to Pentecostalism and healing in 1937 after his wife and infant daughter died of meningitis. He was given to visions, and his revivals took off in 1946, when, he said, an angel visited him and gave him the gift of healing and the gift of discerning the secrets of the human heart. Afterward Branham could detect demons and diseases through vibrations in his left hand and reveal the intimate details of people's lives. Many attested to his miraculous healings, including a former U.S. congressman, who cast aside his crutches, and in his hometown of Jonesboro, Arkansas, it was said that a dead woman returned to life. With tales of his powers spreading far and wide, Branham packed tents, auditoriums, and stadiums across the country. At the height of his fame in the mid-1950s, he denounced all the denominations and veered off into wholly original doctrines. God, he said, had written three works: the Zodiac, the Great Pyramid, and the Holy Bible. Man, he maintained, came of "the serpent seed," for, after eating the fruit in the Garden, Eve had mated with the snake and given birth to Cain. He claimed to have opened the seven seals and said that God had told him that a latter-day Elijah, whom he described as someone much like himself, would come to serve as His messenger to announce the Second Coming. In an echo of the New Order of the Latter Rain, he prophesied that the new Elijah would be empowered to transform saints into their glorified bodies prior to the Rapture. His popularity waned in the late 1950s, but when he died in an auto crash in 1965, his followers held his body in state for four months, hoping to see a resurrection.[9]

In certain circles Branham is still regarded as a prophet, but A. A. Allen, who began his healing ministry three years later, introduced—or popularized—a doctrine that has spread across the planet and is preached by some of the best-known TV ministers in America today. An Assemblies of God pastor—born in poverty to an alcoholic father—he quit his church in Corpus Christi in 1949, hit the sawdust trail, and soon developed a radio program and a magazine. Miracles filled his tent, and in the mid-1950s "miracle oil" began to flow from the heads and hands of people in his audiences. His healings were often unsettling spectacles: cancer patients would cough their cancers into jars, and the demon-possessed would vomit out the evil spirits. One of the first of the healers to develop a television program, he broadcast many of these miracles for viewers at home.[10]

Like many of his fellow healers, Allen taught that God would bring not only healing but also financial success based the laws of faith ("ask and ye shall receive") and divine reciprocity ("give and it will be given to you"). In the mid-1950s, when healing evangelism became more competitive—and more scrutinized by the skeptical—he began to emphasize the prosperity gospel, and by the 1960s his magazine bore more testimonials to financial deliverance than to physical healing. His innovation was what became known as "the word of faith"—or the power to speak things into existence. God, he said, had told him that "Thou shall decree a thing, and it shall be established unto thee." So one day Allen decreed, and all the one-dollar bills into his wallet turned into twenties. "You don't have to believe it," he told his audiences, but "I believe I can command God to perform a miracle for you financially." For divine reciprocity to kick in, he would send believers a "prosperity cloth" for donations of a hundred or a thousand dollars.[11]

Allen prospered, but he could never get rid of the curse that afflicted his father, and in 1970 he died of alcoholism alone in a hotel room.[12]

Oral Roberts, the least troubled and least eccentric of the three, was the most successful of the healers and the only one to go on to a much larger ministry. In his long life he was often ridiculed—in 1980 for his vision of a nine-hundred-foot Jesus—but his influence on the Pentecostal movement can hardly be exaggerated.

By contrast to Branham and Allen, Roberts was the soul of Pentecostal orthodoxy. He was a minister's son, and when he came of age in 1936, he followed his father into the church, and served for ten years as a Pentecostal Holiness evangelist and pastor. In this decade he took courses at a Baptist college and gained a reputation as an effective preacher and writer. In 1948, restless, energetic, and fed up with the church bureaucracy and the tiny salary he earned, he moved to Tulsa and started preaching healing revivals. Like his fellow evangelists, Roberts preached mainly to the working poor: men with calloused hands sitting stiffly in their best suits with women in dowdy dresses at their sides. Many were elderly, and many, Roberts knew, were people "who had fallen upon hard times or are desperately ill." They were, he said, "simple, uneducated, uninhibited" people "to whom God means all." His services were exuberant but nonetheless austere by Pentecostal standards: no entertainment except for hymn singing, no gimmickry, and few extravagant claims. When people filed in front of him at end of a service, he would often simply touch each one and give a prayer for healing. Still, he had authority and a folksy charm, and the crowds in his tent grew larger each year. Forging tirelessly through the South and some of the northern cities he, by the estimate of his associates, spoke directly to eight and a half million souls by 1957.[13]

Roberts's success owed in part to the cooperation he obtained from the Pentecostal churches. The ministers of the larger denominations liked the relative restraint of his meetings and Roberts carefully cultivated relationships with them. His city-wide crusades, he insisted, had to be sponsored by a unified group of pastors or the regional Pentecostal fellowship. Six months in advance his associates would visit the city and negotiate the arrangements. The pastors would be asked to bring their congregations to his revivals and to supply volunteers to put up the tent or to work as ushers or counselors. In return they would take a share of the campaign contributions and hope to gather in some of the converts the evangelist made. Roberts's crusades were never quite as efficiently run as Billy Graham's, but by Pentecostal standards they were very well organized and financially responsible.[14]

Some of Roberts's best-attended crusades came toward the end of the 1950s. By that time the Oral Roberts Evangelistic Association had a seven-story office building in Tulsa and a network of three to five hundred radio and 135 TV stations broadcasting edited versions of his meetings to the United States and Canada. All this was expensive, but, unlike the other healing evangelists, Roberts was a talented fund-raiser with an ability to change with the times. Almost from the beginning, he realized, as Graham had, that the most reliable source of funding came not from the crusades but from direct mail solicitations of the people who wrote to him or subscribed to his magazine. By 1950 he was sending "deliverance cloths" to a hundred thousand people with a suggestion for an appropriate donation for their healing powers. In the mid-1950s the emphasis of his preaching changed from healing to prosperity teaching and evangelism. His magazine, *Healing Waters*, renamed *Abundant Life*, proposed a "Blessing Pact" whereby all those who contributed to saving souls would have the opportunity to share in the "unlimited personal benefits"—"spiritual, physical and financial"—that came to his "faith partners." With the help of his radio and TV broadcasts the number of his contributors rose to a million by 1956.[15]

Not all of Roberts's American faith partners were "simple, uneducated" folk, for along the way Roberts had attracted a number of businessmen, some from the Tulsa establishment, but many from a Pentecostal organization known as the Full Gospel Business Men's Fellowship. Founded by a wealthy California dairy farmer, Demos Shakarian, in 1951, the organization was made up of entrepreneurs, mostly young, who had started auto dealerships, construction companies, and the like, and who had rebelled against the strict prohibitions of their denominations. To these men Roberts offered not just prayer cloths but the chance to spend a few days with him every year at a conference in Tulsa to discuss evangelism at home and abroad.[16]

By the end of the 1950s Roberts's fund-raising pitches centered on his "World Outreach" program that sent religious literature, tape recordings, films, and radio programs abroad. In 1960 he started visiting foreign countries at least once a year. Speaking for the first time of the Communist threat to religion, he visited churches in Warsaw and Moscow and met with Chiang Kai-shek in Taiwan. Subsequently he held a series of crusades in Europe; in 1965 he made an extensive tour of Australia and New Zealand; afterward he campaigned in Brazil, Chile, Indonesia, and Kenya, attracting enormous crowds. Pentecostal missionaries had begun to work abroad not long after the Azusa Street revival, and the movement had spread to Europe and to a number of countries in the global South.

In the 1960s Latin America was going through its second Pentecostal revival, and by the 1980s there were more Pentecostals in Latin America than there were in the United States. But the movement abroad had taken off only after indigenous ministers adapted Pentecostal practices to local cultures, and in many countries—including most of those Roberts visited—American missionaries had become superfluous. Still, foreign crusades attracted support from American believers, who, as always, thought of evangelism as an American task, and many other Pentecostal healers were taking to missions abroad at the very same time. As David Harrell, Roberts's sympathetic biographer, has explained, enthusiasm for tent revivalism in the United States had begun to wane around 1960, and Roberts's audiences were shrinking, along with those of other itinerants. "To some extent," Harrell wrote, "the interest of American revivalists in world evangelism was a ploy to save their decaying organizations. Overseas campaigns were often little more than fund-raising promotions with little, if any, evangelistic impact." [17]

Pentecostal tent rivals died out in the 1960s, and while most of its practitioners simply watched their crowds melt away, Roberts went on to greater endeavors. In 1960 he decided to build a Bible school to train foreign evangelists, but hardly had the construction begun when he changed his mind and decided to build a full-scale American university. His close associates objected that the costs would be astronomical and that his evangelistic mission would founder, but Roberts knew he had to move on. In 1962 he told a Houston reporter that a university would "perpetuate my ministry and multiply it thousands of times, a ministry that otherwise would die." Pentecostal leaders had long been suspicious of academic learning, and at the time the only Pentecostal institution of higher education in the United States, apart from the Bible schools, was Evangel, an unaccredited liberal arts college run by the Assemblies of God. Roberts, however, had a strong feeling that many young Pentecostals wanted an academic education and that they would go to secular universities if they didn't have one of their faith. [18] He had virtually no idea of what a university was or did, but he had, he said, a charge from God, and that was enough for his supporters. Oral Roberts University opened in 1965, its campus centered on a Prayer Tower two hundred feet high. Ten years later it had what *The Chronicle of Higher Education* called "an impressive $60-million collection of futuristic buildings" with state-of-the-art learning technologies and a student body of over 2,500.[19] In the 1980s it looked to me like a Marriott hotel on the moon, but Roberts's intuition had been right.

Roberts brought his crusades to an end in 1968, and even though occupied with his university, he moved his evangelistic enterprise directly into the television studio. "To reach them we have to go where they are, because they are not coming where we are," he said frankly. In the past he had simply filmed his services, as other evangelists did, but television had changed in a decade, and he wanted something more entertaining, something more like the shows people were used to watching on secular TV. Two formats were chosen. One was a weekly half-hour Sunday morning program that had Roberts talking informally with stars such as Pat Boone and Dale Evans, and invariably preaching "Something good is going to happen to you." The other was a quarterly one-hour special for prime time that had the aspect of a variety show. Produced at the NBC studio in Burbank, California, these shows featured very short sermons, ORU singers in modish clothes, and a parade of Hollywood celebrities, including many with no obvious religious connections—Jimmy Durante, Jerry Lewis, and Tennessee Ernie Ford. The venture was risky, and the shows drew a good deal of criticism from religious commentators, but they were an immediate hit with the public at large. Within four years the specials were broadcast over four hundred stations and had audiences in the tens of millions. By 1978 Roberts had annual revenues of $60 million.[20]

Following Roberts's example, other "full gospel" evangelists took to television, among them Pat Robertson, Jim and Tammy Faye Bakker, Jimmy Swaggart, and the Word of Faith preacher Kenneth Copeland. Some, like Robertson, adopted talk show formats; others, like Swaggart, featured gospel music and preaching; while still others like the Bakkers went in for entertainment. Pentecostalism, at least as Roberts and his successors interpreted it, turned out to be made for TV. Other traditions depended on liturgy and/or the exegesis of biblical texts, but Pentecostals could dispense with these drags on the airwaves. Further, they didn't need a church setting, for the move of the Holy Spirit could happen anywhere, including on a glitzy set with singers crooning in the background. Celebrity guests could recount "miracles" of being saved from dreadful accidents, or they could break down weeping as the spirit moved in the studio.

Hosts could announce revelations from God, or they could relay the news that someone in their audience was just being healed of arthritis or a back injury. The shows were exciting, and all about immediate experience—as opposed to rational, linear exposition. (Marshall McLuhan could have predicted their success.) Then, too, miracles seemed fairly normal on television, where even detergents were said have miraculous powers.[21]

The same year Roberts ended his tent revivals, he quit his tiny Pentecostal Holiness denomination and joined the large and tolerant Methodist Church. He had often been at odds with the leaders of the various Pentecostal denominations, and he longed for acceptance in the larger Protestant world. In 1966 he had attended the World Congress on Evangelism sponsored by *Christianity Today* and chaired by Billy Graham. Held in Berlin, the Congress included delegates from over one hundred nations, among them the Emperor Haile Selassie of Ethiopia and a number of Pentecostal ministers from South America. Roberts had hesitated to go because he felt "the healing ministry had not been understood to be an integral part of the mainstream of the Gospel." He was right in the sense that though the National Association of Evangelicals included many Pentecostals, the neo-evangelicals had never accepted glossolalia or healing, and they regarded the tent healers as beyond the bounds of respectability.[22] Arriving in Berlin, Roberts found that the other Americans seemed to walk in big circles around him as if he might have a communicable disease. He went into hiding and ate his meals in his room until a Presbyterian minister took pity on him and introduced him around. When Graham heard of Roberts's plight, he invited him to a dinner and later asked him to address the assembly with a prayer and greeting. Roberts was nervous, but he made a graceful speech of thanks to Graham and Carl Henry for "helping to open my eyes to the main stream of Christianity." The delegates gave him a warm welcome, and Graham agreed to speak at the dedication of ORU the following year. Afterward Roberts told his new Presbyterian friend, "You don't realize what happened out there. Those kind of people never spoke to me before. . . . This is bigger than you understand, because you've lived in these circles all your life and I haven't. I've been on the outside looking in."[23]

The story, as told by Harrell, illustrates not only Roberts's abiding inferiority complex—and his charm—but also the sense many Pentecostals had of second-class citizenship in the evangelical world. At the same time the story speaks to the growing power and influence of Roberts, and Pentecostals generally. In the 1960s Billy Graham's American crowds were shrinking, along with those of all the other itinerants, and he, too, was devoting more of his time to evangelism abroad. He had realized that Pentecostal practices were spreading with great rapidity in the global South, but by the time of the Berlin Congress he had to note that they were gaining ground in America and moving well beyond their denominational bases into mainline Protestantism.

In the early 1960s outbreaks of tongue-speaking began to occur in unlikely places. The first to catch the attention of the national press occurred in 1960 in the fashionable St. Mark's Episcopal Church in Van Nuys, California. Its rector, Dennis Bennett, described as "the epitome of the sophisticated, respectable, slightly worldly clergy of his church," had heard about the baptism of the Holy Spirit from a fellow Episcopal clergyman the previous year. After months of study and prayer with a few members of his congregation, he began to speak in "a new language." Others had the same experience and began shouting "Hallelujah" and "Praise the Lord" in the church office. Their numbers grew to the point where Bennett felt he had to explain. His sermons on Holy Spirit baptism, however, caused an uproar in his very large congregation. "We're Episcopalians, not a bunch of wild-eyed hillbillies," one irate parishioner was heard to say. Bennett was forced to resign and was relegated to a small inner-city church in Seattle. But that didn't stop him. He turned his new church into a hub for Holy Spirit baptisms in the Northwest.[24]

By 1966 Pentecostal practices were being taken up by ministers and lay groups in all the mainline denominations. Episcopalians, Lutherans, Presbyterians, Methodists, and Baptists began to experience all the gifts of the Holy Spirit, among them prophesying, healing, and the discernment of evil spirits, mentioned in 1 Corinthians 12. In 1967 prayer meetings at Duquesne and Notre Dame universities sparked similar outbreaks within the Catholic Church. Many church leaders deplored these practices, but the liberal Protestant denominations—which had long held religion to be based in experience—eventually accepted them, as did the Catholic hierarchy after Vatican II. The movement—first called "neo-Pentecostalism" and afterward "the charismatic renewal"—spread rapidly. According to some estimates, 10 percent of the mainline clergy had experienced the gifts of the spirit by 1970, and four years later Catholic renewalists had 1,800 prayer groups in the United States.[25]

Pentecostal ministers played almost no role in creating this movement, for most considered mainline Protestants and Catholics apostate.[26] The Full Gospel Business Men's Fellowship opened its membership to non-Pentecostals, and Roberts attracted Protestants from other traditions, but generally Pentecostal beliefs seem to have spread, as in the case of Bennett, informally, and, as it were, by osmosis. In any case, the renewalists did not become true Pentecostals. They adapted Pentecostal practices to their own church traditions and rejected what they considered "the cultural baggage" of the Pentecostals, from the "sin list" to their plain folks' style.[27] They called themselves "charismatics"—from *charisma* or divine gift—to make the distinction clear, and Pentecostals initially looked on them with suspicion. Still, to outsiders the difference between the two was not so obvious. Charismatics were also given to ecstatic worship, from quiet, trancelike states to outbursts of weeping, laughing, dancing, and being "slain in the spirit." Like the early Pentecostals, they insisted on a spiritual democracy in which ordinary laymen could manifest a direct experience of God. They aimed to renew the "dry" or "frozen" churches with true spirituality, and they harbored a millenarian, or quasi-millenarian, hope for the soon-coming of Christ.[28]

The sudden explosion of charismata in the Catholic and mainline Protestant churches in the 1960s could be thought of as one of God's mysteries. Still, what is striking about the movement is how much it had in common with many of the countercultural movements of the same period. In the 1960s and '70s young people were taking variously to Buddhist meditation, Hare Krishna chanting, crystal reading, and "channeling." They were joining communes, human potential movements, and consciousness-raising sessions; they were getting high with mind-altering drugs and losing themselves in the great communal melding of rock concerts. Queried by their puzzled elders, some spoke of a desire for authentic experience and authentic spirituality, some about the oppressiveness of institutions, and of the need for liberation from empty hierarchical social conventions. Some railed against the rule of scientific and technological thinking that seemed to be turning people into mechanisms and called for individual autonomy and self-realization. They advocated for peace, love, and genuine community, but unlike their more political contemporaries in the antiwar movement, they tended to turn their attention inward and to see the future in apocalyptic terms. The difference was that the charismatics, like so many other Protestant renewal movements, envisioned going not forward to a new age but back to primitive Christianity. They read the Bible as the inerrant word of God, and most became social and political conservatives.

Most conservative Christians were horrified by the counterculture, but a number of young evangelical ministers, most of them Pentecostals, saw the potential in it for conversions. Preaching the countercultural stance of Jesus, they took to wearing blue jeans, adopted rock and folk music, and urged getting high on Jesus and Holy Spirit baptism. Taking their inspiration from David Wilkerson, an Assemblies of God pastor who in the 1950s had a ministry to New York City gangs, most of them focused on the casualties: the dropouts, the runaways, the homeless, and drug-addicted.[29] In the late 1960s and early 1970s several independent Pentecostal ministries—among them Hope Chapels in Los Angeles and the Bethel Tabernacle in nearby Redondo Beach—established churches, coffeehouses, and homes for transients and ex-dopers. The most compelling of the preachers, Lonnie Frisbee, an art student who converted after freaking out on LSD in San Francisco, was hired by Chuck Smith, the pastor of Calvary Chapel, an independent evangelical church in Costa Mesa in 1969, and built a huge congregation of beach bums and surfers. The spectacle of two thousand kids with bare feet and long hair singing praise songs to Jesus was, of course, made for the media, and the "Jesus movement" became national news. The movement grew to include a confusing variety of different groups. Some of these, like the Children of God, were authoritarian cults, where kids were submitted to harsh disciplines, told to hate their parents and to forsake the rest of the world. Other churches and communes, more conventionally Pentecostal or evangelical, taught biblical literalism, the coming of the end times, and strict moral codes. The movement, never very large, came to an end in the early 1980s, but it made permanent converts, and it lived on in the sense that straight evangelical churches borrowed its coffeehouses, its "Praise the Lords," and its musical styles.[30]

The charismatic enthusiasm in the mainline churches also dimmed in the early 1980s, but the Pentecostal movement continued to grow in other ways. The classical Pentecostal denominations, which had made small gains in the 1960s, took off around 1970, increasing their membership at an enormous rate. The Assemblies of God, for example, went from 625,000 members in 1970 to over a million a decade later. Other denominations, like the United Pentecostal Church and the Church of God (Cleveland, Tennessee), also grew into the hundreds of thousands with converts from the mainline churches.[31] Around the same time charismatic practices began to spread among other evangelicals, giving rise to independent churches and later to whole evangelical denominations claiming some, or all, of the gifts of the spirit. By 1979 a Gallup poll taken for *Christianity Today* found that 19 percent of all adult Americans identified themselves as Pentecostals or charismatics—though only 4 percent spoke in tongues.[32]

Southern Baptists

Southern Baptists flocked to hear Billy Graham, but the Southern Baptist Convention had refused to join the NAE, or any other northern association, and even in the 1960s they refused to take on the label "evangelical." They were Southern Baptists, and that was that. The Convention was, after all, the largest Protestant denomination in the country, the dominant religious force in the region, and so identified with southern culture and history that University of Chicago historian Martin Marty called it "the Catholic church of the south."[33]

The Southern Baptists had founded their Convention in 1845 after a schism with the Northern Baptists over abolition, and, along with southern Methodists and Presbyterians, they had provided biblical justifications for slavery and had supported the Confederacy during the Civil War. After the crushing defeat of the South by the Union armies, they, with their fellow evangelicals, helped revive southern regionalism by propagating the mythology of the Lost Cause: the cult of fallen heroes and the idealization of antebellum white culture as chivalrous, decent, and pure. Recapitulating their old sermons, evangelical preachers proposed that the South was the most spiritual part of the country, the only one to hold to the truth of the New Testament Gospels, a sacred soil and the saving remnant of pure Anglo-Saxon culture. The terrible ordeal of war was, they explained, a part of the divine plan, the judgment of God, not on the sin of slaveholding, as northerners saw it, but on an insufficiency of religious zeal. The defeat, they preached, was a purification process—a baptism in blood—that that would serve to steel them against the worldliness and the apostasy of the North. Thus turning inward, evangelicals once again sanctified the social order, championing states' rights, white supremacy, and the existing economic arrangements. Their message was defensive and isolationist—except for its promise that the South would rise again by fulfilling its God-given mission to Christianize America and bring the Gospel to the rest of the world.[34]

Since the 1830s Southern Baptists had shared their terrain with Presbyterians and Methodists, but in the twentieth century they had become by far the largest domination in the South. The Presbyterians with their elaborate doctrines and their insistence on an educated clergy had established influential churches and seminaries, but their numbers had always been relatively small. In the early days the Methodists with their circuit riders had far outdone the Baptists in the pace of their conversions, but when the episcopal hierarchy gave emphasis to educating its clergy for settled ministries, the rate of conversions slowed. By the end of the nineteenth century the Methodists were generally attracting middle-class people and losing the poor to Holiness and Pentecostal preachers. The Southern Baptist Convention, on the other hand, continued to evangelize in the poor rural areas as well as in the towns. After the end of Reconstruction, Southern Baptists took off across the region from Virginia to Texas, colonizing the countryside, the cities, and the frontiers of settlement. By the end of the century the SBC growth rate exceeded that of the population and its numbers that of the southern Methodist Church. Its ecclesiastical structure—a loose association of independent churches that chose their own pastors—proved well adapted to the decentralized and largely rural South. Its theology took second place to the conversion experience, and its leaders had a passion for spiritual and numerical success that, according to the historian Bill J. Leonard, could not be understood apart from the surrender at Appomattox. Between 1880 and 1925 its membership tripled, from 1.2 to 3.6 million; its share of all southern adherents reached 43 percent, making it by far the largest denomination in almost every state in the South.[35]

Because of its decentralization and its geographical reach, the SBC was always a candidate for schism. It incorporated a variety of theological traditions ranging from the Calvinism of the Regular Baptists of Charleston to revivalist Arminianism of the Separate Baptists of Sandy Creek. By 1850 it also encompassed the Landmark movement of Tennessee and Kentucky, a conservative group whose proponents claimed Baptist churches could trace their lineage directly back to John the Baptist's immersion of Christ in the Jordan River. Denominational leaders, however, held the Convention together. They managed theological differences by establishing doctrinal standards that all could agree upon and resisting the efforts of factions to make them more precise. The Baptist tradition that believers had the right to follow their own conscience, and the evangelical emphasis on individual experience aided them in this regard. They focused on evangelism, and fostered a denominational sense of identity in part by discouraging ecumenical cooperation with other groups. Then, as time went on, they strengthened the denominational machinery.[36]

The SBC had always had annual state and denominational conventions attended by "messengers" from the independent churches. By the twentieth century it had developed numerous agencies: Home and Foreign Mission Boards, colleges, seminaries, benevolent institutions, and a Sunday School Board that published newspapers, books, hymnals, and instructional literature. These agencies had to raise their own money until 1925, when the Convention unified its fund-raising and its budgetary process with the inauguration of the Cooperative Program. Thereafter churches habitually sent a regular portion of their monies to their state conventions, which in turn sent a portion on to the denominational headquarters in Nashville for disbursement to the agencies. An executive committee was empowered to coordinate all of the agency programs and to administer denominational policies. These centralizing measures—and increasing revenues—permitted the Convention to bring some uniformity to religious instruction in the churches—and even to create a calendar of SBC holy days to substitute for the traditional Christian liturgical calendar. As Leonard tells us, these measures helped unify Southern Baptist churches. They also helped to make the SBC the most powerful religious institution in the South.[37]

In the early 1920s fundamentalist agitation roiled the SBC. Apart from the outrageous Frank Norris, none of the fundamentalists charged fellow Baptists with modernism. Rather they insisted that the Convention adopt their own ultraconservative theology, and because they had some influence, the Convention issued its first doctrinal statement, the Baptist Faith and Message, in 1925. The statement, however, generally reaffirmed the Southern Baptist compromise between Calvinism and Arminianism and split the difference when it came to premillennial or postmillennial eschatology. The issue of evolution proved more difficult for the leaders to deal with because popular sentiment had been roused. In 1926 the Convention approved a strong anti-evolution statement and required that all denominational employees subscribe to it. This seemed a victory for the fundamentalists, but the statement was not included in the authoritative Baptist Faith and Message, no denominational employee was ever fired because of it, and the issue eventually faded away.[38]

Until the 1940s the SBC seemed to northerners backward-looking and impervious to change. Its seminaries styled themselves as bastions against the higher criticism and defenders of the truthfulness of the Bible. Victor I. Masters, the head of Home Missions from 1909 to 1921, reflected and influenced denominational thinking when he argued that the North had lost its religion to Romanism and rationalism, and that the SBC's divine mission was to spread "the Anglo-Saxon evangelical faith."[39] As always, the SBC stood as the bulwark against social change. For decades it had enlisted state and local governments to keep the Sabbath laws, and to abolish the liquor traffic and gambling, but when it came to Progressive era and New Deal legislation, favored by many southerners, the SBC invoked the old argument that the Church was a spiritual entity that should not be involved in politics. It took the same position on the Jim Crow laws, and numerous ministers defended them by citing the same biblical verses their forebears had used in defense in slavery. Some ministers deplored white violence and abject Negro poverty, but none could offer anything but the hope that man would renounce his sinful ways. Southern Baptists were comfortable in their social setting, where segregation and inequality were figured as a part of the natural order. Then, too, unchallenged by other theologies, they had come to what the historian Sam Hill calls "a special self-estimate": the view that the SBC had largely attained the simple faith and the pure gospel of the New Testament and embodied the purest expression of Christianity since apostolic times. In 1948 one Alabama preacher called Southern Baptists "the last hope, the fairest hope, the only hope for evangelizing this world on New Testament principles."[40]

The New Deal and the Second World War nonetheless ended the isolation of the South and of southern evangelicals. Under the leadership of its bishops, the southern Methodist church reunited with its northern counterpart in 1938.[41] In the late 1930s a majority of southern Presbyterians made efforts to modify the strict Calvinism of their denomination, and though they failed to muster the necessary three-quarters' vote of the General Assembly, they set up a committee to negotiate a Plan of Union with the northern church. A battle for control over the denomination ensued. In a magazine founded by Graham's father-in-law, Nelson Bell, in 1942, conservatives warned of liberalism in the seminaries and claimed that that reunion with the northern denomination would mean absorption by an apostate church, racial integration, and the loss of the rich southern religious and cultural traditions. Not surprisingly, perhaps, the battle pitted a group of largely rural pastors born in the nineteenth century against a younger, better-educated, and more urban group. In short, the old South against the new. In 1954 the General Assembly overwhelming approved the Plan of Union, but the presbyteries voted against it by the slim majority of 43 to 42. With reunion off the table, the conflict continued over theology and civil rights, ending only in 1973, when the conservatives, having lost their ability to influence the church, broke away to form a new denomination, the Presbyterian Church in America.[42]

The Southern Baptists followed a different path. For them reunion with the Northern Baptist Convention was never an issue. Unlike the more hierarchical Methodist and Presbyterian churches, the SBC had lost all ecclesiastical ties with its northern counterpart. Besides, by 1941 the Convention with 5.2 million members was larger than the northern church—and resolutely anti-ecumenical. In the 1920s and '30s basic Social Gospel notions, such as the responsibility of Christians for institutional reform, filtered into the seminaries, but denominational leaders ignored them, just as they officially ignored the New Deal. It was only the Second World War that roused them from their insularity and convinced them that the church had to take part in the life of the nation and make its influence felt on public policy.[43]

Southern Baptists, like southerners generally, were more supportive of U.S. foreign policy than of the federal government's role in domestic affairs. Their sons had fought in every American war since the 1890s, and in peacetime they had never turned isolationist. World War II seemed to them a global struggle for Christianity, and in its wake the Convention established a sizable fund for world relief, backed the United Nations, and issued a ringing declaration on the need for a world organized on "Christian ideals of brotherhood, justice and truth." The declaration began with a plea for world evangelism, but it included language about the church's responsibility for human welfare and social justice that rang of the Social Gospel. In addition the Convention funded two public policy agencies that had existed in skeleton fashion before the war. One of them, the Joint Committee on Public Relations, represented Baptist positions on religious freedom and the separation of church and state in Washington. A cooperative effort—a singular one—with the Northern Baptist Convention and the largest of the black Baptist conventions, it achieved a degree of independence and sometimes took positions at odds with the SBC. The second, the Social Service Commission—later the Christian Life Commission—had been established to promote "morality in social relations," but its postwar leaders interpreted the mandate as widely as possible.[44]

The first chair of the Commission, Jesse B. Weatherspoon, a seminary professor who understood the conservatism of his denomination, decided to make the Christian Life Commission an educational ministry that would provide information about social problems, discuss Christian responsibilities, and make policy recommendations to the Convention. He likened the agency to a minister who "works behind the lines" inspiring his people to fight for social justice. He and his successors proceeded with caution. Holding conferences and publishing literature, they addressed traditional concerns—alcoholism and pornography—but also introduced other subjects such as labor-management relations and arms control. On many issues their reports were anodyne, but on civil rights they took a series of highly controversial positions. In 1947 Weatherspoon persuaded the Convention to adopt a "Charter of Principles on Race Relations" that began with the command to love one's neighbor and proceeded to such "principles of conduct" as the obligation to protest injustices, to insist on equality before the law, to pay fair wages, and to participate in interracial activities. In 1954 the CLC urged the Convention to accept the Supreme Court's decision in *Brown v. Board of Education*. The ruling provoked outrage through the South and many states resisted integrating their schools. The CLC nonetheless persuaded the Convention to support the decision, and three years later its chairman acted as mediator between President Eisenhower and Governor Orval Faubus in the conflict over admitting black students to Little Rock Central High School. Along with other denominational officials, he took the position that the church should uphold the law of land.[45]

In the postwar period Southern Baptists became in other ways involved with the rest of the country. At a time when church attendance was growing apace, the SBC outgrew all the other denominations, going from five million members in 1941 to ten million in 1961—becoming the largest Protestant body in the country. Most of the growth took place in the South, but not all of it. During the Depression southerners in the hundreds of thousands had begun moving out of the region from Georgia to Oklahoma, abandoning farms that would no longer support them in the hope of a better life in the North or the West. The exodus continued during and after the war as jobs opened in the defense industries of California and booming manufacturing cities of the Midwest. Looking for churches in their new homes and finding none like those they had left behind, Southern Baptists soon began to form their own congregations. In California fourteen of these new churches formed a state Southern Baptist convention, and in 1942 the convention was admitted into the SBC.

Northern Baptists were furious. California stood well outside the territorial limits the SBC had agreed to fifty years earlier with the Northern Convention. Still, the SBC could hardly have handed these churches over to the Northern Convention even if it had wanted to. For several years the SBC honored the old agreement to the extent of holding its missionaries back from the new territories, but in 1950, when the Northern Baptist Convention changed its name to the American Baptist Convention, it dropped all restraint and declared the entire nation its mission field. Its churches proliferated in the new territories at an enormous rate. By sometime in the 1960s there were Southern Baptist churches in every state and nine new state conventions. By 1980 almost two million Southern Baptists lived outside the South—half of them in Illinois and Missouri but many in the Southwest.[46]

While Southern Baptists planted churches across the country, their home territory was undergoing an economic and social upheaval. In the decades following World War II the South went through a process of industrialization and urbanization as rapid as that the North had experienced in the late nineteenth century. In the 1940s a third of the South's workers were employed in agriculture; by 1960 only 10 percent worked on farms. In the 1940s southerners earned 52 cents to every northern dollar; by 1968 they earned 69 percent of what non-southerners earned. The South was no longer outside the sphere of American development, and, virtually for the first time since the 1830s, numbers of northerners arrived as immigrants, most of them settling in cities and towns. In 1950 the South was 63 percent rural and 38 percent urban; by 1970 those figures had almost reversed. In the past southern cities had been small regional centers, homogeneous, and oriented to rural values. With the building of interstate highways and airports many of them grew into large, economically diversified centers, oriented to markets far away. Improvements in higher education and a greater attunement to the national media made city dwellers more cosmopolitan and intellectually diverse. Meanwhile the civil rights movement was overturning the old racial order, and the power of the federal government was manifest everywhere from the highways to the expansion of universities to the enforcement of civil rights laws.[47]

Writing in the mid-1960s the historian Samuel S. Hill foresaw a crisis for the southern church. The SBC had always been a predominantly rural denomination. Before World War II 87 percent of its churches had been in rural communities, and even in the 1960s a half to three quarters of their ministers came from rural churches, though following the general migration pattern Southern Baptists had moved to the cities and suburbs. In the past the SBC had been the equivalent of an established church. In rural areas the local churches had stood as the guardian of community morals and the segregated social order. Attendance at Sunday services was not simply a religious act but was seen as a civic responsibility. Sunday school teachers populated the public school classrooms, and such was the religious homogeneity no one ever seemed to complain of the prayer and Bible reading students did. Rural ministers, few of whom had any higher education, concerned themselves with persuading people to accept the plan of salvation and to follow simple moral rules—just as their predecessors had since the 1830s. Few thought to explain or to justify their interpretations of the Bible because, just like everyone else, they simply assumed their church taught the whole, pure truth of the Gospel. But now, Hill wrote, they and their congregations were moving into a world marked by diversity: diversity of peoples, means of livelihood, social customs, and worldviews. How, he asked, were they to make the transition? So long isolated from the rest of the world, Southern Baptists had no understanding of other religious traditions and no cultural or historical perspective on their own. They had no historical experience of modifying or renewing their message to suit the needs of a changing society, and their success at evangelism had made them supremely un-self-critical. Then, too, their individualism had left them ignorant of complex social forces and unprepared to work with those of different viewpoints for the common good. "Change—dramatic, basic, overarching change," Hill wrote, "is today's ranking fact. Everywhere old moorings are breaking loose, deeply entrenched attitudes are being shaken, traditional patterns of social life are gradually giving way and being replaced by new." The church, he wrote, was in the early stages of experiencing the shock of "a radically different age and climate," and it would confront a full-fledged crisis soon.[48]

8

EVANGELICALS *in the* 1960S

T HE 1960S and early '70s was a tumultuous period, marked by assassinations, war, unruly demonstrations, urban riots, and the resignation of a president. It was also a time of social and cultural upheavals that shook what many conservative Protestants thought of as the foundations of American society. The period began with the election of a Catholic president, the first in the nation's history. There followed two U.S. Supreme Court decisions that banned prayer and Bible reading in the public schools. In 1964 and 1965 the Congress passed President Johnson's two civil rights acts, which for the first time gave African Americans the full rights of citizenship. At the same time came an economic transformation and a social and cultural revolution within the white middle class.

The U.S. economy surged during the 1950s, '60s, and early '70s—the gross domestic product sometimes growing 5 percent a year. World War II had demonstrated the importance of technology to the nation's defense, and around the time of the Soviet development of the atom bomb the U.S. government began to make major investments in science, technology, and education. The Soviet launch of the space satellite Sputnik in 1957 spurred this investment on, and realizing the benefits of modernization private industry contributed. By 1965 the nation was spending nearly 3 percent of its GDP on research and development and employing half a million scientists. The National Science Foundation was pumping money into improving science and social science education in the nation's public schools. Meanwhile, largely because of federal government contributions, expenditures for higher education rose dramatically, going from $5.6 billion in 1960 to $50.7 billion in 1980—almost a tenfold increase in two decades. In that period the student population at colleges and universities almost quadrupled, rising from 3.6 million in 1960 to 12.1 million in 1980.[1]

By the mid-1960s these students came from the baby boom generation—the huge cohort of children born after World War II—a cohort that made the young a larger part of the American population than in any other period in American history. Yet even as the college-age population burgeoned, the percentage of young people who went to college increased, going from 22.3 percent to 35.2 percent between 1960 and 1970 alone.[2] The stresses were considerable. Many of the students were the first in their families to go to college, and many found themselves in mega-universities with tens of thousands of their peers living in high-rise dormitories thrown up almost overnight. Their education alienated them from the world of their parents, and their contact with faculty was often limited to glimpses of professors at the front of large lecture halls.

Left to themselves, the students invented. Around the mid-1960s they abandoned their middle-class clothing, put on the dress of the working man, and took up the music of African Americans. The men grew their hair long, the women took to wearing pants, and together they turned on their elders—Eleanor Rigby and Mr. Jones—accusing them of living lives in thrall to absurd social conventions in little houses made of ticky-tacky. Calling for liberation, they broke major taboos—sex, drugs, and rock 'n' roll. In pursuit of transcendent experience and true community, they tuned in, dropped out, went on journeys with no destination, formed communes, and tried to live off the land. In search of a new consciousness some took up exotic religions, such as Zen Buddhism, some practiced Transcendental Meditation. Rebellious and unimpressed by authority, they challenged their university administrations, marched at Selma, and demonstrated against the Vietnam War. The women then called for liberation from male domination, and in 1969 gay men fought back against a police raid on a bar, the Stonewall Inn in New York City.

In this period American views on major social and cultural issues changed with great rapidity. Polls taken between 1959 and the early 1970s, for example, showed that racial and religious intolerance had declined dramatically; the proportion of the public willing to elect a woman president rose from a third to two thirds; and the proportion that thought premarital sex morally wrong dropped from nearly four out of five to less than one in two.[3] In this period President Johnson not only passed the historic civil rights legislation but attacked structural poverty with his Great Society programs. President Nixon, for his part, tripled outlays for civil rights, oversaw the creation of the Environmental Protection Agency, and signed Title IX, the law granting equality to female student athletes. The Congress passed the Equal Rights Amendment and sent it to the states for ratification. In 1974 the Supreme Court decided for legalized abortion in *Roe v. Wade.*

Most of the college kids of the 1960s eventually put on suits and went to the office, but by the time they did, they had changed American attitudes toward everything from sex and gender roles to child-rearing practices, race, civil liberties, religion, and the natural environment.

That the revolution of 1960s would engender a reaction from a traditionalist party seems in hindsight perfectly predictable. Even in the mid-1970s, however, there was little to suggest one from conservative Protestants. For one thing, evangelicals remained so regionally and theologically divided they agreed on little except on opposition to Catholicism. For another, the most influential evangelicals of the period, such as Billy Graham and the SBC leadership, did not always react to the events of the Long Sixties as might be supposed in retrospect.

John F. Kennedy's candidacy for the presidency in 1960 aroused what the historian Arthur Schlesinger Jr. once pointed out was the oldest prejudice in the nation's history. In the South fundamentalists and other evangelicals reacted much as they had to the candidacy of Al Smith in 1928. "If Kennedy is a good Catholic," Bob Jones Jr. said, "his religion requires him to owe first allegiance to the Pope, and not to the United States." W. A. Criswell distributed ten thousand copies of his sermon warning that a Kennedy election would "spell the death of a free church in a free state and our hopes of continuance of full religious liberty in America." John R. Rice's *Sword of the Lord* published similar dire predictions, as did Southern Baptist periodicals across the South. American liberties, one Southern Baptist editor wrote, would be "whittled away" and the nation "enslaved" by a "ruthless religious totalitarianism controlled by Rome." Even many moderate Southern Baptists imagined the American Catholic Church as a medieval tyranny that controlled its believers and sought power over the state. After several Baptist state conventions resolved that no Roman Catholic could be an acceptable candidate for president, SBC leaders began a campaign to stop Kennedy. The Convention president, Ramsay Pollard, declared that he could not stand by while a man "under the control of the Catholic Church" runs for the presidency of the United States. The Baptist Joint Committee demurred, citing Kennedy's many strong statements on the separation of church and state, but in this case it had little influence. In May 1960 the national convention passed a resolution warning that "when a public official is inescapably bound by the dogma and demands of his church he cannot consistently separate himself from these." This, it declared—descending into near incoherence—"is especially true when the church maintains a position in open conflict with our established and constituted American pattern of life as specifically related to religious liberty, separation of Church and State, the freedom of conscience . . . the perpetuation of public schools and the prohibition against the use of public monies for sectarian purposes."[4]

Northern evangelical opinion on Kennedy's candidacy was not so uniformly apocalyptic. Fundamentalists, as might be expected, took extreme anti-Catholic positions. So, too, did some of the older neo-evangelicals, such as Harold Ockenga, who urged Chistians not to aid and abet "the Roman Catholic domination of America" by electing Kennedy.[5] Younger evangelical leaders had somewhat more tempered reactions. A National Association of Evangelicals resolution, for example, stated, "We doubt that a Roman Catholic president could or would resist fully the pressures of the ecclesiastical hierarchy." It urged the commitment of Catholic candidates to the separation of church and state "because the Roman Catholic Church both as a political and religious organization has for many centuries fostered the policy of church establishment in varying degrees and exerted pressures on public officials to that end." In October the editors of *Christianity Today* opined that the religious issue was "a major factor" in the election and that any Catholic would face "extreme pressure" from the Vatican to make American foreign policy conform to its desires. These statements were not completely out of line with mainline Protestant opinion, for early in the campaign even some liberal leaders, such as G. Bromley Oxnam, head of the World Council of Churches, expressed concern that a Catholic president might have difficulty reconciling his political duties with his obligations to the church on such matters as birth control and aid to parochial schools.[6] Still, what the younger neo-evangelical leaders really thought is hard to say, for on the one hand they feared accusations of religious bigotry and on the other they, as conservative Republicans, opposed Kennedy on political grounds. In September Kennedy assuaged the doubts of liberal Protestants when he spoke to the Houston Ministerial Association and answered a battery of questions about the role his faith would play in his presidency. Neo-evangelicals, however, ignored the event and bent their efforts to electing his opponent, Vice President Richard Nixon. The NAE periodical, *United Evangelical Action*, for example, urged pastors to conduct registration drives outside their churches, and the Wheaton College administration gave free mailing privileges to students who wanted to send out campaign literature for Nixon.[7] Such overt partisanship was new to these organizations, but then the race was far closer than it had been in Eisenhower's two elections.

Billy Graham was certainly troubled by Kennedy's Catholicism, but his one public remark on the subject was that "some Protestants are hesitant to vote for a Catholic because the Catholic Church is not only a religious but a secular institution which receives ambassadors from secular states."[8] His reticence was understandable, for of all the evangelical leaders, he had the most to lose from accusations of bigotry or political partisanship.

During the Eisenhower administrations Graham had developed a close relationship with the vice president, regularly corresponding and playing golf with him. According to his biographer, William Martin, he did his best to allay Eisenhower's misgivings about Nixon's fitness for the presidency. Both before and during the campaign, he offered Nixon a stream of advice about how to woo Protestant voters—suggesting that he pick an evangelical as a running mate, that he go to church regularly, and that he talk more about his faith. On occasion he made statements that left little doubt as to where his sympathies lay. In May 1960 he told a group of reporters, "This is a time of world tension. [It] is a time for a man of world stature. I don't think it's a time to experiment with novices." But, he added, "I'm not taking sides." Nixon, he knew, wanted an official endorsement from him, and he agonized over the matter, giving Nixon assurances, then backing away from them. Meanwhile, he found other ways to help Nixon, such as urging the two million families on his mailing list to use their Sunday schools to get out the vote. In August he convened a meeting of twenty-five evangelical leaders and a guest, Norman Vincent Peale. Whatever its initial purpose, the meeting quickly turned into a strategy session on how to defeat Kennedy. The upshot was that Peale, known for his anti-Catholic views, chaired a conference in Washington sponsored by an NAE affiliate that featured a series of anti-Catholic rants by Nelson Bell and others. Peale was held responsible and pilloried by fellow New York clergymen such as Reinhold Niebuhr and the religious press. The incident apparently frightened Graham, for he claimed he hadn't known of the conference in advance. "We have already witnessed what the Press did to Peale," he wrote Nixon in late September. "I cannot possibly get involved in the religious issue. Not only would they crucify me, but they would eventually turn against you, so I must be extremely careful." In October he wrote a piece praising Nixon for *Life* magazine, but at the last minute he persuaded Henry Luce to cancel its publication. Then in the final week of the campaign he appeared with Nixon at a campaign rally Columbia, South Carolina, and gave the invocation.[9]

Kennedy won the election by a narrow margin, losing heavily among Protestant voters nationwide and losing 53 percent of them in the traditionally Democratic South. A few days before the inauguration Graham accepted an invitation to lunch with the president-elect and afterward told the press that Kennedy's victory had proved that there was not as much religious prejudice as many had feared and probably had reduced forever the importance of the religious issue in American elections. Possibly he simply wanted to please the new president, but a few years later—after Vatican II and a meeting with the amiable Richard Cardinal Cushing—he began to make his peace with the American Catholic Church.[10]

Two years after Kennedy's election, the Supreme Court in *Engel v. Vitale* found prayer in the public schools unconstitutional. The Court had been moving slowly since the 1920s to apply the Bill of Rights to the states through the principle of "incorporation" of the due process clause of the Fourteenth Amendment. In the *Everson* case of 1947 the majority took the unequivocal stance that the establishment and free exercise of religion clauses of the First Amendment applied to the states. Still, the ruling that school prayer violated the establishment clause was a signal decision—and one that after a decade of public religiosity flew in the face of public opinion. According to a Gallup poll taken that year, 79 percent of Americans favored "religious exercises" in the schools. Major Catholic prelates denounced the decision, as did numerous politicians from across the political spectrum. Evangelical leaders, however, did not join the dissent. To the contrary, many of them, North and South, supported the ruling. For one thing, the *Engel* case involved a nondenominational prayer written by the New York State Board of Regents and approved for school use by Protestant, Catholic, and Jewish clergymen. An artifact of the Eisenhower era's civil religion, the prayer, just one sentence long, read, "Almighty God, we acknowledge our dependence upon Thee, and we beg Thy blessings upon us, our parents, our teachers and our country." Evangelicals generally found it inadequate. *Christianity Today* called it a "corporate prayer" that promoted "the least-common-denominator type of religion," and Carl McIntire declared that a prayer without the name of Jesus was simply "pagan." Beyond that, *CT* and other evangelical periodicals echoed the Supreme Court's opinion, writing that the state should not promote religion and that religious education should be left to families and churches. They saw the Court's decision as a way to counter the influence of Catholics, who were waging a prolonged fight for aid to parochial schools. NAE officials worried that *Engel* might lead to further antireligious decisions, but in the hopes it would support their case against federal aid to parochial schools, they hesitantly supported it.[11]

Most evangelical leaders changed their mind the following year after the Court in *Abington v. Schempp* ruled against devotional Bible reading in the public schools. Protestant educators had made devotional reading from the King James Bible a part of the public school curriculum in the early nineteenth century. For Catholics it had been one of the reasons to build parochial schools, and for Protestants it had been a symbol of the nation's Protestant identity. Fundamentalists and northern evangelicals tore into the *Schempp* decision. "We understand that a greater issue is at stake than simply Bible reading in the schools," McIntire wrote. "At stake is whether or not America may continue to honor and recognize God in the life of the nation." Ockenga for his part argued, "A neutral or secular state, while preserving the nation from dominion by a denomination, leaves America in the same position as Communist Russia." Billy Graham claimed that the Court had "misinterpreted our forefathers' intentions" and said, "Personally I think the few atheists who object to Bible reading in schools should be overruled by the majority." The NAE resolved that *Engel* and *Schempp* amounted to "practical atheism" that produces a "religious vacuum" in the land. It called for a constitutional amendment to override the decisions, and in the next two years 111 U.S. congressmen proposed 147 amendments to that purpose.[12]

Southern Baptist leaders, however, dissented from the northern evangelical consensus. Ever since the days of Roger Williams and John Leland, separation of church and state and freedom of religious conscience had been central to the Baptist tradition. That prayer and Bible reading were heard in many southern public schools made no difference in this matter of principle. Some of the same leaders who had raised the specter of Vatican control over the country supported *Engel* and *Schempp* with what they saw as perfect consistency. In 1964 the SBC declared its opposition to all attempts to amend either the establishment or the free exercise clause of the First Amendment. The Convention held firmly to this position, passing eight resolutions to the same effect over the next decade and a half and at least twice lobbying against school prayer amendments in Congress.[13] Meanwhile, the proposed constitutional amendments went nowhere, and the furor over the rulings gradually abated. By 1974 only fundamentalists continued to decry the two decisions; *Christianity Today* positively endorsed them while other leaders, like Graham, simply let the whole issue fade away—while in practice many southern public schools continued to pray and read the King James Bible.[14]

The civil rights movement roiled the entire white South, but when it came to its peak in the mid-1960s, it divided urban and suburban middle-class people from rural whites who had failed to benefit from the prosperity of the "New South." Evangelical leaders reflected this division.

Billy Graham had approached the issue of desegregation cautiously, never supporting the civil rights movement directly or advocating for legislation. Still, he opposed segregation in principle and accepted the federal legislation and court rulings as laws of the land. Fundamentalist leaders for their part fiercely resisted desegregation for an entire decade after *Brown*. Carl McIntire, whose church and radio ministry were in New Jersey, rarely spoke of race per se, but he took two positions in the 1950s and held them resolutely through the 1960s. One was that all the civil rights organizations were infiltrated by Communists and supported by Moscow. He said much the same of the mainline denominations, so this hardly distinguished them. To him the "brotherhood of man" was a "collectivist idea," so it followed that liberals and Communists were causing all of the racial trouble. McIntire's second fixed idea was that in acting against segregation the federal government was encroaching on American freedoms, just as local governments did when they put fluoride in the water. Specifically, he objected to Johnson's 1964 legislation, calling it "the civil wrongs bill." [15]

Southern fundamentalists generally shared McIntire's opinions, but they tended to be more frankly segregationist. As before, many found justification for their position in the Bible, but some skipped the biblical exegesis and went straight to the white southern nightmare. The "supreme goal of this integration campaign," the editor of the Baptist Bible Fellowship newspaper wrote in 1961, is "to make intermarriage between Whites and Negroes as commonplace as black tomcats squalling in back alleys." Billy James Hargis, an Oklahoma radio and television preacher and the founder of the McCarthyite Christian Crusade, proposed that because animals "of widely different characteristics" did not intermingle or cross-breed, segregation was "one of Nature's universal laws." Fundamentalists naturally backed those southern politicians who resisted integration on the grounds of states' rights. After George Wallace made his notorious "stand in the schoolhouse door" in 1963, blocking three black students from registering at the University of Alabama, Hargis's Christian Crusade named the governor "patriot of the year." Bob Jones Jr., who had succeeded his father as president of the segregated Bob Jones University, gave Wallace an honorary degree. [16]

In the Southern Baptist Convention a progressive party emerged on civil rights. Under the leadership of Foy Valentine the Christian Life Commission moved from counseling acquiescence to federal law to promoting racial equality.

In 1964 the Christian Life Commission called upon the SBC to endorse the passage of President Johnson's civil rights bills. The debate over the proposal was heated. Conservatives maintained that any positive response to the civil rights movement would encourage civil disobedience, left-wing politics, and theological liberalism. Others argued that Johnson was going too far, too fast and that race relations would improve when good Christians in the South worked out their differences among themselves. In the end the Convention balked at supporting the bills, but the following year it endorsed a CLC statement condemning the Convention's own "silence and fear" in the midst of the struggle for racial justice and urging Southern Baptists to become actively involved in seeking cures for such racial ills as unfair housing practices, discriminatory employment, and the denial of voting rights. Valentine and his progressive allies never persuaded the Convention to pledge resources to change these conditions—much less to assist the civil rights movement directly, or to intervene when churches or schools resisted integration. Still, they gradually moved the Convention to the position that Christians should not tolerate discrimination. The process culminated in 1968 when, after the assassination of Martin Luther King and a month of urban rioting, the Convention adopted "A Statement Concerning the Crisis in Our Nation." Prepared by the SBC's top officers and executives, the statement made a solemn confession of the Convention's responsibility for condoning the "cultural patterns" that deprived millions of black Americans of "equality of recognition and opportunity" and permitting the social ills that caused the riots. Like its predecessors, the statement offered no specific program of action, but it committed the messengers to combating racism, violence, and injustice.[17]

The adoption of the statement marked an end to the conflict over civil rights at the denomination level. No group dissented, and even the newly elected president of the Convention, W. A. Criswell, signed on. The pastor of the First Baptist Church of Dallas, and one of the SBC's most popular preachers, Criswell had in 1956 told the South Carolina legislature that he "strongly favored racial segregation" and called those blacks who wanted to integrate white churches "infidels, dying from the neck up." By 1968 he had moderated his view, and in 1970 he noted, "I had come to the profound conclusion that to separate by coercion the body of Christ on the basis of skin pigmentation was unthinkable, unchristian and unacceptable to God." [18] Many SBC churches remained deliberately segregated, and struggles over integration rent many other churches, leaving a legacy of bitterness. In some cases ministers who had opened their doors to African Americans had been driven from their pulpits by their congregations or subject to abuse by fellow ministers. In other cases, congregations had split, forcing the minority of integrationists to leave and form fellowships of their own. The outcomes were different across the South, but the conflicts, waged on personal as well as public levels, were everywhere traumatic, and, according to Nancy Ammerman, many of those who worked for change against considerable opposition never forgot the price they paid. Still, by 1968 segregation was no longer a respectable position in the SBC, and influential conservatives never raised the standard again. [19]

The division among evangelicals became obvious during the 1964 presidential campaign. After Barry Goldwater secured the Republican nomination, fundamentalist leaders, among them McIntire, Hargis, and Jones, rallied behind him. The Arizona senator, an Episcopalian of Jewish parentage, came closer to their ideal than any other presidential candidate in the past half century. He wasn't quite conservative enough for them, but he called for a rollback of Soviet power abroad and of the New Deal at home. He had often alleged that the Reds were infiltrating the U.S. government, the media, and the churches, and McIntire called him "the only anti-Communist running." Goldwater favored a constitutional amendment to reinstate Bible reading and prayer in the public schools, and, the first Republican to adopt a "Southern strategy," he opposed federally mandated desegregation and voted against the 1964 Civil Rights Act. Most evangelicals, however, did not share the fundamentalist enthusiasm for a candidate seen by many in his own party as a right-wing radical, who had proposed that NATO commanders should have the power to use tactical nuclear weapons on their own initiative in the event of an emergency. According to a *Christianity Today* poll of evangelical publishers, 62 percent supported Johnson and 38 percent supported Goldwater—a ratio roughly

that of all American voters. New South evangelicals felt comfortable voting for their fellow Southern Democrat, Lyndon Johnson, and in spite of
their Republican sympathies, most northern evangelical leaders avoided
associating themselves with Goldwater and took no part in the campaign.
Goldwater won just six states—his own and the five in the Deep South.[20]

Shortly after Kennedy's assassination, Graham offered his services to
the new president, whom he had known slightly for years, and Johnson,
eager for his support, enveloped him in a bear hug. A few days before the
election, Graham received over a million telegrams and tens of thousands
of other messages urging him to come out for Goldwater. Johnson called
him to say, "Billy, you stay out of politics," and then invited him to spend
the weekend at the White House, where he couldn't read his mail. In July
1964 Graham agreed to join a citizen's committee to oversee the implementation of the civil rights bill, and a month later he and his wife spent
a night at the White House. In the four years that followed Johnson often
invited Graham to the White House and to his Texas ranch. "I almost used
the White House as a hotel when Johnson was president," Graham later
said. "He was always trying to keep me there—he just wouldn't let me
leave." Johnson attended some of Graham's crusades, sought his spiritual
and political advice, and told him little inside stories about foreign heads
of state. He turned Graham into his confidant, and, as he hoped, Graham
supported the Great Society programs as well as the administration's civil
rights initiatives. Just as important, Graham gave his blessing to Johnson's
escalation of the war in Vietnam. Encouraged by the president, he toured
South Vietnam in December 1966 as a guest of General William West-
moreland and announced, "Communism has to be stopped somewhere,
whether it is in Hawaii or on the West Coast. The President believes it
should be stopped in Vietnam."[21]

Like most Americans, evangelicals supported the Vietnam War when
American troops began to pour into the country, and like many others,
they knew little about Vietnam itself but believed the American effort necessary to stop the spread of Communism from China through Southeast
Asia and even to the shores of the United States. In 1966, for example, the
NAE passed a resolution decrying "any action by our government that
would favor Communism under the leadership of Red China"—without

mentioning Vietnam. For fundamentalists and others the domino theory had an extra dimension. Stopping "godless Communism" was, John R. Rice maintained, "a holy and righteous cause." The editor of the Kentucky Baptist Convention's *Western Recorder* wrote, "Communism must be stopped somewhere or this godless darkness will cover the earth." Even Graham initially seemed to see the war in religious terms. "The Communists are moving fast toward their goal of world revolution," he wrote Johnson in July 1965. "Perhaps God brought you to the kingdom for such an hour as this—to stop them. In doing so you could be the man that helped save Christian civilization." [22]

After the Tet Offensive in early 1968, many Americans turned against the war, but evangelicals generally remained steadfast. In its many resolutions on the war, the Southern Baptist Convention never questioned government policies or the morality of the war. The Convention included a small antiwar party, but, according to surveys, the vast majority of Southern Baptist ministers supported the war to the end. Fundamentalists such as Bob Jones Jr., many of the older neo-evangelicals, and many Southern Baptist ministers favored stronger military measures. All the same, many evangelicals harbored doubts about why the U.S. was fighting in Vietnam. The SBC, which in 1967 had resolved support for "the self-determination of peoples of smaller countries" and "the prosecution of a defensive war," made no further mention of American war aims. The NAE as a body fell into silence on the subject, and Billy Graham, who registered popular evangelical opinion, began describing Vietnam as "one of the greatest dilemmas in U.S. history in Southeast Asia." When demonstrators swarmed after his car on the UCLA campus, he submitted, "Vietnam is difficult, confused, complex and perplexing. I can make no moral judgment on whether we should have troops in the first place," but added that because the U.S. had made the commitment, "we should see it through to a satisfactory conclusion." After a second tour through Vietnam at Christmastime 1968, he made the definite statement, "The war is already won militarily. Right now 73% of the Vietnamese people are under South Vietnam's government," only to turn about and say, "I don't comment on Vietnam because it's a complicated problem." Questions about the horrific toll the war was taking on Vietnamese civilians elicited what Marshall

Frady called obtuse little homilies: "We have all had our My Lais in one way or another . . . with a thoughtless word, an arrogant act or a selfish deed." A few days before the 1973 Paris Peace Accords and the withdrawal of the last U.S. troops, he offered a judgment of perfect ambiguity: "I don't think we should fight these long-drawn-out, half-hearted wars."[23]

Unable to explain how a holy war against Communism had turned into a murky conflict in a small, poor country, evangelical ministers generally avoided the subject on Sundays and preached about the disturbances at home. In 1966 and 1967 Graham's radio program, *Hour of Decision*, featured such sermons as "A Nation Rocked by Crime," "Students in Revolt," "Flames of Revolution," "Rioting, Looting and Crime." By the summer of 1967 nearly all of his sermons dealt with "the anarchy" in America. Evangelical organizations also expressed horror at the antiwar protests. A 1966 NAE resolution titled "The New Treason" read, "Believing that the authority of the state is sanctioned by God, the NAE deplores the burning of draft cards, subversive movements and seditious utterances, and prevalent disloyalty to the United States of America." Fundamentalists and others decried the urban riots, blaming them on the civil rights leaders and the acquiescence of liberal politicians, or as Rice put it, "the lawlessness of Martin Luther King and others, and the pussyfooting politicians who want the Negro vote."

The civil unrest of the period alarmed many Americans, but evangelical leaders ran the disturbances together and envisioned a monster that few others saw. In 1969 the NAE spoke of a crisis of "unparalleled proportions . . . a social revolution with economic overtones has made arson, looting, mayhem and murder commonplace in some metropolitan areas." In 1970 the normally stolid SBC gave way to panic about Communist subversion. A month before its June convention the Ohio National Guard had shot and killed four students at Kent State University, but one of its resolutions that year read: "We urge the present administration to continue its vigilant and peaceful efforts to contain radical extremists as well as the encroachment of conspiratorial communism at home and abroad." Another resolution warned: "A break-down in law and order is a weapon being used by some to destroy our form of government in the United States, with the success of these nefarious efforts being evident in many areas of our country." Graham titled one sermon "Can America Survive?" and declared it likely that "in less than ten years there will be internal chaos and a political tyranny in the form of some left-wing or right-wing dictatorship, even if there is no war." [24]

Such statements were on the face of them puzzling, for most Americans believed their democracy strong enough to resist all the buffeting. Evangelicals, however, had a particular respect for authority and a particular fear of disorder. According to fundamentalist tenets, obedience to constituted authority was the cardinal principle of Christian society: children were to obey their parents, wives their husbands, and citizens the state, just as all humans were to obey God. And God, as Graham once said, "does not tolerate disorder." [25] Then, as the 1966 NAE resolution suggested, many evangelicals believed that the government was established by God to preserve the civil order. A 1967 SBC resolution on Vietnam contained the curious sentence, "We uphold in prayer the men who are engaged in restrictive measures against the destructive forces of invasion so that law and order may obtain." For over a century white southerners had looked to government as the guarantor of white rule, preferring order to democracy, and living in constant anxiety about a black rebellion. Such attitudes do not disappear overnight. During the peaceful sit-ins of 1960 Billy Graham had pronounced, "No matter what law may be—it may be an unjust law—I believe we have a Christian responsibility to obey it. Otherwise you have anarchy." [26] By 1969 he and others were predicting not just anarchy but a secularized version of Armageddon.

Richard Nixon made his political comeback in 1968, championing religious faith, strong families, respect for public authority, and the rule of law. Along with his opposition to the busing of public school children to achieve integration, his call for law and order was his "Southern strategy," and it was just what most evangelicals wanted to hear. Northern evangelicals happily returned to their home in the Republican Party, while evangelicals of the New South, turned off by both the Democratic left and the crude racism of George Wallace, voted for Nixon and the social conservatism he espoused. Wallace did well in southern rural counties but Nixon carried many of the suburban counties and five southern states outside the Deep South. Then, during his first term, Nixon continued to court evangelicals by making public displays of his religiosity and attempting to resuscitate Eisenhower's civil religion.[27]

Graham had kept in touch with Nixon through the years of political exile, and Johnson's decision not to seek reelection freed him to support his old friend. As usual, he kept saying he would avoid political involvement, but as the campaign progressed he made so many comments about Nixon's high principles and deep religious convictions as to make a formal endorsement unnecessary. "There is no American I admire more than Richard Nixon," he said while introducing the candidate's two daughters to a crusade audience in Portland, Oregon, that May.[28] Apparently he meant it, for at the Republican convention he virtually joined the campaign, and during Nixon's first term in office he served as Nixon's White House preacher and his ambassador to evangelicals. Not long after the invasion of Cambodia and the Kent State shootings, he invited Nixon to address his crusade audience in Knoxville. Then, after Nixon made his historic opening to China, Graham, briefed by National Security Advisor Henry Kissinger's staff, promoted the new China policy to the Taiwan government and to American evangelicals. During the 1972 campaign he officially endorsed Nixon, advised his aides on political strategies, and encouraged them to regard evangelicals as a potential voting bloc. Increasingly, however, he found himself under attack from within this bloc, for the Nixon years coincided with the emergence of a small but vocal evangelical left.[29]

* * *

In the years after World War II young evangelicals poured into higher education along with the rest of their peers. According to a Gallup poll, one in six evangelicals had been to college by the mid-1970s—a proportion well below the national average but one much larger than in the 1960s. Some went to secular colleges and universities. Others attended evangelical liberal arts colleges, whose size and numbers grew with the same government subsidies that went to secular colleges.[30] Many of these resembled Bible schools in their teaching methods, their narrow curricula, and their efforts to shield students from the larger culture. Still, a number, such as Wheaton and Calvin, a Dutch Reformed college, taught critical thinking and offered a wider range of intellectual fare. Most evangelical students, wherever they went, remained as politically conservative as their parents, but some responded to the reformist causes of the period. On secular campuses many put aside their religion and melded into the various student protest movements. Other students worked to reconcile their faith with social reform and with help from young evangelical scholars rediscovered the social message of the Gospels.[31]

Beginning in the mid-1960s, evangelical student protests occurred here and there across the country. At some of the top evangelical colleges students created small, pale versions of the rebellions on the secular campuses. At Wheaton the student newspaper objected to fundamentalist strictures like bans on moviegoing and card playing, and to compulsory ROTC training for freshman and sophomores. Organizations, such as Americans for Democratic Action, began to crop up, as did informal clothes. By the late 1960s some students were denouncing racism and holding prayer vigils against the Vietnam War. At Calvin College student unrest culminated in 1970 with the presentation of a Youth Manifesto to the local synod of the denomination, the Christian Reformed Church, complaining of racism, male chauvinism, lack of support for conscientious objectors to the war, and the construction of expensive buildings in the face of urban poverty.[32]

In most secular colleges and universities the largest evangelical organization was Campus Crusade for Christ, founded in 1951 by Bill Bright, a conventionally right-wing Presbyterian, to evangelize students and instruct them in conservative religion and politics. Still, on many campuses the InterVarsity Christian Fellowship flourished and became a locus for evangelical dissent. Founded in Britain and rooted in the tolerant English evangelical tradition, the ministry emphasized fellowship and religious studies. It published books, encouraged critical thinking, and gave students leave to raise the issues of their generation, such as racism and the Vietnam War. At the ministry's triennial convention in 1967 students protested the "cultural imperialism" of InterVarsity missionaries and asked why the organization had no African Americans or women on its staff. In the next convention, in 1970, Tom Skinner, a former Harlem gang leader and a star evangelical preacher, delivered a fiery speech about racism in

America, and students voiced indignation about Billy Graham's connection with Nixon—and in particular his celebration of the president at the
Knoxville crusade.[33]

In the early 1970s other centers of the evangelical left emerged. Urban
communes with underground newspapers advocated for causes such as
minority rights, fair wages for farmworkers, and economic justice for developing countries. One such center, the People's Christian Coalition, was
founded by divinity students in Chicago. Its energetic leader, Jim Wallis,
not atypically, came out of the secular student left. Growing up in the suburbs of Detroit, Wallis had rebelled against the middle-class evangelicalism of his family. He went to Michigan State University, where he served
in student government and joined Students for a Democratic Society. As
a senior he helped organize the national student strike after the Cambodia invasion and the shootings at Kent State. When the protests turned
violent, he quit SDS and in disillusionment went to Trinity Evangelical
Divinity School with the thought of becoming a minister. At the conservative seminary he quickly started a heated debate about the Vietnam War
and gathered a group of other rebellious students around him. In late 1971
the group moved out of the seminary, formed a commune, and created
a blend of evangelicalism and New Left politics. Its bimonthly paper, the
Post-American, was dedicated to awakening the evangelical community
from its "folk religion of convenience, conformity and presidential prayer
breakfasts" to a "Christian radicalism" challenging "the corrupt values
of our culture," the injustices of "a racist society," and an "exploitative
system." Later, the group, renamed Sojourners, removed to Washington,
D.C., and Wallis, growing more politically moderate, became the most
recognizable voice on the evangelical left for the next several decades.[34]

Most of this ferment occurred in the North. The civil rights movement had produced a number of committed Southern Baptist activists,
but many of these in bitter disappointment with the churches that had
nurtured them quit the denomination or moved to its fringes. One of
these rebels, a minister in rural Ohio, in 1965 started a small magazine,
The Other Side, dedicated to black civil rights. The magazine, however,
became well known only when his son and two friends from Wheaton
reestablished it in Philadelphia and broadened its focus to gender issues,

global justice, and communal living. In the late 1960s a number of Southern Baptist college students staged antiwar rallies; they called for gender equality and some went to work in inner-city missions for the poor. Many hoped for social progress, but they never challenged Southern Baptist institutions or formed a center for left-wing ideas.[35]

By the early 1970s the northern evangelical left included not just student groups and communes but a number of young academics working on issues of faith and social justice. These scholars belonged to various denominations, but a disproportionate number came from two small groups that had recently moved into the evangelical orbit: on the one hand, the Christian Reformed Church with its roots in Holland and a strong tradition of social and political involvement; on the other, Anabaptist sects, such as the Mennonites and the Brethren in Christ, traditionally pacifist and separated from the world. Some of these scholars were also activists, and one of the most effective was Ron Sider, a Canadian-born son of a Brethren pastor with a Master of Divinity and PhD in history from Yale. In New Haven Sider had worked with InterVarsity and with the NAACP organizing voter registration drives. On graduating from Yale in 1968 he had decided that rather than take up a career at a secular university he would go to a new campus of Messiah College in the inner city of Philadelphia and give his efforts to the urban poor. In 1972 he formed a shoestring group, Evangelicals for McGovern, in support of Democratic antiwar candidates for president and against the Vietnam War and Nixon's efforts to stir up a white backlash. The group raised more press attention than money, but on the strength of it he and other McGovernites decided to hold an interdenominational conference as the first step in building a permanent progressive organization.[36]

The following year fifty evangelicals met over Thanksgiving weekend at a YMCA in downtown Chicago to work out a concise statement of their common beliefs and purposes. Chosen to represent the diversity of the social justice movement, the Thanksgiving Workshop participants ranged ideologically from Jim Wallis to Carl Henry, and included several African Americans and five women. The manifesto that emerged after much debate, the Chicago Declaration of Evangelical Social Concern, began with a confession that evangelicals had failed to defend the rights of the poor and oppressed and had been complicit in racism. It went on to attack the unjust distribution of the nation's wealth, the "pathology of war and violence," sexism, and the "the temptation to make the nation and its institutions objects of near-religious loyalty." Thanks to Sider's efforts, the statement gained publicity and the signatures of many other progressive evangelicals, among them that of Senator Mark Hatfield, the liberal Oregon Republican, who backed women's rights and had been an early opponent of the Vietnam War.[37]

The 1973 Chicago Declaration was in effect SDS's Port Huron Statement of the evangelical left, but it was also the high point of the movement. With the time lag of a decade the evangelical left had missed the glory days of the civil rights movement and most of the Vietnam War. When Nixon brought the last American regular troops home that year, student passions cooled. Having arisen along much the same trajectory as the secular left, the evangelical left fell apart, just as the secular movement did, over ideology and identity politics. The second and third annual Thanksgiving Workshops Sider organized reflected the growing divisions within the movement as a whole.

At the 1974 Chicago meeting blacks and women withdrew into their own caucuses and came back with complaints about racism and sexism. Meanwhile a fight broke out between the Anabaptists and the Calvinists. From the Anabaptist caucus came proposals for a meatless day a week and the commitment of families of four to live on $8,000 a year. Anabaptist theologians, such as John Howard Yoder, maintained that Jesus had rejected political power because the state was inherently corrupt and that entanglement in secular politics was fraught with the dangers of compromise. Christians, they argued, should engage in politics only from the outside: through grassroots organizing and through providing a model of nonviolent resistance and service to the poor. The Calvinists, however, lambasted the approach as naive, impractical, and lacking in "careful and informed reasoning." Christ, they maintained, ruled the entire world, not just the church, thus Christians should involve themselves in every sphere of life from the arts and sciences to labor conditions and electoral politics. At the third Thanksgiving meeting one progressive Calvinist was heard to cry, "All of life is religion. No dichotomy between Church and the world.

No separation of piety and politics." It was like having Gandhi and Marx in the same room, and the meeting broke up a day early.[38]

The hopes for a united evangelical left went unrealized, but out of the ferment came a handful of small progressive organizations, among them Jim Wallis's Sojourners, Ron Sider's Evangelicals for Social Action, and the Calvinist-led Association for Public Justice. Also a number of ground-breaking books, notably Yoder's *The Politics of Jesus*, Sider's *Rich Christians in an Age of Hunger*, and David O. Moberg's *The Great Reversal*, rediscovered northern evangelical engagement in social justice issues before the fundamentalist-modernist split.[39] The number of progressive evangelicals was never great, but as writers and teachers they had enough influence for right-wing leaders such as Bill Bright and Billy James Hargis to consider them a threat to evangelicalism. Their Social Gospel message was, however, drowned out in the late 1970s by a more powerful rhetoric about "the moral issues," such as abortion and homosexuality.

*   *   *

It is a matter of some historical interest that during the Long Sixties established evangelical leaders made little or nothing of the sex and gender issues that later propelled the Christian right. Their tirades about the student rebellions certainly included criticisms of sexual promiscuity, but these generally took a backseat to denunciations of the political and economic "anarchy" abroad in the land.[40] Understandably the national dramas preoccupied them, but there was more to it than that. Particularly after 1957, Billy Graham and other post-fundamentalists were working to rid evangelicalism of the harsh authoritarianism and the innumerable petty taboos that isolated the fundamentalists in the modern world. While insisting on the virtue of obedience, Graham spoke not of punishments but of the love of God for his people, the love of parents for their children and of husbands for their wives. Accompanying this change of emphasis was the notion that sex within marriage should be pleasurable.

At the same time, neo-evangelicals began to rethink the opposition of their fundamentalist predecessors to birth control. In 1959 a Fuller theologian, Edward Carnell, called contraception "one expedient within the creative possibilities of love." That year Ockenga and Graham came out for contraception as a means of family planning and a way to combat "the population explosion" in the world.[41] As for abortion, the neo-evangelicals did not oppose it in principle; indeed, during the 1960s they and the Southern Baptists supported the liberalization of state laws against it.

In 1960 every state had antiabortion statutes on its books that dated from the nineteenth century, but with changing medical practices and social mores, American attitudes about abortion changed with rapidity. The availability of the birth control pill led to a growing acceptance of the idea that women should be able to control their own fertility. In 1962 the famous case of the "thalidomide baby" inspired a grassroots movement for the legalization of abortion in cases of fetal deformity, rape, incest, or a threat to the mother's health. In the mid-1960s Republican politicians led the effort to change state laws to permit what were known "therapeutic abortions." Barry Goldwater supported abortion rights, and in 1967 Governor Ronald Reagan of California became one of the first two Republican governors to sign a bill permitting abortion in cases of rape, incest, or potential damage to the mother's health. In California and other states Catholics—most of them Democrats—lobbied against such bills. The Catholic Church had teachings going back centuries, and recently affirmed by Vatican II, holding that life began at conception and that abortion was murder. American Protestants, however, had no such authoritative teachings—physicians, not Protestant preachers, had campaigned for the nineteenth-century laws—and when the issue came up in the 1960s evangelical, as well as mainline Protestant, discussions centered on the circumstances that would, or would not, justify a "therapeutic" abortion.

In August 1968 Harold Ockenga and Harold Lindsell, the new editor of *Christianity Today*, cochaired a symposium of twenty-five prominent evangelical physicians and theologians to consider the whole issue of controlling human reproduction from a biblical perspective. The participants expressed a variety of opinions in their papers, but the final document showed consensus on certain points, among them that the Bible did not explicitly prohibit contraception or abortion; that contraception was not in itself sinful; and that abortion, while possibly sinful, was necessary and permissible when it served to safeguard "greater values sanctioned by the Scriptures" such as individual health, family welfare, and the social good.

The document, "A Protestant Affirmation on the Control of Human Reproduction," located personhood at birth and spoke with approval of the changes in state laws. Drawn up just a month after the Vatican reaffirmed its opposition to contraception and abortion in *Humanae Vitae*, it was presumably the neo-evangelical response to the encyclical.[42] In the succeeding years discussions about "therapeutic" abortions continued among northern evangelical scholars. *Eternity* magazine, for example, devoted a special issue to the subject in 1971, presenting a range of views about the conditions under which abortion might be considered. The Supreme Court's decision in *Roe v. Wade* defining abortion as a woman's right therefore shocked many evangelical leaders. The NAE immediately deplored the ruling, which, it said, "has made it legal to terminate a pregnancy for no better reason than personal convenience or sociological considerations." *Roe* had rendered the notion of therapeutic abortion legally moot. Still, the NAE went on to say, "we recognize the necessity for therapeutic abortions to safeguard the health or the life of the mother" and to stipulate that other pregnancies, like those resulting from rape or incest, might also require termination. For the NAE, as for most northern evangelicals, abortion was not a woman's right, but it wasn't murder either. The position remained the same even in 1975, when Billy Graham convened a leadership meeting to "determine a proper Biblical response to abortion-on-demand"—as opposed to abortion per se.[43]

The Southern Baptist Convention took much the same approach. In 1971 the Convention called on Southern Baptists to work for the liberalization of state laws to permit abortion not only in cases such as rape, incest, and fetal deformity but "in the likelihood of damage to the emotional, mental and physical health of the mother." The resolution did not please all Southern Baptists. The great majority favored such "therapeutic" abortions, but a small minority objected that abortion was murder, and another small minority argued that it should be legal in all cases. The divide, however, did not fall along the usual conservative-moderate lines, but rather, it seems, along the spectrum of anti-Catholicism. When the *Roe* decision came down, the conservative leader W. A. Criswell praised the Supreme Court's ruling. "I have always felt," he said, "that it was only after a child was born and had a life separate from its mother that it became an individual person, and it has always, therefore, seemed to me that what is the best for the mother and for the future should be allowed." The debate grew more acrimonious, but positions didn't change. In 1974 the Convention voted to reaffirm its 1971 resolution, explaining that it took "a middle ground between the extreme of abortion on demand and the opposite extreme of all abortion as murder." Two years later the Convention made another effort to find a middle ground and found it in self-contradiction. On the one hand its resolution condemned abortion "for selfish non-therapeutic reasons," explaining that "every decision for an abortion . . . must necessarily involve the decision to terminate the life of an innocent human being." On the other hand it spoke of "our conviction about the limited role of the government in dealing with matters relating to abortion" and expressed support for "the right of expectant mothers to the full range of medical services and personal counseling for the preservation of life and health." The SBC reaffirmed this same resolution every year until 1980.[44]

When this "middle ground" position on abortion changed, it changed abruptly, and in tandem with the emergence of the other "moral" issues. What occasioned it was the demise of the evangelical establishments in the North and the South and the rise of new leaders.

Ockenga and his neo-evangelical allies had aimed to forge an interdenominational coalition of evangelicals around a coherent postfundamentalist position, but by the mid-1970s Henry had to admit they had failed. For one thing, much of their success had depended on Billy Graham's domination of the preaching circuits and the political influence he wielded, and Graham was losing both.[45] Graham never used television except to broadcast his crusades. Possibly he and his associates never understood that television favors an intimate one-to-one relationship between the speaker and the viewer—but then he was a revivalist, not a talk show host. In any case, with the waning enthusiasm for tent revivals, and the multiplication of preachers who knew how to use the medium of TV, Graham became one among many popular evangelists. He remained the most respected of them, but his preaching no longer shaped popular evangelical religion as it had in the 1950s—or exerted the same centripetal force. Further, he had lost his taste for partisan politics.

Graham had remained loyal to Nixon long after the thunderclouds of scandal began to gather about the White House. He dismissed the Watergate break-in when it happened, and a year later, just before the Senate hearings, he said, "I don't think anyone, even the President, knows the whole truth . . . I have known him a long time and he has a very strong sense of integrity." That Thanksgiving, after Nixon fired the special prosecutor, the attorney general, and his deputy to prevent the release of the Oval Office tapes, Graham told the press that "the tragic events of Watergate will make him a strong man and a better President." In January 1974 he finally characterized the Watergate break-in and the cover-up as "unethical" and "criminal," but noted that there was no evidence that the president was personally involved. In May after the White House released edited transcripts of the Oval Office tapes showing that Nixon and his top aides had directed the whole operation, Graham remarked only on the constant use of profanity. "I just didn't know that he used that kind of language," he said. Reading the full text of transcripts apparently made him physically sick, but a few days later he pronounced in a press release, "One cannot but deplore the moral tone implied in these papers, and though we know that other Presidents have used equally objectionable language, it does not make it right." [46]

Still, however trivial his response to the scandal seemed to be, Graham had a profound change of heart because of the experience. In July, just a few weeks before Nixon's resignation, he warned an international group of evangelists "not to identify the Gospel with any one political program or culture" and admitted, "this has been my own danger." Thereafter he not only pulled away from partisan politics but also repented that "in my earlier days . . . I tended to identify the Kingdom of God with the American way of life. I don't think like that now." From then on, he often met with presidents and stayed in the White House, but because he had abandoned politics, the press paid no attention, and his influence waned. [47]

What was more, Harold Ockenga, Carl Henry, and their colleagues never managed to create a coherent social and intellectual framework—much less one on which all evangelical scholars could agree. Even they themselves had political differences, and the Vietnam War only increased the tensions. In 1968 Howard Pew and Nelson Bell forced Henry to resign

from the editorship of *Christianity Today* on the grounds that he was insufficiently hostile to what Pew saw as machinations of liberal clergy to
promote their left-wing ideology and to form a voting bloc to take over
the state. Henry's successor, Harold Lindsell, was more to Pew's liking.
A former Fuller scholar who had come to the magazine in 1964, he was,
among other things, a Goldwater Republican who took a hard line against
the student antiwar demonstrators and refused to countenance even the
most moderate members of the evangelical left. By the early 1970s the
center no longer held, and there was nothing Graham could do about it.
Then, too, instead of reaching a theological consensus neo-evangelical
scholars moved farther apart as the years went by.[48]

The Fuller Seminary had been the focus of Ockenga's hopes, but with
the arrival of new leaders in 1962, among them Daniel Fuller, the son of
the founder, the seminary gradually abandoned its mission of refurbish-
ing fundamentalism. The younger Fuller, a theologian who had studied
abroad and returned to become dean of the faculty, rejected biblical inerrancy. For him the issue was quite straightforward: in light of modern
historical scholarship the Bible clearly contained errors that could not be
explained by deviations from the original autographs. It was, of course,
inerrant in its salvation teachings, or in matters of faith and practice, but
not in incidental matters such as cosmological theories or historical detail.
In his view Fuller scholars should just admit the minor errors and get on
with the business of apologetics.

The new president, David Hubbard, took a stand in a different but
related place: that of interpretation. The inerrancy doctrine had always
been inextricably bound to a fundamentalist hermeneutic—or method of
interpretation—that highlighted certain parts of the biblical narrative and
extracted a set of propositional truths from them. It wasn't exactly a literal
reading, but it was what those in the fundamentalist tradition thought of
as the commonsensical way to interpret the text. Hubbard, who came
from a Methodist background, thought that biblical scholarship might
still turn up fresh insights into the meaning of the Scriptures. The new
members of the board approved both positions, and under Hubbard's
leadership the seminary cast off its doctrinal tethers to fundamentalism

and adopted a more tolerant and open approach. Some of the old faculty members quit, but the school was for the first time able to fulfill its second mission of attracting a wide range of evangelical students, among them conservative mainline Protestants, Pentecostalists, charismatics, Mennonites, and Dutch Reformed. With the addition of a School of Psychology and a School of World Missions the emphasis of the whole seminary changed from apologetics to the practical concerns of evangelism and pastoral care. At the same time the students became more attuned to issues of social and economic justice, and some joined the evangelical left. Attendance grew, and by 1982 Fuller had become the largest independent evangelical seminary in the country with a total enrollment of over three thousand students, among them five hundred women and two hundred members of racial minorities.[49]

Fuller was exceptional, but evangelical scholars at other seminaries, among them Bernard Ramm and Clark Pinnock, had also moved away from fundamentalist doctrines. How general the phenomenon was, however, went unnoticed until 1976, when Harold Lindsell launched what Henry called a "theological atom bombing." In his book *The Battle for the Bible*, Lindsell maintained that evangelical Christianity was facing the greatest crisis in its history because of deviations from biblical inerrancy. For a scholar to state that the Bible contained a few errors might seem a small thing, he wrote, but it was the beginning of a slippery slope leading to defections from other biblical truth, such as the virgin birth, and from there into the abyss of apostasy. Such defections, he pointed out, had happened often in the past. They had happened at Union Theological Seminary after Dr. Charles Briggs brought the notion of limited inerrancy back from abroad. They had happened in all the mainline denominations. In fact, history provided no example of a group that had given up on inerrancy when defections from other basic doctrines did not follow. After all, if the Bible could err, it lost its authority. Then who was to say what percent was errant or truthful—and who was to settle the other doctrinal problems? Those who had questioned its complete truthfulness had lost their way and given up their vital interest in evangelism for sociopolitical concerns. The battle today, he wrote, is the same as that fought during the fundamentalist-modernist controversy—only it was happening within the denominations that had not surrendered before. Inerrancy was a watershed issue—and those who denied it were not evangelicals at all.[50]

Lindsell, who had left Fuller in part because of its departure from inerrancy, named the defectors and offered quotations to prove his point. He was, as he later put it, calling for the excision of a cancerous tumor from the body of Christ. Harold Ockenga seemed to concur, for in the foreword to his book he wrote that the evidence that those who surrendered the doctrine of inerrancy inevitably moved away from orthodoxy was indisputable. Therefore those who did "must ultimately yield the right to use the name evangelical."[51]

The book created a storm of controversy, but outside the South it did almost the opposite of what Lindsell hoped. None of the neo-evangelical scholars Lindsell named changed their positions because of it. Northern evangelical institutions were too many and too various to be brought into line. Instead of leading to a purge of noninerrantists, the threat of excommunication merely helped to demonstrate that neo-evangelicals were irreparably divided—and further, not in control of northern evangelicalism. Rather than redefining "evangelical," it showed that "neo-evangelical" had become a meaningless appellation, and the term quickly fell out of use.[52]

Lindsell's main concern was with neo-evangelicals, but his book included chapters on other evangelical groups, two of them very large. One of these, the Lutheran Church—Missouri Synod, a denomination with over two million members, was at the time of his writing going through a serious conflict over inerrancy. One of its two major seminaries had adopted the historical-critical method and refused to obey the directive of the Synod's president to give it up. The issue went to the general convention, and when the conservatives won and the president of the seminary was suspended, the faculty and most of the students left to form a "seminary-in-exile." By 1978, 150 congregations had also quit the denomination, leaving the rest of the Synod in the hands of the conservatives. The other large denomination Lindsell examined was the Southern Baptist Convention, and there his exposure of defectors from inerrancy within the seminaries gave impetus to a growing fundamentalist movement.[53]

9

THE FUNDAMENTALIST
UPRISING *in the* SOUTH

URING THE 1960s and '70s fundamentalist churches proliferated in the South and Southwest at an enormous rate. In her
book *Suburban Warriors* Lisa McGirr, a scholar of the new right
in Southern California, tells us of "fantastic growth" of conservative evangelical churches in Orange County in the late 1960s and '70s. Many were
separatist Baptists, and just one association, the Bible Baptist Fellowship,
founded in 1948, had 1,800 churches and 750,000 members across the South
by the early 1970s. A decade later it comprised nearly three thousand
churches and a million members.[1] Meanwhile a fundamentalist party in
the Southern Baptist Convention transformed the denomination with an
inerrant Bible as its battle cry.

In the course of the 1960s some influential Southern Baptists moved
cautiously out of their intellectual isolation. In the seminaries some
professors engaged with such other currents of Christian thought as
neo-orthodoxy and historical biblical criticism, though usually in a conservative context. That they were doing so became evident in 1961 when
Ralph Elliott, a professor at Midwestern Seminary in Kansas City, published a study of Genesis claiming that the book could not be dated because it relied on stories transmitted by the oral traditions of the Middle
East. Similar claims—old hat in the North—had been timidly advanced
before in Southern Baptist journals, but because Elliott's book was published by Boardman Press, the denominational publisher, it was roundly
attacked by conservatives. The controversy led to Elliott's removal from

his post and a revision of Baptist Faith and Message in 1963. The confession, however, reiterated its 1925 predecessor in describing the Bible as "having truth without any admixture of error for its matter," a phrase that could be variously interpreted. In this way denominational loyalists, as usual, pacified conservatives without adopting their position, and in the following years professors continued to teach views other than inerrancy and to interpret the Bible in ways that conservatives considered suspect.[2]

The controversy flared up again in 1970, when Boardman Press published the first volume of a new series of biblical commentaries written by a British Baptist who used the historical-critical approach on the Old Testament. W. A. Criswell, who the previous year had published *Why I Preach the Bible Is Literally True*, was then the SBC president. At the convention that year his fellow conservatives organized a protest meeting and introduced a motion ordering the volume recalled and rewritten from a conservative point of view. Staffers from the Sunday School Board, which had approved the volume, argued that SBC should have room for a diversity of opinion about the Bible, but most SBC pastors had never questioned the truth of the Bible, and the convention passed the motion by an overwhelming vote. The Sunday School trustees asked the original author to write a revision. Only after the conservatives protested again did they reassign the commentaries, this time to a well-known conservative scholar but one influenced by the historical-critical method, and the Board made arrangements to sell its stock of the original book through another publisher.[3]

Criswell and his fellow conservatives were furious—particularly so because they felt they were losing on another front as well. They had belatedly renounced segregation in part because they had been persuaded that it hampered the SBC's evangelistic mission at home and abroad, but they had begun to think that civil rights advocates within the Convention—principally Foy Valentine and the Christian Life Convention—were moving the Convention away from evangelism to left-wing social concerns, and they feared for the future of their church. Criswell, who had signed the 1968 statement committing the church to oppose racism and injustice, mounted an evangelical rally at the convention the following year to "balance" the attention to social issues. His fellow conservatives attacked on the Christian Life Commission's social and cultural programs, and only a petition from four respected denominationalists prevented them from dismantling the agency. By then the social transformation that had started in the North had made its way into the southern cities. The ambition of the new Southern Baptist leadership had become to restore not just the denomination but the whole country to its traditional Christian ways. Perceiving the changes of the 1960s as the sort of chaos that would erupt when biblical rules were discarded, they found the compromise over the Boardman Bible controversies the last straw. As they saw it, they had won every battle over biblical issues on the convention floor, but still had not managed to halt the dangerous slide toward liberalism abetted by SBC agency staffs and complacent boards of trustees.[4]

Convening a meeting, the Criswell conservatives took the name Baptist Faith and Message Fellowship and voted to start their own publication, the *Southern Baptist Journal*, to awaken the SBC to the dangers of liberalism and return it to orthodox Christianity. What they meant by orthodoxy, it soon became clear, was an uncompromising stand on biblical inerrancy and belief in a literal creation, a literal fish to swallow Jonah, literal miracles, and a literal virgin birth of Christ. Knowing full well that the trustees of the six SBC seminaries would never accept this kind of a doctrinal straitjacket, they founded their own schools: in 1971 the Criswell Bible Studies Center in Dallas and in 1972 the Mid-American Baptist Seminary in Memphis to supplement the inerrantist Luther Rice Seminary in Jacksonville, Florida.[5] They did not call themselves fundamentalists—they insisted they were defending Southern Baptist traditions—but the pattern was a familiar one. A half century after fundamentalist parties emerged in the northern churches, a doctrinaire antimodernist party was forming in the SBC to "do battle royal" with liberal apostasy.

In the mid-1970s, when Harold Lindsell's book appeared, the SBC was, as always, led by moderate conservatives intent on maintaining denominational unity. The fundamentalists—as I will call them—stood to one side.[6] They could muster votes at the annual conventions, but they had small representation on the agency boards and the faculties of the six SBC seminaries. They had their own seminaries, their own journal, their own network, their own conferences, and their churches contributed little to the SBC's Cooperative Program. Still, the dissidents did not see themselves as outsiders. A number of them were popular preachers with enormous congregations and radio and TV ministries. These dominated the Pastor's Conference, an annual display of preaching talents held just before the yearly convention. Speakers at the 1977 Conference, among them W. A. Criswell, denounced the growing influence of noninerrantists in the denomination. That year Paul Pressler, an appeals court judge from Houston with a long Southern Baptist pedigree, teamed up with Paige Patterson, the president of the Criswell Center for Bible Studies, to plan for a "conservative resurgence"—or a "fundamentalist takeover" of the SBC.[7]

Before the 1979 convention Pressler and Patterson crisscrossed the states, speaking at conferences and rallying supporters. At the Pastor's Conference, James Robison, a firebrand evangelist from Fort Worth, told his listeners, "My friend, I wouldn't tolerate a rattlesnake in my house . . . I wouldn't tolerate a cancer in my body. I want you to know that anyone who casts doubt on the Word of God is worse than cancer and worse than snakes." He acknowledged that some of the denominational leaders were "great men," but insisted that others were "just like the government bureaucrats, they're ingrained and they're worse than cancer." Southern Baptists, he trumpeted, should elect a president "who is totally committed to removing from this denomination anyone who does not believe that the Bible is the inerrant, infallible Word of the living God." The crowd cheered. The fundamentalists' choice for president that year was Adrian Rogers, a well-known preacher with a huge church in Memphis. There were five other candidates, but the fundamentalists voted as a bloc, and Rogers won by more than 50 percent of the vote.[8]

Rogers's victory alarmed some at the convention, but the old-guard leaders tended to dismiss it as yet another rightward swing that would wear itself out in a few years. They believed the fundamentalists could be drawn into the Grand Compromise that had always prevailed in the SBC, and they went about inviting them to Bible conferences to show them that the seminaries were not hotbeds of liberalism but benignly conservative. The fundamentalists, however, had no interest in compromise. They had come to believe that the whole nation was in the throes of a cultural crisis, and that to confront it they first had to take over the SBC and bring it into conformity with their own standards of orthodoxy. The plan devised by Pressler involved turning the centralized bureaucracy of the SBC to their own purposes. If they could elect one of their own as president for the next ten years, their presidents could appoint the members of the board that appointed the trustees of the seminaries and denominational agencies; the trustees could then appoint the presidents and directors of these institutions and gradually change their nature. Inerrancy was for them the bulwark against all the tendencies toward liberalism, and the SBC pastors could not but agree to the authority and the truthfulness of the Bible. Thus with inerrancy as their standard, SBC fundamentalists waged a protracted campaign for their denomination. They won election after election, and some years later the purges began.[9]

* * *

The growth of the separatist Baptist churches paralleled the rise of fundamentalism in the SBC, and by the late 1970s Jerry Falwell had set his efforts to awakening his fellow separatists to the dangers of "moral degeneracy" in the country. He became the most important leader of the Christian right in the country in the 1980s, but his major achievement until then was building a church with several thousand members in the small city of Lynchburg, Virginia. One of the hundred largest churches in the country, he had started it with thirty-five people in 1956, and his career tracked the upsurge of separatist Baptist churches in the South. To talk with people in his congregation was to get a sense of what attracted southerners to fundamentalist churches in 1960s and '70s and what it meant to be a fundamentalist at the time.[10]

To many northern liberals the word "fundamentalist" still conjured up the image of a small white church in the mountains filled with backwoods people in overalls. Falwell's church was, of course, nothing like that. Located in one of the middle-class sections of Lynchburg, Thomas Road Baptist Church was a large octagonal brick building with a parking lot of supermarket size. On the Sunday I first visited it in 1979 or early 1980, cars were lined up on the street for blocks trying to get into the lot beside a number of buses. The four-thousand-seat sanctuary inside had baby blue carpeting, comfortable pews, and by the stage up front were television cameras rigged to film the service for *The Old Time Gospel Hour*, which would be broadcast on television through network affiliates and cable stations around the county. The congregation consisted mainly of couples with two or three children, but there were also elderly people and young adults. The men wore double-knit suits and sported gold wedding bands or heavy brass rings stamped with mottos; the women wore demure print dresses and single-diamond engagement bands. The young women were more fashionably dressed. Their flowered print dresses fell to midcalf, but were cut low on the bodice and worn with ankle-strap heels. The young men in white shirts and close-cropped hair looked fresh-faced and extraordinarily clean.

Services normally began with a robed choir singing traditional Baptist hymns. But then Don Norman, an assistant pastor with a pompadour of silver-gray hair, or Robbie Hiner, a cherub-faced young man in a bottle-green suit, would sing inspirational ballads having to do with heavenly love and heavenly riches. A student group called the Sounds of Liberty might follow, the young women with hair flipped in the style of Charlie's Angels snuggling up to their male counterparts. Eventually Falwell would appear at the lectern. Strong-jawed and portly, wearing a thick three-piece black suit and carrying a huge Bible, he looked every inch an old-fashioned Baptist minister. Still, unlike his predecessors in the pretelevision era, he spoke conversationally while making the announcements and preached his sermon without theatrics—though with the authority of a big baritone.

On Wednesdays, when addressing only the Thomas Road congregation, Falwell would often describe his trips to exotic places like New York City, and his meetings with political celebrities, such as Senator Jesse Helms. In his sermons he preached more from the Epistles than from the Gospels, and he often took his text from Timothy I or II, the books in which the Apostle Paul writes to the younger evangelist. On such occasions he seemed an avuncular figure, a dispenser of practical advice to his followers. On other occasions he would put on a threatening display, speaking of the battles Christians were waging with "secular humanists" out to destroy the country. "The war is not between fundamentalists and liberals," he thundered one Sunday, "but between those who love Jesus Christ and those who hate Him."[11]

Falwell had founded his church in an old factory building in a run-down section of Lynchburg. Twenty-three years old, he had just graduated from the Baptist Bible College founded by J. Frank Norris's former lieutenant, G. Beauchamp Vick. The building had recently been vacated by the Donald Duck Bottling Company, and he and his thirty-five congregants had spent several days scrubbing the cola syrup off the walls. A week after the first service Falwell began a half-hour Sunday broadcast for a new local radio station. Not long afterward he started a daily radio program and a Sunday-evening broadcast from a local TV station. Weekdays, he went from door to door visiting houses in an ever-expanding radius from the church. Later, he bought a printing press, a phone bank for telephone evangelism, and television cameras to tape his Sunday services. Following the practice of Oral Roberts, Rex Humbard, and others, he purchased time on TV stations in various parts of the country and set up a direct mail funding operation to defray the costs of production and to build his ministries.

Lynchburg lies on the James River in a country of small farms and wooded, rolling hills at the foot of the Blue Ridge Mountains. A hundred and sixty miles southwest of Washington, it is beyond the gentleman-farming, horse-breeding country and more than halfway to Appalachia. Founded in the late eighteenth century by John Lynch, it began as a tobacco-trading center and an agricultural market town. In the nineteenth century new settlers—many of them Scots-Irish—moved in to build grain mills, an iron foundry, and small manufacturing enterprises. In the late nineteenth century Lynchburg merchants built new foundries, cotton mills, textile mills, and a shoe factory, making Lynchburg one of the few towns in the South with an industrial economy. But it was far from any other urban center, and in 1950 it was still a mill town, most of its factories old-fashioned and its society hidebound, stratified, and segregated. In the mid-1950s, however, it began to undergo the transformation taking place in many other southern cities. A number of major national corporations arrived, attracted by low property taxes, nonunion labor, and relatively low pay scales. Among them were General Electric, Babcock & Wilcox, the manufacturer of nuclear reactors, and Meredith/Burda, a printing enterprise. These corporations stimulated local industry and attracted other large manufacturers from the North and from West Germany. The population grew with immigrants from the countryside.

Lynchburg in 1980 was still a small city—only 67,000 people—but its businessmen could point with pride to a healthily diverse economy, a skilled labor force, and a high employment rate. The median family income remained lower than that of Virginia as a whole, and it had relatively few white-collar jobs. In many ways it remained a conservative place. It had over a hundred churches, and on Sunday mornings the streets were empty, the cars herded up next to the churches. The city voted for Harry Byrd–style Democrats and for Gerald Ford in 1976. Still, it was no longer segregated or hidebound. The new industries had brought new faces into the boardrooms, and in the early 1960s, when black ministers and their congregations conducted a series of sit-ins and demonstrations, they found that the white community was not immovable. Under pressure the companies hired African American workers, and the city's segregation ordinances were stricken from the books. In 1980, 25 percent of its population was African American, and the civil rights movement had left a well-organized black community. Its public education system was one of the best in the state, its integrated schools good enough to send 63 percent of their graduates to college. It also had three well-established private liberal arts colleges, Randolph-Macon, Sweet Briar, and Lynchburg College. These colleges did not generate much intellectual or political ferment, but they did provide the city with voices other than those of its business community. The seven-member city council included four moderate liberals, a woman, and an African American among them, all of whom participated in the amicable consensus that ran the town.

Lynchburg wasn't a physically graceful city. Its old downtown had been supplanted by a series of shopping plazas, and the automobile had cut swaths across it, leaving gas stations and fast-food restaurants to sprout up in parking lot wastelands. Without any real center, it had become a collection of suburbs, its population spread out over many square miles. Still, with the demise of the smokestack industries, it had become a clean city, full of quiet streets and shade trees. Along the James

River, in a section called Rivermont, stately nineteenth-century mansions looked out over wooded parks and lawns. Behind them were streets of white-shingled Victorian houses, and behind *them*, tracts of post–World War II developer-built Capes and Colonials. The developers were still at work, and streets with names as such as Crestview and Forest Park ran through sections of marked-off lots before dead-ending in the woods. There were also poor neighborhoods where cocks crowed in the backyards of trembling wooden houses, and a part of the old downtown had become a depressed area of abandoned factories and boarded-up shops. But there were no real slums, for the city had built low-cost housing with federal funds. There wasn't much crime, and as for the things Falwell spent so much time denouncing, like pornography, drugs, and "the homosexual lifestyle," Lynchburg harbored them quietly, if it harbored them at all.

A number of Thomas Road church members lived in the new developer-built houses on the edges of town: comfortable suburban-style houses set on half-acre lawns, with central air-conditioning and the kitchens resembling those in TV detergent ads—and just as clean. Many had been decorated with shag rugs, wallpaper, and chintz curtains. A woman I visited, Nancy James, had just bought a living room suite, and another, Jackie Gould, had ordered a new set of kitchen cabinets without—she said giggling—consulting her husband. One family had not only a living room but also a family room with a Naugahyde pouf, a twenty-four-inch television, and a sliding glass door looking out over a stone-paved terrace. One Sunday evening, when I was there, this couple gave a potluck supper for twenty neighbors and fellow church members. The man of the house—resplendent in a fitted white shirt, cream-colored trousers, and white shoes—watched a boxing match on television with the other men while his wife organized the dishes of ham, baked beans, candied squash, and potato salad the other women had brought with them. At dinner, around a lace-covered table, the guests joked and made small talk about their gardens, the Lynchburg water system, the problems of giving a Tupperware party, and the advantages of building one's own house. After dinner the men and the women separated, the men going into the living room and the women upstairs for an hour or so of Bible reading and prayers.

In such circumstances it was difficult to see how Falwell could complain so much about moral decay, sex, drugs, and the decline of the family. Conversely, it was difficult to imagine why such people would be drawn to a preacher who spent so much time denouncing pornography—and who once made a point of forbidding his congregation to watch *Charlie's Angels*. But then not all of Thomas Road church members lived in such order and comfort. To go with the pastors on their rounds was to see that the Sunday-morning look of the congregation was in some degree misleading—or in the nature of a Platonic ideal. A number of its members lived in government-financed housing projects or in the neighborhoods of old wooden houses. In one thin-walled apartment a woman sat with her head in her hands gazing dejectedly at four squalling children under nine— the baby crawling naked across the linoleum floor. (The pastor prissily told the oldest girl to put some pants on the baby.) At a church-sponsored flea market I found a number of women with worn faces buying and sell- ing used children's clothing while their husbands squatted in a circle under a nearby tree and talked about boot camp and 'Nam. According to one pastor, many of the elderly people in the church were single women who lived on Social Security allowances of $4,000 or $5,000 a year. And most of them had never traveled outside Virginia.

What is more, to talk to the people who live in the comfortable suburban-style houses was to discover that many of them did not grow up in such middle-class circumstances. William Sheehan, chair of the church's Division of Prayer, became a lawyer late in life. He ran away from home and a drunken father at the age of eighteen and lived for a year in the boiler room of a school in Montana. He married at the age of twenty-one, had nine children, and worked at various manual and clerical jobs. Only when he reached his forties did he have time to study the law at night. He passed the bar, apprenticed himself to an older lawyer, took over a practice in a small Montana town, and eventually moved to Lynchburg. Most of Falwell's parishioners came from closer to home, many from the countryside and the small towns of Virginia and West Virginia. One guest at the potluck supper talked about his childhood in a narrow coal-mining valley of Appalachia, where the preachers handled poisonous snakes and spoke in tongues. He never got used to the Lynchburg traffic, he said, for where he came from, the sound of a car on the road meant that you picked up your shotgun and left by the back door.

To talk with Falwell's parishioners was to see that for many the geography of Lynchburg was symbolic in terms of their lives. As the city stood between Appalachia and Washington, D.C., so the arrival of new industry over twenty-five years made it the transfer point between the Old and the New South. Many Thomas Road members literally made the journey between the underdeveloped countryside and the city with its technologically advanced industries. Many others, however, made a similar journey without moving at all. Growing up in families of poor farmers or unskilled laborers, they became clerical workers, technicians, skilled workers, and small businessmen. Some had Baptist backgrounds, others grew up outside the church, and of these, many I spoke to described difficult, disorganized childhoods—family histories of alcoholism, physical violence, or trouble with the law. They had, or so they said, to struggle with their families and then to struggle with themselves. They credited the Lord for the changes in their lives and dated their success from the time they were "saved."

Falwell talked about his own life in sermons but also in authorized biographies—and later in a ghostwritten autobiography. These accounts differ in interesting ways, but according to all of them, and to his family members, his life followed a trajectory not so different from those of his followers. Falwell and his twin brother, Gene, were born to Carey and Helen Falwell on August 11, 1933. The family, which included two much older children, Virginia and Lewis, lived in a white frame house a mile and a half east of a section of Lynchburg known as Fairview Heights. In a 1979 biography, *Jerry Falwell: Aflame for God*, by Gerald Strober and Ruth Tomczak, the earliest photograph shows Jerry, aged about two, in the arms of a man in overalls with a high-crowned dark hat pulled down over his weather-beaten face.[12] The man was Jerry's grandfather, Charles Falwell, a dairy farmer, whose father had settled in Lynchburg in the mid-eighteenth century. There's also a photograph of Jerry's father, Carey, a slight man in a three-piece suit with a pained expression on his face, and one of his mother, Helen, taken much later, showing an ample-breasted woman with her hair pulled back under a black hat and wearing a printed black silk dress.

Carey Falwell was the oldest in a family of boys. He had only a sixth-grade education, but in the 1920s he started a series of successful businesses—grocery stores, service stations, a gas and oil distributorship, and a bus company serving central Virginia. He also ran a profitable boot-legging operation with his brother Garland. The house where the twins were born was a gentleman's house that Carey had moved piece by piece from Rivermont to the Falwell farm. Carey was, it seems, a shrewd, ambitious, hard-driving man, but by the time the twins were born he had begun to drink too much. In 1931 he had shot and killed his reprobate brother Garland in the heat of an argument in what was judged to be self-defense. According to Falwell, he never got over it. Still, Carey prospered through the Depression, opening an enormous restaurant and dance hall called the Merry Garden, where women came in furs and Tommy Dorsey once played. He ran illegal cockfights and dogfights and kept a bear in a cage. In his autobiography, Falwell tells us that his father was generous to people in need, but that he had "a mean streak." Carey once killed an employee's cat and fed it to him in what he said was "squirrel stew." On another occasion he threw a "tough young drunk" into the cage with the bear. He always carried a gun, and once, when Jerry brought a young friend into the house, he shot a hole in the floor a few inches in front of the boy's shoes, announcing "I've been trying to catch that fly all day." The boy fled, but, Falwell writes, "Dad and I laughed ourselves hoarse." During World War II most of Carey's businesses went bust; he became a serious alcoholic and died of cirrhosis of the liver in 1948, when Jerry was fifteen.[13]

Aflame for God says of Jerry's twin brother, Gene, that he "would follow in his father's footsteps and become an aggressive, successful businessman and, along with his older brother Lewis, consolidate and add to the family's extensive commercial interests." The account could be more accurate. Some of the Falwells did very well in life. Calvin and Lawrence, the sons of Carey's more stable brother Warren, took the businesses they had inherited and built a number of successful enterprises, including a well-drilling company, a trucking firm, and an aviation company. Hard-working and civic-minded, Calvin became one of Lynchburg's city fathers; he was a member of the Chamber of Commerce and the president of the local New York Mets farm team. But Jerry was the only real success in his immediate family. His brother Lewis had an excavation company, and Gene, who lived in the "home place" where they grew up, ran a trailer park on the Falwell land. Calvin, an outgoing man with a soft Virginia drawl, spoke affectionately of Gene. "Aggressive? He's the most easygoing kind of a guy you'd ever want to meet. Never gets mad. Has all the time in the world for you. I suppose he hasn't worn a tie since his mother's funeral. In fact, I'm sure he hasn't. Like someone once said to me, 'I guess Jerry got the other half.'"

The Falwell "home place" wasn't far from a large commercial road, but the white house stood alone in small pasture between two steep wooded hills. Gene was in and out of the house all day, fixing an electrical wire in someone's trailer or helping a brother-in-law prune a maple tree. A homebody who liked to hunt, fish, and farm, he could tell you in detail how to make maple sugar or how people used to make moonshine in a still. He would also tell you unselfconsciously how his grandpa used to make fun of the "colored boys" who worked for him. His wife, Jo Ann, who kept the house with its modern kitchen so clean it looked uninhabited, had clearly not been able to do very much about Gene's clothes or the stubble on his chin. Whereas Jo Ann went to the Thomas Road church, and Calvin was a charter member of a rather more relaxed Baptist church, Gene stayed home on Sundays, like his father and grandfather before him.

The contrast between the twins became obvious in their early years. The boys entered elementary school together, but after a year Jerry skipped a grade. He was good at schoolwork, particularly math and science. He had an almost photographic memory, so he didn't have to work hard, but he did. In his junior year in high school, he entered the state spelling championship; when he lost because a word was unfamiliar to him, he went back and read through an entire college edition of a dictionary. "He didn't like farm work," Gene recalled. "He'd leave me with the chores, and when the time came, he always had something else to do. He never liked to come out trapping with me, either. He'd have his head in a book or he'd be out playing baseball." Jerry liked the sociable, competitive sports. In his senior year in high school, he edited the school newspaper and captained the football team. Gene dropped out of school in his senior year and soon after joined the Navy, but Jerry graduated with 98.6 percent average and was named class valedictorian.[14]

In all the accounts of his life Falwell makes less of his academic record and his athletic prowess than he does of the trouble he got up to during his school years. *Aflame for God* describes him as a "prankster" and tells us that in grade school he set a snake loose in the classroom and once put a large dead rat in the teacher's desk drawer. In high school, it tells us, Jerry and some friends tied up a hated gym teacher and locked him in the basement. Out of school, he and Gene hung out at a café in Fairview Heights with a gang that for fun used to do things like piling a family's porch furniture on the roof of the house. Every so often they would have fistfights with neighboring gangs. In his autobiography, published in 1987 and reprinted by him ten years later, Falwell elaborates on some of these incidents and adds a few others. The rat was alive and the Latin teacher fainted dead away when it jumped out of her desk. Jerry tackled the "prissy" little phys-ed instructor and with two friends wrestled him into a storage room, pulled off his pants, locked him in, and pinned his pants to the school's main bulletin board with a note reading, "Mr. —'s britches." Jerry was not allowed to give the valedictory speech because the school auditors discovered that he and some friends had for a year been stealing cafeteria lunch tickets and handing them out to the football team. As for the Fairview Heights gang, they once thought a neighbor had called the police on them, so they took some old tar-soaked railroad ties and set them alight on the street in front of his house. The asphalt caught fire, and the whole street burst into flame. In a 1981 sermon called "My Testimony" Falwell said that he and a close friend, Jim Moon, used to spend days and nights away from home in "places it's not necessary to talk about, doing things it's not necessary to talk about."[15]

Falwell often exercised what he considered his right as a preacher to tell stories that—to use Dean Acheson's phrase—were truer than the truth. In 1980 he regularly claimed that *The Old-Time Gospel Hour* had 25 million viewers, and he made up an exchange with Jimmy Carter in which he asked the president why he had "practicing homosexuals" on the White House staff, and Carter replied that he had to represent the American people. When confronted by the fact that the exchange never occurred, Falwell said that the story was a "parable," or "an allegory."[16] In other words, it ought to have happened, even if it did not.

Doubtless Falwell's "prankster" tales were based in fact, but the question is why Falwell told them at all, much less elaborated on them as he grew more famous. The born-again sometimes exaggerate how sinful or desperate they were before conversion, but these were not preconversion stories, for Falwell was never punished for his "pranks" and never apologized for them later. Rather, they recalled the practical jokes J. Frank Norris used to play on his associates and the mysterious fires in Norris's church. Then, like Norris, his father had shot a man in what was judged to be self-defense. Jerry, who went to the Bible school led by a former Norris protégé, seems to have been casting himself as a classic fundamentalist preacher: a tough, unpredictable, and somewhat dangerous man that God had laid a hand on to scourge unbelievers.[17] Certainly if Falwell's life were told without these stories, he would seem merely a highly intelligent overachiever. Jim Moon, who became a co-pastor at the Thomas Road church, recalled that Falwell was different from the rest of the gang in that he always knew what he wanted. "I don't remember wanting anything or hoping for anything except to grow up," Moon said. "There weren't many opportunities back then. You could go to work at the hosiery mill, the foundry, or the shoe factory. There wasn't much else. When I was sixteen, I was drinking a lot. But Jerry, he always wanted to be an engineer, and he was willing to do whatever was necessary to be the best."

In 1950 Falwell entered Lynchburg College and began to take courses that would lead to a degree in mechanical engineering. His plan was to transfer to Virginia Polytechnic Institute, and by the end of his sophomore year he had the qualifications to do it: he had the highest math average in the college.[18] But by that fall he was enrolled in Baptist Bible College in Springfield, Missouri, and on his way to becoming a pastor. Exactly why he made this decision he never made clear.

The Falwells were not a pious people. When Jerry was growing up, the men seemed to regard religion as something women did. Jerry's mother, on the other hand, came from a strict Baptist family, and she attended the Franklin Street Baptist Church every Sunday. She took the twins to

Sunday school, though they would often slip out the back and run to their uncle's house to read the comics in the Sunday papers. In his autobiography Falwell tells us that he never went to church in his last years in high school or his first year in college. Still, every Sunday morning he listened—involuntarily—to Charles Fuller's *Old-Fashioned Revival Hour*, which his mother always had on the radio. On one such Sunday morning—January 20, 1952—a new feeling came over him. That evening he went with two friends to Park Avenue Baptist, a Bible Baptist Fellowship church that was said to have preaching like Fuller's and pretty girls. He responded to the altar call along with Jim Moon, and asked Christ to become his personal savior.[19]

So far the story, as he tells it, isn't very remarkable. He was eighteen; his father had died of alcoholism three years earlier, and he had enough of a religious background to respond to the altar call. Further, his conversion occurred in the early 1950s, when people across the country had started going to church en masse. What is surprising is that two months later he decided to abandon an engineering degree and perhaps a future in the family businesses to become a pastor. It's particularly so because he always maintained that he went through no inner turmoil when he made his commitment. "There was no vision. No blinding light. No miracle. No mysterious presence," he wrote in his autobiography. "I didn't even feel particularly emotional." Elsewhere he wrote, "From January to March . . . I got my salvation established, and then from about March to June, I got my call to full-time service established." Perhaps he left something out, but by his account, it was as if, having become a believer, he had to go to the top of the class.[20]

In any case, Falwell seems to have fit right in at the Baptist Bible Fellowship school. He took to evangelism as if he had been born to it, and he relished the aggressive style of his mentors. (One Baptist Bible Fellowship founder, John Rawlings, whom he particularly admired, was, he wrote in retrospect, "more like my dad than anybody I ever met. He was tough, out-spoken, unpredictable, and he refused to be bullied.") On graduating in 1956, he started his Lynchburg church with thirty-five dissenters from the Park Avenue Baptist Church. Among them was the pretty young pianist, Macel Pate, whom he subsequently married. He built his church in the BBF's entrepreneurial style, and in the growing town of Lynchburg, his congregation grew apace. In the late 1960s he began broadcasting the Sunday services in his church and started a bus ministry to bring people in from the far reaches of city and the surrounding counties. According to his figures, weekly attendance went from 1,250 in 1967 to 5,622 in 1972.[21]

In 1980 there was no scholarship on the modern fundamentalist movement, but the emergence of the Christian right spurred scholars on. Since then a number of studies, notably Nancy Ammerman's *Baptist Battles*, a book on the conflict within the Southern Baptist Convention, have done much to explain the rise of a militant antimodernist religion in the South and Southwest during the years Falwell was building his church.

A sociologist, Ammerman conducted extensive surveys of Southern Baptist pastors, deacons, and heads of women's organizations in the mid-1980s. Using strictly theological criteria she found that her respondents fell along a spectrum from moderates to conservatives to fundamentalists, and that there were telling social differences between those at either end. Her findings were roughly these: The moderates, 18 percent of her sample, tended to have grown up in white-collar or professional families and to be well educated with middle-class jobs. Almost all moderate pastors had attended seminaries, and over half of the laity had a college degree or more. The fundamentalists, 33 percent of her sample, provided a contrast. They included both white- and blue-collar workers, but about three quarters had grown up in farming or blue-collar homes. Many of their pastors were Bible school graduates, and only 17 percent of the laity had college degrees. Urbanization was also a factor. Rural people tended to be theologically conservative, but those who had moved from the rural areas into the cities were more likely to fall on the moderate side of the spectrum. Still, this transitional group also included a greater proportion of self-described fundamentalists than did either the stable rural or the stable urban populations. The group had, after all, moved from small traditional communities into modern cities, and fundamentalists tended to be those who experienced the greatest sense of cultural disruption.[22]

The rapid modernization of the South had, it seemed, produced much the same religious reaction that the North had experienced a half century earlier. The crisis that Sam Hill had predicted for Southern Baptists in the mid-1960s had come to pass.

Ammerman then went on to ask what it was about city life—or "modernity"—that created a sense of cultural dislocation among some newcomers and not among others. From interviews she determined that the division had much to do with attitudes toward cultural pluralism and toward change as a fact of life. The theological moderates tended to say they liked the diversity of the cities and thought it important that their children be exposed to a variety of educational offerings so that they could make informed choices and learn how to deal with change. The fundamentalists tended to reject diversity and the idea that their children should be educated for a changing world. But then many of the moderates had college educations, and most of the fundamentalists did not. Fundamentalists, by and large, were not the poorest or the least educated of Ammerman's respondents. Rather they tended to be people with some college education but not a degree, blue-collar workers, and those with incomes in the middle of the scale. They were, in other words, those whose exposure to diversity was high, but whose experience and resources least equipped them to deal with it. It is such people, Ammerman wrote, who "build congregational cultures in which they can be protected from the cognitive challenges of the world, adding schools, Christian media and a network of friends to their organizational armor." [23]

By 1980 the Thomas Road church was a vast and mighty institution with some sixty pastors and about a thousand trainees and volunteer helpers. It had a weekly attendance of some eight thousand people, including tourists and the three thousand Liberty Baptist College students who worked and worshipped in the church. On Sundays it held three general services and Sunday school classes for children of every age group. There was a general prayer meeting every Wednesday night, but it was a center of activity all week long. It had ministries for children, young people, adults, elderly people, and the deaf. The previous year it had added a ministry for divorced people and another for unmarried young adults. Each ministry offered programs of activities, including Bible study classes, lectures, trips, sports outings, and picnics. The ministries also organized groups of volunteers to visit hospitals, nursing homes, and prisons and to proselytize in the community. The organization was so comprehensive that Thomas Road members, old or young, could spend all of their free time in church or church-related activities, and some did just that.[24]

Eldridge Dunn, a former tool-and-die maker for General Electric, ran the Children's Ministry, the largest and busiest of the groups. The purpose of the ministry, he explained to me, was to provide a total environment for children apart from the rest of the world. "Our philosophy is that children should not have to go into the world," he said. "They should not have to get involved with drugs or Hollywood movies. But you can't just tell them not to do things. You have to give them something to do. So we try to provide them with everything that's necessary for children. We take the older kids back-packing. We're renting a skating rink this year. Our idea is to compete with the world." The philosophy, he went on to say, was not unique to Thomas Road, but shared by all churches advocating separation from the world, however extensive or limited their resources. What distinguished his church was its aggressiveness. "I'd like to build a program for every child in Lynchburg," Dunn said.[25]

For those involved in Thomas Road ministries the church had a set of detailed prescriptions for the conduct of everyday life. It had not only prohibitions against such "worldly" evils as drink, dancing, and Hollywood films, but positive prescriptions for dress, child rearing, and family relations. The Liberty Baptist College student handbook, for instance, decreed that men were to wear ties to all classes. "Hair should be cut in such a way that it does not come over the ear or collar. Beards or mustaches are not permitted. Sideburns should be no longer than the bottom of the ear." As for women, "dresses and skirts . . . shorter than two inches [below] the middle of the knee are unacceptable. Anything tight, scant, backless, and low in the neckline is unacceptable." These rules were less formally laid down for the other members of the church.

Prescriptions for the proper relations between husbands and wives, parents and children, were spelled out in *The Total Family*, a book recently written by Edward Hindson, the family guidance pastor of the church. According to Hindson:

The Bible clearly states that the wife is to submit to her husband's leadership and help him fulfill God's will for his life. . . . She is to submit to him just as she would submit to Christ as her Lord. This places the responsibility for leadership upon the husband where it belongs. In a sense submission is learning to duck, so God can hit your husband! He will never realize his responsibility to the family as long as you take it. . . .

Dad, God wants you to be the loving heartbeat of your home by building the lives of your family through teaching and discipline.[26]

In another chapter Hindson dealt with the parent-child relationship and proposed "Five Steps to Effective Discipline." He attacked Dr. Benjamin Spock, modern psychology, and modern public education on the ground that they encouraged children to challenge their parents. Parents founding their authority on the word of God should, he wrote, command absolute authority over their children. Spanking, he explained, is biblically mandated and must be employed if we are not to have another generation of irresponsible, undisciplined adults.[27]

The pastors at Thomas Road defined most relationships outside the family in terms congruent with these. In school, children should not challenge their teachers but should accept instruction and discipline. On the job, a man should work hard, show discipline, and accept the authority of his employer. He should accept the authority of the church and the civil government in the same way. "He does not have the right to break the law, no matter how just his cause may seem," Hindson wrote. In his book an organization chart depicted these relationships. From "God" at the top, two lines of authority descended, one to "local church," the other to "civil authority"; the lines then descended again and converged upon "total family"—father first, then mother, then children. The organization chart was titled "God's Chain of Command."[28]

The pastors at Thomas Road talked about creating a society apart from the world. But by the "world" they clearly meant the evils of the world as they saw them, not American life in general. In Falwell's sermons scriptural lessons on how to become a better Christian often segued into practical advice on how to gain the respect of others and achieve success.

Material wealth, Falwell once said, "is God's way of blessing those who put him first." It was not, then, really paradoxical that many of the pastors' prescriptions for life looked very much like tactics for integrating people into society rather than separating them from it. Most communities, after all, would be happy to have a clean, hardworking family man who respected authority, obeyed the law, and kept off the welfare rolls. A factory manager, a city official, or landlord would find such a man an ideal type—certainly if the alternative was a drinking, brawling country fellow with no steady job, six unruly children, and a shotgun he might consider using against a law officer. Conversely, such a fellow would get nowhere with General Electric, even if he desperately wanted to. As for the Thomas Road women, they might have invented the church, so heavily did the prohibitions fall on traditional male vices like drinking, running around, and paying no heed to the children. To tell "Dad" that he made all the decisions might be a small price to pay to get the father of your children to become a respectable middle-class citizen. On the other hand, the virtues instilled by the church seemed better suited to work in assembly line manufacturing than on software design.

For all of the emphasis the pastors gave to appearances and behavior, there was an otherworldliness about the congregation. To ask a Thomas Road member "What brought you to Lynchburg" or "How did you find this house?" was to hear "God brought me here" or "God found this house for us." Only afterward would come some mention of the family's desire for a warmer climate or the intervention of a real estate agent. I thought of it as a moon-child quality until I realized that Thomas Road people always seemed to know what God wanted—at least in retrospect. God, they would say, had answered their prayers about living in a warmer climate, but he had not given them the new house they wanted because He was teaching them a lesson they needed to learn. As for the future, they were sure that God had a plan for them, and while they sometimes couldn't say what it was, they often had "leadings," or intuitions cultivated in prayer. Falwell, for example, wrote that he decided to start the Thomas Road church because after prayer he felt "a growing conviction that God was pleased I had chosen to stay in Lynchburg."[29] For Thomas Road people nothing happened by chance or because of simple human volition. There was a purpose even behind apparent accidents, and those who prayed and studied their Bible could potentially figure it out. In a 1987 study of a northern fundamentalist church, Ammerman wrote that the church provided believers with "an orderly, well-mapped territory in the midst of an uncharted, chaotic, modern wilderness." In the outside world, she wrote, "the rules are subjective, imperfect, and always changing. Inside, God provides a plan that is clear, objective, and timeless. There are clear rules and understandable answers for all of life's questions." [30]

Certainly Thomas Road people all seemed to know what God wanted for the rest of society. As outsiders soon discovered, there was no point in talking to more than one on a topic of political or social interest because there was one right answer to every question, and any church member could give it to you as well as any of the pastors, unless they happened to lack the specific information. "I'm totally against the ERA," Nancy James told me during a visit I paid to her house. When, for the purposes of discussion, I recited some of the pro-ERA arguments, she listened seriously and apologized for being so ill-informed on the subject. I thought at the time that the arguments had made some impression on her, but later, as I was leaving, she came out after me to apologize again and to say, "I will find out more about the ERA. I know I'm against it. I'm just not sure exactly why."

For Thomas Road people, education—in the broad sense of the word—was not a moral or intellectual quest that involved struggle or uncertainty. It was simply the process of learning the right answers. The idea that individuals should collect evidence and decide for themselves was out of the question. Once Falwell told his congregation that to read anything but the Bible and certain prescribed works of interpretation was at best a waste of time. He said that he himself read all the national magazines just to keep up with what others were saying, but that there was no reason for them to do so. (Most of his church members seemed to follow this advice faithfully; their weakness, if they had one, lay in the realm of television watching.) He and his fellow pastors attacked the public schools for teaching "immorality" and "secular humanism." But what bothered pious members of his congregation was not just that the public schools taught wrong answers; it was that they did not protect children from information that might call their beliefs into question. When I asked Jackie Gould whether she would consider sending her children to something other than a Bible college, she said, "No, because our eternal destiny is all-important, so you can't take a chance. Colleges so often throw kids into confusion." The purpose of education, then, was to progress in one direction to the exclusion of all others.

The way most Lynchburg people met Thomas Road members (or realized they had met them) was through the members' proselytizing efforts. A number of Lynchburg churches engaged in door-to-door evangelism, but Thomas Road was by far the most aggressive of them. Every week pastors organized groups to witness at hospitals, nursing homes, and neighborhoods across the city. In addition many church members spent a good deal of their time proselytizing at checkout counters, baseball games, and restaurants—some requiring only the briefest of conversational openings before asking whether or not their interlocutor had been "saved." Such aggressive evangelism may have annoyed some people, for the pastors often lectured their flock about how to deal with negative reactions. At a briefing session before an organized evangelistic mission one young pastor told his recruits they should prepare for those who would say they hated Jerry Falwell and the church. "But they don't know Jerry Falwell," he explained. "And you can't hate someone you don't know. These people don't hate Falwell, and they don't hate you personally. They hate the Lord Jesus Christ."

Falwell himself often maintained that believers would face nothing but hostility from the rest of the world. "Learn to pay the price. If you are going to be a champion for Christ, learn to endure hardness. . . . You won't always have the applause of men." On another occasion he warned, "You will have Satan as your archenemy. The moment you entered the family of God, Satan declared war on you. The Christian life is to be a competitive, combative life." He frequently made allusions to sports in his sermons, but it was military analogy that was central to his view of the church and its role in the world. "The local church is an organized army equipped for battle, ready to charge the enemy," he said. "The Sunday school is the attacking squad." And elsewhere, "The church should be a disciplined charging army. . . . Christians, like slaves and soldiers, ask no questions." Occasionally Falwell painted evangelism as old-fashioned territorial imperialism. Every pastor, he said in one sermon, has a divine mandate to "capture our Jerusalem for Christ," then "capture the adjacent nations, our Samarias," and, finally, "touch the uttermost part of the earth and likewise capture it for Christ." Often, however, he made a more modern analogy: America is "the only logical launching pad for world evangelization."[31]

In a sense it seemed only natural that Falwell and his people should go into politics. They had, after all, detailed and comprehensive views about the organization of society. They had absolutely no doubt that their way was the correct one, and they had set out to convert the entire world to it. Add to this a man with leadership qualities, and the missionary movement had most of the elements of a powerful political organization. The question, then, might seem to be not why Falwell went into national politics but what took him so long.

There were, of course, impediments. Falwell called himself "a separatist, premillenialist, pretribulationist sort of fellow." He believed, he said, that "this is the terminal generation before Jesus comes," and in a 1965 sermon he had argued most eloquently for the fundamentalist doctrine of the separation of the church from the world. The sermon, called "Ministers and Marchers," was, however, a frontal attack on the civil rights movements.

In the early years of his ministry Falwell was, like most fundamentalist pastors, a segregationist. In the fall of 1958 he preached a sermon ("Segregation or Integration, Which?") against the implementation of *Brown* in which he rehearsed a number of the arguments being made in southern fundamentalist circles: integration was "the work of the Devil" that would lead to the destruction of the white race; "the true Negro" did not want integration, and "We see the hand of Moscow in the background."[32] At the time Governor Lindsay Almond Jr. of Virginia was resisting a court order to integrate public schools with the help of a group known as the Defenders of State Sovereignty and Individual Liberties. The following spring Falwell signed on as chaplain of the Defenders' Lynchburg branch and spoke at one of its meetings—though the cause had been lost in January, when Almond had decided he had to comply with the court order.

Later Falwell denounced President Johnson's civil rights legislation as "a terrible violation of human and property rights" and said "it should be considered civil wrongs rather than civil rights." By the time the legislation was passed, years of sit-ins by local black ministers had brought integration to much of Lynchburg, but in July 1964 one black and three white Lynchburg teenagers associated with a civil rights organization staged a "kneel-in" at the Thomas Road church and were evicted by the police.[33]

Delivered on March 21, 1965, just after the Selma–Montgomery marches, the sermon "Ministers and Marchers" was Falwell's first bid for regional attention, and in pamphlet form it was widely distributed in fundamentalist circles. In it Falwell began by questioning "the sincerity and non-violent intentions of some civil rights leaders such as Dr. Martin Luther King Jr., Mr. James Farmer, and others, who are known to have left-wing associations." He went on to say that the Communists were exploiting the tense situation and that the demonstrations were damaging race relations. Toward the end he talked abut the involvement of church leaders with "the alleged discrimination against the Negro in the South" and asked why they did not concern themselves instead with the problem of alcoholism since "there are almost as many alcoholics as there are Negroes." Much of the rest of sermon was devoted to the doctrine of separation:

> As far as the relationship of the church to the world, it can be expressed as simply as the three words which Paul gave to Timothy—"Preach the Word." . . . Nowhere are we commissioned to reform the externals. We are not told to wage war against bootleggers, liquor stores, gamblers, murderers, prostitutes, racketeers, prejudiced persons or institutions, or any other existing evil as such. Our ministry is not reformation but transformation.
>
> While we are told to "render unto Caesar the things that are Caesar's," in the true interpretation, we have very few ties on this earth. We pay our taxes, . . . obey the laws of the land, and other things demanded of us by the society in which we live. But, at the same time, we are cognizant that our only purpose on this earth is know Christ and to make Him known. Believing the Bible as I do,

I would find it impossible to stop preaching the pure saving gospel of Jesus Christ, and begin doing anything else—including fighting Communism, or participating in civil-rights reforms.[34]

The sermon deserves some examination. For one thing Falwell confined the "the church" to a narrower sphere than the separatist Baptist gospel did. Southern fundamentalists had always engaged in "reforming the externals" within their own ministries—and Falwell was no exception. Further, all the leading Southern fundamentalist pastors from J. Frank Norris to Bob Jones and John R. Rice had denounced the moral ills of society and the menace of Communism in the course of jeremiads about the need for revival, or in warnings that the Second Coming was nigh. Until the 1960s most had drawn the line on criticism of the social and economic arrangements in the South—or precisely where southern evangelicals had drawn it before the Civil War.

However, with the inception of the civil rights movement, they began to preach on domestic political issues, such as desegregation and the federal government's intrusions on states' rights—their change of position being simply a move from support of the racial status quo to opposition. Falwell numbered among them, and in "Ministers and Marchers" he was inveighing against the civil rights movement and Communism—even while maintaining that his gospel didn't permit it.

Falwell gradually reconciled himself to desegregation. He founded the Lynchburg Christian Academy in 1967 as a whites-only school, but a year later it accepted three African American students, and one black family joined the church. Around 1970, when he began to develop a national audience, he recalled the copies of his previous sermons defending segregation so they could not be used against him. "Ministers and Marchers," however, had been so widely distributed that copies were generally available.[35]

By 1980 Falwell moved 180 degrees from his former doctrinal position on the separation of the church from politics. He had vowed to undertake civil disobedience if the Equal Rights Amendment was passed and Congress voted to draft women into the armed forces. When asked about

"Ministers and Marchers" at a press conference in early October, Falwell called the sermon "false prophecy" and asserted that he and his fellow ministers were doing exactly what King and his fellows had done. He and other fundamentalist pastors described their move into politics—and their abandonment of separation—as a response to the national crisis of the late 1970s. Yet clearly the emergence of the civil rights movement had been a turning point. It had shown them that preachers could be politically effective, and it had ended their support of the status quo. Ironically it had benefited white fundamentalists as much as it had benefited blacks in the South. It had given them their voice back on domestic issues, permitting them to speak out against the laws of the land. It had given them their civil rights at no cost to themselves. Further, the success of the movement had removed the obstacle that would have prevented Falwell and other fundamentalist leaders from assuming a role in national politics.

Still, the separation of the church from "the world" was as much a matter of practice as it was of doctrine. It had to do with the dress Thomas Road people wore, the prohibitions they observed, even their manner of speaking. Most Thomas Road people had to spend their workaday week in "the world," but otherwise they kept themselves apart from the life of the city, taking no part in civic organizations or local politics. Lynchburg was otherwise a close-knit community where businessmen, college professors, and ministers—black and white—knew each other and generally cooperated for the common good, but Thomas Road people, feeling secure only under the canopy of their church, tended to regard the rest of the community as no more than a mission field. Falwell for his part actively encouraged the tension between his congregation and the rest of the city, whether in describing the dangers Christians faced when evangelizing or discovering enemies for the church in a local reporter or "the people in City Hall." All the same, he never called for any action against these "enemies" or tried to make the town conform to his own moral standards. He never, for example, campaigned against such local businesses as the discotheques or the theaters that showed Hollywood films or the Lynchburg plant of Meredith/Burda, which for some years printed *Penthouse* magazine. Personally he maintained cordial relations with the local business leaders and city officials, yet civic leaders spoke of his church as if it were a foreign country in the midst of their town. "It's *in* Lynchburg, but not *of* it," one remarked to me.

Wisely, Falwell kept out of Lynchburg politics all his life—thus never fouling his nest—but otherwise he moved to bring "the church" into "the world." The process was a gradual, and to some extent a matter of circumstance.[36]

In the 1960s most of Falwell's energies went into building the Thomas Road church, but he had always wanted to make his mark beyond Lynchburg, and in the early 1970s his electronic ministry—once just a means of bringing people into his church—took on a life of its own. Through radio and television he could preach to more souls than Lynchburg possessed. Buying TV airtime was expensive, but Falwell, and some of the other televangelists, developed sophisticated fund-raising techniques and employed a company to help to him. Using computerized direct mail, he made a variety of appeals, some for mission work, some to build his newly conceived college to train "young Timothys," and some to keep *The Old-Time Gospel Hour* on the air. The appeals were always changing. Those who ran his finances were, however, less than expert, and in the early 1970s he had a run-in with the Securities and Exchange Commission over a faulty bond prospectus. This was his luck, for after his ministry was put into the nonprofit equivalent of receivership, five top Lynchburg businessmen put his affairs in order and the *OTGH* revenues skyrocketed, going from $7 million to $22 million in four years. By 1979 Falwell had two million people on his computerized mailing lists and $35 million in receipts. Yet, notably, most of the funds—five cents for every seven he raised—went into maintaining and expanding the reach of *The Old-Time Gospel Hour.*[37]

To find backers and to promote the show Falwell traveled the country every week in a succession of ever-larger and ever-faster church-owned airplanes, speaking at churches, Bible schools, pastors' conferences, and revivals.[38] His stable of writers turned out sermons, pamphlets, books, and magazines. Pastors were important to his enterprise, and along the way he met hundreds of them, many from the fundamentalist Baptist networks, such as the Baptist Bible Fellowship and those of Bob Jones Jr. and John R. Rice.[39] In the early 1970s he and his associate Elmer Towns wrote sermons and two books on church growth for them. In the sermons, he urged them to stop fighting over minute ecclesiastical or doctrinal differences and to unite for the sake of evangelism.[40] This was in his interests as a TV evangelist, and according to former associates he eventually discovered that he could reach a far wider audience by talking about "family" issues than by talking theology. In any case, around the mid-1970s the emphasis of his preaching changed.[41]

In the first seven months of 1975 Falwell led a road show with the Liberty Baptist College chorale raising money from *OTGH* audiences at banquets and rallies to fill a shortfall of $3 million. The following year, that of the nation's Bicentennial, he led a much more extensive tour with busloads of LBC singers, this one dubbed "I Love America." At rallies with American flags flying behind them, his students sang religious and patriotic songs, and he delivered a rousing stump sermon calling upon America to return to God.[42]

Falwell's timing was serendipitous, for 1976 was also a presidential election year, and evangelicals were constantly in the news. The Democratic presidential nominee, Jimmy Carter, was a devout Southern Baptist, a deacon of his church, and a Sunday school teacher, who spoke frankly about his "born-again" experience. President Gerald Ford, an Episcopalian, described himself as a born-again, and in competition with Carter for the South, he became the first sitting president to address the SBC convention. Charles Colson, one of the Watergate conspirators, emerged from prison with a best-selling memoir, *Born Again*. CBS did a prime-time documentary of the same title, and all the leading national magazines ran feature stories on evangelicals. A Gallup poll queried Americans about their faith and found that over a third described themselves as "born-again" Christians. An additional third—which translated into fifty million adult Americans—agreed that "the Bible is the actual word of God to be taken literally, word for word." Citing the poll, a *Newsweek* cover story of October 25 called "the emergence of evangelical Christianity into a position of respect and power" the "most significant—and overlooked—religious phenomenon of the '70s." The publicity gave fundamentalists, Pentecostals, Southern Baptists, and other evangelicals a sense of their collective importance, and many leaders, including Falwell, cited the Gallup poll as evidence that evangelicals had become the largest religious group in the country.

Amid all of this excitement Falwell's "I Love America" tour attracted enormous crowds. On platforms festooned with red, white, and blue bunting he spoke of America's religious origins and the country's declension into unbelief and sin. "This is a Christian nation," he proclaimed. "What has gone wrong? What happened to this great republic? We have forsaken the God of our fathers. The prophet Isaiah said that our sins separate us from God. The Bible is replete with stories of nations that forgot God and paid the eternal consequences." According to Gerald Strober and Ruth Tomczak, his account of the parlous state of nation included mention of "trends in the public schools, the entertainment world and the media" and in addition to "America's economic, political, military, energy and religious problems." He ended with a stirring appeal. "Will you be one of a consecrated few who will bear the burden for revival and pray, 'O, God, save our nation. O, God give us a revival. O, God, speak to our leaders'? The destiny of our nation awaits your answer." [43]

Clearly Falwell was edging into politics via a jeremiad about the need for a religious revival. In one of his crusade sermons he preached, "The idea of 'religion and politics don't mix' was invented by the devil to keep Christians from running their own country." [44] Still, he had yet to take up the main issues that propelled conservative Christians into politics four years later.

10

JERRY FALWELL *and the*
MORAL MAJORITY

I N JUNE 1979 Jerry Falwell launched the Moral Majority, an organization designed to register conservative Christians and mobilize them into a political force against what he called "secular humanism" and the moral decay of the country. "We are fighting a holy war," he said, "and this time we are going to win."

Earlier that year two Southern California pastors, Robert Grant and Richard Zone, formed the Christian Voice to combat the gay rights movement, abortion, and the ERA, as well as the SALT II nuclear arms treaty and the trade embargo on white Rhodesia. The organization issued "moral report cards" for members of Congress and sent out mailings to thousands of evangelical ministers and hundreds of Catholic priests.

In June fundamentalist Southern Baptists secured the election of their champion, Adrian Rogers, and the following year the Convention under their leadership passed resolutions denouncing pornography and homosexuality, rejecting the Equal Rights Amendment, and calling for a reversal of the Supreme Court decision *Roe v. Wade*.

On April 29, 1980, Pat Robertson of the Christian Broadcasting Network and Bill Bright of Campus Crusade for Christ cochaired a Washington for Jesus rally, assembling somewhere between a quarter- and a half-million conservative Christians, many of them Pentescostals and charismatics, on the Washington Mall. A number of the speakers predicted that abortion, homosexuality, and the banning of school prayer would bring God's wrath upon the country. "Unless we repent and turn from our sin," Bright thundered, "we can expect to be destroyed." According to some, the weakening of America's moral fiber and of its military defense was inviting a Soviet attack. "The scream of the great American eagle has turned into the twitter of a frightened sparrow," Adrian Rogers declared. Later the organizers divided the marchers by congressional districts and encouraged them to participate in politics.[1]

The emergence of the Christian right shocked most political observers. Dominant theories of modern politics predicted the decline of religion in public life. The amorphous civil religion of patriotism preached by Eisenhower, and on occasion by Billy Graham, had apparently died in the tumult over the Vietnam War. By 1980 most pundits and pollsters had come to assume that religion was a private matter and politics a secular sphere. After all, John F. Kennedy, and most recently Jimmy Carter, a devout Southern Baptist, had drawn bright lines between their religious beliefs and their public commitments. That the civil rights movement had begun in the churches had been forgotten, or bracketed, as the phenomenon of black Americans using the only networks they had to gain their rights. Also forgotten was that in the past three decades white evangelicals, from Billy James Hargis to Billy Graham, had spoken out on political issues and backed candidates. Still, the Christian right was in many ways different. White evangelical ministers from previously incompatible traditions were attempting to build lay support for political activism across a wide range of issues and calling for a holy war against secularists and liberals. Some were claiming that evangelicals constituted a voting bloc— even something like a party. "Our goal is to influence all viable [presidential] candidates on issues important to the church. We want answers. We want appointments to government," Jim Bakker told a reporter in November 1979. "We have together, with the Protestants and Catholics, enough votes to run the country," Pat Robertson said.[2] Others, such as Adrian Rogers and Bill Bright, claimed they had no political agenda—that they were merely speaking to the moral crisis in the land. Still, all had much the same message, and one that clearly favored Ronald Reagan and other conservative candidates.

The eruption of the Christian right was sudden. Just three years before there had hardly been a hint of it. Most of the issues were new, and preachers taking the lead were not the familiar faces—Billy Graham, Oral Roberts, Carl McIntire—but men largely unknown to the national press. Many, it turned out, had churches with congregations in the thousands. A number, including Pat Robertson, Jim Bakker, and Jerry Falwell, had radio and television programs broadcast across the country, though not on the major networks but on their affiliates, local cable channels, and Christian stations. In effect, they had been hidden in plain sight. Yet in 1980 they seemed to be everywhere, putting on huge conferences and mass rallies, and giving interviews on secular TV shows.

Journalists scrambling to find out where these preachers came from found themselves in a theological puzzle palace. Some, like Falwell, were separatist Baptists—self-described fundamentalists who had always refused to cooperate with others. Some belonged to the Southern Baptist Convention, a denomination whose leaders since the days of J. Frank Norris had regarded the separatists as schismatic ruffians. A few, like D. James Kennedy, a megachurch pastor in Coral Gables, Florida, were right-wing Calvinist Presbyterians. A number, such as Jimmy Swaggart, were Pentecostals, and Pentecostals, traditionally the least political of all evangelicals, were still regarded by most conservative Presbyterians and Baptists as Holy Rollers. There were also figures who didn't fit any of the old categories. Pat Robertson, for example, was a Southern Baptist, but also a charismatic. For journalists and other political observers the confusion was such that they failed to note that most of the preachers—with the exception of Jim Bakker—who inaugurated the Christian Right had certain important things in common. Born in the late 1920s or in the 1930s, they were a generation younger than Graham, Roberts, and McIntire. They preached an inerrant Bible and a literal creation. All were premillenialists. And all of them came from the Sunbelt states of the South and Southwest.

Initially Pat Robertson took the lead. The son of a U.S. senator from Virginia, he had built his own television network in Virginia Beach and appeared on a weekly talk show, *The 700 Club*. In the fall of 1979 he had brought a stream if politicians onto his show and endorsed candidates. After the Washington rally, however, he retreated from the political arena for the rest of the campaign. The other Pentecostals and charismatics also retreated—Jim Bakker never to return—having apparently decided that the risks of partisan political involvement were too great for their TV ministries.

Falwell, on the other hand, persisted. Energetic, he traveled over 300,000 miles that year, holding rallies, recruiting pastors, and giving sermons denouncing abortion, the ERA, homosexuality, drugs, pornography, and "secular humanism." By the fall of 1980 he claimed that the Moral Majority had chapters in forty-seven states and had registered four million voters. Republican politicians courted him, as did TV talk show hosts, who found him genial and pithy of phrase. By then he had become the leading spokesman for the new Christian right and the provocative name of his organization, the Moral Majority, a synecdoche for the movement as a whole.[3]

The new Christian right had no single leader. What was remarkable about it was how it sprang up all at once among networks of pastors across the South from Virginia to Southern California. Still, Falwell had a major role in developing the rhetoric that would take the disparate groups beyond their ecclesiastical differences and weld them into a coherent social and political movement. He also stood as a fair enough representative of the preachers who started the movement. His theology was much the same as that of the Southern Baptist insurgents, and he had close relations with a number of them.[4] He was also well acquainted with many of the other leading figures in the movement, among them the New Right political organizers who put it together. In the 1970s he went through the process that turned right-wing southern evangelical leaders into culture warriors on a national scale. His career, in other words, tracked the development of the Christian right as well as the upsurge of fundamentalism in the Sunbelt that preceded it.

One of the reasons the rise of the Christian right seemed so sudden was that the protests against the cultural revolution of the Long Sixties originated not with those who became its leaders but with Catholics and with conservative Protestants at the grassroots level, some influenced by the old right.

By 1979 protests against the progressive innovations in public school education had been going on for years, particularly in Southern California, where the John Birch Society flourished, and by the early 1960s were encouraging resistance to what was seen as the inculcation of morally relativist values by liberal educators.* Some of these protests had made national news. In 1968 a Catholic housewife, backed by conservative political activists, led a successful two-year-long struggle against sex education in the high schools of Anaheim, California.[5] Other protests involved the introduction of a new generation of textbooks written for a multicultural society and designed to teach critical thinking and modern science. By far the most spectacular of these textbook conflicts took place in Kanawha County, West Virginia, a county that encompassed the city of Charleston and its rural hinterlands. In 1974 fundamentalist pastors and parents protested the introduction of language arts texts they said were un-Christian, unpatriotic, destructive of the family, and an incitement to racial violence. There were demonstrations and a wildcat strike by sympathetic miners. The conflict went on for months; outsiders, including members of the John Birch Society and lawyers from the conservative Heritage Foundation, turned up. Eventually the protests degenerated into vandalism, shootings, arson, and bombings. A committee of the National Education Association investigated the struggle and concluded that the trouble resulted in part from the cultural gap between the school board and the isolated mountain communities within its jurisdiction. The cultural gap, however, turned out to be just as great in affluent suburbs, like Anaheim, where fundamentalists and Pentecostal churches had taken root. In the mid-1970s "concerned citizens" in many parts of the country—including the Northeast and the Midwest—attempted to purge their schools of similar books, protested against sex education, lobbied for the teaching of creationism, and called for a return to old pedagogy of rote work.[6]

As for the Equal Rights Amendment, opposition to it was galvanized by Phyllis Schlafly, a Catholic and a political activist. In 1972, just after the amendment passed Congress, Schlafly had undertaken what seemed to be the hopeless cause of preventing its ratification. The proposed constitutional amendment read simply, "Equality of rights under the law shall

---

* Robert Welch, the founder of the John Birch Society, named the society for J. Frank Norris's convert, John Birch, a missionary and a military intelligence officer who was killed by the Communists in China in 1945.

not be denied or abridged by the United States or by any State on account of sex." It was generally seen as an anodyne measure that would help women overcome discrimination in the job market, and polls showed that two thirds of the public favored it. Both houses of Congress passed it by huge margins, and with the National Organization for Women and other powerful feminist groups lobbying for it, state legislatures hastened to approve it. By the end of 1973 thirty out of the required thirty-eight states had voted to ratify it, and six years remained to obtain the consent of the rest. At the time Schlafly had been one of the few people organizing against it. Working alone out of her house in Alton, Illinois, she founded STOP ERA, a women's organization, and sent out newsletters, arguing that the amendment threatened the traditional family and all the laws protecting women. In a few years STOP ERA had thousands of members, and though most had no previous political experience, it became a sophisticated lobbying group that changed the minds of many state legislators, and, more important, mobilized other women's groups.[7]

Why Schlafly had turned against the ERA was a question that puzzled many feminists and some of her own friends. She had a husband and six children, but as feminists pointed out, she was hardly the traditional housewife. She had taken an MA in government from Radcliffe College at the age of twenty. A few years later she had managed a congressional campaign for a Republican candidate and in 1952 had run for Congress herself on the slogan "A Woman's Place Is in the House."[8] She lost the race, but from then on had played an active role in the conservative wing of the Republican Party, becoming a leader in the National Federation of Republican Women and serving as an Illinois delegate to most of the subsequent Republican conventions. In 1964 she wrote, and privately published, a short book promoting Goldwater's candidacy that caused a sensation at the Republican convention that year. In *A Choice Not an Echo*, she argued that from 1936 to 1960 Republican presidential nominees had been chosen by "a small group of secret kingmakers, using hidden persuaders and psychological warfare techniques." These kingmakers, she maintained, were members of the eastern internationalist establishment who favored the New Deal and Franklin Roosevelt's interventionist policy in Europe. In 1952 they had used a new propaganda weapon, the Gallup poll, to steal the nomination from Robert Taft. They were currently scheming to take the nomination away from Barry Goldwater, though he was certain to win against Lyndon Johnson.

After Goldwater's defeat, Schlafly wrote five books on strategic defense policy with a retired rear admiral, Chester Ward. All of these books, published between 1964 and 1976, made the same argument: certain powerful government officials, principally Paul Nitze, Robert McNamara, and Henry Kissinger, were plotting the unilateral nuclear disarmament of the United States. These "gravediggers," as Schlafly and Ward called them, were Communist dupes intent on the establishment of a world order. Concealing their real intentions, they met at the Council on Foreign Relations and communicated with each other by code in *Foreign Affairs* magazine. The plot might have been invented by Robert Welch, the founder of the John Birch Society, and a supporter of Schlafly's.[9]

In the midst of these efforts to explain why the United States lacked the capability to win a nuclear war, Schlafly ran for Congress again and published a monthly newsletter championing laissez-faire economics and states' rights as well nuclear armament. The ERA was thus a departure from her usual concerns. When a friend asked her to speak about it in early 1972, she replied, "I'm not interested. How about a debate on defense?" At the time she thought the amendment "innocuous and mildly helpful" but after reading the conservative analysis of it, she changed her mind: the ERA was yet another liberal attempt to turn the federal government into a dictatorship. It was also a new issue when anti-Communism no longer had the drawing power it once did. Setting to work, she developed a series of arguments against it. The amendment was unnecessary because the Fourteenth Amendment gave equal protection to "all persons" (even though it denied women the vote). It would entail a vast and expensive increase in the federal bureaucracy and do incalculable harm to the rights of women. The ERA, as she depicted it, would dissolve men's obligations to support their wives and children, force women into the workplace, and relegate their children to day care centers. It would also lead to unisex toilets, the legalization of homosexual marriages, and women on the front lines of battle with men.[10]

The arguments attracted the attention of religious conservatives. Her organization, and the movement as a whole, grew mightily in the South, Southwest, and Midwest, in particular among Mormons and evangelicals. In Texas, Lottie Beth Hobbs, a Church of Christ Bible school teacher and a writer of devotion books, organized a rally of twenty-five hundred women, many of them fundamentalists, at the state capitol and went on to travel the country mobilizing women for her cause.[11] By 1976 the ratification process had stalled, and though the deadline was extended until 1982, the ERA never gained the approval of the necessary thirty-eight states.

The battle against the ERA led to a broader offensive against the feminist movement. In the mid-1970s evangelical women published a spate of books arguing that women were by nature different from men and could achieve fulfillment and true femininity only by surrendering their lives to their husbands. (One of them, *The Total Woman*, made the *New York Times* best-seller list.) In 1975 Schlafly transformed STOP ERA into the Eagle Forum, a group she described as an alternative to "women's lib," and, while still working on nuclear issues wrote an antifeminist book of her own, *The Power of the Positive Woman*. Two years later, when the National Women's Conference gathered in Houston as a part of the International Year of the Woman, she and her evangelical allies held a counter-convention of fifteen thousand people across town, dubbed the National Pro-Family Rally. The gathering caught Falwell's attention, and he attacked the National Women's Conference, calling the ERA "a delusion" and the feminist movement "full of women who live in disobedience to God."[12]

By the 1976 election Catholic right-to-life organizations had made *Roe v. Wade* a major political issue. Both Jimmy Carter and Gerald Ford wanted to keep abortion out of the campaign, as did many other politicians. Carter personally disapproved of abortion, and Ford, when forced to speak about it, took a middle ground of opposing "abortion on demand" but not abortion in the case of rape or harm to a woman's health. Yet such was the pressure that both presidential campaigns had to decide between accepting *Roe v. Wade* or calling for a constitutional amendment to override it. Carter tried to straddle the issue, but in the end he took a pro-choice position, and the Democratic platform, while not directly endorsing abortion rights, opposed amending the Constitution to over-turn *Roe*. The Republican convention convened a few weeks later. Ronald Reagan, who had changed his position and become an opponent of all abortions, was battling Ford for the nomination. Senator Bob Dole (R-KS), Ford's running mate, who had some experience with the issue, persuaded party regulars that Ford had an opportunity to woo Catholics and other social conservatives by opposing *Roe v. Wade*. The Republican platform therefore read: "The Republican Party favors a continuance of the public dialogue on abortion and supports the efforts of those who seek enact-ment of a constitutional amendment to restore the protection of life to unborn children." [13] Thus despite the wishes of many of the politicians in both parties, and the desire of many for a compromise, abortion became politicized: the Democrats would support *Roe*, and the Republicans would oppose it from then on.

Evangelical leaders played virtually no role in this contest. Pat Rob-ertson, for one, called abortion "a strictly theological matter" in 1975. [14] Evangelical right-to-life groups were few and far between, for like Carter and Ford, most evangelicals continued to favor "therapeutic abortions," but not "abortion on demand." Fundamentalist ministers, for whom ev-erything was either right or wrong, never took this middle ground. They had always opposed abortion. On the other hand, they had always seen it in the context of what for them was the larger issue of the natural, God-ordained roles of men and women. By permitting women to control their fertility, abortion threatened the sexual order, traditional morality, and the law of God. John R. Rice, for example, had condemned abortion along with birth control in his 1945 manual on the Christian family, and in a 1971 sermon he connected it with "new morality," and the "license" of "left-wingers" and "civil rights law breakers." [15] As a discrete issue, however, he gave it small attention, and Falwell did no more, even years after *Roe*.

In his 1987 autobiography Falwell claimed that he had preached ser-mons against abortion long before *Roe v. Wade*, and that when "that terri-ble decision" came down, he realized it "meant that something far more drastic had to be done." He began, he wrote, to preach regularly against abortion, comparing it to "Hitler's final solution for the Jews." *Roe*, he con-tinued, led him to realize the seriousness of the other threats to the American family and moved him to get involved in the political process against all of his fundamentalist scruples. However, he wrote his autobiography when abortion had become a major issue for the Christian right.[16] According to his associate Elmer Towns, he wrote his first full-length sermon on abortion in 1978 at Towns's behest.[17] In 1980, when journalists asked him what made him change his mind about preachers in politics, he usually responded with a list of four or five events such as the Supreme Court's school prayer decision and the "pornography explosion," and the list was always changing. In June he said that the 1973 abortion decision had been a turning point for him, but the following January he said that evangelicals (among whom he included himself) had not paid much attention to the issue until three to five years ago—that is, until 1976 or 1978.[18] To the extent that he later engaged in historical revisionism, he was not alone.

Christian right leaders also came belatedly to the issue of gay rights— in part because most found it unimaginable. In the 1960s a gay liberation movement emerged out of the same atmosphere that produced the counterculture, the New Left, and the women's liberation movement. On university campuses gay students defied all conventions by coming out as homosexuals and putting on gay pride events. By the early 1970s this consciousness-raising movement evolved, as the feminist movement had, into a formal civil rights movement lobbying for antidiscrimination measures. Within a few years thirty cities around the country, including Los Angeles and Seattle, had passed ordinances overturning, or forbidding, discriminatory practices. Religious conservatives mounted a few local protests, and in 1976 the SBC passed its first resolution against homosexuality, but it was only when Anita Bryant publicized the issue that evangelicals woke up to the astonishing change in attitudes.[19]

A popular gospel singer, a conservative Southern Baptist, and mother of four, Bryant could hardly believe it when in 1977 her hometown of Miami, Florida, adopted an ordinance that forbid schools, public and private, from discriminating against homosexuals in hiring. Though a political innocent, she began a campaign to rescind the law by a popular referendum. Well known in Florida as singer and a spokesperson for the Florida Citrus Association, she managed within a month to obtain sixty thousand signatures to put her measure on the ballot. Encouraged, she mounted an organization, Save Our Children, and toured the South raising money from evangelical church groups and conservative political PACs. Calling on the televangelists, she appeared on Pat Robertson's *700 Club,* Jim and Tammy Bakker's *PTL Club,* and *The Old-Time Gospel Hour.* Within a few months she made her fight a cause célèbre and turned Save Our Children into an organization that lobbied against gay rights in other states. In November, she collected a hundred influential pastors and put on a rally that brought a crowd of ten thousand to the Miami Convention Center. The gathering made national news, and two weeks later Dade County residents approved her referendum by a margin of two to one.[20]

Bryant's campaign mobilized southern evangelicals and gave rise to anti–gay rights initiatives elsewhere in the country. Falwell took a lead role. He spoke at the Miami rally for Bryant's measure and later backed a statewide referendum put on the 1978 California ballot by a state legislator from Orange County, John Briggs. Known as the Briggs Initiative, Proposition 6 asked voters to give school districts the authority to fire gay teachers, or any teacher who "promoted homosexuality as a lifestyle." Many California politicians, including Ronald Reagan, called it a violation of privacy rights and possibly unconstitutional, but anti–gay rights groups, many of them evangelical, sprang up in Southern California.[21] Falwell spoke at a mass rallies in San Diego and Orange County and sent out letters to hundreds of California pastors. The measure went down to defeat, even in Orange County, but Falwell forged on with the issue. In December, after the mayor of San Francisco, George Moscone, and an openly gay city supervisor, Harvey Milk, were shot and killed by a former supervisor, Falwell preached a televised sermon on homosexuality, declaring that the wrath of God had fallen on San Francisco because of the "sexual mutiny" in the city. That same year he started a "Clean Up America" campaign, sending out fund-raising letters with ballot questions, among them, "Do you approve of known practicing homosexuals teaching in the public schools?" In addition he published a booklet, *How Can You Help Clean Up America?* in which he encouraged readers to boycott local stores that sold pornography and to put anti–gay rights initiatives on local ballots—actions that he himself never took in Lynchburg.[22]

During this period while Falwell was moving step by step into politics, he was sought out by a cadre of young Washington-based political activists who were in the process of creating a conservative movement outside the Republican Party through a network of think tanks, political action committees, and training institutes. The senior member of the group, Richard A. Viguerie—then in his early forties—was a former Goldwater Republican and a direct mail expert whose company, RAVCO, had raised money for George Wallace and many other conservative candidates. Paul Weyrich, ten years younger, had worked as an aide to Senator Gordon Allott of Colorado and in the early 1970s had found backing from the beer magnate Joseph Coors to establish the Heritage Foundation and his own PAC, the Committee for the Survival of a Free Congress. He described himself—accurately—as a "political mechanic," but he was also the visionary of the group. Howard Phillips, also in his early thirties, had come up through the ranks of the Massachusetts Republican Party; he had been hired by the Nixon administration to dismantle the Office of Economic Opportunity, and when the project had to be abandoned, he quit and in 1974 formed a PAC, the Conservative Caucus. The group also included John "Terry" Dolan, a lawyer in his twenties, who founded the National Conservative Political Action Committee, which specialized in negative campaigning, and Morton Blackwell, who had worked at RAVCO and formed the Leadership Institute to train young conservatives to work political campaigns. The group, which called itself the New Right, combined Goldwater's aggressive defense policies and laissez-faire economics with Wallace's blue-collar social conservatism. All opposed abortion, and Weyrich, a Catholic so conservative he joined an Eastern Rite church after Vatican II, saw the issue of abortion as "the Achilles heel of liberal Democrats." By the mid-1970s Viguerie, Weyrich, and Phillips had recognized the potential of the cultural issues to bring evangelicals into their movement. "The next real major area of growth for the conservative ideology and philosophy is among evangelical people," Viguerie told *Sojournors* magazine in 1976. The problem was to find leaders who would bring conservative evangelicals to the polls.[23]

Weyrich and Viguerie, both Catholics, and Phillips, who was Jewish, found their way to Falwell and other southern evangelical preachers through Edward McAteer and Robert Billings. A former sales manger for

Colgate-Palmolive and a Southern Baptist with contacts in many evangelical groups, McAteer had come to Washington in 1974 with the Christian Freedom Foundation and was lured by Phillips to work as the field director for the Conservative Caucus. Billings, a former high school principal and an organizer of the Christian day school movement, ran for Congress in 1976 with Weyrich's encouragement. By one account the group met with Falwell in 1976 and proposed that he create an organization to mobilize evangelicals as voters, but he declined. Two years later they had something that interested him.[24]

In the 1960s conservative pastors, such as Falwell, had begun to build church-run day schools for the children of their parishioners. These private schools, most of them in the South, were known as "segregation academies." Many had been founded in response to the court-ordered integration of the public schools, but they were never simply refuges from racial integration. Certainly by the 1970s when they were multiplying at a rate of one or more a day, the motive for building them was generally to provide the children of conservative Protestants with religious training and to protect them from the contagions of "secular humanism" and the sinful new youth culture. In 1978 the IRS announced plans to revoke the tax exemption of private schools that did not meet certain standards of racial integration, and these schools were white, or predominantly white, because their churches were. The proposed ruling was based on a 1972 district court decision, but Jimmy Carter, who had established the federal Department of Education, was held responsible. Weyrich, seeing an opportunity to mobilize pastors, helped Billings form Christian School Action to organize a response to the ruling, and Billings recruited Falwell to the cause.[25]

The proposed IRS action, once publicized, caused an uproar among advocates of Christian schools. Falwell stumped on the issue. Bakker and Robertson invited school activists onto their television shows. James Dobson, an evangelical psychologist, then becoming known for his books and radio programs on traditional methods of child rearing, used his newsletter and radio show to warn of the threat to Christian schools. Within weeks the IRS, members of Congress, and the Carter White House received hundreds of thousands of letters of protest; a hearing was held, and the IRS and its congressional oversight committee rescinded the proposed ruling. According to several of those involved, the controversy played a pivotal role in the formation of the Christian right. "The IRS ignited the dynamite that had been lying around for years," Billings reported. Later Weyrich told an interviewer, "What galvanized the Christian community was not abortion, school prayer, or the ERA. I am living witness to that because I was trying to get those people interested in those issues and I utterly failed. What changed their mind was Jimmy Carter's intervention against the Christian schools, trying to deny them tax-exempt status on the basis of so-called de facto segregation." Christians, he explained, thought they could insulate themselves and their families in their communities and schools, but the IRS ruling was a direct threat to their interests and it could not be ignored.[26]

In 1979 Falwell resumed his "I Love America" rallies, this time frequently on the steps of state capitols. In each state he would invite local politicians to join him in speaking before an audience of pastors and their congregations. Politicians, such as Senator Paul Laxalt of Nevada, Governor John Dalton of Virginia, and Senator Jesse Helms of North Carolina, would talk about school prayer or national defense and affirm what a great American Jerry Falwell was, and Falwell would reciprocate by affirming the politician's morality. On April 30 of that year he sent out a fund-raising letter beginning, "My heart is burning within in me today. It is about time that Christians here in America stand up and be counted for Jesus Christ. We are 'the moral majority,' and we have been silent for long enough." He asked his contributors to answer three questions: "Do you approve of pornographic and obscene classroom textbooks being used under the guise of sex education? Do you approve of the present laws legalizing abortion on demand that resulted in the murder of more than one million babies last year? Do you approve of the growing trend towards sex and violence replacing family-oriented programs on television?" He promised to tabulate the results of his survey and send the answers to President Carter and to all the legislators, judges, school boards, TV networks, and major advertisers in the country. He went on to say that the campaign to clean up America would cost hundreds of thousands of dollars, but "if we do not accomplish this task, I am afraid that America will face the judgment of God." [27]

Falwell had been speaking with McAteer since January, and in May he had a nine-hour meeting with Weyrich, Phillips, McAteer, and Billings in Lynchburg. The group decided on the formation of a political organization, discussed the issues to be pursued, and talked about plans to influence the Republican platform in 1980. The Moral Majority, incorporated in June, showed the handiwork of the political operatives. It was set up in sophisticated fashion as three distinct organizations: the Moral Majority Inc., a legislative lobby; the Moral Majority Foundation, an educational group; and the Moral Majority political action committee (a legal defense fund was added later). It was formed as an ecumenical group for Catholics, Mormons, and Jews as well as Protestants. Then, as Weyrich proposed, abortion went to the head of its list of issues. Billings became the first executive director, and within a few months the organization had raised $1.5 million in start-up funds. [28]

While continuing his rallies for *The Old-Time Gospel Hour*, Falwell began urging pastors to form state chapters to elect local candidates and to take initiatives on the moral issues. The chapters would be autonomous, each raising its own funds, but the Moral Majority Inc. would provide information on the issues and basic training about the political process. Describing what pastors could do from the pulpit, he said, "You can register people to vote. You can explain the issues to them. And you can endorse candidates right there in the church on Sunday mornings." [29] (A lawyer had apparently told him that pastors as individuals could endorse candidates without endangering the tax status of the church.) In sermons he argued that the nation faced the most serious crisis in its history and that Christians had to act now to save the country. In his 1980 book, *Listen, America!*, he laid out the argument in an extended form.

At the time, journalists read *Listen, America!* for its exposition of Falwell's views on a gamut of issues, ranging from economics and national security to rock 'n' roll. He was, as might be expected, an advocate of rugged individualism and laissez-faire economics. "The free enterprise system," he wrote, "is clearly outlined in the Book of Proverbs." He opposed almost all forms of assistance to the poor, including food stamps, on the grounds that welfare programs sap the biblically mandated work ethic. (His solution to "welfarism" was to return the responsibility of care for the poor to the churches and charitable organizations.) The free enterprise system, he wrote, had been in decline since the New Deal, when federal spending for nonmilitary purposes began to rise and government bureaucracy to intrude on American freedoms. With flourishes of quotations from the economist Milton Friedman, he denounced inflation and deficit spending and concluded that the nation currently faced the worst economic crisis in its history. By his account, the national security crisis was even more serious. Like the Reagan campaign, he insisted that the Communist threat was growing and U.S. defense was on the decline. Citing various right-wing military and intelligence analysts, he charged that government officials had been unilaterally disarming the country in pursuit of the "no-win" strategy of containment. The Soviets, he wrote, had pulled ahead in offensive nuclear weaponry and possessed such effective antiballistic missiles and civil defenses that in the event of a nuclear exchange no fewer than ten Americans would perish for every Soviet life placed at risk. By 1985 the Soviet Union, he wrote, would be totally impervious to any American threat, and America faced with destruction or surrender to the Communists.[30]

Falwell then went on to write of the moral crisis in the nation and the threats to the American family. His list of national sins included sex education, "secular humanist" textbooks, the ERA, feminism, abortion, and homosexuality—as well as pornography, drugs, and TV soap operas. "We are," he wrote, "very quickly moving towards an amoral society where nothing is absolutely right or absolutely wrong." The list is of interest because it stands as a historical milestone in the evolution of conservative evangelical views about what is absolutely wrong. Divorce, for example, didn't make the list, and rock 'n' roll and women working outside the home have dropped off it since.[31]

Falwell's discussion of all these issues was, however, embedded in a larger argument, the jeremiad he had been developing since the mid-1970s about the need for Christians to take action against social ills. Made up of biblical and secular rhetoric, his larger argument deserves particular attention, for it was probably his most important contribution to the formation of the Christian right.

In his book, as in his sermons, Falwell was addressing fundamentalists and other conservative evangelicals, many of whom had been taught that they, the "saving remnant," should separate themselves from "the world" in its inevitable descent into corruption, fulfill the Great Commission to evangelize, and wait for the Rapture to come. But fundamentalists, as Marsden tells us, had another tradition, which was that they, as the "saving remnant," had the ultimate responsibility for the country and for civilization itself. In his jeremiad Falwell was calling upon this latent tradition and rhetorically turning fundamentalists from outsiders into the very people who would save the nation in its time of need.

The classic jeremiad is this: The people have fallen into evil ways and committed sins that jeopardize their covenant with God and risk His judgment upon them. But His wrath may be stayed if there is a spiritual revival and the people repent and return to God. When Jonathan Edwards and subsequent revivalists used the form, they were speaking to the people in front of them about their individual sins. Falwell, however, adopted the Old Testament version in which whole nations sin and are judged by God. In *Listen, America!* he maintained that Rome fell when it descended into corruption and warned that this country was on a similar path to destruction. America, he preached, was a Christian nation, settled by people seeking religious freedom and founded by "deeply religious men" who had fought heroically to free the country and establish a nation "under God." But Americans had turned away from their heritage of freedom and the faith of their fathers, and sin permeated the land. The decline began long ago (the 1930s was the period Falwell looked back to with nostalgia) but the real plunge came in the 1960s and '70s. America now faced the most serious crisis in its history, and Christians must act or lose their freedom.

When I first read *Listen, America!* I thought it merely an indication of Falwell's priorities that he put the manly issues of economics and national security before such domestic concerns as sex and schooling. I later realized that Falwell made a causal relationship between the two, and it was the reverse of the usual one. In the 1950s and '60s fundamentalist leaders, including Billy Graham in his early crusades, figured international Communism as the threat to American freedom and to the American family. Some—Billy James Hargis, Carl McIntire, and Falwell himself—spun elaborate conspiracy theories about Satanic Communist infiltrators in the liberal churches, the government, and the civil rights movement. But Falwell, in what might be called his Moral Majority jeremiad, turned the sequence around: the decline of American economic and military might owed to the growing moral decay and godlessness of American society ("We are economically, politically and militarily sick because our country is morally sick"). The reversal had the effect of empowering his audience. Ordinary people, after all, couldn't do much about Communist subversion, but in this sequence, they could make "personal moral decisions" that would determine the fate of the nation. Falwell's new formulation sounded more like the Edwardsian jeremiad, but it wasn't, for the sin lay not in the souls of his congregation, but in outside forces. The enemy, as before, was the Other. In this case it was "the immoral minority," composed variously of feminists, humanists, homosexuals, liberals, pornographers, Supreme Court justices, and government bureaucrats. This minority was conducting "a vicious assault on the family," and the only sin of the majority was in allowing it to continue. Christians, said Falwell, have been silent too long. We must provide America with strong moral leadership. "The choice is ours, we must turn America around or prepare for inevitable destruction."[32]

At the end of Listen, America! Falwell provided a "biblical plan of action" that included prayer, national repentance, and mobilization for political action. Interestingly, he prefaced the call for action by praising the nineteenth-century evangelical reformers William Wilberforce and the Earl of Shaftesbury in England, and Charles Finney and Lyman Beecher in the United States. In effect he appropriated prefundamentalist evangelicals as ancestors along with the Puritans. He might have taken a page out of the scholarship of the evangelical left—except that he ended the list with Billy Sunday, whom he credited with leading the nation to Prohibition. He went on to date "the turning point in Christian involvement in social action" to the repeal of Prohibition in 1933, when Christians concluded they had "no business trying to legislate Christian morality on a non-Christian society." Having thus skipped over the whole history of the

Jonathan Edwards (1703–58), the most important theologian of his period, began the revivals of the First Great Awakening. He had studied Enlightenment science and philosophy at Yale and used its methods to reform Calvinism. *Wikimedia Commons*

George Whitefield (1714–70), an Oxford graduate and itinerant English evangelist, came to America and in 1740 preached revivals all up and down the Eastern Seaboard. Endowed with a powerful, melodious voice, he drew crowds of thousands in the cities, and preaching a "new birth" in Christ, created an outburst of evangelical fervor and the first national movement in America. *© John Collet / Getty Images*

A camp meeting circa 1829. After the Revolution, a new wave of revivals, more powerful than the first, led principally by Methodists and Baptists, spread across the country to the lands beyond the original thirteen colonies. *Library of Congress, Prints and Photographs Division*

Charles Grandison Finney (1792–1875), a Presbyterian and the most influential revivalist of the Second Great Awakening, preached not only a "new birth" in Christ, but free will and the responsibility of every Christian to serve humanity and help bring in the Kingdom of God. He formed the first mass constituency for abolition. *Courtesy of the Oberlin College Archives*

Horace Bushnell (1802–76), in most ways a conservative, changed the whole epistemology for the liberal clergy. Words, he wrote, were not thoughts, but only an approximation of thoughts, and the Bible should be seen not as a series of facts and propositions but as a literary work. *Flickr*

Washington Gladden (1836–1918), the most important of the several clergymen who created the New Theology in the 1880s, took Bushnell's theory of language to understand the Bible as a historical record of God's unfolding revelations. He was also an originator of the Social Gospel. *Wikimedia Commons*

Dwight Moody (1837–99), the major revivalist for three decades after the Civil War, aimed to convert the impoverished workers and immigrants and teach them the Protestant virtues of sobriety, thrift, and industry. He preached that all suffering came from the sins of individuals and suggested that conversion itself would bring prosperity. *Library of Congress, Prints and Photographs Division*

William Bell Riley (1861–1947) started the fundamentalist conflict in the Northern Baptist Convention and built the first regional fundamentalist movement. A disciple of Dwight Moody, he preached at the First Baptist Church in Minneapolis. *Courtesy of Hennepin County Library Special Collections*

J. Frank Norris (1877–1952), in an aviator's garb standing next to John Roach Straton. Norris, the Fort Worth preacher, was responsible for bringing fundamentalism to the South. His name is associated with scurrilous attacks on fellow ministers, extremist politics, and scandals of the most lurid sort. Yet he managed the feat of importing militant antimodernism to a region without modernists. *Library of Congress, Prints and Photographs Division*

William Jennings Bryan (1860–1925), for decades the most influential layman in the Presbyterian Church. A social reformer, he worked closely with Washington Gladden until World War I, when he had a sense of crisis about the advance of secularism. To him the principal threat was Darwinism. He participated in the most famous court case of the day. *© Heritage Image Partnership Ltd/Alamy Stock Photo*

Billy Graham (1918–), the most famous and respected evangelist, began preaching just after World War II. A fundamentalist, young and awkward, he preached in a slangy vernacular, telling jokes about "kicking mules." Gradually he became more sophisticated and more moderate theologically. He attracted huge audiences to his revivals and gained the backing of powerful businessmen and politicians. In 1957 he broke with the fundamentalists and called himself an "evangelical." © AP Photo

Billy Graham taking tea with Richard Nixon, whom he supported all through the Watergate affair. © AP Photo

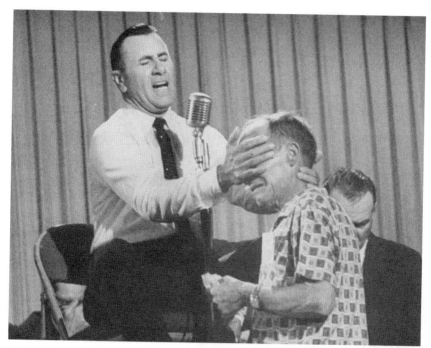

Oral Roberts (1918–2009), a Pentecostal tent revivalist and healer, became a televangelist and built a university of futuristic design with a prayer tower and thousands of students. His attempt to build a hospital ended in failure, and he was mocked for saying he would throw himself off the tower unless he could raise $8 million to complete it. He nonetheless made Pentecostalism respectable for the first time. © *Francis Miller/The LIFE Picture Collection/Getty Images*

Reinhold Niebuhr (1892–1971), the most important liberal theologian of the mid-twentieth century. He attacked the New Theology and the Social Gospel for their sentimental idealism about the perfectibility of man. © *Walter Sanders/The LIFE Picture Collection/Getty Images*

Jerry Falwell (1933–2007), a fundamentalist preacher who attended G. Beauchamp Vick's bible school, built a very large church and Liberty University. In 1980, after he had forsworn segregation, he formed the Moral Majority and led the movement that became the Christian right. Unlike the purists, he made an alliance with Ronald Reagan. © *Bettmann/Getty Images*

Phyllis Schlafly (1924–2016), a right-wing Catholic who came to prominence in the presidential campaign of Barry Goldwater. She made her name by forming anti-feminist organizations that defeated the Equal Rights Amendment. An effective speaker, she became one of the stalwarts of the Christian right. © *Everett Collection Historical/Alamy Stock Photo*

Rousas Rushdoony (1916–2001), one of the two systematic thinkers of the Christian right. A Calvinist, a right-wing Presbyterian, and a controversial figure, he formed a school of thought called Christian Reconstructionism. He envisioned a world ruled by Old Testament law. *Chalcedon Foundation*

Unlike Rousas Rushdoony, Francis Schaeffer (1912–84) was a major intellectual celebrity in the evangelical world as well as a favorite of the Christian right. Though a fundamentalist, he made his reputation by speaking in evangelical colleges about the development of Western civilization in art, architecture, and philosophy. © *Gary Gnidovic*

Pat Robertson (1930–) is a successful Christian broadcaster and a charismatic televangelist. On his show, *The 700 Club,* he has alternated between politics and charismatic practices, such as healing and prophecy. He ran for president in 1988 and afterward formed the Christian Coalition, the most successful Christian right organization in the 1990s. © *Wally McNamee/Corbis via Getty Images*

Robertson clasping hands with President George H. W. Bush during the National Day of Prayer at the White House © *AP Photo*

Ralph Reed (1961–) ran the Christian Coalition. A brilliant political organizer, he devised ways to attract and train members to work in elections and to increase the vote for social conservatives. He also integrated the ranks of the Christian right with the Republican Party. © *James M. Kelly/Globe Photos/ZUMA Press, Inc./Alamy Stock Photo*

Tammy Faye Bakker (1942–2007) and Jim Bakker (1940–) began as itinerant Pentecostal evangelists, spending four years wandering in their broken-down car from Tennessee to West Virginia. Pat Robertson hired them, and they turned out to be naturals on television. In 1974 they started their own network, PTL, where they constructed a Christian Disneyland called Heritage USA. © *Robin Nelson/ZUMA Press, Inc./Alamy Stock Photo*

James Dobson (1936–), a child psychologist, created Focus on the Family, a multimedia ministry that dispensed advice on marriage and child-rearing. His daily radio shows had an audience of five million families in the 1990s, and his books sold sixteen million copies. He formed the Family Research Council and made it the most powerful Christian right lobby in Washington. *Wikimedia Commons*

Dobson praying with his wife, Shirley, and President George W. Bush during the National Day of Prayer ceremony at the White House. © *Chip Somodevilla / Getty Images*

Tony Perkins (1963–), president of the Family Research Council, handpicked by Dobson in 1998, had been a policeman, a television journalist, and a state legislator in Louisiana. In the administration of George W. Bush he put on two televised rallies to support Christian right choices for the Supreme Court. *Wikimedia Commons*

Richard Land (1946–). A part of the "conservative resurgence," Land was appointed head of the Southern Baptist Convention's public policy arm in 1988. Going into the Iraq War, he did President Bush the service of sending out a letter saying that a preemptive strike on Iraq would meet the requirements of a "just war." *© Carol T. Powers/Bloomberg via Getty Images*

Al Mohler (1959–) is the president of the Southern Baptist Theological Seminary, the Southern Baptist Convention's flagship school, and is the denomination's leading public intellectual. A quasi-fundamentalist, he has defended young earth creationism and an inerrant Bible, and has said that Catholicism is a "false religion." He teaches the Calvinism of the seventeenth-century Reformed scholastics. *© Trevor Collens /Photoshot/ ZUMApress/Newscom*

Rick Warren (1954–), the best-known evangelical pastor in the country, whose book *The Purpose Driven Life* (2002) sold twenty million copies worldwide in two years. A second-generation Baptist pastor, he built a 25,000-member church in Saddleback Valley in Southern California. He became known as a church growth expert, but in 2005 he suddenly announced a PEACE plan to eradicate poverty, illiteracy, and disease globally. *Wikimedia Commons*

Warren greets Senator Barack Obama and Senator John McCain at the Saddleback Civil Forum on the Presidency at Saddleback Church. © *Paul Buck/epa european press-photo agency b.v./Alamy Stock Photo*

Richard Cizik (1951–), the former vice-president for governmental affairs of the National Association of Evangelicals, started the first battle between the "new evangelicals" and Christian right leaders. Today he runs the New Evangelical Partnership for the Common Good, which supports action on climate change, reconciliation with American Muslims, and gay marriage. © *Scott J. Ferrell/Congressional Quarterly/Getty Images*

Joel Hunter (1948–) a pastor in Orlando, Florida, who preaches to twenty thousand people in his church, in satellite churches, and over the Internet, is a progressive evangelical who works for social justice and action on climate change. He's opposed to the death penalty. He doesn't believe in abortion, but he's not for outlawing it. He's against gay marriage for theological reasons, but he believes that the government should treat all citizens equally. Formerly a Republican, he gave the benediction at the Democratic Convention in 2008 and became one of President Barack Obama's spiritual advisors. *Courtesy of Northland, A Church Distributed*

Bill Hybels (1951–) is the founder and pastor of the Willow Creek Community Church, in South Barrington, Illinois, for a long time one of the largest of the megachurches. In 1992 he started the Willow Creek Association, which now has twelve thousand churches. He has engaged his own congregation and many others in working for racial reconciliation and antipoverty efforts. Although he doesn't involve himself in politics, he was one of President Bill Clinton's spiritual advisors. *Willow Creek D/CH*

David Gushee (1962–) has been a Distinguished Professor of Christian Ethics at Mercer University since 2007. A prolific and often controversial writer, he coauthored the "Evangelical Declaration Against Torture" during the George W. Bush administration. *© Alice Horner*

Jim Wallis (1948–), the grand old man of evangelical progressives. Born an evangelical, he joined the Students for a Democratic Society at Michigan State University, became disillusioned, and took a degree in theology. He formed a commune known as Sojourners, and since then has worked in Washington as an advocate of peace and social justice. © *Yuri Gripas/UPI/ Newscom*

Russell D. Moore (1971–) is the successor to Richard Land as the president of the Ethics & Religious Liberty Commission of the Southern Baptist Convention. He's a theological conservative, but a political progressive when it comes to race. He was one of the first to insist that South Carolina remove the Confederate flag from the state capitol grounds after the killing of African Americans in a church in Charleston. He was also the most determined foe of Donald Trump's candidacy for president. © *Ethics & Religious Liberty Commission of the Southern Baptist Convention*

fundamentalist movement, he asked whether "we have forgotten that we are still our brothers' keepers" and proposed that the turn against social action was an abdication of Christian responsibilities.[33]

In his call to action Falwell spoke of the need for "a coalition of God-fearing moral Americans to represent our convictions to our government." This part of his program, he knew, would be meet with objections, for separatist pastors had always refused to cooperate with those of other faiths lest they compromise their own. He dealt with the potential protests directly. "As a fundamental, independent, separatist Baptist," he wrote, "I am well aware of the crucial issues of personal and ecclesiastical separation that divide fundamentalists philosophically from evangelicals and liberals. I do not believe that it is ever right to compromise the truth in order to gain an opportunity to do right." But "it will take the greatest possible number of concerned citizens to reverse the politicization of immorality in our society." Our ministry, he wrote, "is as committed as it ever has been to the basic truths of Scripture, to essential and fundamental Christian doctrines. But we are not willing to isolate ourselves in seclusion while we sit back and watch this nation plunge headlong toward hell."[34]

There was yet another objection he had to deal with. Fundamentalists traditionally interpreted national crises, such as Falwell described, as a sign that the end times had begun, the Rapture was nigh, and reformist efforts were useless. In the summer of 1980 Falwell gave a series of sermons on the end times in biblical prophecy with videos from a trip to Israel showing himself pacing out the area where the battle of Armageddon would be fought, and warning that the Tribulations might be at hand. In one of these sermons he preached, "I believe that between now and the rapture of the Church, America can have a reprieve. God can bless the country and before the rapture I believe we can stay a free nation." In other words, he resolved the apparent contradiction between his eschatology and his reformism by opening up time between the current crisis and the beginning of Tribulations. His friend Tim LaHaye, a San Diego pastor and prolific writer on prophecy, put much the same idea this way: the reign of "secular humanists" in America constituted a "pre-tribulation tribulation" that was not predestined and therefore could—and must—be averted. Falwell added that if Christians acted now, they could preserve "the last logical

(not mentioned) 310
Support Israel

launching pad for world evangelization" and could do what the Bible required of them, namely, spread the gospel throughout the world. He had,
in other words, reversed the valence of the Great Commission, so that
instead of requiring separation, it made political action an urgent task.[35]

The response from the separatist Baptist clergy seems to have been
generally positive. Some felt that pastors shouldn't engage in politics, and
a few, like Bob Jones Jr. and his son Bob Jones III, all but called him the
Antichrist for opening the Moral Majority to Catholics.[36] Falwell, however, had already written the strict separationists off, and he had a number
of powerful allies. Among them was Tim LaHaye, who had started an
anti-pornography lobby and worked for the Briggs Initiative. Though well
known for his anti-Catholicism, LaHaye joined the board of the Moral
Majority, as did Greg Dixon, Falwell's Baptist Bible Fellowship classmate
and pastor of the Temple Baptist Church in Indianapolis. Falwell had not
been alone in taking incremental steps into politics, nor was he the first
pastor to form a political organization.[37]

Six months before the founding of the Moral Majority, Robert Grant,
an independent Baptist minister from Southern California, had formed
the Christian Voice out of his own anti–gay rights organization and several other "pro-family" groups. Largely made up of fundamental Baptists and Pentecostals—and much touted on Robertson's *700 Club*—the
Christian Voice also looked for nonevangelical support. Among the 37,000
clergymen it had on its mailing list in 1980, three hundred were Catholic priests. Its Washington lobbyist, Gary Jarmin, a Southern Baptist,
had once belonged to Reverend Sun Myung Moon's Unification Church,
but mainly he was a New Right political operative, who had worked for
Moon's Freedom Leadership Foundation and for the American Conservative Union. (When hired by a predominantly evangelical organization,
he rejoiced, telling a reporter, "The beauty of it is that we don't have to
organize these voters. They already have their own television networks,
publications, schools, meeting places and respected leaders who are sympathetic to our goals."[38]) Christian Voice spokesmen maintained that they
wanted to elect "Christian statesmen," but in practice they targeted six
liberal Democratic senators for defeat without regard for the religion or
the personal morality of their challengers. In the "Moral Report Card" the

organization released in late 1979 senators and congressmen lost points not only if they supported gay rights, but also if they backed the SALT II nuclear arms agreement or any other insufficiently anti-Communist initiative. One Florida congressman, Richard Kelly, received a 100 percent rating even though he had been involved in the ABSCAM bribery scandal.[39]

Other televangelists, too, were making their moves. Not just Robertson and Bakker but others theologically closer to Falwell. In the spring of 1979 D. James Kennedy, pastor of the Coral Ridge Presbyterian Church in Florida, spoke on political issues in televised sermons, and Charles Stanley, pastor of the First Baptist Church in Atlanta, sent out hundreds of thousands of videotapes of a sermon urging Christians to become more active in politics. Both joined the board of the Moral Majority, and Stanley later invited scores of Georgia preachers for a "Campaign Training Conference" for instruction by Weyrich and others. In Dallas James Robison, a populist Southern Baptist preacher, was also edging into the fray. In February the local ABC affiliate WFAA had pulled his nationally syndicated television program off the air after he charged that homosexuals recruited and murdered young boys. In June Falwell attended a rally for him at the Dallas Convention Center, as did Weyrich and Phillips. Criswell spoke at the rally, and pressure from powerful Southern Baptists soon persuaded the station managers to put Robison back on the air. Robison, however, concluded that the whole society required reformation. He joined the Moral Majority and a few months later became the chief spokesman for the Religious Roundtable, an organization founded by McAteer with a view to bringing Southern Baptists and other mainstream evangelicals into the Christian right.[40]

For Falwell and his allies the task of organizing was helped by the disaffection of many Southern evangelicals from the Carter presidency. In 1976 Carter and Ford had split the evangelical vote, but Carter had won every southern state except Virginia and had taken 56 percent of the national white Baptist vote. Though he called Reinhold Niebuhr his favorite theologian and said he wasn't sure he accepted the Apostle Paul's injunctions about the role of women, many conservative Southern Baptists had seen him as one of their own. He had spoken at length about the erosion of the American family, and he promised to hold a national conference to consider ways the public and private sectors might better support the family. He was personally conservative on abortion and what he called "the homosexual lifestyle," but in line with his stance on black civil rights, he came out for gay rights and *Roe v. Wade* as well as the ERA, and by the time the conference finally took place in the summer of 1980, the battle lines had been drawn. These issues, once seen as separate, had fused and Carter became identified with northern liberals and feminists.[41] At the same time Carter, who hoped to hold the military budget down after the vast expense of the Vietnam War, was painted as weak on defense, and events abroad from the Ayatollah Khomeini's Islamist revolution in Iran and the taking of American hostages to the anti-American Sandinista victory in Nicaragua to the Soviet invasion of Afghanistan seemed to conspire to demonstrate that the nation had lost its strength and its credibility in the world. Worse still, the United States was suffering from economic stagnation, oil shortages, and high inflation—and southern evangelicals were not alone in blaming Carter for this state of the affairs.

In early 1979 Falwell and his allies began looking for a Republican candidate for president. Not yet well attuned to the art of the possible, they lit first upon Congressman Phil Crane, a conservative ideologue from Illinois, and then upon John Connally, the former governor of Texas, who had a swaggering tough-guy image.[42] Ronald Reagan, who had nearly beat Ford in 1976 and had been running for president ever since, was the odds-on favorite for the nomination, but he was a divorced former Hollywood actor who rarely attended church, and Falwell couldn't see this affable, sixty-eight-year-old as a leader.[43] Reagan, however, knew he needed the southern states, and like Goldwater and Nixon before him, he pursued a "Southern strategy" of backing states' rights and using racial code words such as "welfare queens." He opened his campaign at the Neshoba County Fair near Philadelphia, Mississippi, where three civil rights workers had been murdered in 1964. He spoke at Bob Jones University. He called for tax tuition credits for students attending private schools and complained that the Supreme Court had "expelled God from the classroom."[44] Endearing himself to Catholics as well as fundamentalists, he apologized for his decision as governor to support "therapeutic abortions" and called for a Human Life Amendment. In addition he called for a massive military buildup to stop the Russians from acquiring the means "to take us with a phone call" and vowed to reduce taxes and shrink the size of the federal government.

Reagan preached the old civil religion of American exceptionalism, and when talking with evangelicals displayed a command of "born-again" speech. As the campaign went on, the Christian right leaders came around to him, turning from skeptics into enthusiasts. In the spring of 1980 he won all the southern primaries and all but five outside the South. Afterward his campaign hired Billings as its religious liaison and established a Family Policy Advisor Board that included evangelical antifeminists like Lottie Beth Hobbs and Beverly LaHaye.[45]

The Republican platform, hammered out at the national convention in mid-July, reflected the rightward trend of the party in its embrace of the South. It failed to support the ERA, and as in 1976, it called for a constitutional amendment to overturn *Roe v. Wade*, but this time suggested that the appointment of federal judges be conditioned on opposition to abortion. It called for tax reductions, tax tuition credits, voluntary school prayer, and a halt to the IRS "vendetta" against private schools. In addition it warned that the Soviets were acquiring the means "to blackmail us into submission," and recommended that the United States achieve "military superiority over the Soviet Union." Falwell, who attended the convention and was invited to meet with Reagan, remarked that the platform "could easily be the constitution of a fundamentalist Baptist church."[46]

In August the Religious Roundtable put on a two-day National Affairs Briefing in Dallas, led by James Robison, which attracted 2,500 pastors from all over the country and enough local churchgoers to fill the seventeen-thousand-seat Reunion Arena. The speakers included Falwell, Weyrich, Phillips, McAteer, LaHaye, Schlafly, and Pat Robertson, as well as Texan politicians and the one presidential candidate to accept the invitation to speak, Ronald Reagan. Because of Reagan, the gathering drew journalists from the major newspapers and television networks, putting the Christian right on display before the nation. Reagan thrilled the crowd. In a press conference before his address he urged that the biblical story of creation be taught in the public schools as an alternative to evolution and later said that "all the complex questions facing us at home and abroad" have their answers in the Bible. He sat on the platform in his usual relaxed fashion while Robison delivered a paint-blistering attack on "radicals and perverts." He then rose to his feet and told the pastors, "I know you can't endorse me, but . . . I want you to know that I endorse you and what you are doing."[47]

This triumph for the Christian right was flawed by one remark. Dr. Bailey Smith, the president of the Southern Baptist Convention, was delivering a sermon when he mused, "It's interesting at great political rallies how you have a Protestant to pray, a Catholic to pray, and then you have a Jew to pray. With all due respect to those dear people, my friends, God Almighty does not hear the prayer of a Jew." His comment, reported by all the major newspapers, created a furor. Smith, a preacher from Del City, Oklahoma, was shocked when even some of his fellow Southern Baptists accused him of hateful anti-Semitism. He was, after all, only stating what for him and for most of the pastors in the hall was a basic piece of theology. "How in the world," he had gone on to say, "can God hear the prayer of a man who says that Jesus Christ is not the true Messiah? That is blasphemy. It may be politically expedient, but no one can pray unless he prays through the name of Jesus Christ." He refused to apologize, and the scandal virtually brought down the Religious Roundtable.[48]

The incident showed how isolated fundamentalists remained from the larger world and how difficult the path Falwell wished to travel, holding both to theological purity and to ecumenical politics. The month of the Dallas meeting Falwell told *The Washington Post*, "I am not one of those who use the phrase 'Christianizing America.'" He had not used that phrase, but he had often spoken of the need to turn the country back into a "Christian nation." Then, Bailey Smith's remark dogged him. On October 3 Reagan traveled to Lynchburg to speak at the National Religious Broadcasters' convention held at Liberty Baptist College. Asked if he shared Smith's opinion, Falwell told a press conference, "I believe that God answers the prayer of any redeemed Jew or Gentile, and I do not believe that God answers the prayer of any unredeemed Gentile or Jew." He had shifted terms in a way likely to confuse journalists, but the Virginia B'nai B'rith reported that he had said in essence what Smith said. The following week Falwell met with Rabbi Marc Tanenbaum of the American Jewish

Committee in New York. In a statement later released by Tanenbaum, Falwell said, "It grieves me that I have been quoted as saying that God does not hear the prayer of a Jew. . . . God is a respecter of all persons. He loves everyone alike. He hears the heart cry of any sincere person who calls on him." [49] The price of ecumenical politics was apparently the renunciation of a fundamental tenet of faith. Alternatively, it was the maintenance of two separate audiences.

Over the summer and fall Falwell appeared on major television talk shows and gave interviews to the national newspapers and newsmagazines. In the interviews he appeared to have moderated his views on a number of subjects. He had always denounced drinking, but the week Reagan came to Lynchburg in October he denounced "excessive" drinking. Earlier he had told *The Washington Post*, "I have no objection to a homosexual teaching in the public classroom as long as that homosexual is not flaunting his life style or soliciting students." He added that heterosexual teachers should act with the same propriety. (That statement was rather different from the one going out with his fund-raising letters for the Moral Majority: "Just look what's happening here in America: Known, practicing homosexual teachers have invaded the classrooms.") In the same *Washington Post* interview Falwell said, "It looks like we're coming on like religious crusaders of the Dark Ages, rule or ruin. That is the last thing the people I work with have on their minds, but we've got to prove that by action. . . . I think we have a P.R. job on our hands to prove that we are human beings who love people but who have convictions about what is right and wrong." [50]

The difficulty was that the new audience Falwell had sought would not go away when he talked to his constituency in his old tone of voice. In August at a rally in Harrisburg, Pennsylvania, he presented a slide show made for his earlier "Clean Up America" campaign. According to the *New York Times* reporter present, the show featured "repeated images of Charles Manson, Times Square sex-film marquees, atom bombs exploding, young men with their arms around each other and unbreathing fetuses lying in bloody white ceramic hospital pans," and a quote attributed to the former head of the American Communist Party: "I dream of the hour when the last Congressman is strangled to death on the guts of the last preacher." [51]

Around the same time journalists discovered that Falwell in speaking to audience in Alaska had made up an exchange with President Carter about "practicing homosexuals" on the White House staff.

The period of the campaign was a difficult time for Falwell. There were conflicting demands on him. His own people were asking for the old truths and the old ferocities; Republican politicians were asking him to look like a tolerant, conservative sort of fellow; and journalists were asking him to be consistent and accusing him of breaking the commandment against false witness when he was not. At the same time Democrats, liberal clergymen, and moderate Southern Baptists were accusing him of violating the principle of separation between church and state. Some, including the president of the National Council of Churches, compared him to the Ayatollah Khomeini.[52] Then, too, contributions to *The Old-Time Gospel Hour* seemed to be declining.

In a fund-raising letter for his TV show dated October 10 Falwell wrote:

> I have become the victim of a vicious, orchestrated attack by liberal politicians, bureaucrats, and amoralists. . . .
>
> The liberals and amoral secular humanists have tried to destroy my character and my integrity.
>
> And sadly enough, some of my friends who once supported the Old-Time Gospel Hour have believed some of these false reports and charges made in the Press.
>
> I have burned the bridge behind me. You will never read in the newspaper Jerry Falwell quit. You may read that someone killed me— but that is the only way I can be stopped. . . . Opposition is becoming more and more violent. Our enemies are hitting us from every side. . . .
>
> In fact, if I am not able to raise 5 million dollars within the next thirty days . . . I may be forced to begin taking the Old-Time Gospel Hour off the air, city by city.[53]

The election results cheered Falwell up a good deal. Running against Carter and the independent candidate, John Anderson, Reagan took a majority of the popular vote and won by a landslide in the electoral college, sweeping all the southern states except for Carter's home state of Georgia. Republicans picked up thirty-five seats in the House and gained a majority in the Senate for the first time since 1954. Several prominent liberal Democrats, among them Senators George McGovern, Frank Church, John Culver, and Birch Bayh, went down to defeat and a new group of Republican social conservatives, such as Dan Quayle, Don Nickles, and Jeremiah Denton, moved into the Senate. "It was my finest hour," Falwell said apropos of President Carter's early concession speech. On behalf of the Moral Majority, he took credit for a number of Republican victories across the country, and he delightedly told his congregation about all the "important people" who had been calling to congratulate him.[54]

Subsequent analysis, however, showed that although Reagan won 67 percent of the evangelical votes—or 9 points better than Ford—he had also picked up mainline voters and made inroads into every Democratic constituency, except for African Americans and Hispanics. His victory thus did not depend on any one particular group. Further, the Moral Majority did not live up to the claims made for it. It failed to attract Catholics or even a spectrum of conservative Protestants. Almost all of the Moral Majority state chairs were fundamental Baptist pastors, and more than a half of them belonged to Falwell's own Bible Baptist Fellowship network. The national headquarters claimed to have chapters in forty-seven states, but in practice only eighteen chapters were functioning organizations, most of them in the Sunbelt. Still, the Moral Majority did have some successes in the Republican primaries for Congress in Oklahoma, Alabama, and Alaska, thus helping to move the party to the right.[55]

Looking back at the election, a number of political scientists, noting the hostility Falwell engendered and the disparity between his extravagant claims and the results, essentially wrote off the Moral Majority as a political force.

They were right in the sense that Falwell had failed to create an effective organization, and in 1987 he virtually shut it down. Still, Falwell had done something far more important: he had played the lead role in founding a political movement. In the late 1970s he and his allies had ridden the growing wave of fundamentalism in the Sunbelt and steered it into national politics by harnessing the sense of cultural breakdown that resulted from the social revolution of the 1960s and the urbanization of the South. Along the way, Falwell had provided a new political agenda and the justification separatist Baptists were looking for to join the national debate. Not all at once but gradually, he led the most marginalized of religious groups into mainstream politics. Further, he and his fellows started the process of convincing fundamentalists, Pentecostals, and conservative Southern Baptists that they and others could work for common goals without compromising their theology or even making a formal alliance. In addition, he introduced the fundamentalist sense of perpetual crisis, and of war between the forces of good and evil, into national politics, where the rhetoric has remained ever since. *pre G.W. Bush/pre Trump*

II

THE POLITICAL
REALIGNMENT *of the* SOUTH

T HE LEADERS of the Christian right looked upon Reagan's inauguration as the beginning of a new era. They had high hopes and a full legislative agenda packed by New Right operatives into a bill known as the Family Protection Act.

Two days after the inauguration the president invited Falwell and fellow ministers to meet with him, and that was just the first of many invitations to the White House. "We now have a government in Washington that will help us," Falwell said. Ed Dobson, Falwell's closest aide, later remembered thinking the meetings with high officials "meant we were somebody, that we mattered, that we cared, that we were making a difference, that all of the years in the back woods of the culture were over. We had come home, and the home was the White House." The omnibus Family Protection Act contained thirty-one items that began with curbing abortion, restoring school prayer, and giving tuition tax credits for children in private schools. It went on through the Christian right wish list all the way down to forbidding the use of federal money to pay for educational materials that did not "contribute to the American way of life as it has been historically understood." Such was the euphoria that Falwell actually thought the bill might pass.[1]

The Reagan administration, however, had other things to do. In its first year it launched an economic program of enormous tax cuts, unmatched by domestic spending reductions, and accompanied by a tight monetary policy. It also embarked on the largest peacetime military buildup

(Reagan agenda)

in American history. It rejected détente with the Soviets, abandoned the arms control talks, and announced "the Reagan doctrine" of support for the contra rebels in Nicaragua and anti-Communist forces around the world. In promoting his $1.5 trillion spending request Secretary of Defense Caspar Weinberger used wartime rhetoric: the Soviets, he said, were building their forces as Hitler did in the 1930s. He insisted that the Soviets held strategic superiority, and he spoke of the need for the U.S. to attain the capability to fight a "protracted" nuclear war.[2]

Intent on passing Reagan's economic and defense program, White House officials decided to put the social issues aside. They refused to back a bill introduced by Senator Jesse Helms designed to eviscerate *Roe v. Wade* or a constitutional amendment sponsored by Senator Orrin Hatch that would have left the issue of abortion to the states; they let tuition tax credits go down to defeat; and they wouldn't touch the Family Protection Act. Then, because of objections from civil rights groups and Republican legislators, Reagan had to abandon his promise to preserve the tax-exempt status of religious schools that discriminated on the basis of race. When a vacancy on Supreme Court opened in the summer of 1981, Reagan nominated Sandra Day O'Connor, an Arizona judge favored by powerful Republicans, but who, when serving in the state senate, had fought for the ERA and supported legalized abortion.[3]

New Right social conservatives grew increasingly testy as the months went by. Weyrich took to warning Republican Party officials that they couldn't take the New Right's allegiance for granted and that social conservatives would not be content with merely rhetorical support. Reagan's Supreme Court nomination struck them as the ultimate betrayal. Along with right-to-life groups and a number of Christian right pastors, they protested vociferously. James Robison by his own account "hollered at" White House staffers, and with the help of Ed McAteer mounted an anti-abortion, anti-O'Connor rally in Dallas on Labor Day.[4]

Falwell, however, took a different tack. In the early days he voiced support for Reagan's economic plan and for the priority the White House gave it. "I don't think the President is side-stepping the moral and social issues. . . . I think he wants to give it [the economic program] the full shot." He endorsed the administration's aggressive anti-Communist rhetoric and had nothing but praise for Ronald Reagan. When the news of the O'Connor nomination leaked out, Falwell in a statement released to press complained that the president either lacked the necessary information about the judge, or had simply ignored it. Then just before the official announcement, Reagan called him personally to assure him that O'Connor represented the values and views he had run upon and asked him to back off until the hearings. Falwell uttered not another word of criticism, and the Moral Majority did not campaign against O'Connor. "I am very, very happy with this President," Falwell reported as the Senate debated the nomination. Reagan, he said, is "the greatest President we've had in my lifetime and history may say the greatest President ever."[5]

Weyrich was disgusted. He thought Falwell and his fellows simply wanted to go the White House and be photographed with the president. "What overshadowed all their concerns was simply the pleasure of being able to get in. . . . They didn't want to do anything to jeopardize that." They had, he said, put aside their entire agenda "to safeguard meaningless access." In seminars and workshops he tried to instruct the naive Christian activists on the corruption of the political process and to convince them that they had to force politicians to do what they ought to do. Possibly he had forgotten that Falwell had always put free market economics and anti-Communism on a par with the social issues. In any case, Falwell paid no heed, and a year later Reagan's liaison to conservative religious groups estimated that he had more contact with the president than any other religious leader.[6]

By the fall of 1982 the president needed the help of Christian right leaders. The administration's unprecedented military buildup, the lack of arms control negotiations, and loose talk about nuclear weapons from Weinberger and his aides had called forth a major antinuclear movement in Europe and the United States. In the U.S. the movement centered on "the Freeze"—a simple and symmetrical proposal that the two superpowers "end the testing, production, and deployment of all nuclear weapons" as a first step to "lessening the risk of nuclear war." The liberal Protestant churches and sixty-nine Catholic bishops backed the proposal, as did congressional Democrats and a huge majority of the public.[7] In June three quarters of a million people had rallied for the Freeze in New York's

82 Peace rally failed to mention Israel's war on Palestinians

Central Park. In August the Freeze resolution had failed in the House by only one vote. The National Council of Catholic Bishops was preparing a pastoral letter, "The Challenge of Peace," that, as was widely known, condemned the arms race and all but pronounced deterrence immoral by condemning the implied threat to use nuclear weapons. Billy Graham, who had recently made a number of evangelistic trips to the Soviet Union and Eastern Europe, was calling for the two great powers to move from SALT II to SALT X and the elimination of nuclear weapons. White House officials feared that evangelicals might follow his lead. As they saw it, the defense buildup—and conceivably Reagan's reelection—was at stake.[8]

Falwell loyally answered the call. Adopting Reagan's own slogan, "Peace Through Strength," he embarked on an eighteen-month-long campaign to combat the Freeze. Criticized for spending too much time on defense and not enough on the social issues, he said that "unless America survives as a free nation, all other issues will become historically moot." When the Freeze movement reached a new peak the following spring, he went to the White House for a tête-à-tête with Reagan and a briefing from his national security aides. Soon after he published a glossy booklet based on the briefing with charts purporting to show the enormous advantage the Soviets held in strategic nuclear weapons and took out advertisements in major newspapers. Freeze activists, he said, were "robots" doing the bidding of Moscow.[9]

On March 8, 1983, Reagan gave a stirring address to the National As-sociation of Evangelicals during which he called the Soviets "the focus of evil in the world." Coming just two weeks before he announced the Strategic Defense Initiative, popularly known as Star Wars, the speech was ridiculed by Democrats as "the Darth Vader" speech. Largely overlooked was the rest of the address. In remarks prepared with the help of NAE director Robert Dugan, Reagan spoke in evangelical terms of a "spiritual awakening and moral renewal" taking place in the country. He decried those who had turned to "modern-day secularism" and were attempting to "water down traditional values and even abrogate the original terms of American democracy." He mentioned administration efforts to prohibit discrimination against the religious speech of public school students and to make certain that "the rights of parents and the rights of families take

No mention of Israel (Lebanon War (Sabra/Shatila massacre) Reagan's alliance w/ pro Israel interests Reagan's political use of religion

precedence over those of Washington-based bureaucrats and social engi-
neers." He spoke passionately about abortion "taking the lives of up to
one and a half million unborn children a year" and vowed that he would
"never rest" until the Congress passed "human life legislation ending this
tragedy." Only toward the end did he mention the Soviet Union—and
then in the context of the problem of "sin and evil in the world." Quoting C. S. Lewis, Whittaker Chambers, and the prophet Isaiah, he called
upon his audience to speak out against those who "would place the United
States in a position of military and moral inferiority" in what was essentially a "spiritual battle." In effect, he was borrowing Falwell's rhetoric,
just as Falwell was borrowing his.[10]

In the NAE speech Reagan promised to reintroduce a constitutional
amendment on public school prayer that had been proposed by the White
House and shelved by the Congress the previous year. School prayer still
polled well with the public, but as all Washington insiders knew, the
amendment hadn't a chance of getting the necessary two thirds of the
vote in both houses of Congress, much less of surviving the arduous process of ratification by the states. Reagan's White House advisors never
put the full weight of the presidency behind it, and the amendment went
down to defeat in the Republican-led Senate the following year.[11]

By the time of the 1984 election Reagan had given several more stirring
addresses to evangelical groups, the National Religious Broadcasters Convention and the Baptist Fundamentalism Convention '84 among them.
Vice President George H. W. Bush had for his part addressed the SBC
convention and Falwell's Liberty Baptist College.[12] Still, in spite of their
promises and their biblical quotations, they delivered very little on the
social issues: Reagan's "Mexico City policy," which withheld USAID funds
from NGOs that performed, or promoted, abortion as a method of family
planning abroad, and the Equal Access Law, which gave student religious
groups the right to hold meetings on public school property. White House
officials never fought for anything more.

Politically speaking, Reagan's advisors had done the exactly right thing.
In the 1980 election the issues most important to all segments of Reagan
voters had been the economy, foreign policy, and defense. White evangelicals had switched from Carter to Reagan in large numbers, but according

to later studies they did so for the much the same reasons that other voters did. Northern evangelicals tended to vote Republican anyway, and a large percentage of southern evangelicals voted for Democrats in other races. More important, the Christian right's social agenda continued to be highly controversial within the Republican Party. In spite of the party's platform, many prominent Senate Republicans, from the libertarian Barry Goldwater to moderates such as Chuck Percy of Illinois, adamantly opposed efforts to amend the Constitution to outlaw abortion—or to reinstate school prayer. Most congressional Republicans supported the gains made in women's rights; and a vast majority of Americans, including a majority of evangelicals, did not want abortion outlawed.[13]

Reagan's first term was nonetheless a period of huge excitement for conservative evangelicals and Christian right activists. "Monarchists at heart," as two of Falwell's closest aides later called them, the activists believed Reagan would change America into the Christian nation it had once been. Meanwhile, grassroots groups sprang up across the country to reform their public schools or to support conservative candidates for office. At the same time a number of powerful ministers geared up new organizations, ready to assume Falwell's position if he faltered. One of them was the San Diego pastor Tim LaHaye.[14]

A graduate of Bob Jones University with long-standing ties to the John Birch Society, LaHaye had since the late 1950s built a large church, a system of ten Christian schools, and a college. He had also established the Institute for Creation Research with Dr. Henry Morris. A biblical literalist and a professor of hydraulic engineering, Morris had in 1963 written the founding document of the modern creationist movement, *The Genesis Flood*. Adapting the idea of an early-twentieth-century Seventh-day Adventist, George McCready Price, that the earth was no more than ten thousand years old, he proposed that Noah's flood had covered the entire earth and sorted the corpses of animals into the strata in which their fossils were found. The book and the institute he ran with LaHaye revived evangelical interest in young earth cosmology and introduced the notion that creationism was a science that should be taught in the public schools.

In 1978 LaHaye had made his way into politics as an ally of Falwell's in the battle for the anti–gay rights Proposition 6 in California and became one of the original members of the Moral Majority board. The following year his wife, Beverly, founded Concerned Women for America, an anti-feminist organization of "kitchen table activists" that became one of the pillars of the Christian right. Composed of women organized into prayer circles of seven, and prayer chains of fifty, the Concerned Women for America asked that its members to pay a small sum in dues and to commit to writing a few letters or making a few phone calls every year. With a newsletter and lobbying office in Washington, the national organization focused on "pro-family" issues, but sometimes went as far afield as aid to the Nicaraguan contras. Its chapters independently engaged in local issues, such as efforts to remove "obscene" books from the public schools. Its reported membership grew larger than that of the National Organization for Women, and unlike many other Christian right organizations, it survived into the next century.[15]

After publishing *Battle for the Mind* in 1980, Tim LaHaye left his pulpit for writing and political activism. The following year he and Nelson Bunker Hunt took the lead in forming the first successful—and enduring—umbrella group for the right. Originally conceived as a steering committee that would set policy for movement conservatives, the Council for National Policy evolved into a forum for movers and shakers of the American right with closed meetings and a secret membership. When its directories leaked out in the mid-1980s, the CNP was found to have around four hundred members. Among them were the notables of the Christian right: Falwell, Robertson, Kennedy, Dobson, Bright, Bob Dugan of the NAE, Henry Morris, both LaHayes, Paige Patterson, Paul Pressler, and others. But that was hardly all. The membership included Weyrich, Viguerie, the rest of the New Right operatives, and Phyllis Schlafly; it also included the leaders of the John Birch Society, the head of the National Right to Work Committee, former military officers such as Oliver North and John Singlaub, and an assortment of administration officials. According to the historian Allan Lichtman, 44 percent of its members were businessmen, almost all of them entrepreneurs or heads of family firms who came from the South and the West. The CNP held three meetings a year in undisclosed locations, and in them the group discussed issues, such as abortion, the Strategic Defense Initiative, a return to the gold standard, secular humanism in the public schools, and how to elect conservatives. In the hallways pastors met with generals, the heads of hungry organizations found donors, and think tank presidents plotted strategy with Texas oil men.[16]

LaHaye, who served as the first president of the body, found his appetite for politics whetted. In 1983 he founded the American Coalition for Traditional Values, an organization similar to the Moral Majority, whose goal was to mobilize churches, register a million voters for that year's election, and recruit Christians to run for office. The Reagan campaign recruited him to coordinate Christian right voter registration projects.[17]

Reagan, however, had no need of Christian right votes in 1984. By the time of the election the economy had made a strong recovery, thanks in part to tax cuts, deficit spending, and lowering of interest rates. In addition Reagan found his way out of the difficulty Defense Department hawks had created for him by declaring that America had regained its military might, calling for arms control talks, and speaking of the elimination of nuclear weapons with the defensive shield of Star Wars. His campaign was relentlessly positive and far more centrist than his previous presidential bids. In speeches he confined himself to the theme struck by his television ad, "Morning in America," celebrating the restoration of national power and prosperity. He made few proposals on domestic issues and avoided Christian right social issues altogether, leaving them to the party platform.[18]

In November Reagan won by a landslide, carrying all but one state, winning 60 percent of the popular vote, and receiving the largest electoral vote in U.S. history. White evangelicals gave him about 75 percent of their votes, but their votes, along with the domestic concerns of the Christian right, were buried in the landslide. In his second term Reagan, preoccupied by U.S.-Soviet relations and the Iran-contra scandal, did even less for social conservatives than he had in his first.

The larger Christian right organizations went into decline. Even before the election the Christian Voice had lost many of its leaders, some in disputes over tactics; the Religious Roundtable had lost its pastor-leader when James Robison, seeing another light, found his salvation in charismatic Christianity and quit. By 1984 neither organization was much more than a shell.[19] The Moral Majority was the only one that could claim an increasing membership, but it had its problems. Its state chapters were independent, and after the 1980 election they went off in different directions. Some of them fought local battles on gay rights, sex education, and the teaching of evolution; others made forays into state politics, with mixed success. The large Virginia chapter, for example, managed to force Republican politicians into such extreme positions that Democrats won in a Republican-trending state. Still other chapters veered entirely off the tracks. The Maryland chapter tried to bring pornography charges against a bakery that sold anatomically explicit gingerbread men; more ominously, the leader of the Santa Clara, California, chapter called for a law making homosexuality a crime punishable by death. (Falwell said he had never met the "gentleman" in charge and had no way of controlling him.) The Moral Majority claimed to have registered two and a half million voters for the 1984 election, but it had few active chapters below state level, and it remained a largely separatist Baptist group run by pastors incapable of bringing those of other evangelical traditions into their organizational fold.[20]

After Reagan's landslide reelection, donations to large Christian right organizations dropped off precipitously. Reagan's "Morning in America" campaign had convinced many religious conservatives that his presidency had succeeded in restoring the nation to Christian values, and that it was no longer necessary for them to "save" America. Primarily an office with a mailing list, the national Moral Majority was ill-equipped to survive the dropoff in funds. Falwell did not help his cause. He raised liberal ire by calling AIDS "the wrath of God on homosexuals" and by saying that all those with AIDS should be quarantined. In 1985 he made a number of overseas trips and supported the most unpopular—and the most ill-fated—of Reagan's overseas allies: Ferdinand and Imelda Marcos in the Philippines, the brutal right-wing regime in El Salvador, and the white supremacist government in South Africa. (He called Bishop Desmond Tutu "a phony" on his arrival back home.) Increasingly, he became a target for liberal organizations and Democratic politicians. By 1986 public opinion polls showed that a substantial majority of the public, and more than two fifths of Reagan voters, viewed him unfavorably.[21]

LaHaye fared no better. After Reagan's reelection, he claimed victory and held a major conference for conservatives, "How to Win an Election." However, an investigation by *Mother Jones* magazine showed that one of the biggest contributors to his American Coalition for Traditional Values was Sun Myung Moon's Unification Church. Moon was then going to jail for fraud, and evangelicals considered the church heretical. After the 1986 election in which the Democrats regained control of the Senate, LaHaye closed ACTV down. The same year Falwell backed away from the Moral Majority by folding it into a new entity, the Liberty Federation; in November 1987 he resigned as president, and contributions continued to fall. By the end of the Reagan administration many political observers judged that the Christian right had run its course and would gradually expire.[22]

The obituary was premature. In the course of the next decade the Christian right developed into the most significant political movement of the period and played a lead role in a fundamental reshaping of the American political landscape. Since the New Deal, the two parties, both composed of various religious groups, had divided largely along economic lines, but by the end of the 1990s the two had come to look much more like the European parties of the 1950s, one religious and the other secular. The analogy is imperfect, but certainly the Republicans came to represent religious conservatives and the Democrats religious and secular liberals—while both drew from the white working and middle classes. The Republican Party attracted religious conservatives of all traditions, but white evangelicals became the largest element its coalition, displacing the northern mainline Protestants that had been its base since the Civil War.

The transformation came about in part because of the changing religious composition of the country over four decades. The 1950s had seen a huge increase in the numbers of churchgoers in all traditions, but by 1960 the postwar revival was over, and afterward the percentage of Americans affiliated with churches dropped off sharply. The decline, however, affected only the mainline Protestant churches and the Roman Catholic Church, not the evangelical denominations. According to the Princeton sociologist Robert Wuthnow, the mainline denominations lost between a quarter and a third of their membership between the 1960s and 1980. In the same period the Catholic Church lost a third of its regular attendees. In the early 1970s mainline Protestants constituted well over 25 percent of the population, but by the end of the century they were down to 18 percent or less. The percentage of Catholics actually grew during the same period, going from 22 percent to 24 percent of the population, but that was because many who never went to mass continued to identify as Catholics, and because the wave of Hispanic Catholic immigrants replaced a quarter of them in the pews. White evangelicals, for their part, constituted perhaps a quarter at the beginning and 26 percent at the end. Given that the whole population grew by eighty million people, or 40 percent, between 1972 and 2002, the figure represents a huge increase in the numbers of white evangelicals.[23]

In the 1970s the dominant hypothesis about the growth of evangelical churches was that people were moving to "strict" churches from those they thought had become too lax. But this was little more than a guess.[24] Better evidence showed that the decline of one tradition and the growth of the other owed largely to demographics. Mainline Protestants, better educated and better off than the rest of the population, married later and had fewer children than the national average. By the 1980s they were hardly replacing themselves.[25] Evangelical Protestants, less advantaged, kept marrying young, having larger families—and more than replacing themselves. Evangelicals also had more success in retaining the next generation in their churches than mainliners. According to Robert Wuthnow, inertia plays an important role in retention rates, and during this period evangelicals in their twenties were more likely to remain in their home communities than young people from mainline churches, many of whom went to college and then had to move again to find jobs they were suited for.[26] In addition, higher education in itself seemed to have a secularizing effect on young people. Certainly from the 1960s on, droves of young mainliners dropped out of organized religion altogether (as did many Catholics and Jews), and the dropouts tended to have significantly more education and occupational prestige than those who remained religiously affiliated.[27]

According to the sociologist Mark A. Shibley most of the growth in church membership during the 1970s and '80s occurred within the southern-based evangelical denominations and churches. This made sense for a number of reasons. In the early 1970s some 60 percent of all white evangelicals lived in the South and another large percentage in the neighboring states of West Virginia, Kentucky, Missouri, and Oklahoma. This general region contained some of the poorest states in the country, where early marriages and large families were prevalent and relatively few young people left for college. Further, the region as a whole had always been the most religious part of the country, where people identified themselves by the churches they attended, and sermons filled the airwaves all Sunday long. In this Bible-soaked atmosphere even the mainline Protestant churches maintained, or increased, the size of their congregations, defying the trends elsewhere. In addition there was far less religious diversity in the South than in other regions. The northern evangelical churches had to contend with religious pluralism, but the southern evangelical churches had little competition except from each other. Then, too, the southern diaspora continued and the southern evangelical denominations to follow it across the country, in particular into the lower Midwest. Between 1965 and 1995 the Southern Baptist Convention grew from 10.8 million adherents to 15.4 million—an increase of almost 100 percent in thirty years—becoming the largest Protestant denomination. Some of the white Pentecostal denominations also burgeoned in this period. The largest of them, Assemblies of God, more than doubled its numbers in two decades, reaching 2.38 million by 1995, and soon afterward its adherents outnumbered those of the Episcopal Church.[28]

In addition to the growth of the evangelical population, the Christian right benefited from the move of the South into the Republican Party. The most important change in American politics since the New Deal, the shift owed largely to the general southern reaction to the federal civil rights laws, but evangelicals—who made up two fifths of white southern voters—played a critical role, particularly from the late 1970s on.[29]

The white South had voted for the New Deal in part because in the 1930s few were rich enough to pay federal taxes, and FDR permitted the South to confine many New Deal laws to whites. The realignment began with Truman's cautious espousal of civil rights, and in 1956 a small majority of white southerners voted for Eisenhower, but more than three quarters of them identified as Democrats and voted Democratic in state and local races, as they had since the Civil War. The move into the Republican

Party took off quite abruptly in the late 1960s after Johnson's civil rights acts and the "Southern strategy" pursued by Goldwater and Nixon. Race was not the only factor. In states such as Virginia the growth of an upper middle class put some into the Republican camp for economic reasons. Nonetheless, Nixon's decision to break with much of his party by cam-paigning for states' rights and by using race-coded slogans like "law and order" and "forced busing," drove many black southerners into the Dem-ocratic Party and many southern whites out of it. In 1968 only 50 percent of southern whites identified themselves as Democrats; the rest divided themselves almost equally between independents and Republicans. The South had become a contested zone. Nixon won almost 80 percent of white southern votes in 1972, but Carter brought most of them back again in 1976.[30]

Next came the reaction to the other events of the Long Sixties from the Vietnam War to feminism and the division of the two parties over the "the social issues." In his 1980 campaign Reagan appealed to southern whites on many grounds: more defense, lower taxes, less government, school prayer, an affirmation of states' rights, and the use of "dog whistle" words. Reagan became the first postwar Republican candidate to take conserva-tive positions across the board, while Carter, and later Walter Mondale, the 1984 presidential candidate, identified the Democratic Party with lib-eral positions, not just on domestic spending but on defense, affirmative action, busing, the ERA, and abortion. In 1984 Reagan won his reelection with 72 percent of the white southern vote, but more important, the per-centage of white southerners identifying as Republicans rose sharply. His presidency proved the turning point in the realignment of the South. His vice president, George H. W. Bush, though less personally attractive to southerners than Reagan, won 70 percent of the white southern vote in his run for the presidency in 1988. That year exit polls showed only 34 per-cent of white southerners identified as Democrats, while 45 percent called themselves Republicans—nearly double the percentage of 1982.[31]

From 1984 on the white South turned increasingly Republican in the down-ticket races. This took some time because many southern Dem-ocratic politicians remained conservatives. In the 1980s the Republicans won about a third of the senatorial and gubernatorial races; in the early

1990s they won about 40 percent, but between 1994 and 1997, after many conservative Democrats had turned Republican, they won 73 percent of these races. In 1994 Republicans took their first majority of the southern U.S. House and Senate seats, and when Bob Dole left the Senate to run for president in 1996, southern Republicans assumed the leadership of both houses. The *Campaigns and Elections* study of 1994 showed that the Christian right held a dominant influence in eighteen state parties (including all of those in the South) and a substantial influence in thirteen others.[32]

The evangelical clergy played a strong role in the party realignment of the South. In a series of surveys taken between 1980 and 1992 the political scientist James L. Guth found that the Southern Baptist clergy joined the Republican Party earlier than white southerners as a whole and voted more heavily for its presidential candidates. According to one survey, the ministers identifying with the Republican Party, or leaning toward it, mounted with great rapidity from 27 percent in 1980 to 66 percent in 1984 and from there to 80 percent in 1996. In every presidential election from 1984 to the end of the century around 80 percent of the clergy voted for the Republican candidate, and in some years more than half actively supported the candidate. In polling random samples of the eighty thousand ordained ministers on presidential election years, Guth found that the interest of the SBC ministers in politics compared favorably with that of the mainline clergy. Even in 1980 more than 80 percent of SBC ministers voiced approval for certain types of political activity, such as urging congregations to vote, and taking public (but not pulpit) stands on political issues. The ministers' political involvement increased over time, and the younger ministers were more active than their elders. By 1992 almost all of the SBC clergy polled had taken public stands on issues, led petition drives, and contacted public officials. Around 80 percent had endorsed a candidate, though not from the pulpit, and preached a whole sermon on an issue; about a quarter had organized a political action group, and a fifth had joined a protest march.[33]

In the civil rights period the most theologically liberal SBC ministers had been the ones most likely to engage in politics. The conservatives had been the ones to insist that their sole duties were to save souls and to maintain the doctrinal purity of the church. The relationship, Guth found, had gone into reverse: the most theologically conservative of the SBC clergy had become the most politically active. Asking what accounted for the change, Guth discovered that conservatives had adopted what he called "the civic gospel": the view that America had been founded as a Christian nation, but had fallen away, and that Christians had to take aggressive political action to protect their own rights, to buttress private and public morality, and to restore the American Constitution. In surveys conservative activists also reported that there was only one Christian view on political issues, and that political liberals could not be true Christians.[34]

In turning to political activism the conservative SBC clergy did not simply ride the groundswell of popular reaction to the social revolutions of the 1960s; they helped create it. The activists, Guth found, did not overly concern themselves with the approval of their congregations. Most believed that the clergy had "great potential to influence the social and political attitudes of their congregations." And those who regarded themselves as more conservative than their congregations tended to be more active than the rest.[35]

The political activism of the SBC clergy grew in parallel with the change in their denominational leadership and during the battle royal of fundamentalists against progressives and moderates.

After winning their first victory with the election of Adrian Rogers to the presidency in 1979, Paul Pressler, Paige Patterson, and their allies went about the task they had set themselves of electing fundamentalists to the presidency over a ten-year period, and through the appointment of nominating committees changing the governing boards of all the SBC agencies and seminaries. They had the advantages of surprise and unity of purpose. A few progressive ministers realized the threat, but they found it difficult to organize an opposition. The SBC clergy was spread across a narrow theological spectrum, and few were ready to attack biblical inerrancy outright, lest they be accused of not believing in the Bible. The progressives were also conscious that many of their views, like their support for the ordination of women, their interest in social justice, and their lack of interest in traditional southern prohibitions such as those against drinking and dancing, would put them in the minority. Their recourse was therefore to the Baptist doctrine of "soul liberty," and to the SBC tradition of tolerance for a measure of diversity. After five years the progressives managed to put together a coalition and bring their allies to the annual conventions, but their coalition was never a cohesive movement that could act with the single-mindedness of their opponents. Some denominational loyalists still believed in the traditional strategy of compromising, or giving in, and waiting until the fuss blew over. In 1986 six seminary presidents issued what was for most of them an astonishing statement, saying that the Bible was "not errant in any area of reality." [36]

The fundamentalist leaders, however, had a much larger agenda and refused to be conciliated. They made no secret of their social and political views. Some had thrown in their lot with the Christian right in the 1980s, and powerful preachers, such as James Robison, Bailey Smith, and Charles Stanley, gave thunderous sermons about the moral decay of the country as a part of their denominational campaigns. In the mid-1980s the annual conventions drew tens of thousands of messengers—some 45,000 in 1985—and there were acrimonious fights, but every year Pressler and his allies succeeded in electing presidents who would put their own people on the nominating committees. The battle was essentially over by 1985, but few outside the movement recognized it until 1988, when the committees appointed new members to the boards, and the boards in their turn made decisive changes in policy and personnel. Moderate seminary professors and agency officials were replaced by hard-line conservatives, and once they were gone, the standard of inerrancy insured against the return of any kind of liberalism. [37]

One of the principal conservative targets was the Christian Life Commission, long the voice for SBC progressives on civil rights, economic justice, and a woman's right to choose abortion in cases of rape, incest, or danger to her health. Another was the Baptist Joint Committee on Public Affairs, an agency supported by nine Baptist denominations, whose Southern Baptist president, James Dunn, aggressively defended the separation of church and state. Well known for his feisty independence, Dunn opposed school prayer as "state-sponsored religion in the public schools," and often sided with the ACLU. In 1988 the new SBC leaders drove the moderate president of the CLC from office and appointed a new one, Richard Land, an inerrantist and social conservative. They expanded the mission of the CLC to include church-state issues, "defunded" the Joint Commission and, renaming the CLC the Ethics & Religious Liberty Commission, they made Land the sole voice of the SBC in Washington. In the 1990s Convention resolutions became fully aligned with the Christian right agenda, and Land's Ethics & Religious Liberty Commission distributed voter guides clearly favorable to Republican candidates.[38]

The SBC clergy provided an enormous corps of activists for Republicans, and in their opinion they influenced not only their congregations but public attitudes generally.[39] They were not, however, without assistance from other evangelical ministers, including separatist Baptists and Pentecostals. The southern-based Pentecostal denominations, historically the poorest and the least politically engaged of evangelical groups, were also the most socially conservative. In the 1988 presidential election the clergy of the Assemblies of God voted almost unanimously for the Republican candidate, Vice President Bush.[40] That many rural and relatively poor white southerners made their way into the Republican Party owed much to a fear that government spending would help only the blacks and cost them money. Still, their steady movement into the GOP attested to the power of the evangelical clergy in persuading voters that cultural issues should trump pocketbook concerns.

The majority of northern evangelicals had always voted Republican, just as mainline Protestants had, but when joined by southerners, evangelicals generally became a key Republican constituency. By the late 1980s they had become as numerous as mainliners, and they had begun to vote in similar percentages. Republican politicians had to listen to them, and as they did the party turned further right on social issues. In consequence, mainline Protestants began fleeing the party, thus reducing their influence even more. In this self-reinforcing cycle, evangelicals gained increasing strength within the GOP and voted even more consistently Republican. In the 1994 midterm elections some 75 percent of evangelicals voted Republican—compared to only 56 percent of mainline Protestants—and contributed three out of ten Republican votes.[41]

At the same time the "social issues" created another kind of shift in voting patterns. In the past Americans had voted largely according to their religious (and regional) traditions: Catholics had voted Democratic, mainline Protestants Republican, Jews Democratic, and so forth. In the 1980s, John C. Green and his fellow social scientists began to see political divisions emerging between the more and less observant in every religious tradition: those who attended services regularly and held conservative religious views tended to vote more heavily Republican than others within their tradition, while those less connected to religious institutions and more secular in their outlook tended to vote more heavily Democratic. In the three-way presidential election of 1992, for example, 56 percent of all evangelicals voted for Bush, while 70 percent of the highly committed evangelicals did.[42] The trend continued, and after the 2004 presidential election, a Pew survey found that Americans of all traditions who went to services more than weekly gave 64 percent of their votes to the Republican candidate, while those who never went to services voted just as heavily Democratic.[43] The shift was not as dramatic as the South changing parties, but the phenomenon known as the "God gap" was something new in American history.

12

THE THINKERS
of the CHRISTIAN RIGHT

THE CHRISTIAN right hadn't much truck with intellectuals. Few of its leaders had, for example, read Carl F. H. Henry, the leading theologian and social ethicist of the neo-evangelical tradition. A populist movement led by pastors and televangelists, it had an inbuilt hostility to seminary theology—not to mention to secular academic thinking. Its leaders had a great regard for educational credentials. (The Bible school graduates liked to call themselves "doctor" as in "Dr. Falwell" and liked to add honorary degrees, like DD or LLD, after their names.) But, preachers and activists, they listened to their audiences and changed their messages on the basis of what moved people and what spurred them to action. They operated inside their own theological traditions, but they borrowed from here and there and made their own additions. Picking up on what attracted, and what was usable for their purposes, they gradually altered their traditions, ignoring philosophical inconsistencies and gaps. In the general orbit of the Christian right there were very few systematic thinkers or men regarded as intellectual authorities. Indeed there were only two of cross-denominational importance, R. J. Rushdoony and Francis Schaeffer, and both had an outsized influence on the Christian right.

Both men, not surprisingly, belonged to the intellectual Presbyterian tradition: that of J. Gresham Machen and his fellow separatists at Westminster Theological Seminary. In the 1960s and '70s both men produced large bodies of work of history, theology, philosophy, and social criticism; both lectured extensively; and in the late 1970s and early 1980s both ap-

XIV Reconstructionism — Rushdoony

peared on *The Old-Time Gospel Hour, The 700 Club*, and other Christian right TV programs. Schaeffer had a wide evangelical audience—one that went far beyond the Christian right. His books were avidly read by a generation of evangelical students, and two of them were made into popular films. His biographer, Barry Hankins, a Baylor University professor, wrote in 2008 that it was hard to find an evangelical from the northern or northwestern United States between the ages of fifty and seventy who was not influenced by Schaeffer.[1] Many eventually discarded, or moved past, his teachings but continued to give him credit for opening their students' eyes. Rushdoony, by contrast, was always a controversial figure. His vision was original—not to say outlandish—and his school of thought, called Christian Reconstuctionism, ran counter to prevailing fundamentalist doctrines. His major work was difficult to read, and his central thesis so generally rejected that those who adopted parts of his philosophy had to deny it. His ideas, thus detached from their author, became difficult to track. Still, floating free, they made their way into a variety of Christian right circles whose members adopted those they found useful for filling in intellectual gaps.

Of the two, Rushdoony was the more systematic thinker. His central proposal, conceived in the early 1970s, was a radical, and entirely novel, program of social reconstruction. His vision, as one scholar said, was of a society, not reformed but rather razed and rebuilt, where the people of God would exercise dominion using biblical law as a blueprint for a totally "reconstructed" and holy social order. A minister with an unusual biography, Rushdoony came to this vision building from premises he constructed while writing his earlier, and equally influential, books.[2]

Born in 1916, R. J. (Rousas John) Rushdoony grew up in California of Armenian parents who could trace the ministers in their family back to the fourth century. He went to public schools, then to the University of California, Berkeley, where he took a BA in literature and an MA in education. He went on to a liberal seminary, the Pacific School of Religion. Ordained in the Presbyterian Church USA, he served for eight years as a missionary to desperately poor Native Americans on the Duck Valley Indian Reservation in eastern Nevada. After his return to California in 1952, he became a strict Calvinist and eventually joined the Orthodox

Presbyterian Church, founded by J. Gresham Machen.[3] His first book, *By What Standard?*, published in 1959, was a study of the philosophy of the Dutch Reformed theologian Cornelius Van Til, a Princeton seminarian who went on to teach at Westminster when Machen founded it in 1929. Van Til, who retired only in 1972, had a particular approach to apologetics, known as presuppositionalism, and Rushdoony adopted it.

The apologetics of Gresham Machen and most Princeton scholars, based on Common Sense Realism, sought to prove the truth of Christianity through factual evidence. Van Til, by contrast, held that facts did not speak for themselves but were meaningful only within some presupposed framework of interpretation. The truth, he held, lay only in God's framework as revealed in the Bible. Natural law, or autonomous human reason, reflected only man's fallen state, and the attempt by nonbelievers to create their own coherent interpretation of reality was doomed to failure. (His interpretation of the Bible was nonetheless based on Common Sense Realism.) Rushdoony took this notion farther, arguing that there could be no common intellectual ground between believers and nonbelievers. Then, while Van Til avoided the social and political consequences of presuppositionalism, Rushdoony did not. In the 1960s he became an early advocate of home schooling, arguing that education was not theologically neutral, and the state had no business imposing its own truth and its own religion on the American populace. His book *The Messianic Character of American Education* examined the philosophy of the major American educators from Horace Mann to John Dewey, and provided an academic-style resource for leaders of fundamentalist schools and home schooling parents. In the 1970s and '80s he served as an expert witness in numerous cases involving home schooling rights, creating the first network of home schooling parents and convincing many pastors that the state was actually preaching a religion while claiming to be neutral.[4]

A voracious reader and a prolific writer, Rushdoony in the mid-1960s wrote two books on American history. Dwelling on the legacy of the Puritans, he argued that the intellectual roots of the American Revolution were purely Calvinist and owed nothing to the Enlightenment. He challenged the propriety of calling the defensive war against Britain "a revolution"; he called it "a conservative counter-revolution" to preserve American liberties and religious heritage. The Constitution, he maintained, was a secular document in appearance only. It was a minimalist framework regulating only with process and fashioned by men whose primary concern was to ensure the vitality of local governments. It did not include a confession because the states were already Christian establishments with biblically based laws, such as those prohibiting blasphemy and those establishing the Sabbath restrictions. The First Amendment, he argued, was designed to protect the states from interference by the federal government. Article VI, prohibiting religious tests for office, he did not explain. In any case, he held that the Founders had no need to establish the Christian religion because it was already established at local levels. The early American Republic, he maintained, was an orthodox Christian nation with an economic and social Protestant feudal system. By 1860, however, only the South had a Christian system, and in the Civil War the Union troops destroyed it. Quoting a southern Presbyterian clergyman of the period, he asserted that the northern assault on the Calvinist South was inspired by Unitarians and free-thinkers, who, unlike the northern clergy, were abolitionists and "statists": the same men who championed women's suffrage, the Negro vote, mesmerism, the peace movement, vegetarianism, and socialism. The South, he wrote, had a right to defend slavery because the radical reordering of its society by atheists was a far worse alternative.[5]

Possibly Rushdoony had absorbed Machen's defense of the antebellum South and his libertarian opposition to centralized political structures and laws that intruded on personal freedoms. However, he was writing at the time of Lyndon Johnson's civil rights acts, and the clergyman he was quoting was Rev. Benjamin Morgan Palmer, who on Thanksgiving 1860 had urged the South to secede, holding that it had a religious duty to defend the cause of God and to perpetuate the institution of slavery. Along with Rev. C. Gregg Singer, a schismatic southern Presbyterian also writing in the mid-1960s, Rushdoony rediscovered the works of Palmer and two other leading Presbyterian defenders of the Confederacy and used them to argue that the Civil War was essentially a "theological war"—and the civil rights movement anti-Christian.[6] Rushdoony found both the Thirteenth and Fourteenth Amendments unconstitutional and nothing but an effort to impose the power of the federal government on the states. By

RS RACISM

his account, it was downhill from there on, with increasing federal power and increasing racial and religious diversity. "Minority groups," he wrote in 1965, "hold the balance of power in many states—Negroes, Catholics, Zionist Jews, pensioners, and the like. . . . Only by restoring localism, by amending the Constitution to require the coincidence of the electoral college and its vote with the structure of Congress, can minority rule, with its attendant evils, hatred and injustice, be checked."[7] Rushdoony's America was white and Calvinist, and at the heart of his politics was not just racism but an all-purpose, full-service bigotry.

In the 1950s and early 1960s Rushdoony, a pastor in Santa Cruz churches, took up with political right-wingers, social conservatives, and economic libertarians. He became a close friend of Robert Welch, the founder of the John Birch Society. His history books were subsidized by the Volker Fund, the leading libertarian organization of the period. Under the direction of the founder's nephew, the fund had spread the influence of the Austrian school of economics to the United States by bringing Friedrich Hayek to the University of Chicago and helping to support Ludwig von Mises and others. Rushdoony acquired an abiding admiration for the Austrian School economics.[8]

Biblical law

In 1965 Rushdoony with the help of a few wealthy friends founded the Chalcedon Foundation (named for a fifth-century ecumenical council), whose main purpose was to allow him to write.[9] Eight years later he published his major work: an eight-hundred-page volume, *The Institutes of Biblical Law*, in which he drew out what he saw as the full legal and political implications of Van Til's rejection of autonomous human reason. "Neither positive law nor natural law," he wrote, "can reflect more than sin and apostasy of man: revealed law is the need and privilege of Christian society. It is the *only* means whereby man can fulfill his creation mandate of exercising dominion under God." Christians, he proposed, must seek a regime based exclusively on biblical law. God, he held, had given Moses the law at Sinai not just for Israel but for all nations at all times, and Christians had taken up the covenant that Israel had broken. The Great Commission therefore meant not just evangelism but the institution of biblical law across the globe. As one protégé, David Chilton, put it, "The Christian goal for the world is the universal development of Biblical theocratic republics, in which every area of life is redeemed and placed under the Lordship of Jesus Christ and the rule of God's law." The goal, once achieved, would, Rushdoony promised, lead directly to Christ's return and His millennial reign on earth.[10]

Christian Reconstructionism, then, rested on three central concepts: presuppositionalism, theonomy (or rule by God's law), and postmillennialism. In the *Institutes* Rushdoony fleshed out his conception of theonomy and the Kingdom of God on earth. The Bible was to be the governing text for all areas of life, from government to education and the arts. In the "kingdom society" there was to be no room for diversity or tolerance of another religion, not even Judaism, for the Jews failed to live up to the covenants. With God on their side, Christians had no need for majoritarian politics, or for compromise and accommodation to reach their goal. Rushdoony was completely straightforward in rejecting democracy. "Christianity is completely and radically anti-democratic; it is committed to spiritual aristocracy," he wrote, and only "the right have rights." What a reconstructed society would look like was not entirely clear, but he was quite specific about certain issues of its governance. Bible law in his view required a radical decentralization of government under the control of the righteous. Once defenses were no longer needed, federal governments would wither away, and local governments would cede power to the basic institutions of government: the patriarchal family and the Church. With no property or income taxes, government services would be confined to building roads, ensuring weights and measures, and the like, while families and churches would provide all social services, including education, health, and welfare. Government would have no control over the economy, but then the society he envisioned was agricultural, and the economy was to be cash or gold-based with little or no debt.[11]

"I'm close to being a libertarian," Rushdoony said brightly on a Bill Moyers program in 1987. Wearing a banker's suit, his white beard brushed and shining, Rushdoony spoke to Moyers in clipped, precise sentences. Moyers raised his eyebrows at the word "libertarian," for they had just been talking about the government's responsibility for enforcing religious law.

In Rushdoony's reconstructed society criminal justice was to be based on Old Testament laws—except for those specifically abrogated in the New Testament. Capital crimes were to include homosexual behavior, adultery, lying about one's virginity, incorrigible juvenile delinquency, blasphemy, witchcraft, and apostasy. The biblically approved methods of execution included stoning, burning at the stake, hanging, and "the sword." Punishment for most noncapital crimes involved whipping and restitution in form of indentured servitude or slavery. To Moyers, Rushdoony said he didn't like everything in the Bible—"some of it rubs me the wrong way"—but the Bible was God's word. End of story. Nothing could be left out. As his student Greg Bahnsen wrote, "*Every* single stroke of the [biblical] law must be seen by the Christian as applicable to *this* very age between the advents of Christ." In Reconstructionist circles this led to arcane disputes over the contemporary application of ceremonial laws respecting diet, menstrual purity, and ritual sacrifice.[12]

Rushdoony attracted several disciples, among them Bahnsen, David Chilton, Gary DeMar, and George Grant. The most important of them was Gary North, who met Rushdoony in 1962 when he was twenty and married his daughter in the early 1970s. Without North, as one scholar of the movement wrote, there might have been no Reconstructionism, for North popularized Rushdoony's ponderous volume and reached across sectarian boundaries dividing ultraconservative Presbyterians from the rest of the evangelical world.[13]

The son of an FBI agent and a youthful contributor to Fred Schwarz's Christian Anti-Communist Crusade, North took a PhD in history from the University of California, Riverside, in 1972, specializing in economic history. For Rushdoony he researched the relationship between biblical law and the laissez-faire economics of von Mises and Hayek. He reached out to active political conservatives, and through Congressman Larry McDonald, a former head of the John Birch Society, he found a job as a researcher for Congressman Ron Paul of Texas in 1976. When Paul lost an election, North formed the Institute for Christian Economics and began a grassroots effort to spread Reconstructionist ideas among disparate southern church groups, many of them Pentecostal or charismatic, with the goal of forming a network for political action.[14]

North and Rushdoony had a falling-out in 1981 and never spoke again.

The split between two orthodox Christians would not seem a good auspice for the future of the global Reconstruction, but the advantage was that the movement developed two centers, the Chalcedon Foundation in Vallecito, California, and North's institute in Tyler, Texas, and the two competed in churning out publications. The result was an avalanche of literature and a series of breathless announcements of new insights into biblical law. Rushdoony's foundation published the monthly *Chalcedon Report* and the more scholarly *Journal of Christian Reconstructionism*, and issued books.[15] The Institute for Christian Economics with the same institutional logorrhea published a newsletter, a journal, and books. North himself wrote dozens of books, numerous articles, and countless blogposts. The two leaders agreed on basic principles, but they disagreed on the ways to reach the goal of Christian dominion.

Rushdoony led the purist wing of the movement. Apparently exhilarated by the rise of the Christian right and Reagan's victory, he joined the Council on National Policy founded by Tim LaHaye and Nelson Bunker Hunt in 1981, but he rarely went to meetings, and in the late 1980s he pulled out completely. He was not a man for collaboration. The sovereign God of history, he was sure, would bring victory without need for compromise, and he urged patient efforts at evangelism, education, and politics. The changes would come by regeneration, not revolution, and he was willing to wait. Over thousands of years, he wrote, God's grace would regenerate enough men so that the society would submit to God's law. David Chilton's estimate was 36,000 years.[16]

North was more impatient. While Rushdoony put the emphasis on persuasion, North thought in terms of conquest. "Jesus' ministry," he wrote, "restored the inheritance to His people. He announced a world-wide ministry of conquest, based on preaching the gospel of peace. Christians are required to pursue the same program of world dominion which God originally assigned to Adam and reassigned to Noah." Rushdoony thought political control necessary but not sufficient; North focused on politics, and the takeover of government by the righteous. "The long-term goal of Christians in politics should be to gain exclusive control over the franchise," he wrote. "Those who refuse to submit publicly must be denied citizenship." Rushdoony for all of his optimism—or perhaps because of it—saw the world as sliding into anarchy. "You can have two kinds of law," he said, "theonomy—God's law, or autonomy—self-law. . . . Autonomy leads to anarchy, and which is what we are getting increasingly." On the Bill Moyers program he announced that the state was a bankrupt institution and that a worldwide breakdown was under way. North, more specific, made numerous predictions about a crash in the global economy (including YK2 in 2000). Incessantly warning that American society would collapse under the weight of massive foreign debt, military over-stretch, and internal decadence, he strove to prepare godly men to step forward at the moment of cataclysm. In book after book he advised Christians to think of Noah's preparations for the Flood, and he instructed them on how to live debt-free, how to avoid electronic surveillance, and how to develop the skills necessary for surviving economic collapse. His vision was of a medieval world with very few people in it. Needless to say, he favored Birchite conspiracy theories about the plan of Eastern Establishment bankers to create a world socialist superstate. In 1985 he wrote the prologue and the epilogue to the revised edition of the genre classic, *None Dare Call It Conspiracy,* by two former members of the John Birch Society. But then Rushdoony himself maintained that "the view of history as conspiracy . . . is a basic aspect of . . . orthodox Christianity." [17]

In the 1980s North had high hopes for the spread of Reconstructionism. "Christians are rallying to support Falwell and others like him who stand up and fight," he wrote early in the decade. "In doing so, they are steadily abandoning premillenialism, psychologically if not officially." Pentecostals, he said, were asking, "If God can heal a sick person, why can't He heal a sick society?" In a newsletter of 1984 he described what he called "the three legs of Christian Reconstruction's stool." First came the Presbyterian scholars in the tradition of Machen and Rushdoony. "Presbyterians supply the ammo," he wrote. "They shoot, too, but there just aren't enough of them to make much difference." [18] Second, the Christian schools, which in "molding the minds of the next generation of Christian leaders," constituted "the knife at the throat of monopolistic humanistic schools." In his view the very act of a starting a school often changed "the psychology of conformism and capitulation." "When a parent pulls his child out of a public school," he wrote, "he has broken institutionally and psychologically with the statist order." The schools gave formerly "pietistic" pastors the motivation to fight, and "pressure from state boards of education and local truancy officers provide the fight." The third leg of the stool was the charismatic telecommunications system: "The holy rollers," he wrote, "are rolling less and broadcasting more." Pentecostals, he explained, were taking advantage of the technological miracle of satellite transmission and renting inexpensive time to broadcast their programs. Pastor Robert Tilton, for one, had one thousand churches hooked up by satellite to his ministry, and if others, such as the Full Gospel Business Men's Fellowship . . . and Maranatha campus Ministries, ever got their own scheduled satellite broadcast, "the technological foundation of a comprehensive revival will be established." [19] Technology, in other words, was going to lead the way back to a medieval world.

Some Reconstructionists, however, realized they faced an uphill battle. When critics harped on the Old Testament penal laws, as they invariably did, leading evangelical personalities sidled away. North was apparently oblivious of the public relations problem. He once pronounced group stoning the preferred method of execution, saying that stones were cheap and plentiful, and because no one could tell who struck which blow, the method established collective responsibility. Then, while North often spoke of a coalition of evangelical groups, he seemed no more likely than Rushdoony to create one. Attack was his usual rhetorical mode, and his propensity was to insult the very people he imagined would join the coalition. He published a series of attacks on proponents of the premillenial Rapture. He described "pietists" as "mush-mouthed, spineless, lily-livered milksops," and called Presbyterians the brains of the movement and charismatics "the feet." On top of that, his always unfulfilled predictions of economic disaster alienated those who had bought gold or otherwise followed his survivalist instructions. [20]

In itself the idea of reinstating Mosaic Law was enough to ensure that the number of full-fledged Reconstructionists remained too small to fill a large living room. One of the few of note was Howard Phillips, the Jewish-born head of the Conservative Caucus, and later the founder of the U.S. Taxpayers Party (renamed the Constitution Party) and a three-time candidate for president. Others were Colonel Doner of the Christian

Voice after he became disillusioned by Reagan, and Randall Terry, the anti-abortion activist, after he left Operation Rescue. Reconstructionist books turned up in Christian bookstores and in some fundamentalist and charismatic college libraries. North took to distributing them free, but many readers—literally or figuratively—hid them under their beds. Reconstructionist ideas nonetheless circulated in bits and pieces or in watered-down forms. By the end of the 1980s a few theologically informed observers, such as the Lutheran-turned-Catholic scholar Richard John Neuhaus, reported that Reconstructionist doctrines were making their way into circles whose members would not be comfortable with calling themselves theonomists, and many of whom had no notion of where the doctrines came from. In particular they seemed to be cropping up among fundamentalist political activists, home schooling congregations, and charismatic ministries, sometimes using the title Dominion Theology.[21]

Later journalists and dedicated opponents of the Christian right began finding Reconstructionist ideas under every theological bush, sometimes plausibly, sometimes not. (Some of them attributed traditional fundamentalist notions to Rushdoony, and some took North's claims about his constituency for reality.) The influence of Reconstructionism was thus overstated. Still, Rushdoony made explicit the prejudices that some southern white evangelicals continued to harbor and enhanced the mythology of the Lost Cause. In addition certain Reconstructionist ideas had their attractions for those who were in any case antistatist and antisecular humanist: among them, the critique of the presupposition of nonbelievers, the importance attributed to the Puritans in the founding of the United States, and the focus on the issue of Christianity and law. Then, as Neuhaus noted, the Reconstructionists had the optimistic, can-do American spirit sorely lacking in premillennialism—especially when it came to the long-term potential of Christians to change the world.[22]

*   *   *

Unlike Rushdoony, Francis Schaeffer was a major intellectual celebrity in the evangelical world. From the 1960s to his death from cancer in 1984 he lectured extensively at evangelical colleges, addressed conventions of the SBC and the Lutheran Church–Missouri Synod, made two best-selling documentary series, and published over thirty books and booklets with combined sales in the millions. In a 1997 article in *Christianity Today* the historian Michael Hamilton called Schaeffer "evangelicalism's most important public intellectual in the twenty years before his death." In the late 1970s he was taken up by Christian right leaders, from D. James Kennedy to Pat Robertson, and by Jack Kemp and other powerful Washington Republicans. President Reagan invited him to the White House, and after his death Reagan wrote in a condolence note to his wife, "He will long be remembered as one of the great Christian thinkers of our century." Falwell and LaHaye often referred to his work, and since then a succession of Christian right leaders from Charles Colson to Richard Land—right down to Michele Bachmann—have testified to the profound influence his works had on their thinking. Schaeffer, however, had made his reputation among evangelical students who wouldn't have been caught dead listening to a Falwell or a Robertson.[23]

Schaeffer came upon the American scene in the mid-1960s, lecturing on Christian apologetics at evangelical colleges and at InterVarsity chapters at secular universities. He had been living in Switzerland for twenty years, and he cut an exotic figure. With long hair and a shaggy goatee beard, he usually appeared in a Nehru jacket, mountain climber's knickers, and boots. His lectures were not the usual fare of theology interlaced with biblical quotations. Instead he spoke of the development of Western civilization in art, science, and philosophy, making connections between, for instance, Kierkegaard and Salvador Dalí. His theme was the gradual erosion of Christian thought by humanism and the kind of secular thinking that confined reason to the world of natural phenomena and assigned the realm of meaning and values to "unreason," or pure subjectivity. The consequence of what he called "the existential methodology" was the modern dilemma of people trying to live with the presupposition that there was no ultimate truth or meaning.

Schaeffer's knowledge of Western culture seemed encyclopedic. In a review of his 1968 lecture series at Calvin College, George Marsden, then an assistant professor of history at Calvin, wrote that Schaeffer might in a typical hour "present the thought of Antonioni, Aquinas, two Francis Bacons, the Beatles, Bergman, Bernstein, Camus, Cezanne, Cimabue,

Francis Crick, Leonardo da Vinci, Eliot, Fellini, Gauguin, Giotto, Hegel, Heidegger, several Huxleys, Jaspers, Kierkegaard, Leary, Henry Miller, Picasso, Rousseau, Marquis de Sade, Sartre, Terry Southern, Schlesinger, Tillich and Zen Buddhism."[24] The students were dazzled. "What an electric moment it was," a future professor said of an early lecture. "It energized a lot of us to believe you could be an intellectual and be a Christian." Marsden, somewhat less impressed, remarked dryly, "Intellectual modesty is not Schaeffer's long suit." Still, Marsden praised Schaeffer for sketching a map of the intellectual currents in the Western world and making "Christianity appear intellectually relevant to the contemporary era."[25]

Schaeffer often spoke of popular culture. He would describe Fellini or Buñuel films and quote the lyrics of Jimi Hendrix or Led Zeppelin. What surprised students was not just how much he seemed to know about contemporary artists, but the appreciation he showed for their work and the sympathy he seemed to have for the counterculture of the day. Brought up in a society with no values except for personal peace and affluence, the young, Schaeffer often said, were rejecting the "plastic" world of their "bourgeois" parents and desperately searching for spiritual meaning in music, drugs, free love, and Asian religions. Most evangelical students had never thought of drugs or sex in that way. Schaeffer did insist that Christianity was the only answer, but the lesson most students seemed to have learned was not just "the relevance of Christianity to contemporary culture," but rather, as Marsden also noticed, the opposite. At a time when they were fighting to watch Disney movies, Schaeffer told them they had to go into the great outdoors of art, science, and literature if they wanted to understand the world they were living in. Further, they could leave their antiseptic shelters and listen to "dirty words" and watch Italian "dirty movies" without fear of catching a communicable disease.[26]

When Schaeffer was not on the lecture circuit, he was holding forth at L'Abri ("the shelter"), an evangelical community that he and his wife, Edith, had founded in 1955. An independent ministry supported by American donors and housed in chalets in a small Alpine village not far from Lausanne, L'Abri offered hiking, hearty meals, Sunday church services, informal seminars, and long evenings of talk. The Schaeffers initially brought in English students attending local boarding schools and the University of Lausanne, but by the 1960s L'Abri was attracting visitors from England and the United States: a combination of university students, indigent travelers, and the rebellious children of the evangelical aristocracy sent by their parents in hopes they might be saved. Warm and hospitable, the Schaeffers accepted everyone, including unwed mothers, homosexuals, interracial couples, atheists, and the occasional Jesus freak. Francis came to believe he couldn't save non-Christians by quoting the Bible and using a language foreign to them. Certain that he could prevail by reason, he took to lecturing on European civilization, and his tape-recorded lectures were turned into books. Word of his lectures spread, and by the late 1960s, L'Abri had become a stop on the magical mystery tour that took hipsters and "seekers" from communes in San Francisco to ashrams in India. Timothy Leary paid a visit, as did Jimmy Page of Led Zeppelin, and guests smoked pot outside on the grass. Schaeffer, his son Frank later wrote, "had evolved into a hip guru preaching Jesus to hippies." [27]

In this period Schaeffer wrote *Pollution and the Death of Man* (1970), calling for care for the environment and framing environmentalism in evangelical terms. He often called for "the compassionate use of wealth," but he never addressed the subject of business directly. Like Billy Graham, he took American capitalism as a given and never thought about how it might be contributing to the secularization of the country.

Schaeffer had come a long way from his religious training. Born in Germantown, Pennsylvania, in 1912, he had converted at the age of eighteen, gone to a Presbyterian college, and married Edith, the daughter of a China missionary. Introduced to the work of J. Gresham Machen, he went in to Westminster Seminary in 1935. By then Machen had been expelled from the Presbyterian Church for creating an Independent Board of Foreign Missions. In the two years he spent at Westminster, Schaeffer lived through not only the aftermath of the fundamentalist-modernist controversy but also through the battles between the strictly Calvinist Machen faction and the fundamentalist McIntire faction over dispensationalism, the use of alcohol, and control over the Independent Board. Schaeffer sided with McIntire, and when Machen died, he completed his studies at McIntire's new Faith Seminary in Wilmington and joined his breakaway Bible Presbyterian Church. Becoming a separatist from the separatists, he served as a pastor in a series of Bible Presbyterian churches until 1947, when McIntire sent him to Europe to establish the Independent Board and the international arm of his American Council of Christian Churches on the Continent. He and Edith settled near Lausanne and served the cause of militant fundamentalism until 1955, when he broke with McIntire (as just about everyone did). His years abroad having convinced him that Europeans had no interest in intramural American squabbles, and that the real problem was unbelief, he formed his own independent ministry to evangelize the younger generation brought up on modernist thinking without a "Christian base." [28]

In 1974 a film producer and the Schaeffers' youngest child, Frank, then twenty-two and longing to escape the confines of L'Abri, convinced Schaeffer to turn his lectures into a series of documentary films. The two raised money from evangelicals such as Nelson Bunker Hunt and Richard DeVos, the founder of Amway, advertising the project as an answer to the BBC series *Civilisation* written by the eminent art historian Sir Kenneth Clark. The ten-episode series, *How Should We Then Live?*, directed by Frank, appeared two years later accompanied by a book of the same title. In his biography of Schaeffer, Barry Hankins wrote that the book "brought together Schaeffer's entire intellectual and cultural project" and that it was the best thing he had written thus far. [29]

In the survey of Western intellectual history from Roman times until the present, Schaeffer tracked the disease of humanism as it made its way from Aristotle to the works of Acquinas and Dante, infecting the entire Italian Renaissance. The Reformation held back its progress, but it continued through into the Enlightenment and from there into modern thought. What Schaeffer calls the "line of despair"—or the division between Christian and post-Christian "thought-forms"—appeared, he tells us, in Europe with the works of Rousseau, Hegel, Kant, and Kierkegaard. After that, it was all over on the Continent: belief in a universal truth and the capacity of reason to grasp it gave way to humanistic "relativism." What followed was the fragmentation of thinking reflected in the works of Monet, Cézanne, Picasso, and the existential despair of the late Beethoven quartets, the works of Arnold Schoenberg, Camus, Sartre, and Marcel Duchamp. Only in the United States did the Reformation continue to reign until the 1930s, but as the lyrics of Dylan, Hendrix, and the Jefferson Airplane demonstrated, it was finished now.[30]

To read the book, or watch the film series, is to wonder at pronouncements such as "Apathy was the chief mark of the late [Roman] Empire," delivered without any doubt or a ray of humor, or "the development of the Renaissance in the south could have gone in a good direction or a poor one. But humanism took over—all was made autonomous and meaning was lost." It is also to have the suspicion that Schaeffer never actually read Aquinas, much less Hegel or the rest of the philosophers and theologians he cited. Hankins gives him the benefit of the doubt, but all the evidence he discovered makes the case. "Schaeffer," he writes, "was a voracious reader of magazines and the Bible, but some who lived at L'Abri and knew him well say they never saw him read a book." In Hankins's view it was highly likely that Schaeffer had learned almost everything he knew about Western intellectual history from the students who had dropped out of European universities—and the rest from the consultants and editors who worked on his films.[31]

How Should We Then Live? is a testament to the innocence of the evangelical student audiences of the period. Today the most interesting thing about the series is the struggles Schaeffer had with his own intellectual upbringing and with the "thought-forms" he shared with students from fundamentalist backgrounds. For example, Schaeffer shows a real appreciation for Italian Renaissance art and architecture. In one film he dwells lovingly on Masaccio's frescoes and Brunelleschi's dome; he doesn't flinch before of paintings of nudes, or depictions of non-Christian gods. But after a word or two about the formal elements in each work, he flings aesthetics aside for the "worldview" expressed in the art—or rather the "worldview" he attributes to its creator. Leonardo, he writes, was a genius, but he was a humanist who tried to paint "the universal . . . out of his observation of the particulars" and failed. Dürer, on the other hand, a product of the Reformation, succeeded: "His beautiful watercolors of flowers, rabbits, and so on were a clear exhibition that God's world has a value, a real value." Why Leonardo's portraits or his fresco of the Last Supper failed to do likewise, Schaeffer doesn't explain. It's a triumph of

ideology over the sight of what was in front of him—and a perfectly philistine position that viscerally he did not feel.[32]

Schaeffer criticized almost everything written or painted after the
mid-nineteenth century. It wasn't just that he disapproved of the works
of non-Christians or that he didn't understand modernism. The problem went deeper than that. Of the Impressionists he wrote, "These men
painted *only* what their eyes brought them, but this left the question as
to whether there was a reality behind the light waves reaching the eyes."
Clearly he believed there was a "reality" to naturalistic pictures of flowers
and rabbits beyond the paint on the canvas. He had similar difficulties with
what he understood of Hegel. He quotes a commentator: "According to
Hegel, the universe is steadily unfolding, and so is man's understanding of
it. No single proposition about reality can truly reflect what is the case."
His conclusion was, "truth, as people had always thought of truth, had
died." The idea that "reality" exists in some absolute form independent
of perspective or time was seventeenth-century Scottish Common Sense
Realism preserved flawlessly in American fundamentalism.[33]

The film series, released in 1976, was an enormous success. To watch
it on YouTube in the twenty-first century is to see an embarrassment of
actors dressed up in 1950s B-movie style as gladiators, martyred Christians, Galileo, or Martin Luther. Many evangelicals of the 1970s (including Michele Bachmann) loved it. Frank took it on a fifteen-city tour, and
films went on into churches and meeting halls, making his father into a
major star.[34]

The conclusion of *How Should We Then Live?* was, however, not a
part of Schaeffer's recent "intellectual and culture project" but rather a
reversion to type. In the last segment Schaeffer imagined the future of
an America without "a Christian consensus." Changing tone abruptly, he
spoke of the apathy that followed the student rebellions and a new climate
of "degeneracy, decadence, depravity and a love of violence for violence's
sake" taking over the land. Condemning "determinist" science and social
science, he warned that humanist elites in the media, universities, and government would exploit a coming crisis—economic collapse, world war,
chaos, and terrorism, or the growing shortage of natural resources—to

persuade apathetic Americans to accept a "manipulative authoritarian government" for the sake of their own personal peace. Clearly the Antichrist was on its way. Still, like Falwell, who began his crusades the same year, Schaeffer concluded with the hope that Christians could bring the nation back to its "Christian base." [35]

While the films were in production, Schaeffer had found disputes over biblical inerrancy cropping up, as they had in the 1920s, but this time within the evangelical world. As his son Frank later wrote, he girded on his fundamentalist armor and went into battle against all those who claimed that the Bible contained errors or that Genesis should be understood metaphorically. Like Harold Lindsell, whose book he read in draft, he held that those who found a jot or a tittle of error had started down the slippery slope—and were not evangelicals at all. In his books on the subject he attacked biological evolution and modern geology on the grounds that the theories were weak and the facts probably wrong. His books brought him invitations to speak to the Southern Baptist Convention and the Lutheran Church–Missouri Synod, where inerrancy had become the fundamentalist rallying cry. Once enlisted in the American conflict, he began to turn his attention to politics—though he kept returning to the defense of inerrancy and a literal reading of the creation story for the rest of his life. [36]

In one segment of *How Should We Then Live?* Schaeffer denounced *Roe v. Wade.* According to Frank, he hadn't wanted to mention it because it was "a Catholic issue," but Frank, who felt strongly that abortion was murder, had argued him into it. The segment attracted the attention of Dr. C. Everett Koop, a leading pediatric surgeon, a Reformed Presbyterian, and one of the few evangelical antiabortion activists of the period. An old friend of the Schaeffers', Koop traveled to L'Abri and with Frank's help persuaded Francis to do a book and a film series defending the sanctity of life. The result, *Whatever Happened to the Human Race?,* appeared in 1979. [37] In the book Schaeffer goes off into disquisitions about biblical inerrancy and changing worldviews, but Frank made the films dramatic. The four-part series begins with Koop doing surgery on a newborn with Schaeffer's voice in the background talking about the decline of the Judeo-Christian tradition and the rise of indifference to human life. Koop describes in graphic detail how abortion procedures end the life of a fetus. In an arresting shot the camera shows him standing on the salt flats of the Dead Sea (where the city of Sodom once stood) with hundreds of plastic dolls lying broken around him. Abortion, Koop reports, has devalued human life; it has inclined many doctors to allow infants to die, though even severely deformed children can be saved by heroic medical measures and grow up to lead full lives. (The camera shows him sitting in a living room with several grown men and women who owed their lives to his surgery.) Passive infanticide and passive euthanasia, he argues, already occur in many hospitals, and if tolerated along with abortion, they will inevitably lead to state-mandated infanticide and the euthanasia of unwanted individuals and groups. Frank interpolated with darkly lit images of shackled blacks, old-world Jews, elderly people, and handicapped children while the voice-over created an equivalence among slavery, the Holocaust, abortion, infanticide, euthanasia, and state control.[38]

To the Schaeffers' surprise the films of *Whatever Happened to the Human Race?* tanked. Frank had organized two-day "seminars" in venues as large as Madison Square Garden, but he could hardly fill the first rows, and the producers lost a good deal of money. A *Christianity Today* reporter, noting the poor attendance, asked, "Do Christians really want to know that much about euthanasia, infanticide or abortion?" The answer apparently was no. Some pastors discouraged their congregations from attending, for even in 1979 the antiabortion movement was viewed as Catholic and thought highly controversial. Schaeffer later blamed "the evangelical establishment" for the empty seats, claiming that pietism and "over-spiritualized Christianity" had prevented its leaders from recognizing the social evils around them. Still, the films moved many people who had never thought about abortion or euthanasia before. Koop and the Schaeffers kept promoting the series, and slowly it gained an audience in conservative churches, then it took off, and within a few years it had become a nation-wide phenomenon.[39]

Schaeffer's next book, *A Christian Manifesto*, was a general call to arms. Schaeffer's answer to *The Communist Manifesto*, it described the historical advance of humanism in the United States and exhorted Christians to turn back the tide. Used to collaboration, he wrote it with research furnished by John Whitehead, a young lawyer introduced to him by Frank who be-

longed to the circle around Rushdoony. Schaeffer had had some acquaintance with Rushdoony's works. He never took his ideas about Mosaic Law
seriously, and he lost interest when he found out that the author was a
postmillennialist. In 1964, however, he had given an informal seminar on
Rushdoony's *This Independent Republic* at L'Abri and had filled his students
with enthusiasm for the idea that the Constitution was a religious document that owed nothing to the Enlightenment.[40]

In *A Christian Manifesto* Schaeffer maintained that the only governments in human history "with a balance of form and freedom" were
those in Northern Europe and its former colonies in North America,
Australia, and New Zealand. These governments, he claimed, derived
uniquely from the Reformation, where authority resided in Scripture
and "God's written law." In the case of the United States, he explained,
the Founding Fathers took their political theories from the English Puritans. Instead of offering up his usual vague notion of "worldviews," he
specified that they came from *Lex Rex*, the work of Samuel Rutherford,
a seventeenth-century Scots Presbyterian divine. John Witherspoon, the
Scots Presbyterian president of Princeton and a signer of the Declaration of Independence, he claimed, had drawn directly on *Lex Rex*, while
Thomas Jefferson had gathered the same ideas from John Locke, who had
simply secularized Rutherford's work.[41] Building on this novel notion, he
concluded, much as Rushdoony had, that the Founders had no intention
of establishing a secular state, or of using the First Amendment to remove the influence of religion on government. "And now it's all gone!"
he wrote. "Today the separation of church and state in America is used
to silence the church."[42]

Unlike Rushdoony, Schaeffer didn't blame secularism on the Unitarians
or celebrate the Confederacy. The move away from the Constitution, he
wrote, came in two waves. The first was the arrival of immigrants with
views not shaped by the Reformation (i.e., Catholics and Jews), and the introduction of the concept of "pluralism." The second was the emergence
of humanism: a total worldview with a "material-energy-chance concept
of reality" standing in complete antithesis to the Christian worldview. Humanists, he wrote, used the concept of "pluralism" to mean that there is
no right and wrong: everything is acceptable and personal preferences

are all that matter in ethics or in law. Where, he asked, were "the Christian lawyers" when law, and especially the courts, became "*the vehicle to force* this total humanistic way of thinking upon the entire population?" And where were the theologians? The Presbyterian Church expelled Dr. Charles Briggs in 1893 for teaching humanistic liberal theology, but after that it gave up. Some of us, he wrote, may think the Moral Majority has made mistakes, but it has done one thing right: "it has drawn the line between one total view of reality and the other total view of reality and the result this brings forth in government and law." [43]

At present, he continued, there were two tracks open to Christians. First, the conservative victory in the 1980 election had opened a window in which Christians could try to roll back the "total entity" of humanism. But if the window closed, the majority of the Silent Majority, concerned only for their personal peace and affluence, would doubtless accept some form of "elite authoritarianism"—possibly a technocrat elite, or the judges of the Supreme Court. What then should Christians do? The lesson from the early church and the Reformation, he wrote, was that Christians had a duty to resist a government that acted against God's law. He later spoke of the sanction given by the Founding Fathers in the Declaration of Independence to throw off an oppressive, authoritarian state, ending with a flourish: "What is needed at this time is to take the steps necessary to break the authoritarian hold which the material-energy-chance concept of reality has on government and law." The result, he wrote, would be freedom, and freedom for Reformation Christianity "no longer subject to hidden censorship," to compete in the free market of ideas and show its unique value for "individual salvation and for society." [44]

Schaeffer went to some lengths to say that he was not calling for a theocracy.

> We must make definite that we are in no way talking about any kind of a theocracy. Let me say that with great emphasis. Witherspoon, Jefferson, the American Founders had no idea of a theocracy. That is made plain by the First Amendment.

And:

There is no New Testament basis for a linking of church and state
until Christ, the King returns. The whole "Constantine mentality"
from the fourth century up to our day was a mistake. . . . Through
the centuries it has caused great confusion between loyalty to the
state and loyalty to Christ, between patriotism and being a Christian.
We must not confuse the Kingdom of God with our country. To
say it another way: We should not wrap Christianity in our national
flag.[45]

Here Schaeffer is clearly differentiating himself from Rushdoony and,
as he did elsewhere, chiding Falwell for confusing patriotism with Christianity in his "I Love America" rallies.

On the other hand Schaeffer wrote that the Constitution was not a
secular document, and that the Founding Fathers took their political theories entirely from the Reformation, and specifically from Samuel Rutherford. In *Lex Rex* Rutherford had indeed advocated resistance to illegitimate
authority, but the authority he had in mind was the Catholic monarchy,
and whether Schaeffer knew it or not, he had also written a book proposing that a "Christian" civil government should not tolerate heretics or
schismatics from the Presbyterian Church, but put them to death by the
sword.[46] Then, too, Schaeffer condemned pluralism in the United States,
and bemoaned the arrival not just of non-Christians but of all Christians
outside the Reformed tradition. He did say that, with humanism vanquished, Reformation Christianity would compete in "the free marketplace of ideas." But he added that Reformed Christianity had "a unique
value for individual salvation and for society." As George Marsden wrote,
the American Calvinists traditionally believed that their own ideas would
triumph in a free society.[47]

Schaeffer called "secular humanism" a "total entity," and a total "worldview" that had *forced* its way of thinking onto the entire population and
that would inevitably lead to state tyranny. As an example of what he
meant, he cited a 1981 lawsuit in which he said the ACLU was contesting
an Arkansas state law allowing the teaching of creationism in the public
schools, and "acting as an arm of the humanist consensus" was trying to
force its view "on the majority of Arkansas officials." Unfortunately for his

argument, he had his facts wrong. As it happened, George Marsden was testifying for the ACLU in the case. Arkansas, he pointed out, was not just "allowing" the teaching of creationism, as Schaeffer had it, but "requiring" it, and thus in Marsden's view imposing the views of a small group of Christians on all public school children. Then, while misunderstanding the case, Schaeffer wrote that if the federal appeals court ruled in favor of the ACLU, the state government should protest and refuse to submit. He did not say exactly how the state of Arkansas should resist the federal government, but he did not seem to remember that in 1957 federal troops were called in to allow nine African American students to attend Little Rock Central High School.[48]

In general Schaeffer's counsel about the means Christians should use to resist "secular humanism" was opaque or ambiguous. His son Frank, who mutatis mutandis became a novelist and critic of the Christian right, said of his father in a PBS interview in 2009, "Here you had a guy who's having lunch with the President calling for the overthrow of the U.S. government, and he just gets invited for afternoon tea. No one says a word."[49] When a journalist later wrote that *The Christian Manifesto* called for a "violent overthrow" of the government to stop abortion, a Schaeffer defender—an editor of Neuhaus's magazine *First Things*—responded indignantly that anyone who had read the book would know it said nothing of the sort: Schaeffer had explicitly called for nonviolent civil disobedience to end abortion. True, he spoke of the use of force throughout the book, but he had carefully defined "force" as "compulsion or constraint exerted upon a person (or persons), or an entity such as the state," and he had added, "Two principles . . . must always be observed. First, there must be a legitimate basis and a legitimate exercise of force. Second, any overreaction crosses the line from force to violence. And unmitigated violence can never be justified."[50]

In fact Schaeffer never advocated the "violent overthrow" of the U.S. government in so many words, and in the case of abortion he plainly called for civil disobedience. On the other hand, he wrote, "What we face is a totality. . . . It is not too strong to say that we are at war, and there are no neutral parties in the struggle." Then he compared the current situation to the American Revolution in which "the colonists used force in defending themselves." His definition of "force" raised more questions than it answered. Where did "compulsion" end? And what was a "legitimate basis" for the use of it? At one point he took the Reformation as a model for legitimate Christian resistance, explaining that its use of force included violence. ("In almost every place where the Reformation had success, there was some form of civil disobedience or armed rebellion.") Disquietingly, Schaeffer described with approval the sixteenth-century wars of religion, failing to note that Protestants as well as the Catholics destroyed the opposing church and its adherents wherever they won. At another point he wrote of the sanction given by the authors of the Declaration of Independence to throw off an oppressive authoritarian state. Was he recommending that present-day Christians put "secular humanist" heads on pikestaffs? Or calling for a revolutionary war against the U.S. government? Doubtless not. Probably it was just that political history and political theory were not his long suits. In any case, his argument was incoherent and open to different interpretations.[51]

A Christian Manifesto sold 290,000 copies in its first year, 62,000 of them bought by Falwell as gifts to his contributors. Thereafter Schaeffer often appeared on television with Falwell and Robertson and spoke from the pulpits of such pastors as D. James Kennedy. According to Frank, he thought the TV evangelists "plastic" and "power hungry," but he developed a relationship with Falwell and took it as his mission to set the Moral Majority on the right path. After he died of cancer in 1984, Newsweek called him the intellectual guru of the Christian right. Writing in 2005, Marvin Olasky, the editor of the conservative World magazine, called him the central figure in the political mobilization of conservative Christians from 1980 on.[52]

Few Christian right activists would have agreed with Olasky. According to Frank, Falwell and Robertson invited his father to speak mainly because of his aura of respectability. Still, Schaeffer reached an audience that the populist TV evangelists could not, and conservative evangelicals did listen. His call for engagement with the culture, for example, found resonance not just at colleges such as Calvin and Wheaton, but also to some degree in the more conservative institutions, such as Liberty University. Then, three of his themes became of central importance to the Christian right movement. The first and most obvious was his big idea about the total opposition between the Christian and the humanist-materialist worldviews. Schaeffer was hardly the first to warn of the threat of humanism, but in jeremiads, such as Falwell's, it was only one of the national sins. In his last years Schaeffer often complained that the Christian right saw only discrete issues, such as pornography or the breakdown of the American family ("the bits and pieces"), when they should have been looking at the whole. Tim LaHaye, among others, seized upon "secular humanism" as an all-encompassing explanation for all that had gone wrong. In his best-selling book *The Battle for the Mind* (1980) he put Schaeffer's idea in a more familiar form, figuring humanists as a conspiratorial group intent on destroying the Christian faith, family values, and democratic freedoms. For the Christian right "secular humanism" soon replaced Communism as the prime ideological enemy and became foundational to the notion of a "culture war" between two totalistic worldviews. Even in moderate evangelical circles the notion of a "Christian worldview" became an accepted part of the conversation, if not a truism.[53]

Similarly, Schaeffer's claim that America had been a Christian nation was hardly original. Whether it meant that the American population was largely Christian, or whether it meant that the nation itself was Christian, the phrase "Christian nation" had inhabited evangelical and civil religion rhetoric from the nineteenth century through the 1950s, and fundamentalists had long ago put it in the past tense. What Schaeffer did—following Rushdoony's work—was to make a detailed historical argument about the intellectual roots of the American Revolution and the founding documents. Appalled by his argument, George Marsden and two younger evangelical historians, Mark A. Noll and Nathan O. Hatch, felt compelled to write a response. In *The Search for a Christian America* (1983) they demolished his intellectual history and in the process instructed their students in the demands of historical scholarship. (Noll found documents to show that Witherspoon's political theories came directly from secular Enlightenment thinkers.) Their book did its work within the elite evangelical colleges, but not in popular right-wing circles. In the wake of Schaeffer's *Manifesto*, making up the beliefs of the Founders, often with the help of invented, or out-of-context, quotations, became a small industry. The lead practitioner, David Barton, whose only academic credential was his 1976 degree in Christian education from Oral Roberts University, churned out books, school texts, and videos for many years, purporting to show that the Founding Fathers, including Jefferson, were Christians who aimed to create a Christian nation. A favorite on Christian right talk shows and praised by Newt Gingrich and Senator Sam Brownback (R-KS), he became according to *Time* magazine in 2005 "a hero to millions," though no academic historian took his work seriously.

Probably the most influential of Schaeffer's works was *Whatever Happened to the Human Race?* In the early 1980s the issue of abortion was still not settled in northern evangelical circles or in the ranks of the SBC. Some continued to favor "therapeutic abortions," and some would have left the choice to individuals. The films Schaeffer made with Koop—later Reagan's surgeon general—are credited by historians with turning the tide of popular evangelical sentiment.[54] Previously Christian right preachers had linked abortion with promiscuity and with feminist efforts to subvert the male headship of the family. In the early 1980s Jim Wallis told a Wheaton audience that he opposed abortion but that he didn't like the antiabortion movement because it was anti-women and anti-poor. *Whatever Happened* made an argument unencumbered by sexual politics: abortion was murder—a holocaust—and the beginning of a slippery slope to the killing of society's outcasts. The films with their powerful imagery and the connection Schaeffer made between the Bible and respect for human life proved so persuasive that Christian right preachers added their rhetoric to their own. Abortion shot to the head of their list of national sins, and opposition to it became known as the "traditional" evangelical position. According to polls, many evangelicals continued to hold other views on the subject, but these were rarely expressed in public, and eventually evangelicals became more Catholic than the Catholics in opposing abortion and *Roe v. Wade*.[55] As a matter of politics, abortion, once framed as murder, made it almost impossible for any evangelical leader to argue against those who insisted the faithful must vote Republican.[56]

One of those directly inspired by Schaeffer's work was Randall Terry, who founded the most militant of the antiabortion groups. As a student in a Bible college, Terry had seen *Whatever Happened* and sobbed, "God, please use me to fight this hideous crime." After reading *The Christian Manifesto*, he remembered that "one of the things it did for me was legitimize the idea that there was a higher law, that God's law is above man's law." By the mid-1980s he and his wife were picketing abortion clinics with right-to-life groups, and in 1987 he formed Operation Rescue and introduced a new set of confrontational tactics. His people surrounded clinics, blockaded doors, and forced themselves on pregnant women to convince them not to have abortions. Many were sent to jail for violating local ordinances, but Terry persisted and for a time he was celebrated by Falwell, D. James Kennedy, and others on the Christian right for leading a new civil rights movement. Thousands of young evangelicals enlisted, and their efforts sometimes temporarily overwhelmed local police forces. Operation Rescue's most notable action was in Wichita, Kansas, in 1991, where a group of protesters carried out a forty-six-day siege on the three abortion clinics, blocking cars, chaining themselves to clinic doors, and haranguing abortion doctors. The protesters were pledged to nonviolence, but as time went on speeches became more inflammatory, and Operation Rescue distributed "wanted" posters for abortion doctors. When protesters bombed abortion clinics and gunned down doctors outside their clinics, the movement was discredited, and after President Clinton signed the Freedom of Access to Clinic Entrances Act in 1994, the blockading of clinics had to stop for a while.[57]*

---

* As surgeon general, Dr. C. Everett Koop decided he should not use his office to campaign against abortion because *Roe* was the law of the land. His main concern soon became the threat of HIV-AIDS. The Reagan administration muzzled him for five years, but he finally was able to sound the alarm with a report that Phyllis Schlafly said might have been edited by the Gay Task Force.

13

PAT ROBERTSON:
POLITICS *and* MIRACLES

I N RETROSPECT the critical decade for the Christian right was the
mid-1970s through the mid-1980s, from the time the movement
began until the evangelical tide turned in favor of the Republicans. In
this period the Christian right owed the most to Jerry Falwell. He not only
put the issues together but he created an organization and persisted when
others dropped out or turned their attention elsewhere. By the time he
effectively retired the Moral Majority in 1986, some judged his effort a failure. He hadn't built an effective political organization; he hadn't forged the
coalition Paul Weyrich had envisaged; and he hadn't persuaded President
Reagan to weigh in on any of the "pro-family" legislation the Congress
might have passed. Nonetheless, he did several important things in the
early 1980s. In a period when journalists, political scientists, and pollsters
had a minimal understanding of the forces at work among evangelicals,
he had kept the Christian right movement in the spotlight and insisted
on its vote-getting power. After the 1984 election, when evangelicals gave
75 percent of their vote to Reagan, he made the cover of *Time* magazine,
and a poll in *U.S. News & World Report* ranked him as the fourteenth most
influential person the country, just after Vice President Bush. Even when
unmasked as a political Wizard of Oz, he remained the person journalists went to for quotes and continued to appear regularly on national TV
talk shows. Few evangelicals other than Separate Baptists ever joined the
Moral Majority, but he made the organization a touchstone for the emerging movement among Southern Baptists and helped to set its agenda.[1]

Weyrich was right that Falwell failed to use what leverage he had to pass "pro-family" legislation, but when Weyrich accused him of putting his agenda aside for the sake of "meaningless access" to the White House, he was missing the point. Beside the fact that photo ops with the popular president helped the preacher enlarge his audience, Falwell's decision to remain loyal to the president showed Reagan Republicans that the Christian right was not just a special interest group ready to bolt if its leaders did not get what they wanted but a loyal constituency. In effect, Falwell provided a half of the epoxy that cemented the Christian right and the Republican Party. Then, as he doubtless realized, the president didn't have to sign any social legislation to endear himself to evangelicals. Reagan just had to give one of his speeches about traditional values, and he would do more to spread the Christian right message than Falwell ever could. In a sense, Reagan, his counterpart, provided the other half of the epoxy.

Falwell appeared on *The Phil Donahue Show, CBS Morning News, Nightline,* and others. Normally affable, often witty, he was sometimes completely outrageous. In 1985 his solution to the AIDS epidemic was legal documentation of all those who carried the AIDS antibody and manslaughter charges against any AIDS carrier who knowingly infected another person. When liberal organizations such as Norman Lear's People for the American Way sprang up to oppose the Christian right, he used their literature in jujitsu fashion to increase his own visibility and to turn himself into a martyr for the cause. On occasion he reached way over into the liberal camp for debating partners. He invited Senator Ted Kennedy to speak and debated Rev. Jesse Jackson on *Nightline,* attracting attention from both the left and the right.[2]

After Falwell folded the Moral Majority, some journalists and scholars predicted the death of the Christian right. The second wave, however, began almost immediately. Taking place while the South was moving decisively into the Republican column, it was characterized by grassroots political mobilization and electoral successes. The voting strength of the movement came from rural areas, but most of the activists came, as before, from conservative areas experiencing rapid modernization like the suburbs in the Sunbelt, where upwardly mobile traditionalists confronted an influx of cosmpolitan people. The dedication and the zealotry of the activists became legendary. Christian right organizations proliferated, most at local, state, or regional levels. By the mid-1990s prominent regional and state groups included the American Family Association in Mississippi, the Traditional Values Coalition in California, Citizens for Traditional Values in Michigan, and Citizens Alliances in Oregon and Washington. In Texas, a state grown increasingly socially conservative, the groups included Concerned Texans and the Associated Conservatives of Texas. In many states, chapters of Concerned Women for America and affiliates of James Dobson's Focus on the Family made their appearance, as did specialized groups, such as Citizens for Excellence in Education and home schooling associations. In 1996 the political scientist John C. Green and his colleagues estimated the number of activists at 200,000 and the core support of the Christian right as one sixth or one fifth of the entire electorate.[3]

Much of the success of the Christian right in the 1990s owed to the one truly national organization, the Christian Coalition. Led by laymen, rather than by ministers, the Coalition succeeded in bringing together evangelicals from a wide range of denominations. Focused on electoral victories and lobbying, it enlisted members of other Christian right groups and worked with Catholic right-to-life organizations and Schlafly's Eagle Forum. Its pragmatic and politically astute leadership turned political naïfs into trained operatives capable of mobilizing voters and winning elections. In some states its activists badly split the Republican Party, but in others they joined, or actually took over, local GOP organizations. Either way the Coalition became a force that every Republican candidate for president had to reckon with in the primaries and at convention time.

The Christian Coalition was work of Pat Robertson, the most curious and contradictory of all the Christian right leaders. The standard-bearer for the movement for over a decade (1987–98), Robertson was well known to millions of television viewers, and though many were sure they understood him, he confounded supporters and opponents alike. Rob Boston, the director of Americans United for Separation of Church and State, called Robertson "the most dangerous man in America," but even his own constituency found that hard to believe. Robertson had none of Falwell's aggressiveness. Broad-faced with smile crinkles next to his eyes, he had an easy, open manner and rather than a domineering father, he seemed an affable, indulgent uncle. He dressed in well-cut suits and spoke with the soft drawl of a Virginia gentleman—yet out of his mouth came astonishing pronouncements: God told him that someone in his TV audience was being cured of bone spurs; his prayers had averted a hurricane; Cuba had Soviet nuclear missiles in the 1980s. Francis Schaeffer, according to his son, regarded him as "a certified lunatic."[4]

Robertson, however, was one of the most successful entrepreneurs in the history of television—as well as a formidable political organizer. His network, CBN, one of the first in the cable market and the first with satellite links to Latin America, Asia, and Africa, changed the whole system of religious broadcasting. His own show, *The 700 Club*, with an audience in the millions, was by the twenty-first century the longest-lived religious program on the air. CBN made some billions of dollars, and Robertson made a personal fortune in the hundreds of millions. As the recognized leader of the Christian right, he spoke at the Council on Foreign Relations and consorted with President George H. W. Bush. In the 1990s Republican senators and presidential candidates flocked to the annual Christian Coalition conventions, and such was Robertson's power in the GOP that conservative intellectuals, from William Buckley to Norman Podhoretz, excused his most bizarre conspiracy theories. Then in 1997 he deserted the party leaders and his Christian right allies, deciding they had become unrealistic about the impeachment of President Clinton.

Most Americans viewed Pat Robertson in a political context, but throughout his long career he was also a nexus in the Pentecostal/charismatic movement. In the late 1950s, Robertson witnessed the last revivals of Pentecostal tent healers such as William Braham and A. A. Allen.[5] Later he became well acquainted with men like Oral Roberts, Demos Shakarian, Vinson Synan, and David du Plessis, the modernizers who brought Pentecostal beliefs to a wider public. As his television empire grew, CBN became the network for the next generation of Pentecostal televangelists, from Jim Bakker to Jimmy Swaggart, and a powerful force in the new charismatic movement at home and abroad. On *The 700 Club*, Robertson hosted leaders of all the various theological schools, as positive confession and spiritual warfare, and entertained many of their ideas. To follow his career is thus not just to see the evolution of the Christian right but to follow the currents and cross-currents in the most inventive and unstable of religious movements in modern American history.

In the fall of 1980 Pat Robertson had removed himself from politics, telling a reporter that his focus was now "on the spiritual mission of reaching people for the Lord Jesus, and helping to bring a spiritual-moral revival in America." Yet in February 1981 he formed the Freedom Council, an organization with a mission to defend Christian liberties and to "encourage, train and equip Americans to exercise their civil responsibility to actively participate in government." Little was heard from the Council until 1986, when it suddenly surfaced in Michigan. The Michigan Republican Party then had a system whereby precinct-level elections began a complex process of choosing delegates to the national convention two years later. Normally only party regulars bothered to run, and many precincts went unrepresented. But in May Freedom Council members flooded the precincts and put up four to five thousand candidates—almost half of the total—shocking the state Republican establishment and the well-organized George H. W. Bush campaign.[6]

On September 17 Pat Robertson took the stage in Constitution Hall in Washington and announced that he would explore a run for the Republican nomination for the presidency of the United States. Falwell, La Haye, Robison, and others had hoped to mobilize voters and gain influence with the president and the Republican Party, but Robertson was going right for the top. A year later he declared his candidacy, gave up his ordination as a minister, and plunged into the primary campaign, eventually spending more money than any of his opponents except for Vice President Bush.[7] But then he had certain advantages that the others lacked.

Unlike Falwell, Robertson came from a prominent Virginia family. His ancestry, which he often referred to as "noble," went back to one of the members of the Jamestown colony, to the Harrisons, who provided a signer of the Declaration of Independence and two presidents, plus the first Duke of Marlborough and others in Winston Churchill's family. His father, A. Willis Robertson, a lawyer and a conservative Democrat, had served in the U.S. Congress from 1932 to 1946 and in the Senate for the next twenty years. An opponent of the New Deal and of desegregation, he had been a fixture in the Virginia political establishment from the time Pat was born until he was thirty-six. The son of a Baptist preacher, an avid hunter and a conservationist, Willis, it was said, had prayed or shot with everyone in Virginia. Though always overshadowed by Harry Byrd, he had made his mark as chair of the Senate Banking Committee, where he claimed credit for removing billions of dollars from the federal budget. His wife, Gladys, a distant cousin and well-brought-up southerner, was not the best of political wives. She didn't like Washington and at some point in the 1950s became a self-described fundamentalist and afterward rarely left her house. On the other hand, she was an adoring mother, and Pat, the younger of her two sons and a mischievous, sociable boy, was her favorite. Brought up in Lexington, Pat went to private schools and then to Washington and Lee, where he graduated magna cum laude, even while specializing in fraternity house drinking and road trips to women's colleges. He served as a Marine lieutenant during the Korean War, and after his discharge in 1952 he went to Yale Law School, where he took courses in tax and corporate law. He spent a summer working for the Senate Appropriations Committee and hanging out in his father's Senate office. Apparently he intended to go into business and into Virginia politics, and he was building the perfect résumé for both when his life began to go off course.[8]

At Yale Robertson for the first time encountered students better than he was. His grades were mediocre, and on graduating he failed the New York State bar exam. By that time he had secretly married Dede Elmer, a Yale nursing student from a well-off conservative Ohio family, who gave birth to their first child just ten weeks later. Thanks to his father's connections he went to work for W. R. Grace and Company, but not content with a climb up the corporate ladder, he quit after a few months and took a flier at starting a company to sell an electrostatic loudspeaker. When the venture went belly-up, as his father had predicted, he fell into a depression and decided to become a minister. His mother, who had been sending him gospel tracts with all of her letters, insisted that he must first become a believer. She introduced him to a fundamentalist evangelist, whose tract society she was supporting, and over dinner in an expensive Philadelphia restaurant, Pat became a born-again Christian.[9]

In 1956 Robertson went to the Biblical Seminary in New York (later the New York Theological Seminary), a small fundamentalist Bible school that trained students for domestic and foreign missions. The course work was not demanding, and he fell in with a group of spiritually hungry students whose quest pointed them to the miraculous gifts of the Holy Spirit. In New York in the mid-1950s Pentecostalism was still an underclass religion practiced in storefronts and dilapidated buildings, most of them in African American neighborhoods and unknown to the white denominational churches. With the assistance of an older minister, Harold Bredesen, the students roamed the city and listened to Pentecostal congregations shouting, weeping, and speaking in tongues. Apparently Pat and his friends saw this as a raw, authentic religion, and the expressive, emotion-filled worship seemed attractive, given the doctrinaire fundamentalism they were learning in school. Certainly it was a spiritual adventure and made all the more exciting because once the students began speaking in tongues, they had, like the early Christians, to worship in secret. For two years this clandestine fraternity met behind the locked doors of a church, where they heard God speaking to them and discovered personal spiritual powers.[10]

After graduating in 1959 Pat moved his family—Dede and their three children—to a friend's mission in the Bedford-Stuyvesant section of Brooklyn, but neither Pat nor Dede was made for inner-city work, and their parents were frantic. After three months they left for Portsmouth, Virginia, where Pat had found a defunct UHF television station up for sale. The building was a shell and the signal weak, but Pat decided to buy it and to spread his new religion through the airwaves. His father, thinking it another harebrained scheme and repelled by his son's charismatic vocabulary, did nothing to help. While trying to raise the money from other sources, Pat took a job at a Southern Baptist church, whose pastor was a friend of his parents, and was duly ordained. He had, however, determined on religious broadcasting, and in the two years it took him to put the station on the air he looked far beyond in the dingy one-camera studio and incorporated his new venture as the Christian Broadcasting Network.[11]

In the beginning there wasn't much to watch on the station: a few improvised programs, two paid religious broadcasts, and a filler of travel documentaries. Money was a serious problem. In 1963 Robertson held a telethon pleading for 700 viewers to contribute just $10 a month to keep the station on the air. The results were dismal. By his account, his mother called to say that she had seen a vision of him kneeling in prayer with his arms outstretched to heaven and a packet of banknotes of large denominations floating down from heaven into his hands. The vision was surely prophetic but nothing of the kind happened until 1965, when he hired Jim and Tammy Faye Bakker to do a children's show.[12]

Two diminutive persons, then in their early twenties, Jim and Tammy were itinerant Assemblies of God evangelists from rural Michigan. For the past four years they had been wandering in broken-down cars from Tennessee to West Virginia holding revivals in small Pentecostal churches and earning only what contributions came into their plate. Jim had just one year of Bible school, and Tammy not even that, but both charmed their audiences. Jim preached, Tammy sang, and they put on puppet shows for Sunday school children. Hired by Robertson, the Bakkers turned out to be made for TV. Warm, high-spirited, and completely natural, they were much more in tune than Pat with the lives of their viewers and far better at expressing their emotions. In their children's show Jim acted as host and straight man while Tammy, described by a CBN press release as "cute as a button," worked the puppets and through them spoke about the conflicts in her feelings. The show was an immediate hit and made them both local celebrities. In *The Jim and Tammy Show*, which succeeded it, the two turned everything, including their choice of detergents, into a major drama. She had a scatterbrained humor, much like that of her heroine, Lucille Ball, and Jim, expressing a childlike faith, could go from a flight of rapture to the depths of despair in a matter of moments.[13]

The financial turning point for CBN came during the 1965 telethon. Jim joined Pat on the set, and late in the evening, when it seemed that their fund-raising goals would not be met, Jim broke down and wept, declaring that all was lost. His spontaneity electrified viewers. Callers jammed the telephone lines, pledges rolled in, and with everyone in the studio laughing or crying in "the move of the spirit," the telethon went on into the small hours of the morning. For days afterward people continued to call in pledges, and in a new development, to ask for prayer and to report miracles that had taken place during the broadcast. The event brought in all the money the station needed for the following year, and Robertson had learned a lesson. From then on the annual telethons were pitched as the ultimate crisis for his ministry and attended by "the move of the spirit." Often featuring celebrity guests, the telethons raised increasing sums of money: $400,000 in 1968. After the initial success, Bakker proposed to host a nightly talk show with viewer call-ins: a program of prayer and ministry that would allow the move of the spirit every evening (and raise money as well). Robertson was dubious, but he soon found that the format worked, and, taking over the role of cohost, he named the show *The 700 Club.*[14]

Knowing the Southern Baptists in Virginia, Robertson had initially played down such "gifts of the spirit" as tongue-speaking, but Jim had no such inhibitions, and in the late 1960s, CBN became aboil with charismatic teaching and worship. The timing was good, for Pentecostals were just then becoming respectable, and charismatic practices were finding their way into other Protestant denominations and the Catholic Church. On *The 700 Club* Bakker might speak in tongues, or Robertson, declaring a "word of knowledge" from God, might cry out that someone in the television audience had been cured of gout, arthritis, or a broken ankle. One evening, according to Vinson Synan, a Pentecostal minister and historian, the spirit moved with such intensity that entire CBN staff was "slain in the spirit"—the technicians apparently falling down with their headsets on. Occasionally the broadcast went on into the middle of the night with Pat praising Jesus and people calling to accept Christ or to receive the baptism of the Holy Spirit over the phone. After one such evening four hundred people reported that they had been saved.[15]

The Bakkers quit CBN in 1972. For years there had been friction between Jim and Pat with both vying for the spotlight and Jim throwing temper tantrums. Jim then went to Trinity Broadcasting Network, a new charismatic venture, and after failing to take it over, he formed a network of his own, called PTL for Praise the Lord—or People That Love—in Charlotte, North Carolina. In the next decade he raised huge sums of money, some of it by imitating the moves Robertson was making in the television industry.[16]

In the business of media, Robertson proved a serious and innovative entrepreneur. Falwell had never done more than syndicate *The Old-Time Gospel Hour*, but Robertson by the late 1970s had assembled a small empire consisting of radio and TV stations and a cable network. Borrowing money—and repeatedly going into debt—CBN acquired several ailing radio and TV stations in venues from upstate New York to Dallas, Texas, and turned them around. CBN bought time on its own TV stations as well as on other VHF and UHF stations, and by 1977 *The 700 Club* was appearing on thirty-six commercial stations, among them channels in New York, Los Angeles, and San Francisco as well as the CBN channels in Boston, Atlanta, and Dallas. In addition CBN entered the nascent cable market, distributing its programming free to community operators hungry for content. Even in 1979, before the enormous expansion of cable, the network reached five million households. In the early years the videotapes of CBN programs had to be "bicycled" to each TV station or cable operator, but in 1977 Robertson presciently bought an earth-to-satellite station to broadcast his programs around the United States and abroad. By 1985 the satellite network reached thirty million households, and other stations were buying time on his delivery system. CBN became the third largest satellite network in the country after HBO and the Turner Broadcasting Network, and it had outlets in Latin American and Asia.[17]

The 700 Club remained CBN's flagship program, and through telethons, regular donations from Robertson's "Faith Partners," events staged for larger donors, and its associated charity, Operation Blessing, CBN raised $20 million in 1977 and over $50 million in 1980. Still, Robertson made his real money in secular programming. His first TV station in Portsmouth had of necessity to run travelogues, but after he bought the small religious station in Dallas he saw that family entertainment shows—along with sports coverage—brought in twenty times more viewers than strictly religious programming. Wholesome family programs, he concluded, were the key to reaching a wide audience for *The 700 Club*—and they could sell advertising. In the late 1970s and early 1980s CBN enlarged and diversified its secular offerings with reruns of westerns, quiz shows, children's programs, and sitcoms like *Leave It to Beaver* and *The Brady Bunch*. In 1978 the state of Massachusetts sued CBN under a law requiring charities to disclose their finances. In response Robertson spun off his stations and the cable network into a for-profit entity called Continental Broadcasting. Though wholly owned by CBN, Continental gained more flexibility in programming and advertising, and three years later it eliminated most of its religious programming. The for-profit entity soon made as much money as *The 700 Club*, and much more was to come. In 1978 Robertson founded a university, CBNU, with a graduate school of communications and a seminary; the following year CBN moved into a new headquarters in Virginia Beach—just twelve miles from where the Jamestown settlers had landed—with two enormous brick buildings and state-of-the-art television facilities.[18]

In the late 1970s, *The 700 Club*, too, began to move into a more secular vein. By the early 1980s it had a tightly programmed magazine format, beginning with news from CBN's Washington bureau, celebrity appearances, and interviews with politicians and commentators on public policy and world affairs. Using his new cohost, Ben Kinchlow, an African American charismatic, as his foil, Robertson himself often lectured about topics from supply-side economics to nuclear fusion. Half of the show remained religious, and toward the end Robertson would preach on the Scriptures and declare a "word of knowledge" that God was curing a cancer or healing a woman with deafness in one ear. Still, the new secular material caused considerable confusion within the audience and the CBN staff, and Robertson often found himself having to justify it. On occasion, when asked about the religious significance of an interview with an expert on credit cards, or a congressman plugging the gold standard, he explained that the interviews explored "fiendish practices"—presumably debt and inflation—that were "infecting the whole population." Christians, he added, would call for prayer and healing, but "what about the whole population coming under the Anti-Christ?" On other occasions he explained that he wanted to bring secular people to the gospel—or to make an impact on "people in all walks of life," including those in business and government. According to his biographer, David Edwin Harrell Jr., *The 700 Club* ratings had been flat or in decline for a few years, and Robertson heeded ministry polls showing that adults—particularly young males—wanted more news. Whatever Robertson's reasoning, he was clearly enjoying himself—doing just what he wanted to do. He had, after all, been his father's son, then his mother's son, and now he was in the process of combining the two.[19]

Why Robertson decided against political involvement in 1980 was unclear at the time. The explanation favored by some was that in January he had prophesied that 1982 would see the start of the end times when the Soviet Union invaded the Middle East, seized the oil reserves, and caused the collapse of the global economy. In retrospect other explanations seem more plausible. For one thing, Robertson usually hedged his bets on end times prophecies with an "if" or a "might," and of all the end times prophecies he delivered in his long life, he never acted on one of them. In 1980 he was in the midst of major business expansion—and looking to the future of cable TV. Possibly his unsettled business affairs were one of his considerations, but there were good political reasons to stay out the fray. Pentecostals had always been less politically active than other evangelicals, and many remained Democrats, as he did by family connections and registration. Then, too, Jerry Falwell was well out ahead of him in political organization, and he was not going to take second place to a fundamentalist. In the early 1980s he widened his circle of Washington acquaintances by lobbying for the school prayer amendment and serving as president of the Council on National Policy, but he continued to preach revival and demonstrate the gifts of the Spirit on his show.[20]

In 1982 Robertson published a book, *The Secret Kingdom*, which he said outlined "the fundamental principles of human life," principles "given to me by God." Written with Bob Slosser, the executive vice president of CBN and a former assistant national editor of *The New York Times*, the book was nearest he ever came to systematizing a religious message. Addressing a general evangelical audience, he never mentioned the words "Pentecostal" or "charismatic," though the book lies solidly in the tradition. *The Secret Kingdom*, he later said, "sets forth the keys to a stable, prosperous and satisfying life." Indeed, much of it was Robertson's version of the prosperity theology, the teachings that in the early 1980s were gaining ground among charismatic televangelists and putting them on the top of the religious TV charts. Still, it had a public policy dimension foreign to the genre. Subtitled "A Promise of Hope and Freedom in a World of Turmoil," the book begins with a quasi-Falwellian jeremiad about the rise of military and economic threats to the nation (with an emphasis on nuclear weapons, energy shortages, and debt), the moral declension of the country, the rise of "secular humanism," and the near inevitability of chaos or dictatorship. The book then switches to advice on how Christians might find success in their individual lives, but now and then it reverts to the life of the country. The interest is how it explains the workings of the supernatural in both spheres, for "logically" (as Robertson was wont to say), the explanation did for Pentecostals what Falwell and LaHaye did for fundamentalists with their concept of a pre-Tribulation Tribulation.[21]

Like many charismatics, Robertson interpreted Jesus' words "the Kingdom of Heaven is at hand" to mean that God's kingdom is "an invisible spiritual reality" that "undergirds, surrounds, and interpenetrates" the visible world. To Robertson, however, this "secret kingdom" was no mystery: it had "principles" as immutable "as the laws of thermodynamics or gravity" that could be found in the Bible and put to use in the visible world. The Bible, he wrote, "is not an impractical book of theology, but rather a practical book of life containing a system of thought and conduct that will guarantee success." Indeed, it was "a workable guidebook for politics, government, business, families, and all the affairs of mankind." He then laid out eight "broad overriding principles" he had adduced that would allow Christians to reach into the kingdom and find "true success, true happiness and true prosperity." The kingdom of heaven was, in other words, a rational and predictable system that could be used for the attainment of practical personal ends.[22]

Justin Watson, a scholar of religion, wrote that the book "reflected a widespread tendency in evangelicalism to accommodate the cognitive style of modernity."[23] It also reflected a tendency in the world of charismatic TV preachers to domesticate "the gifts of the Holy Spirit," and to make the task of acquiring them something like reading the instructions on a Lionel train set. In his chapter "How the Kingdom Works" Robertson had this to say: "Once we are born-again and have our sins forgiven, we can communicate with God through the Spirit. It's a bit like tuning into a radio or television station. You get on the right frequency, and you pick up a program." After God speaks to us, "we are to speak to him, and if we do, miracles occur." With faith we can "translate the will of God in the invisible kingdom to the visible situation that confronts us. We speak to money, and it comes. We speak to storms, and they cease. We speak to crops, and they flourish." According to Robertson, "positive thinking will more often than not lead to successful action."[24]

This was Robertson's version of the concepts of "word of faith," or "positive confession," developed by Oral Roberts and Kenneth Hagin—though a version certainly influenced by Norman Vincent Peale, who gave the book a quote for the jacket. In one passage Robertson answered the usual objection about the existence of suffering in the world. "I am convinced," he wrote, "that if a person is continuously in sickness, poverty, or other physical and mental straits, then he is missing the truths of the kingdom. He has either failed to grasp the points we have been making . . . about the operations of the kingdom or is not living according to the major principles we will be exploring." In other words, go back to the instruction book.[25]

Robertson's eight "Laws of the Kingdom" codified some of the age-old Protestant rules for success: work hard, use the talents you have, persevere, fulfill your responsibilities, and lead by serving others. (For each of these laws Robertson provided an inspiring example from his own career.) His "Law of Reciprocity," however, included Oral Roberts's "seed faith," or the promise that if you give to the Lord, your money will be returned to you many times over. Then there was the "Law of Miracles," a category under which Robertson put those gifts of the Spirit he claimed as his specialties: "word of knowledge," or a supernatural knowledge of God's miracles in the present, and "word of wisdom," or a prophecy about the future.[26] Noticeably missing were the less generally acceptable Pentecostal practices like tongue-speaking and the driving out of demons—though these were certainly in Robertson's repertoire. Also missing were the traditional Pentecostal prohibitions, or any mention of punishment for sin. In Robertson's book the Lord is a "partner" with whom "it is possible to have total favor"—if you follow the rules of the kingdom.[27]*

Robertson wrote that these "kingdom principles" applied to nations as well as to individuals. By the "Law of Reciprocity" the South had cursed it-

---

*When Robertson's prophecies were disconfirmed, he tended to blame the problem on something like interference—or noise—in the channel between himself and the Lord. ("If I am hearing him correctly.") Harrell, pp. 316–17.

self by enslaving others and suffered for a hundred years, but once it freed black people, provided them with education, and helped lift their standard of living, its economy prospered as never before. On the other hand America had neglected the "Law of Unity." It had been founded as a Christian nation, but since the 1960s it struggled under a "social philosophy of pluralism" with the result that it was heading toward fragmentation. As for the "Law of Responsibility," he wrote, the nation has flouted it since the 1960s by deficit spending, borrowing from foreign banks, and giving insufficient effort to stopping Communism in Africa and Latin America. Frankly, he wrote, we need leadership at every level, but evangelicals, concerned almost exclusively with their personal salvation, have neglected their public responsibilities. Unlike the British in the nineteenth century, he concluded, "we have no national fiber of noblesse oblige." [28]

Minus the last remark his observations added up to a political platform, but Robertson did not suggest political action. In 1982 his solution was spiritual revival and the general application of the laws of the secret kingdom. God, he wrote, wanted mankind to "prepare the way" for His return. And if Christians generally applied His laws, they could expect some of His millennial blessings: peace, plenty, and freedom. Specifically, Robertson wrote, if Christians acted, "it would be reasonable to see" the world transcend "many of the limitations we are experiencing now," such as shortages of energy and food. Sooner or later, "God may give one or more of His people" a concept for running cars on hydrogen, for developing new building materials, inventing new foodstuffs, and perhaps creating a new living space to accommodate vast populations. In addition to these technical fixes Robertson promised that if people loved their neighbors as themselves, there would be no need for standing armies or tariff barriers; there would be no extremes of wealth or poverty, no crime, no pollution of air, water, or land, and huge governmental bureaucracies would disappear. (To be sure, he added, lawless renegades would still have to be punished and rogue nations disciplined, but that did not violate the "Law of Reciprocity.") [29]

Robertson always insisted that he was a premillenialist, but his promise of "millennial blessings" within the current era did not fit the Darbyite prophecy of continual decline, and his end times scenario, set out in the book's last chapter, can only be described as pre- and postmillennialism.

Most of his narrative follows the fundamentalist script: a coalition led by the Soviet Union—Gog and Magog—marches into the Middle East and invades Israel; Europe's economy is devastated; and the Antichrist emerges in a successor kingdom to the Roman Empire. And so forth. (In his version the Antichrist comes from within the European Economic Community, imposes a "new economic order," and using computer technology implants a microchip in everyone's hand or forehead with the capacity to debit accounts instantly.) But Robertson was no dispensationalist. His end times prophecies never included the Rapture, for his premise was that the kingdom of heaven is always at hand and ready to emerge into the visible world. There was thus no complete break between the current age and the next. In *The Secret Kingdom* he waxed optimistic about the future of life on earth. Citing Scripture, he wrote that God might save Israel from the Soviet Union and give her ascendancy for seven years. Meanwhile all those who chose to live under His rule could do so until Christ returned (thus avoiding the Tribulations). The thousand-year reign of Christ that followed he described as a "transition period" in which "food, water and energy will be ample," and the "trillions of dollars" spent on weaponry will go for "parks, forests and scientific advances as yet beyond imagination." After that half-worldly period, God would defeat Satan and create His "ultimate and eternal kingdom." [30]

According to Robertson, his campaign for president was God's idea. "I had everything you could ask for," he said in 1988, "but . . . I heard the Lord saying, 'I have something else for you to do. I want you to run for president of the United States.'" God, he indicated, had said this to him in the mid-1980s. If so, He gave him ample time to prepare. [31]

In 1984 Robertson changed his registration to Republican and attended the Republican National Convention. Soon afterward the Freedom Council, financed by CBN, began organizing Republican campaign workers in states across the country, and Robertson began traveling to meet with ministers, volunteers, and conservative groups. In early 1985 *The Saturday Evening Post* as much as launched his campaign with an interview with him on politics, describing his "Agenda for Public Action," and quoting Paul Weyrich and others as saying what a fine president he would make.

He later appeared on *Face the Nation* and *Good Morning America* and spoke at the National Press Club.[32]

His victory in the Michigan precinct elections came as an unwelcome surprise to Republican Party officials. There and in other states Freedom Council organizers had recruited in Pentecostal and independent charismatic churches and from *The 700 Club* donor list. Most of the members were new to politics, and they were advised to remain anonymous. According to sociologist and author William Martin, a Minnesota Freedom Council instruction sheet warned that "experience has shown it is best not to say you are entering politics because of your Christian beliefs." A similar set of instructions in Iowa read, "Give the impression you are there to work for the party, not to push an ideology" and "Try not to let on that a close group of friends are becoming active in the party together. . . . Hide your strength." That Freedom Council members had a religious identity became obvious only after the Michigan election, when a fund-raising letter announced, "THE CHRISTIANS HAVE WON!"[33]

At his rally at Constitution Hall in September 1986 Robertson promised to enter the presidential race if by the following September three million registered voters signed petitions pledging to pray and work for him. "What is God's will for me in this?" he said. "Let me assure you I know God's will for me."[34] He hired Connie Snapp, a born-again executive from the advertising firm of Young & Rubicam, to obtain the signatures and to help the public understand why he was qualified for the presidency. The spring of 1987 was, however, not the best time to begin introducing a televangelist to the public. First, Oral Roberts attracted ridicule when he climbed to the top of his prayer tower and announced that if his supporters didn't send him $8 million, God would "call him home." Then began the seemingly endless unfolding of scandals at PTL when *The Charlotte Observer* revealed that Jim Bakker had engaged in a tryst with the church secretary, Jessica Hahn, and had arranged to pay her $250,000 in hush money. There followed stories of a Ponzi scheme perpetrated on PTL donors, the Bakkers' extravagant spending, Tammy's problem with drugs, Jim's sexual exploitation of male employees, and on and on. The stories occupied the national media for months, and Robertson was often asked about his former association with Bakker, and nearly every major television ministry, including his own, experienced a sharp drop-off in contributions.[35]

In September 1987 Robertson announced he had gathered more than three million signatures and was going to run for the presidency. He resigned his ordination, severed his ties with CBN, and on the advice of Connie Snapp began to describe himself as a conservative businessman with a law degree from Yale, a Marine who had served in Korea, a TV broadcaster, and the host of a news and information show—but not, not a televangelist.[36]

The image he wished to project was, however, hard to sustain. His television appearances were often preceded by clips from *The 700 Club*. In a fifteen-year-old videotape he exhorted, "We come against cancer now and declare it gone in the name of Jesus! Come out now! . . . Bone spurs are being taken away right now by Jesus! Thank you Jesus! Thank you Jesus!"[37] In a later clip he cried, "Praise the gum diseases being healed by the power of God, several people being healed of hemorrhoids and varicose veins, the Lord is healing you of this."[38] Often shown were clips of him in 1985 commanding Hurricane Gloria in the name of Jesus to turn away from the Virginia coastline, and taking credit when the hurricane turned north and spared Virginia Beach. Journalists refrained from pointing out that Hurricane Gloria had devastated New York's Long Island, but they did ask how his particular beliefs might affect his presidency. Did he think prayer could stop Soviet missiles? Would he take God's advice in making specific political or policy decisions? The questions were fair enough, but instead of answering them, Robertson would try to change the subject and finally in exasperation accuse the reporter of religious bigotry.[39]

He ran into other problems as well. Journalists found that he had been lying about his wedding date for years in an effort to conceal the fact that his wife was more than seven months pregnant when the ceremony occurred. They also found, though he claimed to be a combat veteran, he had never seen combat in Korea. Congressman Pete McCloskey of California, who had served in the same unit as he had, charged that Willis Robertson had used his influence to keep his son out of combat. Pat sued McCloskey for libel, but dropped the suit when he found that the trial date was the day of the Super Tuesday primaries.[40]

Reporters nonetheless had to take him seriously. By the time of his announcement he had raised $11 million, just slightly less than the sum raised by Bush. He had won the straw poll in Iowa, beating the three major Republican candidates: Vice President Bush, Senator Bob Dole, and former congressman Jack Kemp. What reporters called his "invisible army" was on the march in other states as well, among them Hawaii, Virginia, and South Carolina. In February he passed the first real test of the campaign in the Iowa caucuses. Bob Dole, who came from the neighboring state of Kansas, won as expected, but Robertson came in second, beating Kemp and the vice president. Again the Republican establishment went into an uproar. After the New Hampshire primary that month came the Super Tuesday primaries, all of them in southern states, where Robertson could be expected to do well among evangelical voters. Journalists piled into Robertson's press buses and began to ask him new questions about his policy views.[41]

Robertson's campaign slogan was "Restore the Greatness of America Through Moral Strength," but while he talked to supporters about moral decline, he otherwise put his economic and foreign policy position front and center.[42] Most of them seemed conventionally conservative Republican policies. In retrospect what is interesting about them is how difficult it is to tell whether he was taking a position for religious or secular reasons—and how great was the overlap between the two.

For example, many of his economic positions sounded much like Reagan's in 1980: smaller government, lower taxes, deregulation of business, abolition of the Department of Education—plus a major military buildup. He also attacked social welfare programs and called for a partial privatization of Social Security. Reagan for all his 1980 rhetoric had presided over a 300 percent increase in the national debt, and Robertson gave special emphasis to ending the annual deficits by radical means, among them a balanced budget amendment to the Constitution, a return to the gold standard, and restricting the role of the Federal Reserve. According to David Harrell, Robertson regarded federal deficits as both "fiscally and morally wrong." Neil Eskelin, his first CBN producer, wrote that he believed that both government and individuals should operate on a bare minimum of credit and, echoing a refrain of the Christian right, said that governments should balance their budgets just as families do. The idea that debt was ruinous and immoral for individuals lay deep within the evangelical tradition, and many churches offered "financial stewardship" courses, whose main counsel to parishioners was to stay out of debt. Robertson, however, had built his own business by borrowing large sums of money and purchasing on credit, and apparently he saw nothing immoral about it. Then, while no economist, he had learned enough to know that corporate and government finances had little in common with family budgets. Effectively, his proposals would have reduced the federal government—except for the Pentagon—to something like the size it was before the New Deal. His father, a states' rights advocate, had spent his entire political career trying to do just that, and not incidentally Pat also called for less federal government interference in state and local affairs.[43]

On foreign policy Robertson opposed arms control talks with the Soviet Union, called for forceful measures to free Eastern Europe, and urged the defeat of Marxist regimes in the Third World. He often denounced "Godless Communism" and said he would never negotiate with Communists or terrorists. Still, he made an exception for the People's Republic of China, saying that a "close relationship" between the United States and China would be conducive to peace and serve the interests of both nations. In regard to the Middle East he strongly supported Israel and claimed it had the right to retain the West Bank. He called the United Nations "an exercise in futility" and "a sounding board for anti-American, anti-Western, and anti-Israeli propaganda." In a speech before the Council on Foreign Relations in January 1987, he urged a reduction of funding for the U.N. and for putting the savings into a new organization of democratic countries that would advance "the global struggle of freedom against totalitarian tyranny."[44] In Central America he called for breaking relations with the leftist Sandinista government in Nicaragua and supplying the contra rebels with U.S. military aid. Right-wingers in the Reagan administration held similar views, but this was Robertson—and all of these positions accorded with his eschatology or with his view of the Great Commission. The Soviet Union was potentially the Beast, but China was the historic mission field for American Protestants, and Robertson was hoping to broadcast into the People's Republic; the West Bank was a part of ancient Israel—Judea and Samaria; the U.N. was the harbinger of a world government ruled by the Antichrist.

As for Central America, it had seen a wave of conversions to Pentecostalism, or charismatic evangelicalism, in recent decades. In the early 1980s Robertson, along with Jimmy Swaggart, had expanded his broadcasting operations to Central America. He often visited the region, and whether motivated by missionary zeal or ideology, or both, he became an active supporter of the right-wing generals and Reagan administration policies. By 1984 CBN had become the largest private donor to the Nicaraguan contra camps in Honduras and one of the most energetic campaigners for the contra aid in Washington.[45] Robertson also supported the brutal right-wing regime in El Salvador, whose victims included a Catholic archbishop and four American nuns. (He called Roberto D'Aubuisson, the head of the death squads, "a very nice guy.") His closest associate in the region was the Guatemalan general Efraín Ríos Montt, a charismatic who belonged to a California-based Jesus movement group, Gospel Outreach. After the coup that brought him to power in 1982, Ríos Montt led the Guatemalan army to new heights of violence and was later tried for genocide against the indigenous Maya Ixil people. In the seventeen months of Ríos Montt's reign of terror Robertson repeatedly gave his personal assurances that Ríos Montt was not a thief or a butcher like his predecessors but a Christian who "has not allowed his army to kill, rape and torture."[46] After Ríos Montt was deposed, Robertson supported his successor, and in June 1984 delivered $1 million in supplies to the Guatemalan government.[47]

Robertson's most controversial positions involved church-state relations and his reading of the Constitution. In 1985 he told a *700 Club* audience that only Christians and Jews were qualified to serve in government, but during the campaign he retracted the statement. Robertson had lobbied for the Reagan administration's school prayer amendment, and not surprisingly his official campaign statement said of the candidate, "He favors the return of traditional Judeo-Christian values to the school curricula and supports voluntary prayer as a legitimate freedom guaranteed by the First Amendment." In interviews he went further than that, taking issue with the modern Supreme Court's interpretation of the establishment clause of the First Amendment. In an interview with *Southern Partisan* in 1987 he said, "I think the popular conception of the separation of church and state is one of the great fictions that have been foisted upon us by those who do not like religion." On other occasions he put his contention in a more polemical form: "It's amazing that the Constitution of the United States says nothing about the separation of church and state. The phrase does, however, appear in the Soviet Constitution." When elaborating, he maintained that the First Amendment did prevent the creation of a state church, but asserted that the only intention of the framers was to separate the church as an institution from the apparatus of government. Even more surprisingly he claimed that the First Amendment applied to the federal government but not to the states. On a *700 Club* broadcast on April 11, 1986, he said of the First Amendment, "There is never in the Constitution at any point anything that applies to the states, none at all." This was not just a chance remark to supporters. At a meeting with editors and reporters of the *Atlanta Journal and Constitution* in the summer of 1987 he asserted flatly that the Bill of Rights did not apply to the states. On a *700 Club* broadcast Robertson said by way of explanation, "The Supreme Court has done it over repeated attempts by the Congress which have been beaten back to do such a thing." [48]

What he meant is hard to tell, but there was, as he suggested, a legal history to the matter. Many of the congressional supporters of the Fourteenth Amendment, adopted just after the Civil War, had argued that the amendment incorporated the Bill of Rights and applied them to the states. The Supreme Court had disagreed for decades. After 1925, however, it had ruled in a long string of cases that the Fourteenth Amendment incorporated the First Amendment, as well as all the relevant sections of the rest of the Bill of Rights. [49]

Like the other Republican candidates, Robertson came out against abortion. He had changed his mind since 1978, when he called it a "purely theological issue." Abortion, he said, was "murder," and he vowed to appoint Supreme Court justices who would reverse *Roe v. Wade*. On the other hand he seemed to see no need for new justices. At a meeting at *The Washington Post* in June 1986 a reporter asked him if, as president, he would abide by *Roe* since the decision was "the law of the land." Robertson contradicted him. "A Supreme Court ruling is not the law of the United States. The law of the United States is the Constitution, treaties made in accordance with the Constitution, and laws duly enacted by the Congress and signed by the president." I am bound, he said, "by the laws of the United States and all fifty states . . . [but] I am not bound by any case or any court to which I myself am not a party. . . . The Congress of the United States . . . can ignore a Supreme Court ruling if they so choose." According to David Broder, he added that *Roe* was "based on very faulty law," and he made no promise to enforce it if elected president.[50]

The origin of these startling legal theories seemed to lie in the evolving version of American history taught by the Christian right. Robertson's claim that the U.S. Constitution said nothing about the separation of church and state, which while literally true, had by the mid-1980s become a part of the polemic and was on its way to gaining currency as a corollary to the idea that the United States was a Christian nation at the time of the Founding Fathers but had fallen away.[51] Tim LaHaye and others often blamed the decline of the "Judeo-Christian tradition" on a small minority of people. In his speech at Constitution Hall in September 1986 Robertson put it this way: "During the last 25 years an assault on our faith and values" has been launched by "a small elite of lawyers, judges and educators." In *The Christian Manifesto* Francis Schaeffer had delivered a tirade about modern jurisprudence, and the year Schaeffer's book came out Robertson had paraphrased him: "Today under the assault of secular humanism, a new rule of law is emerging. No longer do judges seek to make decisions based on the Bible, the Constitution, natural law, or historic precedent. Instead they impose as a rule of law whatever seems sociologically expedient or whatever reflects the prevailing sentiment of the ruling humanistic elite."[52] Apparently Robertson, as a lawyer, had followed this train of thought and developed the novel legal theory that all modern Supreme Court decisions were illegitimate.

The theory was, however, no novelty. Writing in *The Washington Post* at the time, Garrett Epps showed that Robertson's father had held much the same view of the Constitution. In 1962 Willis had passionately denounced the school prayer decision, arguing that the courts had misunderstood the First Amendment. "Clearly, the words 'establishment of religion' in the First Amendment were intended to mean the establishment of a particular denomination—Methodist, Baptist or Catholic—as the national religion," the Virginia senator said. "And clearly the Fourteenth Amendment was not intended to apply the establishment clause of the First Amendment to the states." If, he continued, "the courts continued to apply the First Amendment to the religious affairs of the states, they would undoubtedly sweep us down the broad and easy highway of secularism."[53]

Born in 1887, Willis grew up before the incorporation of the Bill of Rights into the Fourteenth Amendment was settled law, and as a devout Southern Baptist he may well have been shocked by the decision to ban official prayer from the public schools. Still, his objection to the federal courts went deeper. Standing on the floor of the U.S. Senate on March 3, 1960, Willis declared, "The decision of the Supreme Court is not the supreme law of the land, because the Constitution provides what is the supreme law of the land." As Epps pointed out, this view of the Constitution—which flew in the face of settled law since *Marbury v. Madison* of 1803—was not uncommon among southern politicians after *Brown v. Board of Education*. Willis was arguing that the school integration decisions of the Supreme Court could legally be overturned by acts of Congress. Pat Robertson was, in other words, using the legal arguments of southern segregationists and defenders of states' rights.[54]

Robertson's campaign went downhill after the Iowa caucuses. In February Jimmy Swaggart, one of the most popular televangelists and gospel singers in the country, was photographed taking a prostitute into a motel room near New Orleans. After he made a tearful confession on television, the scandal grew to national dimensions, reinforcing the notion that all televangelists were hypocrites, charlatans, or worse. Robertson, who had gone to some pains to get Swaggart's endorsement, found his already high-polling "negatives" jump another 20 points.[55] He accused the Bush campaign of leaking the details of the scandal—he just knew it, though he was wrong. He made more serious gaffes as well. In New Hampshire, where the press corps was for the first time treating him as a viable candidate, he told reporters that there were Soviet missiles in Cuba. He also said that CBN News had learned the location of several American hostages in

Lebanon and suggested that the Reagan administration could have rescued them if it had listened to the news report. In both cases President Reagan felt obliged to respond, saying that there hadn't been any Soviet missiles in Cuba since the early 1960s, and that if Robertson thought he knew the whereabouts of the hostages in Lebanon, he had kept it to himself.[56]

Paul Weyrich later pointed out that Robertson had for years been "doing a television show where nobody challenged what he said. . . . He used to get on his program and make statements about things he had heard; maybe they were true, maybe they weren't, but nobody challenged him." Certainly Robertson wasn't used to press scrutiny, and without any other defense, he increasingly portrayed himself as a victim of persecution by religious bigots in the secular press.[57]

In the New Hampshire primary Robertson came in a weak fifth. In South Carolina he took only 19 percent of the vote. Vice President Bush, who had won both states, swept all nine primaries on Super Tuesday, six of them in key southern states and the others in Missouri, Texas, and Oklahoma.[58] Robertson's campaign was effectively over, and Bush the unofficial nominee. Robertson pulled out of the race in May and threw his support to Bush. He had done well in caucus states, scoring victories in Hawaii, Alaska, Nevada, and Washington and making respectable showings in Iowa, Michigan, and Minnesota. Still, though he had raised $30 million in contributions and federal matching funds, he had won around a million votes—or just 9 percent of the total Republican votes cast.[59]

Surprising to some political observers was the relatively poor showing Robertson had made among evangelicals. On Super Tuesday he took 14 percent of the vote, though approximately 40 percent of the voters were born-agains. A later study showed that he had taken just over a quarter of the born-again vote in the primaries while Bush had taken almost 50 percent. Certainly some evangelical voters preferred Bush's moderate conservatism to Robertson's full-blown right-wing program, yet even Christian right leaders refused to support him. Early in the campaign, he had called on Falwell, LaHaye, D. James Kennedy, James Robison, Charles Colson, and James Dobson, but all had politely declined to endorse him. Falwell campaigned for Bush, and the LaHayes became cochairs of the Jack Kemp campaign. When Robertson put out a list of a hundred Christian ministers who supported him, almost all were Pentecostals and charismatics; just three, Paige Patterson, Bailey Smith, and Jimmy Draper, were Southern Baptists. Apparently the theological differences were unbridgeable, for as later studies showed, Robertson's voter support came not from Southern Baptists or Moral Majority fundamentalists, but overwhelmingly from Pentecostals and charismatics.[60]

Bush turned the Robertson campaign to his advantage. After Michigan, the Yankee Episcopalian paid special attention to the evangelical vote, and his evangelical organizer, Doug Wead, developed sophisticated strategies to counter Robertson's appeal, even in the Assemblies of God churches. Once Robertson came out for him, Bush gave him a speaking slot at the Republican Convention. He persuaded Robertson to campaign for him, then he hired a number of his campaign staffers and took his list of three million voters in exchange for paying off some of his campaign debts. He chose Senator Dan Quayle, a social conservative, as his running mate, and appealed to the southern vote by accusing his rival, the liberal Massachusetts governor Michael Dukakis of opposing the Pledge of Allegiance, coddling criminals, and supporting the ACLU. In the general election white evangelicals gave him some 78 percent of their vote, becoming the single largest voting bloc for Bush.[61]

Robertson's campaign nonetheless had consequences for the Republican Party. After Super Tuesday Robertson told reporters: "We are going to place Pat Robertson people on city councils, school boards and legislatures all over this country. . . . That's His plan for me and for this nation." This time he was right. Robertson had won several state party caucuses, and in a number of states that had gone for Bush his supporters packed postprimary precinct meetings and district conventions in an effort to elect delegates, draft platform statements, and control the party machinery. In Arizona, Robertson supporters joined with backers of Governor Evan Mecham to write a state platform declaring the United States a "Christian nation" and asserting that the Constitution had created "a republic based on the absolute laws of the Bible, not a democracy." The Oklahoma platform read like Robertson's on social issues: it opposed homosexual marriage, surrogate motherhood, New Age influence in education, school-based health clinics, and sex education. In these and other states the newcomers caused pandemonium among party regulars and were called everything from "a bunch of kooks" (this from Barry Goldwater) to "freaks from outer space." Many, however, were in the party to stay.[62]

Robertson in Context

After the campaign Robertson said: "In 1985 I was two people. One believed and taught the miracle power of God. . . . The other was being scrutinized by the secular public as a potential political leader. If I prayed the way I knew how to pray, the secular world would say I was a religious fanatic. If I didn't pray as was needed, the storm would hit us and the faith of millions would be damaged."[63]

The remark says much about Robertson. He realized that he had two audiences—believers and nonbelievers—and such was his understanding of both, he was in a sense two people, one looking at the other. Falwell, too, realized that he had a secular audience, but the chasm between believers and nonbelievers was much greater in Robertson's case. Secular people and many other Christians disliked the fundamentalist gospel, but Robertson's they found incomprehensible—if not completely lunatic. A part of the difficulty they had was with the basic Pentecostal belief that the supernatural could break through into the natural world through prayer. Still, many Assemblies of God preachers took issue with some of Robertson's religious ideas and practices, for Robertson was no classical Pentecostal but a charismatic of the movement that began in the 1960s. As such, he belonged to a continually shifting world, whose preachers came up with novel and sometimes radical ideas. As a televangelist, he swam in all the spiritual currents, and buffeted about, he pushed back against some and went with others. There was no anchor—no completely acceptable position—for an independent such as himself.

In the first half of the twentieth century the Pentecostal denominations developed firm ecclesiastical structures, sets of fixed doctrines, and routinized styles of worship. In the Assemblies of God congregants understood they couldn't disrupt the services with ecstatic outbursts or surprise the pastor with novel prophecies. (The spirit would move them only in certain prescribed ways.) The healing revivalists of 1940s and '50s had broken through all of these strictures. Asserting that God was speaking directly to them and giving them miraculous powers, they preached all kinds of new revelations and prophecies. According to William Branham, Eve produced Cain in mating with the snake, and Los Angeles would fall into the sea in 1977. The New Order of the Latter Rain ministers spoke of the restoration of the fivefold ministry with apostles and prophets, and they looked to the arrival of human "overcomers" who would dethrone Satan and usher in the Kingdom of God on earth. Pentecostal denominations barred the door, pronouncing these revelations unbiblical. But on what authority? Fundamentalists maintained their doctrines were objective truths derived rationally and logically from the Bible, but the basic teaching—and the distinguishing mark—of Pentecostalism was that the revelations from God didn't end with the Bible and any believer could receive them as personal subjective experience. Most of the revivalists' revelations died with their creators, but some that had been considered eccentric—if not heretical—found an audience in the next generation.

The charismatic renewal movement that began in the 1960s inaugurated another period of religious excitement and instability. The Pentecostal gifts of the spirit found a new audience: Catholics and mainline Protestants but also other evangelicals, who by the 1990s made up almost half of the charismatic constituency. Many Catholics and mainline Protestants remained within their churches, but evangelicals generally had to leave theirs, and the ferment gave rise to a host of independent teachers claiming heavenly authority and a proliferation of nondenominational churches and ministries with no ecclesiastical authority to police them. "There's a great deal of wildfire [in the charismatic movement]," Robertson said in 1974, "there's a great deal of what passes for prophecy, which is just foolishness." What in particular outraged him, and many of the older established charismatic leaders such as Oral Roberts, David du Plessis, and Demos Shakarian, was a phenomenon known as the Shepherding Movement.[64]

Born out of an association of five popular charismatic leaders working together in the Christian Growth Ministries in Fort Lauderdale, Florida, the movement centered on their teaching that in order to develop spiritual maturity, believers from laymen to pastors had to have a personal, submitted relationship to a "shepherd," or pastoral authority. The Christian Growth Ministries leaders also emphasized the fivefold ministry and the appearance of apostles and prophets in the present day. Seen as a response to the chaos of independent churches and the "individualistic, subjective spirituality" of charismatics, the movement grew rapidly. By 1975 the CGM publication, *New Wine*, was the most widely circulated charismatic publication in the country and 4,700 pastors attended that year's National Men's Shepherding Conference. Some thousands of pastors submitted themselves to the new apostles, the "Fort Lauderdale Five," and built networks of churches and prayer groups based on their teachings. With shepherding, or discipleship, at every level, they built a pyramidal structure of authority where tithes went up to the five founders, and discipline went down to the "sheep." Oral Roberts and others suspected that the five were engaged in a "power grab," but given human nature, the single pyramid quickly divided into numerous pyramids, some large, some very small. "Shepherding," however, came to involve a "covenant relationship" in which committed members had to submit all their life decisions to a "personal shepherd" and to believe that he spoke with the authority of God. Chaos had given way to authoritarianism, and predictably this led to many cases of abusive behavior. At Oral Roberts University one twenty-year-old "shepherd" was found to be taking tithes from other students; in other ministries "shepherds" split up families when a husband or wife refused to submit to their discipline.[65] Robertson denounced the movement as "cultic," and in 1975 he along with others confronted the leaders in an explosive meeting, but accomplished little. The "Fort Lauderdale Five" broke up a decade later, and two of them repented, but the practice of shepherding continued at least into the 1990s in a number of parachurch organizations, among them the Maranatha Campus Ministries, a group with Jesus movement zeal, an enthusiasm for politics, and seventy chapters on college campuses in the U.S. and abroad.[66]

At the far end of the charismatic spectrum lay the phenomenon of Jim and Tammy Bakker and the most open, tolerant, and disorderly of ministries, PTL. In October 1989 Jim Bakker was convicted in a federal court of twenty-four counts of fraud and conspiracy, the prosecutors having made their case that he had bilked his followers out of $158 million and taken $3.5 million for himself out of ministry funds. When the verdict was announced, two television networks interrupted their regular programming to show Jim and Tammy walking out of the courthouse. The scene was, after all, the epilogue to the long-running drama known as Gospelgate that had riveted the country's attention when Robertson was trying to run for president.[67]

In March 1987 Jim had resigned from PTL. He had discovered that Jimmy Swaggart had found out about his tryst with the church secretary, Jessica Hahn, and the hush money the ministry had paid her, and he believed that Swaggart would use the story to destroy him and to take over PTL. He resigned to quiet the scandal and asked Jerry Falwell to become the chairman of PTL, apparently hoping that Falwell, the fundamentalist, would keep his distance from a Pentecostal ministry. Falwell accepted because he knew that unless he saved PTL all television ministries would suffer from the fallout. Yet when a reporter tipped him off to the financial malfeasance at PTL, he had to go to the account books and then to expose the other scandals, including Bakker's habit of having sex in the form of mutual masturbation with male staff members.

Of course, what most people knew about the Bakkers had less to do with the court case than with what made the Bakkers perennial favorites with *People* and the *National Enquirer.* The Bakkers had built a Christian Disneyland called Heritage USA near Charlotte, North Carolina, with a 163-foot waterslide and a fourteen-foot-high fiberglass moose. At the Heritage Grand Hotel they had a suite with gold-plated bathtub fixtures and a fifty-foot walk-in closet. They also had luxurious houses in three resorts and a fleet of automobiles, including two matching antique Rolls-Royces. Both Bakkers had so many clothes that once the ministry hired a private jet to fly the clothes from North Carolina to California. Tammy, who explained she had a "shopping demon," often gave away boxes of dresses with the price tags still on them. She had an air-conditioned doghouse, and once she held a wedding ceremony for a poodle and Yorkshire terrier, complete with bridal gown and tuxedo. On one of Jim's birthdays she announced she had bought him two giraffes as presents. Never without false eyelashes and makeup an inch thick, she cried easily on the set, her mascara running down her face with her tears. Toward the end she gained weight, swallowed pills, and had to be taken to the Betty Ford Center.[68]

The actual charges against Bakker were pallid by comparison: mail fraud and wire fraud and conspiracy to commit both. The government's case centered on a money-raising device Bakker had used for three years to support his ministry. On television he had offered "lifetime partnerships" for donations of $1,000 or more—partnerships that entitled donors to three free nights' lodging per year at Heritage USA for the rest of their lives. According to the prosecution, Bakker had sold tens of thousands more partnerships than he said he would and failed to build the accommodations he advertised. Most of the money had gone into the operating expenses of PTL and some of the rest into his own pocket. In a book published later Charles Shepard, the *Charlotte Observer* reporter who had broken all the major stories from 1984 to 1987, reported that the financial chicanery at PTL was far more extensive than the court case revealed, and far longer-lived.[69] According to his authoritative account, PTL had been badly managed from the start. Almost every year since Bakker founded it in 1974, the ministry had been plagued by financial crises, overdue bills, tax problems, and an appalling waste of funds. On television Bakker was always talking about some worthy new plan: he would build a university, start a school of evangelism, or put PTL on the air in Italy and Brazil. None of these projects ever materialized, but money poured in and poured out just as quickly, most of it for real estate and construction. Bakker would break ground for a new building when the PTL treasury was empty, raise some money, then move on, leaving the old one half finished. When a building was actually completed—often at double the estimated cost—he would invariably find some fault with it, and order the offending piece of construction torn out and redone. By 1984 Heritage USA stretched over 2,300 acres, and only Disneyland and Disney World drew bigger crowds. PTL was bringing in $66 million a year, but with as many as nine hundred people on its payroll, it had staggering expenses and often huge debts. It was in this context that Bakker began to sell his lifetime partnerships—while at the same taking larger and larger amounts of money for himself.

Jim Bakker wasn't the only minister ever to be caught with his hand in the till, but what made him unique was that almost nothing he did was ever a secret. For one thing, Shepard and his colleagues at *The Charlotte Observer* had reported on most of the financial scandals more or less contemporaneously. Year after year they wrote about the bad management and fiscal irresponsibility at PTL; they exposed the fact that the huge sums Bakker had raised for foreign missions never went to missions, and they chronicled all of his major purchases, including a condo in Florida and an estate in Palm Springs, California. Bakker sometimes displayed the *Observer* headlines on television to demonstrate the hostility of the secular press to his ministry. The stories, however, seemed to make no impression on his donors. In 1986 the publisher of the *Observer* wrote in an in-house memo, "PTL's givers—the people our coverage is primarily intended to enlighten—have not shown us in any substantial way that they appreciate our revelations. Rather, they seem to endorse the show-biz lifestyles of the Bakkers and to admire the creation of Heritage USA."

The lack of response to the hard work of investigative reporting disappointed the *Observer* staff, but then almost everything Jim did was in more or less plain sight anyway. To his television audience he preached a religion based on faith in financial miracles and in heaven here on earth with a waterslide and luxury hotels. It was a religion of celebrity, showmanship, and fun; its standard was excess and its doctrines tolerance and freedom from guilt—or any accountability. A third-generation Assemblies of God evangelist, Jim had taken all the harsh prohibitions of the early Pentecostal church and turned them upside down—and slightly askew. Tammy with her huge hairdos, thick makeup, flashy outfits, and jewelry presented almost a caricature of all that had once been forbidden to Assemblies of God women. (Many nonreligious gay men adored her and held gender-bending look-alike contests in her honor.)[70] On the Bakkers' TV show the guests were often Hollywood stars, and the emphasis was always on dramas and spectacle, rather than on Bible teaching. The Bakker religion was certainly charismatic, and yet there was always something off-centered and transgressive about it. To Pentecostals the aberrancy would have been obvious not just on the television show but in the design of Heritage USA.

Take the waterslide, for example. In the Pentecostal tradition falling water is associated with the baptism of the Holy Spirit and with the gifts of the spirit that rained down upon the apostles on the day of Pentecost. In Palestine the physical rains come in the fall and in the spring; Pentecostals call the Pentecost "the early rain," which planted the church and, look to "the latter rain," which brings the harvest that is the return of Christ to earth. Most Pentecostal ministries, if they are affluent enough, have some flowing water about them. Oral Roberts University in Tulsa always had fountains and decorative pools laid out in straight lines along the avenues of approach to the central buildings. Jimmy Swaggart's television ministry and Bible school in Baton Rouge had a series of indoor fountains. Flowing water is welcome in the heat of Tulsa and Baton Rouge, and the very abundance of it in both complexes not only demonstrated the wealth of the ministries but symbolized the abundance of the Holy Spirit around them. But Jim Bakker's water park with its acres of swimming pools surely contained more water than all Roberts and Swaggart pools put together. The curious thing about it was that the water came not in the form of a garden but in pools designed for swimming—for the pleasures of the body—and a 163-foot slide and sluiceways designed for thrills. The message of this was surely not lost on most of Bakker's life partners.

The message was certainly not lost on Jerry Falwell. Some months after he had assumed control of PTL, he found it politically necessary to take a plunge down the waterslide himself. A memorable photograph of the occasion shows him on the chute, a few feet from the top and a few seconds after he has let go. He is wearing what he always wore in public—a black Baptist suit—and his arms are folded over his chest in the manner of corpse in an open coffin. In fact the photograph suggests he is doing it over his own dead body. Now, Jerry Falwell liked swimming as much as the next person, indeed he had a swimming pool at his house. But the fundamentalist Baptist was plunging into a Pentecostal pool, and it is precisely the waters of the Holy Spirit that separate Pentecostals from their parchy-dry fundamentalist cousins. So Falwell had to show that he did not enjoy the plunge.[71]

The rich metaphor of the water park, which Falwell, as it were, fell into, suggests the kind of sensibility at work in Andy Warhol's Campbell Soup cans. Possibly Bakker's was the richer art, for while Warhol was playing with the conventional boundaries between art and commerce, Bakker was playing more dangerous games. In his television show and in his theme park, he was playing with the boundaries of the sacred and the profane, good and evil, heaven and hell, now you see it, now you don't. To speak of fraud in such a context might be to make the same category mistake a philistine might make looking at Warhol construction labeled "Campbell's" and saying it wasn't art but an imitation soup can. Or maybe not.

Heritage USA, when I visited it in September 1987, seven months after the Bakkers left, seemed a parody of the once forbidden world beyond the church, a postmodern concoction with hints of mockery about it. The Heritage Grand Hotel, for example, turned out to be a "Colonial" brick building fronting on the water park and attached to the Victorian facade of a street in some imaginary southern town with pastel-colored grillwork and balconies. Under the white-columned porte cochere a doorman in a uniform dripping with silver braid leaped from one car to another, crying "God loves you" and "Have a nice day." In the four-story atrium inside, an elaborately trimmed Christmas tree surrounded by presents rose almost to the ceiling—though Christmas was still three months away. Under the tree a pianist in a dinner jacket, who looked the young Liberace, tinkled on the keys of a gold piano. A passageway from the atrium led to a shopping mall, where to judge from the temperature and a cloudy blue skyscape painted on the ceiling, it was still midsummer. The shops behind the Victorian street facade included a bakery, the "Heavenly Fudge Factory," and stores with an overwhelming—indeed almost encyclopedic—array of knickknacks, gifts, and mementos, many of them inscribed with homiletic mottos. There was also a dress shop, a jewelry store, and a toy store with fancy dollhouses and seriously expensive china dolls. Nearby was an amphitheater with a castellated facade where the PTL passion play was staged at night, complete with special effects, including fire-and-brimstone explosions when the Devil appeared. In another part of the grounds was a family entertainment center, which once had featured a carousel, a little red train that Bakker loved to drive, and miniature village where mechanized gnomes bobbed up and down in time to winking lights and religious music coming from loudspeakers. Other notable sights on the grounds included the actual house where Billy Graham had spent his childhood, a brick building that had been disassembled, moved, and reconstructed. The house, however, contained no sign of Graham, not even a photograph.

On television the Bakkers preached their own particular version of prosperity theology. Oral Roberts taught that if you gave to God you would be repaid many times over, and that if you prayed with enough faith, and if God willed it, your prayers would be answered. For the Bakkers there was nothing conditional about this promise. "If you pray for a camper, tell God what color," Bakker once advised his audience. Otherwise, he said, you were asking God to "do your shopping for you." In her 1978 autobiography, *I Gotta Be Me*, Tammy wrote about buying a trailer that broke down and the miracles of a passerby photographing the defect and the manufacturer replacing the trailer with a new and better one. Later, of course, miracles like this happened to the Bakkers all the time. Only the quantities changed. "It's important to recognize I didn't start out on a level of faith working with millions of dollars," Bakker once wrote. "I started out by believing God for a newer car than the one I was driving. I started out by believing God for a nicer apartment than I had. Then I moved up." Later Bakker just had to pray on television, and millions of dollars floated out of envelopes at PTL. Bakker claimed no credit for raising the money: that was God's work and a sign of His anointing. How, then, could Bakker behave like an accountant, or be expected to behave like one? Miracles could not be predicted or saved up for a rainy day. And if Bakker acted on impulse, or changed his mind about what to do with the money, that was the way the Spirit moved him. Apparently it was not God's plan for him to give money to missions or to finance a PTL broadcast in Italy; it was God's plan that he build what he called "the campground of the 21st century," complete with a waterslide and a luxury hotel. "Why should I apologize because God throws in crystal chandeliers, mahogany floors, and the best construction in the world?" Bakker once asked.

Many people who watched the Bakkers for the first time after the scandal broke found it impossible to understand how anyone could listen to this kind of talk. It sounded so shockingly materialistic. Why would God be involved with Bakkers' décor? And how could He be asked to deliver a camper that was, say, burgundy, as opposed to navy blue? The answer was that a believer could look at it from the opposite point of view: it was not that the supernatural was mundane but that the material world had a miraculous, God-filled quality; the chandeliers were spiritual chandeliers and the burgundy camper that came in answer to prayer was a sign of His presence in the world. It could, of course, be argued that a God who bothered to throw in some chandeliers was not recognizably Christian. But then Bakker was hardly alone in espousing prosperity theology—and to name the point at which the sacred became profane was to draw a doctrinal line in the sand.

During his last year at PTL Bakker spent a good deal of airtime advertising Heritage USA. Sometimes his pitches were purely secular, but sometimes he interlaced the ads with hymns and Scripture reading, creating surreal video collages. On one program PTL singers sang "We are the army of the Lord," over photos of teenagers in scanty bathing suits floating down the sluiceways of the water park on inner tubes. The PTL promotional picturebook spoke of a Heritage Village Church, a Heritage Village Church Sanctuary, a Heritage Grand Ministry Center, and a World Outreach Center. But there was no church building anywhere. The sanctuary turned out to be an auditorium in PTL's television studio complex, the Ministry Center an indoor swimming pool that was used for baptisms once a week, and the World Outreach Center the administrative offices of PTL. There was no Bible school and no educational institution of any kind—unless you counted a counseling center in which therapists dispensed advice on marital problems and what to do about feelings of unworthiness. The promotional book went some way to accounting for these absences. "What is a church?" it asked rhetorically. "Not just a building. Not just a ritual, not a set of dogmas, not just an institution or a hierarchy. . . . Heritage Village Church shows that the church can be encompassing, not a part or a compartment of life, but life itself, all of life with nothing left out."

The church was, then, the world. And Heritage Village Church was everything that happened at Heritage USA. Bakker had simply pasted the label "church" on all of it. He may have done that for tax purposes, but clearly he had made the label stick, for in my two days there, I heard several people say, "This is heaven on earth." They seem to have meant it literally, for when the Bakker verdict of guilty came down, a man amid the cluster of Bakker supporters outside the courthouse cried out: "They don't treat murderers like they treated him. I've been to Heritage USA, and I felt like I was in heaven. You were on holy ground there."

The people I saw at Heritage USA seemed as diverse as most crowds in Disneyland. I kept expecting the question put to strangers in Falwell's domain, "Are you saved?" The question that served as a challenge: Are you one of us or one of them? But the question never came. Tolerance reigned in Bakker's kingdom. His soundstage was an equally open and tolerant place. It wasn't racist or politically partisan, and over and above the musicians and Hollywood celebrities, PTL shows included a good many women, and even women preachers. The tolerance was in fact such that from time to time strange incidents occurred. Once a woman appeared on the show maintaining that wifely submission wasn't Christian. There was some awkwardness, and she disappeared. On another occasion Robert A. Schuller (the son of the televangelist) was heard to say, apropos of his own divorce, that divorce was merely a social and cultural situation and not a moral problem at all. In December 1986, a PTL announcer said that among the forthcoming events to be held at Heritage USA was a conference of Christian hairdressers.

According to Charles Shepard, Bakker had once preached the fire-and-brimstone sermons he had no doubt been brought up on. But at PTL he preached only the love of God: God healed, God answered prayers, God forgave. At the close of his show Bakker would say, "God loves you, He really, really does." That was PTL's main slogan, and it could be found embossed or engraved on items throughout the gift shops of the park. PTL promotional literature elaborated on this theme: "God is love. God is a God of restoration. Our ministry focuses on that simple, central truth." Bakker's audience could have chosen to believe that Bakker simply decided to emphasize the positive and the rest was understood. Yet since Bakker preached only a half of the Christian message, who was to say that he believed in the other half? And whatever he privately believed, he preached an unbalanced equation. God might be love, but if He was only love, then He had no judgment and there was no such thing as sin. Bakker did not come right out and say that, but he and his fellow pastors so neglected the topic of sin that his audience apparently didn't even notice when, in the summer of 1986, with the Jessica Hahn scandal threatening to surface, he and other PTL pastors segued into messages that were purely antinomian.

On one show that summer Bakker began the discussion by reading the Epistle of Paul to the Galatians, Chapter 5: "Stand fast in the liberty wherewith Christ hath made us free . . ." Paul's message in this chapter, he maintained, was that Christ had made men free of the Hebrew law. What he omitted to mention was Paul's conditions: "if ye be led of the Spirit" and "use not the liberty for an occasion to the flesh." Possibly it was a Freudian slip—though possibly not—for Paul is very specific about "the flesh" in this chapter; indeed, he gives a list of fleshly sins, which include adultery and fornication. On the same program Bakker quoted the phrase "Love covers a multitude of sins," explaining, bizarrely, that it meant that Christians should cover up the sins of others. There were other strange messages during the year. At the end of May, an attractive couple, a young church musician and his wife, appeared on the show with the unlikely story that she was a reformed prostitute and he was a reformed homosexual. In August Bakker gave a rip-roaring sermon, of the sort he had given up, proposing that those who judged would go straight to hell because judging others was worse than any other sin. Clearly the message was aimed at Swaggart.

By then Jimmy Swaggart had had PTL in his sights for a long time. From 1985 on he, the traditionalist Pentecostal, had waged a relentless campaign against what he saw as the false doctrines of popular charismatic preachers. He denounced positive confession as having more to do with positive thinking, or with some New Age cultish practice, than with Christianity; he deplored ecumenism and the violation of the traditional boundaries between the church and the world. What seems to have raised his doubts about Bakker in the first place were the Hollywood stars on his show. PTL was by no means his only target but it represented just about everything he despised. In 1987 he accused "Christian broadcasting" of featuring " 'get-rich-quick' schemes, psychological philosophies, rock n' roll music, and all the way down to the exhibition of homosexual guests." He had learned of the Jessica Hahn affair more than a year before, and had confronted Bakker's co-pastor, Richard Dortch, with the story and with the rumors he had heard about Bakker's homosexual activity. Dortch denied everything. Swaggart said nothing in public about the Hahn affair, though he did warn the Assemblies of God presbyters against Bakker. By March rumors of the Hahn incident had leaked out from other sources. *The Charlotte Observer* made frequent calls to Bakker asking about the hush money, and there was a move afoot among Bakker's fellow televangelists—Swaggart included—to confront Bakker with the story.

Bakker resigned. He must have panicked. The year before Swaggart had destroyed the career of a rival, Marvin Gorman, a New Orleans pastor and a rising Pentecostal televangelist, over an adulterous affair. Still, not long after Falwell took over as chairman of PTL and *The Charlotte Observer* broke the news of the Hahn affair, Bakker announced he was ready to come back to PTL because God had already forgiven him. Apparently God had not had the heart to put Bakker through the intermediate steps, the admission of sin and repentance. "Forgiven" was PTL's last slogan, and it appeared on bumper stickers and baseball caps all over Heritage USA and its environs. Falwell, however, could not let Bakker return, and by then not all the people in Bakker's audience were ready to swallow this new lesson in faith—or to forgive Bakker as quickly as he claimed God had done. All the same, those who had sat quiet for months listening to his strange messages were in no position to charge Bakker with hypocrisy. Bakker had not violated his own rules; rather he had changed them in plain sight.[72]*

*   *   *

Pat Robertson had kept a distance from Bakker ever since Bakker left CBN. Apropos of the Shepherding Movement he had said, "In the move of God across America it often happens . . . that teachers will teach upon a truth and then will push it to such a degree that it becomes unbalanced, and, in some cases, heretical."[74] He might have said the same of Bakker, but, unlike Swaggart, he never criticized him on religious grounds.

In his biography of Robertson, David Harrell tells us that Robertson was a theological "moderate." But what did that mean exactly in the context of the modern charismatic revival? So many new ideas and practices

---

* The Bakkers divorced while Jim was in prison, and both later remarried. Tammy embraced the gay men who supported her, started attending gay pride events, and in 1996 became the cohost of a syndicated television talk show with an openly gay actor. She acted in a few movies, and had a film and musical made about her. She died of colon cancer in 2007. Jim repented of prosperity theology, saying that he had never read through the Bible before he went to prison. In 2003 he started a new broadcasting ministry in Branson, Missouri, and in 2008 he moved to Blue Eye, Missouri, where he broadcasts from a studio in a residential/retail complex bankrolled by a developer who claims Bakker saved his marriage.

Jim and Tammy had two children, a boy and a girl. The boy, Jay Bakker, who was thirteen when his father went to prison, didn't finish high school, took up drugs and alcohol, and covered himself in tattoos and piercings. Gradually he found his faith and started his own ministry, the Revolutionary Church. In 2006 he took his ministry to New York, where he preached at a hip bar in Brooklyn. A social liberal, he became an ardent supporter of gay rights, including gay marriage. In 2013 he went to Minneapolis to found a second Revolutionary Church.[73]

As for Swaggart, he was brought down by Marvin Gorman, the very preacher whose career he had ruined by exposing Gorman's adulterous affair. Gorman, who was suing him for defamation, photographed him going into a motel with a prostitute a few hundred yards from his New Orleans church. As the New Yorker reporter Lawrence Wright wrote, it was as if he were courting his own destruction and asking for punishment. He repented tearfully, but refused to follow the Assemblies of God presbyters' instructions to step down from his television ministry for a year and spend another year in probation. He was defrocked, and when he returned to his pulpit after three months, his enormous ministry was already in ruins. In October 1991 he was caught with another prostitute in California. He and his wife and son managed to hang on and to continue broadcasting on local stations.

were swirling around outside the denominational boundaries. Among them was the form of positive confession known as "name it and claim it" in which God did the will of believers; and on the other hand John Wimber's teaching that the purpose of Christians until Christ's return was to manifest the Kingdom of God to the world through evangelism and righteous social action. There was a school of thought, associated with Frank Peretti and C. Peter Wagner, holding that demonic "principalities and powers" were waging a cosmic war, and that believers using spiritual warfare could drive the demons from specific geographical areas such as Kansas City or Colorado Springs. There was also Kingdom Now, a variant of the postmillennial Latter Rain theology, in which apostles and prophets would lead a new generation of spiritually empowered Christians to take dominion over all the major institutions of the world and run them until Christ's return. In addition there were a number of "anointed" healers. The most famous of them—and a friend of Robertson's—was Benny Hinn, a latter-day healing revivalist, who in his televised crusades hissed and "fired" at afflicted believers, and who once promised to raise the dead. Plus there were a number of self-appointed prophets, among them Mike Bickle, who claimed to hear an assortment of revelations from God. From time to time preachers would ignite a revival that went on for months. Such was the Toronto Blessing of 1994, which drew 600,000 charismatics—American Catholics, English Protestants, and many others—to a Toronto church, where, overcome by the Spirit, people roared, barked, growled, jerked, laughed uncontrollably, or fainted dead away. Then, too, Reconstructionism, shorn of its insistence on Mosaic Law, penetrated this experience-oriented and theologically ungrounded world.[75]

Robertson rejected some of these novelties, such as the fivefold ministry and Bickle's personal visions. He endorsed the Toronto Blessing. He flirted with others. "We are not coming up against just human beings to beat them in elections. We're going to be coming up against spiritual warfare," he said at a Christian Coalition conference in 1994. He was a positive confession teacher, and he never called down the fraudulent practices of friends such as Robert Tilton and Benny Hinn. He was a premillennialist, but he did more than flirt with the postmillennialism in *The Secret Kingdom*. Swaggart hesitated to endorse his candidacy for president because of it. Robertson knew Rushdoony. He interviewed him on *The 700 Club* in the 1970s, and agreed with him when he spoke about reclaiming the Puritan heritage. Apparently viewers reacted, for he later put out a public statement distancing himself from what he called "the extremes of Dominion Theology." [76]

Robertson, of course, had a show with hundreds of hours a year to fill. He needed to keep in touch with his viewers and needed to interest and entertain them. Then as a charismatic televangelist, he was in show business of the Spirit, as opposed the literal Word business of Falwell and other fundamentalists. Like Jim and Tammy, he had his own specialties: his hurricanes, his yearly pronouncements about disasters ahead, and his "word of knowledge" that God was curing someone out there of bunions. Often he seemed to embrace novel doctrines, but as with his predictions of the end times, he generally left himself an escape hatch, or simply dropped them later on. His involvement with Reconstructionism, however wasn't just a matter of showmanship, for he hired a quasi-Reconstructionist, Herbert Titus, to found his law school, and during his seven years at CBN University Titus had a major impact.

Titus came to CBNU in 1986. A Harvard Law School graduate, he had worked at four state university law schools during the 1960s and '70s, where he supported abortion and gay rights and became an affiliate lawyer of the ACLU. He had a crisis conversion in 1975, and for the following two years he studied with Francis Schaeffer at L'Abri. He read Rushdoony's work, and when he returned in 1977 he invited the author to speak at the University of Oregon, where he was a tenured professor. Two years later he left Oregon, and though no charismatic became founding dean of the law school at Oral Roberts University (where he taught Michele Bachmann, among others). When Roberts had to close his law school down, he donated his law library to CBNU (later renamed Regent University) and Titus migrated with it to become the founding dean of Regent's law school and its school of public policy. [77]

Titus was not a Reconstructionist in the sense that he didn't insist that "every single stroke" of Deuteronomy and Leviticus had to be observed. But he did insist that God's law, as revealed in the Scriptures, was the law.

Fixed, unchanging, and uniform for all nations from the beginning, this Law had to be discovered—rather than invented by man. In his major work, *Biblical Principles of Law*, he wrote that God's law had been ignored by men and nations with the outstanding exception of America in its first two hundred years. (That is, from the early seventeenth century to the early nineteenth.) Having come to America to propagate Christianity, the early settlers had adopted covenant law; America's revolutionary leaders had made the same choice when they justified their separation from the mother country by calling on "the laws of nature and nature's God." America's "constitutional commitments" linked her to the covenant God made with Israel; and both the nation and the states were linked to God's law through biblically based English common law. Since then the concept of man-invented law had brought the nation to the brink of chaos or totalitarian rule. But, Titus wrote, "With such a biblical heritage, Christians have been given a foundation for reconstruction not only of America's legal system but of the legal systems of all nations."[78]

Titus maintained that the Constitution was not "a living thing" open to interpretation, but he did not belong to the school of "originalism" that held it was necessary to interpret the Constitution according to the intentions of the Founders. He wrote that the Founders were biblically wrong to permit slavery but biblically right to eliminate state laws against blasphemy and heresy. Similarly, while objecting to most modern jurisprudence, he found that some modern laws, such as that against drafting women into the military, accorded with God's law. (He judged that women had the right to own property, to vote, and to hold public office, but not the right to equality within the family.) The final authority he looked to was not the Constitution, or "biblically-based common law," but the Scriptures—or the Scriptures as he interpreted them. In his chapter "Restitution and Punishment," he wrote that "an eye for an eye and a tooth for a tooth" was never meant to be taken literally. God never sanctioned revenge. What *lex talionis* meant was restitution for wrongs according to the principle of proportionality. Titus then invoked the Eighth Amendment to the Constitution, claiming that the Founders in speaking of "cruel and unusual punishment" had no intention of outlawing whipping; the Thirteenth Amendment, he maintained, allowed "involuntary servitude" as restitution for crimes such as theft.

Thanks perhaps to Schaeffer, Titus's theory of law had the advantage over Rushdoony's of sounding more familiar to Americans; its disadvantage was its total incoherence. God's law was not what the Scriptures actually said, and the Constitution, while not "a living thing," was not what the Founders actually agreed to, or what subsequent jurisprudence resolved. The Law was simply what Titus said it was. As might be expected, Titus railed against what the Christian right considered the outrages of modern jurisprudence: *Roe v. Wade*, gay rights, affirmative action, the legality of "adultery and fornication," and the state's interference with the affairs of the church and the family. He followed Rushdoony in calling for an end to public education and to government welfare programs. ("To tax a person to support a government program to help the needy under threat of civil or criminal prosecution . . . is the very antithesis of Christian charity.") He also advocated the substitution of "the divinely guaranteed benefits of corporal punishment" for the incarceration of criminals. Much of his book, however, concerned economic issues: the divine sanction for free enterprise, the church's authority to govern contracts, the biblical permission for businesses to charge any amount of interest on loans ("usury" didn't mean what most people thought), and illegitimacy of the redistribution of wealth by the government. "Aid to dependent children, to the disabled, to the unemployed, and to the handicapped, retirement funds and Medicare for the aged financed by tax revenues," he wrote, "violate the law of love."[79]

A forceful personality and thought of as brilliant, Titus attracted broad support among students, faculty, and alumni at Regent University. While heading the school of law and government, he was made vice president for academic affairs, and many assumed he was next in line for the presidency. The law school, however, year after year, failed to obtain the accreditation from the American Bar Association that Robertson badly wanted. By Harrell's account, Titus's recourse was to sue the ABA for $600 million. "He wanted to fight all the time," Robertson complained, and after years of frustration he came to the not unreasonable conclusion that the main obstacle to accreditation was Titus. Finally in 1993 he fired Titus as dean, and though he offered him a well-funded chair at the law school, the dismissal caused a rebellion among students, faculty, and alumni. Titus threatened to sue; eight of the fourteen law professors resigned, or had to be fired, and the dispute went on for two years. At some point Robertson began to feel that Titus had "an extraordinarily narrow view of Christianity." He decided that the dean had become "essentially a cultist" who had surrounded himself with a coterie intent on controlling the university.[80]

It wasn't the first or the last time that Robertson went from the wilder shores of charismatic belief to worldly pragmatism.*

---

*Titus went on to join a private law firm and in 1996 ran for vice president of the United States on the U.S. Taxpayer's Party ticket with Howard Phillips. He became the lawyer for the Gun Owners of America, an organization far to the right of the National Rifle Association.

14

THE CHRISTIAN COALITION
and the REPUBLICAN PARTY

A FTER THE 1988 election Robertson returned to CBN and *The 700 Club*. He hadn't planned to, but the telescandals—and his absence—had taken a toll on ministry finances. Contributions declined by a third over a two-year period, the receipts reaching their lowest level since the early 1980s. Other television ministries reported similar drop-offs, and some never recovered. Falwell, whose finances had never been well managed, eventually had to pull *The Old-Time Gospel Hour* off the air in all but a few local stations. *The 700 Club* continued, but donations remained low throughout the 1990s.[1] The nonreligious CBN cable network became the financial anchor of all CBN activities. Renamed the Family Channel, it reached more than forty million subscribers in the late 1980s. Attracting advertising and charging cable stations for its broadcasts, it became so profitable that by 1990 CBN had to spin it off to maintain its own nonprofit status. Robertson and his son Tim formed a company with CBN as a major shareholder and bought it for $250 million. They took it public in 1992, and with the proceeds they bought entertainment companies with collections of old movies and TV shows. In 1997 they sold the company to Fox Kids Worldwide for $1.9 billion.[2]

Robertson, however, had hardly given up on politics. "This campaign is not a one-shot attempt to win one office," a Robertson staffer said in 1988. "It is designed to start a permanent restructuring of American politics, particularly Republican politics." The vision was that of his boss. In January 1989 Robertson asked Ralph Reed, a twenty-seven-year-old Republican

activist from Georgia who was taking a PhD in American history, to pro-
pose a plan for a political organization—as yet nameless and undefined.
The following year Robertson and some of his chief campaign supporters
launched the Christian Coalition and hired Reed as its executive director.
Billing itself as a nonpartisan organization aimed at making "government
more responsive to the concerns of Evangelical Christians and pro-family
Catholics," the Christian Coalition started up quickly with financing from
Robertson's 134,000-member donor base—and a contribution of $64,000
from the Republican Senatorial Committee. "The Christian Coalition will
be the most powerful political organization in America," Robertson wrote
in 1991. By the time of the 1992 presidential election, its budget had risen
to over $8.5 million, and it claimed a quarter of a million members and
more than a thousand chapters in the fifty states. The membership figures were highly exaggerated, but by recruiting activists already mobilized
at the local level, the Coalition soon became the largest Christian right
organization—and the most politically effective.[3]

Unlike the Moral Majority, the Christian Coalition did not recruit pastors but worked with lay evangelicals of different traditions and made alliances with other Christian right groups at the local level. Its core mission
was "to mobilize and train Christians for effective political action." In Robertson's vision the Coalition would recruit five or more activists in each
of the nation's 175,000 precincts; it would start with elections for school
boards, county commissions, and other local races, where a small percentage of the registered voters could make the difference. It would work up
from there to congressional races and the White House.[4] Ralph Reed, who
ran the operations and served as the public face of the Coalition, had what
was often called "choir boy looks," but he was a political engineer. He had
battled his way to the top of the College Republicans and attended Morton Blackwell's Leadership Institute, making friends with two important
lobbyists, Grover Norquist and Jack Abramoff. After a religious experience
in an upscale pub on Capitol Hill in 1983, he had founded a Christian right
student organization, campaigned for Senator Jesse Helms, led antiabortion protests at family planning clinics, and worked for Jack Kemp in 1988.
Articulate and techno-savvy, he put together a sophisticated organization
with a newspaper, the *Christian American*, a website, and a monthly tele-

vision program. Under his direction the Coalition held training seminars across the country, and an annual "Road to Victory" conference, where activists were given specific guidance on how to identify and mobilize voters and how to be a candidate.[5]

In the early years Reed and other Coalition leaders often recommended stealth tactics of the sort the Freedom Council had used. They urged their members not to attract attention and to avoid using the name of the organization in Republican circles. Reed sometimes described his voter mobilization program as a covert military operation. "I want to be invisible," he told the *Virginia Pilot* in November 1991. "I do guerrilla warfare. I paint my face and travel at night. You don't know it's over until you're in a body bag. You don't know until election night."[6] Stealth tactics dovetailed with the theme of religious persecution ubiquitous in Coalition literature: Democrats, gays, feminists, the Supreme Court, and the media were attacking religion and people of faith. In one letter signed by Robertson, America was said to have become "a largely anti-Christian pagan nation" and our government "has become a weapon the anti-Christian forces now use against Christians and religious people." In some instances Coalition members won local elections with stealth tactics, but the Coalition soon became far too well known to conceal its activities. In its first two years it made a noisy, well-financed attack on the National Endowment for the Arts for supporting "obscene art," and lobbied for the confirmation of Clarence Thomas to the Supreme Court.[7]

Coalition literature stated: "The Christian Coalition is not affiliated with any political party and does not endorse candidates." The Coalition had applied to the IRS for status as a tax-exempt "social welfare" organization, a 501(c)(4), and claimed to operate within the statute that allowed such groups to engage in politics as long as partisan politics was not their "primary activity."[8] The statute was sufficiently vague to make stepping over the line from "pro-family" advocacy into partisan politics difficult to prove, but Robertson himself never made any secret about which party the Coalition intended to work through. "We want . . . to see a majority of the Republican Party in the hands of pro-family Christians by 1996," he told reporters in 1992.[9] Reed geared his tactics to doing just that.

One of the Coalition's major efforts was the distribution of voter guides, which, like those of the Christian Voice, clearly favored their candidates and often distorted the records of their opponents. In 1990, when Senator Jesse Helms was lagging behind a Democrat in the polls, the Coalition distributed three quarters of million voter guides in churches across North Carolina the weekend before the election, and Helms won by 100,000 votes. The Democratic Party and organizations such as Americans United for the Separation of Church and State and Norman Lear's People for the American Way took notice. In 1992, when the Coalition printed forty million voter guides for races around the country, they raised objections. The Democratic Party filed a complaint with the Federal Election Commission, accusing the Coalition of raising money as a tax-exempt group but spending it on Republican Party activities. It was only the first of such complaints.[10]

Reed introduced a number of sophisticated methods to identify "pro-family" people who would vote Republican. One was to cross-reference conservative church membership lists with the list of registered Republicans in a given area. Another was to call voters in selected precincts to ask if they were Republicans, and if they were, to find out what issues they felt most important. (If they said they were Democrats, their names would be discarded.) The survey information would be coded and stored in a database, and later the identified voters would mysteriously receive computer-generated letters from the Republican candidate with issues tailored to each individual. Coordination between a 501(c)(4) and a political campaign was illegal, but because many Coalition members joined Republican campaigns or took party posts, the two were often the same. In effect, while skirting the law, Coalition leaders were melding the Christian Right with the Republican Party in a way the Moral Majority never had.[11]

During the presidency of George H. W. Bush the Christian right was more in evidence in the states than in Washington. Democrats controlled both houses of Congress, and of necessity Bush focused on foreign policy. The Berlin Wall came down in his first year in office, and afterward one Eastern European country after another threw off their Communist regimes and broke away from the Soviet Union. In 1991 the Soviet Union itself disintegrated. Foreign policy experts gave Bush high marks for his deft handling of the reunification of Germany, of the Soviet regime as its empire fell apart, and of the negotiations for the control of nuclear weapons. In the midst of these historic developments, Saddam Hussein invaded Kuwait. Gaining the consent of the U.N. Security Council and the U.S. Congress, Bush sent U.S. and coalition troops to the Persian Gulf and drove the Iraqi armies from Kuwait with few Coalition casualties. He spoke of a "new world order" of justice, peace, and security, and after the Gulf War he put a major effort into peace process between the Israelis and the Palestinians. Domestically, Bush had less room for maneuver. To pass a budget reducing the deficits left by Reagan, he had to renege on his pledge not to raise taxes. He passed the Clean Air Act, and the Americans with Disabilities Act, but except for the nomination of Clarence Thomas to the Supreme Court, he did nothing of substance for the Christian right.

Robertson criticized Bush for raising taxes and called his 1990 strategic arms treaty with the Soviet Union a move toward "unilateral disarmament," but according to Harrell his relationship with Bush was the closest he had with any president. In January 1991 Bush invited him to the White House "for the purposes of encouraging him and praying for him with regards to the Persian Gulf Crisis." The next day he wrote Robertson a note of thanks for his prayers and his words of support. At the approach of the 1992 presidential election with the power of the Christian Coalition becoming more visible, he wrote Robertson a number of other personal notes, one in March thanking him for coming to an "enjoyable" meeting and assuring him he looked forward to having the benefit of his counsel in the months ahead.[12]

Yet in 1991 Robertson published a book that suggested he was extremely cross with the president. First, he charged Bush of being taken in by the apparent disintegration of Communist control over the Soviet Union and Eastern Europe, claiming that totalitarianism was reasserting itself in these countries in a more "deceptive and dangerous form." Then, he accused Bush of waging war against Saddam Hussein for the sole purpose of ceding American sovereignty to the United Nations. But that wasn't all. Bush and "other men of good will" were, he charged, unwittingly doing the bidding of those who aimed to replace the "Christian social order" with "an occult-inspired world socialist dictatorship . . . under the domination of Lucifer and his allies."[13]

Robertson's book *The New World Order* wasn't just an attack on Bush or another end times scenario. It was the revelation of a vast and sinister conspiracy that had shaped world history from the French Revolution through the Cold War. A classic example of what Richard Hofstadter called "the paranoid style," the book delineated the course of this conspiracy through two centuries of European and American history with the pedantry common to the form: the bibliography, the documentation, and the laborious accumulation of facts—or what appeared to be facts. Little in it was new. In essence it was a compendium of conspiracy theories hatched over the decades by fundamentalists and the secular hard right, updated and with the addition of Robertson's case for Latin American dictators. Its central characters were the usual suspects: the Council on Foreign Relations, the prestigious Trilateral Commission, the Rockefellers, the Wall Street banks, and the Eastern Establishment as a whole. Previously the best-known conspiracy theorists, Joseph McCarthy and Robert Welch of the John Birch Society, had proposed that top government officials, and the Establishment generally, were riddled with Communists, but by 1991 it was too late for that. Robertson's book took up a secondary but persistent theme in the literature: that a cabal of corporate internationalists was waging a sustained conspiracy to control the world economy and to create a one-world government. President Bush's speech of September 1990 to a joint session of Congress, "Toward a New World Order," galvanized conspiracy theorists, but Robertson's book was ahead of the curve. In his version the Eastern Establishment had since World War I used its influence to promote the Communist takeovers in Russia and China as an intermediate step to establishing an atheistic, socialistic world government. It had created the United Nations and promoted huge Cold War expenditures in order to put the U.S. government in debt to the banks, and to weaken the American economy and American sovereignty.[14]

Tracing the course of the one-world conspiracy under both Democratic and Republican presidents from Woodrow Wilson to George H. W. Bush wasn't hard, he wrote, but more difficult was explaining why these "well bred, highly refined, quite wealthy" leaders had been destroying the world economy and subverting American national sovereignty for most of the twentieth century. Simple greed or lust for power could not explain it. No. "There has to be some other power at work," for "impulses of that sort do not spring from the human heart" but "from the depth of something that is evil."[15]

The occult power Robertson identified was also familiar: the Illuminati. The object of American conspiratorial fantasies for two centuries—and a favorite of the early fundamentalists such as Reuben Torrey—the secret society of Illuminati was said to have infiltrated Free Masonry, caused the French Revolution, inspired Marx and Engels, and fostered the Bolshevik movement. How Robertson connected the Illuminati with the Council on Foreign Relations involved, among other things, Cecil Rhodes's dream of empire and Woodrow Wilson's decision to create the Federal Reserve Board. Noticeably, though, at every juncture in Robertson's tortuous chain of historical causality, influential Jewish bankers appeared as what he called the "missing link." Among them, by his account, were the Frankfurt Rothschilds, who had joined the Illuminated Free Masonry; Jacob Schiff, who had financed the Bolshevik movement and Cecil Rhodes's adventures in Africa; the "European economic powers" who "wanted to get their tentacles into the American economy"; and Paul Warburg, who succeeded when he established the Federal Reserve. As sources for these "facts," Robertson cited and quoted from the works of two notorious anti-Semitic conspiracy theorists: Nesta H. Webster, a British Fascist of the interwar period, and Eustace Mullins, an American, who had worked for Senator Joseph McCarthy and taken his inspiration from Ezra Pound in the lunatic asylum.[16]

Robertson went on to report that only a "vital, economically strong, Christian United States" could "prohibit a worldwide Satanic dictator from winning his battle." Satan's strategy was to make "a frontal assault on Israel"—and that was the plan of "the presently-constituted new world order." Satan would also "launch a war against the Christian people"— and already the very techniques the Nazis had used against the Jews were being used against Christians. Still, "With America free and at large, Satan's schemes will at best be only partially successful." The Christian Coalition, he continued, was launching an effort to "rebuild the foundation of a free, sovereign America from the grassroots" that would "sweep the one-worlders out of contention in the public policy arena in a short time." The time has come, he exhorted, "to mount an all-out assault on the ultimate power of the Establishment through its control of the money supply." [17]

When *The New World Order* appeared, a *Wall Street Journal* columnist called it "a predictable compendium of the lunatic fringe's greatest hits . . . written in his energetically crackpot style." The book quickly rose to fourth place on the *New York Times* best-seller list, eventually selling half a million copies. The secular press, however, paid it no further attention until 1995, when *The New York Review of Books* ran pieces by Michael Lind and Jacob Heilbrunn describing Robertson's references to Jewish bankers and tracing them, word for word, to their anti-Semitic sources. The columnist Frank Rich wrote about Lind's piece in *The New York Times*, and Robertson wrote the *Times* protesting that he was a strong supporter of Israel and certainly not anti-Semitic. [18] He said a researcher had come up with the anti-Semitic sources, but failed to explain what the material from Webster and Mullins was doing in his book—or why, given his upbringing, he was peddling Eastern Establishment conspiracy theories.

According to Harrell, Robertson had flirted with the same conspiracy theory off and on for years. Presumably it was in the air he breathed. In 1976 he wrote a supporter who had inquired about rumors of plots involving the Trilateral Commission and the Rockefellers, "Even if some of these things were true, which they probably aren't, I believe that we as Christians will worry ourselves to death looking for plots instead of spending our time shining the light of God's love into the darkness of the world. I do believe that we must accord a measure of trust to our leaders, and that includes trust in their motives." Still, writes Harrell, the more he edged toward political involvement in the late 1970s, the more he entertained the conspiracy theory. In 1980 he warned, "The major thrust of the CFR [Council on Foreign Relations] and the Trilateral Commission is to destroy nationalism in favor of an interdependent one-world government." [19] He toned this theme way down during the 1988 campaign, but on launching the Christian Coalition, he turned it up full volume. Galvanizing his supporters was, perhaps, more important at that point than pleasing the readers of *The New York Times*.

In later years Robertson continued to defend *The New World Order*, but not always with much conviction. In a private letter he told a supporter, "I'm a writer and not a bad writer. . . . If you are going to write it so people want to read it, you have to set a little sense of drama in it." The whole concept of the new world order, he maintained, was "the plan," but he added, "I am not interested in conspiracies, but one would have to be blind to ignore the 'good old boy network' that for many years dominated American policy." [20]

The new attention to Robertson's book was occasioned by the prominence the Christian Coalition had gained since the book appeared.

Just after the Gulf War President Bush's approval ratings stood at 89 percent, but because of a recession, they sank into the 30s in the following year. Seizing the moment, Pat Buchanan, a right-winger and a newly born isolationist, launched a presidential campaign, and to the shock of the Bush team took 37 percent of the vote in the New Hampshire primary. Robertson decided to support Bush, even though the vast majority of his supporters favored Buchanan. [21] Strategically, as Reed saw, he had made the right decision. To regain the loyalty of conservative evangelicals, Bush and Quayle reached out to the NAE and the SBC and ran on the social issues. [22] The Republican platform reflected Christian right positions. It called for a ban on abortion with no exceptions, for opposition to any civil rights laws for homosexuals, and for an end to public funding of "obscene" art. It endorsed home schooling and school prayer and opposed making contraceptives available in public schools. Ralph Reed called it "the most conservative and the most pro-family platform in the history of this party." The Coalition and its allies held over a third of the seats at the Republican National Convention, and "culture war" became the theme of the convention with hard-line speeches by Robertson, Marilyn Quayle, and most notably Buchanan, who on the opening night declared, "There is a religious war going on in this country. It's a cultural war as critical to the kind of nation we shall be as the Cold War itself. This war is for the soul of America." Later Quayle spoke at a Christian Coalition "God and Country" rally in Houston, and Bush at the organization's second Road to Victory Conference in Virginia Beach. The election, however, was fought on the economy, and in the three-way race with Bill Clinton and Ross

Perot, Bush received only 38 percent of the popular vote. Still, he took 63 percent of the white evangelical vote, or proportionately more than he had in 1988.[23] And the Christian right did well in down-ticket races. People for the American Way estimated that up to five hundred "pro-family" candidates were elected at local levels—mostly school boards and state legislatures—and that 40 percent of the candidates the Christian right backed in state and local campaigns won their elections.[24]

After the election of Bill Clinton, the Coalition, along with other Christian right groups, experienced an explosive growth in membership and financing. A baby boomer, Clinton seemed to embody everything religious conservatives hated about the 1960s from his youthful experimentation with marijuana to the professional career of his wife. He began his term by instituting a "Don't Ask, Don't Tell" policy for gay men and women in the military and planning for a national health care system. On top of that, he was a liberal Southern Baptist who could talk "God talk" naturally with blacks and whites. In just three years the Coalition went from reporting 250,000 "members and supporters" to reporting 1.6 million of them in 1,600 local chapters and an annual budget of $25 million.[25]

In the midterm elections of 1994 the GOP gained a major victory, picking up eleven governorships, eight Senate seats, and fifty-four seats in the House. The election gave Republicans control of the lower body of Congress for the first time in forty years and inaugurated more than a decade of Republican dominance in the House. Exit polls registered the historic shift of the white South into the Republican Party and the importance of the evangelical vote. White evangelicals had moved decisively into the Republican camp, giving GOP congressional candidates 70 percent of their vote; they had also turned out in record numbers, contributing heavily to the nine-million jump in the GOP voter turnout from the 1990 midterms. According to John C. Green and his colleagues, the Christian right had probably mobilized four million voters and reached fifty million people— or as many as the gun lobby or the labor unions.[26] The Christian Coalition had played a major role in the effort. It had worked in 120 congressional races, and according to Americans United for the Separation of Church and State, 114 House members and 26 senators in the new Congress had either received perfect scores on the Coalition's scorecard or had won with its backing. Even more important, it had come to dominate the Republican Party apparatus in a dozen states, including Texas and Florida.[27] In April 1995 Robertson made the cover of *U.S. News & World Report*; in May, Reed, often described as the political wunderkind of the evangelical right, made the cover of *Time* under the headline: "The Right Hand of God."[28]

The question was what the Coalition would do with its newfound power. By the logic of *The New World Order*, the Coalition had to detach itself from the Republican Party. There could, after all, be no compromise with the forces of Lucifer, and according to Robertson, every administration that came to power, including those of Reagan and Bush, harbored secret agents of a one-world order. However, the author of *The New World Order* was also the man who had spoken at the Council on Foreign Relations and who had twice supported Bush for president. Furthermore, Ralph Reed was clearly trying to move the Coalition toward the Republican mainstream.

In his first two years as executive director of the Coalition Reed had recognized that the Christian right (or what he called "the pro-family movement") remained a small minority of the voting public. He had larger ambitions for it, and shortly after Clinton's election, he had called for a change of course. In the January 1993 issue of the in-house publication, *Christian American*, Reed advised Coalition members to "avoid hostile and intemperate rhetoric." We must, he wrote, "acknowledge the opinions of others and the sincerity of their beliefs. We must emphasize inclusion, not exclusion. . . . We must be tolerant of diverse views and respectful of those who express them." He also wrote, "We have allowed ourselves to be ghettoized by a narrow band of issues like abortion, homosexual rights and prayer in school."[29] The following summer he outlined a strategy for growth in the Heritage Foundation's *Policy Review.*

In his piece, "Casting a Wider Net," Reed noted that frequent church attenders and families with children were "the most predictive demographic characteristics of conservative voting behavior," but that the "pro-family movement" still had "limited appeal" to the forty million evangelicals and conservative Catholics. The challenge, he wrote, was to develop a broader issues agenda, for "without specific policies designed to benefit families and children, appeals to family values or America's Judeo-Christian heritage will fall on deaf ears." He quoted a recent poll indicating that only 12 percent of all voters—and only 22 percent of evangelicals—listed abortion as the key issue in their voting decisions. Abortion and homosexuality, he maintained, were "vital moral issues," but "to win at the ballot box and in the court of public opinion . . . the pro-family movement must speak to the concerns of average voters in the area of taxes, crime, government waste, health care and financial security." With such an agenda, he wrote, "a social movement until now largely composed of white evangelicals can win allies among Catholics and racial minorities." He ended by quoting the Apostle Paul: "I have become all things to all people that I may by all means win some." [30]

"Casting a Wider Net" caused a stir when Reed wrote an op-ed in *The New York Times* citing the poll on abortion. Still, in the first two years of the Clinton administration the Coalition hardly seemed to be changing its tactics. Bill Clinton was just too tempting a target. The Coalition attacked his proposal to lift the ban on gay men and women in the military and charged that his health care plan concealed a "radical social agenda" of promoting abortion, homosexuality, and sex education. However, the Coalition refrained from the scurrilous attacks on the Clintons mounted by Falwell and other Christian right leaders. [31] Then, during the midterm elections Reed supported the House Republicans' legislative blueprint, "Contract With America," although the Speaker of the House Newt Gingrich had on purpose excluded the contentious social issues, such as abortion and school prayer. After the momentous Republican victory of 1994, Reed said with satisfaction, "Our movement is now in many ways thoroughly integrated and enmeshed into the machinery of the Republican Party." [32]

In May 1995 Reed unveiled his "Contract With the American Family," a series of proposals designed to add "pro-family" legislation to the Republican agenda. In introducing it he figured the Christian right as an interest group with limited aims. "As religious conservatives," he said, "we have gained what we always sought—a place at the table, a sense of legitimacy and a voice in the conversation." Reed's Contract included a myriad of familiar Christian Right proposals, such as a school vouchers, the abolition of the Department of Education, and an end to public funding of the National Endowment for the Arts. It also proposed measures that Reed had suggested in *Policy Review*: an expansion of IRAs for homemakers, a tax credit for children, and "in concept" a flat tax. It recommended an end to the Legal Services Corporation, which provided lawyers for the poor, and a welfare reform that eventually would turn over government programs to private charities. Following tradition, it called for a constitutional amendment to legalize organized prayer in public places, including schools. Strikingly, however, it hardly mentioned homosexuality, and though it proposed further hindrances to abortions and a ban on a procedure known to opponents as "partial birth abortion," it did not call for a constitutional amendment to overturn *Roe v. Wade*.[33]

The ACLU denounced the Contract as "dangerous and radical," but, as a sign of the times, one of Reed's Christian right allies called it "unduly modest," and Pat Buchanan asserted, "The Coalition has given away any boldness in a search for popularity and consensus."[34] Presumably Reed thought at least some of the legislation might actually pass in a Congress controlled by white Southern Republicans.

In his effort to cast "a wider net" Reed formed the Catholic Alliance, a division of the Coalition specifically geared to Catholic voters, and courted Orthodox Jews. Despite the name of his organization, he criticized the notion that religious conservatives spoke for God in matters of public policy and any idea that the Coalition rejected religious pluralism. "America is not solely a Christian nation," he wrote, "but a pluralistic society of Protestants, Catholics, Jews, Muslims and other people of faith whose broader culture once honored religion, but today increasingly reflects a hostility toward faith in the public sphere." In a speech before the Anti-Defamation League he decried the long history of Christian anti-Semitism and "the blatant wrongs" of the few who claimed "this is a 'Christian nation,'" suggesting that others might not be welcome." These speeches got him some good press, but they failed to allay suspicions that the Coalition was essentially a sectarian organization. Some thirty thousand Catholics joined, but only a handful of Jews. Reed also attempted to reach out to Latinos and African Americans through conservative ministers with offers of charity, but he made little headway. A "rainbow coalition," he finally admitted, would take a generation to build.[35]

With the approach of the 1996 presidential election Reed made it clear that the Coalition would back Bob Dole, the centrist candidate, over the fiery and divisive Pat Buchanan, even though Dole resisted pressing the issue of abortion. In his book *Active Faith*, published that year, Reed suggested not only that most voters lacked "the biblical world view" to understand the Christian right's condemnation of homosexuality, but that the Republican plank on abortion should be revised. Rather than a call for a constitutional amendment, the plank, he wrote, should be a "morally compelling statement," such as "We will seek by all legal and constitutional means to protect the right to life for the elderly, the infirm, the unborn and the disabled." His reasoning was pragmatic: abortion was not a major concern for most voters, and a constitutional amendment couldn't pass.[36] Somehow Reed had failed to see that abortion had become the central issue for the Christian right.

Sensing a rift in the movement, *Newsweek* published an excerpt from the book in May, and *The New York Times* ran a front-page story quoting Reed as saying that he would "reluctantly" permit exceptions to an abortion ban for victims of rape or incest—as well as for saving the life of the mother.[37] Immediately Reed's whole world erupted. The Buchanan camp, right-to-life groups, Jerry Falwell, Coalition members, and the rising powers on the Christian right, James Dobson of Focus on the Family and Gary Bauer of the Family Research Council, vied with each other in denouncing him. Reed braked and reversed. In the July/August issue of *Christian American*, he wrote, "We will oppose with every fiber in our being any effort to include a rape and incest exception in the pro-life plank or to drop a call for constitutional and legal remedies such as an amendment to the Constitution."[38]

During this period many on the Christian right worried that Robertson had withdrawn from the Coalition and was paying no heed as Reed destroyed his political legacy. Liberal critics on the other hand surmised that Reed was constructing an elaborate facade, behind which lurked his boss Robertson and his intent to impose a sectarian religion and morality— and some said, a theocracy—on the nation. Both groups had reason to wonder. In a message in 1992 Robertson had insisted that America was at a crossroads and said, "Either she returns to her Christian roots and then to further greatness, or she will continue to legalize sodomy, slaughter innocent babies, destroy the minds of her children, squander her resources and sink into oblivion." He continued to call for the restoration of a moral Christian America, and he never ceased to maintain that "diversity" and "pluralism" led only to chaos. He nonetheless backed Reed in all that he did.[39]

According to Harrell's research, Robertson watched every move his executive director made. Many of Reed's initiatives were originally his, and the rest he approved. For example, it was his idea that to grow the Christian right had to shed its extremist image and its fixation on the "moral issues": it had to broaden its agenda and cast a wider net for conservative voters. In 1990 he told Coalition supporters: "People care about their pocketbook. Jobs, taxes, educational issues are important to them. We can't just focus on abortion, gay rights, pornography, and prayer in the schools without being labeled as a fringe group identified with single issues." Making political allies of conservative Catholics had been his goal from the start. In spite of some anti-Catholic bias at CBN, he hired Catholic charismatics for executive jobs, and he had a private audience with Pope John Paul II. He also made an effort to recruit Orthodox Jews, and he approved Reed's speech to the ADL.[40]

Robertson often fielded criticisms of Reed from his right-wing allies. When Reed's piece with the poll on abortion appeared in 1993, Senator Jesse Helms wrote Robertson, "If he's going to be in charge of 'Christianizing' the Republican Party, he can count me out. And frankly I suspect he will do you more harm than good. If he wants to try to secularize the Republican Party, that's his business—but he ought to leave the word Christian out of his sales pitch." Robertson gave the letter to Reed, who made a conciliatory reply. After *Newsweek* published the excerpt of *Active Faith*, Congressman Robert K. Dornan (R-CA), an early Christian right activist, wrote: "What in heaven or hell is going on? . . . Honestly Pat, if conservatives won't raise the issue of abortion, homosexuality and Bill Clinton's character . . . then we'll be stuck with him for another four years. . . . Ralph's 'big tent' rhetoric will not bring anyone closer to truth, goodness or decency." James Dobson for his part contributed a dense five-page letter of objections to the excerpt, maintaining that in suggesting a change in the Republican plank on abortion Reed was making a thinly veiled effort to help Bob Dole. Robertson, however, had read a draft of *Active Faith*, made changes, and then approved the book. It was Robertson who had decided to support Dole, and it was under his direction the Coalition gave the Republican establishment candidate the considerable support he needed to win the South Carolina primary. Replying to Dobson after Dole had won the nomination, Robertson wrote that he knew the Republicans would not compromise on the abortion plank, but, he added, "We must be careful not to allow ourselves to be diverted by what is intended to be a non-issue at the convention. The key is party unity." Then, in late 1998 he announced that a ban on abortions was not achievable, and that the Coalition should work to limit them through further restrictions.[41]

Robertson hoped the Christian right would eventually dominate the Republican Party, and certainly his support for Dole, like his support for Bush in two elections, was a tactic to maximize its influence. Still, unlike some on the Christian right, he knew how to compromise, and he liked to have "a place at the table." In 1994 he wrote a supporter, "Regrettably elections in the United States are never between perfection and less than perfection but between two fallible human beings." [42] Politics, in other words, was not as he had described it in *The New World Order*, a contest between perfect good and perfect evil, but rather as a fallible human undertaking where compromises were inevitable. Robertson was not a simple man. As a preacher he continued to hold out the promise of a restored America, whose only sovereign was Jesus Christ, but as the president of the Coalition he practiced interest group politics.

Dole lost the election badly, taking only 41 percent of the popular vote. The evangelical turnout was lower than it had been in 1992, and Clinton took a surprising 36 percent of the churchgoing born-again vote. The Republicans retained control of both houses of Congress, but the Democrats picked up eight seats in the House. Christian right leaders blamed the poor results on Dole, but misreading the 1994 election House Speaker Newt Gingrich and the other Republican leaders had moved aggressively to cut the domestic budget, and to weaken environmental regulations and consumer protection laws—all actions highly unpopular with the electorate. A battle over the budget had led to a shutdown of the government in late 1995, and Gingrich and his fellow Republicans were blamed. Reed argued, not implausibly, that the loyalty of conservative evangelicals at the state and local levels had stood as a firewall to a complete meltdown for Republicans.[43] As for the Christian right, one poll showed it had the sympathies of 50 percent of white evangelicals, and only 19 percent expressed unfavorable views. According to John Green, the core constituency of the Christian right remained somewhere between one sixth and one fifth of the electorate, depending on the measurements used. During the election year it won important primaries and made further gains in state and local Republican Party organizations. Its strongest supporters in the House had won reelection as often as other Republicans, and the resignation of a number of moderate senators had resulted in the election of members sympathetic to the movement. At the same time it deeply divided the party, threatening a shift of northern moderates into the Democratic Party.[44]

In terms of federal legislation the Christian right did slightly better after 1994, but most of what the Coalition called "victories" came on issues where its views coincided with those of economic conservatives, such as limitations on the Legal Services Corporation and an important welfare reform bill supported by Clinton. The Congress did pass a few minor abortion restrictions; it also passed a law against "partial birth abortion," but it couldn't muster the votes to override Clinton's veto. Then at a time when gay marriage lay beyond the horizon, it passed the Defense of Marriage Act stipulating that marriage would be recognized only if it were between a man and woman.[45] For a movement the size of the labor unions, its gains on the federal level were few.

In April 1997 Reed took his leave from the Christian Coalition to form his own political consultancy. He resigned with only praise for Robertson, and there was nothing to suggest a rift between the two. Apparently he just wanted to go into mainstream Republican politics and to make some real money as a lobbyist. In announcing his departure, he reported that the Christian Coalition had grown to a peak strength of 1.9 million members and supporters and its budget had increased to $27 million. Still, as he knew, the growth in membership had leveled off, and the Coalition faced major financial challenges.[46]

In June Robertson announced that Don Hodel, a businessman who had been secretary of energy and secretary of the interior in the Reagan administration, would become president of the Coalition and that he himself would move to the newly created post of chairman of the board. Hodel was to take on most of Reed's responsibilities, including the day-to-day management of the organization. Randy Tate, a thirty-one-year-old Washington state politician who had gone into politics as a Robertson supporter in 1988 and one-term congressman who had acted as a deputy to the Republican whip, Tom DeLay, was to serve as his assistant with the title of executive director. Both were evangelical conservatives, and Robertson said the two appointments "would link the Reagan Revolution with the rising influence of active people of faith." "My dear friend," he told Hodel, "I want to hold out to you the possibility of selecting the next president of the United States." [47] By the end of the Clinton presidency, however, both men had resigned, and the Christian Coalition had become a shell of its former self.

In July 1996—a year before Reed left—the Federal Election Commission had filed a civil suit charging that the Coalition had illegally aided a number of Republican campaigns in the 1990, 1992, and 1994 elections. Based on complaints from the Democratic National Committee, it charged that the Coalition had acted in coordination with the campaigns of Republican candidates, and that its distribution of voter guides constituted "in kind" contributions to the Republicans. Robertson hired a team of expensive lawyers to fight the suit, and in 1999 a federal judge threw out most of the FEC's case, allowing the Coalition to continue distributing voter guides. [48] The IRS case was more serious. Ever since 1990 the Coalition had been acting as if had the tax-exempt status of a social welfare organization, a 501(c)(4), even while engaging in what seemed to be partisan political activity. Given the difficulty of proving that the Coalition's work was "primarily" political, the IRS had delayed taking action, but in 1998 in response to complaints by Americans United and People for the American Way, it rejected the application and insisted that the Coalition had to pay back taxes from 1990 on. The Coalition immediately took shelter under its Texas chapter, which already had a tax-exempt status, but Robertson wanted to win. [49] He asked conservative Senate leaders to start an inquiry into the IRS's "selective enforcement" of its rules and vowed to sue the IRS. The Coalition's chief counsel, Jay Sekulow, advised Robertson not to litigate, warning that some of the actions of the Coalition had allowed the IRS to "make a forceful argument that the organization acted outside of the constraints of a (c)(4)." Robertson paid no heed. He sued the IRS in 2000 and won, forcing it to grant the Coalition tax-exempt status from 1990 on.[50] He proclaimed a great victory, but by that time, the Coalition had paid lawyers hundreds of thousands of dollars in fees.

While fighting these legal battles, the Coalition went on with its business, and in 1997 the business of all Christian right organizations became the impeachment of the president of the United States.

In June 1997 at a secret meeting at the Council for National Policy Christian right operatives discussed impeachment with the congressional members of the group. Many CNP members had long wanted to drive Clinton out of office on one ground or another, and at the meeting they drew up a resolution of impeachment that Congressman Bob Barr (R-GA) introduced in November charging that the president's reelection campaign had received illegal donations from Chinese sources.[51] The resolution went nowhere, but after evidence of Clinton's sexual relationship with White House intern Monica Lewinsky surfaced in early 1998, and Clinton denied any wrongdoing on the witness stand, Gingrich and the other House leaders believed they had grounds for impeaching Clinton on charges of perjury and obstruction of justice.

The House authorized an impeachment inquiry in early October, and by that time the Christian right had long been up in arms. After Clinton's reelection, Robertson, who had previously steered clear of personal attacks on the president, had become increasingly vitriolic about "the poster child of the 60s sexual revolution."[52] When the House released the report by the independent counsel, Kenneth Starr, with the lurid details of Lewinsky performing oral sex on the president, he delivered a tirade to a cheering crowd at the Coalition's Road to Victory conference and called for the immediate impeachment of the president.[53] The hearings, with the Lewinsky affair on an endless loop, were scheduled to continue through the November election, and Gingrich, who had been largely responsible for the Republican losses in Congress in the last election, predicted that the party would pick up eight to thirty seats in the House. It was a serious miscalculation. On November 3 the Republicans lost five more seats in the House, and Gingrich had to resign as speaker under pressure from his colleagues.

After that things went from bad to worse for the Republican right.

On December 18 the full House convened to consider the impeachment of a president for the first time in 130 years. The following day the speaker-designate, Bob Livingston (R-LA), resigned after admitting to adultery. He became the fourth GOP congressman, including Henry Hyde, the chair of the Judiciary Committee, who had recently confessed to marital infidelity when confronted with the evidence by journalists. (Gingrich, who left his second wife the following year, later admitted what was known to House Republican leaders at the time, that he had been having an extramarital affair during the hearings.)[54] The House nonetheless voted for impeachment along party lines in a lame-duck session. By the time the Senate trial began in early January, Clinton's approval rating, high since the 1996 election, had risen to over 70 percent, and it had become perfectly obvious that the American people—many Republicans included—did not want their president convicted for denying that he had had an affair.

Pat Robertson became disgusted with what he regarded as strategic mistakes of the Republican leaders, in particular their failure to block Clinton from giving the State of the Union address. On *The 700 Club* he said in anger, "From a public relations standpoint, [Clinton] won. . . . They might as well dismiss this impeachment hearing and get on with something else, because it's over as far as I am concerned." The remark, widely quoted, caused a rebellion among Coalition activists. Robertson said he was only stating the obvious: conviction required a two-thirds vote in the Senate, and Democrats were not going to vote to throw their popular president out of office. Indeed on February 12 the Senate voted for acquittal. However, in January the Coalition activists were lobbying hard for a conviction. True believers, they saw it as their duty to fight on to the end. Don Hodel told Robertson that he should apologize to his supporters, but Robertson refused.[55] For Hodel that was the last straw. He'd clashed with Robertson several times before when Robertson as "a private citizen" endorsed candidates or made statements on *The 700 Club* that conflicted with official

Coalition positions—and the views of many in the ranks. (One of the statements may have been the recommendation that the Coalition should stop calling for a total ban on abortion—a recommendation Robertson made for a second time in early 1999.) Hodel had never been able to persuade his boss to see the problem, and this time he resigned.[56]

Robertson reassumed the presidency of the Coalition, and when Randy Tate left a few months later he called in Roberta Combs, the head of the South Carolina Coalition, to run the organization day-to-day. In March he announced a major new initiative geared to the next presidential election: a $21 million fund-raising drive, a tenfold expansion of the Coalition's national field staff, and the training of a million and a half volunteers. Critics derided the project as a publicity stunt. After Clinton's reelection, the Coalition's income had plunged from $25 million to $17 million in a year, and bills from the lawyers were coming in fast. Both Robertson and Hodel put money into the organization to keep it afloat, and they were beginning to get its finances stabilized when the controversies surrounding the impeachment split the activists and drove donors away again. By the spring of 1999, the organization was $2.5 million in debt; its net revenues were 49 percent below budget, and it was losing over $35,000 a day. It had to cut 20 percent of its national staff, and according to its officials it had only seven strong state affiliates left because of turnover in the local leadership.[57] Robertson surely thought that a major initiative was the only hope of reviving the Coalition—and he may have been right. The problem was that he didn't have anyone to carry it off. Roberta Combs had run a successful state chapter, but she lacked the skills to run the national organization. She wasn't good at raising money; the staffers disliked her, and when she questioned their loyalty there were mass resignations. The organization went into a downward spiral. Robertson campaigned energetically, but in the election year of 2000 the Coalition raised only $3 million, and debts piled up. At the end of the following year he suddenly resigned as president and quit the board, leaving the Coalition in a welter of acrimony, lawsuits, and unpaid bills.[58] Laurie Goodstein of *The New York Times* reported that, according to disaffected Coalition officials, the Coalition had fudged the membership figures for years by counting every individual who once called its 800 number, or signed a petition, and by keeping dead people, duplications, and wrong addresses on the roles. Its watchdogs at Americans United and People for the American Way estimated that even at its peak in 1996 the Coalition had only somewhere between 300,000 and 500,000 dues-paying members plus a list of a million names.

Robertson had other things to do. His university was growing; he was extending the global reach of CBN as the charismatic faith gained ground in Latin America, Africa, and Asia; he was also investing in new businesses, among them gold and diamond mines in Africa with permits from dictators he befriended.[59] His *700 Club* continued to attract hundreds of thousands of American viewers a day, but with the demise of the Christian Coalition his political power drained away, and journalists looked to others to represent the Christian right.

15

THE CHRISTIAN RIGHT
and GEORGE W. BUSH

The New Christian Right Leaders

By the start of the 2000 presidential campaign season the Christian right was in complete disarray. In 1994 activists had helped the congressional Republicans win a historic victory, and they turned out in force two years later, determined to elect a Republican president. Yet the man they called the self-indulgent baby boom liberal had won reelection handily, taking 36 percent of the evangelical vote. After the Lewinsky affair surfaced, many were outraged, and along with the House leadership they had bent their efforts to driving the president out of office. Certain that the salacious details revealed in the Starr report gave them a winning hand, they had high expectations for the 1998 congressional elections, but not only had the Republicans lost five seats in the House but a number of Christian right allies had gone down to defeat as well. Clinton's continuing popularity bewildered them. Even before the election, James Dobson wrote his supporters: "What has alarmed me throughout this episode has been the willingness of my fellow citizens to rationalize the President's behavior, even as they suspected, and later knew, that he was lying. I am left to conclude that our greatest problem is not in the Oval Office. It's with the people of this land."[1]

Pat Robertson, too, had foreseen the defeat of the drive for impeachment, but his effort to reconcile his supporters to the inevitable had caused his chief lieutenants to resign in protest. The Senate vote to acquit Clinton left Christian right activists, as well as secular right-wingers, in stunned disbelief. One close observer later wrote that it was a "devastating blow" and that "People need to know the depth of the disappointment." [2]

In February Christian right leaders began taking stock of their situation, and some despaired. In a widely circulated letter, Paul Weyrich, the strategist for the Christian right, wrote, "I believe we have probably lost the culture war. That doesn't mean the war is not going to continue. . . . But in terms of society in general, we have lost." That's why, he wrote, that "even when we win in politics, our victories fail to translate into the kind of policies we believe are important." [3]

Weyrich was referring to the paradox noted by the social scientists John C. Green, Mark Rozell, and Clyde Wilcox. The Christian right had a greater institutional influence in the GOP than any other movement: it dominated eighteen state parties; it had virtual control over the party platform and veto power over the selection of vice presidential candidates, and yet it had made little progress on its policy agenda. Many movement leaders blamed the Republicans in Congress, but as Weyrich suggested, polls showed that the movement had failed to change attitudes on the social issues. Indeed, after two decades of Christian right political activity, the public was not more conservative on abortion than it had been before, and substantially more liberal on gay rights and women's roles. [4]

Having declared the culture war lost, Weyrich went on to propose that a legitimate strategy would be separation from "the institutions that have been captured by . . . the enemies of our traditional culture," as the home schooling movement had done. "If we expend our energies on fighting on the 'turf' they already control," he wrote, "we will probably not accomplish what we hope, and we may spend ourselves to the point of exhaustion." Later, clarifying his position, he wrote: "The question is not whether we should fight but how . . . in essence, I said we need to change our strategy. Instead of relying on politics to retake the culturally and morally decadent institutions of contemporary America, I said that we should separate from those institutions and build our own." [5]

Weyrich, though a Catholic, was advising much the same course of action that the fundamentalists had followed in the 1920s. Shortly after his letter appeared, Cal Thomas and Ed Dobson, who had been Falwell's chief lieutenants in the Moral Majority, published a book questioning not just the efficacy of political action but the righteousness of the enterprise. In *Blinded by Might* they argued that in the process of trying to win elections conservative Christians had been seduced by the lure of power. What had begun as an effort to restore Christian values to the nation had degenerated into an unbridled partisan struggle, creating an atmosphere in which it was assumed that Democrats could not be Christians and that Bill and Hillary Clinton were the Antichrist. Ultimately, they argued, Christians in committing themselves to politics had lost their ability to serve as prophetic witnesses.[6] Weyrich's letter and reports of the book coursed through the evangelical media, giving rise to an acrimonious debate. Many Christian right activists felt a sense of futility, even despair, and yet many had spent their lives working in politics and had become an integral part of the Republican Party at local and state levels. According to one scholar, the Christian right at the turn of the century was not simply a social movement but "in part an interest group and in part a faction of the GOP." As for the heads of the Christian right organizations, they harshly attacked Thomas and Dobson for having the temerity to suggest that some self-criticism might be order—and respectfully argued with Weyrich's position.[7] But the question was what to do next.

The immediate problem was whom to back in the presidential election. The potential candidates initially included such friends to the movement as Pat Buchanan, Dan Quayle, and Senator John Ashcroft of Missouri, but all of them soon took themselves out of the running. By the start of the primary season Governor George W. Bush of Texas was the clear favorite to win. Bush, who had managed to bridge the ideological divisions in the Texas GOP and to attract Hispanic voters, had become the establishment candidate, and Pat Robertson had endorsed him early on. The younger Bush, however, wasn't much known outside Texas; for conservative evangelicals he carried the baggage of his father's presidency, and his early statement that "America is not ready to ban abortion" had drawn a rebuke from James Dobson. Activists warmed up when he talked about his life-changing born-again experience, and how prayer and Bible study had strengthened him. They warmed up further when Bush in a December debate among GOP candidates said that Jesus was his favorite philosopher "because he changed my heart." Still, his campaign mantra of "compassionate conservatism" seemed to mark him as one of those middle-of-the-road Republicans who had always disappointed them.[8]

They were still hesitating, when to the surprise of Republican Party leaders, Senator John McCain of Arizona beat Bush soundly by 49 to 30 percent in the New Hampshire primary. McCain, a well-known maverick, had attracted the support of Republican moderates and independents, and he was playing to his strength. In the Senate he had a perfect antiabortion record, but in New Hampshire he suggested that the GOP was a big tent that could accommodate the pro-choice. That was enough for the Christian right. During the South Carolina primary that followed, Robertson and Falwell attacked him on television and privately. Robertson called his campaign manager "a vicious bigot." Dobson questioned his fitness as a moral leader, pointing to the adultery he acknowledged that he had committed before divorcing his first wife twenty years earlier. Ugly rumors circulated, among them that the Bangladeshi child he and his wife had adopted was his illegitimate daughter.[9]

South Carolina had a number of strong Christian right organizations, among them Roberta Combs's state chapter of the Christian Coalition and a group from Bob Jones University that dated from the 1970s. In courting them Bush spoke at Bob Jones University without so much as mentioning its ban on interracial dating and its deep-dyed anti-Catholicism. (It defined the Roman Catholic Church as a "cult.") After the McCain campaign made an issue of the speech, Bush publicly apologized to John Cardinal O'Connor, but not until after the South Carolina primary, when conservative evangelicals voted for him in overwhelming numbers, and he prevailed—when a loss in that primary might have ended his campaign.[10]

McCain won the Michigan primary with Catholic support, and in Virginia he made what one observer characterized as a "Hail Mary pass." While Bush was still on the defensive over the Bob Jones speech, McCain addressed a large rally in Virginia Beach and made a deliberate attack on the best known of the Christian right leaders, Falwell and Robertson, calling them "agents of intolerance" and "corrupting influences on religion and politics," comparable to "union bosses" who "desire to preserve their own political power at all costs." He drew a distinction between Christian conservatives and their values on the one hand and "their self-appointed leaders" on the other, but he said the Republican Party is "the party of Lincoln, not Bob Jones," and he accused Bush of "pandering to the outer reaches of American politics." [11] He also attacked what he called "the tired Republican establishment," in effect calling for a party that excluded the Christian right. Republican commentators lambasted him for crossing the line of legitimate criticism and attacking people of faith. Social conservatives, Catholics as well as evangelicals, deserted him, and after Super Tuesday his campaign was over.[12]

In the general election Christian right activists supported Bush with more enthusiasm than they had Dole, and some 80 percent voted for him over his opponent, Vice President Al Gore. Nonetheless, John C. Green estimated the number of activists working in the campaign had dropped to 150,000 from the 200,000 working in 1996, and the percentage of the electorate that identified as members of Christian right declined from 17 percent to 14 percent. Even more dismaying, the turnout of white evangelicals dropped six points below the turnout for Dole with no corresponding decline among Catholics or mainline Protestants. Bush won an estimated 68 percent of evangelical vote, but he lost the popular vote and won the electoral vote only narrowly after the Supreme Court voted to halt the recount in Florida. Karl Rove, Bush's chief political strategist, later said that the victory was closer than he had expected because four million evangelicals failed to vote, and he speculated that evangelicals might be returning to their belief that politics was corrupt and they shouldn't participate.[13]

The Christian right seemed to be losing its base of support, and once again pundits occupied themselves with writing its obituary. Five years later, however, the movement had not just rebounded, but reached a new height of strength and a new degree of influence in Washington. George W. Bush proved the most sympathetic president the movement had ever experienced and hugely popular with its base. In the wake of the 2004 election the movement could claim to be a major player in the Republican victory. The evangelical turnout had risen dramatically; Bush had taken 78 percent of the evangelical vote as well as substantial majorities among all regular churchgoing voters.[14] By and large movement allies had won their races for House and Senate, adding to the Republican majorities in both houses of Congress, and at the start of 2005 movement leaders were looking forward to the passage of their agenda and, more important, to changing the nature of the third branch of government: the courts.

Behind these victories lay two major forces. One was the Southern Baptist Convention and the other network of organizations assembled by James Dobson.

The Southern Baptist Convention was not a political organization, but after the ultraconservatives took control of its seminaries and its bureaucracy it began to act like one. In the 1970s the leadership of the Convention had reflected a certain range of theological and political views, but the leaders of what some called "the fundamentalist takeover" and others "the conservative resurgence" appointed only biblical inerrantists and social conservatives to the boards of trustees. In the seminaries there were years of struggle between the trustees and the faculties, but by the early 1990s what one professor called "the Firm" had appointed the presidents of the six seminaries as well as the heads of the agencies and mission boards. The few liberals and a number of moderates hived off into two new associations, the Alliance of Baptists and the more centrist Cooperative Baptist Fellowship. A few state conventions remained in the hands of moderates, but the SBC became so conservative that Jerry Falwell affiliated his church with it in 1996, and its conventions annually passed resolutions that lined up with the Christian right agenda.

The final steps in transforming the denomination came toward the end of the century. In 1998 the SBC convention passed an amendment to its official confession of faith, the Baptist Faith and Message, stating a wife should "submit herself graciously" to her husband's leadership, and the husband should "provide for, protect and lead his family." The amendment startled many observers. It put the SBC to the right of many evangelical churches and of Pope John Paul II, who had characterized the relationship between husbands and wives as one of "mutual subjection." [15] An outcry followed. Moderate Southern Baptists protested, and Jimmy Carter, who had remained a Southern Baptist through all the years of the "conservative resurgence," saw the amendment as the last straw and left his denomination. Two years later the SBC revised the Baptist Faith and Message to include the amendment and a statement that only men should serve as head pastors of churches. In a section called "The Christian and the Social Order," the confession, previously confined to general theological statements addressed sex and abortion. "Christians," it declared, should oppose "all forms of sexual immorality, including adultery, homosexuality and pornography" and it called for Christians to "speak on behalf of the unborn and contend for the sanctity of all human life from conception to natural death." [16]

The ultraconservatives had always intended not just to change the denomination, but to reverse the tide of secularization and cultural decay they saw as overwhelming the nation. The first generation of SBC activists had been independent megachurch pastors and televangelists, such as Adrian Rogers, Jerry Vines, and James Robison; the second were SBC officials who had gained institutional power and acted with substantial support from clergy and laymen.

One of the two most influential of these was Al Mohler, the young president of Southern Baptist Theological Seminary, the SBC's flagship school, and the denomination's leading public intellectual. Since his appointment to the presidency in 1993, he had been instrumental in shaping SBC theology and policies; he had also gained a public platform. On his weekly radio show and blog, he spoke out on issues from the higher biblical criticism to abortion. Articulate, he argued in a reasoned and well-mannered fashion attractive to the mainstream media. He wrote for the *Washington Post*'s "On Faith" column; he appeared on *Larry King Live* and other talk shows. In 2003 *Time* magazine called him "the reigning intellectual of the evangelical movement in the U.S.," though he was more theologically conservative than some on the Christian right. Unlike Robertson, for instance, he defended young-earth creationism and called Roman Catholicism a "false religion." [17]

How Mohler came to have such opinions puzzled many of his acquaintances, including the former president of Southern Seminary, Roy Honeycutt, a moderate who had hired Mohler as his assistant in the 1980s. In one account of his spiritual journey Mohler said he had been born in Lakeland, Florida, in what he described as an "intact culture" where "the messages I was receiving at home and church were the same messages I was receiving in public school." At the age of fifteen, in 1975, he moved with his family from central Florida to Pompano Beach in the south, where he recalled sitting next to Roman Catholics and the children of rabbis in school. Apparently this caused him a good deal of spiritual confusion, for his youth pastor took him to D. James Kennedy, whose church was just down the highway in Fort Lauderdale. Kennedy gave him a volume of Francis Schaeffer's work, which assured him there were "legitimate Christian answers" to all his questions. Reading Schaeffer was, Mohler said, "a determinative life experience." Having discovered religious pluralism, he apparently rejected it. He nonetheless went to the moderate Samford University and in the 1980s to Southern Seminary for his master's and doctoral degrees. He joined the staff of Southern while still a student and worked for Honeycutt, who was doing his best to negotiate between the faculty and the hard-line trustees. When the SBC passed its first resolution rejecting the ordination of women 1984, Mohler led student protests against it. Three years later he assumed the key post of director of Capitol Funding. In his telling he had another determinative experience toward the end of his studies when Carl Henry, the neo-evangelical theologian and a serious scholar, came to the campus and rebuked him for thinking that an egalitarian view of gender roles was compatible with the inerrancy of the Scriptures. Reading Henry's work, he grew convinced of the idea Schaeffer had taken from Cornelius Van Til of the Westminster Seminary that the assumptions behind Christianity were fundamentally at odds with those undergirding the secular worldview.[18]

In its insistence on the influence of two famous figures, Mohler's narrative recalls the Old Testament stories, such as that of Elisha and Elijah, in which the young preacher inherits the prophetic mantle from the elder prophet—a claim familiar in the evangelical world. Still, it makes sense that he had learned from northerners who had spread the doctrine of biblical inerrancy to the South. In any case, by the end of his studies, Mohler had adopted the classical fundamentalism of the 1920s. Not all in his seminary knew it. When Honeycutt resigned in 1992, weary of the struggles between the faculty and the trustees, the search committee with Honeycutt's support appointed Mohler, then just thirty-three, on the assumption that he could resolve the differences better than candidates from the outside. Instead, Mohler moved the seminary abruptly to the right, adding positions on abortion, homosexuality, and women in the ministry to the litmus test for future professors and causing turmoil in the faculty. In 1994 he forced the resignation of the most prominent woman professor, Molly Marshall, by accusing her of heresy and not informing her of the charges prior to a hearing.[19] Then, two years into his presidency, he made it clear the seminary would teach Reformed theology, or rather that particular strain of Calvinism passed down by the nineteenth-century Princeton theologians from the seventeenth-century Reformed scholastics to the Westminster fundamentalists. Strict five-point Calvinism was a minority position in the SBC, and one not shared by revivalists such as Adrian Rogers, but Mohler called it the most robust defense of inerrancy and "a structure of thought that's more comprehensive than merely a deck of cards with all the right doctrines." This glorious architecture of rationality, he believed, was uniquely impervious to the corrosive forces of modern life.[20]

Interviewed in 1997, Mohler told Barry Hankins that his Reformed perspective gave him a sense of cultural crisis deeper that than of other conservatives. "I don't think the fixes that most conservatives propose would fix anything," he said. "I don't think bringing back in the props of official Christianity is going to get at the darkness at the center of all this." To him the Christian worldview had become just too remote in America, and worse, millions of Americans denied the very notion of the objective truth. Like many other conservative evangelicals at the end of the century, Mohler spoke of "postmodernism" rather than "secular humanism" as the condition of godless modern America. For most it was just a newer and fancier word for relativism, but Mohler had actually read Jacques Derrida and could parse the French destructionists.[21] Still, his real quarrel was with David Hume and with any notion that the truth was not universal, objective, and eternal.

Mohler told Hankins he hadn't much hope for political reform because the culture was just too far gone. Evangelicals, he said, had to concentrate on building localized Genevas, Calvin's Reformed city, before they could even think of re-Christianizing the nation. The task was thus to train future pastors to interpret the culture and to stand against it. Mohler, however, was not consistent on this score, and on occasion he engaged in politics himself.[22] In pointedly dismissing political reform Mohler may have been taking a swipe at Richard Land, the other major figure in the second generation of conservative activists. The president of the Ethics & Religious Liberty Commission (ERLC), Land was the SBC's chief policy maker and lobbyist in Washington. In the years of the "conservative resurgence," he had transformed the Christian Life Commission (later ERLC) into a formidable power in the nation's capital—a power he was well equipped to use.

A sixth-generation Texan, and fifteen years older than Mohler, Land had grown up in Houston in the late 1950s and early 1960s, when his father, a Navy welder, had returned with his mother, a devout Southern Baptist from Braintree, Massachusetts. He went to Princeton University on scholarship, and then took a master's degree from the conservative New Orleans Seminary, and a doctorate from Oxford University in English Puritan history. An ordained minister, he pastored churches in New Orleans and Oxford, and he, too, discovered Schaeffer and Henry. On his return to Texas in 1975 he went to Criswell College, where he served as a professor of church history and a vice president for academic affairs, and he bided his time. On a leave of absence from Criswell in 1987–88, he worked as an administrative assistant to the Republican governor, Bill Clements, acting as his senior advisor on issues such as abortion, drugs, and pornography. In Texas he struck up friendships with Paige Patterson and Paul Pressler, the architects of the "resurgence." He also met Karl Rove and George W. Bush, who was drumming up support for his father's presidential campaign.[23]

Well connected and politically experienced, Land was a natural to head the Christian Life Commission after the last moderate president was forced out in 1988. In his installation address he compared the situation of evangelicals to that of the early Christians "immersed in a world dominated by pagan idolatrous philosophies and life styles." Within a few years he had brought the agency to heel, and when the SBC pulled out of the Baptist Joint Committee on Public Affairs, he assumed responsibility for church-state issues as well as the rest of the SBC's public affairs agenda. To overcome the traditional Southern Baptist reluctance to exert political power in Washington, he traveled widely, visiting SBC churches and seminaries. In 1993 he became a finalist for the presidency of Southern Seminary in competition with Mohler.[24] The two might easily have changed places. Their views on the cultural crisis were virtually identical, except that Land held the government to be the chief culprit in the advance of secularism. In 1995 he held a conference titled "War of the Worlds: The Struggle for the Nation's Soul" to galvanize his constituency, and Mohler spoke on what he called "the homosexualization of America." In the late 1990s both steadily gained influence in the SBC, their success marked by the fact both served on the small committee that revised the Baptist Faith and Message. Land, however, was a diplomat. In his role as lobbyist, he spoke the language of politicians and worked with members of other religious groups. Better educated than the populist SBC preachers, he became well informed about foreign as well as domestic affairs. By the end of the 1990s he had made alliances with many Republicans in Congress, who thought him more reasonable and reliable than the leaders of most of the Christian right organizations.

As the head of the ERLC, Land's strength was that he represented the largest Protestant denomination in the country—with sixteen million souls—and had no need to raise money. On the other hand he was not a completely free agent, and the SBC as a denomination had never engaged in mobilizing voters. Precinct politics remained the province of the Christian right groups, and by the end of the 1990s James Dobson had built a network of organizations that rivaled the Christian Coalition. Dobson's own force of personality and his appeal to evangelicals across traditions made him the most influential leader the movement ever had.

A child psychologist with a PhD from the University of Southern California, Dobson had since the 1970s won a huge following by dispensing practical and "Bible-based" advice on child rearing and marriage. Beloved by many for helping them through the trials of parenting and troubled marriages, he had built a media empire, Focus on the Family. His daily radio program, carried on more than two thousand stations in the United States and hundreds overseas, had a domestic audience of over five million families. His fourteen books, including *Dare to Discipline* and *What Wives Wish Their Husbands Knew About Women*, had sold over sixteen million copies. His filmed lectures, distributed through television stations and church-sponsored screenings, had reached a far wider audience. Perhaps sixty million people had watched just one of his lecture series, *Where's*

Dad? A marketing genius, he had expanded his ministry to include a variety of radio programming, video productions, and instructional materials. In addition Focus published ten magazines and newsletters for different audiences, ranging from teenage girls to physicians, with a combined circulation of three million. With donations averaging more than $100 million a year, the organization had 1,300 employees, many of them fielding the ten thousand letters, emails, and phone calls it received every day and entering them into computer databases. A writer or caller would find trained staffers ready to respond to questions about anything from potty training to adolescent drug use, and even to offer temporary financial help in an emergency. The eighty-eight-acre campus of Focus in Colorado Springs, Colorado, had its own zip code, its own exits off the Interstate, and about 200,000 visitors a year.[25]

Dobson had an abiding interest in public policy. Not long after the establishment of Focus on the Family he heard about Jimmy Carter's White House Conference on Families, and when he asked his listeners to write the executive director, he received an invitation. At the meeting he and eight other conservative evangelicals decided to form a Washington lobby for "pro-family" policies. Three years later he founded the Family Research Council, an organization designed to monitor legislation and government policies on family affairs. During the Reagan administrations Dobson spent almost a year in Washington, serving on six different commissions, including Attorney General Edwin Meese's Commission on Pornography. When the Reagan presidency came to an end, he, like Pat Robertson, moved to fill the political vacuum left by the demise of the Moral Majority. He brought in Gary Bauer, who had worked as a top domestic policy advisor to Reagan, to broaden the scope of the Family Research Council, and within a decade Bauer turned the FRC into the most powerful Christian right lobby in Washington with half a million people on its mailing list. Then, while reviving the FRC, Dobson developed a public policy division within Focus on the Family to plant independently financed state-level Family Policy Councils across the country to serve as proxies for Dobson and Focus on local issues and to raise grassroots support for their initiatives in Washington. Focus published a politically oriented magazine, *Citizens*, sent out a newsletter, and produced a radio program, *Family News in Focus.* By 1998 the Focus network claimed thirty-four state affiliates and more than two million members, or as many as the Christian Coalition.[26]

Still, Dobson's most powerful tool was his own radio audience. When he called upon listeners to support or oppose some piece of federal legislation, letters and phone calls would pour into the White House or into congressional offices by the hundreds of thousands. During the 1980s Dobson lobbied for items on Reagan's agenda from the school prayer amendment to the confirmation of Robert Bork to the Supreme Court. He also promoted Reagan's 1985 tax proposals and opposed a civil rights bill because he said it would force religious organizations to hire homosexuals. After Reagan left office, he struck out on his own, often backing highly controversial causes. In 1992 he joined a campaign to pass an amendment to the Colorado state constitution to prohibit antidiscrimination laws on behalf of homosexuals, including those already on the books. Denounced by Colorado newspapers, Amendment II seemed to political analysts to have no chance of passage, but after Dobson devoted a program to it and Focus produced commercials for it, the campaign took off, and the amendment passed by 100,000 votes. (It was later struck down by the U.S. Supreme Court.) Two years later he joined with Michael Farris, president of the Home School Legal Defense Association, to defeat a bill that would have required home schooling teachers—mostly parents— to be certified in the subjects they taught. Focus on the Family became known as the best platform for Christian right activists in the country, and Dobson himself went on to enlist his radio audience in campaigns against Clinton administration policies from his veto of antiabortion legislation to his education bill.[27]

Much of Dobson's effectiveness as a Christian right leader came from the perception that he was simply a family advisor concerned about the moral issues. Politically he kept a low profile, rarely speaking to the press, and then portraying himself as reluctant warrior forced to stand up to some unprecedented threat to the family. However, guided by Gary Bauer and a new friend, Charles Colson, the born-again Nixon operative who upon emerging from prison after Watergate founded the Prison Fellowship ministry, he went about making high-level contacts among

Republicans in Washington. In the run-up to the 1996 election he began to intervene directly into Republican politics. In addition to objecting to Ralph Reed's attempt to soften the platform language on abortion, he carried on a correspondence and a series of public exchanges with Haley Barbour, the chair of the Republican National Committee. Once, on reading an RNC magazine describing party positions, Dobson complained that there wasn't a word about abortion, homosexuality, or family values. "You are being watched much more closely than you think you are," he wrote, "and you will not be permitted to waffle on those issues. If you do, I believe there will be a third party in 1996—which won't win. But neither will you." When Barbour declared the party a "big tent" that included those who disagreed with the party's hard-line position on abortion, Dobson sent an eight-page letter to his supporters and a special mailing to 112,000 clergy, 8,000 politicians, and 1,500 members of the media, informing them that "a struggle [is] under way for the soul of the party, [and] I am committed never again to cast a vote for a politician who would kill one innocent baby." Apparently his threat had the effect intended, for almost every Republican presidential hopeful either traveled to Colorado Springs or met with him in Washington—often more than once—to seek his blessing. When Bob Dole became the nominee, Dobson had a three-hour meeting with the candidate and again suggested that evangelicals might launch a third-party candidacy if Dole didn't speak out on the moral issues. Dole paid no heed, and Dobson for the first time deserted the Republican Party and voted for Howard Phillips, the Reconstructionist candidate of the U.S. Taxpayers Party.[28]

Unlike Falwell and Robertson, Dobson seemed to have no intention of integrating the Christian right into the Republican Party. He was, John C. Green tactfully wrote, "a purist." To his followers he made it clear that he would brook no compromises. When the Defense of Marriage Act came up, for example, and Senator Ted Kennedy attached an amendment to outlaw discrimination against homosexuals in the workplace, Dobson, as expected, told his listeners to support DOMA and to oppose the Kennedy amendment. But then he added that if the amendment could not be stripped from the bill, they should tell their senators to vote against DOMA, though he knew the failure of the bill would have meant that all state governments would have had to recognize gay marriage if it were approved by only one state. He prided himself on standing on principle. Dobson, his friend Charles Colson remarked, saw every issue as crystal clear: there was a black and a white, a right and a wrong. Politics, Colson said, "are loaded with nuances, and he's never met a nuance that he liked. He's not a nuanced guy." In his Focus office Dobson had a painting of Winston Churchill on the wall and sometimes quoted Churchill's famous dictum, "Never give in, never, never, never." [29]

Dobson's success as a Christian right leader came in part from the fact that, unlike Falwell and Robertson, he was not an ordained minister. When quoting Scripture, or invoking the deity, as he often did, he spoke a generic evangelical language, with no talk of miracles or end times prophecies. Richard Land once called him "the most influential person in evangelical life since Billy Graham." [30] Dobson was nonetheless deeply rooted in a Holiness denomination: the Church of the Nazarene. For three generations his ancestors had been Nazarene preachers, and for much of his early life his father worked as an itinerant evangelist traveling the Deep South and the Southwest conducting revivals. For someone who assumed "the traditional family" meant two parents living at home, he knew from experience that families were not always made to the model. Born in 1936, he was an only child. Until he was seven his parents left him with relatives, and even after the family moved into a house outside Oklahoma City, his father, whom he worshipped, was often away. [31] (Where indeed was Dad?) The Church of the Nazarene was a small denomination, founded in 1908, with only 350,882 members sixty years later. Wesleyan in origin, its perfectionist theology stressed constant efforts after conversion to lead a pure and righteous life, and with the help of the Holy Spirit to achieve a second blessing, or entire sanctification in this life. When Dobson was growing up, striving for holiness meant going to church every time the door was open and following a strict code of behavior: no moviegoing, no card playing, no taking the newspaper on Sunday, and no wearing of jewelry, not even a wedding band. "The church emphasized what you *didn't* do much more than what you *did* do," Dobson's cousin, a pastor, said. Perfectionists, such as the Nazarenes, had to stand out as models of righteous living, and were, in the words of church historian Sydney Ahlstrom, "almost by definition censorious of the worldliness of others." Asked about the distinctive Holiness doctrine of entire sanctification, Dobson explained that no one can avoid sinning in the sense of having no flaws or shortcomings, but that from the Wesleyan perspective sin was *"willful* disobedience to a *known* law."[32] Possibly he thought he had reached that second stage, for one day after his radio cohost casually remarked, "Well, one thing for certain is that we are all sinners," Dobson motioned to the engineer to stop the recording and said, "We are not all sinners."[33]

Exceptionally for a Nazarene preacher of his generation, Dobson's father believed in the importance of education, and he saved up enough money to send his son to Pasadena College, a Nazarene institution in California. One of his professors introduced him to the idea of biblically based psychology, and Dobson pursued it. Highly ambitious, with what one classmate said was a sense of being divinely guided, he went on to the University of Southern California and took a PhD in educational psychology. In 1966 he joined the faculty of the Children's Hospital in Los Angeles and three years later was made associate clinical professor of pediatrics at the USC School of Medicine. At the same time he taught an adult Sunday school class and spoke on parenting issues at Nazarene churches in the area. An evangelical publisher invited him to write a book, and the result was *Dare to Discipline*, a loose collection of essays, part pop cultural analysis and part parenting guide. Published in 1970 while he was still at USC, *Dare to Discipline* decried the collapse of traditional morality where "all at once, there were no definite values. There were no standards. No absolutes. No rules." Dobson bemoaned the rise of a youth culture of sex, drugs, and violence, and attributed it to the permissiveness of modern child rearing practices and lack of discipline in the schools. His advice to parents was, reasonably enough, to teach children self-discipline and responsibility, but though he admired Dr. Benjamin Spock, his method relied more on B. F. Skinner's training of pigeons. To liberals what stood out in his system of training children was his insistence on physical punishment for the rebellious child, specifically spanking, or twisting a neck muscle. "Pain is a marvelous purifier," he wrote in an echo of his Nazarene upbringing. Yet he cautioned against child abuse and recommended giving children love and emotional support.[34]

His timing was good, for in 1970 many evangelical parents were struggling with the cultural upheavals of the 1960s and the new "child-centered" parenting advice, when most were innocent of psychology. The book reassured them that the real problem lay not in their own values but in the decline of morals in the society at large. It also gave them a simple entrée into psychological thinking. The book quickly sold two million copies; Dobson took to the lecture circuit and wrote two more books on family issues. In 1977 he left academia and started a radio program, *Focus on the Family*. With that he forsook behavioral science for pop psychology—and for preaching morals, much as his father and grandfather had done.

A tall man with sandy hair, blue eyes, a slight southern drawl, and the demeanor of a kindly family doctor, Dobson had a gift for engaging his audience. On the air he spoke casually, as if including his listeners in a conversation. On the podium he seemed to be speaking extemporaneously. In fact, said a longtime associate, "You are watching a man work harder than any public speaker you know." His radio broadcasts were rehearsed over and over and edited sentence by sentence. When preparing a major speech, he would spend weeks, or even months, deciding on the stories, testing out phrases and gestures before smaller audiences and getting the rhythms right. He ran his organization in much the same way and set a frantic pace. Neglecting his own advice to "Dads," he often stayed late in the office, leaving his wife and two children to have dinner without him. He demanded that his employees do the same, and from them he wanted no surprises and no independent decision making. A micromanager, he instituted a system of oversight to check up on every detail of the lowliest employee's work. His theory was that at any given moment something was going wrong, and that the task of managers was to patrol the company sniffing the air for the "smell of smoke" that would alert them to employee misconduct. Sometimes he would walk the corridors late at night and randomly open his employees' desk drawers, searching for evidence of some misdeed. If he found, say, a bill unpaid, he'd bring it to the next executive meeting and wave it about angrily, telling his managers that they weren't doing their jobs. He did not like to be crossed, and he found no one indispensable. When his three top lieutenants decided to move on, worn down by his controlling style, he expressed no regret but said simply,

"God has a plan. . . . And when he's through with things as they are, he changes them." [35]

As a Christian right leader, Dobson was not an original thinker. What changes he made to the agenda were mostly matters of emphasis. In terms of economics and national security, Dobson called simply for a strong national defense, law and order, free enterprise, lower taxes, and a smaller government that left welfare to churches and families. He had, however, a strong interest in education and church-state issues. He supported the teaching of creationism, silent school prayer, and "parental rights" in public schools. In 1994 he cofounded the Alliance Defense Fund, a legal advocacy group much like the Rutherford Institute and Robertson's American Center for Law Justice, whose stated purpose was "to fight for believers' rights in precedent-setting cases around the country." [36] Naturally, he paid most of his attention to "family" issues. Feminist organizations were often his target. He called the 1995 World Conference on Women in Beijing, attended by Hillary Clinton, "the most radical, atheistic, anti-family crusade in the history of the world" with "a plan to get rid of traditional sexuality in order to destroy patriarchy." He knew that a large majority of American women worked in the paid labor force, but he continued to describe the family in Victorian terms: the strong, silent husband, the breadwinner; and emotionally expressive and needy wife bound to spend her time with her children at home. By "learning to yield to the loving authority . . . of his parents," a child learns "to submit to other forms of authority . . . his teachers, school principal, police, neighbors and employers." [37]

Dobson's position on abortion stiffened as time went on. In the 1970s he had made the usual exceptions for rape, incest, and the mother's health, but in the 1990s, after Operation Rescue had radicalized the Christian right, he, like many of his fellows, made no exceptions at all. He also took a harder line on homosexuality as the gay rights movement gained ground. In 1998 Focus launched Love Won Out, an annual series of conferences around the country, in an aggressive attempt to counter what Dobson called "the gay agenda" and its threats to "the traditional family" and religious freedom. At conferences speakers condemned homosexuality as both sinful and abnormal, at once invoking the Bible and psychologists who claimed homosexuality owed to child abuse, unhealthy family dynamics, or gender identity confusion. In any case, speakers assured their audience, homosexuality was preventable and changeable, and thus homosexuals could not claim to suffer discrimination. Love Won Out supported Exodus International, a collection of "ex-gay" ministries that claimed to help men and women overcome "unwanted same-sex attractions" through prayer and "conversion therapy." [38]

In speeches Dobson gave voice to all the familiar themes of the Christian right: the past in which Americans lived "in harmony with the Scriptures"; the present assault on churches and families by an elite conspiracy of "secular humanists"; the rise of moral relativism; and the decline Western civilization. He often cited Francis Schaeffer, and he used the rhetorical devices of a fundamentalist minister: the jeremiad, the choice between good and evil, the slippery slope, and the martial music. His close associates often compared him to an Old Testament prophet, and as badly as the notion accorded with his self-description as child psychologist with a PhD, he once said, "I really do feel that the prophetic role is a part of what God gave me to do." [39]

Two years before Pat Buchanan gave his famous "culture war" speech at the 1992 Republican convention, Dobson wrote in his book *Children at Risk*:

> Nothing short of a great Civil War of Values rages today throughout North America. Two sides with vastly differing and incompatible worldviews are locked in bitter conflict that permeates every level of society.
>
> Bloody battles are being fought on a thousand fronts, both inside and outside of government. Open any daily newspaper and you'll find accounts of the latest Gettysburg, Waterloo, Normandy or Stalingrad.

It is, he wrote, "a war over *ideas*. And someday soon, I believe, a winner will emerge and the loser will fade from memory."

The situation, he went on to say, resulted not from "a casual and random drift of social mores, shifting over time" but from "a coordinated, well thought out strategy." "Secular humanists," he wrote, "have a particular objective in mind for the future. They hope to accomplish that goal, primarily by isolating children from their parents. . . . It will then be relatively easy to "reorient" and indoctrinate the next generation of Americans."[40]

With chapters written by Gary Bauer, *Children at Risk* was an advertisement for the newly formed Family Research Council and the Focus Policy Councils. In the concluding chapter Dobson urged readers to get personally involved and to clean house in Washington. By his estimate 20 percent of the Congress was solidly pro-family, 40 percent committed to the liberal position, and 40 percent in the "wishy-washy middle." All you need to do, he wrote, is to retire 10 to 20 percent of Congress, and perhaps six senators, and the rest would get the message.[41]

In 1998 with Ralph Reed gone from the Christian Coalition Dobson began a campaign to change the relationship between the Christian right and the Republican Party. In an address to the Council on National Policy in early February he made a fierce attack on Republican congressional leaders. Citing Scripture, he accused them of doing nothing less than defying God's law and ignoring the nation's "severe moral crisis." Social conservatives, he said, had swept them into office in 1994, but for the past three years Republicans had done nothing but "insult" them. In toting up the congressional failures, he excoriated a long list of conservatives: Newt Gingrich for inviting the "pro-abortion" Christine Todd Whitman to respond to Clinton's State of the Union speech; Senator Jesse Helms for approving a $900 million appropriation to Planned Parenthood; Senators John Ashcroft and Rick Santorum for failing to speak out on homosexuality and sex education. "Where," he asked, "are the Republican leaders who stand up and say this is outrageous. We will not stand for it!" He continued, "Does the Republican Party want our votes? No strings attached? To court us every two years, and then to say, don't call me, I'll call you? And to not care about the moral law of the universe? . . . Is this the way it's going to be? If it is, I'm gone. And, if I go . . . I will do everything I can to take as many people with me as possible."[42]

The speech received a standing ovation.

Dobson next sent out a letter to every Republican in Congress—and to the news media—outlining his legislative priorities: ending the funding of

Planned Parenthood and the National Endowment for the Arts, requiring parental consent for minors seeking abortions within federal programs, and several other specific items. He demanded action on objectives that he said "are so obvious that they require no elaboration, such as a ban on partial birth abortion, the defense of traditional marriage, and opposition to any legislation that would add 'sexual orientation' to any civil rights law." Finally, he wrote, "I would strongly recommend to all Republican leaders that they abandon the use of the phrases 'Big Tent' and 'Litmus Tests.' These terms are only trotted out when the beliefs of conservatives are about to be trampled." [43]

On March 18 Dobson dined with two dozen conservative House Republicans and their wives in the basement of the Capitol. In an after-dinner talk he repeated his threat to abandon the party if Republicans did not vote on the Christian right agenda. He said he planned to meet the next day with reporters from *The New York Times* and *The Washington Post* to deliver his ultimatum in public. The congressmen tried to explain that the legislative process was complicated, and that obstacles—such as Clinton's veto—stood in the way of advancing his agenda. Around midnight one of the wives broke into tears as she told him that she and her husband had come to Washington to work for the causes he believed in and that his criticisms had hurt their family. Dobson promised to cancel his interviews for the next day. [44]

Dobson kept his promise, but shortly thereafter he gave an exceptional number of interviews to the media. On *Meet the Press* he once again threatened a walkout, and when asked about the consequences said, "It would be the Democrats in the White House and the Congress, so that would be unfortunate. But you never take a hill unless you are willing to die on it. And we will die on this hill if necessary." [45] In a cover story in *U.S. News & World Report* Michael Gerson, a Wheaton College graduate, reported that Dobson was considering two possibilities. He might take periodic leaves of absence from Focus on the Family—thus keeping its tax status—to campaign for social conservatives. Gary Bauer had found forty races in the fall elections where he might weigh in for one candidate or another. Or Dobson might "go nuclear." It wouldn't, Dobson told Gerson, take many votes to end the GOP control of the House. "Just look at how many people are there by a hair [who won their last election by] 51% to 49%, and they have a ten or eleven vote majority. I told Tom DeLay, 'I really hope you guys don't try to make me prove it, because I will.'" [46]

Dobson's outbursts seem to have galvanized other Christian right leaders, for as Laurie Goodstein of *The New York Times* reported, the talk among them in conferences, radio call-in shows, and a private meeting in Paul Weyrich's office was of frustration and a sense of betrayal. The Republican candidates they had worked so hard for had promised action but failed to deliver, constantly pushing the social agenda to the back burner. "There is virtually nothing to show for an 18-year commitment," lamented Gary Bauer. The strategy of compromising with moderate Republicans had been a failure. "The get-along, go-along strategy is dead," said Richard Land. "No more engagement. We want a wedding ring, we want a ceremony, we want a consummation of the marriage." [47]

Under pressure the House Republican leaders, Speaker Newt Gingrich, Majority Leader Dick Armey, and Majority Whip Tom DeLay convened a "values summit" with top Christian right leaders, among them Dobson, Randy Tate of the Christian Coalition, Richard Land, and officials from Concerned Women for America. Gingrich, who went into the meeting grumbling about the difficulty of legislating the Christian right program, went out sounding enthusiastic about moving the agenda forward. DeLay, a born-again former alcoholic, who gave Dobson's film *Where's Dad?* the credit for his conversion, quickly set up a permanent forum for movement activists and congressmen. Known as the Values Action Team, the forum allowed activists to learn about legislative strategy and socially conservative congressmen to call upon them when they needed support on key votes. In late spring and summer Christian right initiatives crowded the House schedule. Republicans introduced bills to fund a pilot program of school vouchers, to ban human cloning, to prevent gay couples from adopting children, to cut off funding for the National Endowment for the Arts, and to make it illegal to bring an underage girl across state lines to obtain an abortion without her parents' consent. Representative Ernest Istook (R-OK) introduced an amendment to the Constitution to allow organized school prayer, and the House voted to ban "partial birth abortion" for the third time in three years. Most of the bills went nowhere, but then by September the House leadership with Christian right support had begun the process of impeaching Clinton.[48]

In the midterm election Dobson and Bauer worked energetically for socially conservative candidates, raising money and making endorsements, but their efforts were counterproductive. Some of their candidates hadn't a chance. For one, they backed Randall Terry, who was running for Congress in upstate New York, calling for the abolition of property taxes, federal income taxes, and Social Security. Some won their primaries against Republican moderates and were quickly dispatched by Democrats. The impeachment of Clinton had energized Democrats and organizations such as People for the American Way, and Christian right–backed candidates were routed in all regions, even the South. In the long list of those defeated by Democrats were Lauch Faircloth of South Carolina, one of the staunchest of the social conservatives in the Senate; Governor David Beasley of South Carolina; and Governor Fob James of Mississippi, whom Dobson, Falwell, and Schlafly had rescued from defeat in the primary.[49]

Dobson nonetheless refused to give in to Weyrich's despairing view that the Christians had lost the culture war. In the pages of *Insight*, a conservative journal, he wrote, "I believe we should fight all the harder to reclaim territory we've lost." The problem, he said, was a matter of intensity: people on the left pursue their agenda with fervor, while many on the right "don't bother to get involved in public policy, and some don't bother to vote." That Gingrich and the Republican leadership had accomplished very little wasn't, he wrote, "because the public demanded it but because the left did, and the GOP leaders . . . had no stomach for a fight." Citing "encouraging social trends," such as the decline in abortions, he declared that "neither the political nor the culture wars are lost" and quoted Winston Churchill: "Never give in, never, never, never."[50]

The platform of the Republican Party in 2000 reflected Christian right views, but Dobson had no candidate. He thought it necessary to see that John McCain lost, but George W. Bush, who said as little as possible about the controversial social issues, did not please him. When Dobson pressed the Bush campaign to say exactly what the candidate would do about abortion and gay rights, he got no answers. Deciding that Bush had adopted a "big tent" strategy, he gave him only tepid support.[51]

After the election, the Christian right went into a period of quiescence. The Christian Coalition was disintegrating; Beverly LaHaye had stepped down from the presidency of Concerned Women for America; Bauer had left the Family Research Council to run—briefly—for president, and because he later joined the McCain campaign, Dobson refused to let him back. For Christian right organizations money was hard to raise after the dot-com bubble burst and with a Republican in the White House. The FRC lost a third of its revenue, and the funding of Focus on the Family dropped off sharply. Dobson also had to cope with a scandal: the "ex-gay" director of Love Won Out had been found in a gay bar. He was hardly heard from for the next two years.[52]

President Bush and his political strategist, Karl Rove, however, were keenly aware of the importance of conservative Christians. The Christian right had saved Bush's candidacy in South Carolina. Evangelicals had constituted 40 percent of his vote in the general election. The "God gap" had increased. Observant evangelicals, mainline Protestants, and Catholics made up over a half of Bush's vote.[53] Rove, who attributed the tightness of the race to four million evangelicals voters who had failed to go to the polls, said, "It's something we have to spend a lot of time and energy on."[54] Bush understood he was more dependent on conservative Christians than Reagan, or than his father in 1988, and the lesson he drew from his father's defeat in 1992 was that a Republican president must attend to his conservative base. Rove, a direct mail expert, knew how to count, and Bush knew what conservative evangelicals wanted to hear.

"A Wedding Ring"

George W. Bush, unlike his father, had grown up in Texas, where even mainline Protestant churches tended to be conservative, and where the Christian right grew more rapidly than in any other state.[55] At a dim point in his career, when his oil business was floundering, he was drinking too much and his wife was ready to leave him, he became born-again. Unlike most converts, he never said that the experience happened at a certain date. In his campaign autobiography, *A Charge to Keep*, he wrote that a talk with Billy Graham had planted a "mustard seed" in his heart. He went on to describe a gradual transformation in which he quit drinking and joined a Bible study group and recommitted himself to God, church, and family. This was in 1985 and 1986. A year later, when his father decided to run for president, he became the campaign liaison to the Christian right. Working closely with Doug Wead, an Assemblies of God minister and a longtime political operative, he met the important evangelicals and learned how to win their support by showing that he spoke their language and shared their values.[56]

In *A Charge to Keep* Bush tells us that he had another life-changing experience. In January 1999, after he had won his reelection as governor, the pastor of his Methodist church in Dallas preached a sermon, taking his text from Exodus 3–4. In telling the familiar story of God appearing to Moses in the burning bush and calling him to free Israel, the pastor, Mark Craig, emphasized that Moses had initially hesitated, feeling himself unworthy. Connecting this critical moment in sacred history with concerns of the present, he said, Americans are hungry for leadership, moral courage, and faith. Good men could not hesitate. This prompted Barbara Bush to inform her son, "He's talking to you." Addressing his readers, Bush modestly demurs: "The pastor was, of course, talking to us all, challenging each of us to make the most of our lives."[57]

As the religious historian Bruce Lincoln points out, the story can be read in two ways. Bush had heard a thoughtful sermon about the need for commitment to vocation, or he had heard a divine call, issued through an inspired minister, to become the American Moses. His speeches, Lincoln writes, often had the same kind of double coding, and the faithful who heard such speeches felt they had special relationship with him.

A Charge to Keep—the title taken from a hymn written by Charles Wesley—later became the main text for discussions of the president's religion. In *The Faith of George W. Bush*, a hagiography published in 2003, Stephen Mansfield made much of the pastor's sermon and Barbara Bush's response. He added that Bush soon thereafter summoned James Robison to his office and told the televangelist, "I've heard the call. I believe God wants me to run for president." Richard Land, who went to the governor's mansion the day of his second inauguration, heard something similar: "Among the things he said to us was, 'I believe God wants me to be president.'" According to Mansfield, Robison could not resist the appeal of a politician with such a deep personal faith. Bush, however, does not seem to have spoken of God's call to nonevangelicals.[58]

As governor, Bush had avoided identification with the Christian right, but he had cultivated important conservative Texan ministers. As he began his run for president, a number, including Robison, John C. Hagee, a Pentecostal televangelist from San Antonio, and Ed Young Sr., the pastor of Houston's largest Baptist church and a past president of the SBC, formed a network of pastors to promote his candidacy. The Sunday morning he announced his presidential exploratory committee he addressed Young's ten-thousand-member Second Baptist Church, saying, "Faith gives us purpose—to right wrongs, to preserve our families and to teach our children values. . . . Faith changes lives. I know, because it has changed mine. I grew up in the church but I didn't always walk the walk." According to the aide, not one of the hundreds of journalists waiting for him to announce he was going to run for president reported on his sermon. What they had missed was one of the many occasions that Bush gave his testimony to evangelical leaders and church groups, and as the aide wrote, that was all they needed to hear: he was a redeemed sinner, a brother in Christ, and naturally he would do the right thing.[59]

Once elected president, Bush faced a real challenge. He was more dependent on social conservatives than Reagan or his father had been, but a half of his votes had come from other Republicans, and the two wings of the party had grown increasingly antagonistic. As John C. Green put it, he faced pressure from zealous social conservatives but could not afford to alienate moderates, and the closeness of the election—plus the 50-50 tie in the Senate—made his situation acute.[60] His choice of cabinet officers and his early policy decisions seemed an effort to strike a balance. After some lobbying by Christian right organizations, he appointed John Ashcroft, a devout Pentecostal and well-known social conservative, as attorney general; on the other hand he appointed Colin Powell and Christine Todd Whitman, both pro-choice moderates, and both of whom had openly opposed the Christian right. One of his first acts as president was to reinstate Reagan's Mexico City policy, abrogated by Clinton, the so-called gag rule that prohibited federal funding of international family planning agencies that provided abortion services or abortion counseling of any kind. He also began increasing funding for abstinence-only education in the U.S. and abroad. Gay rights fared better than reproductive rights. Bush had run on tolerance, and with the help of the gay Republican group, the Log Cabin Republicans, had taken an estimated 25 percent of the openly gay vote. To head the Office of National AIDS Policy, Bush appointed a leader of the Log Cabin Republicans; he chose another gay activist for the job of screening civilian applicants for Pentagon positions and continued Clinton's "Don't Ask, Don't Tell" policy for military personnel.[61]

In the campaign Bush had pledged to cut taxes and to reform federal education policy. He had also promised to promote charitable giving and to expand the role of religious and other private groups in the provision of social services. The proposal on charities had been the centerpiece of his claim to "compassionate conservatism," and "compassion" took up the longest section of his Inaugural Address. In late January he announced the formation a White House Office of Faith-Based and Community Initiatives and satellite centers in cabinet-level departments with much fanfare. Every major newspaper and newsmagazine ran long pieces about what they called "the religious initiative," but while all had opinions, no one knew what Bush had in mind for it.[62]

"Compassionate conservatism" had been one of Bush's double-coded phrases. To most it meant simply that he was not going to tear up the social security net, but to many conservatives it had an entirely other meaning. During the campaign Bush had written the introduction to the book *Compassionate Conservatism* by Marvin Olasky, the editor of *World* magazine and an author well known in right-wing circles. Newt Gingrich had read Olasky's previous work, *The Tragedy of American Compassion*, in 1994 and had been so impressed that, as the new majority leader of the House, he had distributed it to every freshman Republican congressman. A history of American welfare, *Tragedy* maintained that government policies had been a disaster since the 1930s and proposed as a model the nineteenth-century system in which churches and private individuals, dis-

pensing aid and religion together, had been entirely responsible for helping the poor. Olasky was a true believer. Coming from a Russian Jewish
family, he had abandoned his faith at Yale College to become an atheist and a Marxist, and in graduate school in 1972 he joined the American
Communist Party, when there was hardly anyone left in it. A year later he
quit the party, and after reading Francis Schaeffer turned to conservative
evangelicalism and later to the nearest Christian equivalent to Stalinism.
Hired by the George Grant, the former director of D. James Kennedy's
Coral Ridge Ministries, as an editor of *World*, he joined the Presbyterian
Church of America and wrote books heavily influenced by Rushdoony.
Poverty in his view resulted from moral failure, and the poor could be
helped only by spiritual regeneration and discipline in personal responsibility. "The early Calvinists," he wrote in *The Tragedy of American Compassion*, "knew that time spent in the pit could be what was needed to save a
life from permanent debauch." [63]

Gingrich and his allies weren't ready to go that far, but *The Tragedy of
American Compassion* bolstered their argument that government welfare
policies had led to dependency and social pathology. In the debate over
welfare reform they maintained that "compassion" was leading them to
slash federal spending for the poor. They discarded Senator Dan Coats's
bills to fund modest charitable programs, but Senator John Ashcroft did
manage to attach a "Charitable Choice" amendment to the welfare bill,
though without any money attached to it. In any case, Olasky, then a professor of communications at the University of Texas, Austin, became a
talk show star. Governor George W. Bush consulted him while promoting
legislation that encouraged "faith-based" social programs in Texas, among
them a ministry run by Colson's Prison Fellowship. [64]

During the presidential campaign Bush proposed to spend $8 billion
a year to promote religious and private charities, most of it in tax credits
for donors, but $1.7 billion for programs to aid the poor and $200 million for the Compassion Capital Fund to help small charities expand their
work with the poor. [65] Olasky was one of his advisors, but he had others,
principally John DiIulio, a generally respected professor of government
administration at the University of Pennsylvania. A "born-again" Catholic, DiIulio believed that, according to the principle of "subsidiarity,"

"You always try to solve serious social problems as close to the people as possible." In papers he argued that inner-city churches had the power to alleviate social ills, but that ministries could not replace public assistance programs. He also differed with Olasky in that he wanted to channel aid to churches to do social work, not to proselytize and, as he once said, "I strongly believe in the separation of church and state." These issues were hammered out in a meeting in the early stages of the campaign, and in his first major speech on the initiative in an Indianapolis church Bush split the difference between the two. Charities, he said, should make demands and use "severe mercy," and "Sometimes our greatest hope is not found in reform. It is found in redemption." But he added, "Government cannot be replaced by charities." [66]

Christian right leaders had good reason to back Bush's Faith-Based Initiative, but they became wary when Bush appointed DiIulio to direct the White House Office of Faith-Based and Community Initiatives. Pat Robertson worried that the government would have to fund "aberrant" religious groups, such as Hare Krishna and Scientology, while Jerry Falwell thought it might fund Muslims. Others, including Richard Land, worried that "with government shekels come government shackles"—or that Christian groups might be forced to lose their religious character if they took government grants. Given that SBC hospitals, colleges, and overseas aid programs had been receiving government grants and subsidies since World War II, it seemed a strange thing for Land to worry about.[67] But what he meant became clear when the Congress began its debate on the appropriations bill early in the year.

The House bill, known as HR-7, was shaped by conservatives such as Tom DeLay, and backed by the Christian right. It went through various iterations, but it centered on three provisions: the bill would allow government funding to groups that proselytized with no restrictions—in effect subsidizing religious conversions; it would change numerous large federal grant programs into voucher programs so that individuals could choose to fund proselytizing groups; and it would give all religious groups receiving public funds the right to hire and fire people based not just on their religious affiliation, but on whether they lived according the "practices" of their religion. That is, such groups could hire or fire people if they weren't, say, "Buddhist enough" or "Baptist enough." Certainly it would permit conservative Christian groups to discriminate against gays and lesbians.[68]

Civil rights and civil liberties organizations quite naturally opposed the bill, charging that all three provisions were unconstitutional. The ACLU, People for the American Way, Americans United, the Human Rights Campaign, the largest LGBT rights group, the Unitarians, and Reformed Jews launched an intensive lobbying campaign against the bill. Congressional Democrats balked, and to DiIulio's surprise the White House did not even try to pressure DeLay and his allies to back off from their extreme positions and write a bill that could pass.[69] The bill predictably stalled in the Senate. The Christian right then lost interest and turned their attention to other issues.

Meanwhile Bush had more success with legislation on education and taxes, but neither bill made the Christian right happy. His signature education bill, No Child Left Behind, passed with bipartisan support, but had no provision for school vouchers and would expand the federal government's role in the public schools. Then the bill the White House put its greatest effort into passing was the first round of tax cuts, a bill that in lowering the rates for income, capital gains, and estate taxes added up to $1.35 trillion in cuts.

During the spring low grumbling noises could be heard from Christian right quarters. Dobson, sulking in his Colorado headquarters, called Bush's decision to appoint a gay activist to head the office of AIDS policy "unwise." The March issue of *Citizen* asked: "Is there any reason to expect bold policy stances on family values issues from someone who for two months has peppered his speeches with phrases like 'bipartisan consensus' and 'common ground'?" Bauer, who had formed a group called American Values (and a PAC, Campaign for Working Families), said he was pessimistic. The criticism, however, remained muted. When the administration unveiled the education bill, Christian right leaders kept their peace, and to the surprise of those who had heard Dobson berate Gingrich for putting economic policy first, Dobson actively supported the tax bill. The lather the activists had worked themselves into three years before had cooled.[70]

The Christian right was, of course, in a weakened state, and in no position take on a newly elected Republican president—the first from the South—and particularly one popular with evangelical voters. Still, its leaders had other reasons for keeping silent about the policies that disappointed them. For one thing, the White House gave them more access than they had ever had, and not just when the president needed their help, but consistently. Karl Rove, who was an Episcopalian—and thus rumored to be an atheist—had set up a religious outreach team in his Office of Public Liaison, headed by Tim Goeglein, an evangelical who had served as press secretary for Senator Dan Coats and as spokesman for Gary Bauer in the 2000 campaign. That spring White House officials gave Christian right representatives in Washington much the same treatment they had their business allies, inviting them to regular private meetings downtown and asking their advice on legislation. From then on Goeglein's office set up conference calls, weekly or more, with conservative evangelical leaders to brief them on events and solicit their opinions. Often Rove himself was on the phone. The regulars on the calls that year included Tom Minnery, head of public policy at Focus on the Family; Ken Connor, Bauer's replacement as president of the Family Research Council; Jay Sekulow, president of Robertson's American Council for Law and Justice; Janet Parshall, a Christian radio talk show host; Richard Land of the Southern Baptist Convention; and Ted Haggard, a megachurch pastor and the president of the National Association of Evangelicals. Goeglein also dispensed special invitations to the White House and small favors, such as cuff links or passes to be in the crowd greeting the president when he arrived on Air Force One.[71]

Land, whom the White House staff much preferred to Dobson, said he had weekly talks with administration officials and two to three conversations with the president a year.[72] Weyrich, who had been in Washington since the early 1970s, judged that "the effort to communicate with conservatives and to understand our concerns and address our concerns and involve us in the process is the best of any of the Republican administrations, including Ronald Reagan." In fact, he said, "it's far superior to Ronald Reagan."[73]

In other ways, too, Bush hugged conservative Christians close to his chest. He spoke at gatherings such as the National Religious Broadcasters' convention, saying prayers with the audience, while Rove gave pep talks at the Family Research Council's annual meeting, which had replaced Christian Coalition conferences in Washington. In the White House he surrounded himself with conservative Christians. Forty percent of his staff attended regular Bible study or prayer meetings. (A speechwriter, David Frum, reported that to his discomfort Bible study attendance was "if not compulsory, not quite *uncompulsory,* either.") Bush's chief speechwriter and senior policy advisor, Michael Gerson, was an evangelical, who before a brief stint with *U.S. News & World Report* had worked at the Heritage Foundation and had ghostwritten one of Charles Colson's books. Every year a few of the coveted White House internships went to students from Patrick Henry, a small, unaccredited college founded in 2000 by the home schooling activist Michael Farris.[74]

Then, too, the Bush administration brought more conservative Christians into the federal bureaucracy than any previous Republican administration. One of Bush's first appointments was that of Kay Coles James to head the U.S. Office of Personnel Management, the agency that oversaw the whole federal government workforce. An African American, James was recruited from Robertson's Regent University, where she had served as the dean of its school of government. Known as one of the most articulate of antiabortion advocates, James had been on the board of Focus on the Family and a senior vice president of the Family Research Council. A few reporters noted her appointment, but then she was forgotten until 2007, when, because of a scandal involving a lawyer in the civil rights division of the attorney general's office, reporters found that the administration had hired 150 graduates of Regent University's law school—then still one of the lowest-ranking schools in the country.[75] But that was hardly all. Under James's supervision religious conservatives were appointed to rank-and-file posts in a number of federal agencies and commissions, notably those involved with health and human services. For the first time prayer groups were discovered deep in the federal bureaucracy, and members of Christian right organizations could be found among neoconservatives, flat tax economists, and lawyers who belonged to the Federalist Society. Connie Mackey, the lobbyist for the Family Research Council, told the group's annual gathering in 2002, "The good news is that with President Bush in office a lot of FRC people are in place" and "that makes our life a lot easier." Lobbying, she said, "now works from both ends of Pennsylvania Avenue and everything in between, and that means all the federal agencies." Interviewed by *The Washington Post*, Ralph Reed said that the religious conservative movement "no longer plays the institutional role" it did before the Bush administration. "You're no longer throwing rocks at the building; you're in the building."[76]

In his first six months Bush managed to pacify both social conservatives and social moderates by doling out appointments on both sides and splitting his policy decisions between the two. In June, however, he had to face an issue of real contention: federal funding of research on human embryonic stem cells. According to scientists, the research, begun in the late 1990s, held the promise of cures for Parkinson's, Alzheimer's, diabetes, and other intractable diseases. Earlier in the year eighty Nobel Prize winners wrote the president calling the discovery of stem cells "a significant milestone" with the potential to save millions of lives. Groups such as the Juvenile Diabetes Foundation and many congressional conservatives, among them Senator Orrin Hatch and Vice President Dick Cheney, urged Bush to fund the research. On the other hand many antiabortion groups, including the U.S. Conference of Catholic Bishops and the Southern Baptist Convention, condemned the use of human embryos, even those produced in vitro, on the grounds it amounted to the destruction of human life.[77]

Bush gave a great deal of time to the issue, meeting with groups on either side of the dispute, though not, it seems, with scientists involved in the research. On August 9 in a prime-time address to the nation he acknowledged that there were ethical concerns on both sides of the issue and announced a compromise: he would approve funding for research on the existing sixty stem cell lines, but not for developing new stem cell lines from live embryos. "This," he said, "allows us to explore the promise and potential of stem cell research without crossing a fundamental moral line." Scientists, however, reported that there were fewer than twenty-two usable lines in existence.[78] Those who supported the research concluded that Bush was ready to sacrifice science to religion—or that he had no idea what he was talking about. On the other hand the spokesman for the National Right to Life Committee expressed delight, and Dobson wrote his

Focus members that he was "elated" that "contrary to our fears, Mr. Bush was planning to act on behalf of unborn life." The applause from the social conservatives was, however, far from unanimous. Organizations including the FRC, Concerned Women for America, and the U.S. Conference of Catholic Bishops vigorously opposed the decision and continued to call for a total ban on stem cell research.[79]

The question of whether Bush could keep his Republican coalition together by trying to split the difference between the two sides was mooted by 9/11. The terrorist attacks made him into a wartime leader. His polls soared and remained high through the midterm election, when Republicans picked up eight seats in the House and took control of the Senate. The tendency of Americans to rally behind a wartime president proved particularly strong among evangelicals. According to surveys, evangelical identification with the GOP, following a decline during the Clinton years, rose sharply.[80] The reaction of the Christian right was striking.

In the months that followed the attacks Christian right spokesmen were for the first time heard to say that God had put George Bush in the White House. In December, after Robertson quit the presidency of the Christian Coalition, Gary Bauer told *The Washington Post* that Robertson had stepped down because the position was already filled. "Bush," he said, "is the leader now." There was, he added, "already a great deal of identification with the president . . . in the world of the Christian right, and the nature of this war is such that it has heightened the sense that a man of God is in the White House."[81]

Certainly Bauer's promotion of Bush to the leadership of the Christian right came in a rough patch for two of its own leaders. Two days after the Twin Towers came down Falwell, appearing on *The 700 Club* with Robertson, declared, "The abortionists have got to bear some burden for this because God will not be mocked. And when we destroy 40 million little innocent babies, we make God mad. I really believe that the pagans, and the abortionists, and the feminists, and the gays and the lesbians . . . the ACLU, People for the American Way, all of them have tried to secularize America. I point the finger in their face and say, 'You helped this happen.'"

"Well, I entirely concur," Robertson responded.[82]

Predicting that "secular humanists" would bring God's wrath on the country had been a staple of Christian right rhetoric since the 1970s, and doubtless Falwell expected his audience to concur, as Robertson had, but in the firestorm that ensued, none of his fellow ministers defended him. The White House reprimanded him, and eventually he apologized. It was an interesting moment, for, as it turned out, even conservative evangelicals proved unwilling to believe that the country had been so corrupted that God was punishing the nation.

With his outburst Falwell had not just discredited himself and Robertson but for the moment the entire movement. Bush on the other hand turned himself into the leader the Christian right had been looking for.

On 9/11 Bush, initially struck almost speechless, struggled to comprehend and describe what had happened. In his third speech of the day he found the themes he would develop in the days and weeks that followed. Describing the attacks as "evil, despicable acts of terror," he reassured Americans that "our country is strong. A great people has been moved to defend a great nation." By contrast to Falwell, he figured the nation as the City on the Hill. "America was targeted for attack because we're the brightest beacon for freedom and opportunity in the world. And no one will keep that light from shining." He went on to characterize the situation with stark moral simplicity. "Today our nation saw evil, the very worst of human nature, and we responded with the best of America, with the daring of our rescue workers, with the caring for strangers and neighbors who came to give blood and help in any way they could." He used the word "evil" four times in the short speech and promised that "we"—a united America—would "go forward to defend freedom and all that is good and just in our world." If there ever was a time to invoke the nineteenth-century evangelical notion of American goodness and innocence in a fallen world, it may have been that. Bush, however, continued to explain the disaster in the same Manichaean terms: an evil force had attacked a free and godly country. In a speech on the South Lawn of the White House on September 16, he turned defense into offense, declaring, "We will rid the world of evil-doers. This is our calling." The war on al Qaeda had become a spiritual war, and the president had a divine calling from God to fight it.[83]

In his major address to a joint session of Congress four days later Bush explained that the al Qaeda terrorists practiced "a fringe form of Islamic extremism," and were attacking America because "they hate our freedoms, our freedom of religion, our freedom of speech, our freedom to vote and assemble and disagree with each other." Promising a long war on terrorism, he said, "Freedom and fear, justice and cruelty have always been at war, and we know that God is not neutral between them." When speaking extemporaneously to employees of the FBI—without the help of speechwriters—Bush put the matter more simply: "I see things this way: The people who did this act on America, who may be planning a future one, are evil people. They don't represent an ideology, they don't represent a legitimate political group. They are flat evil. That's all they can think about is evil. And as a nation of good folks, we are going to hunt them down."[84]

Many Americans understood "evil" as just an another descriptor, like "really bad"; some found Bush's repeated use of a theologically loaded word offensive, and some were tempted to ask if ridding the world of evildoers was a feasible foreign policy objective. To conservative evangelicals, however, Bush's use of the word signified moral clarity. "We don't inhabit that relativist universe" of European leaders, Richard Land said. "We really believe some things are good and some things bad."[85]

For Bush to say the terrorists had no ideology and no reason to attack America apart from their evilness made the situation clearer still: the "good folks" of America were at war with agents of the Devil himself. And George Bush was leading them. Then, as Steve Waldman, the editor of the religious website Beliefnet, wrote, Bush's rhetoric had a resonance that went beyond foreign policy: when he called al Qaeda evil, he was indirectly talking to evangelicals about abortion, gay marriage, and whatever else they might think was evil, for if he had moral clarity, he could fight American cultural rot as well as terrorism.[86]

By December conservative evangelicals were offering up choruses of praise for Bush. Magazines, publications, radio and TV shows resounded with them, and several Internet sites offered prayers for the president's safety and success. The popular radio broadcaster Janet Parshall said, "I think that God picked the right man at the right time for the right purpose." Preachers reminded their flocks that Bush might have lost the election and called his victory an act of God. Interviewed by *The Washington Post*, Ralph Reed reported, "I've heard a lot of 'God knew something we didn't,'" and he explained, "In the evangelical mind the notion of an omniscient God is central to their theology. He had a knowledge nobody else had: He knew that George Bush had the ability to lead in this compelling way." [87]

Not only Bauer but also other Christian right leaders felt that Bush had taken over the role they had played. "He's the leader of the Christian right," Marshall Wittmann, a former Christian Coalition figure at the Hudson Institute, said of Bush. "As their institutions peel away, he can go over the heads" of religious conservatives. The Christian right organizations were in a weakened state, but another factor was surely what Ed Dobson and Ed Hindson said of evangelicals: "We tend to be monarchists at heart." In the face of an unprecedented terrorist attack on American soil, the president, this one a Christian like themselves, became the protector of the country and the focus of hopes for the future. [88]

★　★　★

On November 5, 2003, President Bush addressed a cheering crowd of four hundred in an auditorium in the Ronald Reagan Federal Building. In addition to members of Congress and administration officials the gathering included Catholic right-to-life advocates and a full complement of Christian right leaders, among them James Dobson, Richard Land, Adrian Rogers, former president of the Southern Baptist Convention, Jerry Falwell, Jay Sekulow, Michael Farris, Lou Sheldon of the Traditional Values Coalition, and a newcomer, Rod Parsley, a Pentecostal televangelist from Columbus, Ohio. The crowd had gathered for the signing ceremony of the Partial-Birth Abortion Act, the first federal ban on any abortion procedure since *Roe v. Wade*. "Every person however frail or vulnerable has a place and purpose in this world. Every person has a certain dignity," Bush said. "The right to life cannot be granted or denied by government because it does not come from government, it comes from the Creator of life." His remarks were interrupted by standing ovations, and according to a National Right to Life member, the audience was giddy with joy "and obvious affection and love" for the president. [89] Afterward Christian right activists described the event as one of the greatest moments in the

history of the pro-life movement. The Family Research Council called
the signing of the bill "a turning point in the debate over abortion," and
Concerned Women for America "one of the most important milestones
in the thirty-year struggle to regain legal protection for right to life." On
his Focus broadcast Dobson declared, "The president is more committed
to the unborn and to life in general than any other president in our history,
including Ronald Reagan and President Bush's own father. It is incredible
the stand he has taken. And he means it, and he believes it, and you could
see it on his face."[90]

For all the excitement the act was not much of a legislative achievement. The same bill had passed both houses of Congress twice in the mid-
1990s after right-to-life groups had circulated graphic charts and drawings
of the late-term abortion procedure in which the fetus is partially extracted live from the womb and its head crushed in. According to the
American College of Obstetricians and Gynecologists, the procedure was
seldom used, but was a gruesome sight, and 70 percent of the public had
turned against it, as had many pro-choice members of Congress. Clinton
had twice vetoed the bill because it made no exception for the health of
the mother and because the bill was so vaguely worded it might apply to
other procedures; and the Supreme Court had subsequently ruled identical state bills unconstitutional on the same grounds. Still, the Democrats
had never been able to muster a defense of the procedure. Sixty-three
House Democrats and seventeen senators had voted for the current bill.
Bush had signed it, knowing that it would be contested in the courts. Indeed a federal district court judge immediately put a hold on it, assuring
that it would go up to the Supreme Court again.[91]

The bill was nonetheless the first significant legislative victory Bush
had achieved for antiabortion advocates, and he made the most of it.[92]
Before the signing ceremony he invited Dobson, Colson, Michael Farris,
Don Hodel, and Tony Perkins, the new president of the Family Research
Council, to meet with him in the Oval Office and to join him in the motor-
cade to the Ronald Reagan building. Afterward he invited another small
group that included Jerry Falwell; Richard Land; Jack Graham, president
of the SBC; Ted Haggard, president of the National Association of Evangelicals; and Frank Wright, president of the National Religious Broad-

casters. Falwell reported that the president had asked them to join hands and pray. Not long before Bush had repeated his campaign statement that America was not yet ready for a total ban on abortion.[93] This time, however, not even Dobson took him to task for it. At some point after the election even the most hard-line Christian right leaders had tacitly abandoned any attempt to pass a constitutional amendment to reverse *Roe v. Wade* under the Bush presidency.

Christian right leaders were quieter about the Faith-Based and Community Initiatives. By then all supported it, but the program had become almost a covert operation, and to the extent it attracted press attention journalists found it hard to fathom.

DiIulio had resigned in August 2001, and not long afterward Bush and his White House advisors gave up on passing a bill and ran the program by executive order. Congress passed a small appropriation for a single program, Compassion Capital Fund, to provide technical assistance to small charities to allow them to compete for federal dollars, but as journalists discovered, money was flowing out of the executive branch in quantity and turning up in abstinence education programs, crisis pregnancy centers, and evangelical youth groups—and later faith-based drug treatment programs and churches.[94] Pat Robertson's Operation Blessing, whose goal was "world evangelization," received a $1.5 million grant over three years from the Compassion Capital Fund to help other charities. Charles Colson's Prison Fellowship ministry, whose programs involved "biblically based" therapies, was chosen as one of the four "national non-profit partners" and given $22.5 million for a workplace reentry program for ex-offenders.[95] These grants were never announced, and journalists found it impossible to discover the extent of the program.

The White House had created faith-based centers in ten cabinet departments, and with no appropriation for the program, the departments were diverting existing funds and writing their own specific regulations. How much money there was, and where it went, no one seemed to know. Each department had various kinds of funds to spend, and each faith-based center distributed them in different ways. Some grants went to the states, some to intermediary groups, and some directly to charities. The White House Office of Faith-Based and Community Initiatives kept no central records, and even the cabinet departments had no idea what happened to the money after it went to the states or to the intermediaries.[96]

Many Democrats and civil libertarians were scandalized by these revelations. As they saw it, the federal funding of organizations that promoted sectarian religion was an unprecedented breach in the wall of separation between church and state. As a matter of practice, though, there was hardly anything new about it. Since World War II the federal government had made religious organizations integral to U.S. international aid programs, and had subsidized religious as well as secular hospitals, colleges, and universities. With the War on Poverty it had, rather than increase the size of the federal bureaucracy, poured money into nongovernmental organizations, some of them small, and many of them religious. Federal laws and regulations, it was true, barred religious groups taking federal money and mixing religion with social service, but the rules were often honored in the breach. A survey conducted in the mid-1990s found that almost three quarters of the religiously based foreign aid agencies openly engaged in religious practices, such as worship, instruction, and proselytizing. And the same was true of 77 percent of religious family and child-centered agencies, and 91 percent of religious colleges and universities, many of which made worship mandatory. The federal government had allowed this to happen by devoting few resources to monitoring the policies of religious groups it funded and rarely intervening in the case of suspected violations. This pattern of "benign neglect" had been established at the beginning of the Cold War when religion was seen to bolster anti-Communism and strengthen the fabric of American society. It had continued as the U.S. government increasingly relied on NGOs for the provision of domestic social services, and religious groups gained more leverage. Then in the 1990s in a period of Republican dominance in the Congress the government had funneled ever more federal money for domestic programs through block grants to the states and through voucher programs to individuals, reducing the ability of the federal government to regulate its programs. At the time scholarly researchers found that Washington officials had no government-wide overview of federal support to religious groups and little statistical data.[97]

Bush's faith-based initiative followed these established practices. In addition, it relied on legislation written in the mid-1990s: the Charitable Choice amendment to the welfare bill sponsored by John Ashcroft. Passed with little examination by the Congress, the amendment loosened the existing federal laws and regulations on religious groups receiving public money. For example, it allowed states to use federal funds in contracting with charitable and faith-based organizations without the usual elements of federal oversight. It abandoned the requirement for religious social service agencies to be separately incorporated as a condition for receiving federal funds; it permitted government aid to go to pervasively religious organizations, such as churches, if the providers agreed to follow a few guidelines keeping religious and nonreligious elements distinct in their programs. Then, because houses of worship and certain other religious groups are free to hire only those who share their faith, Charitable Choice permitted government-funded organizations to hire only their coreligionists.[98] The amendment received small attention because the Clinton administration and most state governments regarded its central provisions as unconstitutional, and never used it. Bush, however, had used Charitable Choice in Texas to contract with evangelical agencies, among them Colson's Prison Fellowship ministry.[99]

In 2002, unable to pass a bill for his faith-based initiative, Bush issued executive orders hailed by Robertson and Sekulow as bold actions to ensure "fair and equal treatment for religious organizations" and roundly criticized in the press as bypassing Congress to ease requirements for the funding of faith-based charities.[100] The orders allowed federal funds to go directly to churches, permitted "coreligionist hiring," and further limited the ability of the state to interfere with the religious content of social services, but in essence they put the Charitable Choice law into practice.[101] The only real novelty of the faith-based initiative was the political use put to grants going to religious organizations.

By 2003 it became clear that the Bush administration meant the faith-based initiative to serve two ends. One of them was to please the Christian right. This was easy enough to do. The political appointees that ran the faith-based centers in cabinet departments selected groups of conservative Christians to review the applications for grants and, not surprisingly, they chose many Christian right organizations, such as those led by Colson and Robertson.[102] David Kuo, a devout evangelical who worked in the faith-based initiative office in the White House, was shocked by the favoritism he saw in the grants of the Compassion Capital Fund. One of them, he noticed, went to an organization called Jesus and Friends Ministry, which was little more than a post office box. "The initiative," he wrote, "was purely about paying off political friends for their support." Kuo, however, worked on the second political goal of the faith-based initiative, which, as Ken Mehlman, the director of political affairs in the White House, put it, was to "bring new African-American faces and voices into our party." This was a bit more difficult, but DiIulio's successor, Jim Towey, presented a plan to Mehlman: Republican congressional incumbents facing tough races in the midterms would host "nonpartisan" events for minority community groups to tell them about the grants available to help the poor. With Mehlman's approval he and staff members put on meetings for twenty candidates in targeted races and a regional conference in Atlanta with full houses of clergy and community leaders eager to learn how they could apply for grants. Only one reporter figured out that the Republicans were using the faith-based initiative to court black voters, but no one picked up on his piece.[103] DiIulio, however, noticed. He had long been critical of how the White House had handled the initiative, and in the December issue of *Esquire* Ron Suskind quoted him as saying, "There is no precedent in any modern White House for what is going on in this one: a complete lack of a policy apparatus. What you've got is everything—and I mean everything—being run by the political arm. It's the reign of the Mayberry Machiavellis." [104]

The faith-based initiative never reached the front pages because by 2003 the war on terror and the war in Iraq overshadowed all else. And more than any domestic policy issue, the wars cemented the alliance between the president and Christian right.

In early February 2003, a month before the invasion of Iraq, 64 percent of evangelicals—and 70 percent of those who identified themselves with the Christian right—registered support for the invasion, compared with 59 percent of the public as a whole. Evangelical support for the war rose to 79 percent in July, and remained high long after other Americans had given up hope for success.[105] The reaction was not surprising. Most evangelicals were Republicans, many were southerners with a tradition of support for the U.S. military, and many evangelicals thought Bush one of their own. Richard Cizik, vice president of governmental affairs for the National Association of Evangelicals, said in February, "They trust this president, George W. Bush and his assessment of the nature of the threat. . . . Evangelicals resonate to George Bush's leadership because of the language that he uses, which is often theological."[106] Richard Land was of the same opinion. "There was a very high level of trust among white evangelicals and George W. Bush," he said a year later. "If he said that's what we needed to do, then they were willing to give him the benefit of the doubt."[107] But that was not all.

Anti-Muslim sentiment ran high among conservative evangelicals. Immediately after 9/11 Billy Graham's son, Franklin, who had given the invocation at Bush's inaugural, pronounced Islam "a wicked and evil religion," and Robertson described the Koran as "teaching warfare so at the core of this faith is militant warfare." The president, who repeatedly said Islam was a religion of peace, failed to criticize them for suggesting that Islam as a whole was responsible for the attacks. In the next two years the vitriol only increased. Robertson said Muslims "were worse than the Nazis," Falwell called the Prophet Muhammad "a terrorist . . . a violent man, a man of war," and Jerry Vines, a former president of the SBC, said at the convention of June 2002, that the Prophet was "a demon-obsessed pedophile."[108] At the National Religious Broadcasters convention Islam was denounced a pagan religion—the revival of an ancient Babylonian religion—and an influential evangelical charismatic, C. Peter Wagner, called Allah "a high-ranking demon." Men like Dobson and Land blamed only "radical Islam" or "violent factions" within Islam, but as they never spoke of any other kind of Islam, it came to much the same thing.[109] A *New York Times* reporter found that lectures and books gaining currency in evangelical seminaries and missionary training institutes presumed that the world's two largest religions were headed for a confrontation—with Christianity representing what was good, true, and peaceful and Islam what was false and violent. Richard Cizik of the NAE worried aloud that evangelicals had "substituted Islam for the Soviet Union" and that "Muslims have become the modern-day equivalent of the Evil Empire."[110]

Notably some Christian right leaders called for an invasion of Iraq well before the fact. Just nine days after 9/11 Gary Bauer signed a statement calling for the overthrow of Saddam Hussein.[111] The SBC passed a resolution in June 2002 calling on the U.S. government to "protect our people against rogue nations in their quest for weapons of mass destruction." That fall, just as the administration had begun to marshal its arguments for an invasion, James Dobson said on *Larry King Live*, "Saddam is a tyrant . . . out of the mold of Hitler, Stalin and the others. And you can't negotiate with a tyrant. One who is bloodthirsty, one who's willing to kill innocent people. I think there's only one thing to do, and that's to go in there and confront him."[112] In early October Richard Land released a letter he had written to Bush signed by Charles Colson, Bill Bright, D. James Kennedy, and Carl Herbster, president of the American Association of Christian Schools, making a case that a preemptive strike on Iraq would meet the requirements for a just war.[113]

The Land letter came as boon to the president. In the months leading up to the war Christian leaders in the United States and Europe sent up an outcry against the proposed invasion. Pope John Paul II appealed to Bush to refrain from going to war, citing just war theory, and a Vatican spokesman declared preemptive war "a crime against peace." The U.S. Conference of Catholic Bishops added their protests, as did the leaders of all the American mainline Protestant denominations, including Bush's own United Methodist Church. The National Council of Churches held vigils and tried, but failed, to get Bush to receive a delegation of fifty leading ministers. The Mennonites opposed the war, and the National Evangelical Association, clearly divided, made no official comment.[114] The letter, nonetheless, accepted as fact the administration's claims that Saddam Hussein was harboring al Qaeda terrorists and gaining weapons of mass destruction. "We believe," it said, "your stated policies . . . are well within the time-honored criteria of just war theory."[115]

In his letter to Bush, Land had appealed to generally accepted moral principles, but evangelicals tended to see the Middle East through the lens of the Bible, and as he later suggested, many evangelicals, himself included, had their own religious reasons for supporting the war.

Comparatively few evangelicals were theological dispensationalists, though their numbers had grown among charismatics and Southern Baptists in recent years, but in times of conflict in the Middle East many others consulted the prophetic literature, such as Hal Lindsey's *The Late Great Planet Earth*, for an explanation of current events.[116] One of the key signs of the end times had always been the return of the Jews to Palestine, or the land given by God to Abraham. The creation of the state of Israel had been seen as a first step toward the fulfillment of prophecy, and Israel's annexation of the West Bank and the Old City of Jerusalem during the 1967 War was seen as the second. Since the 1970s popular American prophecy writers and preachers had closely monitored events in the region. Falwell, Robertson, and many other dispensationalist preachers had made numerous trips to Israel, some to pace out the battlefield where Armageddon would be fought.[117] Dispensationalists saw Jewish settlements on the West Bank—or Judea and Samaria—and the future rebuilding of Solomon's Temple on the site sacred to Muslims, the Temple Mount in Jerusalem, as the next steps in God's unfolding plan. Christian Zionists, they supported the most hard-line expansionist groups in Israel, and although Darbyite prophecy spelled out annihilation of all Jews who had not converted to Christianity before the final days, many Likud leaders had welcomed their support. On his trip to the United States in 1998 Prime Minister Benjamin Netanyahu went to a meeting Falwell had arranged with over a thousand evangelicals before going to see President Clinton. That year John Hagee, one of Bush's Texas supporters and a popular dispensationalist televangelist, wrote: "We are racing toward the end of the time, and Israel lies in the eye of the storm. . . . Israel is the only nation created by a sovereign act of God, and He has sworn by His holiness to defend Jerusalem, His Holy City. If God created and defends Israel, those nations that fight against it, fight against God."[118]

In the modern dispensationalist scenario the Islamic world was allied against God and would be totally destroyed during the last days. Ever since Iraq's invasion of Kuwait in 1990, prophecy writers had identified Saddam Hussein as the possible Antichrist, pointing out that Iraq was the site of Babylon, the city described in the book of Revelation as "the great whore" and doomed to annihilation by fire.[119] Like Pat Robertson, many dispensationalists had not seen the Gulf War as a part of God's plan, for

George H. W. Bush had assembled a coalition that included many European and Arab nations they regarded as allies of the Antichrist, and he had spoken of creating a "new world order." George W. Bush, by contrast, had decided to go into Iraq almost unilaterally, and in his State of the Union address had portrayed Saddam Hussein as a quasi-demonic figure who could one day unleash "a day of horror like none we have ever known."

Christian Zionism, with its vision of Islam as the enemy, found support not just among dispensationalists, but also among the much greater numbers of evangelicals who believed that God still had a covenant with Israel and that He had promised the restoration of Jews to the Holy Land. Evangelical groups, such as Christian Friends of Israel, Bridges for Peace, and the International Christian Embassy Jerusalem, contributed millions of dollars a year to the settlement of Jews in Israel and for Jewish settlements on the West Bank. In the 1990s *Christianity Today* found an "enormous network" of small Christian Zionist organizations springing up across the country. With the rise of Israeli-Palestinian violence, the breakdown of the peace process, and the erosion of European and American liberal Protestant support for the Israeli occupation of the West Bank, evangelical Zionists became more important to Likud and to its American supporters. Christians' Israel Public Action Campaign lobbied with its Jewish counterpart, American Israel Public Affairs Committee. Gary Bauer, a Christian Zionist, was asked to join the Project for a New American Century, a neoconservative think tank founded in 1997 to create a coalition to advocate for a military buildup and an aggressive assertion of American power. Its members soon included Dick Cheney, Donald Rumsfeld, Paul Wolfowitz, and Elliott Abrams, and in letters to President Clinton and the Republican congressional leadership they argued that the only way to protect the United States and its allies from weapons of mass destruction was to remove Saddam Hussein from power.[120]

After 9/11 Christian right leaders, who were not dispensationalists, and who normally kept a distance from foreign policy, began to take a new interest in the Middle East for both theological and geopolitical reasons. Dobson's reaction was not untypical. "I feel very strongly about Israel," he said on *Larry King Live* in 2002. "You know it's surrounded by its enemies. And it exists primarily because God has willed it to exist, I think, according to Scripture, but also because America has stood with Israel. If we ever abandon it, it's gone. There are six million Jews in Israel. There are 400 million Muslims around them that hate them . . . and want to drive them into the sea. That's a major concern to me. It's the only democracy in the Middle East." [121]

Rabbi Yechiel Eckstein, who had founded the International Fellowship of Christians and Jews in 1983 to raise evangelical support for Israel, saw his membership burgeon. In 2002 the Fellowship had 330,000 Christian donors who gave $20 million for projects in Israel and millions more for the settlement of Jews in Israel. [122] That year he created Stand for Israel and brought in Ralph Reed and Gary Bauer to mobilize leadership and grassroots support in the evangelical community. [123] Bauer, many of whose Project for a New American Century colleagues had taken high posts in the administration, had by then signed two open letters to President Bush calling for regime change in Iraq. The first, sent just a few days after 9/11, maintained that even if there was no evidence linking Saddam Hussein to al Qaeda, a failure to move against Iraq would constitute "an early and perhaps decisive surrender in the war on international terrorism." The second, of April 2002, called Yasir Arafat and his Palestinian Authority a part of the "terrorist network" and insisted that "if we do not move against Saddam Hussein and his regime, the damage we and our Israeli friends have suffered until now may someday appear but a prelude to much greater horrors." In the vision of Project for a New American Century members, the overthrow of Saddam Hussein was to be a demonstration to the "terrorist network" and to other "rogue states" in the Middle East that they could not resist American military might. [124]

Then, in the years before 9/11, evangelical missionary organizations evinced a new and intense interest in Muslim countries. In the 1990s many decided to focus on what they called "the 10/40 window," or that part of the world between the 10th and 40th parallels north of the equator in Africa, the Middle East, and Asia, where much of the world's Muslim population lived. In Africa the 10th parallel was the dividing line between the Muslim north and Christian and animist south. Among others, Franklin Graham, a Southern Baptist who headed a large relief organization, Samaritan's Purse, had worked in Sudan at the juncture between the world's two great proselytizing religions.[125] More conservative theologically and politically than his father, he saw the Arab world with its "evil" religion as the next target for conversion. He was not alone. In 2000 the SBC reorganized its International Missions Board to focus on Islamic countries. Shortly afterward, a collection of evangelical mission groups formed Windows Network International to target Muslim countries in the 10/40 window. A number of other groups gave crash courses to train evangelicals to convert Muslims to Christianity. According to *The New York Times* the number of missionaries in Muslim countries quadrupled between 1990 and the early 2000s. Still, many window countries, many of them in the Arab world, were off-limits to missionaries because of laws against religious conversion efforts.[126] Iraq was one of them, and according to Jim Brady, the coordinator of the SBC's International Mission Board for the Middle East and North Africa, "Southern Baptists had prayed for years that Iraq would somehow be open to the gospel." [127]

As soon as the invasion began, some of the most aggressive evangelical missionaries readied themselves to move in behind the U.S. troops. In early April representatives of the International Bible Society were already in Iraq watching the bombs fall and distributing tracts and videos. The SBC's International Mission Board announced that eight hundred missionaries had volunteered to distribute food and shelter and to "help Iraqis have true freedom in Jesus Christ." Samaritan's Purse had staff members in Kuwait and Jordan preparing water-purifying equipment and medical supplies and ready to spend some of the charity's $194 million budget on Iraq. Graham declared himself "poised and ready" to send his staffers into Iraq as soon as possible.[128] Speaking to *The New York Times*, he emphasized that his group's principal purpose was to help people who were sick or hungry or who had lost their homes, but he added, "God will always give us an opportunity to tell others about his Son. We are there to love them and save them." In public SBC officials also stressed humanitarian relief aid, but internal fund-raising documents emphasized mission work. "Southern Baptists," wrote the International Mission Board's Jim Brady, "must understand there's a war for souls underway in Iraq." And he told the *Baptist Press* that he was witness to "a pivotal moment in history." The Missouri Baptist Convention was sending volunteers, and its executive director, David Clippard, exulted, "With Iraq, God has opened a door into the very heart of the Muslim world for us!" and "We must step through this historic opportunity—an unprecedented ministry opportunity of epic proportions." [129] Soon their purposes became apparent on the ground in Iraq. On the tens of thousands of boxes of dried food brought by SBC volunteers appeared the words of John 1:7 in Arabic: "The law indeed was given to Moses; grace and truth came through Jesus Christ." One Mission Board bulletin reported that aid workers were handing out copies of the New Testament and praying with Muslim aid recipients. In addition teams of independent missionaries were handing out tracts and Jesus videos in Baghdad. [130]

To many observers the presence of such missionaries in Iraq seemed a poor idea. Some worried about the safety of the American troops and wondered why the Bush administration did nothing to stop them. A University of Virginia expert on Islam said in April, "The Iraq War is being interpreted in religious terms by Muslims around the world as a war against Islam, and this is dangerous." In many Muslim countries, John C. Green told a *New York Times* reporter, the American military and its dominant religion appear inseparable. True or not, he said, "you have the image of a deeply religious president essentially giving Christians a green light to come into Iraq." To some evangelicals the problem was just the opposite. Robert Pyne, a theologian from the conservative—and dispensationalist— Dallas Theological Seminary, worried that Muslims and others would identify the Iraq War as the cause of Christ. "We may," he said, "need to truly distance ourselves as Christians from what is perceived around the world as a national agenda." Leaders of the NAE did not object to evangelizing in Iraq but called the anti-Islamic statements of evangelists such as Franklin Graham "dangerous" and "unhelpful." Dr. Clive Calver, the head of the NAE's aid and development agency, World Relief, said that Graham's comments had circulated widely among members of the Red Crescent, the Muslim agency he worked with. "It's used to indict all Americans and used to indict all Christians," he said. He and other NAE leaders expressed concern for the safety of Christian missionaries and for indigenous Christian groups in predominantly Muslim countries. [131]

As it turned out, their worries were somewhat misplaced. Graham,

Brady, and others assumed, like many in the Bush administration, that the American troops would quickly end the resistance, and that peace would descend on Iraq. Instead the violence mounted, and those missionaries who went into Iraq were caught up in guerrilla and sectarian warfare. In March 2004 four SBC volunteers were killed and one was wounded. In November the SBC stopped distributing food boxes, and by January 2005 it and the other missionary groups had quietly sidled out of the war zone.[132] Subsequently the sectarian war forced indigenous Christians to flee their country, and by the time the American forces pulled out, there were a million fewer Christians in Iraq than had been before.

But all of that came later. In February 2003 the National Religious Broadcasters association passed a resolution commending Bush on his performance as commander in chief and saying, "We recognize that God has appointed President George W. Bush to leadership at this critical period in our nation's history."[133]

The Marriage Amendments and the 2004 Election

In the 2004 election Bush focused his campaign on national security, devoting fully half of his speeches to the war on terrorism, presenting himself as the leader most capable of keeping America safe. His opponent, Senator John Kerry, countered by criticizing the war in Iraq and by emphasizing the economy and jobs. The candidates hardly mentioned social issues, such as abortion and gay rights. It thus came as a shock to many when the national exit poll showed that a plurality of voters chose "moral values" as their most important priority. Because most of these had voted for Bush, it appeared that the hot-button issues had trumped both war and the economy just three years after 9/11. That Bush had won with only 50.7 percent of the popular vote meant the Christian right might have given Bush his narrow margin of victory over Kerry.

The poll caused a huge controversy. Critics argued that the term "moral values" was much vaguer and more encompassing than the other options on the questionnaire, like Iraq or health care, and that it could apply to a wide variety of matters such as the personal characteristics of the candidates or social justice issues. A series of post-election surveys, including one by the Pew Research Center, however, produced similar results and showed that almost nine out of ten voters, whatever option they chose, defined "moral values" as related to the social issues or to "traditional" or "family" values. In other words, a large minority of the electorate—perhaps 25 percent—had found "moral values" more important than economics or foreign policy, and to almost everyone the term "moral values" had come to mean exactly what the Christian right said it meant.[134]

The Democrats had not seen this coming. The Christian right had been left for dead, but in just two years its desiccated organizations had revived and swollen like some desert plants after a rain. For the first time in its history movement leaders had put their differences aside and created a united front, mobilizing new groups of pastors and gaining new allies among conservative Catholics, Mormons, and others. The Bush campaign had meanwhile organized religious conservatives of all traditions more effectively than had any previous campaign. Its efforts, almost invisible, had melded with those of the Christian right.

The revival of the Christian right began one day in June 2003, when Paul Weyrich and Rev. Don Wildmon convened a meeting of movement leaders in an apartment building in Arlington, Virginia. Wildmon, a Christian broadcaster and the founder of the American Family Association in Tupelo, Mississippi, had suggested such a meeting to Weyrich months before. Christian conservatives, he argued, had helped Republicans take control of Washington and they didn't have enough to show for it, while at the same time the Republican victories had drained the grass roots of motivation. Conservatives, he insisted, had to coordinate their strategies. Weyrich agreed with Wildmon, but he was dubious. A political junkie, he had not been able to leave the fray, but he had tried putting Christian right groups together before and failed because, as he later wrote, "Some Christian right groups were rivals . . . and on the right there's a streak of individualism which causes leaders of groups not to want to cooperate with other leaders." He had nonetheless called the meeting, and fourteen people, including those he called "the heavyweights"—James Dobson, Richard Land, and Gary Bauer—showed up in the apartment complex where Sandy Rios, the president of Concerned Women for America, had a condo. All thought the movement was in trouble. "Things had not been going well with us in the past couple of years," Weyrich later wrote. "The movement had not been gaining members, it has not been winning battles—with the exception of the pro-life issue, and those were marginal battles." Other participants admitted that the movement was in financial straits and had no single compelling message. "There was a little bit of a burn-out," Bauer remembered.[135]

Other movement leaders and impartial observers also thought their situation critical. "Obviously in some ways Christians are losing the culture war," D. James Kennedy said in an interview. "It's time to reexamine the situation we're in." John Green, a skeptic when it came to predictions about the movement's demise, said of Christian right leaders, "They're at a moment when they have to reinvigorate themselves or reinvent themselves, or they'll just slowly fade away."[136]

The meeting in Arlington had no agenda. "All we knew," Wildmon told a *Times* reporter, "was we were going to get together and find if there were some issues of concern we could agree on and combine our efforts." The first thing that came up, he said, was the Federal Marriage Amendment— or the bill in the House designed to make gay marriage unconstitutional.[137]

At the time gay marriage seemed almost inconceivable to most Americans, but religious conservatives had taken the prospect of it seriously for almost ten years. Legal challenges to Hawaii's marriage law had been filed in the early 1990s, and in 1996 the Hawaii Supreme Court ruled that the state had no compelling reason to deny same-sex couples the right to marry. In June that year the SBC had passed a resolution that spluttered with outrage. Homosexual relationships, the resolution read, were "a gross abomination . . . sinful, impure, degrading, shameful, unnatural, indecent, and perverted." Any action by the government to give homosexual unions the legal status of marriage would, it said, "jeopardize seriously the favor of Almighty God on whom the security, welfare and stability of every nation, even Gentile nations, ultimately depends." In the backlash that followed the court's decision Hawaiian voters passed a constitutional amendment allowing the state legislature to ban same-sex marriage; the U.S. Congress and thirty-five states passed defense of marriage acts limiting marriage to a union between a man and woman. National gay organizations had not supported the gay marriage litigation in Hawaii, and working on state legislatures to grant domestic partnership benefits, they saw the legalization of same-sex marriage as far in the future.[138]

Still, the Hawaii court decision had persuaded a small group of legal scholars at the conservative Ethics and Public Policy Council in Washington to draft an amendment to the U.S. Constitution to ban gay marriage. Among them were Robert P. George, a prominent Catholic conservative from Princeton University; Robert Bork, whose nomination to the Supreme Court had failed; and Gerald V. Bradley of Notre Dame law school. "People involved in those early discussions thought same-sex marriage in the courts was going to happen soon," George told Dan Gilgoff of *U.S. News & World Report*. "But we had a lot of trouble convincing other people to take it seriously. It seemed too distant and unlikely. And politicians weren't going to cross that bridge until they'd come to it." The scholars, however, found an ally in Matt Daniels, a young lawyer who headed Focus on the Family's family policy council in Massachusetts. In 1999 Daniels founded the Alliance for Marriage in Washington, and careful not to identify it as a Christian right organization, he chose an ecumenical group of clergy to serve on his board. While lobbying on other issues, he sought the help of congressional aides in completing the draft of what became known as the Federal Marriage Amendment. Three years later he found congressional sponsors for the bill, just two sentences long, which limited marriage to a union between one man and one woman.[139]

By the summer of 2003 the matter of a marriage amendment had taken on greater urgency for Christian conservatives. They had been losing the battle on gay rights. Some 80 percent of the American public favored equal opportunity in employment; major corporations had extended benefits to the partners of gay employees; the states of Vermont and California had adopted laws permitting civil unions, conferring legal benefits for same-sex couples. An appeals court in Canada had just ruled a gay marriage ban unconstitutional, and the Massachusetts Supreme Court was due to rule on gay marriage in the fall. In July the U.S. Supreme Court handed down a decision in *Lawrence v. Texas* finding a Texas law criminalizing sodomy unconstitutional, and in a blistering dissent Justice Antonin Scalia wrote that the Court had just decreed the end of all morals legislation and made gay marriage the logical next step.[140]

In their discussion of how to revive the movement the Christian right leaders assembled in Arlington thought a federal marriage amendment might just be the issue they needed. The general public had not yet realized the imminence of a decision on same-sex marriage, but once what Daniels called "the marriage bomb" went off, many religious people would react. The problem was the wording of the bill. The Federal Marriage Amendment then in the Congress would bar the courts from discovering a right to same-sex marriage in the Constitution but would leave state legislatures the right to create civil unions and domestic partnerships. Daniels believed it was the only amendment that had a chance of passing. Most Christian right groups, however, opposed the granting of any legal rights to homosexual couples. The SBC resolution adopted that June opposed "all efforts by any court or state legislature to validate or legalize same-sex marriage or other equivalent unions." Michael Farris, the head of the home schooling defense association, said: "I don't care if you call it civil unions. I don't care if you call it domestic partnership. I don't care if you call it cantaloupe soup, if you're legally spouses at the end of day, I am not willing to do that." [141]

In his book *The Jesus Machine*, Dan Gilgoff tells us the issue caused a rift between Dobson and Ken Connor, the head of the Family Research Council. Two years before Connor had asked his staff to study the Federal Marriage Amendment and had concluded that the bill protected only the semantic definition of marriage. A memo released by the FRC in May 2002 proposed a tougher bill barring state legislatures as well as the courts from conferring any legal benefits on gay couples. It also warned that "the long effort to amend the Constitution to protect unborn human life" should serve as caution to those who believed the proposed amendment offered "a panacea for the protection of marriage." Connor thought the Christian right would do better to press for the appointment of conservative judges and to pressure Congress to strip the courts of their jurisdiction over same-sex marriage cases than to undertake a futile struggle to pass a constitutional amendment. [142] Dobson on the other hand supported the Federal Marriage Amendment with total conviction. Six months after the FRC released its memo, he invited Daniels onto his show and asked his listeners to support Daniels's bill. In a Focus newsletter of 2003 he called the legalization of same-sex marriage merely a ruse by gay activists, whose goal was to end marriage entirely. Harking back to the gay liberation movement of the 1970s, he wrote, "Most gays and lesbians do not want to marry," and "the legalization of homosexual marriage for gay activists is merely a stepping-stone on the road to eliminating *all* societal restrictions on marriage and sexuality." The very survival of Western civilization was at stake, and its best hope, he insisted, lay with the Federal Marriage Amendment. "This effort," he wrote, ". . . is our D-Day, or Gettysburg or Stalingrad." [143]

Gary Bauer had always deferred to Dobson when he headed the FRC, but when Connor came to Washington he thought that the FRC had become independent of Focus. On paper it was, but he did not know Dobson. A board member, Dobson wielded an outsized influence and controlled other seats. On this issue he had an ally in Robert George, an author of the Federal Marriage Amendment, who in 2001 had become the first Catholic to join the board. A month after the Arlington meeting Connor was forced to resign, and by the end of the summer, the FRC had a new president handpicked by Dobson. [144]

Tony Perkins, the new FRC president, had a long history in the Christian right movement and knew Dobson well. A graduate of Falwell's Liberty University, he had settled in Baton Rouge, Louisiana, where he had headed a chapter of the Christian Coalition while working in a local TV station. Elected to the state legislature in 1995, he spent much of his time combating abortion and gay rights.

Not overly scrupulous about his allies, he had, as the campaign manager for a Republican senatorial candidate, paid $86,500 for the mailing list of the former Ku Klux Klan leader and state representative David Duke. [145] When the Coalition fell apart in 1998, he cofounded the Louisiana Family Forum, one of Focus's Family Policy Councils, and often appeared as a guest on Dobson's radio show. In 2002 he ran in a crowded Republican primary for the U.S. Senate and came in fourth with 10 percent of the vote. Too much of a right-winger even for Louisiana, he was in Dobson's eyes ideal for the Family Research Council. Just forty years old, and an ordained minister in a nondenominational evangelical church, he had telegenic good looks and experience as a speaker. He understood Dobson's power in the Christian right. When he arrived in Washington, he not only put the Federal Marriage Amendment at the head of the FRC's agenda but made it the sole issue for the organization in the coming year.[146]

In the fall Christian right activism against gay marriage heated up with organizations redirecting their resources from abortion and school voucher fights to a campaign for a marriage amendment. The group of leaders that had met in Sandy Rios's apartment building was rapidly expanding. Now called the Arlington Group, it met for the third time since June and declared October 12–18 Marriage Protection Week. Richard Land predicted that if the Massachusetts court permitted gay marriage, the federal Defense of Marriage Act, and those of the states, would crumble. "We need a firewall," he said. In November, after months of internal debate, the group decided to support an amendment that would bar state legislatures from approving civil unions or domestic partnerships. That month members representing twenty organizations went to Capitol Hill and in a stormy meeting with Representative Marilyn Musgrave of Colorado and other sponsors of the Federal Marriage Amendment, Sandy Rios took the lead in pressing for a tougher bill. Musgrave refused to budge. A stronger bill, she and others insisted, would never pass the Congress, much less the state legislatures. With that the consensus in the group began to shift, and at the urging of Dobson and Perkins, the Arlington Group got behind the Daniels amendment.[147]

In November the Massachusetts Supreme Court ruled 5–4 that gay marriage was permissible under the state constitution and gave state lawmakers 180 days to pass the enabling legislation. In Washington the Senate immediately took up the House bill, and Christian right leaders, along with their congressional allies, pressured the president to support it. Bush was reluctant. He had always opposed gay marriage and civil unions, but he had taken the position that marriage law should be left to the states. States' rights were important to Republicans, and he was loath to alienate the gay voters in his party or to appear intolerant.[148] In July, when asked if he supported the bill, Bush had avoided giving a direct answer. "I think it's very important for our society to respect each individual, to welcome those with good hearts, to be a welcoming country." On the other hand he said, "I believe a marriage is between a man and a woman. And I think we ought to codify that one way or the other."[149]

Put on the spot after the Massachusetts court decision, Bush took another step in the direction of endorsing the amendment, saying he would do what was "legally necessary to defend the sanctity of marriage."[150] Christian right leaders were not satisfied. They planned to make the amendment the central issue for the 2004 campaign, and they wanted a clear endorsement from Bush. As the date for the State of the Union address approached, well-known members of the Arlington Group, such as Dobson and Land, telephoned Rove reminding him of the importance of Christian voters. Rove, who needed no reminder, assured the group that the president favored the amendment. In his address Bush struck a tone of outrage. "Activist judges . . . have begun redefining marriage by court order, without regard for the will of the people and their elected representatives," he said. "If judges insist on forcing their arbitrary will upon people, the only alternative left to the people would be the constitutional process. Our nation must defend the sanctity of marriage."[151] His remarks led the Log Cabin Republicans to drop their support for him, but Christian right leaders thought he still hadn't made a firm commitment to the amendment. In a direct mail appeal to his supporters Dobson wrote, "The homosexual activist movement is poised to administer a devastating and potentially fatal blow to the traditional family. And sadly very few Christians in positions of responsibility are willing to use their influence to save it."[152]

In early February the Arlington Group decided to press the White House once again. According to *The New York Times*, its members gathered around a speakerphone as Land questioned Rove. Would the president support the amendment publicly? If so, would he do it with the vigor he showed fighting for the Medicare prescription drug benefit—an entitlement expansion conservatives opposed? Rove told them that the president was fully behind the amendment and was looking for an appropriate moment to make a public announcement. Still Bush hesitated. Public opposition to gay marriage had grown since July, but Americans, including evangelicals, were evenly divided on a constitutional amendment, and a number of Republican senators thought it would never pass. Then on February 12 the mayor of San Francisco, saying he was upset about Bush's attempt to divide the nation over gay marriage, instructed city officials to issue marriage licenses to same-sex couples. In just ten days three thousand couples flocked to get married, and the extensive media coverage made gay marriage a reality to the American public for the first time. On February 20 Bush in a short statement said, "After more than two centuries of American jurisprudence and millennia of human experience, a few judges and local authorities are presuming to change the most fundamental institution of civilization." He called on Congress to pass a constitutional amendment defining marriage "as a union between a man and a woman," while "leaving state legislature free to make their own in defining legal arrangements other than marriage." [153]

By then Christian right organizations were in midst of a major campaign against gay marriage with radio and TV broadcasts, daily emails, direct mail fund-raising, and two websites. Richard Viguerie, the direct mail specialist, told *The New York Times* that his company would send out ten million appeals for several social conservative groups in the coming months, and he believed gay marriage would make a more effective fund-raising issue than abortion. Movement leaders from Sandy Rios to Richard Land had sworn to make gay marriage a litmus test in the 2004 election. The Family Research Council had distributed a Marriage Protection Pledge asking all federal and state elected officials to sign it. [154] Dobson had resigned from the presidency of Focus on the Family to fight gay marriage "on a political level." Already the campaign had "reinvigorated" the movement. The Arlington Group was on its way to including seventy organizations, among them the National Religious Broadcasters and the National Association of Evangelicals. Chaired by Dobson and meeting every six weeks in off-the-record sessions in the offices of the FRC in Washington, the Arlington Group allowed member organizations to coordinate their strategies and combine their strengths. [155] Movement leaders had also found co-belligerents. The U.S. Conference of Catholic Bishops had come out in support of the Federal Marriage Amendment, and most conservative religious groups, including Mormons, Orthodox Jews, and Muslims, opposed gay marriage. A large majority of African Americans also opposed gay marriage, and the Arlington Group succeeded in recruiting a few popular black pastors.[156]

Looking to the November election, Christian right leaders thought they had found a winning issue. They had been losing badly on gay rights, notably among younger voters, most of whom had grown up with gay people among their acquaintances and on their favorite TV shows. Since the 1990s religious homophobic rhetoric had only served to marginalize them, but gay marriage was a new issue for the public, and the amendment allowed them to be *for* something. "Millions of people," Gary Bauer said, "understand that it's not bigotry to believe that marriage is between a man and a woman."[157] For first time in years the American public was behind them. According to a Pew Research Center survey of February 2004, two thirds of the American public opposed gay marriage, and within this group, gay marriage surpassed abortion and gun control as a "make-or-break voting issue"; 34 percent would not support a candidate who did not share their view, and that number rose to 55 percent among the evangelicals.[158] "I've never seen anything that has energized and provoked our grass roots like this issue, including *Roe v. Wade*," said Land in February.[159] Bush's endorsement of the Federal Marriage Amendment had been crucial, for the leading Democratic candidates for president opposed gay marriage, but they also opposed a constitutional amendment, saying that marriage law should be to the left to the states. Just as the presidential campaign began, Bush had made marriage a partisan issue.

In the spring the Arlington Group lobbied for the amendment, while working to put state constitutional amendments banning same-sex marriage on ballots in the November elections. The amendment, predictably, did not get very far in the Senate.[160] After the House, voting largely on partisan lines, failed to give it the required two-thirds majority, movement leaders blamed Bush for not having lobbied hard enough. Some in the media called the vote a big election-year defeat for Bush.[161] The failure of the amendment, however, spurred Christian right leaders to redouble their efforts to stop gay marriage in the states—efforts that dovetailed with their work for the Bush-Cheney campaign.

For Christian right leaders there was never any question about their choice for president that year. Bush had no primary challengers, and the

winning Democratic candidate, Senator John Kerry, a Massachusetts lib-
eral with a perfect pro-choice record, was certainly no alternative. Like
John F. Kennedy, Kerry was a practicing Catholic, but whereas evangel-
icals had opposed Kennedy in 1960 because they feared he would follow
Vatican teachings, they opposed Kerry for the very opposite reason. Pope
John Paul II took a hard line on abortion. The archbishop of St. Louis told
Kerry he could not take communion if he went to mass in his diocese, and
Cardinal Joseph Ratzinger (who became Pope Benedict XVI the following
year) later instructed the American bishops to deny communion to Catholic politicians who were "consistently campaigning and voting for permis-
sive abortion and euthanasia laws." [162] Amazingly from the perspective of
1960, *Christianity Today* called it "certainly appropriate" for the bishops to
expect a Catholic president to submit to Vatican authority on values matters, especially abortion. Gary Bauer went farther, saying: "When John F.
Kennedy made his famous speech that the Vatican would not tell him
what to do, evangelicals and Southern Baptists breathed a sigh of relief.
But today evangelicals and Southern Baptists are hoping the Vatican *will*
tell Catholic politicians what to do." [163] When in the second presidential
debate Kerry said his religion would not influence his public policy positions, Land called him "a functional atheist." [164]

In the months before the election Christian right leaders had nothing
but praise for the president. Dobson told Sean Hannity, "George Bush is
one of the most conservative presidents we've ever had. He's the strongest pro-life president we've ever had. He had the courage to stand up for
family and for marriage." [165] In an interview on PBS Land compared Bush
favorably to Reagan. "Now we have a president who [Southern Baptists]
feel really sees the world the way they see it, understands them, is sympathetic to them and has an administration that understands they are a very
important part of a governing coalition." This, he added, "is the Reagan
administration without the drag of those old country-club Republicans
who disdained social conservatives. . . . This president not only thinks
we're important; he shares our concerns." In listing Bush's achievements
Land mentioned his decision on embryonic stem cell research, Dobson
spoke of his cutting taxes on families, and said of Kerry, "I'm afraid he will
turn the country over to the United Nations, certainly the military." [166] In

the campaign season neither mentioned what Bush had failed to do for the Christian right. Being realists, they felt they could persuade him to do better if they turned out the four million evangelical voters that Rove said were missing in 2000. Then, both thought that the critical issue was the makeup of the courts. "More is at stake in this election than merely the influence of chief-executive policies for a four-year term," Dobson said. "Judicial appointments made by the president can directly impact our culture and our families for half a lifetime or more."[167]

One or two vacancies on the Supreme Court seemed likely to open up in the next four years, and Bush would surely nominate conservatives. Republican presidents had denounced "activist judges" before, but he was the first to pay no attention to the recommendations of the American Bar Association, and many of his nominees to the circuit courts were of such an ideological cast that Senate Democrats, led by Minority Leader Tom Daschle, had taken the unusual step of filibustering ten of them. The experience of the past year had shown Land and Dobson that even changes to the state constitutions might not stop gay marriage. "The states are not going to determine the definition of marriage," Dobson told Hannity. "The courts are going to do that."

Both Dobson and Land thought the stakes were high. If Bush were reelected, and if they could replace Senate Democrats with Republican social conservatives, they might change the nature of the courts and reverse the trend not just on gay rights but on the secularization of the country that in their view had been going on at least since the school prayer decisions of the 1960s.[168]

Bush and Rove for their part knew the election would be close. At the Republican convention they chose speakers to appeal to moderate Republicans and independents, and Bush said little about Christian conservative issues in his acceptance speech, or later when speaking to the general public. At the same time the Bush campaign put a high priority on mobilizing conservative Christians. As always Tim Goeglein, Bush's emissary to evangelicals, and Rove made weekly phone calls to Arlington Group leaders such as Land, Dobson, Colson, and Ted Haggard. In midsummer Ken Mehlman, chair of the Bush-Cheney campaign, and Ralph Reed, who had been appointed the southeastern regional coordinator, started making regular calls to Land and Dobson, for both had plunged into the campaign.[169]

The Southern Baptist Convention had never taken part in an election before, but this year, the twenty-fifth anniversary of the "conservative resurgence," was different. In the spring Land, as the head of the Ethics & Religious Liberty Commission, the SBC's public policy arm, mounted an "I Vote Values" initiative, a voter registration and education effort, with a website and an eighteen-wheel tractor trailer that drove from church to church with advice on how to register people to vote. The website contained information on what the candidates stood for and what Christians ought to consider when they voted. "We want people to vote their values and convictions over economic issues," Land said. The registration drive was completely nonpartisan, he told *The New York Times*. It would undoubtedly pick up some Democratic voters because 20 percent of Southern Baptists had voted Democratic in the last election, but, he added, he expected even more Republican voters this year.[170]

At the SBC Convention in June, where Land advertised his "I Vote Values" effort, President Bush appeared on a live telecast and gave a short campaign speech emphasizing his pro-life stance and his support for the Federal Marriage Amendment. The next day Jack Graham, the departing president of the SBC, and three other prominent Southern Baptists hosted a Bush-Cheney "pastors' reception" at a hotel next to the convention site paid for by the Bush campaign. According to the *Times*, a campaign aide collected signatures and addresses of a hundred pastors who pledged to endorse Bush publicly, to register voters, and to organize "a party for the president" nearer election time. At the reception Ralph Reed explicitly asked the pastors for their help, telling them, "You can make sure that everyone in your circle of influence is registered to vote." Collared by the *Times* reporter, Jack Graham said he was attending the reception as an individual and not as the president of the Southern Baptists. When asked about the potential benefits of his personal endorsement of Bush, he said, "You can connect the dots. I don't mind if you connect the dots. You can't separate what you believe from the political process."[171]

James Dobson also flung himself into the campaign.

The previous year he had left the presidency of Focus on the Family, giving the day-to-day operations over to the ubiquitous Don Hodel, while remaining chairman of the organization and continuing his broadcasts. In May he created Focus on the Family Action, a 503(c)(4), that could play a larger political role, saying, "The attack and the assault on marriage is so distressing, I just feel I can't remain silent." Dobson had never been known for his silence, but this time he campaigned for candidates, spoke at dozens of anti–gay marriage rallies across the country, and took such a public and partisan role that Hodel had to tell journalists that "the brand of Focus" remained "evangelical outreach to the family." [172]

In the campaign Dobson used all of his institutional resources. Focus on the Family joined the Ethics & Religious Liberty Commission's initiative and sent out "I Vote Values" kits that included registration forms and instructions on promoting causes, such as the Federal Marriage Amendment, to twelve thousand churches across the country. Focus's pastor outreach ministry encouraged the more than 100,000 pastors on its mailing list to preach on the social issues, and its director traveled to ten states working to convince pastors that avoiding controversial political stances would be dereliction of duty. [173]

Dobson had worked hard to pass the Federal Marriage Amendment, putting full-page ads in the hometown papers of opponents, and when the amendment failed, he supported efforts to put constitutional amendments banning gay marriage on state ballots. By the fall thirteen states had amendments on their ballots, and nine with language broad enough to be interpreted as forbidding civil unions and domestic partnership benefits. Focus affiliates, the Family Policy Councils, led all but two of the initiatives, and Dobson frequently plugged the amendments on his radio program. His new organization, Focus Action, coordinated signature-gathering efforts in five states where petition drives were necessary, distributed sample sermons to pastors, and sent cash contributions to affiliates in Michigan, Oregon, and Ohio. The Alliance Defense Fund, which he had helped found, sent out letters encouraging pastors to involve their churches in organizing, addressing fears that sermons on a ballot issue might jeopardize the church's tax-exempt status, and pledging legal support. [174]

In the months leading up to the election Focus Action, the FRC, and the American Family Association sponsored anti–gay marriage rallies around the country, some of them in stadiums with thousands of people, some in megachurches, where the events were syndicated live to hundreds of other churches and carried by Christian radio stations and cable networks. Dobson, Perkins, Colson, and Bauer were regular speakers and often were joined by special guests, such as House majority leader Tom DeLay and Senate majority leader Bill Frist.[175] These events culminated in a "Mayday for Marriage" rally on the Mall in Washington, D.C., on October 15. Addressing a crowd of tens of thousands of people, Dobson offered to get down on his knees to beg the audience to go the polls. Arguing that the federal courts were the real threat to marriage, he called them "unaccountable," "unelected" "arrogant," and "imperious." "We can't get our hands on the courts," he said, "they're out of reach . . . but we can reach the Senate. . . . We must change the make-up of the Senate. We must get the Senate to limit the power of the court, one way or another. We must turn out the vote." [176]

Meanwhile Dobson was making his own efforts to change the Senate. In April he tried to unseat Arlen Specter, a moderate and the ranking Republican member on the Senate Judiciary Committee, by supporting his GOP opponent in the Pennsylvania primary with radio commercials and personal appearances, but Specter won. In the general election Dobson took on South Dakota's Tom Daschle, the Senate minority leader, who was running for reelection against the Republican John Thune, a fresh-faced graduate of Biola University (formerly the Bible Institute of Los Angeles) and the state's only congressman. In the Republican-leaning state the race was hotly contested, and Dobson mounted two "Stand for the Family" rallies in the last three months of the campaign, blaming Daschle for blocking Bush's circuit court judges.[177] In addition he stumped for three social conservatives who were running for the Senate for the first time. One was a South Carolina congressman, Jim DeMint, a deacon of a Presbyterian Church in America congregation, and close to Christian right organizations, including Focus on the Family.[178] Another was David Vitter, an old friend of Tony Perkins's from the Louisiana House of Representatives and the Louisiana Family Forum. A U.S. congressman, he had dropped out of the race for governor in 2002 amid allegations that he had patronized prostitutes, claiming that marital difficulties alone forced him to end his campaign. Louisiana Republicans accepted his explanation, and two years later he was running for the Senate with the help of a "Stand for the Family" rally and a personal endorsement from Dobson.[179] The third was Tom Coburn of Oklahoma, a former board member of the FRC and one of the most conservative members of the House. An obstetrician, Coburn had sponsored the first "partial birth abortion" bill, and had said that he favored the death penalty for abortionists.[180] His Democratic opponent, Brad Carson, was a conservative who opposed abortion and favored the anti–gay marriage amendment in Oklahoma, but Coburn said, "This is a battle for the culture of America, and I would describe it as a battle of good versus evil." Dobson campaigned hard for Coburn, arguing that a vote for Carson was a vote for a Democratic Senate run by such liberals as Tom Daschle, Ted Kennedy, and Patrick Leahy and asking voters to fast and pray on the weekend before the November 2 election.[181]

Not just Land and Dobson but the entire Christian right worked enthusiastically on the campaign. Opposition to gay marriage gave the movement a focus, and this time activists strongly supported Bush. The existing organizations, such as the American Family Association, gained momentum, new groups sprang up in the states, and the press gave the movement a new level of attention. In addition, pastors who had never been involved in an election before took active roles in mobilizing voters. Rick Warren, the author of the best-selling *The Purpose Driven Life* and a newcomer to public policy, wrote a letter to 136,000 fellow pastors urging them to compare the candidates' positions on five "non-negotiable" issues: abortion, same-sex marriage, stem cell research, human cloning, and euthanasia. Jay Sekulow, chief counsel of the American Center for Law and Justice, sent mailings to 45,000 churches encouraging their clergy to tell people to vote their convictions and giving legal advice. After the election he told *The Washington Post* he believed that thousands of clergy members gave sermons about the election and that many went farther than they ever had before.[182]

At the same time the Bush-Cheney campaign put an unprecedented effort into securing the votes of religious conservatives. After the poor showing in 2000, Bush strategists, according to Gilgoff, believed they couldn't count on the Christian right to get out the evangelical vote. Four years before they outsourced their efforts, but this year they brought evangelical organizers directly into the campaign. Ralph Reed, whose consulting firm, Century Strategies, they had hired in 2000, became a campaign official. His title was chair of the southeast region, but more than a year before the election, he had built a national network of religious volunteers—some 300,000 by his count—that was virtually another Christian Coalition, but this one inside the campaign. Focusing on the battleground states, he appointed state chairs, who in turn appointed regional and county chairs to recruit teams of volunteers at the precinct level. The Bush campaign later augmented his network and used it to reach out directly to churches and church members across the country. The project was never announced, but its scale was suggested by an email, discovered by *The New York Times*, from a Pennsylvania campaign official saying that the national headquarters had asked them to identify 1,600 "friendly congregations" and a volunteer in every church.[183]

Bush's religious networks, it appeared, had a variety of tasks, some of which skirted the IRS rules for the tax exemption of churches. In Pennsylvania, according to the email, volunteers were to distribute voter registration materials and campaign information "in a place accessible to the congregation." In Florida Gilgoff found that the state chair's main objectives were to persuade churches to host registration drives and to convince pastors to preach on the social issues and encourage people to vote their values. A *Washington Post* reporter in July found a detailed plan of action distributed by the national Bush-Cheney headquarters to religious volunteers across the country. The instruction sheet listed twenty-two "duties" to be performed by specific dates, among them, hosting at least two campaign-related potluck suppers with church members and distributing voter guides. The sheet also asked volunteers to "send your church directory to your state Bush-Cheney 04 Headquarters or to a BC04 field representative."[184]

The revelation that the Bush campaign was asking for church directories caused an outcry among clergy members, including some of those associated with the Christian right. Richard Land said he was "appalled" by the strategy. "To share the church directory with anyone outside the church body," he said, "is a violation of the sanctity of the body."[185] With protests coming from influential figures like Land, it was widely, but wrongly, assumed that the campaign halted the practice. In many localities there were no objections, and the Bush campaign found the church lists an important part of the data they were collecting to identify and contact religious voters. In television ads the campaign avoided mention of the hot-button issues, but with church lists correlated with voter registration files, it could narrowly target messages about religious and moral issues. According to a study, most of the religiously oriented mail sent out by the Bush campaign concerned abortion, same-sex marriage, the nomination of judges, and family values. One Republican Party mailer sent out to households in Arkansas and West Virginia claimed that liberals wanted to allow same-sex marriage—and to ban their Bibles.[186]

In addition the GOP continued its efforts to enlist African American pastors through the faith-based initiative. During the campaign season Jim Towey organized more than a dozen large conferences in battleground states, including two in Florida, where he advertised the availability of federal funds for church-related social projects to some twenty thousand clergy and community leaders. In Ohio and other states the faith-based initiative was promoted at rallies and ministerial meetings. As reporters discovered, four prominent African American church-based organizations in contested states, whose pastors backed Bush, received grants of over $1 million. At one conference Towey called the initiative a flashpoint in the "culture war" between people of faith and the secular world. Pointing to abortion, gay marriage, and federal rules that had excluded churches from grants, Towey said, "African-Americans are starting to question some of the fundamental precepts that the Democratic Party is there for them."[187]

Later it became a matter of debate in scholarly journals whether the Bush campaign or the Christian right had proved more effective in getting out the religious vote.[188]

The two groups, however, overlapped, and in parts of the Bush campaign they melded to the point where they were almost indistinguishable. Ralph Reed, the former Christian right leader, called on a number of Christian right activists to staff the campaign's religious network. In Florida his state chair for evangelical outreach led the Florida Prayer Network, a ministry that had held a fast for Bush in 2000. Reed also called on activists who had already made their way into the GOP. In St. Louis, one Bush team leader was an Assemblies of God church member who had served as state chair of the Christian Coalition and as a state Republican Party official. Whether a campaign worker was primarily a Republican or a Christian right activist was often difficult to tell. That was certainly the case of David Barton, whom the Republican National Committee hired as a political consultant for the campaign.[189]

A former vice chair of the Texas Republican Party, Barton had worked on Bush's gubernatorial campaigns in the 1990s. He was also an activist, who by 2004 had published dozens of books, CDs, DVDs, and CD-ROMs, arguing that the Founding Fathers were evangelical Christians and that the United States had been a Christian nation until the twentieth century.[190] During the campaign he gave "briefings" at three hundred Republican National Committee–sponsored lunches for pastors around the country. In an interview with Beliefnet he said that he and the RNC official who co-ordinated the luncheons "make it very clear that we are not partisan per se but biblical." Asked about his briefings to pastors, he said, "I show them the historical role of pastors being involved in civil government . . . and then I show them the issues that are at stake from a biblical point of view and the voting records that pertain to those [issues]." In a briefing attended by Gilgoff he told pastors that the Bible "takes a very clear position" against the capital gains tax, the estate tax, the progressive income tax, and the minimum wage. "All these," he said, "are economic issues that we should be able to shape citizens' thinking on because of what the Bible says."[191]

The Christian right made its most impressive showing in Ohio, a piv-otal state, where the election was predicted to be close, and where an anti–gay marriage amendment on the ballot faced considerable opposi-tion. A demographic microcosm of the nation, Ohio resembled the coun-try in its religious makeup, with white evangelicals making up a quarter of the population, Catholics just less than a quarter, and the other religious groups in proportion to their numbers in the country as a whole. The Christian right had always had a presence in the state—a chapter of the Moral Majority, state and local chapters of the Christian Coalition, and other "pro-family" groups—but its influence over the Republican Party had never been strong. The state was just too diverse. After the Republican Party took over the state government in the early 1990s, the Christian right was able to pass a few items on its agenda, such as a ban on partial birth abortions, but essentially it remained just one interest group among others. In 2004, however, it took off as a movement, inspiring evangelical pastors beyond its usual reach to get involved in the election and making common cause with other religious groups.[192]

The main agent of the Christian right resurgence in Ohio was Phil Burress, a longtime activist who headed the Cincinnati-based Citizens for Community Values. A union negotiator for truck drivers in the 1970s, Burress had a born-again experience in 1980 after what he described as a two-decades-long addiction to hard-core pornography that ruined two marriages and estranged him from the evangelical church of his youth. Shortly after his reconversion, he joined Citizens for Community Values, an evangelical anti-porn advocacy group that with the growth of the Christian right took on a larger agenda. A decade later he retired from the two small businesses he had started and became the full-time director of the CCV. With an advisory board that included the Catholic archbishop of Cincinnati, retired judges, and respected businessmen, the CCV in the 1990s had considerable success combating pornography in the city. At its core it was always the Christian right, and Burress at one time or another led most of the movement organizations in the state, including the Christian Coalition and the American Family Association. Homosexuality began to preoccupy him. In 1993 he led a successful ballot initiative that amended the Cincinnati city charter to prohibit anti–gay discrimination ordinances. Two years later he took on a much more ambitious project. While the Hawaii Supreme Court was considering the gay marriage case, he assembled a national coalition of conservative Christian leaders to draft and promote what became the Defense of Marriage Act, the federal law signed by Bill Clinton in 1996 and the model for laws passed in thirty-six states. His name rarely appeared in the national press, but after the passage of the DOMAs, it became well known in Christian right circles. Focus on the Family made Citizens for Community Values its Ohio Family Policy Council, and in 2003 Burress became an early member of the Arlington Group.[193]

Ohio had never adopted a defense of marriage act but when the Massachusetts Supreme Court legalized same-sex marriage in November, Christian right organizations put intense pressure on the Ohio General Assembly to pass one, and in February one of the toughest acts was signed into law. Not satisfied, Burress and other Christian right leaders proposed putting the law into the state constitution. As a member of the Arlington Group, he favored amending the U.S. Constitution and the state constitutions to prevent the courts from ruling against the defense of marriage acts. The Ohio legislature, however, demurred, for the amendment, known as Issue One, would require a three-fifths vote in both houses, and the GOP was divided because the language of the amendment, like that of the federal DOMA, was so broad it could be interpreted to bar all forms of domestic partnership benefits. Public universities and state agencies would have been affected, and possibly private companies.[194]

Burress then decided to mount a petition drive to put the measure on the ballot directly. The task was daunting, for it meant gathering 323,000 signatures in a just a few months. Under the banner of "Ohio Campaign to Protect Marriage," Burress and Citizens for Community Values went to work with other state Christian right groups and with considerable assistance from national organizations. Focus on the Family sent petitions to its 65,000 Ohio constituents, and Burress used the mailing lists of the American Family Association and Gary Bauer's PAC, Campaign for Working Families. Within a few weeks he had six thousand volunteers. He also hired more than fifty people from a professional signature-gathering firm with funds provided by the Family Research Council. By the final deadline in September the CCV had collected 350,000 valid signatures and registered 54,000 voters.[195]

Issue One divided Ohio. Opposition came from the mainline Protestant clergy, liberal religious groups such as the Unitarian Universalists and Reform Jews, gay rights groups, Democratic leaders, and prominent Republicans, including the governor and both U.S. senators. On the other hand the Roman Catholic Church endorsed the amendment, as did groups of African American pastors; and the usually apolitical Eastern Orthodox and Amish communities actively supported it. The organizing drive, however, came from the Christian right.[196]

Burress and his allies began with their contacts in the white evangelical community, but they also aspired to enlist black congregations. One of Burress's first phone calls was to J. Kenneth Blackwell, Ohio's secretary of state and an African American, who attended a Pentecostal church in Cincinnati. The only successful conservative Christian politician in the state, and a member of the Arlington Group, Blackwell was at once the official in charge of election procedures and an honorary cochair of the Bush-Cheney campaign. When Burress asked him to serve as spokesman for the Issue One campaign, he accepted immediately. He was planning to run for governor in 2006, and during the campaign he preached in support of Issue One from the pulpits of black churches, gave pastor briefings, and taped spots for African American radio stations. On occasion he toured the state with Rod Parsley, a white Pentecostal televangelist with a multiracial megachurch outside Columbus and ministries to the inner cities. Parsley, who had, he said, been inspired at Bush's signing ceremony for the Partial-Birth Abortion Ban Act to join the august company of Christian right leaders, was rallying pastors, black and white, around Issue One.[197]

Burress's campaign for Issue One had many of the elements of a political campaign. It involved extensive television and radio advertising, direct mail, yard signs, and get-out-the-vote efforts. Citizens for Community Values hired a firm to call every household in the state to identify Issue One supporters, generating a list of 850,000 households to call again before Election Day. The campaign recruited hundreds of white evangelical pastors to hold voter registration drives, preach sermons on traditional marriage, and urge their congregations to vote. It held ten briefings for clergy members and numerous rallies, including a September 19 "Marriage Sunday" rally—a simulcast of Christian right leaders heard in many Ohio churches. Just before Election Day it sent church bulletin inserts to seventeen thousand congregations (or virtually all Christian churches in the state) and called ten thousand churches with electronic messages encouraging congregations to go to the polls. The CCV reportedly spent a total of $3.5 million on petitioning and the general election campaign, most of it provided by Focus Action and the FRC. Other national groups, such as the Alliance for Marriage, contributed hundreds of thousands of dollars for get-out-the vote materials; and the Alliance Defense Fund and Sekulow's American Council for Law and Justice offered legal advice to clergy members. For some, like the FRC, it was the biggest investment they made in any state that year.[198]

Christian right leaders of course knew that Ohio was a key swing state and that their campaign for Issue One might provide the turnout Bush needed to win it. At one rally Burress said that a polling firm told him the amendment would give the president a 3 to 5 percent margin over Kerry. That he would make the connection clear was hardly surprising, for many Christian right members in the state were working directly for Bush's reelection. A revitalized Christian Coalition chapter distributed two million voter guides; other groups, such as the Concerned Women for America, worked at the grass roots, while many activists joined the Bush campaign through the Republican Party or through the campaign's religious network. According to John C. Green, the activist corps involved in the election, numbering in the thousands, was substantially larger than in previous years. As for the Bush campaign, it registered voters with the help of church directories, and targeted "values" voters with direct mail and automated calls from figures such as Franklin Graham. But then the presidential contest in Ohio was intense. George W. Bush made eighteen visits to the state, John Kerry twenty-three, and a record total of $150 million was spent on the election.[199]

When the results came in on November 2, Christian right leaders were elated. Bush had not won by a landslide, but he had done better than he had in 2000, winning the national popular vote by a small majority (50.7 percent) and the electoral college by a clear majority. Evangelicals had voted in record numbers, their turnout jumping by 9 percent, or 3.5 million voters—almost what Rove had hoped for. Almost 78 percent of evangelicals who went to the polls had voted for Bush, making up 35 percent of his electorate. Catholics, too, gave more of their vote to Bush: 52 percent versus 47 percent in 2000. Only mainline Protestants voted less Republican, this time splitting vote their between Kerry and Bush. As before, frequent church attenders in all traditions voted more heavily Republican than others in their traditions, but this year the "God gap" was larger than ever. Bush took more than 60 percent of all frequent church attenders and over 70 percent of white voters who went to church weekly or more. "Moral values" had been the top priority for nearly a quarter of all voters. Then, too, the outcome of the election had very possibly turned on the issue of gay marriage.[200]

Gay rights groups had not been prepared to mount a forceful campaign for same-sex marriage and had allowed the Christian right to frame the issue as the "destruction of traditional marriage." The anti–gay marriage amendments—two of which were decided in elections before November 2—passed by overwhelming margins (from 57 percent in Oregon to 86 percent in Mississippi). In most of the eleven states where they were on the November ballot the votes made no difference to the presidential election. Eight were in any case locked in for Bush; two of them, Oregon and Michigan, went for Kerry, but the election, as predicted, had come down to Ohio. Bush's victory had depended on Ohio's twenty electoral votes, and he had taken the state by a mere 118,000 votes. Concerns about the war and the economy had certainly influenced Ohio voters, but Issue One had passed by 62 percent of the vote, and according to several postelection studies, the marriage amendment had at the very least contributed to Bush's narrow victory.[201] White evangelicals had been the amendment's strongest supporters—more than 80 percent had voted for the amendment—and they had given Bush 75 percent of their vote. Catholics, in particular weekly church attenders, had voted for the amendment and for Bush. African Americans had given Bush 16 percent of their vote—a gain of 7 points over the 2002 election—and frequent churchgoers accounted for much of the increase. Thus one thing was certain: the groups targeted by the Christian right and the Bush campaign in Ohio had been critical to the success of Issue One and crucial to Bush's narrow victory.[202]

The Arlington Group principals didn't wait for the analysis. Bush had won, evangelicals had turned out in record numbers; all thirteen marriage amendments had passed, and the Republicans had picked up five seats in the Senate. Tom Daschle had been defeated by John Thune, and the three other candidates Dobson had stumped for had won. "The President rode our coattails," Burress said of the Ohio vote.[203] Not since the Republicans swept the Congress in 1994 had movement leaders felt they had such a triumph. Falwell called the election a "slam dunk" for Christians and Dobson "a resounding victory in the battle for American families."[204] "Make no mistake," Viguerie wrote in a memo to fellow activists, "conservative Christians and values voters won the election for GWB and the Republicans in Congress."[205] "Before our strength was a question mark," Weyrich told a reporter. "Now it's an exclamation point."[206]

An Exclamation Point

For the first time since the movement began in the 1970s Christian right leaders could claim to have handed a Republican president his margin of victory, and they were quick to demand their reward. "Now that values voters have delivered for George Bush, he must deliver for their values," said D. James Kennedy just after the election.[207] "As we say in Texas, he's going to dance with the one who brung him," Land told *Newsweek*. "We haven't come to this place to go home and not push our values and our beliefs."[208] To *The New York Times* Dobson divulged that he had issued a warning to "the White House operative" who had called to thank him, saying he told the caller that many Christians believed that the country was "on the verge of self-destruction" but that "God has given us a reprieve." I believe, he added, "it's a short reprieve." Conservatives, he said, had four years to pass an amendment banning same-sex marriage, to stop abortion and embryonic stem cell research, and most of all to remake the Supreme Court. "I believe the Bush administration now needs to be more aggressive in pursuing these values, and if they don't do it, I believe they will pay a price in four years."[209]

Dobson had been issuing similar warnings to Republicans for a decade, but by the end of 2004 the movement had become a virtual echo chamber. The day after the election Tony Perkins gave much the same warning to congressional Republicans. "I think that the voters spoke with a clear voice . . . on the issue of marriage, which speaks more broadly to the issue of judicial activism," he said, adding, "I think if they do not hear that voice on the Hill, they're deaf."[210]

A test of their hearing came immediately. In a post-election victory speech Senator Arlen Specter, who was due to move to the chairmanship of the Judiciary Committee, warned that Bush had not won a large enough majority to change the courts in a radical fashion. "If you have a race that's won by one or two percent, you have a narrowly divided country, and that's not a traditional mandate." Observing that the Senate Democrats had already filibustered some of Bush's nominees and were likely to resist efforts to install antiabortion Supreme Court justices, he called *Roe v. Wade* as difficult to overturn as *Brown v. Board of Education.* Perkins quickly sent out a bulletin asking supporters to call the Senate majority leader, Bill Frist, and insist Specter not be allowed to head the Judiciary Committee, saying that Specter's comments were "the height of arrogance and ingratitude." Dobson, who had tried to defeat Specter in the primary, accused the senator of "arrogant grandstanding," and said he "must be derailed."[211] Along with Phyllis Schlafly and others, he repeated Perkins's appeal to supporters, and within a few days the phone lines of the Republicans on the committee were overwhelmed with calls. Specter issued a statement saying, "I have never, and would never, apply any litmus test on the abortion issue," and "I expect to work well with President Bush on the judicial confirmation process in the years ahead." Only after making a few similar pledges to his Republican colleagues did they allow him to take the chair of the Judiciary Committee.[212] Frist, however, soon added two Christian right allies, Senators Sam Brownback and Tom Coburn, to the committee.

Bush, however, disappointed them. His second Inaugural Address overflowed with biblical imagery, but he said nothing about the social conservative agenda except for one oblique reference to abortion. His domestic priorities, it soon became clear, would be making the tax cuts permanent and partly privatizing Social Security. In an interview with *The Washington Post* Bush signaled he would not make much of an effort to pass the Federal Marriage Amendment, saying "nothing will happen" because the senators don't see the need for it.[213] Arlington Group members, including Dobson, Land, Bauer, and Falwell, sent Karl Rove an indignant letter, dated January 18, asking, "Is [the president] prepared to spend significant political capital on [privatizing Social Security] but reluctant to devote the same energy to preserving traditional marriage?" If so, they wrote, "it would create outrage with countless voters, . . . including an unprecedented number of African-Americans, Latinos and Catholics who broke with tradition and supported the president solely because of this issue." And they warned, "When the administration adopts a defeatist attitude on an issue that is at the top of our agenda, it becomes impossible to unite our movement on an issue such as Social Security privatization where there are already deep misgivings."[214] A White House spokesman quickly assured them that Bush had been talking about the situation in the Senate and not his personal commitment or his willingness to support the amendment.[215] But they had heard him correctly the first time. The Federal Marriage Amendment, as even its congressional backers admitted, still did not have the votes needed to pass the Senate, and Bush, intent on partially privatizing Social Security, did nothing to press the issue.

Dobson, among others, was not happy, but as he had recently told a *New York Times* reporter, he was prepared for some disappointments from Bush. "He does not take the bully pulpit and use it effectively," but he was, he said, confident that the president would do the right thing in nominating social conservatives to the courts.[216] In a letter to his supporters he had promised "a battle of enormous proportions from sea to shining sea" if Bush failed to appoint "strict constructionist" judges or if the Democrats filibustered conservative nominees. Recalling Senator Daschle's defeat in November, he told the *Times* he had singled out six vulnerable Democrats up for reelection in 2006 and threatened that they would be "in the bull's eye" if they continued to block conservative judges. His political energies, he said, would be concentrated on the courts because, as he later told *Time* magazine, "religious liberty and the institution of the family [and] every other issue we care about is linked in one way or another to the courts."[217]

In an aside to the *Times* reporter Dobson said he had begun working on Daschle's defeat ever since August 2003, when he had attended a rally for Chief Justice Roy Moore of Alabama and saw the depths of the resentment toward the liberal court decisions.[218] The comment was revealing, for the Moore case was in many ways a touchstone for the views of Christian right leaders. Moore had installed a two-and-half-ton granite monument engraved with the Ten Commandments in the rotunda of the judicial building in Montgomery and had been refusing a federal court order to remove it. "Roy's rock," as many called the monument, had become a favorite subject for cartoonists, but the case was not just about the Ten Commandments on a four-foot-tall rock. To reporters Dobson spoke of replacing liberal with conservative judges, but the case Moore made in refusing to remove the rock involved the meaning of the First Amendment and the separation of church and state established by forty years of Supreme Court jurisprudence. Supported by Alabama politicians, the rallies for Moore in 2003 had the elements of a southern populist rebellion against the federal government, such as those waged against the civil rights acts.

The saga of Moore and "Roy's rock" had begun several years earlier. As circuit court judge in Etowah County, Alabama, in the early 1990s, Moore hung a wooden plaque he had hand-carved with the Ten Commandments over his bench and began court sessions with prayers. Neither practice was at all uncommon in the Deep South at the time, but the local ACLU had, after a warning, brought suit in 1995, declaring both of them unconstitutional. The Alabama governor, Fob James, had instructed Assistant Attorney General Bill Pryor to file suit on Moore's behalf, but to the surprise of many in Alabama, a colleague of Moore's, a state court judge, had ruled for the ACLU.

Moore appealed the ruling, declaring that the judge could take his job or jail him for contempt, but the Ten Commandments would stay as long as he was in the courtroom. The governor went farther. After listening to Richard Land at an SBC prayer luncheon denounce the Supreme Court decision against school prayer and exhort his listeners to resist the intrusion of the government into spiritual affairs, Fob James got up and said, "The only way those Ten Commandments and that prayer will be stripped from that court is with the force of arms."[219] Later on the radio he dared the judge to enforce the ruling, promising that the state troopers and the National Guard would be there to greet him. His threat of force soon brought a swarm of national newspaper and TV reporters to Montgomery, and while James held center stage, Moore appeared on the *Today* show and Pryor on Dobson's radio program.[220]

Governor Fob James, best known for reinstituting prison chain gangs, and for mimicking an ape when declaring his faith in the biblical account of creation, had always made the state's business leaders cringe, but Moore was no rural Alabama innocent. A West Point graduate who has served as the captain of a Military Police battalion in Vietnam in the early 1970s, he had lived out of state for many years. Defeated twice in elections for circuit court judge in the 1980s, he had, after his appointment to fill the seat of a judge who had died in office, won his first election in 1994 on the strength of his defiance of the ACLU warning. His refusal to take the plaque down made him a folk hero in Alabama. A 1996 poll showed that almost 90 percent of Alabamans supported his right to display the Ten Commandments. The Alabama House of Representatives overwhelmingly passed a resolution supporting the display.[221]

The case also made Moore something of a celebrity in the Christian right. D. James Kennedy's Coral Ridge Ministries raised $100,000 for his legal defense fund, and he appeared on *The 700 Club*. The Alabama Christian Coalition and the American Family Association organized a rally for him in Montgomery with thousands of people from around the country and speakers who included the national heads of the two organizations, Ralph Reed, Don Wildmon, as well as George Grant and the perennial candidate for the presidency, Alan Keyes.[222] Richard Land, however, was not among them. Southern Baptists had a long tradition of support for the separation of church and state, and nine Alabama pastors, including the pastor of the First Baptist Church in Auburn, filed a brief opposing Moore on the grounds that the government should not be promoting religion. Land, apparently torn between opposing groups in the SBC, took the convoluted position that he would not support prayer in a courtroom unless people were given the option to leave the court and prayers of other faiths were accepted.[223]

In 1998 the Alabama Supreme Court dismissed the case on technical grounds, and two years later, petitioned by the Alabama Christian Family Association, Moore ran for chief justice of the Alabama Supreme Court.[224] Campaigning on the need to "return God to our public life and restore the moral foundation of our law," he won easily, defeating the candidate backed by the state's business establishment.[225] By his account, he immediately contracted with a sculptor to build a granite monument depicting the Ten Commandments to place in the rotunda of the judicial building in Montgomery.[226] On its installation he gave Coral Ridge Ministries video photographers exclusive access to the rotunda that night, and D. James Kennedy advertised the videos for $19 on his television show for the Moore defense fund.[227]

As expected, the ACLU filed suit, along with Americans United and the Montgomery-based Southern Poverty Law Center. By the time the case came before a federal district judge in October 2002, Moore had hired Herb Titus, Robertson's former law school dean, as one of his lead attorneys and adopted a new defense strategy. In answer to the charge that the monument promoted religion, he argued the Ten Commandments had to be in court because God was the foundation of American law and religious liberty. On top of that he argued in essence that the country was a Christian nation because the Founders had intended the establishment clause of the First Amendment solely to protect diversity among Christian sects by preventing the establishment of any one of them.[228]

When the federal district judge Myron Thompson rejected his arguments, Moore appealed the decision to the Eleventh Circuit Court of Appeals and came up with another argument: the purpose of the First Amendment, he claimed, was to prevent the federal government from interfering with the worship of God by the states and the people, and therefore in this case the federal court had no authority over the justice system of Alabama.[229]

The Circuit Court upheld the district court's opinion, and on August 5, 2003, Judge Thompson ordered the monument removed from the rotunda by August 20. On the 14th Moore announced that he had no intention of removing the Ten Commandments and "the moral foundation of our law." This time he had no help from the state government: a new governor had taken office, and Attorney General Bill Pryor, who had been nominated for a federal appeals court judgeship, no longer supported him. Undeterred, Moore, riding the new wave of press attention, hired a media spokesperson and appeared on *Hannity and Colmes.* On the 16th a rally organized by Rick Scarborough, a Texas pastor and the head of a Christian right organization, Vision America, brought two thousand people from across the country to join a local crowd in Montgomery. Alan Keyes, Jerry Falwell, Howard Phillips, and Scarborough gave speeches on the steps of the state capitol, and for the next two weeks people gathered in and around the judicial building—some kneeling by the monument in protest. When the Supreme Court rejected an emergency appeal, twenty-two people were arrested in the rotunda. The deadline for the removal of the monument passed, a Judicial Inquiry Commission suspended Moore, and on August 27 the monument was removed to a storage room. The next day more than 1,200 people gathered to hear Dobson and Keyes speak from the steps of the judicial building. Dobson warned the crowd that "the liberal elite and the judges at the highest level and some members of the media are determined to remove every evidence of faith in God from this entire culture." People, he said, should send a message to Congress that the federal courts needed to be "reined in. . . . Let Congress know this is not going to continue." Dobson compared Roy Moore's act of civil disobedience to that of Rosa Parks, who had launched her bus boycott just blocks away.[230]

Of course, had Dobson come to the rally on the 16th and spoken on the steps of the capitol, he might have trod on the bronze star that marked the spot where Jefferson Davis took his oath of office. Dobson might also have looked around and found himself amid Christian Reconstructionists, such as Titus and Phillips. He might also have noticed the absence of other Christian right leaders, such as Land and Jay Sekulow, both of whom had urged Moore to obey "the rule of law." [231]

Moore was removed from office, but the case continued to reverberate in Christian right and southern Republican circles. In 2004 Moore and Titus in consultation with Howard Phillips wrote a bill introduced by Alabama representatives into both houses of Congress.[232] The Constitution Restoration Act, as the bill was known, sought to strip federal judges of their power to hear cases dealing with any state or local government's "acknowledgment of God as the sovereign source of law, liberty and government." In other words the First Amendment did not apply to state or local governments—an argument that came right out of Moore's defense. Citing Article III of the Constitution (which created the federal court system), the Constitution Restoration Act provided that federal judges could be impeached for taking religious liberty cases forbidden by the bill. Further, it restricted federal judges from recognizing foreign or international law in their opinions.[233] Though the bill died in committee, the Republican platform of 2004 explicitly supported the legislation. It called for using Article III of the Constitution "to limit federal court jurisdiction," in such instances as "when judges are abusing their power by banning the use of 'under God' in the Pledge of Allegiance, or prohibiting depictions of the Ten Commandments, and potential actions invalidating the Defense of Marriage Act." "Additionally," it declared, "we condemn judicial activists and their unwarranted and unconstitutional restrictions on the free exercise of religion in the public square."[234]

The Constitution Restoration Act was reintroduced in the spring of 2005, this time with thirty southern Republican cosponsors, and in early April, Moore, Titus, and Phillips appeared as featured speakers at a conference Rick Scarborough convened in Washington titled "Confronting the Judicial War on Faith." Scarborough had written a booklet, *In Defense of Mixing Church and State*, and a flyer for the conference read: "We have come to perceive activist judges as the greatest threat to life and liberty. When the courts abandon their legitimate role as impartial arbiters, and seek to impose their will on a nation, a free people must respond."[235] The two hundred activists assembled included Christian right stalwarts, among them Jerry Falwell, Tony Perkins, Michael Farris, and Phyllis Schlafly, but also Christian Reconstructionists such as Michael Peroutka, a member of the Confederate League of the South, and the presidential candidates for Phillips's Constitution Party in 2004.[236] To the surprise of some Washington reporters these "fringe figures" were joined by several Capitol Hill aides, two congressmen, and on a video screen by Tom DeLay, the House majority leader. Appearing via satellite from Rome, where he had gone to attend the funeral of Pope John Paul II, DeLay spoke of a judiciary "run amok" and said that to rein it in Congress had to reassert its "constitutional authority over the courts."[237]

During the conference tempers ran high. Perkins called the judiciary "more of a threat to representative government than terrorism," and Alan Keyes called it "the focus of evil."[238] Speakers proposed various methods of stripping the courts, many of them making Titus and Moore's bill look reasonable. Farris said he would block judicial power by abolishing the concept of binding judicial precedents and by allowing Congress to vacate court decisions.[239] Schlafly called for a constitutional amendment to allow Congress to overturn Supreme Court rulings and term limits for federal judges.[240] Michael Schwartz, the chief of staff to Senator Tom Coburn, argued that judicial review of congressional laws went "counter to the very

basis of the Republic" and should be abolished.[241] Several participants asserted the right of the president and Congress to disregard court decisions
they think are unconstitutional.[242] Some claimed Congress could abolish
the federal courts or simply defund them, yet on the whole, the most
popular solution to "judicial tyranny" was impeachment. Some speakers
named particular circuit court judges, and some called for mass impeach-
ments of those who believed in "a living Constitution."[243] Still, the favorite target was Justice Anthony M. Kennedy, the Reagan appointee who
had often disappointed them. In one session Schlafly said that Kennedy's
opinion forbidding capital punishment for juveniles was "a good ground
of impeachment," and amid cheers and applause Farris called the justice
"the poster boy for impeachment" for citing international norms in his
opinions.[244] Next, Edwin Vieira, a constitutional lawyer, accused Kennedy
of relying on "Marxist, Leninist, satanic principles" in his opinion in striking down the Texas anti-sodomy statute. Then in what might have been an
effort at a joke, he said that his "bottom line" for dealing with the Supreme
Court came from Joseph Stalin. "He had a slogan and it worked very well
for him, whenever he ran into difficulty: 'no man, no problem.'" (The full
quote, as the *Washington Post* reporter Dana Milbank later pointed out,
was "Death solves all problems: no man, no problem.") The audience
laughed, and Vieira repeated, "No man no problem," adding, "This is not
a structural problem we have; it's a problem of personnel."[245]

The frenzied atmosphere of the conference had much to do with the
case of Terri Schiavo, a Florida woman who had been brain-dead for fifteen years. The case had occasioned a very strange moment in Washington. Three weeks before Republican leaders under pressure from the
Christian right had called Congress back in the midst of Easter recess to
pass a bill on behalf of Schiavo, and the president had rushed back from
his Texas ranch to sign it in the middle of the night.

The Schiavo case had been a cause célèbre for the Christian right
for some years, though in essence it was a family dispute between the
woman's husband and her parents. In 1990 Schiavo at age twenty-six had
gone into cardiac arrest as the result of an eating disorder, and had suffered massive brain damage. She was diagnosed as being in a "persistent

vegetative state." Her husband, Michael, had taken her to a variety of doctors for experimental therapies with no result, and eight years later he had petitioned a Florida court for authorization to remove her feeding tube so she could die, as she had requested, and not have to live in her condition. Her parents, Robert and Mary Schindler, objected, claiming she was a devout Catholic who would not wish to violate the Church's teachings on euthanasia. They filed suit against Michael, and litigation went on for five years with a series of court decisions for her husband. In 2003 the Florida Supreme Court upheld the original ruling by the circuit court judge, George Greer, and the feeding tube was removed.

At that point the Schindlers decided to wage a public campaign. With money provided by right-to-life groups, they hired Randall Terry and showed homemade videos of their daughter appearing to smile and respond to her mother. Soon enough Dobson and other Christian right leaders took to the airwaves to protest Schiavo's fate. Under pressure Governor Jeb Bush, the president's brother, hired Ken Connor, a Florida trial lawyer and the former head of the Family Research Council, and filed a federal court brief on behalf of the Schindlers. The petition was denied. Next, the Republican-dominated state legislature, with Christian right groups tying up the phone lines, passed what was known as "Terri's Law," allowing the governor to intervene, and the feeding tube was reinserted.[246]

In September the following year the Florida Supreme Court ruled "Terri's Law" unconstitutional, and in January 2005 the U.S. Supreme Court declined to hear the case. As the case went back to Judge Greer, an outcry came from the Christian right. On *Hannity and Colmes*, Dobson said if the feeding tube were removed, "I'd consider it murder."[247] By that time all kinds of rumors had circulated—Schiavo's husband had beaten her, marks of abuse had been found on her body, there was a conspiracy to kill her—and Christian right leaders found themselves in possession of "facts" that contradicted the testimony of dozens of doctors, and that of the guardian appointed by Governor Bush. "She is not," Dobson said, "in a coma. She is not on life support. She is not in a vegetative state. She is being supported by food and water. If they take that away, she is going to suffer a very painful death." Judge Greer was a conservative Republican and a Southern Baptist, but Richard Land claimed that the judiciary had "condemned her to death" on nothing but "hearsay evidence" from her husband. "Terri Schiavo is in fairly good health," Land said.[248]

For the Christian right Schiavo had become a symbol not just of all victims of euthanasia and abortion but of Christianity crucified by judges. She "has become the poster girl for whether or not our people are going to force the legal system to give us the society we want," Land said on *Meet the Press*. "We're seeing this in case after case with homosexual marriage, with abortion, with the Terri Schiavo case. Are we going to have a government of the people, by the people and for the people, or a government of the judges, by the judges and for the judges?"[249]

Ken Connor, knowing that nothing more could be done at the state level, took the case to Washington. He persuaded Congressman Dave Weldon, a Florida Republican, to introduce a bill on Schiavo's behalf, and a week later Senator Mel Martinez, an ally of Governor Bush and former member of President Bush's cabinet, agreed to join Weldon. Not all Republicans liked the idea of congressional intervention, and there was a good deal of back-and-forth. Meanwhile time was running out.[250] Judge Greer had ordered the feeding tube removed on Friday, March 18, and a few days before the deadline, Tom DeLay and Bill Frist, the majority leaders of the House and Senate, took charge of the legislation. On the 16th the House passed a bill by unanimous consent offering a right to review in federal courts in cases when the family cannot agree on care for "incapacitated individuals." Frist, unable to rush a similar bill through the Senate, had his staff write a "private relief bill" allowing Schiavo's parents to appeal the case to the federal court. Amid growing friction among Republicans, an aide to Senator Martinez circulated a memo saying, "This is an important moral issue, and the pro-life base will be excited that the Senate is debating this important issue," and "This is a great political issue because Senator [Bill] Nelson of Florida has already refused to become a cosponsor, and this is a tough issue for the Democrats."[251] The Senate passed the bill on Thursday the 17th, but only after the House adjourned for a two-week Easter recess, and the bills were irreconcilable.[252]

As it happened, the Family Research Council was holding its annual meeting at the Willard Hotel. Senator Bill Frist addressed the group by telephone on Thursday, saying he had serious questions about Schiavo's diagnosis, and promised not to leave Washington the next day "until we do everything we can and ultimately save the life." [253] At Connor's urging, an FRC lobbyist called DeLay's office and said the House leader should take the extraordinary step of reconvening the House to pass the Senate's "private relief" bill and that a failure to do so would be "something we would not forget." [254] DeLay scrambled. His office floated ideas, such as staging a meeting in Schiavo's hospital room or subpoenaing Schiavo, her husband, and her doctors to testify before Congress, to prevent the removal of the feeding tube, but all were unrealistic. [255] The next day, Friday, March 18, DeLay turned up almost unannounced at the Willard Hotel and told an audience that included the leaders of Focus's state Family Policy Councils that he would do everything in his power to save Schiavo and would remain in Washington until the case was resolved. [256]

At the time DeLay was under investigation by a Texas prosecutor for shady campaign financing, and the Republican-dominated House Ethics Committee had reprimanded him for shaking down a corporation for campaign funds and attempted bribery. In his remarks he denounced what he said was a liberal campaign to destroy him and the entire conservative movement. "I tell you, ladies and gentlemen," he said, "one thing that God has brought to us is Terri Schiavo to elevate the visibility of what is going on in America. This is exactly the issue that is going on in America, of attacks against the conservative movement, against me and against many others." [257]

The following day, Saturday, the two Republican leaders negotiated a bill confined to the Schiavo case and called the House back from recess. "Every hour is incredibly important to Terri Schiavo," said DeLay, and Frist urged, "Remember Terri is alive, Terri is not in coma." The Senate majority leader acknowledged that the congressional action was highly unusual. "These are extraordinary circumstances that center on the most fundamental of human values and virtues: the sanctity of human life." The Senate with only a few members on hand approved the legislation by a voice vote on Sunday, but some House Democrats raised objections. Insisting on a roll call vote, they sent Republican leaders scurrying to summon lawmakers back to Washington to provide a quorum. DeLay called an extraordinary night session, and when the debate began at 9 p.m., some members likened the atmosphere to a vote to go to war. Representative F. James Sensenbrenner (R-WI), the chair of the Judiciary Committee, opened by saying that Ms. Schiavo needed to be protected from a "merciless directive" from a state judge, and that no constitutional right was "more sacred than the right to life." Democrats responded that these "gut-wrenching decisions" happened every day, and that Congress was overstepping its authority by inserting itself into a family matter better left to the states. The recall of Congress, they said, was an "unseemly" political move, and the bill a violation of the separation of powers. The bill passed at 12:01 a.m. Monday, and Bush signed it at one o'clock in the morning.[258]

Over the weekend the Schiavo case eclipsed every other story in Washington, including the Iraq War and the budget. Even small newspapers and local TV stations around the country covered the extraordinary congressional sessions and the return of the president to sign a bill that he could have signed in Texas a few hours later. While investigating the case, journalists discovered certain contradictions in the Republican behavior. Bill Frist, a Harvard-educated heart surgeon, had concluded that Schiavo was conscious by doing no more than watching her on the home video circulated by her parents. DeLay, who had called Michael Schiavo's decision "an act of barbarism," had, after his sixty-five-year-old father had been left brain-dead by a freak accident in 1988, joined the family consensus to let his father die. Then, as governor, George W. Bush had signed an end-of-life bill that, had the case been brought in Texas, would have given the Schiavo decision to her husband and doctors.[259] Newspaper columnists wrote scathingly that DeLay was trying to divert attention from the ethics charges against him and that Frist, whom many expected to run for president, was currying favor with the Christian right. Editorialists called the passage of the Schiavo bill "massive government meddling in the affairs of the states" and "a blow to the rule of law."[260]

Republicans had been prepared for some unfavorable press, but they were not prepared for the polls. An ABC poll released on Monday, the 21st, showed that 70 percent of the public said that the congressional action was inappropriate, and 67 percent said that lawmakers had become involved for political advantage rather than for principle. According to the survey, conservatives and evangelicals were more likely to support federal intervention than other groups, but in neither group did the support reach a majority. Then, 63 percent said they supported the removal of Schiavo's feeding tube, including 46 percent of the evangelicals surveyed. Moreover, the intensity of public opinion was on the side of Schiavo's husband, with more Americans strongly supporting the removal of the feeding tube than strongly opposed it. Republican spokesmen dismissed the survey, but in a CBS poll taken the following week, the proportion of those who thought the Congress and the president should have stayed out of the case reached 82 percent. Bush's favorability rating slid to 45 percent and that of Congress to 34 percent.[261]

*   *   *

Washington Republicans began to worry that they had become too closely associated with the Christian right, and many in Congress were furious with Frist and DeLay. The former majority leader Dick Armey, a libertarian conservative who had never liked DeLay, called "the Terri Schiavo thing" "pure, blatant pandering to James Dobson."[262] Frist began avoiding journalists. DeLay and his Christian right allies, on the other hand, blamed the public reaction on the liberal media and, continuing to believe that conservative Christians supported them, pressed their attack on the courts. The Schiavo case, Bauer said, will "bring more emotion into the view held by many conservatives already that the courts are rewriting the Constitution to suit their own value system."[263] After a federal appeals court rebuked the Congress for intervening, and the U.S. Supreme Court refused for the fourth time to take the case, fury at the courts redoubled. Senator John Cornyn (R-TX) mused about how a perception that judges are making political decisions could lead people to "engage in violence," and DeLay ominously declared that "the time will come for the men responsible for this to answer for their behavior."[264]

Schiavo died on March 31 after Judge Greer dismissed the last appeals. At the "Judicial War on Faith" conference a week later, the Schindlers' lawyer, David Gibbs, described Terri sobbing in her mother's arms after the courts condemned her to death, and Michael Peroutka called the removal of the feeding tube an act of "state-sponsored terrorism."[265] Michael Schwartz called for the impeachment of the two federal appellate judges who had ruled against the Congress. "I hope they serve long sentences," he said.[266] Phyllis Schlafly told the audience, "People who have been speaking out on this, like Tom DeLay and Senator Cornyn, need to be backed up." After Vieira's quotation of Stalin, "no man, no problem," Dana Milbank of *The Washington Post*, who was covering the conference, warned that the anti-judge furor had the potential to turn ugly. A judge in Atlanta and the husband and mother of a judge in Chicago had been killed in recent weeks. Judge Greer was under armed guard after death threats, and the SBC church he had belonged to for years had asked him to leave the congregation.[267] Toward the end of the conference the participants got down on the floor to pray. From somewhere in the audience a preacher started up, "Father, we echo the words of Apostle Paul, because we know Judge Greer claims to be a Christian. So the Apostle Paul said in First Corinthians 5, in the name of our Lord Jesus, when you are gathered together, with the power of our Lord Jesus Christ, deliver such a one to Satan for the destruction of the flesh that his spirit may be saved in the day of our Lord Jesus."[268]

Judge Greer survived the imprecatory prayer. DeLay, on the other hand, had to fight for his political life as a cloud of political scandals enveloped him. Then, while Republican strategists hoped the Schiavo affair would just go away, public disapproval continued to mount, even among evangelicals. Indeed, a Pew survey taken four months later showed that 69 percent of evangelicals and 68 percent of conservatives opposed the intervention of Congress and the president in the Schiavo case.[269] In Congress the backlash spurred Democrats and moderate Republicans, who had been cowed by the apparent strength of "values voters" in the November election, to resist the Republican leadership on ideologically driven initiatives.[270] Christian right leaders, however, enclosed in their echo chamber, paid no attention to the public verdict.

Dobson had not appeared at Scarborough's conference, but he didn't disagree with the participants. At the Family Research Council annual meeting he suggested the federal courts should be stripped of funding. "Very few people know this," he said, "that the Congress can simply disenfranchise a court. . . . All they have to do is say the 9th Circuit doesn't exist anymore, and it's gone." [271] Still, for him and his close allies, the immediate issue was the threat of another Democratic filibuster against Bush's most conservative nominees to the federal appeals courts. Conservatives had for some time been urging Frist to end the filibuster by a parliamentary procedure that Senator Trent Lott had dubbed "the nuclear option." Senate rules specified that sixty votes were required to end a filibuster and sixty-seven to change a rule, but the procedure would allow the Senate to override a rule, or a precedent, such as a filibuster, by majority vote, thereby depriving the minority of its traditional power to halt a vote. The Democrats had vowed to shut down all Senate business if the Republicans invoked the "nuclear option," and overhanging the Schiavo case had been the possibility of a constitutional crisis. [272]

Frist, no ideologue, was torn between the Christian right and business side of his party, which did not want a shutdown of the Senate. In his phone call to the FRC meeting about Schiavo, he had spoken of the need for "good judges" and of his commitment to ending the filibuster. [273] Later he had, however, distanced himself from DeLay's attack on the courts, saying, "I believe we have a fair and independent judiciary today." [274] He also said he hoped to avoid a fight over Senate rules, and Dobson, who was spending $1 million through Focus Action on radio and newspaper ads to pressure a handful of moderate Republicans to support the "nuclear option," feared he might accept a compromise. [275] With Chief Justice William Rehnquist ill with thyroid cancer, the decision would affect not just the circuit courts but the Supreme Court.

In late April Tony Perkins convened "Justice Sunday," a rally in a megachurch in Lexington, Kentucky, to protest the filibuster. Organizers of the event said they were hoping to enlist conservative Christians at the grass roots for the imminent Senate battle and that they hoped to reach a million people by distributing a telecast to churches around the country and to local cable stations and Christian radio and television networks. [276] Frist had agreed to appear on the telecast, though Perkins had billed the rally as a protest against anti-Christian discrimination. On the FRC website Perkins had written, "For years activist courts aided by liberal interest groups like the ACLU have been quietly working under the veil of the judiciary, like thieves in the night, to rob us of our Christian heritage and our religious freedom." A flyer for the rally read, "The filibuster was once used to protect racial bias, and now it's being used against people of faith." [277]

On the evening of Sunday, the 24th, television cameras were trained on the stage at High View Baptist Church, where enormous portraits of Bush's nominees surrounded the podium. The speakers included Dobson and Colson; Bishop Harry Jackson, an African American Pentecostal preacher from Maryland; plus William Donahue, the head of the Catholic League for Religious and Civil Rights; and Al Mohler of the SBC's Southern Seminary, whose church it was. [278] Dobson gave the most aggressive speech of the rally. Apparently oblivious that the evening was on the second day of Passover, he said, "The biggest Holocaust in world history came out of the Supreme Court." [279] He called federal judges "unelected and unaccountable and arrogant and imperious and determined to redesign the culture according to their own biases and values," and he railed against the "six or eight very squishy Republicans" who might not vote to end the filibuster. [280] Most of the speakers, however, stuck to the familiar theme of the victimization of Christians by Democrats and liberal judges. In calling for the confirmation of Attorney General Bill Pryor of Alabama, a Catholic, William Donahue argued that Senate Democrats were practicing "de facto" discrimination against Catholics by "setting the bar so high with the abortion issue" that no "real Catholics" could get over it. [281] Despite his theological anti-Catholicism, Al Mohler held up Pryor as someone who had been discriminated against because of "a deeply held personal belief that human life is sacred from the moment of conception." [282]

Then Mohler said something more interesting. In effect he explained the Christian right view of "strict construction." Asking rhetorically how the justices had found "a constitutional right to sodomy" in the *Lawrence v. Texas* decision, he answered, "by reading into the Constitution what they wanted to find"—as opposed to what the framers intended—and "by expanding the Constitution by reinterpretation." Now, he said, "of all people, we ought to be the folks who understand that. Because we as Christians have had to understand there are people who will take the word of God and say it's really not about the text. It's about what's behind the text. . . . And God's people have had to learn to discern and say no, the text is the inerrant and infallible word of God. It's what God says it is, and what God revealed it to be." But now, he said, "there are judges who are using the same exercise of interpretation to find in the Constitution what's not there." [283]

In making a parallel between reading the Bible and reading the Constitution, Mohler had come dangerously close to suggesting the Constitution was a sacred text. Explicitly he was saying that both texts have a fixed meaning and an objective truth. Here was eighteenth-century Common Sense Realism rearing its head at the beginning of the twenty-first century. Here was the willed innocence that allowed inerrantists, such as himself, to believe that, unlike liberal ministers and judges, they did not favor certain parts of the text above others or engage in any kind of interpretation. They knew what God and the framers intended; no one else's point of view was admissible, and there could be no compromise.

The evening culminated with the appearance of the Senate majority leader on a big screen above the audience. Frist did little more than reiterate his commitment to ending the filibuster, but he was introduced as a "friend of the family," and when he had finished, Perkins rushed onstage to tell viewers to call their senators. Meanwhile the names and phone numbers of Senators John McCain, Dick Lugar, and other "squishy Republicans" scrolled across the screen. [284]

A few weeks later seven Republican senators—including some of those that Dobson had spent a million dollars trying to pressure—joined with seven Democratic senators in reaching a deal to avert a crisis. Taking the matter out of Frist's hands, the so-called Gang of 14 agreed that three of Bush's nominees would get an up-or-down vote, ensuring their confirmation, and that two others would not, and would have to be withdrawn. The senators also agreed not to block future judicial nominees by filibuster except in "extraordinary circumstances." The agreement made no one completely happy, but the compromise was a tactical victory for conservatives in that the candidates the senators chose to confirm were the three most controversial of Bush's nominees still before the Senate, Janice Rogers Brown, Priscilla Owen, and William Pryor, the Alabama attorney general involved in the Ten Commandments case. Whether the agreement would extend to nominees to the Supreme Court had not been decided, but with the illness of Chief Justice William Rehnquist the Republicans had agreed to take the "nuclear option" off the table—at least for a while.[285]

Dobson could hardly believe it. When John McCain made the announcement, he said, "The Senate agreement represents a complete bailout and betrayal by a cabal of Republicans and a great victory for united Democrats."[286] Soon afterward he taped a broadcast with Tony Perkins and Gary Bauer to mourn the decision. "This one hit me personally harder than anything ever has coming out of Washington," he said. "I literally went home and hugged Shirley [his wife] and pulled over the covers and went to bed."[287] Bauer said, "I felt like someone had punched me in the stomach," and Perkins confessed that when he heard the news, he and his coworkers "began to pray about the situation, but I'll tell you what, I wanted to cry."[288]

In early July Justice Sandra Day O'Connor announced her retirement from the court, and Dobson was considerably relieved when a few weeks later Bush nominated John Roberts, a judge on the U.S. Court of Appeals for the D.C. Circuit, who had served in the Justice Department of the Reagan administration. Roberts, a Catholic, did not have a long record of speeches or opinions on issues the Christian right cared about, but Jay Sekulow and Leonard Leo, the head of Catholic outreach for the Republican Party, had, at the behest of the White House, spent a year quietly reassuring conservative Christians about him. They had, they said, become comfortable that Roberts would fit the president's standards of a jurist in the mold of Antonin Scalia and Clarence Thomas and that he would be a good bet for their side on abortion, same-sex marriage, and public support for religion. Sekulow personally vouched for him, as did Professor Robert George of Princeton. After his nomination, George and Dobson joined a conference call with reporters. "I think we know a lot about Judge Roberts," Dobson said, and "we believe the issues we care about will be handled carefully by this judge."[289]

Perkins then began to organize another "Justice Sunday," to support Roberts, sending out a mass mailing asking for donations to combat "a secret liberal strategy" to destroy Roberts. But then on August 4 the *Los*

Angeles Times revealed that Roberts, when in private practice, had worked pro bono for a gay activist group. That would have been bad enough, but he had also helped prepare the argument in the Supreme Court case against the Colorado law of 1992, passed in a ballot initiative Dobson had supported, that would have permitted landlords and employers to discriminate against homosexuals. The case, *Romer v. Evans*, had resulted in a landmark Supreme Court decision for gay rights. Immediately some of Dobson's allies abandoned the Roberts cause. The editor of *WorldNetDaily* criticized the plans for the second Justice Sunday rally and Gary Bauer denounced Bush for picking "a stealth nominee," and demanded that the White House produce the files on Roberts it had not released to the Judiciary Committee. On *Hannity and Colmes* Dobson said the *Romer* case "was perhaps one of the most egregious decisions ever handed down by the Supreme Court," and "to have Judge Roberts be part of that in any way was troubling." Still, he reassured the audience that "he had a very minor role," and August 14, Justice Sunday II, sponsored by the FRC and Focus Action, took place as planned.[290]

Held in Two Rivers Baptist, an SBC megachurch in Nashville, Tennessee, the telecast rally featured many of the same speakers as the first. Frist had not been invited because, deliberately distancing himself from the Christian right, he had made a floor speech calling for more federal funding for embryonic stem cell research. DeLay took his place, along with five other House Republicans.[291] In opening the event Perkins took pains to say that Justice Sunday II was not a rally to support John Roberts but "to raise awareness of why every American should be concerned about who sits on the Supreme Court."[292] A photograph of Roberts nonetheless loomed large on a screen in the auditorium, and Dobson in a video appearance urged viewers to defend Roberts "from the likes of Senators Edward Kennedy and Patrick Leahy" by calling, emailing, or faxing their senators. "It looks like John Roberts is, we think so, a strict constructionist," he said, somewhat tentatively. Perkins urged viewers to be in prayer right up until Roberts's nomination hearings.[293] Other speakers mentioned Roberts only in passing, for the central theme of the evening was an attack on the Supreme Court.

In now familiar rhetoric speakers condemned activist jurists "legislating from the bench," "unelected, life-time appointed" persons in black robes, and the decisions on abortion, sodomy, and pornography. "That is not judicial independence," DeLay roared. "That's judicial supremacy. That's judicial tyranny." [294] Dobson also went on about "judicial tyranny" and said, "America's court system is tearing at the very fabric of the nation." [295] On this occasion he suggested no remedy, but others did. DeLay questioned the power of the Supreme Court to strike down laws passed by Congress it found unconstitutional. Donahue, after warning Democrats not to discriminate against Roberts because of his Catholic faith, argued that ruling any congressional law unconstitutional should require a unanimous vote by all nine justices. [296] Curiously, the speakers made no distinction among Supreme Court justices, nor did they even try to explain to viewers why they were at the same time supporting a Bush nominee and attacking the judicial system itself.

As usual, the victimization of Christians was a constant refrain, but this time it was more than matched by its complement, triumphalism. Bishop Harry Jackson, the one African American preacher there, spoke of "the black church" teaming up with white evangelical churches and the Catholic Church and said, "We need to tell both parties, 'It's our way or the highway.' You and I can bring the ruling reign of the cross to America." [297] Donahue, apparently unable to stop himself, charged that "the left" had forced Christians "to sit at the back of the bus," and then declared, "It's time we moved to the front of the bus and that we took command of the wheel!" [298] In the last speech of the day Jerry Sutton, the pastor of High View Baptist Church and first vice president of the Southern Baptist Convention, urged the pastors in the audience to get involved. "It's a new day," he said in closing, "Liberalism is dead. The majority of Americans are conservative." [299]

Contrary to Perkins's and Dobson's view that liberals were out to destroy Roberts, Democrats on the Judiciary Committee did not oppose Bush's nominee, thanks in part to the Gang of 14's compromise. When William Rehnquist died in early September, Bush nominated Roberts for chief justice, and a few weeks later, on September 27, Roberts was confirmed by a bipartisan vote of 78–22. Christian right leaders still did not know what to make of Roberts, and for them the crucial question remained who would succeed Sandra Day O'Connor, the justice who had often been the swing vote on the Court.

*   *   *

While the Christian right agitated in Washington, a wave of attacks on the teaching of evolution rolled across the country in school boards and state legislatures from Alabama to Wisconsin. The No Child Left Behind Act with its mandatory testing had prompted states to rewrite their curricula, giving anti-evolutionists an opportunity to challenge them.

The case that attracted the most attention was in Kansas, where the November election had put a majority of religious conservatives on the state school board. In three days of hearings in May the board heard from twenty-three witnesses, many of them from the Discovery Institute in Seattle testifying that Darwinian evolution relied on too many unproven assumptions and that living organisms were so complex they could not be explained by natural causes. None cited Genesis or claimed the earth was only six or ten thousand years old. In 1987 the Supreme Court had held that the teaching of creationism was a constitutionally impermissible introduction of religion into public education. Since then scholars at the Discovery Institute had developed a new approach. Resting their case on microbiology, they claimed that the complexity of design inherent in organisms, such as an eye, could be explained only by invoking an "intelligent designer." They did not ask that the schools ban the teaching of evolution; they did not ask them to adopt their own concept of "Intelligent Design," explaining that while it was a robust frontier of science, that it wasn't yet ripe for students. Instead they asked that the schools teach that there was a controversy between evolution and Intelligent Design. Not to do so, they said, would be a breach of academic freedom and the endorsement of an ideology.[300]

The approach was poll-tested and seemed to hold promise. Asked whether the schools should "teach the controversy," almost 70 percent of the American public agreed. The movement gained ground with the success of the Christian right in the election, and by late summer of 2005 the National Center for Science Education had recorded seventy-eight clashes in thirty-one states in school districts and state legislatures—or twice the usual number. Three states, Ohio, New Mexico, and Minnesota, adopted the "teach the controversy" approach, and George W. Bush endorsed it, saying that both evolution and Intelligent Design should be taught in schools "so people can understand what the debate is about."[301] The Kansas case brought local and national scientific organizations out to protest, but without success, for in the wake of the hearings the state school board adopted new standards, including Intelligent Design as an alternative to evolution but without endorsing it, as the Discovery Institute had advised, providing a definition of science that was not strictly limited to "natural explanations."[302]

Students in Kansas were thus going to be taught that the supernatural was a part of science. At least until the next school board election.

On October 3 Bush in a surprise move nominated his White House counsel, Harriet E. Miers, to succeed O'Connor. A lawyer with no judicial experience, Miers had joined the White House staff in 2001, and she had been leading the search for judicial nominees, including nominees to the Supreme Court. Before the end of the day conservatives, among others, were asking serious questions about her qualifications. Rove, who was clearly expecting trouble, started calling Christian right leaders to ward off conservative opposition even before the president made the announcement at 8 a.m. Throughout the day White House representatives made calls and held teleconferences with Dobson, Land, Colson, Weyrich, Perkins, Bauer, Falwell, Robertson, and others.[303] In one teleconference with thirteen members of the Arlington Group's executive committee, Justice Nathan Hecht, a conservative on the Texas Supreme Court and an old friend of Miers's, said that the nominee attended a very conservative evangelical church in Dallas and that he knew she was personally opposed to abortion because she had attended pro-life events with him.[304] Leonard Leo, an official on leave from the Federalist Society, circulated a memorandum saying that she was a friend and that in the early 1990s she had pushed for the American Bar Association to retract its support of abortion rights.[305]

By the end of the day Dobson and Richard Land declared themselves satisfied, as did Falwell and Robertson. Land said, "If the president trusts Harriet Miers . . . then I trust Harriet Miers."[306] Dobson told *The New York*

Times that he supported Miers partly because of her faith and partly because "I have reason to believe she's pro-life." He declined to discuss his conversations with the White House. "Some of what I know, I'm not at liberty to talk about," he said.[307]

The reaction from other conservatives was one of disbelief. The president had ignored the list of conservative judges and legal scholars they had carefully prepared and chosen someone with no legal record on abortion, gay rights, or religion in public life.[308] "Conservatives feel betrayed," Viguerie said in a statement. Bauer told *The New York Times* that conservatives had been advising Bush for weeks not to pick Miers and warned that the ramifications would be felt not just by Bush but by the Republican Party. Perkins called off the Justice Sunday he had planned to support the new nominee.[309]

Conservative commentators, among them George Will and William Kristol, wrote scathingly of Miers's lack of legal credentials and her close ties with Bush.[310] Miers, as some noted, had been in private practice until she joined the White House staff. She'd headed a large law firm in Dallas, and the Texas Bar Association. She had met Bush through Hecht, and in 1994 had joined his gubernatorial transition team. The following year she had become his personal lawyer, and Bush had appointed her to head the Texas Lottery Commission. She worked on his first presidential campaign and joined him in Washington. She had served as assistant to the president and deputy chief of staff for policy until 2004, when Bush appointed her to succeed another old Texas friend of his, Alberto Gonzales, after he had appointed Gonzales attorney general. In his column in *The Washington Post* Charles Krauthammer wrote, "If Miers were not a crony of the President of the United States, her nomination to the Supreme Court would be a joke as it would have occurred to no one else to nominate her."[311] More troubling for her nomination, conservative Republican senators, among them Sam Brownback, John Thune, and Trent Lott, started expressing doubts about her legal views and her qualifications. "Trust but verify," said Brownback, echoing Reagan on arms control.[312]

The following day, Wednesday, Dobson devoted his entire Focus on the Family broadcast to the Miers nomination. Saying he knew that many Christian conservatives were "angered and disillusioned," he explained that he supported Miers because he knew the church she went to and was sure of her religious faith. "I know the person who brought her to the Lord. I have talked at length to people who know her, and have known her for a long time." He also suggested the White House had given him privileged information. "When you know some of the things I know— that I probably shouldn't know—you'll know why I say with fear and trepidation . . . that I believe Harriet Miers will be a good justice."[313] On Thursday he joined a White House conference call to hundreds of conservative activists across the county in which he, Land, Colson, Sekulow, and a few other conservative evangelical leaders argued for Bush's trustworthiness on Miers.[314]

Within the week Senator Arlen Specter and Democrats on the Judiciary Committee were threatening Dobson with a subpoena. "If Dr. Dobson knows something he shouldn't know, or something I ought to know, I'm going to find out," Specter said on ABC's *This Week*. "If there are backroom assurances and deals . . . I think that's a matter that ought to be known by the Judiciary Committee and the American people."[315] When press queries and calls from conservatives overwhelmed the switchboard at Focus, Dobson said he would devote a broadcast to disclosing what the White House had told him.[316]

On his next program Dobson said that Karl Rove had given him clearance to reveal what he could not before. Miers was an evangelical "from a very conservative church that is almost universally pro-life." She had challenged the American Bar Association's pro–abortion rights position, and she had been a member of the Texas Right to Life organization.[317] In other words, Rove had told him nothing about Miers's legal views, and nothing more than had been in the press—though, if he were quoting his source accurately, Rove had given him some misinformation. (As the head of the Texas Bar Association, Miers had challenged the ABA only on its procedures in dealing with controversial issues, and it was unclear whether she had ever been a member of Texas Right to Life.) It also transpired that Dobson had never spoken directly to Miers's pastor, or to Hecht, as he claimed he had.[318]

In their preliminary meetings with Miers, the members of the Senate Judiciary Committee found her ill-prepared and uninformed on the law.

After she handed back the usual questionnaire about her career and the cases she had handled involving constitutional issues, Senators Specter and Leahy called the answers inadequate. "The comments I have heard range from 'incomplete' to 'insulting,'" Leahy, the ranking minority member, said in a news conference on October 19.[319] In an embarrassing slip, Miers had written of "the proportional representation requirement of the Equal Protection Clause," when proportional representation was nowhere in the Constitution. Specter asked her for a more detailed response to the questionnaire saying she must provide "amplification on many, many of the items."[320] Announcing plans to begin the confirmation hearings on November 7, he said it would be an "unusual hearing" in which all eighteen senators would have "probing questions."[321] At that point Senators Lindsey Graham and Sam Brownback gave Miers an exit strategy by drafting a letter asking the White House to turn over legal memoranda she had written for Bush, knowing the memos were protected by executive privilege and she could refuse to proffer them.[322]

On October 26 *The Washington Post* reported on a speech, provided to the Senate Judiciary Committee, that Miers had given to a group called the Executive Women of Dallas in 1993. Miers, it seemed, was a libertarian. On issues such as abortion and school prayer she endorsed a principle of "self-determination." In the course of the speech she remarked, "The on-going debate continues surrounding the attempt to once again criminalize abortions, or to once and for all guarantee the freedom of the individual . . . to decide for herself whether she will have an abortion." She went on to assert, "We gave up . . . legislating religion or morality," adding, "When science cannot determine the facts, and decisions are based on religious beliefs, then the government should not act."[323]

Tony Perkins went ballistic. "Miss Miers' words are a close paraphrase of the infamous *Roe v. Wade* decision," he wrote on the FRC website. "Her use of terms like 'criminalize abortion' . . . should have sounded alarms in the White House during the vetting process." Concerned Women for America demanded that Miers withdraw her nomination.[324] When Miers took the exit Graham and Brownback had opened for her, saying the senators' requests for confidential documents were potentially damaging to the independence of the executive branch, Dobson issued a statement welcoming her decision. He said he was dismayed to learn about the speech Miers gave in 1993. Claiming that he had expressed only "tentative support" for her nomination, he said, "Based on what we now know about Miss Miers, it appears that we would not have been able to support her candidacy."[325]

Three days later the White House announced the nomination of Samuel Alito, a federal circuit court judge with a reputation for taking a methodical and cautious approach to the law and a fifteen-year record of opinions that conservatives could embrace. In January Alito was confirmed in a narrowly partisan vote, and afterward Alito sent Dobson a note of thanks.[326] But the damage was done.

By the end of October it was hard to say whether Dobson or Bush had taken the bigger beating from the Miers episode. Bush looked a fool, or worse, for nominating an unqualified crony. Bush's words of support for her—"I know her heart"—inspired Stephen Colbert to invent the word "truthiness." When "trust me" wasn't enough, he had flirted with the constitutional prohibition on religious tests for office by selling her candidacy on the basis of her evangelical faith. Even Miers's withdrawal did not help because Democrats could make the point that she had been forced out because of insufficiently right-wing views on abortion and that the Christian right had a disproportionate influence on the Bush White House.

As for Dobson, his credibility with supporters and others on the Christian right had always rested on his claim to stand up for principle independent of politics, and he had badly compromised it. Richard Land, Charles Colson, and Jay Sekulow had also joined the White House efforts to convince other conservatives to support Miers, and Dobson surely believed, as Sekulow had put it on *The 700 Club*, it was "a big opportunity for us . . . that share an evangelical faith in Christianity, to see someone with our positions put on the Court."[327] Still, as Bauer had said, there was no evidence that Miers shared their positions on the law. Dobson had made a spectacle of himself by claiming that Rove had given him privileged information that Miers would oppose *Roe v. Wade*. That he had none suggested that he was simply boasting of his access to the White House. Falwell and Robertson, too, had dropped hints that they had inside information about Miers, but Dobson had most obviously given way to the temptation to show himself off as an intimate of the president. Possibly he feared losing his access to Rove. Whatever was the case, the public perception was that he had been carrying water for the White House. And he was conscious of it, for on the same broadcast when he claimed to have inside information, he had insisted that he was not acting as "a shill" for the Bush administration.[328]

The Miers episode might have passed into history as an aberration but instead it confirmed what many Americans saw as a pattern. Just three weeks before Miers withdrew, Michael Brown, the head of FEMA, the Federal Emergency Management Agency, and another Bush crony, had resigned in disgrace. His attempt to cope with the devastation of New Orleans after Hurricane Katrina had been hopelessly inept, and Bush had become the object of political satire for his feckless ("Brownie, you're doing a heck of a job") response to the hurricane that killed 1,400 people on the Gulf Coast. Iraq was in turmoil, and by then it had become clear that Saddam Hussein had no weapons of mass destruction, and the Bush administration had failed to plan for the aftermath of the invasion. Two thousand servicemen and -women had been killed since Bush had announced "Mission Accomplished," and while administration officials continued to issue rosy pronouncements, the violence continued to mount with no end in sight. Then, the Miers episode recalled the Schiavo affair and the absurd deference of the president and the Republican congressional leadership to the Christian right.

At the beginning of the year both Bush and the Christian right had claimed victory and a clear mandate, but by December the mandate had disappeared. Bush's approval rating had gone steadily downward to less than 40 percent. His priority second-term program—the partial privatization of Social Security—had proved almost universally unpopular and had vanished without a trace. As for the Christian right, it had not a single legislative achievement to point to. The Iraq War and Katrina largely accounted for the decline in Bush's polls, but the Schiavo affair had begun a shift in the balance of power in the Congress. The backlash had emboldened Democrats, who had feared that moral and religious issues had carried the election for the Republicans. It also convinced moderate Republicans that they could break ranks with their leadership without cost when they needed to. Before the Schiavo affair, a number of Democrats had helped the Republican leadership pass a number of ideologically charged bills, such as that permitting oil drilling in the Arctic National Wildlife Refuge, but after it their support for most Republican initiatives evaporated. Along with moderate Republicans, they forced House leaders to reduce spending cuts for Medicare, food stamps, and education, and to abandon drilling in the refuge. In addition the Republican caucus began to shy away from Christian right issues. "The Schiavo case absolutely made the leadership reluctant to take up controversial social issues," Weyrich told the *St. Petersburg Times*.[329] The Christian right had expected—and the congressional leadership had planned for—votes on constitutional amendments banning gay marriage, banning the desecration of the U.S. flag, and promoting prayer in public schools, but all the amendments were put off. They had also expected various bills limiting abortion, such as one requiring pregnant women to be told that a fetus could feel pain and another requiring them to view an ultrasound image of the fetus, but by December the bills had gone nowhere. "Everyone was talking about 'values voters' last year," Tony Perkins wrote on the Family Research Council website in December, but "What has the GOP done for 'values voters' this year? We're still waiting for action on marriage. We're still waiting for stronger pro-life initiatives."[330]

The answer was the Republicans had given the Christian right what it had fought the hardest for: two more conservative justices that put them in reach of a reliably conservative majority on the Supreme Court. As for the rest, they would have to wait for some time. By the end of the year the Texas prosecutor had indicted DeLay for criminal conspiracy and money laundering related to illegal campaign financing, and the U.S. Justice Department had made him a target of a probe into the scandals surrounding the former lobbyist Jack Abramoff. DeLay was forced to leave his post as majority leader, and his resignation ended the rule of "the Hammer" and the most powerful ally the Christian right had ever had in Congress.

To many Democrats and moderate Republicans, the White House and the Republican leadership had seemed to have become a captive of the Christian right. To many evangelicals the opposite seemed to be the case: the Christian right had become a function of Republican politics.

16

THE NEW EVANGELICALS

F OR MOST of the year after the 2004 election the power of the
Christian right in the Bush administration, the demonstrations
for Roy Moore, and the Kansas School Board decision created
what one critic called "an evangelical scare" among journalists and others. Some writers raised the specter of a Christian right intent on taking
over and making America a Christian nation. The sociologist Sara Diamond and journalists such as Chip Berlet, Fred Clarkson, and Michelle
Goldberg claimed the Christian right subscribed to Reconstructionist ideology of "dominionism," or the belief that "Christians had a God-given
right to rule all earthly institutions."[1] (By their account, "soft dominionists" were Christian nationalists who stopped short of wanting to sup-
plant the Constitution, while "hard dominionists," wanted the U.S. to be
a theocracy.[2]) A documentary film, *Jesus Camp*, nominated for an Academy Award, showed a charismatic summer camp where, according to its
leader, children were to be "indoctrinated into Christian values" to serve
as "the army of God." Kevin Phillips, the former Republican strategist
who had once triumphantly announced the emergence of a Republican
majority with its base in the South, titled his new book *American Theocracy*,
writing that "the substantial portion of Christian America committed to
theories of Armageddon and the inerrancy of the Bible has already made
the GOP into America's first religious party" and is creating "a gathering
threat to America's future."[3] Chris Hedges, a former *New York Times* reporter and a liberal Christian, titled his 2006 book simply *American Fascists:
The Christian Right and the War on America*. Meanwhile Sam Harris, Rich-

ard Dawkins, and Christopher Hitchens made what was called "the new atheism" fashionable.[4]

The year 2005, however, turned out to be the apogee of Christian right influence in Washington. By the end of Bush's presidency the political landscape had changed. The Republicans had lost control of the Congress, and the Christian right for the first time faced challenges from within the evangelical community.

In late September 2006 at the approach of the midterm election Dobson addressed two thousand activists at the annual Values Voters Summit convened by the Family Research Council in Washington. He celebrated the confirmation of "two new and very, very exciting" Supreme Court justices,[5] but expressed frustration that the Congress had failed to enact "values voters" legislation for the past two years.[6] That spring he and his colleagues had given the Republican leadership a list of bills and what amounted to an ultimatum before the midterms. The House had passed a few of their bills, but all of them had stalled in the Senate. Even with a Republican president and ten-vote Republican majority in the Senate, the Federal Marriage Act had gone down to defeat, and there had been no further legislation to restrict abortion.[7] Still, Focus on the Family launched a major midterm election effort with county coordinators in eight states encouraging pastors to speak out, hold registration drives, hand out voter guides, and help get out the vote. That year eight more states had anti-same-sex marriage amendments on their ballots; Dobson held Stand for the Family rallies and appeared at a Liberty Sunday rally in Boston.[8]

Dobson had found considerable enthusiasm in Ohio. After the passage of the marriage amendment that helped elect Bush, the Christian right had been on a victory march. Ken Blackwell, the secretary of state, was running for governor, and two pastors who had worked on Issue One with Phil Burress had set themselves ambitious goals. Russell Johnson, the head of a nondenominational evangelical church in Lancaster, had launched the Ohio Restoration Project with the aim of recruiting two thousand "Patriot Pastors," each to register three hundred new voters by the 2006 election. Rod Parsley, the Pentecostal televangelist and the leader of a twelve-thousand-member church on the outskirts of Columbus, had started a campaign, Reformation Ohio, and promised to bring

100,000 Ohioans to Christ, register 400,000 new voters, and create "a culture-shaking revolutionary revival." Both were careful not to endorse politicians from the pulpit, but both were clearly supporting Blackwell, who was running on Christian right issues and had come out for a law banning abortion without exception for the life of the mother. Johnson held seven Patriot Pastors meetings featuring Blackwell. Parsley mounted a rally outside the statehouse: a multimedia event with music and videos, where Blackwell spoke, along with Senator Brownback, about the need to bring God and morality back into government. "Sound the alarm," Parsley boomed. "A Holy Ghost invasion is taking place. Man your battle stations, ready your weapons, lock and load." In May Blackwell had won the Republican primary with 56 percent of the vote, unnerving the moderate Republican establishment.[9]

The November election, however, was a crushing national defeat for the Republican Party and the Christian right. The Democrats captured the House and Senate, and won a majority of governorships and state legislatures. Missouri passed a ballot initiative funding stem cell research; South Dakota rejected a ballot initiative designed to test *Roe v. Wade* by banning abortion. Arizona became the first state to reject a gay marriage ban, and while the marriage amendments passed in the other seven states, they proved of small help to Republican candidates. Many Christian right favorites lost their races. Rick Santorum of Pennsylvania, the most prominent social conservative in the Senate, lost to a Democrat; Katherine Harris of Florida, the former secretary of state and a conservative evangelical, lost her bid for the Senate, repudiated by many other Republicans after she spoke at D. James Kennedy's "Reclaiming America for Christ" meeting and told a Baptist publication, "If you're not electing Christians, then in essence you're going to legislate sin."[10] Ralph Reed had lost the Republican primary for lieutenant governor of Georgia, and Roy Moore had lost the gubernatorial primary in Alabama. In Ohio Ken Blackwell took only 36 percent of the vote against Congressman Ted Strickland, a Methodist minister and a progressive Democrat.[11]

Midterm elections tend to be driven by local issues, but in this one national issues predominated. Voters had turned against the war in Iraq, which had claimed three thousand American lives and had devolved into a sectarian conflict. They were disgusted by what the Democrats called "the culture of corruption" in Washington. Lobbyist Jack Abramoff, as it turned out, had tentacles that stretched across the capital. One congressman, eight congressional aides, and five Bush administration officials had pleaded, or were found, guilty of crimes; others, such as Tom DeLay, had been indicted; and still others, including Ralph Reed and Grover Norquist, president of Americans for Tax Reform, had been implicated in one way or another in the scandals. Then, a month before the election it appeared that Mark Foley, a Florida congressmen, had been sending lewd emails to male congressional pages and that the Republican leaders had known but had done nothing to stop him. Many voters were furious. Some 60 percent disapproved of the Republican-led Congress, and four in ten voters said they were voting against Bush. Voters did not like Bush's handling of Hurricane Katrina, Social Security, and above all the war in Iraq (only a third thought it had made the country safer). Republicans generally remained faithful to the party, but independents deserted it: nearly 60 percent of them voted for the Democrats.[12]

In two years Republicans had lost votes in every religious group, including among white evangelicals, but they took just about as many votes from every white Christian group as they had in the 2002 midterms. White evangelicals remained the Republicans' strongest supporters with 72 percent of them voting GOP. Voters who attended church at least weekly voted less Republican than they had in 2004, but only by 4 percentage points. Where the Republicans had lost most decisively was among the less faithful and non-Christians. Compared with 2002, the Democrats had gained 10 percentage points among infrequent churchgoers, 12 among nonchurchgoers, 25 among Jews, and 7 among those of other faiths. The so-called God gap, which had been growing ever since the two parties divided over the social issues, had widened in an unprecedented fashion during the Bush administration.[13]

For Dobson and other Christian right leaders the election was bad news, but after all it was just another election, and they could, as Lou Sheldon of the Traditional Values Coalition did, blame it on the unpopularity of the war in Iraq and the spate of scandals in Washington. But something new was happening that posed a direct threat to their power.

Before 2004 only three white evangelical leaders had publicly challenged the Christian right: Jim Wallis of Sojourners, Tony Campolo, a
well-known Baptist preacher, and Ron Sider, the president of Evangelicals
for Social Action. All three had founded activist organizations in 1970s,
but as energetic and articulate as they were, their constituencies seemed
permanently confined to a small progressive minority. Yet in the two years
after Bush's reelection, half a dozen prominent evangelicals published
books denouncing the Christian right for what they saw as its confusion of
religion and politics, its equation of morality with sexual morality, its aggressive intolerance, and its unholy quest for power. Some of the authors,
like former president Jimmy Carter and Jim Wallis, had already been dismissed by the right as liberals or "pseudo-evangelicals," but the first, and
the most powerful, critique came not from anyone on the evangelical left
but from Reverend Gregory A. Boyd, the head of a large conservative
church in St. Paul, Minnesota.

A theologian from a small denomination that had its roots in Swedish
pietism, Boyd had built a five-thousand-member congregation. He wrote
that during the 2004 campaign Christian right activists and members of
his own congregation pressured him to "shepherd" his flock into voting
for "the right candidates" with "the right positions." He was asked to hand
out leaflets, announce political events, and have church members sign petitions. He kept refusing, and some grew so irate he wrote a series of sermons explaining why the church should not join the right-wing political
chorus.[14]

In his sermons, as in the book he published in 2005, *The Myth of a Christian Nation*, Boyd challenged the idea that America had been, or ever could
be, a "Christian nation." Taking his text from the Gospels, he reminded
evangelicals that Christ's kingdom was "not of this world," and worldly
kingdoms were the domain of fallen man. Evangelicals, he wrote, speak
of "taking America back to God," but the Constitution said nothing about
a Christian nation, and America never remotely looked like the domain
of God, certainly not in the days of slavery or of Jim Crow, and not today.
A nation may have noble ideals and be committed to just principles, but
of necessity it wields the "power over" of the sword, as opposed to the
"power under" of the cross—which is that of Jesus' self-sacrificial love. To

identify the Kingdom of God with that of any version of the kingdom of the world is, he wrote, to engage in idolatry. The myth of a Christian nation, he continued, has led to the misconception that the American civil religion is real Christianity. Evangelicals, he wrote, spend our time striving to keep prayer in the public schools, "In God we trust" on our coins, and the Ten Commandments in public places. Might it not be, he asked, that the effort to defend prayer before civic functions reinforces the notion that prayer is a perfunctory social activity? And what if we spent all that energy serving each other with Christ-like love? We could, he wrote, feed the hungry, house the homeless, bridge the "ungodly racial gap," and side with others whose rights are routinely trampled.

Evangelicals, Boyd continued, are tempted to see ourselves as the moral guardians of the country, keeping it from cutting its tether to a Christian heritage, and invariably we set up lists of sins in which our sins are minor and theirs major, opening ourselves to charges of self-serving hypocrisy. For example, we talk about "the sanctity of marriage" in condemning gay marriage, when evangelicals have the highest number of divorces in the nation, and the Bible says a good deal more about divorce and remarriage than about monogamous gay relationships. Further, he argued, America is a pluralist country, and while the apostle Paul expected Christians to live consistently with their faith, Paul said he had no right and no ability to judge those outside the church. In Boyd's view Christians should bear witness to injustice, but they should not try to enforce "their righteous will on others."

Boyd also tackled the evangelical support for the Iraq War. Borrowing from John Yoder, the Anabaptist theologian, he made the case that since the Emperor Constantine made Christianity the official religion, the history of the church was for centuries that of the coercion of others, and violence in the name of the glory of God. The militant mind-set, he wrote, carried over from the late Roman Empire to the Reformation and the conquest of the New World. Indeed, whenever the leaders of so-called Christian nations felt the need to defend or expand their nations, they could often count on the church to call on God to bless their violent campaigns. America today, he continued, is a largely secularized country, but many still believe we fight "for God and country," and leaders continue to use this faith to their advantage. President Bush, he wrote, could have argued that the war on Iraq and the war on al Qaeda were in the national interest—a claim some would accept and others reject—but instead he called America the "light of the world" that "darkness" could not extinguish, quoting Scripture (John 1: 1–5) to imply that Americans are of God and our national enemies of Satan. Instead of being disturbed by this "idolatrous association," evangelicals applauded it, demonstrating the unholy fusion they had made between the United States and the Kingdom of God. Boyd went on to attack Christian Zionism and fundamentalism per se, charging "an escapist apocalyptic theology . . . in the name of fulfilling biblical prophecy . . . that directly or indirectly encourage[s] violence, possibly on a global scale." [15]

Boyd's sermons caused an uproar, and 20 percent of his congregation, or roughly a thousand people, left his church.[16] Evangelicals were not used to hearing any criticism of the Christian right, for a sense of communal solidarity, or a fear of ostracism, had made it all but taboo. Yet just a year later at the height of furor over Terri Schiavo and the Supreme Court nominations, journalists in Washington began noticing prominent evangelicals making direct or indirect criticisms of the Christian right and Bush administration policies.

During 2005 a group called the Evangelical Alliance of Scientists and Ethicists turned up in Washington to protest the Republican-led attempt to rewrite the Endangered Species Act, its ad featuring a picture of Noah's Ark adrift after the deluge.[17] Another group attended the G-8 summit of the world's wealthiest nations calling for debt relief and financial aid for the world's poorest countries.[18] Rick Warren, the megachurch pastor who had in 2004 sent out a letter calling on pastors in his network to vote against abortion and gay marriage, sent out another asking them to urge Bush to double his spending to fight AIDS and extreme poverty around the world.[19] "It's time that the church be known for what it's for" rather than what it's against, he told the Baptist World Centenary Congress in England.[20] World Vision, the largest evangelical relief and development agency, campaigned against the Central American Free Trade Agreement because it lacked protections for workers and farmers in the region. Jim Wallis found his new book, *God's Politics*, criticizing the Christian right, on the *New York Times* best-seller list. *Christianity Today* editorialized, "George W. Bush is not the Lord. The American Flag is not the Cross. The Pledge of Allegiance is not the Creed. 'God Bless America' is not the Doxology." [21] Even more surprising was the reaction at Calvin College to a visit by the president.

In March Karl Rove had engineered an invitation for Bush to give the commencement address at Calvin through a local congressman, effectively bumping the scheduled speaker two months before the event. A small evangelical college situated in the strategic Republican stronghold of Grand Rapids in the key state of Michigan, Calvin seemed a perfect place for the president to give his usual speech to graduates, encouraging them to work hard and to do good. Yet two days before Bush arrived, an open letter signed by eight hundred faculty members, students, and alumni appeared in a full-page advertisement in the *Grand Rapids Press* saying, in part, "Your deeds, Mr. President—neglecting the needy to coddle the rich, desecrating the environment and misleading the country into war—do not exemplify the faith we live by." The next day the *Press* ran a longer letter signed by one hundred out of the three hundred faculty members objecting to "an unjust and unjustified war in Iraq," actions "that favor the wealthy of our society and burden the poor," and policies that have "harmed creation" and "fostered intolerance and divisiveness." [22] Calvin, unbeknownst to Rove, was one of the most politically progressive of the evangelical colleges. On commencement day the students politely applauded the president, but a few demonstrators held up signs saying, "Where Has Calvin College Gone?" and "No More Blood for Oil." [23]

Of longer term consequence, the National Association of Evangelicals at its annual March meeting in Washington considered a position paper called "For the Health of a Nation: An Evangelical Call for Civic Responsibility." Passed unanimously by the board the previous October, the document laid out ten principles for political engagement. It called upon all evangelicals to seek justice for the poor, to protect human rights, to seek peace, and to protect God's creation—as well as to preserve religious freedom, to protect the sanctity of human life, and to nurture families. Carefully drawn up so as not to provoke right-wing opposition, the document had been approved by Dobson, Colson, and other non-NAE members, but it gave official sanction to the more progressive leaders to move, at a national level, beyond the Christian right agenda. At the luncheon held on Capitol Hill, Ron Sider, who had helped draft the document, told the members, "Evangelicals have sometimes been accused of having a one- or two-item political agenda. This document makes it very clear that a vast body of evangelicals today reject a one-issue approach." Several speakers said they welcomed the document because it could change the tenor and direction of the evangelical movement. "There's a consensus here, but some of us haven't had the nerve to do what needs to be done," said John Holmes, the director of government affairs for the Association of Christian Schools International.[24]

The document, however, had papered over deep differences. The previous day Richard Cizik, the vice president for governmental affairs, had taken the opportunity to invite experts to brief the assembly on climate change. At the luncheon Tom Minnery, vice president of Focus on the Family, stood up and warned, "Do not make this about global warming. The issues of marriage, the issues of pro-life . . . define us to this day." Other speakers voiced concern that the new position paper could dilute the focus of the movement, one warning the NAE not to travel the route of the mainline denominations. Diane Kippers, president of the conservative Institute on Religion and Democracy, who also helped draft the document, warned Democrats not to try to hive off the evangelical left, but several speakers, including some who identified themselves as Republicans, said the document was necessary because evangelicals risked being seen as merely a Republican voting bloc.[25]

Asked about the NAE document, the historian Mark Noll, who had praised the statement, said it's "an effort to bring out of the background things that have always been there but have been overshadowed by the concentration on life issues."[26] It was also a reaction against the Christian right and its alliance with Bush's Republican Party. As Noll said in the same interview, "Evangelicals don't want themselves identified as the Republican Party at prayer." His old friend David Wells, a theologian at Gordon-Conwell Theological Seminary outside Boston, told the same reporter that the effort to broaden the agenda came in part from "a fear that the fundamentalistic hard right has so far been the only voice in national affairs." And that that has resulted in a misrepresentation of "what the vast majority of evangelicals think" on issues beyond abortion and same-sex marriage.[27]

These dissenters came from an evangelical constituency largely unknown to the rest of the country. The Christian right had for so long dominated the public discourse, the dissenters seemed to be coming out of nowhere. Some, as Noll suggested, had been there all the time: in international aid agencies, colleges and seminaries, denominations and independent churches. Indeed, to visit evangelical churches in the northern cities was often to find pastors who had been expressing discontent with the right, or departing more or less radically from the right-wing agenda, for years.

Rich Nathan, for example, the senior pastor of the Vineyard Church in Columbus, Ohio—a megachurch not many miles from Rod Parsley's—had long preached that the Christian message could not be reduced to issues of sex or private morality, and the emphasis should be on Jesus' teachings about the poor and about peacemaking. "Our focus in this church is on racial reconciliation and issues of poverty," he told me in 2006. "It's not about charity. It's about getting to root causes of poverty and correcting injustices, such as racial and gender discrimination." His church supported "fair-trade coffee," an international program that sought to ensure that living wages were paid to coffee growers around the world, and had a free legal clinic for those needing help with their immigration status, domestic violence, or tenant-landlord disputes. "The Vineyard Association," he said, "has 650 churches in the country, and you won't find one of them that's not involved with the poor." Nathan said he believed that churches should stay out of politics—that they shouldn't campaign for candidates or lobby for legislation—but he spoke his mind on what he considered the moral issues.[28] After the revelations of Abu Ghraib, he preached against torture, and later he called the Iraq War "a senseless slaughter" and asked how Christians could claim to follow the Prince of Peace and yet "be led so easily into war." [29]

Other pastors had taken up the cause of the poor more recently. Of these by far the best known was Rick Warren, the pastor of a huge church in Orange County, California, who had sprung into view after the phenomenal success of his book *The Purpose Driven Life*. In 2005, just after he had written the letter calling on Bush to cancel the debts of the least developed countries, he announced a plan he called PEACE to eradicate poverty, illiteracy, and disease worldwide.

His move came as a surprise, given his background and career. Unlike Rich Nathan, whose church was a part of an association of politically progressive churches born out of the charismatic renewal movement of the 1970s, Warren was a Southern Baptist with a not untypical background for an SBC pastor of his generation. Born into a family of poor sharecroppers from West Texas, his father, James, had built and pastored a number of small churches in Northern California, and Rick had devoted his life to the church even before he left high school in 1972. His decision to become a pastor, as opposed to a crusading evangelist, came after he listened to W. A. Criswell, the fiery orator with the largest SBC church in the country. He attended the Southwestern Baptist Theological Seminary in Fort Worth at the beginning of the "conservative resurgence," but he avoided the denominational disputes and focused on the practical side of ministry.[30]

At age twenty-six he and his wife, Kay, also from a Southern Baptist family, founded the Saddleback Valley Community Church with seven people in the living room of their rented house with the vision of building a congregation of twenty thousand. His methods, unorthodox at the time, came in part from Rev. Robert Schuller, who had pioneered techniques for attracting nonchurchgoers and had built a towering edifice, the Crystal Cathedral, in Garden Grove, California, and in part from Peter Drucker, the famous management consultant, who served as his mentor for two decades.[31] Warren chose the site for his church by studying the U.S. Census to find the fastest-growing tracts in the relatively unchurched parts of the West. Finding one in Saddleback Valley in Orange County, he canvassed door-to-door with a questionnaire to ascertain the "felt needs" of the community and advertised his future church through direct mail.[32] From Donald A. McGavran, a former missionary and the founder of an institute for church growth at the Fuller Seminary, Warren had learned that it was more effective to evangelize what McGavran called "people groups"—tribes, castes, clans, or tightly knit segments of society—rather than individuals, who might have to leave their own cultures to become converts. The idea contradicted the evangelical belief that conversion was an individual decision to accept Christ, but it fit with Warren's own view that people came to church more readily when they saw people like themselves in the congregation. Accordingly he focused on one large group in the Saddleback Valley: young, unchurched white-collar couples, and specifically couples in their thirties or forties with two children, college degrees, good jobs but stressful lives, mindful of health and fitness and skeptical of organized religion.[33] To bring such people to church he designed what became known as "seeker-sensitive" services with contemporary music and sermons that, avoiding religious jargon and controversial topics, gave positive, practical messages, such as "How to Survive Under Stress" and "How to Feel Good About Yourself." His church was Southern Baptist in affiliation and doctrine, but Warren did not advertise it as such lest the name turn off suburbanites from outside the South. He took care to make the church an informal, comfortable place for newcomers, and cemented the congregation with small groups designed to give a sense of "fellowship, personal care and belonging."[34]

Ministering to "felt needs" with "seeker-sensitive" services, pioneered by Robert Schuller and adopted earlier by Bill Hybels, the pastor of a megachurch in the suburbs of Chicago, raised controversy at the time. The guardians of evangelical orthodoxy, many of them Calvinists, complained of slick marketing techniques and therapeutic, feel-good messages that minimized the hard truths of the Gospel. "Marketing savvy demands that the offense of the cross must be downplayed," wrote John MacArthur, a well-known Los Angeles pastor. "Consumer satisfaction means that the standard of righteousness cannot be raised too high."[35] God, wrote David Wells, "becomes transformed into a product to be sold, faith into a recreational activity to be done, and the Church into a club for the like-minded."[36] Still, Warren had the fastest-growing church in the region, and McGavran's successor, C. Peter Wagner, invited him to teach at Fuller's Institute for Evangelism and Church Growth. His classes evolved into conferences at Saddleback that drew hundreds of pastors every year, and in 1995 he published *The Purpose Driven Church*, a practical church growth manual for pastors that sold 100,000 copies in its first year alone.[37]

With his reputation as church growth expert, Warren formed the Purpose Driven Ministries, a network of pastors from a variety of denominations in the U.S. and abroad who looked to him for advice on practical and religious matters. In 2002 he followed up on his first book with *The Purpose Driven Life*, a combination devotional guide and self-help book that he promised would teach "God's purpose for your life" as well as "reduce your stress, simplify your decisions, increase your satisfaction, and, most important, prepare you for eternity." Published in September and initially distributed through his now extensive network of pastors, the book took off, and reaching the *New York Times* best-seller list for advice books after five months, stayed there for 118 weeks, selling 800,000 copies a month. Two years after publication, the book had sold twenty million copies worldwide, and according to *Publishers Weekly* it was "the fastest-selling book of all time, and the best-selling hardback in American history."[38]

Previously almost unknown outside the evangelical world, Warren suddenly became a celebrity. Appearing on TV talk shows, he was blizzarded by invitations to speak and by requests from businessmen, sports stars, and politicians to give them his advice and blessing. He also earned what he described as "a ton of money": $9 million by his account, in just one quarter of 2003, and $25 million by a *Forbes* estimate in 2006.[39] Later he often spoke of how he faced the problem of what to do with this new "affluence and influence." Knowing he would be under scrutiny, the first decision he made was to take no salary from the church but give back all he had earned in the past twenty-five years and "reverse tithe," giving 90 percent of his income away.[40] Then, by his account he went to South Africa in mid-2003 with his wife, Kay, who had become involved with the HIV-AIDS pandemic in Africa. After seeing a village struck by AIDS and a young pastor who said he had no training other than reading Warren's sermons on a public computer an hour and half by foot away, he asked himself what were the biggest problems on the planet, problems that affected billions of people and seemed impossible to solve. He drew up a list of five: spiritual emptiness, self-serving leadership, poverty, pandemic disease, and illiteracy. On his return home he drew up a list of ways to attack "these great global giants" under the acronym PEACE:

Plant new churches (later, "partner with churches" or "promote
  reconciliation")

Equip servant-leaders

Assist the poor

Care for the sick

Educate the next generation

He and his associates then thought out a strategy to achieve his five
objectives. The plan was to send teams from American churches on short-
term missions to distribute kits that would equip Christians in the global
South to plant churches, and start small businesses or literacy programs or
preventive health care clinics. The kits, which Warren called a "clinic in a
box" or a "school in a box," would contain rudimentary instructions and
materials, such as medical or school supplies. In 2004 over four thousand
people from his congregation, he said, fanned out to forty-three countries
to test the approach.[41]

The plan seemed improbable to development experts, but it had few
critics. Evangelical churches had been sending out people on short-term
missions for years with the hope they would fund mission work and not
harm the local effort too much. The aid agencies had ceased to pay much
attention.[42] As for journalists, some thought Warren naive, but they were
far too interested in Warren himself and the effect he was having in the
United States even to ask about the "boxes."

In other respects Warren knew exactly what he was doing.

As the PEACE plan developed, he hired a "strategic outreach" staff
to help him get to know people outside his own networks, among them
businessmen and politicians, to increase his range of influence. Because
of the business contacts he made, he went to Rwanda at the invitation of
its president, Paul Kagame. When it became clear that he could bring corporate executives to invest in the country, Kagame entertained him like
royalty and proposed to make Rwanda the first "purpose-driven nation."[43]
In April 2005 Warren officially announced his PEACE plan to a crowd of
thirty thousand assembled for the twenty-fifth anniversary of his church.
In the spring he went on a speaking tour, traveling to conventions and to
intellectual institutions—Harvard, Oxford, Cambridge, the Aspen Ideas

Festival, and the Council on Foreign Relations—often describing PEACE and his own conversion to the cause of global poverty. Warren always thought large-scale, and that summer he told the Baptist World Alliance that PEACE would engage ten million churches and a billion Christians. What we need, he said, is "a reformation not of creeds but deeds," for "a non-serving Christian is a contradiction." [44] Whatever support he managed to build for his plan, he himself became almost as well known as Billy Graham. Church leaders in polls chose him the first or second most influential among them, and *Time* magazine called him "America's pastor." [45]

At a Pew Forum on Religion and Public Life meeting that May Warren spoke to religion writers from publications, such as *The New York Times, The New Yorker*, and *The Atlantic*, laying out his views in some detail and answering tough questions. Most found him charming. As one wrote, he is an "utterly likeable guy with a hearty and generous laugh and a manner so casual he wears a suit only once a year—on Mother's Day to honor his wife." (Warren had a habit of wearing Hawaiian shirts over his imposing frame.) With the Christian right still taking up all the oxygen in Washington, Warren began by saying that the first trend reporters should watch for was the return of evangelicals to their nineteenth-century roots of "compassionate activism." Since the split in Protestantism, he explained, the mainline churches had tended to concern themselves with social morality—caring for the sick, the poor, the dispossessed, and racial justice—while fundamentalists and evangelicals concerned themselves with personal morality and personal salvation. "But they really are all a part of the total gospel—social justice, personal morality and salvation," he said. "And today a lot more people, evangelicals, are caring about those issues." Taking his PEACE plan as a case in point, he predicted that the embrace of such issues would lead to a second reformation in the Church, and that, whereas the first Reformation had been about beliefs and creeds, the second would be about deeds, or about what the Church does in the world. The new reformation would in turn lead to a new spiritual awakening, a third Great Awakening in America and the world. "The Bible calls the Church the body of Christ," he said, "and what's happened in the last 100 years is that the hands and feet have been amputated, and the Church has just been a mouth, and primarily it's been known for what it's against." [46]

The other trend he said they should watch was the evolving alliance between evangelicals and Catholics. Dismissing the Protestant mainline as the "sideline" today, he said that because Catholics represented 25 percent of the population and evangelicals 28 or 29 percent, together they would have a majority in America. Asked about his views on issues such as abortion and gay marriage, Warren said that he was "firmly a cultural conservative," but he didn't want the evangelical movement "pigeon-holed" into three or four "primarily personal moral issues." Few, he said, understand the difference among evangelicals, fundamentalists, and the religious right, but "I'm an evangelical. I'm not a member of the religious right. I'm not a fundamentalist." On the subject of politics, he said that most of his congregation voted Republican ("I'm in Orange County, what do you expect?"), but that he was a pastor, not a politician or policy maker. "I don't think we need a God party," he said.[47]

Asked about his PEACE plan, he said that he had come to a turning point in his life two and half years ago, when he read Psalm 72, wherein King Solomon prayed for more influence so that he could support widows and orphans, care for the oppressed, and defend the defenseless. Warren had, he said, to repent to God for never having thought about the poor and the marginalized. "I've had four years in Greek and Hebrew and I've got doctorates. How did I miss the 2,000 verses in the Bible where it talks about the poor?"

Warren's sincerity was obvious in part because his performance before a nonevangelical audience was neither slick nor seamless. For all his desire to make a bridge across faiths, he did not give up on his theology of salvation only through belief in Christ. He would often speak as if the evangelical church was the entire church, and occasionally he would come out with one of the shibboleths of the right. Walter Rauschenbusch, he said, did not believe in Jesus, and the Social Gospel was "Marxism in a Christian form."[48] In speaking of gay marriage, he said he believed in a pluralist America, where everyone had the right to state his or her case, and though he often didn't get his way when it came to a vote, he accepted the verdict of majority. "What I worry about," he said, "is the tyranny of activist judges, who keep throwing out what the majority said. Are we a democracy or not?" When one journalist asked what if the majority passed laws that codified the majority's religious beliefs, and another asked if he didn't think that judges and the Constitution protected the rights of minorities, he didn't seem to understand what they were getting at.[49]

Clearly Warren was closer to the conservative evangelical position than Gerald Boyd or Rich Nathan, but as the best-known pastor in the country, he was making a major statement by insisting he was not a part of the Christian right. Simply by putting issues of poverty and social justice ahead of the culture war issues, he was breaking a taboo and making a breach through which other conservatives could go. In the following years Warren grew bolder in challenging Christian right politics, as did many others.

For a time the opposition centered in the leadership of the National Association of Evangelicals, an organization then said to include fifty-one denominations, 45,000 churches, and thirty million members.[50] Its members were not united in their understanding of the implications of the "Call to Civic Responsibility," but in pursuing the issue of global warming, its leaders created the first serious conflict with the Christian right.

Since the 1980s the NAE had always been a good deal more moderate than the Southern Baptist Convention, both theologically and politically. It included several southern-based Pentecostal denominations, such as the Assemblies of God, but its strength was largely in the North, and it comprised the Vineyard Association and a number of Anabaptist and Reformed denominations from which the old left had come. Its leaders—ever since Harold Ockenga and Billy Graham—had been Republicans and during the Cold War fervent anti-Communists. In the 1980s Robert Dugan, its vice president and representative in Washington, consulted with Reagan's staff over speeches, and the NAE mounted a registration drive before the 1984 election. In the same period the organization took up the antiabortion cause under the influence of Francis Schaeffer and supported much of the Christian right's family and church-state agenda, including tax credits for religious schools. Still, the NAE, and *Christianity Today* (always close to it), eschewed polemics and the demonization of secularists and Democrats. After his 1992 election President Clinton courted its leaders, and its then president Don Argue called for evangelicals to distance themselves from partisan politics, saying, "We are in danger of becoming, if not already, identified as the political arm of one party, a very dangerous position to be in." The NAE opposed Clinton's gay rights initiatives and health care plan, but it did not call for Clinton's impeachment, saying that not all evangelicals agreed on the values involved, or on the definition of "high crimes and misdemeanors."[51]

In 1997 Richard Cizik succeeded Dugan as vice president for governmental affairs. An ordained Presbyterian minister brought up on a cherry farm in Oregon, he had served in the Washington office for seventeen years as a researcher. He considered himself a Reagan Republican, but unlike Dugan he had experience abroad, and in the late 1990s in the wake of the Cold War he undertook to extend the NAE's agenda to foreign affairs. The issues he chose stemmed from traditional evangelical concerns, but he managed to get the board to overturn a long-standing policy of noncooperation with non-Christian groups. In coalition with Tibetan Buddhists, liberal Jews, as well as Dobson and Colson, the NAE lobbied successfully for the International Religious Freedom Act of 1998. Two years later Cizik joined with Gloria Steinem and other feminists to pass the Victims of Trafficking and Violence Protection Act and later with the Congressional Black Caucus to pass the Sudan Peace Act. The NAE also allied with Senator Ted Kennedy, the NAACP, La Raza, and Human Rights Watch to pass legislation targeting rape in prison.[52] In 2001 the Executive Committee commissioned the Evangelical Project for Social Engagement that three years later produced the document "For the Health of a Nation," drafted by Cizik, David Neff, the editor of *Christianity Today*, Ron Sider, and Diane Knippers.

In the summer of 2002 Jim Ball, a Baptist minister and the head of the Evangelical Environmental Network, took Cizik to a conference on climate change in Oxford, where the keynote speaker was Sir John Houghton, a British evangelical, an atmospheric scientist, and the former head of the scientific working group of the Intergovernmental Panel on Climate Change. Cizik, who said he had to be "dragged" to the meeting, had what he called a "conversion" that he likened to an altar call. "I realized all at once, with sudden awe, that climate change is a phenomenon of biblical proportions."[53] Two years later, the NAE joined Ball's Evangelical Environmental Network and *Christianity Today* to convene a meeting of thirty evangelical leaders in Sandy Cove, Maryland, for Houghton to make his case that climate change was a Christian issue. After much prayer and Bible reading, the group covenanted to "engage the evangelical community" on climate change and produce "a consensus statement" within a year.[54]

The EEN, a ministry of Sider's Evangelicals for Social Action, was founded in 1993 as the evangelical representative on the National Religious Partnership for the Environment, an association of the U.S. Catholic Conference, the National Council of Churches, the Coalition on the Environment and Jewish Life, and a number of African American denominations. The EEN was mainly an educational outreach group, but it had participated in a campaign to prevent the weakening of the Endangered Species Act, and in 2002 Ball and Sider had mounted a campaign called "What Would Jesus Drive?" asking Christians to see their transportation choices as moral choices because the pollution from vehicles had a serious impact on human health and the rest of God's creation, because it contributed to global warming, and because U.S. reliance on imported oil was a threat to peace and security. By 2005 Ball had formed partnerships with twenty-three moderate and progressive evangelical organizations, including InterVarsity Christian Fellowship and World Vision.[55]

All knew that global warming was a contentious issue among evangelicals. For one thing, as Cizik noted, many evangelicals distrusted science in general. "There is a basic formula that goes: science supports evolution, evangelicals oppose evolution, ergo there's a conflict between science and evangelicals. Evolution is like the third rail—if you touch it, you die—sorta like Social Security."[56] In addition some evangelicals thought the world was doomed anyway, and many thought of environmentalists as tree-huggers, practitioners of New Age religions, advocates of population control, people who put plants and animals ahead of humans, or simply godless liberals. Then because evangelicals tended to look to individual salvation as the cure for social ills and to favor states' rights, many opposed big-government solutions and regulation of businesses. "We are preternaturally free-market-oriented," Cizik said. "The backbone of the local church is the local businessman."[57]

Cizik took heart from the fact that a recent Pew poll showed a slight majority of evangelicals would support strict rules to protect the environ-

ment even if it cost jobs or resulted in higher prices.[58] He decided to keep
a distance from the secular environmental organizations for the moment,
involve leaders that evangelicals trusted, and frame the issues in terms
they could appreciate. The EEN and other evangelical environmental
groups, such as Cal DeWitt's Au Sable Institute, had long described environmental protection as "creation care," and global warming as a threat
to humans, particularly the poor, who faced the greatest danger from
droughts, hurricanes, and flooding. Christians, they said, were called to
protect God's creation, love their neighbors, and to care for "the least of
these." In January 2005 Ball and Cizik appeared at an antiabortion march
in Washington with a banner reading, "Stop Mercury Poisoning of the
Unborn," distributing flyers saying that one in six babies was born with
dangerous mercury levels, and urging participants to demand improvements in the Clear Skies Act.[59]

Still, Cizik and Ball knew they would face opposition from the Christian right. Already a group of religious conservatives, mainly evangelicals
and Catholics, had founded the Interfaith Stewardship Alliance to promote a counter-agenda to the Evangelical Environmental Network and its
partners, the U.S. Catholic Conference, the National Council of Churches,
and a coalition of Jewish organizations. Its defining document, the Cornwall Declaration, written largely by E. Calvin Beisner, a professor of ethics
at the conservative Knox Theology Seminary, conceded that some environmental issues posed problems, but that the threats of global warming,
rampant species loss, and overpopulation were "largely hypothetical" and
that "public policies to combat exaggerated risks can dangerously delay
or reverse the economic development necessary" to "improve . . . human
life." Arguing that the greatest environmental threats were local in nature and largely confined to the developing world, it maintained that free
markets and technological advance offered most effective solutions and
the best ways to help the poor. "Wise stewardship," it reported, should be
exercised by limited government "at the lowest level possible."[60] Though
its mention of the fate of the poor demonstrated the success of the EEN
and its allies, the Interfaith Stewardship Alliance had gained the support
of numerous Christian right leaders. The statement that Tom Minnery,
the vice president of Focus on the Family, issued after the NAE meeting,

when Cizik introduced the subject of global warming, incorporated some of the claims made in the Cornwall Declaration, such as that radical environmentalists would stifle advances that would benefit the lives of people the world over.[61]

Cizik and Ball hoped that the NAE board and other evangelical leaders would make a strong statement on climate change and come out in support of the bill sponsored by Senators John McCain and Joseph Lieberman to reduce the emission of greenhouse gases by a business-friendly cap and trade system that would allow industries to buy and sell emissions allowances. *Christianity Today* had endorsed the bill shortly after the Sandy Cove meeting. The Bush administration, however, opposed all mandatory controls on CO_2 emissions, and the bill had failed to gain traction among congressional Republicans. The chair of the Senate Environment and Public Works Committee, James M. Inhofe, Republican of Oklahoma and an evangelical, called global warming "the greatest hoax ever perpetrated on the American people." Still, Cizik expressed optimism that evangelicals, if mobilized, might persuade the Bush administration to change its policy.[62]

The draft statement, however, took more than a year to complete, and though the NAE's president, Ted Haggard, the pastor of a charismatic megachurch in Colorado Springs, favored a strong statement, it seemed there were disagreements in the board. In January 2006, as the announcement of the initiative neared, Haggard received a letter on Interfaith Stewardship Alliance stationery from a who's who of the Christian right "respectfully" requesting that the NAE not adopt any position on climate change. "Global warming," it read, "is not a consensus issue" and "individual NAE members or staff should not give the impression they are speaking on behalf of the entire membership." The letter reminded Haggard that the central issues had always been those like protecting traditional marriage, and that evangelicals were to be "first and foremost messengers of the good news of the gospel to a lost and dying world."[63] Most of the signatories, such as Charles Colson, James Dobson, D. James Kennedy, Richard Land, Donald Wildmon, Louis Sheldon, David Barton, and John Hagee, were not NAE members, but such was the power of the Christian right that in early February the NAE's executive committee passed a motion "recognizing the ongoing debate" on global warming and "the lack of consensus among the evangelical community on the issue." Reluctantly Haggard and Cizik had to say that the NAE would not take a position on the issue. Still, they and Ball had done their work well.[64]

On February 8 a group of eighty-six evangelical leaders announced the Evangelical Climate Initiative and issued a "Call to Action," declaring that climate change was real, human-induced, and that "millions of people could die from it in this century." Christian moral convictions, they said, demanded a response, and the need to act was urgent. Businesses, churches, and individuals could do their part, but the most important immediate step was to pass a federal bill reducing carbon dioxide emissions through effective market-based mechanisms. The group included the presidents of thirty-nine evangelical colleges (Calvin and Wheaton among them) and the deans of three divinity schools. Another large contingent was made up of the CEOs of international aid agencies, including the national commander of the Salvation Army. The signatories also comprised the heads of several denominations, such as the Christian Reformed Church, the Vineyard Association, and the International Church of the Four Square Gospel, and a few megachurch pastors—including Rick Warren, though he had often expressed skepticism about evolution.[65] The group planned a campaign of radio, TV, and newspaper ads in states with influential legislators, discussions with energy companies, and events at churches and colleges.[66]

An uproar ensued. Right-wing publications, such as *World* and *Citizen* magazines, denounced the initiative as an abandonment of the central moral issues. The SBC voted for a resolution saying that "environmentalism is threatening to become a wedge issue to divide the evangelical community" and warning members not to rely on "extreme environmental groups" or support solutions based on "questionable science."[67] The Interfaith Stewardship Alliance (renamed the Cornwall Alliance), this time with the backing of several scientists, denounced the Evangelical Climate Initiative for refusing to accept the scientific truth. Ball was not impressed. The Cornwall Alliance had found a few assistant professors from evangelical colleges and several well-known climate change skeptics, eight from organizations receiving funds from ExxonMobil.[68] In December the NAE and the Center for Heath and the Environment at Harvard Medical School convened a conference of fourteen evangelical leaders and fourteen scientists, including the Nobel laureate Eric Chivian, E. O. Wilson, and James Hansen, the leading American climate scientist, and issued an "Urgent Call to Action," promising a joint effort to address climate change before it was too late.[69] Meanwhile Cizik and his allies persisted in their campaign of speaking out, publishing ads, and lobbying congressmen.

The dispute between the Christian right and the NAE broke out into the open in March 2007. Just before the annual NAE board meeting Dobson and over twenty other leaders, including Paul Weyrich and Gary Bauer, sent a public letter to the NAE board—this one considerably less polite than the last—accusing Cizik of waging a "relentless campaign" over global warming and calling on the board to silence him or demand his resignation. Cizik, they wrote, puts forth "his own opinions as scientific fact" and "regularly speaks without the authorization" of the NAE, extending its mandate beyond its statement of purpose. "More importantly," they wrote, "we have observed that Cizik and others are using the global warming controversy to shift the emphasis away from the great moral issues of our time, notably the sanctity of human life, the integrity of marriage, and the teaching of sexual abstinence and morality to our children," displacing them with "a divisive and dangerous alignment with the left." The signatories also expressed dismay that the emphasis on global warming was "contributing to a growing confusion about the very term 'evangelical,'" suggesting the term should signify "conservative views on politics, economics and biblical morality."[70]

This time, Cizik lacked the protection of his friend Ted Haggard, who had been found to frequent a male prostitute and had to resign. Still, the board stood its ground. It refused to rebuke Cizik and reaffirmed its 2004 statement of purpose. It said nothing about global warming. On the other hand, it endorsed a document drafted by the Evangelicals for Human Rights condemning the use of torture as a tactic in the war on terror and calling for changes in the laws that permitted ongoing violations of the human rights of U.S.-held detainees.[71]

The board's decision to support Cizik was much criticized by the right. Richard Land said that the NAE's failure to address Cizik's claims should not be interpreted to mean that a consensus had been reached among evangelicals on global warming. "Most evangelicals," he said, "have their own positions on global warming and do not take their marching orders from the NAE. Southern Baptists certainly do not."[72] Jerry Falwell in a televised sermon on global warming called environmentalism "Satan's attempt to redirect the church's primary focus."[73]

A defense of Cizik came from an unexpected quarter: Ken Connor, the former Family Research Council president and the lawyer for Governor Jeb Bush who had brought the Terri Schaivo case to national attention. Not long after the meeting Connor wrote a piece in the *Christian Post*, saying that while he sympathized with the emphasis Dobson and others put on abortion and marriage, "unfortunately these leaders are inadvertently suggesting that the scope of Christ's concern is fairly narrow. . . . Can't we admit that Christ came to redeem all things" and that "a comprehensive Christian worldview should cause us to be concerned about suffering and injustice in all areas?" People, he wrote, have callings to different causes, like AIDS in Africa, or the protection of the environment, and they should be free to pursue them. Some leaders, he argued, worry that to expand the "'issue set' beyond abortion and gay marriage will harm the pro-life and pro-family cause," but this was not necessarily true. Giving Mother Teresa as an example, he wrote, "The pro-life witness of the Christian Church may actually be strengthened when men and women are free to pursue their calling."[74]

The fury of Christian right leaders at the NAE, however, came not just from their view that global warming distracted from "the great moral issues," but, as the SBC resolution suggested, that such causes would divide the evangelical community, giving movement leaders less sway over evangelicals and their claim to represent them in Washington.

In the past, movement leaders had been able to prevent others from challenging their authority, but by 2007 they saw their power to control the agenda slipping away.

New issues, such as the Bush administration's tolerance of torture, kept cropping up, and in November 2006 Rick Warren invited the young senator Barack Obama to speak at his second conference on AIDS with Senator Sam Brownback. "I think," Michael Gerson wrote, "there's a little bit of an element of revolt against the tone of some political engagement of the religious right in the past, which seems quite harsh."[75] It was more than that. Many evangelicals knew the Christian right had become deeply unpopular with most Americans and that evangelicals had become thoroughly identified with the Christian right. In April 2006 a *Christianity Today* editorialist suggested that evangelicals stop calling themselves "evangelical" because the label carried such negative connotations. "To the unchurched and people of other faiths," he wrote, " 'evangelical' is increasingly shorthand for: right-wing US politics—an arrogant loud mouth who refuses to listen to other people's opinions."[76] Confirmation of this view came in 2007, when the Barna Group, an evangelical research firm, released a study showing that most young Americans (ages sixteen to twenty-nine) had extremely negative views of Christians, and of evangelicals in particular. What was more, evangelicals knew it, for over 90 percent of them reported that Americans were becoming more hostile to Christianity. Among the results of the Barna survey: only 3 percent of young non-Christians expressed favorable views of evangelicals— compared with 25 percent in the previous generation. More than three quarters of the non-Christians thought Christians "judgmental," "hypocritical," "old-fashioned," and "too political." Furthermore, about half of young churchgoers agreed with them, and huge proportions of both thought Christianity anti-homosexual. More alarming to the pollsters, young born-again Christians frequently expressed the same sentiments, and 22 percent said that Christianity "no longer looked like Jesus."[77] In other words, the Christian right had done its work all too well: it had managed to convince Americans that all evangelicals, if not all Christians, belonged to their movement. And many evangelicals wanted out. In the opinion of Geoff Tunnicliffe, the Canadian head of the World Evangelical Alliance, Warren was "trying to rebrand American evangelicalism" for the future.[78]

Even many Southern Baptists understood they had to untangle themselves from the Christian right. Interviewed by Nina Easton of *The Boston Globe* in 2005, Jimmy Draper Jr., the head of the SBC's publishing arm, said, "Southern Baptists seem to be known in recent years for what we're against. The public perception is that we're mean and negative." Bobby Welch, the president of the Convention, added, "I'm deeply concerned that evangelicals put too much of a priority on the political and not enough on the spiritual. I think it's a complete error to allow that sort of image to arise in the public's eye." That year the SBC dropped its boycott of the Walt Disney Company for producing what it said were movies that "promoted infidelity" and for putting on special days for gays and lesbians at its theme parks.[79] The following year the Convention elected a new president, Frank Page, age fifty-four, an almost unknown candidate, opposed by the conservative establishment but supported by a network of young Baptist pastors, who spread their views via blogs. The bloggers had objected to the increasingly narrow definition of the Baptist faith and the close relationship between SBC leadership and Bush's Republican Party. One Oklahoma pastor, Paul Littleton, blogged, "I'm conflicted because I am a part of an American evangelical Christianity that's almost entirely and uncritically in bed with the Republican Party who will support them as long as they support capitalism and oppose homosexual marriage. Do that, and we'll vote for you, we'll go to war with you, we'll let you spend the country into oblivion and we'll be silent when you make sexual advances to minor pages. I don't go for any of that stuff." A pastor from Texas, Benjamin Cole, wondered why "the most ardent supporters of the conservative resurgence somehow see global warming . . . [as] somehow apart from any Christian concern, but they think the Second Amendment right to keep and bear arms as very much an issue of religious liberty. . . . I've been a card-carrying of member of the so-called 'Religious Right' since I first voted for Pat Buchanan in the 1996 primaries," he wrote, but "I am sick and tired of the Religious Right. . . . As a Southern Baptist, I don't want to wake up any more in the morning and look on the pillow beside me and find an elephant."[80]

After his surprise election Page, a mild-mannered South Carolina pastor, told reporters he had not been elected "to somehow undo the conservative resurgence," but that the spirit he hoped to embody was quite different from the angry, politicized preacher who had become a stock figure in American life. "I believe in the word of God," he said, "I'm just not mad about it." Page promised he would "reform the operations" of the SBC so that it did not seem "closed and intolerant," and that he would speak to both the Democratic and the Republican presidential candidates in the next election.[81]

In just two years the number of influential evangelicals who had publicly separated themselves from the Christian right had grown exponentially. Yet no one knew how many there were, or even how to characterize them. The movement, if it was a movement, had no single charismatic leader, no central organization, and no fixed set of policies or programs, such as the right had developed. Some offered simply a different style of leadership and a less politicized church. Others proposed a new agenda, and among them many lacked the entire complex of attitudes descended from fundamentalism and had a different vision of the relationship between evangelicals and the rest of the society. For lack of a better term, these became known as "the new evangelicals," though some had been waiting for years to have their voices heard. They included theologians, professors, representatives of international aid agencies, and pastors. Prominent among them was Richard Mouw, a Dutch Reformed theologian whose Calvinism stood in opposition to that of Al Mohler. The president of Fuller, who had signed the Chicago Declaration of 1973, Mouw had transformed the seminary by attracting international students and making it more socially conscious and more aware of other evangelical traditions. Another was Brian McLaren, a college English teacher who founded a nondenominational church in the Baltimore area and a made a third career as an author and speaker. An intellectual rebel, he challenged many of the orthodoxies of evangelicalism from its methods of interpreting the Bible to its social and political conservatism. Yet another was David Gushee, a Southern Baptist professor of Christian ethics at Mercer University's school of theology in Atlanta, who had studied with Ron Sider, and who had written the declaration against torture with his mentor, Glen Stassen, an ethicist at Fuller. A pivotal figure in the movement, David Neff, the editor in chief of *Christianity Today*, had changed his flagship magazine from a conservative publication to one that had taken the lead in discussions of sensitive subjects, such as divorce and global warming.

The movement included several powerful pastors, including Bill Hybels, whose Willow Creek Community Church in South Barrington,

Illinois, had the fourth largest congregation in the country. Over fifteen years he had built an association of twelve thousand churches with an annual leadership conference that, telecast to the churches, had a virtual audience in the tens of thousands. He had served as a spiritual advisor to Bill Clinton, and as his stature had grown, he became more willing to buck the conservatives in and out of his congregation. He had preached against the Iraq War, and in 2007 he horrified many by inviting Jimmy Carter and a secular filmmaker to speak at his Global Leadership Conference, saying evangelical leaders could benefit from "a whole world of information, a world of powerful ideas that God could use to challenge [them], to stretch them." He considered politics "a heartache and a disappointment" for a Christian leader, but he put his congregation to work on racial reconciliation in the Chicago area, the global AIDS epidemic, and poverty in Africa. His message to the Willow Creek Association was that churches had to try to transform their communities through working on racial and educational injustice.[82] Like Hybels, many "new evangelical" pastors preferred to work in their own communities. But a few were willing to work with others on the development of a new public policy on a national level.

One of these was Dr. Joel C. Hunter, the pastor of the nondenominational Northland Church in Orlando, Florida, who preached to ten thousand people a week in his church, in its satellites in other parts of Orlando, and over the Internet. A board member of the NAE, Hunter signed the Evangelical Climate Initiative statement, and as a megachurch pastor in a state vulnerable to climate change, he was chosen to do a nationally broadcast television spot for the initiative. Before that Hunter had been active in community affairs for many years, working with his congregation on issues like homelessness, and making alliances with the Catholic and Jewish clergy to help the city government with job training for the poor. He became friends with the head of the local Muslim association, Imam Muhammad Musri, and after 9/11 he invited him to speak at his church and the local Reformed seminary to ward off the anti-Muslim sentiment that seemed to be growing among evangelicals. A science buff, he required no conversion to the idea of global warming, and in spite of some resistance from his board, he soon became a lead exponent of the climate change initiative. Working closely with Cizik, he met with scientists, lobbied Congress, and helped to publicize *The Great Warming*, a documentary designed for religious audiences. "One thing led to another," he said.[83] In April, when the issue of immigration came up in the Congress, he signed a letter to Bush with a number of other evangelicals, including Rev. Samuel Rodriguez, the head of the National Hispanic Leadership Conference, urging the president to work for a "comprehensive and humane" immigration bill. Bush favored such a bill, but 63 percent of evangelicals regarded immigrants as "a threat to U.S. customs and values," and in an FRC poll the previous spring 90 percent chose forced deportation for all undocumented immigrants.[84]

Not long afterward Hunter published a new version of *A New Kind of Conservative,* which he'd written in 1988, when Pat Robertson was running for president, in which he argued, much as Boyd did, that the evangelical right confused the power of the Cross with the coercive power of government and misunderstood the nature of American democracy. In looking back "to the good old days when Christians ran things," evangelicals, he wrote, failed to understand that the purpose of checks and balances in the Constitution was to prevent majorities from becoming too powerful. Evangelicals, he wrote, should participate in politics—indeed as citizens and Christians, they had a duty to do so—but they should understand they constituted a special-interest group, one of many in a pluralist society, and should act accordingly, recognizing the need for cooperation for the common good.[85] He called for civility in political discourse and wrote, "A voice of biblical values cannot be in the pocket of one party."[86]

Not long after Hunter's book was published, Roberta Combs, an acquaintance, asked him to succeed her as president of the Christian Coalition. His friends were flabbergasted, but Combs, her organization in dire financial straits, was making small steps to broaden its agenda by lobbying for a bill on Internet neutrality, supported by the ACLU. Hunter accepted on the condition that he could transform the Coalition from a Washington-based advocacy group into grassroots organization to get churches involved with the environment and poverty. The Coalition's board agreed in July, but already the state chapters had begun breaking away from the national organization. In March the Iowa chapter left, followed by the chapter in Ohio, and when it became known that Combs and

Hunter favored pressing for a raise in the minimum wage, and that he opposed the death penalty, John Giles, the head of the Alabama chapter, said "The Coalition is drifting left. There's a new vision and we're not a part of it."[87] He quit and formed a new organization, as did the head of the Georgia chapter. In November, just a month after the Coalition officially announced the appointment of a new president, the board backed away from its commitment, and Hunter abruptly resigned. "When we really got down to it," he explained, "they said, 'This just isn't for us. It won't speak to our base, so we just can't go there,'" adding that "some evangelical leaders" were "deathly afraid of being labeled a liberal by other Christians, the media, talk radio."[88]

The episode spoke to the division in evangelical ranks and the ambivalence that many evangelicals, such as Roberta Combs, felt about it. As for Hunter, it brought him national press attention and gave him a larger platform to speak out on the issues he cared about, such as global warming and reconciliation between evangelicals and Muslims. The following February he attended the U.S. Islamic World Forum, an annual gathering of American and Muslim leaders in Qatar, sponsored by the Brookings Institution.[89] When he discovered that even the American diplomats assumed that all evangelicals believed that Israel had a biblical right to the Palestinian territories, he and eighty-three colleagues, including Ron Sider and Richard Mouw, wrote an open letter to President Bush, calling for a two-state solution and justice for both the Israelis and the Palestinians.[90] The statement was "hardly revolutionary," Hunter said with a grin, "but it was subversive," meaning subversive of the Christian right.[91]

"We're at a watershed in our history," Hunter said in an interview in Orlando. "What has passed for an 'evangelical' up to now is a stereotype created by the people with the loudest voices. But there's a whole constituency out there that it doesn't apply to. Now something is happening. You can feel it like the force of tsunami under the water."[92]

Hunter was no one's stereotype. In his early sixties, trimly built, not tall, and usually clad in a gray suit and a conservative tie, he was so unassuming that it was hard to imagine him as a megachurch pastor. On the days he preached, he parked his car in the lot farthest from the church so others were not inconvenienced, and in staff meetings he listened a good deal more than he spoke. He often opened his sermons with folksy stories, but he was something of an intellectual. In the study of his small house he had stacks of books piled on the floor. Getting up at four in the morning to have some privacy, he would, after making his devotions and answering emails, read eclectically in philosophy, science, history, and current affairs. Hunter, who does not like to be thought of as earnest, said he was having more fun than he had since college. "This is the most idealistic and vision-ary time in my life." In fact, he had brought together the two parts of his life that had been separated since the 1960s.[93]

Born in 1948 in Shelby, a small county seat in northern Ohio, Hunter grew up outside the evangelical orbit. His father, a decorated World War II veteran, died of cancer when he was four, and his mother married a devout Catholic, who worked in a carbon-paper factory. Joel attended a Methodist church with his grandparents, and went to public school. In 1966 he enrolled in Ohio State University, where he majored in history and government, and was swept up in the student activism of the period. He didn't demonstrate against the Vietnam War because there were many military men in his family, but as he remembered, that was the exception. "If the mashed potatoes were lumpy in the cafeteria, we were out there with placards." He believed his generation would change the world, and idolized Martin Luther King Jr. and Bobby Kennedy. When they were as-sassinated and the student movement split into angry factions, Hunter's disillusionment was profound. He turned to the religion of his youth and went to seminary.[94]

Hunter spent fifteen years in the United Methodist Church, pastoring a small rural church and then one in a growing suburb of Indianapolis, where under his leadership the congregation burgeoned. Inspired by one of his professors, he had become a theological conservative, and though the Methodist Church harbored many evangelicals at the congregational level, he became increasingly uneasy. At the age of thirty-seven with a wife and three children, he left what had become the second-largest church of its denomination in the state and accepted an offer from Northland, a nondenominational evangelical congregation of two hundred that had just lost its pastor. Ten years later he was preaching seven services every weekend to accommodate five thousand congregants.[95]

Many megachurches (defined as those with over two thousand in the congregation) have sports facilities, a day care center, a school, and social clubs, but Northland never had such amenities, and it never used marketing techniques to attract seekers. It grew mainly because of its worship services. Hunter is a populist preacher in the sense that he's a good storyteller, witty and down-to-earth, but according to Reggie Kidd, a professor at the Reformed Theological Seminary near Orlando, his great gift is the ability to find the profound in simple things and to explain difficult theological concepts in ways that are easy to understand. His emphasis is on the New Testament, and on the Gospels more than on the epistles of Paul. The church, he said, relied too much on doctrine and not enough on the life of Christ—his ministry to the poor, the outcast, and the peacemakers. In 1996, when he felt the congregation was ready, he changed the emphasis of his preaching from individual faith and mutual service to service to the community as a whole. "He pushed us out," Lori Droppers, a physical therapist who had been going to Northland with her husband and children for ten years, said. "It's not a church that wants to gather you in with people of the same mind-set." Sometimes, she said, "I do long for the 'holy huddle,' but it was the right thing to do."[96]

In other ways Hunter differed from the Christian right and quasi-fundamentalists such as Al Mohler. No biblical literalist, he understood the Bible as a number of different kinds of literature. On the question of salvation he said, "I go back to John 14:6 where Christ says, 'I am the way' . . . but I know the limits of my understanding of Christ. [And] the more friends I have who are Jewish or Muslim, the more I hope I am wrong or can't see the fullness of God. . . . The only assurance I have is the Cross, but I'm sure hoping God works out another deal" [for non-Christians]. On what he called the "below the belt" issues, Hunter believed that sex should be confined to marriage, and that homosexuality was a sin—a sin like so many others—but he didn't believe in imposing Christian views on non-Christians. He opposed abortion, but he didn't believe in overturning *Roe v. Wade* or limiting abortion by legal means. Further, he believed abortion to be a part of an ethical continuum. Since the 1970s some on the evangelical left, like Jim Wallis, had adopted Joseph Cardinal Bernardin's idea of consistent pro-life ethics, or "the seamless garment of life." Hunter did, too, but he didn't like to use fancy theological terms. He said, "The problem has become that we have paid so much attention to the human being in the womb that we forget about the human being out of the womb." [97] To him such things as the death penalty, poverty, AIDS, and global warming were also life issues. "Precious lives are lost from abortion," he once said, "but if we don't address climate change, there will be even more." [98]

By then the issue of school prayer was essentially dead. The Southern Baptist Convention, however, supported it, and Land had developed a complicated formula whereby minority religious groups could choose the daily prayer in proportion to their numbers. Hunter, however, was very clear: all school prayer was of necessity government-sanctioned, and the majority had no right to impose its religious views on others.

Asked why the Christian right had retained its hold over evangelicals for a quarter of a century, Hunter began by evoking the sense of alarm that evangelicals felt during the cultural upheavals of the 1960s. "When you're angry or afraid," he said, "the loudest voices carry the day." Speaking of the Jerry Falwells and the Pat Robertsons, he compared them to "guys like Eldridge Cleaver and H. Rap Brown," who made people say to themselves, "I can't believe how this could be happening in our country!" There wasn't, he said, "a lot of thinking," but because "these guys held the microphone, everyone said, 'Well, there's a leader, and let's mobilize around that because at least we'll get this done.'" The Falwells, he said, gathered large constituencies because people were afraid, they sounded confident, and they created "a common enemy." Radio and television broadcasters, they built powerful organizations, and that was intimidating. "Who in the world was going to stand up to Jim Dobson?" Hunter asked. Everyone knew how many people listened to him and no one wanted to stand up and say, "I'm not sure he's right on this," certainly not the pastors who were still building their churches. "They were the last ones who wanted to introduce any kind of controversy." Now, he said, "It's really funny because people are saying, 'We were never that kind of person . . . we weren't angry all the time! We were always compassionate.'" In Hunter's view it took not just a change in evangelical attitudes but the emergence of a new generation of pastors, such as Warren and Hybels, with power bases of their own to challenge the Christian right.[99]

★   ★   ★

In May 2007 Jerry Falwell died, followed by Bill Bright and D. James Kennedy, all of them in their seventies. At Kennedy's funeral Dobson lamented, "Many giants of the church are coming to the end of their journeys and leaving this earth one by one." And now, "the passing of Dr. D. James Kennedy poses serious concerns about the future of the conservative Christian movement." Who, he asked, "will defend the un-born child? Who's going to fight for the institution of marriage . . . [or] teach young people the dangers of both heterosexual and homosexual promiscuity? Who in the next generation will be willing to take the heat when it's so much safer and more comfortable to avoid the controversial subjects? Who's going to defend traditional morality and a culture that's spinning into moral decline? Who will call sin by its name and lead a na-tion to repentance and holiness?" I pray, he said, "that the Lord will anoint another generation of Jim Kennedys—courageous men and women who will never waver one inch in defense of righteousness."[100]

Dobson was not alone in asking what would become of the conserva-tive Christian movement. "The fiery old guard who helped lead conser-vative Christians into the Republican Party are aging and slowly receding from the scene," reported The New York Times.[101] The rest of the original movement leaders were also in their seventies, and Dobson was think-ing of retiring from the chairmanship of Focus on the Family. "I just don't see in the next generation of so-called evangelical leaders anyone as politically activist-minded" as Falwell, Robertson, or Dobson, said the historian D. G. Hart. Most of them, he said, were pastors, as opposed to the heads of advocacy groups, making them reluctant to plunge into politics and risk alienating their congregations.[102] "The evangelical move-ment as a political force is in a serious state of transition," Frank Page told The Washington Post. "With the passing of Jerry Falwell, evangelicals are struggling to try to find the kind of cohesion he represented." We are, he said, "in a time of real doubt and a disturbing lack of loyalty to causes. We see people having a hard time pulling together."[103] Rick Scarborough, who was barnstorming the country with a Falwellesque "Seventy Weeks to Save America Tour," had to agree, "We are somewhat in disarray right now."[104]

As Page suggested, the dissent was coming not just from the pulpits, but from the pews. For example, Dobson presumably thought he was speaking to a sympathetic audience at the funeral, but Kennedy's congregation had already moved on. While their preacher was in the hospital, his political arm, Center for Reclaiming America, which two years before had launched a plan to open a Capitol Hill office and recruit activists in all of the 435 congressional districts, had closed its doors.[105] After his death, his congregation chose to merge with a nearby Presbyterian church pastored by Tullian Tchividjian, the grandson of Billy Graham, who preached the faith and avoided divisive issues.[106] Similarly in Wichita, Iowa, the three pastors who had led the Christian right and the antiabortion protests had retired, or been asked to leave, having experienced various degrees of resistance from their congregations and from their young associate pastors.[107] In Ohio, Russell Johnson, who had attempted to mobilize Patriot Pastors and had preached virtually nothing except politics before the 2006 election, had left his church, and Parsley had grown quiet on the subject.[108]

Analysts of evangelical politics agreed that the Iraq War and the overreaching by the Christian right during the Bush presidency had set off the reaction, but that there were longer-term trends that led to the decline of the movement.[109] In forty years evangelicals had made significant gains in income and education. Moreover, as John C. Green said, "The social-issues arguments are the first manifestation of a rural outlook transposed into a more urban or suburban setting," but once people had been there for a while the culture shock had worn off, and "hard-edged politics no longer appeals to them." They still "care about abortion and gay marriage, but they are also interested in other, more middle-class arguments," he said.[110] Similarly, Mark Pinsky, a veteran religion writer then at the *Orlando Sentinel*, observed that the Sun Belt evangelicalism was very different from that of the Bible Belt: suburban families trying to get their kids into college didn't believe that the earth is only a few thousand years old, and they didn't join crusades to post the Ten Commandments in courthouses.[111] Then, too, as Hunter had pointed out, the generational change was important. The baby boomers were less afraid of secularism than those brought up entirely within an evangelical subculture, and for many the older concerns had receded. As for the young, they had moved even farther into the secular world. Thanks in part to the new media, they had absorbed many of the social changes of the past forty years, and they shared many of the interests of the rest of their generation. Cameron Strang, who published the glossy magazine *Relevant* in Orlando for young evangelicals, ran stories about pop stars as well as about young preachers and specialized in new music by secular and cross-over Christian artists. According to polls, the young were much more inclined to worry about the environment than their elders and to be more in favor of an active government at home. Abortion was the defining issue for them—even more so than for their parents—but homosexuality was not. Many had grown up with openly gay friends, and one in three favored same-sex marriage, as opposed to one in ten of their elders. On the whole they were more tolerant of the views of others, and over 40 percent said a person can be moral without believing in God.[112]

Looking to the next election, Christian right leaders saw little that gave them hope. Bush's approval ratings among evangelicals had dropped by 28 points between 2002 and 2007. Among the young they had fallen precipitously, from 87 percent to 42 percent, and the percentage of young evangelicals who identified with the Republican Party had dropped by 15 percent.[113] Furthermore, the movement leaders had no candidate. According to Land, the only candidates with wide appeal for evangelicals were Senator Sam Brownback and Governor Mike Huckabee of Arkansas, but neither appeared to have a chance of winning. As for the major candidates, all had strikes against them. Rudolph Giuliani, former mayor of New York City, was thrice married, pro–gay rights, and pro-choice. Governor Mitt Romney took all the positions they favored, but he was a Mormon, and in his past races in Massachusetts had supported gay rights and legalized abortion. Senator John McCain had a fraught relationship with the Christian right; he had been part of the Gang of 14 that had created a compromise over the issue of judges, and he had resisted a constitutional amendment to ban gay marriage.

In the early fall opinion polls showed Giuliani in the lead with Romney and McCain running far behind him. Even 25 percent of evangelicals supported Giuliani.[114] Pat Robertson, who was becoming more unpredictable all the time (he had changed his mind on global warming to admit that it was human-induced), came out for Giuliani on the grounds that he would be the best one to fight terrorism. Dobson and his allies, on the other hand, decided that if Republicans nominated a social liberal like Giuliani, they would create a third party.[115] Richard Viguerie argued that social conservatives should stay out of presidential politics until the Republicans had more to offer them, but Richard Land worried that a victory for Giuliani could crack the united front that had backed Bush in 2004 and give the Democratic nominee "a license to go hunting for evangelical votes."[116]

In September McCain's polls and financial support melted away, and Fred Thompson, the actor and former senator from Tennessee, joined the race. With a perfect antiabortion record in the Senate, he courted social conservatives, hoping to be the candidate for those who had their doubts about Romney, but he had to admit he was not particularly religious and didn't go to church every week. The National Right to Life Committee supported him, and Land, while he could take no official position, made no secret of his preference for the former senator.[117] Dobson, however, spoke of him sarcastically. "He's apparently the Great White Hope that burns in the breasts of many conservative Christians. Not for me, my brothers, not for me."[118]

Christian right leaders gave small attention to Huckabee, though in many ways the former Southern Baptist pastor seemed the ideal candidate. He held by far the strongest antiabortion record of all the candidates, and many thought him fresh and appealing. A near unknown with a cash-starved campaign, he had come in second in the Iowa straw poll and the Values Voters Summit poll behind Romney, who had spent millions of dollars rounding up voters. He expected that Southern Baptist leaders would support him—after all, he had headed the Arkansas Baptist State Convention—and he was disappointed when Pressler and Land did not. But then he had not joined the "conservative resurgence," and he had a liberal streak. As governor he had successfully worked to get health insurance for lower-income children, and he had made a try at getting in-state college tuition rates for the children of undocumented immigrants. He had raised taxes to improve roads and schools, and pardoned or reduced the sentences for over a thousand people, saying they deserved a second chance.[119] During the campaign he took a hard line on immigration, saying that all illegal immigrants should be deported, but he criticized Bush's foreign policy and called for diplomacy in the Middle East. His website gave just as much space to the need to fight poverty, to increase funding for the arts, and to reform health care as to opposing abortion and gay rights. Telling reporters that evangelicals had widening political concerns beyond the hot-button issues, he spoke of the need to protect the environment, gain energy independence, improve education, and create jobs. Emphasizing his humble economic roots, and calling the Club for Growth "the Club for Greed," he attracted young working-class evangelicals.[120] Some called him a "compassionate conservative," and some said he was not a conservative at all. *The Wall Street Journal* editorial page called him "the tribune of the 'religious left,'" though he made a point of going to Hagee's church and appearing with Tim and Bev LaHaye.[121]

In their review of the candidates' positions just before the start of the primaries in January on the Focus Action and the Family Research Council websites, Tom Minnery and Tony Perkins had nothing good to say about Giuliani or McCain, and they were surprisingly harsh about Huckabee. They called the former pastor "fairly good on values voters' issues," but Minnery suggested that Huckabee did not understand the cause for which American soldiers were dying in Iraq, and Perkins said that he lacked the fiscal and national security credentials necessary for a conservative president. "Huckabee has got to reach out to the fiscal conservatives and security conservatives," he said. Only Romney came in for praise—and for what amounted to an endorsement—even though more than a third of evangelicals said they would not vote for a Mormon. "He has staked out positions on all three areas we have discussed," said Perkins. "I think he continues to be solidly conservative." Romney, Minnery said, "has acknowledged that Mormonism is not a Christian faith, but on the social issues we are so similar." Land averred that Mormonism was not a "cult," as some in the SBC called it, but "the fourth great Abrahamic religion."[122]

In December Romney addressed his "Mormon problem," just as JFK had addressed his "Catholic problem," in a speech in Texas. Like JFK, he promised that no authority in his church (whose name he did not mention) would exert any influence on the decisions he made as president, or on his obligations to the Constitution and the common cause of the people of the United States. But he said he would never distance himself from his religion, because all religions taught the "the great moral principles that unite us," and religion should never be a purely private affair because it formed the basis for American values, such as human equality, the obligation to serve one another, and a steadfast commitment to liberty. In other words, he ignored the divisions created by religion in the United States, and particularly those involved with the relationship between church and state. Dobson praised his speech as "a magnificent reminder of the role religious faith must play in government and public policy."[123]

The primaries did not go at all as the Christian right leaders expected, exposing a split between the leaders and grassroots evangelicals. In early January Huckabee won the Iowa caucuses with the help of the home schooling network, local pastors, and a sudden burst of enthusiasm among evangelicals. Days later McCain staged a comeback by winning in New Hampshire over Romney. He and Huckabee virtually split the vote in South Carolina, and Thompson, who desperately needed to win the heavily evangelical state, came in a disappointing third and dropped out of the race. In Florida, where Giuliani had put all his resources, McCain beat Romney, and Giuliani, who tied for fourth with Huckabee, withdrew the next day. Romney won Nevada, but Huckabee prevented him from sweeping up the social conservative vote in other states. On Super Tuesday McCain was the big winner, taking almost enough delegates to cinch the nomination, but Huckabee won five southern states. Evangelical Republicans divided their vote almost evenly among the three top candidates, but Romney, the candidate of Christian right leaders, could not beat McCain or Huckabee in any Bible Belt state, and he had to drop out a few days later.[124] Dobson was furious. "Should Senator McCain capture the nomination, as many assume, I believe this general election will offer the worst choices for President in my lifetime."[125] He threatened not to vote, then came out for Huckabee when it was too late to make a difference.[126] On March 4 McCain sewed up the nomination, and Huckabee had to concede.

All this time the Democrats had been working to pick up religious voters and narrow the "God gap." Knowing the Democrats were seen as hostile to religion, the Democratic National Committee convened an advisory council of sixty religious leaders, and the three major candidates, Senators Hillary Clinton, Barack Obama, and John Edwards, hired religious outreach teams.[127] A number of new progressive faith organizations, such as Catholics in Alliance for the Common Good, Faith in Public Life, and Tony Campolo's Red Letter Christians, tried to help them close the breach. The Third Way, a centrist Democratic think tank, brought secular progressives and evangelicals, such as Joel Hunter and David Gushee, together to try to find common ground on the most divisive of the culture issues such as abortion, and House Democrats put together a bill designed to reduce the number of abortions through increased funding for the prevention of unintended pregnancies, support for women who couldn't afford to bring their pregnancies to term, adoption awareness, and child care.[128] Jim Wallis, who had often criticized the Democrats for not "getting religion," put on a nationally televised forum in June 2007 in which the candidates spoke of how their faith informed their politics and personal lives before an audience of 1,500 clergy. All three had religious backgrounds, and to many the forum sounded like a religious revival. None gave way on *Roe v. Wade* or gay rights, but they acknowledged that abortion was a "moral" issue, and Clinton in answer to a question from Joel Hunter said it should be "safe, legal, and rare."[129]

When the primary season got under way, journalists speculated that the Democrats might pick up substantial numbers of evangelical votes.[130] Democratic strategists were more cautious, and scholars of the subject, such as John C. Green, said it might take a generation to change voting patterns. Still, the polls suggested that the new evangelical movement was gaining ground. A Beliefnet survey conducted in January showed that the top issues for evangelicals were the economy and cleaning up government. Almost 60 percent said they favored a more progressive agenda, focused on protecting the environment, tackling HIV-AIDs, and alleviating poverty. Of those who said that reducing abortion was a high priority, 69 percent said that the best way to do it was "changing the culture through education and other means."[131] A Pew survey showed that 15 percent of evangelicals under thirty were moving away from the Republican Party and 5 percent were becoming Democrats.[132] In February, after Edwards had dropped out, Faith in Public Life, whose spokesmen had complained that exit polls asked only Republicans if they were evangelicals, sponsored a Zogby survey to find out how evangelicals were actually voting. The poll, taken on Super Tuesday, showed that in Tennessee and Missouri 30 percent of evangelicals had voted in the Democratic primaries, and a majority of them ranked the economy and jobs as their top concerns with abortion and gay rights way down the list. "The new [evangelical] agenda is in full swing," Jim Wallis told the press. "I would say all the data . . . shows the evangelicals are leaving in the Religious Right in droves."[133] Asked if the polls did not show that evangelicals were returning to the pre-Bush period, when Bill Clinton won 30 percent of the vote, Wallis said evangelicals were not changing one partisan allegiance for another, but becoming more independent. "Younger evangelicals who previously were committed to Religious Right organizations are defecting because they are as concerned with issues like global warming, poverty and the Iraq war as with saving unborn children."[134]

Wallis did not need the polls to tell him that. The previous year the SBC had passed a resolution urging Southern Baptists "to proceed cautiously in the human-induced global warming debate in light of conflicting scientific research" and to weigh "the effects on economics and impacts on the poor when considering programs to reduce CO_2 and other greenhouse gas emissions."[135] But in March Jonathan Merritt, a twenty-five-year-old seminary student, caught the attention of the media when he released "A Southern Baptist Declaration on the Environment and Climate Change" saying our "current denominational engagement with these issues has often been too timid, failing to produce a unified moral voice. Our cautious response to these issues in the face of mounting evidence may be seen by the world as uncaring, reckless and ill-informed. We can do better."[136] The declaration was signed by forty-six prominent Southern Baptists, including his father, James Merritt, a past president of the SBC; Jack

Graham, another former president; and the current president, Frank Page. It was unusual to make an end run around Richard Land, who normally made public policy for the SBC, but Jonathan said he had had an epiphany: "God reveals himself through Scripture and in general through his creation, and when we destroy God's creation, it's similar to ripping pages from the Bible." [137]

Even members of the Christian right were calling for a broader agenda. In a piece for *WorldNetDaily* Rick Scarborough wrote that he supported Huckabee because as "values voters we must include social justice" and "as stewards of God resources, there needs to be a fresh look at [the environment.]" [138] More surprising, Tony Perkins and Harry Jackson launched their book *Personal Faith and Public Policy* in a bid to succeed the older generation of the Christian right, saying, "The issues facing our nation have broadened, and we have to grow with the issues," including "immigration, poverty, justice, the environment and global warming." Some, Perkins added, "argue that evangelicals lose influence when they fail to vote as a bloc, [but] the ability to seed both parties and act as a 'free agent' could prove to have a much greater impact on public policy [by making them] more faith friendly." [139] The book turned out to be a collection of right-wing bromides about the virtues of self-reliance and the vices of government intervention in a free economy. It was nonetheless an homage to the new evangelical movement.

The hard-fought contest between Clinton and Obama lasted until June. Several primaries showed Clinton winning the white Catholic and the white evangelical vote, but an informal poll of *Christianity Today* readers showed Obama winning, and when in January, Cameron Strang's magazine for young college-educated evangelicals asked whom Jesus would vote for, a plurality of readers chose Obama over all the Republican and Democratic candidates in the field. [140] The Christian right, for its part, seemed more worried about Obama than Clinton. In his "Call to Renewal" speech in 2006, Obama had chastened Democrats "who dismiss religion in the public square as inherently irrational or intolerant" and emphasized the centrality of religion to progressive politics. [141] He also seemed more comfortable talking about his faith than Clinton or McCain. Referring to Rev. Jeremiah Wright, the former pastor of his home church in Chicago, he told a church audience, My pastor "introduced me to someone named Jesus Christ. I learned that my sins could be redeemed. I learned that those things I was too weak to accomplish for myself, he would accomplish if I put my faith in him." [142]

The problem came when clips of his pastor's sermons appeared on YouTube in which Wright, who espoused a form of black liberation theology, said, "God damn America for treating our citizens as less than human. God damn America as long as she acts like she is God, and she is supreme." [143] Understanding the threat, Obama gave a speech four days later denouncing the pastor's remarks without condemning his old friend, and putting the controversy in the context of race and religion in America. His speech, "A More Perfect Union," was widely praised in the press, but some feared he had lost many blue-collar white voters, who might think that he, too, was "an angry black man." A month later McCain had his own pastor troubles. Rev. John Hagee and Rod Parsley, who had been among the few well-known pastors to support him, were found to have made a series of offensive remarks. Hagee had said there was "a clear record of history linking Adolf Hitler and the Roman Catholic Church in a conspiracy to exterminate the Jews," and Parsley, who had always been anti-Muslim, had called for Christians to wage war against the "false religion" of Islam and destroy it. [144] McCain had to publicly reject their endorsements, offending some Pentecostals and showing just how little he and his staff knew about evangelicals—even though they had given Bush 40 percent of his vote. [145]

After his nomination in March, McCain was slow to assemble religious outreach staff, and by May Christian right organizers, such as Michael Farris and Phil Burress, were complaining that they had never been contacted by the McCain campaign and might sit out this election. They were furious about his reluctance to talk about the "moral issues" and his own faith. [146] In June McCain hired staffers devoted to religious outreach, but Marlys Popma, an experienced evangelical organizer, said it was the most difficult campaign she had ever worked in, for evangelicals were dividing into "movement conservatives" and "young evangelicals" who wanted to broaden the agenda to global warming and poverty and felt that the conservatives' talk about abortion and same-sex marriage was too divisive and off-putting. She finally decided she had to have separate conference calls because the mistrust between the two groups was just too great.[147] McCain himself went to see Billy Graham and, guided by Gary Bauer, met privately with skeptical Christian right leaders, stressing his record as a conservative and his pro-life and anti-same-sex-marriage credentials.[148] Apparently he succeeded, for in early July eighty Christian right activists, including Phyllis Schlafly, the LaHayes, and representatives from the largest national organizations, assembled in Denver, and most decided to support him. According to David Barton, there was some grumbling about the bills he had sponsored on campaign finance and immigration reform, but they agreed that although he was not a "pure candidate," he would support their core issues, and they did not want Obama picking judges.[149] Still, a number of conservatives, among them Phil Burress, warned him that if he did not pick a pro-life running mate, he would lose the evangelical vote.[150]

The Obama campaign was faster off the mark. A week after Obama won the nomination, he assembled a group of thirty religious leaders for a private talk in a conference room in Chicago. The group included mainline Protestants, leading African American preachers, conservative Catholics, and white evangelicals, ranging from Joel Hunter and David Neff to Franklin Graham and Stephen Strang, Cameron's father and the conservative publisher of *Charisma*, who sat on the board of Hagee's Christians United for Israel. The meeting was off the record, but some of the participants found it so surprising that a Democratic candidate would reach out to all of them they described it in blogs and to the press. Obama apparently talked about his faith journey and answered their questions. According to Strang, Obama was "warm and personable" and "obviously very intelligent," and when asked how as a Christian he could support abortion, Obama gave a fifteen-minute answer, convincing Strang that he was "more of a centrist that I would have expected."[151] Franklin Graham was apparently more aggressive. He asked about the Muslims in Obama's family and whether he had been raised as Muslim in Indonesia. Obama calmly explained that he had no Muslim background, and others at the meeting changed the subject, and one got up and lectured on McCain's lack of religious commitment.[152]

Obama's strategy, it seemed, was to let these leaders get to know him and to diffuse the hostility of conservatives, who thought all Democrats "secular humanists." He took another opportunity to do the same in August, when Rick Warren invited him and McCain to Saddleback for a televised "Civil Forum on the Presidency." The event had much advance publicity, for it was the first time two presidential candidates had come to the same stage before the conventions and the first time contenders had met in a church with a pastor as a moderator. Obama and McCain appeared separately, and Warren asked them the same questions with different follow-ups, depending on their responses. To the expected questions, McCain gave succinct, blunt answers, such as "At the moment of conception," while Obama had to make lengthier explanations, and when asked when a baby acquired human rights, he joked that the question was "above my pay grade."[153] McCain clearly won over the Saddleback audience, and doubtless many evangelicals who watched the program, but Obama showed he was a thoughtful, religious man.[154]

During the summer the Obama campaign reinforced its religious affairs team, hiring half a dozen full-time staffers, and continued its practice of making weekly conference calls to leaders in every religious community. Under the direction of Joshua DuBois, a young African American Pentecostal minister, the team held hundreds of "faith forums" in local communities and "American values" house parties, targeting mainly Catholics, mainline Protestants, and moderate evangelicals. Capitalizing on the excitement on the campuses, the campaign visited ten evangelical colleges, often with Donald Miller, a best-selling author among young evangelicals. The Mathew 25 Network, a PAC run by Mara Vanderslice, who had helped elect Democrats, such as Ted Strickland in 2006, raised money, ran ads on the evangelical media, and took on the task of pushing back at the Internet rumors that Obama was Muslim.[155] As for the Democratic convention, it held more religious gatherings than the four previous conventions combined. The program began the Sunday before the convention with a large interfaith service in which Christians, Muslims, and Jews read from their sacred texts and prayed together. It continued with a luncheon in which politicians talked about their faith, and a series of "faith caucuses" and "faith panels" in which participants discussed how the Democrats could integrate serious moral considerations with policy and how the campaign could attract people of faith.[156] Publicly the emphasis was on diversity, but behind the scenes Democrats worked the hardest on attracting Christian "values voters."[157] Those in charge of writing the abortion plank consulted with leaders of the Catholic Alliance for the Common Good and a number of evangelicals, such as Joel Hunter, Tony Campolo, and Jim Wallis. The plank had stronger language about a woman's right to choose than the previous platforms, but it spoke of the need to reduce the number unintended pregnancies and abortions. It also had a new sentence, saying "The Democratic Party also strongly supports a woman's decision to have a child by ensuring access to, and the availability of, pre- and post-natal care, parenting skills, income support and caring adoption programs."[158] The plank did not please Catholics and evangelicals who wanted legal sanctions against abortion but Joel Hunter defended it as "a historic and courageous step towards empowering women for an expanded range of choices and saving babies' lives by supporting the mothers whose will and conscience tell them to take their babies to term."[159] Donald Miller gave the invocation to the convention and Hunter the benediction the day Obama accepted the nomination.

The Republican convention, by contrast, held no religious gatherings, but McCain's choice of Sarah Palin as his running mate was *the* religious event of the convention. The governor of Alaska, Palin had grown up in an Assemblies of God church, and although she called herself "a Bible believing" or "a non-denomination Christian," she continued to go to Pentecostal and charismatic churches, one of which cast out demons and another that held an event for Hagee's Christians United for Israel, as well as a nondenominational "Bible church."[160] When McCain picked her, 250 Christian right leaders were meeting in Minnesota, and according to Land they jumped to their feet and cheered. "There wasn't a pro-life activist in the country who didn't know exactly who Sarah Palin was," Land said.[161] A few days later Dobson, who had declared he would never vote for McCain "under any circumstances," reversed course and said on a radio program, "If I went into the polling booth today, I would pull the lever for John McCain."[162] "She's one of us," said Land.[163] The choice of Palin, a former beauty queen with five children, the youngest with Down syndrome, caused considerable excitement among conservative evangelicals. "People have gotten off the fence. They're ready to work now," said Chris Long of the Ohio Christian Alliance. "All that was unknown until the Palin pick." [164]

After the convention McCain for the first time pulled ahead of Obama in the polls, but the post-convention "bounce" did not last long. When Palin muffed her interviews on foreign policy and many other subjects, she became fodder for Jon Stewart on his show and Tina Fey on *Saturday Night Live* and on the whole a liability for McCain. In mid-September the Wall Street crash made the economy the primary issue for voters, and in part because people normally blame the party in power, the economic crisis benefited Obama. At the same time the Obama campaign became increasingly optimistic about "redrawing the map" of religious voters by attracting moderate evangelicals in battleground states like Colorado, Ohio, and Michigan. Indeed, so confident had the campaign become, Obama took his message of "hope and change" directly into McCain stronghold states such as Indiana and North Carolina. His Joshua Generation project designed to court young evangelicals never materialized in the eight weeks he had after the convention, but he made direct appeals to young religious voters on Facebook and other social media. His polls continued to rise, and journalists again speculated that he might take a substantial number of evangelical votes.

In October Christian right leaders launched a series of attacks on Obama, predicting doomsday if he were elected. More than the usual jeremiads, they seemed to be signs of desperation. Stephen Strang titled one of his weekly emails to readers, "Life as We Know It Will End if Obama Is Elected," writing that gay rights and abortion rights would be strengthened, taxes would rise, and "people who hate Christianity will be emboldened to attack our freedoms." [165] Focus Action published a lengthy "Letter from 2012 in Obama's America," imagining what the future would look like if Obama won. In its crystal ball it saw:

- The U.S. Supreme Court with a liberal majority has forced the Boy Scouts to disband because of its decision they would have to "hire homosexual scoutmasters and allow them to sleep in tents with young boys."

- Tens of thousands of Christian teachers in public schools have quit or been fired; private Christian schools have been closed; home schooling is all but outlawed; and many parents have taken their families to Australia and New Zealand.
- Health care has been nationalized with long lines for surgery and no access to hospitals for people over eighty.
- Because of Obama's reluctance to use force, terrorists have attacked four American cities; Iran has exploded a nuclear bomb on Tel Aviv; and Russia has captured and occupied the Baltic States and Eastern Europe.
- Conservative talk radio has been shut down; dozens of Bush officials have been imprisoned; and Obama has repressed dissent to the point that "hardly any brave citizen dares to resist the new government policies anymore."[166]

The letter was clearly targeted at evangelicals, and specifically at young evangelicals, for it said, "Christians share a lot of the blame. In 2008 many evangelicals thought Senator Obama was an opportunity for a 'change,' and they voted for him . . . [and] younger evangelicals actually provided him with the needed margin to defeat John McCain."[167]

In an interview Strang voiced optimism, saying that a last-minute push might help McCain, as it had Bush in 2004. Phil Burress, however, said that the dynamics were different from 2004, when conservative evangelicals were motivated by enthusiasm for Bush, but now there was less excitement about McCain than fear of Obama. "It reminds me," he said, "of when I was a school kid, when I had to go out in the hall and bury my head in my hands because of the atom bomb."[168]

When the results came in, it appeared that Obama had not changed the religious map of country, but in a landslide victory he had swept all but one of the battleground states, and made incursions into the red states. The Democrats had gained a more substantial majority in the House and a supermajority of sixty votes in the Senate with two independents voting with them. In an election with the highest percentage of voter turnout since 1968, Obama's greatest supporters were non-white Americans and the religiously unaffiliated, both of whose numbers had grown in four years, and the young, who turned out in droves, giving Obama 60 percent of their vote. Obama did better among most religious voters than Kerry, winning a majority of Catholics, and reducing the "God gap" by gaining the vote of 44 percent of those who went to houses of worship weekly or more—a 9 percent gain over Kerry.[169] White evangelicals, however, remained faithful to the Republican Party, with 74 percent of them voting for McCain and 24 percent for Obama (or 3 percentage points over Kerry).[170] As for younger evangelicals (ages eighteen to twenty-nine), they gave Obama 32 percent of their vote, or double the percentage they gave Kerry but about the same percentage all evangelicals gave Clinton in 1992.[171]

Many wondered why Obama hadn't done better among evangelicals, when many of them were lukewarm about McCain and worried about the economy, and some embraced traditionally Democratic issues such as poverty and the environment. One of the answers, as Amy Sullivan in *Time* magazine pointed out, was that half of all evangelicals lived in the South, and the South was never in play.[172] According to Mara Vanderslice, the Obama campaign had never made an aggressive outreach to white Southern Baptists living the South. It had concentrated on moderates in the swing states like Florida, Michigan, and Ohio. In such states, Obama's gains were much larger than the national average. In Michigan he took 33 percent of the white evangelical vote; in Colorado 29 percent; in Indiana 30 percent, the latter giving him enough votes to win one of the reddest states.[173] "There is a different flavor to evangelicalism in the South," said John C. Green.[174] Obama's gains among Catholics were driven by Hispanics and the white working class, but low-income white evangelicals in the South voted for McCain. Even in the states Obama carried, such as Virginia and North Carolina, his white evangelical vote was much lower than in the northern states.[175] As for the Deep South, party politics was segregated in the sense that almost all people of color voted Democratic, and apart from a few liberals, almost all white people voted Republican. There, certainly, the vote against Obama was as much racial as it was theological.

As for younger evangelicals, the divide in their vote may have been a matter of class as well as geography. For example, the Pew poll of early 2007 had shown that young evangelicals took conservative positions on a variety of issues, including abortion, the death penalty, and the war in Iraq. The *Relevant* poll, however, showed almost the opposite. *Relevant* readers opposed the war in Iraq, felt that the government should support national health care, and put gay rights at the bottom of their list of important topics. Only on the issue of abortion was there any agreement between all young evangelicals and the college-educated subscribers to *Relevant*.[176]

17

THE TRANSFORMATION
of the CHRISTIAN RIGHT

I F OBAMA was disappointed by the evangelical vote, he hardly showed it. He chose Rick Warren to give the inaugural benediction, though his choice caused consternation among gay activists because Warren had sent his congregation an email backing Proposition 8, the successful California ballot initiative to reverse the State Supreme Court's ruling permitting same-sex marriage. He also invited Joel Hunter to give the blessing at a private service in St. John's Episcopal Church before the inauguration. The two men liked each other—they were temperamentally quite similar—and Obama made Hunter one of his spiritual advisors.[1]

A few days before Obama took office, a group of evangelical leaders working with progressives of the Democratic-leaning think tank Third Way gave the transition team a memo designed, as the Third Way spokesman put it, "to serve as roadmap of how to put an end to culture wars." The memo, a consensus agenda, had four elements. First, a plan for reducing abortions without restricting abortion rights through programs such as sex education that included abstinence as well as contraceptive education, improved access to contraception for low-income women, expanded health care for pregnant women and new families, plus new tax credits for adoptions. Second, the memo proposed federal prohibitions against workplace discrimination for gays and lesbians with a "clear exception" for religious organizations. The agenda also called for laws against torture and advocated comprehensive immigration reform, including a path to earned citizenship for undocumented aliens.[2] The last two proposals had been easily agreed upon, but the drafters of the memo, who included Joel Hunter, Ron Sider, David Gushee, and Samuel Rodriguez, head of the National Hispanic Christian Leadership Council, had struggled to find a consensus with the Third Way liberals on abortion and gay rights. When the draft was done, they circulated it and gained support from a handful of liberal advocacy groups, including NARAL Pro-Choice America, and a number of evangelical leaders, among them, Richard Mouw, Tony Campolo, Jim Wallis, and Jonathan Merritt.[3] The consensus document had been long in the making, but it dovetailed with Obama's own proposal to reduce abortions and his desire to find some solution to the conflict between gay rights and the rights of religious institutions.[4]

When the memo was introduced to the press in a conference call, reporters asked why the group had made proposals on the hot-button issues when the president was focused on a major economic crisis. "We have to address these wedge issues now so they don't keep coming up again," Rodriguez said, "and they will come up again in 2010 if we don't find common ground."[5] In his endorsement of the plan Richard Mouw wrote, "One of the miracles recorded in the gospels is the healing of paralysis, and we need that kind of miracle today. We are paralyzed in polarization regarding many of our most pressing issues."[6]

To many Democrats, and particularly the young, Obama's election brought a sense of euphoria, a sense that change would come, that all was possible. Some evangelicals had the same sense. Taylor Wigg-Stevenson, a thirty-one year-old Baptist minister, formed the Two Futures Project to promote nuclear disarmament, envisioning verifiable reductions in nuclear arms of all the nuclear powers that would lead to global disarmament. David Gushee and Glen Stassen of the Fuller Seminary, and other members of the National Religious Campaign Against Torture, pressed the Congress to close the Guantánamo Bay military prison, as Obama desired, and to end U.S.-sponsored torture forever.[7]

Christian right leaders saw the prospects of an Obama administration differently, but their response was subdued. Land said little, though the Ethics & Religious Liberty Commission prepared a defensive agenda: opposition to legislation that relaxed restrictions on abortion, opposition to bills like the Employment Non-Discrimination Act for federal employees, which ERLC said would "normalize homosexuality," and opposition to adding sexual orientation or gender identity to categories protected by the hate crimes act lest it criminalize preaching against homosexuality.[8] As for Dobson, his response was uncharacteristically muted. "I want to admit, I'm in the midst of a grieving process at this time," he said on his radio show. "I'm not grieving over Obama's victory but over the loss of things I've fought for for 35 years." He mentioned abortion, gay rights, and the Supreme Court, then said, "Our hope is in the Lord. He hasn't lost control of things. He understands our fatigue and maybe our disappointment."[9] Possibly Dobson just didn't want to attack the first black president before he took office because he congratulated Obama on his "stunning victory," which he called a historic accomplishment. Possibly, however, he was thinking about himself and his future.[10]

In February 2009 Focus on the Family announced that Dobson was stepping down as chair of the organization. It was no surprise. The finances of Focus were a good deal more transparent than those of many other media ministries, and Focus had been losing money since 2001, or about the time Dobson and his Arlington Group allies began to complain that they were losing the culture war. Dobson had raised money for Focus Action for the political battles of 2004, but the annual income of his entire ministry had dropped off from a high of over $150 million and the number of its employees had begun to sink from a high of 1,400.[11] In November 2008 Focus had approximately 950 employees and announced it was laying off another 202.[12] In December *Time* magazine reported that Focus's expenses had exceeded its revenues for the years 2005 and 2006 and that the income from the purchases of books and tapes had declined from $678,000 in 2002 to $269,000 in 2006.[13] Worse, according to Dan Gilgoff, Dobson's listenership had remained flat since 2000, the average age of his listeners had risen to thirty-eight in 2005, and the average age of his constituents on Focus mailing lists to fifty-two.[14] Clearly the decline was a long-term trend with no end in sight because Focus listeners were getting older, and Dobson, age seventy-three, was unable to attract the younger generation. Furthermore, because he had dominated Focus, the organization had no resources to do it, and Jim Daly, whom he had handpicked for president in 2005, said as much. "The people that have connected with him, they've aged right along with him. We've got to reach a very different twenty-something parent, and to the degree we need to communicate with them differently, that will be the stretch for us."[15] The problem was that Dobson was the star, and Focus had hardly any identity without him. The board therefore compromised and replaced him with Daly as chair but let him keep the daily Focus radio show.[16]

The new chair of the board did what he could to reach the next generation. Daly, who had been orphaned as a child, moved Focus into more hands-on social services, like a program that found families to adopt children from foster care. He otherwise tried to shift the organization away from politics and back to its original mission of helping marriages and families. "We tend to shut down the ears of people to hear the Gospel because they only see you in political context, or as a conservative," he said. "Christianity must transcend politics in order to change culture and politics."[17] Early on Daly praised Obama for his devotion to family and later hailed the president for his attention to human trafficking. He opposed abortion and gay marriage, but he maintained a moderate tone, and expressed willingness to work with Democrats on issues on which they could agree. Dobson, however, regained his voice and attacked Democrats and "secular humanists" with his usual vitriol, and a year later in February 2010 the board asked Dobson to resign from Focus's flagship radio show.[18]

Dobson had to leave Focus, but instead of retiring he began a new radio show with his son Ryan called *James Dobson on the Family*. The Focus board gave it its blessing, and, it was said, a million dollars in start-up costs, though the program would be in direct competition with the Focus show.[19] Hard as it would have been to imagine Dobson going off the air into a gurulike silence, many supposed that he had started the new show for his son. Adopted in infancy, Ryan had had a troubled youth with attention-deficit/hyperactivity disorder. A tattooed surfer and skateboarder, Ryan, age thirty-nine, had become a youth preacher and had co-authored a book, *Be Intolerant: Because Some Things Are Just Stupid*, which according to *Publishers Weekly* had "all the subtlety of a two-by-four to the side of the head."[20] He had also been divorced, which made him ineligible to act as the voice of Focus on the radio.

Dobson seems to have had some difficulty integrating his son into a family advice show, but it was nothing like the difficulty his replacement had in trying to move Focus into the twenty-first century. Focus officials told one reporter they wanted to join the growing movement to broaden the agenda and to frame their political work as an inspirational call to do good, not just to oppose the sinful.[21] Daly launched a youth organization, Rising Voice, in an effort to reach young adults with issues such as sex trafficking, poverty, and the environment. At Christmas, instead of complaining about people saying "Happy Holidays," Rising Voice went so far as to ask consumers to consider organic or eco-friendly clothing and fair trade products.[22] That year, however, Daly had to reduce Focus's budget to $105 million and slash the staff to seven hundred, or half what it had been at its peak. According to visitors, Focus began to have the air of a ghost town.[23]

Such transitions were taking place throughout the conservative evangelical world at the time. From megachurch pastors to the heads of media empires, Christian right leaders were dying or retiring, and giving way to a new generation. In some cases, like that of Focus on the Family, the transitions were politically or personally wrenching, in others much easier. One of Falwell's two sons, Jerry Jr., took over Liberty University, proving a far better administrator than his father and remaining faithful to his political legacy. The other son, Jonathan, became head pastor of Falwell's Lynchburg church.[24] Don Wildmon bequeathed the American Family Association and his two hundred southern radio stations to his son, Tim, but Bryan Fischer, the director of public policy and an outspoken culture warrior, often seemed to be in control.[25] Bev LaHaye retired from Concerned Women for America, leaving the organization to her deputies, and Bill Bright died, allowing Campus Crusade for Christ to serve the more liberal millennial generation. In no case did these transitions bring forth new national Christian right leaders, and no new media empires or large political organizations appeared to replace Dobson's or Robertson's. In some states, like Washington and Ohio, the Christian right movement simply collapsed with its leaders retiring or getting out of politics, and finding no successors.[26]

In 2009 Rick Warren declared the Christian right dead.[27] He was correct in the sense that the Christian right was no longer a movement, or even an independent entity, with sway over evangelicals, as it had been for thirty years. Its remnants survived only by making alliances with groups more powerful than themselves, one of them with the American Catholic bishops.

* * *

In September 2009, Charles Colson, who had been a long-term advocate of rapprochement between evangelicals and conservative Catholics, joined up with Robert George, the Princeton University law professor, and Timothy George, the dean of the evangelical Beeson Divinity School, to produce a document known as the "Manhattan Declaration: A Call of Christian Conscience."[28] Unveiled in November and signed by 148 evangelical, Roman Catholic, and Orthodox leaders, the document called for taking a firm stance on the sanctity of life, traditional marriage, and freedom of religion. In the sense that all its examples of threats to religious freedom involved abortion or same-sex marriage, the document was no novelty, but still there were several surprising things about it. First, the signatories included not just the usual right-wing evangelical and Catholic activists—such as Colson, Land, Mohler, Dobson, Perkins, and William Donahue—but nine Roman Catholic archbishops and the primate of the Orthodox Church in the U.S. They also included several centrist evangelicals, such as David Neff of *Christianity Today*, Ron Sider, and Leith Anderson, president of the NAE. Second, the "Manhattan Declaration" provided a theological justification for its stances that blended evangelical with Catholic themes—an anathema, one would think, to Mohler at least, who in 2000 had called Catholicism "a false church" that teaches "a false gospel."[29] (In one of its odder passages the Declaration had Martin Luther King referring to Augustine and Aquinas in his "Letter from a Birmingham Jail.") Third, the signatories identified themselves with the early Christian martyrs and threatened civil disobedience if compelled by law to act against their consciences. Vowing that they would not comply with any law that might compel their institutions to participate in abortions, or in embryo-destructive research, or to acknowledge same-sex unions, they wrote, "We pledge to each other and to our fellow believers that no power on earth, be it cultural or political, will intimidate us into silence or acquiescence." The threat, along with heated rhetoric about same-sex marriage leading to polygamy, incest, and the destruction of the institutions of civil society, seemed uncharacteristic of the Catholic bishops—if all too well known on the Christian right.[30]

Asked the purpose of the document at the inaugural press conference, its authors said they wanted to demonstrate to the Obama administration and the Democratic-led Congress that Christians were still a formidable force. They hoped to gather a million signatures in six months, and specifically they aimed to influence the current debates on health care reform, a same-sex marriage bill in Washington, D.C., and the Employment Non-Discrimination Act. Colson added that he wanted to persuade younger evangelicals who had become engaged in issues like climate change and global poverty that there was a hierarchy of issues and that abortion, same-sex marriage, and religious freedom stood at the top.[31] The "Manhattan Declaration" never gathered much more than half a million signatures in five years, but what Colson had done was to hitch what had become the rather small wagon of the evangelical right onto the mighty engine of the American Catholic Church.

The nine archbishops who signed the statement spoke for themselves, but the U.S. Conference of Catholic Bishops had already become heavily involved in the health care reform bill that Obama had put at the head of his new agenda. The Catholic bishops had since John XXIII's encyclical *Pacem in Terris* been the leading advocates for universal health care in the U.S., but since the appointees of John Paul II and Benedict XVI had filled the dioceses, the bishops had become more conservative. Instead of writing on economic justice and nuclear disarmament, as they had in the 1980s, they emphasized abortion and "below the belt" issues, from contraception to gay sex. When discussions of the bill began, they had—to the regret of many liberal Catholics—failed to weigh in with a broad moral case for national health care but rather focused on the threat of federal funding for abortion and what they considered the weakness of the conscience clauses for health care providers. In a statement for the record of one congressional committee, the bishop in charge of the Committee for Domestic Justice and Human Development had written with hardly a preamble, "No health care legislation that compels Americans to pay for, or participate in, abortion will find sufficient votes to pass."[32] In November the abortion issue almost scuttled the House bill. It passed only because Speaker Nancy Pelosi at the last moment, and against her will, allowed an amendment barring any insurance plan purchased with government subsidies—or virtually all of the new ones—from covering abortion. The pro-choice Democrats held their noses and voted for the bill.[33]

When the Senate considered health care reform the following year, the Catholic bishops took extraordinary measures to see that the final bill adhered to their criteria. They not only wrote op-eds in numerous newspapers and letters to the relevant Senate committees, but they distributed background papers and "action alerts" to all nineteen thousand Catholic parishes. When the Senate seemed unresponsive, they distributed information to go into every church bulletin and to be read at mass calling on Catholics to oppose the bill unless their conditions were satisfied. The Obama administration did what it could to find a compromise, but the bishops were adamant, and when the Senate passed the Affordable Care Act without the amendment they desired, the bishops opposed the entire act. They then supported a series of lawsuits for institutional exemptions from its abortion and contraception mandates under the Religious Freedom Restoration Act that went on for years.[34]

The second alliance Christian right leaders made was with a group that from a historical perspective was almost equally unlikely: Republican libertarians. Actually, it was less an alliance than a merger—or a submergence of the Christian right in the tsunami that overtook GOP politics in the first two years of Obama's presidency.

Neither pundits nor pollsters predicted the rise of the Tea Party, but it was hardly surprising that a political reaction would follow the collapse of Wall Street and the economic crisis that hit Main Street just after Obama's election. In the economic earthquake, the worst since the Great Depression, the Dow Jones Industrial Average plunged 54 percent from its 2007 high, wiping out retirement savings; the unemployment rate went into double digits for the first time in twenty-six years; housing prices fell, and home foreclosures soared, bankrupting thousands of families. From the left came the Occupy Wall Street movement, an unorganized series of demonstrations and sit-ins against the "give-aways" to the big banks; from the right came a larger and more durable movement that opposed all government intervention in the crisis and Obama's entire policy agenda.

The Tea Party movement took off on February 19, 2009, when a CNBC business editor, broadcasting from the floor of the Chicago Mercantile Exchange, excoriated Obama's plan to help homeowners avoid foreclosure by refinancing their mortgages, accusing the government of "promoting bad behavior" by supporting these "losers" and suggesting that the Chicago bond traders create a tea party and throw all the derivatives of the mortgages into the Chicago River. The rant went viral, and a week later there were "Tea Party" demonstrations in over forty cities, in which some dressed as Revolutionary-era patriots and some held incendiary signs. Within the year a thousand Tea Party committees had sprung up all over the country calling for a reduction of the national debt, lower taxes, and an end to "wasteful" government spending meant to alleviate the economic crisis. The activists were angry at Washington, and especially at President Obama, whom they said was born in Kenya, brought up a Muslim, and was turning the country toward socialism. The movement came from the grass roots, but it was well funded by corporate titans, principally Charles and David Koch, and reinforced by Fox News, right-wing talk radio, and conservative bloggers.[35] As a result, it was often hard to tell which activities were genuinely grassroots and which "Astroturf" initiated by groups such as the Kochs' FreedomWorks, headed by the former House speaker Dick Armey. The Tea Party, however, remained a decentralized movement with no national leaders, except perhaps for the Fox News broadcaster Glenn Beck and politicians such as Sarah Palin and Michele Bachmann, Christian conservatives who essentially anointed themselves as spokespersons for it.[36]

Tony Perkins and other Christian right organizers were initially skeptical of the Tea Party because its lead organizations appeared to have a libertarian bent, as the Kochs had.[37] They soon realized that in what became known as the Great Recession, even their own supporters were paying more attention to the economy than to the social issues—and that the Tea Party was taking up all the oxygen.[38] On September 12 a coalition of Tea Party groups, including FreedomWorks, the Koch brothers' Americans for Prosperity, and Grover Norquist's Americans for Tax Reform, held a Taxpayer's March on Washington at which a crowd, estimated at 75,000, listened to a roster of politicians, including Senator Jim DeMint and Representative Mike Pence, denounce Obama administration policies, including health care reform and the cap and trade bill.[39] At the FRC's Values Voters Summit the following week, speakers emphasized economic issues, linking freedom with free enterprise, giving ominous warnings about the "march to socialism," and complaining that taxes were too high and largely misappropriated. Other Christian right leaders soon jumped on board. Richard Land admitted the Tea Party's purposes were essentially secular, but said that a lot of people involved were not secular. "I don't see the tea party movement as threat at all—I see it as additional allies and fellow travelers."[40]

What the Tea Party represented—and how big it was—preoccupied the political class in Washington. At first it was thought to be a populist rebellion or a movement of libertarian political independents, such as that of Ross Perot, frustrated and angry about the effects of the recession on their own lives. However, the first major survey—a CBS/New York Times poll of April 2010—showed that those who identified with the Tea Party were overwhelmingly white and middle-class; three quarters of them were forty-five years or older; more were men than women; and all were better educated and wealthier than Americans as a whole. A disproportionate percentage of them lived in the South, and not surprisingly 39 percent identified themselves as evangelicals and 22 percent as Catholics. Most were conservative Republicans who had been active in electoral politics before. In other words, the Tea Party was the Republican right in a new garb. And many sympathized with the Christian right—or were actually a part of it.[41]

The Pew Research Center analysis showed that Tea Party supporters were disproportionately white evangelical Protestants and that most people who agreed with the Tea Party agreed with the "Christian conservative movement," though the two movements were not coextensive. For example, 69 percent of those agreed with the "Christian conservative movement" agreed with the Tea Party, while 42 percent who agreed with the Tea Party agreed with the "Christian conservative movement," though many of the rest hadn't heard of it.[42] According to another study, fully three quarters of those who identified with the Tea Party described themselves as "Christian conservatives," while only 29 percent identified as libertarian. Six in ten of both were less likely to vote for candidates who supported abortion or same-sex marriage.[43] Most polls showed that the Tea Party was larger than the Christian right, though the number of its activists comprised only 4 percent of the population.[44] Subsequent polls showed that the number of people who identified with the Tea Party grew as the year went on. After the election of 2010 Pew reported that 41 percent of registered voters sympathized with the Tea Party, but that younger people were underrepresented.[45]

During the campaign before the midterm elections, the Tea Party dominated the news. *The New York Times* found that it supported 138 candidates for Congress, nine of them for the Senate. Tea Party supporters, as well as their candidates, tended to be conservative on the social issues of the Christian right, but their organizers insisted that the movement keep to the economic issues to maximize its support.[46] The Christian right organizers acquiesced, and of necessity, for according to a Pew study nearly all of those who agreed with the "Christian conservative movement" also agreed with the Tea Party.[47] The American Family Association was one of the first groups to join the Tea Party movement, and afterward came others.[48] Ken Blackwell, who since his defeat for governor of Ohio in 2006 had joined the Family Research Council, told the *Columbus Dispatch* that the Ohio Christian right had found a home in the Tea Party and was being energized to deal with "our common enemy, which is bloated, ineffective and power-hungry central government." The Obama administration policies, he said, were providing "a perfect storm for the resurgence of a conservative coalition that involves social conservatives, economic conservatives and national-security conservatives."[49] David Brody, the savvy senior correspondent for the Christian Broadcasting Network, had coined the term "teavangelicals," and Christian right organizers such as Lori Viars, the executive director of an Ohio antiabortion group, felt that the alliance with the Tea Party was a natural fit. "I definitely consider myself a Teavangelical," she said.[50]

Tony Perkins and Ralph Reed, who had founded the Faith and Freedom Coalition the year before in the hopes of duplicating Reed's success with the Christian Coalition, put on rallies and registered church voters, but while many Tea Party candidates endorsed their issues as a matter of course, economic matters remained front and center. Christian right leaders worried that many evangelical Christians had grown weary of the culture wars.[51] Reed invited Tea Party spokesmen to his annual gathering in Washington. He claimed that, as a number of Tea Party organizers belonged to the Coalition, he had clearly felt it necessary to include them and to move beyond the Christian right to mount an effective campaign, even though it meant taking a subordinate role and disappointing those who continued to believe abortion and same-sex marriage the most important issues.[52]

For the Christian right organizers to reach out to the Tea Party was not as much of an ideological stretch as might be imagined, for not only did most conservative Christians favor a smaller federal government and lower taxes, but according to a study by three Harvard scholars—Vanessa Williams, Theda Skocpol, and John Coggin—the grassroots Tea Party activists did not entirely share the free market fundamentalism and the hostility to government spending that characterized the business elite that financed the movement. Yes, they resented taxes and government regulations, but like many in the Christian right they had a positive view of government programs such as Social Security, Medicare, and veterans' benefits. What they vehemently opposed were programs, such as Obama's Affordable Care Act, which helped the young and the poor. The distinction they made was between government programs they perceived as going to hardworking, productive members of society, such as themselves, and "handouts" that went to undeserving "freeloaders"—a category that seemed largely to be made up of African Americans, Hispanic immigrants, and the young. The context, in the view of the scholars, was an anxiety about racial, ethnic, and generational changes. The attitude, hardly novel, had existed among Nixon's Silent Majority and Goldwater supporters. Apparently the Tea Party was yet another flare-up of resistance to change—along with resentment against those who might take their relatively privileged place in society.[53] Mark Noll, the historian, told *Newsweek*: "I do think this aggrieved sense of a nation having been stolen is stronger now than it was in 1940 and maybe stronger than it was in 1960."[54] Glenn Beck and others had simply changed the threat from "increasing secularization" to "socialism," while insisting on American exceptionalism and the civil religion that, as Gregory Boyd wrote, had marked the Christian right. The feeling that the nation had been stolen from them, the scholars wrote, crystallized in the Tea Party opposition to Obama, who was not just the first black president, but who promised change and reached out to racial and ethnic minorities and the young.[55]

Glenn Beck seems to have understood what else the Christian right wanted of the Tea Party. On August 28, 2010, he held a rally at the Lincoln Memorial on the anniversary of Martin Luther King's "I Have a Dream" speech attracting a crowd of perhaps 100,000—while a few civil rights veterans, gathered elsewhere in Washington, attacked what they saw as a sacrilege. On the stage were 240 clergy members Beck called "the Black-Robed Regiment," after the clergy who supported the American Revolution. The "Restoring Honor" rally, he insisted, was not political but rather a "celebration of America's heroes and heritage," and a call for spiritual renewal. Beck, who was a recovering alcoholic and drug addict, and who had become a Mormon in 1999, had libertarian views except on abortion, but David Barton had helped Beck pick out the regimental members, and among them were James Dobson, Richard Land, Jerry Falwell Jr., John Hagee, and numerous other Christian right figures, along with token Jews and Muslims. The night before the rally Beck had held a "Divine Destiny" event in the Kennedy Center that promised to leave the participants "with a strong belief that faith can play an essential role in reuniting the country." From the stage at the Lincoln Memorial he announced, "Something beyond imagination is happening. Something that is beyond man is happening. America today begins to turn back to God."[56] "It's time to start the heart of the nation again. And put it where it belongs. Our heart with God." He went on in this vein for two hours, managing to infuriate a number of evangelical theologians.[57] In spite of Land's appearance at the rally, Russell Moore, the dean of the Southern Baptist Theological Seminary, wrote on his blog the day after, "It's taken us a long time to get here, in this plummet from Francis Schaeffer to Glenn Beck. In order to be this gullible, American Christians have had to endure years of vacuous talk about

an undefined 'revival.'" The rally, he said, served "at best a generally theistic civil religion and at worst some partisan political movement."[58] Land,
however, told *The Washington Post* that he and other evangelicals who had
met with Beck in the planning stages of the rally had been impressed with
the authenticity of Beck's faith. "He sounded like Billy Graham," he said.[59]

The party in power almost invariably suffers losses in the first midterm election, but the results of the 2010 election came as a stunning blow
to the Obama administration and the congressional Democrats. The Republicans gained sixty-three seats in the House—the largest change in
seats since 1948—recapturing the majority; they also took six more seats
in the Senate, reducing the Democrats' majority to four with two independents caucusing with them. The poor performance of the economy,
it appeared, discouraged Democratic voters from turning out, while encouraging Republicans, and particularly Tea Party members, to vote. The
Tea Party helped the Republicans by increasing the turnout, but it hurt
them because its candidates unseated many establishment Republicans in
the primaries, and in the general election they won in the safe Republican
districts but not in the competitive districts or states.[60] What the Tea Party
did was to push the previously weakened Republican Party sharply to the
right and fill the House with intransigents.

* * *

The "new evangelical" leaders on the other hand paid small attention
to partisan politics, and not all involved themselves with national policy.
Some, like Gregory Boyd, were essentially pastors and theologians who
believed they should preach the Gospel and leave the members of their
congregations to follow its teachings in matters of politics and policy.
Some of the younger ministers, such Chris Seay in Houston, explored
new ways to follow the example of Jesus in working with the poor in their
own neighborhoods. Shane Claiborne, who took on a rock-star status for
young evangelicals, founded the counterculture Simple Way Community
in one of the poorest quarters of Philadelphia, where he worked with city
agencies to build affordable housing, planted gardens in abandoned lots,
and organized barter economies.[61] He went to Iraq in early 2003 with the
Iraq Peace Team to act as a witness to the bombing of Baghdad and to

document the human rights abuses of the war.[62] As for Rick Warren, he withdrew from the public arena after Obama's election, but he continued with his PEACE plan and made efforts to reconcile evangelicals and Muslim Americans in spite of criticisms from the right. Jim Wallis, Joel Hunter, David Gushee, and others, however, waded deeply into national policy, lobbying for issues that they considered morally and biblically important, sometimes with the support of centrist evangelical groups such as the NAE.

In the first two years of the Obama administration, the policy-oriented new evangelicals pressed for the same bills the Obama administration considered priorities beyond the stimulus legislation: health care reform, a cap and trade bill to retard global warming, an immigration reform bill, and the reduction of nuclear weapons as a step toward their abolition.

The health care bill, which came up first, was by far the most difficult for the new evangelicals and by far the most contentious. The Republican right portrayed it as a "government takeover" of the health care industry, and fears spread that it could lead to "rationing" of health care services for the most vulnerable patients, the federal funding of abortion, and euthanasia. There was talk of "death panels," and Richard Land said, "I'm telling you based on everything I know, if we get Obamacare . . . it will significantly lower the quality of life and length of life for your children and grandchildren."[63] Joel Hunter, Jim Wallis, and others felt that a system that did not give insurance to 45 million Americans was profoundly immoral, but they, too, worried about federal funding of abortions. Still, they joined a coalition of thirty-two progressive religious groups put together by Faith in Public Life that included mainline Protestant denominations, liberal Catholic, Jewish, Muslim, and Buddhist groups to support the plan. Known as Faith for Health, the group faced off against an equally formidable coalition, the Freedom Federation, composed of the old Christian Right and Tea Party groups, like Americans for Prosperity. In August Faith for Health gave Obama the opportunity to speak directly to their constituents in a conference call streamed live on the web. Hunter made the opening remarks to an audience of over 100,000 listeners.[64] Faith for Health ran radio and cable TV ads and lobbied Congress while its member organizations conducted grassroots campaigns or prayer vigils and meetings with members of Congress in eighteen states.[65] When Tony Perkins and others brought up the fears about abortion coverage, Joel Hunter, not one to mince words, said, "I do think that abortion is being used as a diversionary or a barrier tactic to slow down, and therefore defeat, health-care reform." Until we have something concrete, some real legislation, he said, it's "posturing."[66]

In the fall the House passed a health care reform act, a bill of mind-numbing complexity, with an amendment, known as Stupak-Pitts, more or less designed by the Catholic bishops, that prevented taxpayer funds from paying for abortions directly, or indirectly by subsidizing private plans that pay for abortions, and gave what the bishops thought of as adequate conscience protections for health care providers. The Senate, responsive to the pro-choice lobby, however, refused to adopt it.[67] When Senator Bob Casey (D-PA) presented a compromise amendment aimed at gaining the support of the antiabortion Democrat Ben Nelson (of Nebraska), to achieve the supermajority needed to stop a filibuster, thirty-nine antiabortion pastors and leaders including Ron Sider, David Neff, Joel Hunter, David Gushee, Glen Stassen, and a number of liberal Catholics applauded the effort to move the debate along, saying the amendment could ensure that the strong conscience-provider protections in the House bill could be maintained, and no federal funds would pay for abortion. The Catholic bishops, the National Right to Life Committee, and Christian right groups on the other hand argued that the way the Casey amendment proposed to segregate public from private funds would facilitate at least indirect taxpayer support for abortion. Mark Tooley, president of the conservative Institute on Religion and Democracy, called it an "unholy compromise" and attacked its supporters for "backing abortion funding."[68] Tony Perkins called the bill "pro-abortion, pro-rationing, pro-tax, pro-death," and the NAE urged the senators to withhold their support.[69] The new evangelicals, in other words, had taken a position to the left of the Catholic bishops and of NAE, to which most of them belonged, putting aside any fears about indirect abortion coverage, in order to see the health care bill passed.

In the end Nelson accepted a somewhat different compromise that permitted the states to opt out of abortion coverage. His vote was the only one that mattered because, as anticipated, the Affordable Care Act passed without a single Republican vote. The NAE opposed the final draft, but Hunter and his colleagues supported it. After the 2010 election, House Republicans voted thirty times to repeal "Obamacare," and in January 2011 Kathleen Sebelius, the secretary of health and human services, appealed to religious leaders for support, and put on a conference call in which Joel Hunter said how grateful he was for the protections the bill afforded the most vulnerable members of his congregation.[70] Hunter later wrote an op-ed in the *Orlando Sentinel* on behalf of the 800,000 working-poor Floridians unable to get health care insurance because of the lack of Medicaid funding, saying, "I pray Governor Rick Scott and House leaders, who have so far refused to consider or propose their own health-care bill, will find the compassion to stop the suffering of so many less fortunate Floridians."[71]

On the cap and trade bill the evangelical groups were similarly divided. The Evangelical Environment Network (which now included World Vision and the InterVarsity Christian Fellowship as affiliates) and Jonathan Merritt's group of Southern Baptists worked hard for it, putting on conferences and asking members to lobby their representatives in Congress.[72] They had, however, lost a powerful ally. The NAE had never taken a position on global warming because of divisions among its members, but the bill had had a strong advocate in Richard Cizik until December 2008. On NPR's *Fresh Air* Cizik had told Terry Gross that his position on gay unions was evolving. "I'm shifting," he said, "I have to admit. In other words, I would willingly say that I believe in civil unions. I don't officially support redefining marriage from its traditional definition, I don't think."[73] Leith Anderson, the president of the NAE, fired Cizik abruptly ten days later, telling him that "his credibility as a spokesman for the NAE was irrevocably compromised."[74] Cizik felt wounded—he had worked for the NAE for twenty-eight years—but he had crossed a red line. The NAE had not endorsed civil unions, and gay marriage was anathema to many of its member churches and denominations. Anderson, who had supported him on global warming, could not save him, nor could his friends on the board. Sixty NAE members, however, wrote Anderson a letter, drafted by Gushee, praising Cizik's performance over the years, signaling their support for Cizik's efforts, and urging the organization to carry on his vision of a broad Christian moral agenda rather than to pull back into the Christian right's two issues.[75] Six months later the NAE appointed Galen Carey the new vice president for governmental affairs. Having worked for World Relief for twenty-six years, Carey supported a broad agenda, but a more cautious man, he respected the doubts about human-induced global warming within the NAE and did not push for the cap and trade bill. For years afterward the NAE said nothing about the causes of climate change, but focused on the plight of the poor and vulnerable who would suffer because of its effects on their environment.[76]

On the other side, lobbying against the cap and trade bill was Calvin Beisner's Cornwall Alliance and the Richard Land's Ethics & Religious Liberty Commission. In response to the Evangelical Climate Initiative the Cornwall Alliance had launched a "We Get It" campaign, financed in part by ExxonMobil and the Koch industries, to show not just that anthropogenic global warming was a flawed scientific "theory" but that the consequences of the actions intended to stem it would be devastating. "Proposed policies," read the Cornwall Declaration of 2009, "would destroy jobs and impose trillions of dollars in costs to achieve no net benefits. They could be implemented only by enormous and dangerous expansion of government control over private life." The two themes played well with the Tea Party as well as the Christian right. Then in answer to the Evangelical Environmental Network's contention that the poor of the planet would be the first to suffer from climate change, the Cornwall Declaration read, "Worst of all, by raising energy prices and hindering economic development, they [these policies] would slow or stop the rise of the world's poor out of poverty and so condemn millions to premature death."[77] Christian right groups, the FRC, and Concerned Women for America signed on to the "We Get It" campaign, and Land used much of the same rhetoric in speaking to SBC audiences about the cap and trade bill.[78]

In the event, the American Clean Energy and Security Act passed the House in June 2009 by a slim margin of 219–212, but then because of the bargaining and logrolling among industries, it had become a thousand pages long and almost as complicated as the health bill. The Senate put off consideration of the bill to the next session, and by the time it came up again, the Democrats had lost their supermajority and Republicans like John McCain and Lindsey Graham who had previously supported a cap and trade bill had turned against it. Senator John Kerry appealed to Joel Hunter to help build support for a bipartisan bill, hoping he might persuade other Republican moderates, such as Senators Dick Lugar and Lamar Alexander, to vote for it.[79] Hunter did what he could, but with the Tea Party on the rise, Senate minority leader Mitch McConnell had decided that to win in November Republicans should refuse to vote for any Democratic legislation.[80] Then, as the Great Recession rolled over Main Street, polls showed declining support for an effort to stem climate change with its significant up-front costs, and even a declining belief in the existence of human-made global warming.[81] Hunter had to admit that his own congregation was just too distracted by personal economic problems to consider global warming.[82] The bill never came to a vote.

Immigration reform suffered much the same fate, but it divided evangelicals in a different way. Since the first bill to overhaul the broken system had been introduced into the Congress in 2007, "comprehensive immigration reform" had meant efforts to secure the nation's borders and a pathway to citizenship for the eleven or twelve million immigrants who had entered the country illegally. The 2007 bill had failed, and in 2009 it had to wait until the health care bill was passed, but by the beginning of the next year there seemed to be some hope for it. On March 19 Senators Charles Schumer (D-NY) and Lindsey Graham wrote an op-ed laying out a bipartisan framework. Evangelicals were important to the bill, and the NAE spearheaded a lobbying campaign to pass it, sponsoring a full-page ad in the Capitol Hill newspaper, *Roll Call*, urging the Congress to pass a bill that united families, secured the borders, and created a pathway to citizenship for those who qualified.[83]

When Obama gave a major speech on the subject, Bill Hybels, who had a Spanish-speaking ministry in his Chicago-area church, introduced him, while Leith Anderson sat in the front row with Samuel Rodriguez, an NAE board member and the head of the National Hispanic Christian Conference. More surprisingly, perhaps, Richard Land also sat in the front row. But the SBC had declared itself for comprehensive reform in a 2006 resolution, and Land had signed the NAE's ad along with Hybels, Joel

Hunter, and others.[84] "Hispanics are religious, family-oriented, pro-life and entrepreneurial," Land said. "They are hard-wired social conservatives unless they are driven away." [85]

Land meant driven away politically, but driving the immigrants away in a more literal sense was just what many of the right wanted to do. A poll taken of Family Research Council supporters three years before had shown that 90 percent had chosen forced deportation as the fate for the eleven or twelve million undocumented immigrants.[86] In April, Arizona passed a law making it a state crime to be an undocumented immigrant and giving the police the power to detain anyone they suspected of being an illegal alien. The law caused an outcry among Hispanic organizations and their supporters, increasing the pressure for the passage of a national legislation. Richard Land charitably—or with an eye to politics—called the Arizona law "a cry for help from a state that has been let down by the federal government"[87] and said the best way to deal with it was to pass comprehensive federal legislation. Rod Parsley, no liberal, said the arguments in favor of the Arizona law "betray a selfish, arrogant and, at times, racist attitude that is incompatible with the Christian's command to love one's fellow man and serve the poor among us." [88] Mathew Staver, founder of the Liberty Counsel and dean of Liberty University's school of law, said immigration was a federal not a state matter. Other evangelicals, however, backed the law. When the ACLU filed suit against it, followed by the U.S. Department of Justice, Jay Sekulow, the chief counsel of the American Center for Law and Justice, filed an amicus brief in support of Arizona, saying, "I think there is a need to reform the system, but I don't support amnesty." Bryan Fischer of the American Family Association said, "What my evangelical friends are arguing is that illegal aliens should essentially be rewarded for breaking the law." In answer to those who worried about the separation of parents from children born in the U.S., who had American citizenship, he said, "We don't want to break up families, so let's help them all return to their country of origin." [89] When a U.S. district court judge ruled the law unconstitutional, Fischer called the ruling "a monstrous display of judicial activism, arrogance and tyranny" and warned of "impending anarchy and vigilantism" that only the state governments could avert.[90]

Much of the Christian right rhetoric against immigration reform had to do with law and order. When the bill came up in 2007, Phyllis Schlafly's Eagle Forum had demanded that the federal government "erect a fence and double our border agents in order to stop the drugs, the smuggling racket, the diseases and the crimes."[91] As the statement suggested, nativism was a powerful factor, and one that Gary Bauer and Tony Perkins had made explicit in a conference on immigration that year. "Hyphenated Americans put other countries and affiliations first, and they drive a wedge into the heart of 'one nation,'" Bauer had said, and Perkins asked, "Do we have an immigration policy that is serving to strengthen the cultural fabric of the nation, which has a great influence on the family? The answer is no."[92]

The division among evangelical leaders had much to do with whether the organizations they headed included recent immigrants or not. The all-white lobbies, such as the FRC, saw immigrants as a menace to the whole American way of life. In effect they were a part of the Tea Party before it came into being. The NAE, however, embraced immigrants, because, as Anderson said, the Bible taught the welcome of "aliens in the land." But then many of its largest members, including the Assemblies of God and other Pentecostal denominations, attracted Hispanics and were growing because of them.[93] Parsley headed a multiracial Pentecostal church. Jim Daly of Focus on the Family refused to commit himself to immigration reform at the time, but two years later Rodriguez had convinced him that the future of his ministry, and perhaps of American Christianity, lay with Hispanics.[94] As for the Southern Baptist Convention, it had maintained its numbers in part by evangelizing Hispanics and Asians, and as its leaders recognized, its prospects for future growth lay in adding more immigrant churches.[95] Further, as Land saw it, Hispanic evangelicals might actually save the Christian right as well. Advocating for immigration reform, he said, might split the "old coalition," but not the "new" one. "And if the new one is going to be a governing coalition it's going to have to have a lot of Hispanics in it," he said.[96] The trouble was that white evangelicals as a whole had a more negative view of immigrants than many of their pastors and denominational leaders, and more than the American population as a whole. Only 15 percent favored a path to citizenship for illegal immigrants.[97] Asked by Senator Charles Schumer if pastors felt negative pressure from their congregations, Rodriguez had to admit, "There's a disconnect between the pulpit and the pews, particularly in the non-ethnic churches."[98] "If white evangelicals," he said, "would have been the staunchest supporters of the immigrant community, the debate would have long been finished."[99]

The Immigration Reform Act of 2010 went nowhere, for with evangelicals divided, and the Tea Party on the rise, the Republican leadership in the Senate saw the road to victory in refusing to pass any Democratic bills, however much support they might lose among Hispanics. McCain, who had once favored comprehensive reform, backed the Arizona law, and Lindsey Graham, who agreed to sponsor the Senate bill, made it clear a month later that he would not support it that year.[100]

After the midterm election with Tea Party and other Republicans pressing for cuts in spending to lower the mounting deficits caused by Bush's unbalanced budgets and Obama's stimulus bills, the new evangelical leaders went into a defensive mode. The Republican-led House was insisting on the reduction of discretionary spending, and in February it threatened to cut $60 billion from the previous year's budget, targeting education, the environment, foreign aid, and a number of programs for the poor in the United States. Sojourners lobbied against it, and Jim Wallis said, "Taking the cutting knife to programs that benefit low-income people while refusing to scrutinize the much larger blank checks we keep giving to defense contractors and corporate executives is hypocritical and cruel. . . . It's not only bad economics, but also bad religion."[101] As the debates on the Hill raged on, Wallis helped put together a coalition of diverse Christian groups to create a "circle of protection" around programs for the poor, the headline on its website reading "What Would Jesus Cut?" The coalition grew to include African American and Hispanic organizations, international aid organizations, the ecumenical Bread for the World, the U.S. Council of Catholic Bishops, and the mainline Protestant National Council of Churches, but not the Southern Baptist Convention. The National Association of Evangelicals, which had passed a resolution, "Lowering the Debt, Raising the Poor," joined the coalition in March with a statement saying in part, "By failing to live within its means, the nation had enjoyed unsustainable prosperity at the expense of future generations. [But] we reiterate our insistence that deficit reduction not lead to an abandonment of our commitments to the poor." [102]

Keynesian economics was not the NAE's forte—many evangelicals continued to see the federal budget as a family budget writ large—nor was it that of the Republican Party. Still, the NAE's decision to come out against cutting "programs that meet the essential needs of hungry and poor people at home and abroad" took some courage. [103] A Pew poll released that February showed that evangelicals were more supportive of cuts to the budget than other Americans in every area except defense, energy, and aid to veterans, and their top choices for the chopping block were economic assistance to needy people around the world, government assistance to the unemployed, and environmental protections. [104] Too, for the NAE joining the Circle of Protection meant an alliance with its historic enemy, the National Council of Churches.

That summer, as House Republicans threatened to shut down the government by refusing to raise the debt ceiling unless Obama gave way on the budget, members of the Circle of Protection met with Senate majority leader Harry Reid, aides to the House speaker John Boehner, and the chair of the House Budget Committee, Paul Ryan. They expressed concern that the latest proposals appeared to make trillions of dollars in cuts over the next several years that would hit the poor hard. Sojourners sponsored a series of radio ads in the home states of Harry Reid and Senate minority leader Mitch McConnell, and Boehner's home district in which local clergy, calling the federal budget "a moral document," quoted the Bible on the need to take care of the poor. Finally, the coalition members met for forty minutes with President Obama, admonishing him to protect Medicaid, food stamps, aid to poor women with infant children, international development aid, and other programs specifically targeted to the poor, in the deal he might have to make to avert a debt crisis. [105]

The coalition had some successes, but because the budget debates continued, the Circle of Protection did not disband. In 2012 the members asked Obama and his opponent for the presidency, former governor Mitt Romney, to make short videos answering how they would protect the poor and the hungry at home and abroad. The following year, when Tea

Party Republicans once again forced the U.S. government to the brink of a default over raising the debt ceiling, they held vigils at the Capitol until the crisis was averted.[106] In addition Sojourners formed the Evangelical Immigration Table, a coalition that included Hispanic groups, the Council for Christian Colleges and Universities, the right-wing Liberty Counsel, the SBC's Ethics & Religious Liberty Commission, the NAE, and the evangelical aid agencies.[107] Samuel Rodriguez finally got Jim Daly to agree to advocate for work visas for undocumented immigrants, and with the support of Focus on the Family, the Table ran radio ads in sixteen states and held hundreds of pastor meetings, prayer events, and press conferences in the next three years, urging the Congress to pass immigration reform.[108] Their advocacy apparently changed the minds of some evangelicals, for in the states where the radio ads ran, opposition to a pathway to legal status for undocumented immigrants dropped from 62 percent to 55 percent among white evangelicals, while opposition from white nonevangelicals increased.[109]

While Jim Wallis and other new evangelicals were making alliances with Hispanic evangelicals and other Christian groups to lobby for programs to help the poor and the undocumented immigrants, the Christian right organizations had coalesced with the Tea Party with the goal of winning the 2012 election and unseating Obama. They had high confidence they would succeed. They had won a record number of congressional seats in the midterms; the Great Recession had only slightly abated; the Affordable Care Act, now known as Obamacare, had yet to gain traction, and anti-immigrant sentiment ran high. In addition Obama had come out for gay marriage after several years of hesitating. Mitt Romney, a Mormon, had beaten the Christian right candidate, Rick Santorum, in the primaries but as Al Mohler explained to fellow pastors in a conference call, a vote for Romney was not "a perfect option" but a "a clear option." Mormonism, he said, was "one of the most insidious false gospels imaginable" and pastors had to denounce it as leading to eternal damnation, but in the election they had to stand up for "the sanctity of human life, the integrity of marriage and the defense of religious liberty."[110] The Billy Graham Evangelistic Association, headed by Franklin Graham, removed from its website a reference to Mormonism as a "cult," and Franklin persuaded his ninety-four-year-old father to help Romney by signing newspaper ads asking voters to support candidates who affirmed "the biblical definition of marriage and the sanctity of life." [111] The Catholic bishops for their part attacked the Obama administration over the mandatory contraception coverage in its health care bill, and one warned his flock of the "intrinsic evil" of the Democratic platform's support of abortion and same-sex marriage. [112] Ralph Reed, who sought to meld the Christian right with the Tea Party through the use of voter turnout strategies, promised he would contact the 27.1 million conservative voters seven to twelve times each to get them to the polls. He claimed he would distribute 25 million voter guides and reach to more than 100,000 churches, promising to bring a dramatic influx of new voters. [113]

At the Republican convention Christian Right and the Tea Party leaders, among them Tony Perkins, David Barton, and Dick Armey, essentially wrote the Republican platform. Phyllis Schlafly said it was the best one ever adopted. [114] As usual, the platform called for a ban on abortion except in cases of rape or incest, but this one called for three constitutional amendments: one to limit marriage to a union between one man and one woman, another to give the fetus the rights of a person, and the third to mandate a balanced budget. The platform also called for the public display of the Ten Commandments, repealing Obamacare, halting illegal immigration, and giving no "amnesty" to the undocumented. In addition there was a great deal of rhetoric about restoring the opportunity society through lowering taxes and free market policies that would deliver the country from a culture of dependency, bloated government, and massive debt. [115]

The results of the election shocked many Republicans, including Karl Rove. Obama won by a majority of the popular vote and by a landslide in the electoral college. Democrats picked up eight seats in the House and two in the Senate, winning Senate races against two strong antiabortion candidates in states where the Republicans should have coasted to victory. Further, three states approved same-sex marriage, and a fourth rejected a constitutional amendment to restrict marriage to opposite-sex couples. Romney had won 79 percent of the evangelical vote—or the same percentage that had voted for Bush in 2004—and a majority of mainline Protestants and white Catholics, but white Christians, who made up 80 percent of his vote, were not enough to win the election. He had lost the nonwhite Catholic vote because three quarters of Hispanic Catholics had voted for Obama, as had many Hispanic evangelicals. Obama had carried 35 percent of the white Christian vote, but his winning coalition rested on minority Christians—blacks, Hispanics, and Asians—plus 70 percent of those who had no religious affiliation.[116]

The Christian right leaders took the election results much harder than they had Obama's first victory, and they didn't bother to hide it. Mohler called the election an "unmitigated disaster"; Mike Huckabee, "a humiliating defeat" that called for repentance; and Tony Perkins, "a bruising day for our movement that no amount of spin can improve."[117] Democratic victories tended to inspire end times rhetoric and this was no exception. Don Wildmon called it "the beginning of the end of Western civilization"; John Hagee predicted global economic chaos that would lead to the reign of the Antichrist; and Glenn Beck advised his audience to go and buy farmland and guns and pull the kids out of public school.[118] The depth of the reaction came from what the election revealed about the trends in American society. As Mohler put it, "Millions of American evangelicals are absolutely shocked by not just the presidential election, but by the entire avalanche of results that came in. It's not that our message—we think abortion is wrong, we think same-sex marriage is wrong—didn't get out. It did get out. It's that the entire moral landscape has changed. An increasingly secularized America understands our positions and has rejected them."[119]

One of Mohler's concerns was that American public opinion was moving rapidly toward the acceptance of same-sex marriage. In 1994, 46 percent of Americans believed homosexuals should not be accepted by society, and in 2003 all major religious groups had opposed same-sex marriage. Even in 2009 more than half of the public opposed same-sex marriage, compared to the 37 percent that favored it, but by 2012 the public was evenly divided, and the numbers who favored it were mounting, for 61 percent of the millennial generation supported it.[120] Almost three quarters of white evangelicals opposed it, but those of the millennial generation were more than twice as likely to accept same-sex marriage as the oldest cohort of evangelicals (43 percent to 19 percent).[121] After all the Christian right's past electoral victories on gay marriage, the 2012 election had, Mohler said, "handed [us] a rather comprehensive set of defeats on the issue of the integrity of marriage."[122] Already, several federal appeals courts had ruled the Defense of Marriage Act unconstitutional, the Ninth Circuit had overturned the same-sex marriage ban in California, and the matter was likely to go the Supreme Court in the next few years.[123]

What also disturbed Mohler, and other evangelicals who read the polls, was that the number of people unaffiliated with any religion was mounting year after year. According to a Pew survey released just before the 2012 election, the number of people who said they had no affiliation with any religion had risen from 15 percent to almost 20 percent in just five years. The growth of the "nones" was largely generational, for 30 percent of those under thirty said they had no religious affiliation, but many older people who had said they seldom or never went to church had included themselves in the category, and with few exceptions the "nones" were not looking for a church to go to. According to the survey, the "nones" overwhelmingly thought religious organizations too concerned with money and power, too focused on rules, and too political. Seven in ten of them had voted for Obama, and nearly three quarters of them supported legal abortion and same-sex marriage.[124] The country, Mohler said, will grow to look more and more like Europe. "It's going to be a chastening, humbling moment for American Christians to realize that we're going to be in the position across the country of speaking as a minority."[125]

Then there was the issue of the Hispanics. The numbers of Hispanic citizens were growing fast; that year Hispanics made up 10 percent of the electorate, and 71 percent had voted for Obama.[126] Clearly the Republican Party and the Christian right had helped drive them away by their treatment of the undocumented immigrants. This had come to bother Jim Daly. Having poured the resources of Focus on the Family into electing Romney by sending out millions of mailers that listed the presidential candidates' positions on the issues that mattered to "values voters," he said that the evangelical community should have been considering immigration reform years ago, "but we were led more by political-think than by church-think." He added, "If the Christian message has been too wrapped around the axle of the Republican Party, a) that's our fault and b) we've got to rethink that." [127] Like Richard Land, he assumed that Hispanics were essentially pro-family Christians, and that if the issue of immigration were out of the way, they would support socially conservative organizations, such as Focus on the Family. In fact Hispanic Catholics—59 percent of the group—favored marriage equality and abortion rights, and Hispanic evangelicals, largely Pentecostals and charismatics, while more socially conservative, had found common ground with Latino Catholics on Obama's health care bill and the Democrats' defense of poverty programs. [128] Rev. Gabriel Salguero, president of the National Latino Evangelical Coalition, had come to the same conclusion as Rev. Samuel Rodriguez. "We believe some difficult decisions need to be made [on the budget] but not on the backs of the poor and the most vulnerable," he said. "For us it's not a political agenda. It's a moral issue. We're Christians." [129]

White evangelicals remained faithful to the Republican Party, but in spite of high voting rates, there were just not enough of them to win national elections, and by 2012 they lacked the allies they needed in other groups. The problem seemed likely to grow worse as time went on, for the new generation was profoundly different from that of its parents. As a whole it was less white and less Christian. Nonwhite voters were already 28 percent of the electorate—up from 26 percent in 2008—and a quarter of the millennial generation had left church altogether. Romney's electoral base of white Christians resembled the religious composition of senior voters while Obama's coalition of some white Christians, minority Christians—blacks, Hispanics, and Asians—and those with no affiliation resembled that of younger voters. [130] Al Mohler put the issue sharply, "If we do not become the movement of younger Americans and Hispanic Americans, and any other number of Americans, we will just become a retirement community." [131] Mohler suggested bending on issues of lesser importance and supporting candidates who had different ideas about the role of government so long as they took the right positions on marriage and life issues. [132] Robert Jeffress, who had succeed W. A. Criswell as pastor of the First Baptist Church in Dallas, concurred. We evangelicals, he wrote, need to remember that we are a diminishing minority in America. If we care about winning elections with candidates who will push back against abortion and immorality, then we have to be willing to compromise on some secondary issues to form a winning coalition with other Republicans. . . . We must differentiate between biblical absolutes and political preferences. . . . Breaking a pledge to Grover Norquist . . . is not tantamount to denouncing Christ. Acknowledging the need for government health care reform does not necessarily pave the way for the rule of the Antichrist. . . . Instead of nominating a candidate who is mute or malleable on social issues but intransigent on political issues, let's try the reverse.[133]

It was a bit too late for such purist solutions. Many conservative evangelicals, including their principal activists, had joined the Tea Party and had elevated opposition to higher taxes and Obama's health care reform to the status of biblical absolutes. Further, they had turned the entire Republican Party to the right on economic issues to the point that Jeffress would have had a hard time finding anyone to compromise with. At the same time, according to one Pew survey, seven out of ten young people said they preferred a bigger government with more services than a smaller government with less services.[134] Then, too, just over a half of young people favored legal abortion and more than 60 percent believed homosexuals should be accepted by society.[135] In other words the Christian right was facing an impasse: with every passing year they were less likely to be able to enlist anyone but other old white conservatives as allies. The prospect was that they would continue to do well in the many districts they dominated, but not in presidential elections.

What was more, the Christian right had to worry about their own evangelical base. Mainline Protestant churches had been hemorrhaging people since the 1960s and evangelicals had attributed it to their liberal theology, but in the late 1990s the evangelical population had plateaued. Some of the Pentecostal denominations attractive to Latinos continued to gain members, as did many nondenominational churches—the prime example being Joel Osteen's 43,000-member multiethnic congregation in Houston. However, the Southern Baptist Convention, the great evangelical powerhouse, second in membership only to the Catholic Church, began to decline after years of spectacular growth. Between 1961 and 1998 its membership had grown by 59 percent—going from fewer than ten million to nearly sixteen million—but in 1998 it had experienced its first drop in membership since 1926. It recovered the next year, but its growth leveled out, and baptisms started falling off. In 2006 SBC reached a peak of 16.3 million members, but after that its membership began declining by a small percentage every year. For a denomination centered on the Great Commission the decline was a matter of profound concern to officials, who each year recommended prayer and more effort at evangelism.[136] Looking to the future, officials calculated that if present trends continued, the SBC membership could fall by a half by 2050 and represent 2 percent of the population, as opposed to the 6 percent it represented in the late 1980s.[137] Thinking to put the issue in context, the *Baptist Press* pointed out that, according to the U.S. Census, the entire white population of the United States was on decline because of lower birth rates, and the falloff matched that of the SBC.[138] It failed to note that the decline in birth rates had hit the middle-class mainline denominations first and only recently had begun to affect the more southern and more rural SBC.

Beginning in the mid-1990s the SBC made efforts to recruit non-Anglo members and churches. The initiative began with a dramatic resolution on the SBC's 150th anniversary in 1995 apologizing for slavery, on which the denomination had been founded. It regretted the SBC's failure to support the civil rights movement a century later and the fact that many congregations had intentionally, or unintentionally, excluded African Americans. Initiated by Richard Land, the resolution denounced racism as a "deplorable sin" and quoted the Bible to the effect that every life is sacred and of equal and immeasurable worth, and that every human is made in God's image.[139] From then on the SBC had some success in attracting black Baptist churches to join it, largely because of the superior resources it possessed. It also founded churches for Latinos and Asians, and between 1998 and 2005, according to its North American Missions Board, the ethnic membership of the SBC, African American, Latino, and Asian, went from 4.2 percent to 7.2 percent of the total.[140]

Still, the total membership numbers kept falling, and according to Ed Stetzer, the head of the SBC's LifeWay Research, the mean age of SBC members was growing higher than that of the general population.[141] In 2012, as the membership descended to 15.8 million, an SBC task force on evangelism reported that SBC churches weren't baptizing the young as they had before, in spite of programs for children, students, and young adults. Sixty percent of the churches reported they hadn't baptized anyone ages twelve to seventeen within the year, and 80 percent reported that they baptized zero or one person aged seventeen to twenty-nine that year. "We are not being effective in winning and discipling the next generation to follow Christ," the task force wrote.[142] Clearly this was the most serious problem the denomination had faced, and there was no consensus on why it was happening. LifeWay Research had suggested the SBC put on special programs for its now large numbers of unmarried young adults and involve them in small groups and social action of service to others.[143] Others within the SBC blamed the increasing numbers of Calvinist ministers coming out of the seminaries that were unpopular with many congregations and, according to Land, bad for evangelism.[144] Outside critics blamed the "conservative resurgence" itself for making the denomination too socially conservative, too political, and too narrow theologically to attract the new generations—an explanation that jibed with the Barna Group survey of 2007.[145]

In any case, Richard Land's behavior did not help. Since 2008, he had taken against Obama—or his own lack of influence in the White House— and had increasingly begun to sound like Dobson or Perkins. Gay rights activists, he said, were "recruiting people for homosexual clubs"[146] and Obama administration officials were "attempting to do on health care, particularly in treating the elderly . . . is precisely what the Nazis did."[147] Then one day in February 2012 he went too far. Trayvon Martin, an African American boy who had who had gone out of the house for candy and juice, was shot and killed by a neighborhood watch volunteer in Sanford, Florida. The volunteer, who claimed self-defense, was not then arrested or charged because of Florida's "stand your ground" law that permitted the use of deadly force by anyone who felt threatened. The case became a national scandal, and as protests erupted in cities around the country,

Land on his radio program called the African American leaders "race hustlers" and said they were using the incident "to gin up the black vote for an African-American president who is in deep, deep, deep trouble for reelection." When Obama remarked, "If I had a son, he would look like Trayvon," Land accused the president of "pour[ing] gasoline on the racialist fires." African American SBC pastors called for Land's dismissal, but Land refused to apologize. "True racial reconciliation means you don't bow to the false god of political correctness." He went on to say that seeing young blacks as threatening was "understandable" since they are "statistically more likely to do you harm than a white man." Apparently unconscious of what he had done, he told the Associated Press, "I have no doubt, based on the e-mails I have received, that a vast majority of Southern Baptists agree with me." A Baptist blogger then discovered that he had plagiarized some of his remarks on the radio from a column in the *Washington Times*.[148]

The SBC was just about to elect its first African American president, and by the time Land tried to make amends with African American pastors and SBC officials, it was too late. In early June the SBC took away his radio show and reprimanded him for his "hurtful, irresponsible, insensitive, and racially-charged words" and for "quoting material without giving attribution." Soon after, Land announced his retirement from the Ethics & Religious Liberty Commission, effective the following October, writing, "My denominational service, while always close to my heart, has to some degree inevitably limited my participation in the culture war's political debates," and vowed to continue "the struggle for our nation's soul."[149] More troubling, when he for the first time endorsed a Republican candidate for president, Mitt Romney, he said that he had the "deep conviction" that the 2012 election was "perhaps the most important in my lifetime, and perhaps the most important election since 1860"—as though reelecting Obama might lead to civil war.[150] Whatever the cause, the SBC lost 200,000 members in 2013–14, 2.75 percent of its weekly worship attendance, and baptisms descended to the lowest rate since the late 1940s.[151] Gifts to the International Missions Board also dropped off to the point that in 2015 the SBC had to cut eight hundred employees, or 15 percent of its overseas staff.[152]

Land retired to head a seminary with 350 students near Charlotte, North Carolina, and Russell Moore, the dean of the Southern Baptist seminary's theological school, a forty-one-year-old protégé of Al Mohler's, took over the presidency of ERLC. Soon after he took the job, Moore told an NPR radio host, "We have to recognize that the people who disagree with us aren't our enemies, they're not our opponents. And so we treat them with the civility made in the image of God." [153] But Moore was no pallid version of Land. He had his own views, and he had very strong views about racism in America. When the police put a choke hold on Eric Garner in New York City, and the grand jury did not indict the officer responsible for his death, ERLC put on a summit meeting on racial reconciliation and the gospel. "Now," Moore wrote, "what we too often see still is a situation where our African-American brothers and sisters, and especially brothers, are more likely to be arrested, more likely to be executed, more likely to be killed. . . . I think we have to acknowledge that something is wrong with the system at this point, and that something has to be done." [154] Raised in Biloxi, Mississippi, he could sometimes look at the world from the perspective of nonwhite Americans. "Often," Moore wrote, "white Christians assume, without even thinking about it, that normal Christianity is white and that we then minister to black people, Asian people and Hispanic people and they're the ones receiving ministry. No, no, no, no, no," he said. "If this is going to change, the way it's going to change is by white people being ministered by those who are called in leadership recognizing that most of the Body of Christ in heaven and on Earth isn't white, isn't American, never [spoke] English." [155] When a white supremacist shot and killed nine people at Bible study in the historic Emanuel AME Church in Charleston, South Carolina, in 2015, Moore was among the first to demand that the Confederate flag be moved off the grounds of the state capitol. "White Christians," he wrote, "let's listen to our African-American brothers and sisters. Let's care not just about our own history, but also about our shared history with them." [156]

Still, racial reconciliation was not social justice, and Moore did not move the SBC to act against the systemic poverty of African Americans in the rural South through pressing for educational funding or an expansion of health care for families. He was too sophisticated to believe that racial disparities were simply a matter of individual sins, or that pastoral care was all that was needed. When asked about it, he said the Bible was clear about the moral and social issues but not about structural economic issues. "No one wants to see a social safety net discarded. We need it," he said. "But these debates aren't settled by Scripture" whereas "opposition to abortion comes directly from the Bible." Subsequently, however, ERLC joined conservative groups in lobbying for federal legislation to reduce the prison population and expand programs to reduce recidivism; it also joined the NAE in lobbying for laws against predatory payday lending.[157]

On issues such as abortion, gay marriage, and the inerrant Bible, Moore was an orthodox Southern Baptist, but he believed that evangelicals lived in "a post–Bible Belt America" in which nominal Christians, who went to church merely for acceptance in their communities, had been "reverse raptured" from the Church. He said he was glad they had gone and that true Christians had to learn to serve as a "prophetic minority" within the larger culture "without simply being absorbed into that culture."[158] He rejected the declinist narrative of the Christian right, and he believed the young had a "visceral recoil" against the culture wars. According to Joel Hunter, he wanted to move the SBC in a progressive direction but he knew he had to do so slowly and sometimes in a roundabout way.[159]

In June 2014 the Supreme Court in a 5–4 decision ruled same-sex marriage legal in all fifty states. For the Christian right, the decision was the worst defeat they had ever suffered. Worse than *Roe v. Wade* because they had fought same-sex marriage, and had fought it hard for a decade with the introduction of the Federal Marriage Amendment into the Congress, in the 2004 campaign, and with their efforts to pressure the Bush administration to nominate justices that would rule against it. Of course some had seen the decision coming—Justice Scalia had predicted it a decade before in his dissent to the *Lawrence v. Texas* decision—and yet the turn of the tide in popular opinion had come so quickly that it shocked even non-believers of the older generations. Once the gay rights organizations had framed the issue as one of equal rights, and Massachusetts had adopted same-sex marriage, the percentage of the American public who favored marriage equality had jumped by 21 percent in a decade. In 2003 no major religious group favored same-sex marriage, but by 2014, 62 percent of mainline Protestants declared themselves for it in polls, as did 56 percent of Catholics despite the opposition of their Church hierarchy. Only 27 percent of evangelicals favored same-sex marriage, but the percentage had risen since 2003 and was continuing to rise with the replacement of the older generations by the younger ones. Having family members, friends, and people in their congregations come out as gay made the difference to evangelicals, as to other Americans.[160] Many ex-gay ministries had folded because people like Russell Moore no longer believed they could change homosexual desires into heterosexual ones.[161] By the time the Supreme Court considered the case, thirty-seven states and Washington, D.C., permitted gay marriage because of judicial rulings or ballot initiatives. Still, the Supreme Court's decision was never a certainty.

From the Christian right—or what was left of it—came the usual cries about the decline of Western civilization and the judgment of God on a people who had gone astray. Tony Perkins declared that he had stopped saying "God bless America," and said that the U.S. should assemble a convention of the states to amend the Constitution because the Supreme Court justices "act like the average American can't even read the plain text of the Constitution." [162] Franklin Graham blamed Obama. "The President is leading the nation on a sinful course, and God will judge him and us as a nation if we don't repent." [163] James Dobson said that the family that had existed since antiquity "will likely crumble, presaging the fall of Western civilization," and the homosexual activist movement was turning America into Sodom and Gomorrah. He predicted that ministers who would not officiate in a same-sex marriage would be threatened legally and might be sent to jail.[164]

The evangelical reaction was far from unanimous. The old Christian right aside, conservatives took a mild, nonconfrontational tone. In a televised stand-up in front of the Supreme Court after the decision came down, Russell Moore said it was not the time to panic because God was still sovereign, and Christians needed to be people who could articulate a vision of marriage and sexuality that would be "increasingly counter-cultural as time goes on." [165] In an apparent rebuke to the Christian right Jim Daly said, "It's time to be light in these dark times. It's not time to be combative and caustic. . . . We must continue to show loving kindness as we talk with our neighbors and friends who see this issue differently." [166] A joint statement organized by ERLC and signed by one hundred evangelical leaders, including Daly, Al Mohler, Samuel Rodriguez, Gabriel Salguero, Richard Mouw, Ron Sider, and a number of Southern Baptist pastors, gave a more substantive response, but notably never mentioned homosexuality. "We believe the Supreme Court has erred in its ruling," the statement read. "We pledge to stand steadfastly, faithfully witnessing to the biblical teaching that marriage is the chief cornerstone of society, designed to unite men, women and children." Christian theology, it said, "considers its teachings about marriage both timeless and unchanging, and therefore we must stand firm in this belief." [167] The National Association of Evangelicals issued a similar statement, and in introducing it Leith Anderson said, "As we respect a legal ruling with which we do not agree, we ask others to respect our faith and practices even when they disagree with us." [168] What concerned some evangelical organizations was not that pastors would be prevented from preaching the Gospel as they saw it but rather that institutions, such as Christian colleges, would lose their accreditation or their tax-exempt status if, for example, they refused to put same-sex couples in their housing for married couples. The ERLC statement therefore warned, "We will not allow the government to coerce or infringe on the rights of institutions to live by the sacred belief that only men and women can enter into marriage." [169]

Some evangelicals on the other hand positively welcomed the Supreme Court decision. Tony Campolo came out for the decision, as did Brian McLaren and David Neff. [170] A group called Evangelicals for Marriage Equality, largely made up of young evangelicals, applauded the decision and maintained that devout, Bible-believing evangelicals could support the right of same-same sex couples to be married under civil law. [171] Like them, Joel Hunter made a distinction between civil rights for LGBT people and the position of the church on marriage. "We must not confuse the roles of church and state," he said in a statement. "It is the responsibility of civil government to defend the rights of all its citizens. . . . It is the responsibility of a religious group to interpret its scriptures and act accordingly, including defining the practice and parameters of holy matrimony." [172] Hunter believed that marriage between a man and a woman was what the Gospels decreed. But there were others who challenged that view. About one hundred evangelical pastors and leaders signed an online letter supporting the Supreme Court ruling, and going one step farther, called on Christians to work for LGBT rights in other areas like housing and employment discrimination. As evangelical leaders, the letter read, "we believe that the gospel of Jesus Christ is a message of good news for all people," and "For far too long, we have been silent and complicit in the discrimination and marginalization of LGBT people around the world. Today we commit to no longer stand by when discrimination and inequity flourish, but to lift our voices on behalf of all God's children." The letter, released by the evangelical RISE network, included signatures from Randy Thomas, a former leader of the defunct ex-gay ministry Exodus International, and Richard Cizik, the founder of the New Evangelical Partnership.[173] David Gushee, who also signed the letter, had gone through a conversion when his sister after years of depression came out as a lesbian and became a vocal advocate of LGBT rights. Gushee, who had become well known because of his articulate books, articles, and blogs, told an interviewer, evangelicals "claim such an unparalleled authority for the Bible, but tend to be resistant to recognizing the forces that affect how the Bible is read, including personal loyalties and life experiences." Then, contradicting the Southern Baptist doctrine of inerrancy, he added, "There's often a refusal to recognize that we don't just have scriptural texts, we have traditions of interpreting those texts" and even "the selection of which texts will be important and which texts will drop to the periphery."[174]

Still, the Supreme Court decision opened up a new political battlefield in which opponents of same-sex marriage argued that individuals or businesses with religious objections should not be compelled to participate in acts that would validate same-sex marriage. Not just the Christian right but conservative evangelicals, such as Russell Moore and Rick Warren, called for the "religious liberty," meaning not just the liberty to worship in freedom, but the ability of individuals to carry religious objections from their private lives into their public roles as small business owners, service providers, and even government officials. (For example, a baker need not bake a cake for same-sex couples if he had a religious objection.) Some twenty states passed laws based on the Religious Freedom Restoration Act, a federal bill passed almost unanimously during the Clinton administration to protect the rights of Native Americans to participate in peyote ceremonies, and in states where the Republicans controlled the state legislatures, this new concept of "religious liberty" was often adopted as law. Some made specific exemptions for clergymen and others, and some wrote their laws so broadly as to seem merely thinly veiled efforts to discriminate against all gay men and lesbians. Indiana, for example, passed a law permitting individuals or companies to assert that their free exercise of religion has been "substantially burdened" as a claim, or defense, in a lawsuit, even if the government was not a party to it. Gay rights organizations objected that such a law would permit discrimination in public accommodations, housing, employment, and the like. Large businesses, such as Apple and Walmart, saw it the same it way, and their objections had a good deal of weight with state officials. The legislature passed an amendment with some antidiscrimination provisions, but not enough of them to prevent business conventions and sports teams from deciding not to go to Indianapolis, and the state lost millions of dollars in revenue.

After that, proposed RFRA laws roiled politics in many other states. Most eventually shied away from them, but in 2016 North Carolina passed a law that would require transgender people to use only the public toilets of their birth gender. Much was made of this ridiculous, unenforceable law, but more important, the small print precluded cities and town from passing their own antidiscrimination ordinances and prevented workers from bringing discrimination cases to the state courts. Again there was much resistance from big businesses on the grounds that many of their employees, suppliers, and customers would not live in a state that legalized discrimination against LGBT people.[175] Such battles would continue in the absence of a legal standard to show where religious liberty, with all of its importance to American society, became antithetical to the common good or curtailed the rights of others.

The fraught issue of same-sex marriage brought out the divisions within the evangelical leadership and demonstrated what had occurred within the evangelical community since 2005. Fifteen years earlier the Christian right would have been the only voice speaking for evangelicals, but the backlash against it had led to the emergence not only of the progressive evangelicals but of conservatives, such as Russell Moore and Jim Daly. The progressives saw themselves not as part of an embattled subculture but as part of a pluralistic society with a Christian duty to work for the common good. They worked on such issues as poverty and global warming, and they understood the importance of structural change. They had also begun debates on the most sensitive subjects, such as gay rights, and the question of how to reduce abortions without legal restrictions. The conservatives did not go that far. They took a traditional stance—and emphasis—on the "below the belt" issues, but they dreamt no more of a "Christian nation," and showed themselves open to compromise and working with others. How large a constituency either one represented remained to be seen, but according to polls, their positions appealed to much of the younger generation. The Christian right, for its part, represented the generation that had reacted to the social revolution of the Long Sixties. It maintained considerable power in the southern states, but it had no national leaders. The Republican Party had absorbed its issues to the point where reporters looking for spokesmen found mainly elected politicians, most of them also members of the Tea Party. In other words, the Christian right was no longer a movement but simply a faction within the Republican Party.

EPILOGUE

URING THE ascendency of the Christian right very few other Americans connected evangelicals to the nineteenth-century Protestants who, after the revivals of the Great Awakenings, exerted a dominant influence on American society. That is, the society that made its way across the continent, and some of whose characteristics, such as individualism, and the idea that one could change one's life, seem typically American. Evangelicals, however, remained closer to that society and culture than anyone else. In fact, it's impossible to understand the Christian right without realizing that most of its religious beliefs, preserved as if in amber by fundamentalists, originated in the nineteenth century. It's that that gives its theology its exotic cast. For conservative evangelicals religion permeates the whole of life, and seen through biblical lenses, Israel is not so much a country as the land of the Old Testament or the site of the future battle of Armageddon. For them the first chapter of Genesis is to be interpreted literally. Even today two thirds of evangelicals say they believe that humans have existed in their present form since the beginning of time.[1] Dispensationalism, in which the future of the planet is predicted in the books of Daniel and Revelation, came from a society in which many thought humans just a part of a cosmic struggle between Christ and Satan. Similarly, conservative evangelicals remain with the belief, developed in a nonindustrialized society, that the conversion of individuals to evangelical Christianity can solve all social ills. That these beliefs lasted so long surely had something to do with the ferocity with which the fundamentalists reacted against modernist thinking.

The Christian right was an equally forceful reaction, not against liberal theology, but rather against the social revolution of the 1960s. Its dominant theme was nostalgia for some previous time in history—some quasi-mythological past—in which America was a (white) Christian nation. But which time exactly? Would its leaders have been content with reversing the Supreme Court decisions made since the 1960s? Or would they have insisted that America must be by law a Christian nation? Naturally there were differences among them, but by failing to specify how far they would go to reverse the process of separating church and state, men like Pat Robertson and James Dobson allowed their opponents to charge that they wanted a theocracy.

In the 1990s the Christian right was a powerful movement, but mainly because of those who had lived through the Long Sixties. Later generations had absorbed some of the shocks of the women's movement and the gay rights movement, and were less fearful and angry about them. After the turn of the century, the Christian right maintained its power largely because of the further shock of same-sex marriage. In other words, the decline of the Christian right began earlier than assumed. Then, by allying themselves too closely with the unfortunate George W. Bush, they created a backlash among evangelicals as well as among others. Emboldened, the "new" evangelicals broadened the agenda, and in a sense came full circle with a return to the reformist imperatives of the antebellum evangelicals, such as Lyman Beecher and Charles Finney. The Christian right tried to resist, but the younger generation was not with them except on abortion. The death or retirement of the older leaders was a sign of the changing regime.

In electoral campaigns Christian right leaders invariably put the "moral" and "pro-family" issues front and center, and journalists and scholars invariably toted up their wins and losses on these issues. After thirty-five years, they had clearly lost on the issue of gay rights, and they had failed to convince a majority of Americans of the need to reverse *Roe v. Wade*. However, they had always taken a stance on economic policy and national security, as did their constituency. From this perspective it was not at all surprising that many evangelicals supported the Iraq War, and that after Obama's election many joined the Tea Party. What *was* surprising was the number of evangelicals who voted for Donald Trump in the 2016 Republican presidential primaries.

Before the start of the primary season, Tony Perkins helped to corral the old guard of the Christian right for a secret meeting to decide which candidate they should support. Several candidates, including Mike Huckabee, Rick Santorum, the neurosurgeon Ben Carson, and Senator Marco Rubio of Florida, had the religious and political qualifications to claim their support, but the old guard had determined to present a united front to lead social conservatives to victory. After some deliberation, they agreed on Senator Ted Cruz of Texas, a Southern Baptist and a right-winger who had spent his term in the Senate blocking Obama's initiatives and accusing the Republican leadership of being too soft. Possibly because of his father, a fiery Pentecostal preacher, Cruz often used the familiar jeremiad: America was once a devout Christian country, but it had drifted away from its Christian moorings. "Awaken the body of Christ," he declared, "that we might pull back from the abyss." [2] He gave them reason to believe that he would fight abortion and gay rights in the states and nominate justices who would oppose the Supreme Court decisions on marriage and *Roe v. Wade.* Indeed, Cruz would have seemed an ideal candidate for conservative evangelicals—and Donald Trump the very opposite.

A thrice-married real estate mogul and a star on reality television, Trump had written that he got to sleep with "some of the top women in the world." He claimed the Bible was his favorite book, but he did not seem to remember even a verse of it. He had, he said, never asked God for forgiveness, but that he felt "cleansed" when "I drink my little wine" . . . and "have my little cracker." He was pro-choice until recently, and he still praised Planned Parenthood for having done "very good work for many, many—for millions of women." He was not interested in the conservative evangelical social agenda and, unlike previous Republican candidates, he did not pretend to be.[3] His only concession until late in the primary season was to promise that when he was elected, "Merry Christmas" instead of "Happy Holidays" would be heard in the stores.

At the start of the campaign Trump had said that all illegal immigrants should be deported from the United States and that a wall would be built between the United States and Mexico because Mexican immigrants were "criminals and rapists." Mexico, he said, would pay for "this beautiful wall." After a terrorist attack by two Muslim radicals in San Bernardino, California, he said there should be a moratorium on all Muslims entering the United States. He also said he would use waterboarding and other "stronger" interrogation techniques on suspected Islamic terrorists, and kill their families. "Torture," he said, "works."[4]

Christian right leaders with a few exceptions, such as Jerry Falwell Jr. and Robert Jeffress, W. A. Criswell's successor as the senior pastor of the First Baptist Church in Dallas, opposed Trump. James Dobson said he would never vote for a "kingpin" of casino gambling, and several cited Trump's reported comments about his daughter's figure, "If Ivanka weren't my daughter, perhaps I'd be dating her." Progressive evangelicals opposed Trump not only because of his libertinism but also because of his xenophobia and bigotry. *Christianity Today* accused Trump of "fear mongering and demagoguery" and "Nietzsche-eque notions of power." Still, the strongest criticisms of Trump came from Southern Baptist leaders; Al Mohler, and in particular Russell Moore, kept after him throughout the primary campaign. In an op-ed in *The New York Times* in September 2015 Moore compared Trump to a "Bronze Age warlord" in his attitude toward women and said he built his career off gambling, "a moral vice that oppresses the poorest and most desperate." Later Moore wrote that deporting eleven to twelve million people "would take a government so big it would nearly be a police state." When Trump proposed closing the United States to Muslims, Moore wrote, "Anyone who cares one iota about religious liberty should denounce this reckless, demagogic rhetoric." Make no mistake, he continued, "a government that can shut down mosques just because they are mosques can shut down Bible studies just because they are Bible studies." We cannot, he said, "say we're for religious liberty and then be silent when we have calls for an entire group of people to be banned from the country based on their religion." Mohler said Trump was running "on a dangerous mix of populism and nationalism," and Moore accused Trump of "the spewing of profanities in campaign speeches, race-baiting and courting white supremacists, boasting of adulterous affairs, debauching public morality and justice."[5]

By mid-March an average 36 percent of evangelicals in twenty states had voted for Trump, though there were several other candidates in the race. Mohler could hardly believe it. Trump's "entire mode of life," he said, "has been at odds with American evangelical conviction and character." Moore, equally disgusted, said Trump could win only in a "celebrity-focused mob-ocracy in which sound moral judgments are replaced by a narcissistic pursuit of power." In fact, Mohler and Moore cared more about the evangelicals who supported Trump than about the candidate himself. "Have evangelicals lost their values?" Moore wondered. "Trump's vitriolic—and often racist and sexist—language about immigrants, women, the disabled, and others ought to concern anyone who believes that all persons, not just the 'winners' of the moment, are created in God's image." He had, he wrote, temporarily stopped calling himself "an evangelical" because the "ugly election" had turned the word meaningless. He would call himself "a gospel Christian" until the word could be redeemed.[6]

White evangelicals made up 48 percent of the Republican primary voters, and by the end of the primaries, when only Cruz was still in the race, the average of evangelicals who voted for Trump rose to 40 percent. The exit polls showed that Trump's support among evangelicals was highest among those who went to church rarely or never, but this was small consolation because a plurality of regular churchgoers across the Bible Belt, as well as elsewhere in the country had voted for Trump.[7]

Evangelical leaders, journalists, and pundits debated why this happened, and many theories were advanced. Some thought that since 1980 the Christian right had turned ever more secular, putting politics before theology. Evangelicals, they said, were becoming less evangelical. Some thought Trump appealed to prosperity gospel preachers. (And he did. Word of Faith preacher Kenneth Copeland and televangelist Paula White gave him their blessings.) Some said evangelicals like someone who stands up to the media and makes no apologies for "politically incorrect" statements even if they included profanity or misogyny. Still, the simplest explanation was that those evangelicals who voted for Trump had affinities with the Tea Party. Those who went to church rarely if ever were the poorest and least educated evangelicals (35 percent of evangelicals had household incomes of $30,000 or less) who worried about jobs more than about abortion or gay marriage.[8] Illegal immigrants, they felt, should be deported, and they believed Trump when he said high tariffs would stop China from taking away American manufacturing. They and others feared that American culture was being overwhelmed by immigrants of color, and all wanted a strong, aggressive leader to protect them from the threats of terrorists and liberals. Trump seemed to them a strong leader because, like George W. Bush, he appeared very self-confident. Appealing to their nostalgia, he promised them that "America will be great again." And he reassured them about his selections for the Supreme Court.

The question for the two Southern Baptist leaders was, What to do next? Some Christian right leaders, such as the president of Concerned Women for America, were already deciding that Trump wasn't so bad: at least he wasn't Hillary Clinton. Mohler, however, said a Trump-Clinton race would pose a "dilemma" for Christian voters, and that demanded a "fundamental rethinking of what we believe about the purpose of government and the character of political leadership." We will, he said, "have to spend a great deal of time thinking and praying together about what faithfulness will look like in a way we never have before." Moore was less ambiguous. Christians, he said, "should vote for a third party or a write-in candidate, rather than settle for the lesser of two evils." He could not support a candidate who was for abortion, and he could not support a pro-life candidate who was for racial injustice, war crimes, "or any number of other first-level moral issues."[9]

As many commentators saw it, the Trump victory had shown that the Christian right had lost its power. Even when united, its leaders could not influence evangelicals to reject what Jonathan Merritt called an "immodest, arrogant, foul-mouthed, money-obsessed, thrice-married" man "who was pro-choice until recently." Merritt suggested that the Christian right had become so fractured that it could no longer mobilize itself. It was true that some, such as Jerry Falwell Jr., Robert Jeffress, and Franklin Graham, had broken ranks, but the main problem seemed to be that the Christian right was not as big or influential as many of its leaders liked to believe. They had lost the progressives a decade before, and with the departure of Richard Land they had lost the Southern Baptist leaders as well. They had no significant national organizations, as they had in the past. They could swing some primaries or caucuses for Cruz, but not determine the Republican nominee, even if his opponent was someone like Trump.[10]

Where the Christian right still did have power was in the South and other states dominated by the Republican Party. The state "religious freedom" laws that discriminated against LGBT people were opposed by big business, and only a bare majority of evangelicals (51 percent) approved of them. Thus most were vetoed. The antiabortion legislation was, however, much more successful. From 2011 to 2016 the states passed more than three hundred antiabortion regulations from mandatory ultrasounds to rules for the burial of fetal remains. The number of freestanding clinics that provided most of the abortions declined at a record rate. Five states had only one clinic. The most successful antiabortion tactics were the laws adopted in Texas, and in part in twenty-three other states, which required clinics to build hospital-like surgical centers and doctors to have admitting privileges to local hospitals. The cost of building to hospital standards was just too high for most of the clinics, and the major medical associations judged it unnecessary. The requirement for doctors was impossible to meet in smaller cities, where clinics used visiting doctors. When the law went into effect in Texas, the number of clinics sank from forty-one to eighteen, and poor women in rural areas were the hardest hit because large portions of the state had no clinic. The Fifth Circuit, the most conservative of the circuits, upheld the law, but in 2016 the U.S. Supreme Court overturned it, the majority opinion ruling that unnecessary health regulations placed an "undue burden" on women seeking abortions. Because the ruling might eventually apply to all abortion laws that involved unwarranted claims about the dangers to women's health, abortion opponents then directed their efforts to passing restrictions on abortions they alleged would entail fetal pain.[11]

Meanwhile evangelical and Catholic nonprofits sued the government because the Affordable Care Act required their insurance to cover contraception and abortion for their employees. The Department of Health and Human Services had already agreed that they need not pay. All they had to do was to submit a notification to the government, and it would deal with the insurance companies, but many refused to do even that. In addition thirty evangelical colleges and universities were petitioning the U.S. Department of Education to receive exemptions for Title IX requirements related to sexual orientation and transgender identity, claiming their religious liberty gave them the right to discriminate.[12]

The culture war was certainly not over. Perhaps it would never end, or perhaps it would slowly die away. In any case, it was nothing like it was in the 1990s, and never would be again, if only for reasons of demography. In 1998 white evangelical Protestants were 22 percent of the American population and in 2014 only 18 percent. That was largely because of the rapid growth of the Latino population. In 2000, it was about 12 percent and by 2014 it was 17.4 percent of the whole population. (The growth didn't depend entirely on immigration but also on the fact that Latinos had more children and were generally younger than non-Hispanic whites.) Many Latinos, most of whom were born Catholic, joined denominations or churches in the white evangelical tradition, and racial and ethnic minorities made up 24 percent of evangelicals in these churches in 2014, compared to 19 percent in 2007. In 2016 Russell Moore wrote another op-ed in *The New York Times* titled "A White Church No More," in which he said, "The vital core of American evangelicalism can be found in churches that are multi-ethnic and increasingly dominated by immigrant communities." Jesus, he wrote, "will keep his promise and build his church. But he never promises to do that solely with white, suburban institutional evangelicalism. . . . A vast majority of Christians, on earth and in heaven, are not white and have never spoken English." Moore castigated those who responded to the "cultural tumult with nostalgia," but he failed to note that Latino evangelicals, as well as Latino Catholics, tended to vote Democratic.[13]

Then, the millennials were the largest of all living generations, and not only more ethnically diverse, but less conservative than their parents' generation. According to one Public Religion Research Institute/Brookings survey of 2013, 23 percent of eighteen- to thirty-three-year-old Americans were progressives, compared to 12 percent of sixty-six- to eighty-eight-year-olds. The young had a more favorable view of the federal government than their elders, and of immigration. Millennial churchgoers were far more ready to accept gays, lesbians, and transgender people and, of course, other ethnic minorities, than their elders. However, a large proportion of millennials were unaffiliated with any church—35 percent compared with 23 percent of the whole adult population. That meant there were more "nones" than evangelicals in that generation. And "nones" were known to vote Democratic. In addition the numbers of evangelicals were dwindling. From 2007 to 2014, according to a PRRI analysis, the number of white evangelicals nationwide had slipped from 22 percent to 18 percent. The same analysis showed that while nearly 30 percent of senior Americans (age sixty-five and above) were evangelicals, only 10 percent of millennials were. Even in five southern states the number of evangelicals had declined in six years, ranging from 5 percent in Louisiana to 11 percent in Kentucky. Evangelicals had an outsize presence in such states because of the high turnout of older evangelicals in elections, and the decline would not be noticed for a while because Hispanics, the religiously unaffiliated, and the young were less likely to vote, but it would eventually.[14]

Evangelicals might continue to vote Republican, but the demographic changes were already registering in the major evangelical organizations. The National Association of Evangelicals and the Southern Baptist Convention were taking on more social justice issues. Immigration was certainly one of them. When conservatives called for a border wall, Russell Moore remained a part of the Evangelical Immigration Table, and the Ethics & Religious Liberty Commission launched a $250,000 ad campaign to advocate for immigration reform with a path to citizenship. When refugees came streaming out of Syria during the intense fighting of 2015, the NAE issued a statement calling for the resettlement of Syrian refugees in the United States, a policy that thirty Republican governors and all of the Republican presidential candidates opposed. World Relief, one of nine agencies approved by the State Department for the resettlement of refugees, stood ready to help them. Moore, for his part, signed a letter asking Congress to reject "damaging changes to the US refugee resettlement program," and the SBC in opposition to Trump approved a resolution calling upon Southern Baptist churches and families to welcome the refugees. In 2016 the NAE held a conference on "racism and racialization"—a different matter from its usual talk about "racial reconciliation." Moore had spoken frequently about racism, especially after the murder of nine people in a Charleston Baptist church by a white supremacist, and the SBC approved a resolution asking Southern Baptists to discontinue the display of the Confederate flag. Then the NAE and ERLC joined other religious and civil rights groups in asking a court to support a Muslim group in New Jersey that had been trying to build a mosque for ten years but could never get the approval of the town's planning board.[15]

The NAE had come out against torture during the Bush administration, and just before Obama's visit to Hiroshima 2016, it came out for the reduction of U.S. nuclear weapons with a view toward their eventual elimination worldwide; in addition it finally endorsed the Evangelical Climate Initiative of 2006, which said that climate change was real and human-induced—a Democratic position but not a Republican one. "World poverty and climate change," it said, "need to be addressed together."[16] Of particular note was the NAE's 2015 resolution on the death penalty. White evangelicals had historically been the most favorable to capital punishment of all large religious groups. The previous resolution of 1973 had supported the death penalty, and this one did not reverse it. However, it recognized that some evangelicals opposed the death penalty, and gave the biblical and theological arguments for both sides: on one hand the just character of capital punishment in extreme cases, and on the other the sacredness of all life, including the lives of people who perpetrate serious crimes but have the potential for repentance and reformation. The change seemed modest, but as Robert P. Jones reminds us, most evangelical statements have a high degree of moral certainty—given their concerns about "moral relativism"—but this one affirmed a commitment to "both streams of Christian ethical thought." Just as striking, the resolution recognized "systemic problems in the US" that challenged the just implementation of the death penalty. Evangelical statements characteristically rejected systemic factors, but this one even connected capital punishment to the broader issue of criminal justice reform, calling for the elimination of "racial and socio-economic inequities in law enforcement, prosecution and sentencing of defendants." Again, another modest step, but as Jones rightly reports, the resolution "added a lens for perceiving systemic injustice and greater tolerance for sincere moral disagreement." [17]

Joel Hunter and other members of the NAE executive board had long opposed the death penalty, but, recognizing the changing demographics, the board had recently included a few younger white evangelicals, an African American preacher, and Samuel Rodriguez, president of the National Hispanic Leadership Conference. According to Rodriguez, millennials and nonwhites were driving the anti-death-penalty message. And some had been influenced by Catholic teachings about the sanctity of all life. "This is coming from very conservative evangelicals, who are staunchly pro-life," Rodriguez said. "They don't see it as a liberal issue." Nonetheless many millennials and nonwhites believed it was an issue of justice, for DNA tests had recently shown that a disproportionate number of nonwhites had been put to death for crimes they did not commit.

Presidential election votes might seem to belie it, but evangelicals were splintering. For more than thirty years Christian right leaders had held evangelicals together in the dream of restoration and in voting for the Republican establishment and policies that favored the rich in exchange for opposition to abortion and gay rights. No more. Evangelicals no longer followed their leaders. Some right-wingers had branched off into the secular politics of economic nationalism and opposition to immigration, while others continued to put abortion and gay marriage first. Many millennials had left the church because of what they saw as the Christian right's intolerance and bigotry. Conservative leaders, such as those in the Southern Baptist Convention, did not believe in the dream of "Christianizing" America through legislation—though with exceptions for "religious liberty." Some were also expanding the number of "first level moral issues" to racial injustice, war crimes, and more, instead of just "below the belt" issues. Progressive leaders went further. Understanding they lived in a pluralist society, they made alliances with other ethnic and religious groups for the common good. They recognized moral ambiguities and knowing that their positions were not that of the majority, they made their position on the separation of church and state as strict as that of the ACLU. The millenial churchgoers tended to support social justice and to differ with the Christian right. All the same, the victory of Donald Trump with 81 percent of the evangelical vote, and a Republican Congress, might mean the Christian right would come to power in Washington and nominate a new and sympathetic Supreme Court. In that case, the hope of the progressives lay in the future, when Latinos and the younger white evangelicals had enough strength to vote their representatives out.

GLOSSARY

Evangelical—from the Greek *euangelion*, meaning good news, or the Christian gospel. Today it applies to Protestants with beliefs summarized by the British historian David Bebbington as Biblicism, or reliance on the Bible as the ultimate religious authority; crucicentrism, or a focus on Christ's redemption of mankind on the cross; conversionism, or the emphasis on a "new birth" as a life-changing experience; and activism, or concern with sharing the faith with others.

Evangelicals come from many different religious traditions, from Calvinist, or Reformed, churches to Holiness churches. Pollsters count evangelicals either by self-identification or by the membership in those churches they have identified as evangelical.

An evangelist is one who disseminates the gospels by zealous preaching. Evangelism is the act of spreading the gospels. Evangelicalism is the religion.

Amillennialism—the rejection of the idea that Christ will have a literal thousand-yearlong physical reign on earth. Christ's reign during the millennium (of Revelations 20) is spiritual in nature, and at the end of it He will return in the flesh to render judgment and to create a new heaven and a new earth. Episcopalians, among others, believe in this doctrine.

Arminianism—the doctrine of Jacobus Arminius (1560–1606) and his followers that humans have free will and can choose salvation or not. Each person can decide for himself, and it's possible to lose your salvation. Arminians believe that Jesus died for all people's sins, and not just those of Christians. Methodists, among others, come from the Arminian tradition.

Calvinism—the religious doctrines of John Calvin (1509–1564) that emphasize the omnipotence of God and the salvation of the elect by God's grace alone. It focuses on God's sovereignty, meaning that God is able and willing by virtue of his omniscience, omnipresence, and omnipotence to do whatever He desires with His creation. It also maintains that within the Bible are the following teachings: that Jesus died for the sin of Adam; that by His sovereign grace He predestines the elect for salvation; and that it would be impossible to lose your salvation. Many churches, Baptists and others, have some admixture of Calvinism in their theological make-up. Some are pure, or five-point Calvinist, known by the acronym: T.U.L.I.P.

Total Depravity (also known as Total Inability and Original Sin)

Unconditional Election (God does not choose the elect based on any merit)

Limited Atonement (Jesus died only for the elect)

Irresistible Grace (when God calls his elected to salvation, they cannot resist)

Perseverance of the Saints (also known as Once Saved Always Saved)

Charismatics—believers from outside the Pentecostal denominations who have adopted the Pentecostals' belief that God can work miracles today and have adapted it to their own denominational traditions. For most glossolalia is a private prayer language. Charismatics can be Catholic, mainline Protestant, or evangelical.

Dispensationalism—the premillennial doctrine promulgated by John Nelson Darby in the nineteenth century that divides all history into seven dispensations in each of which God treats humans differently. It posits that the Jews, the earthly people, have from Adam on failed to keep their covenant with God. The seventh dispensation is that of the Christian church, and it has not yet ended. It offers the hope that all true Christians, "the spiritual people" will be "raptured" and meet Christ in the air before the tribulations begin.

Fundamentalist—a member of a militant evangelical movement bent on combatting Protestant liberalism and secularism. Most believe the Bible inerrant (or true in every detail) and claim to interpret it literally. George Marsden joked that a fundamentalist is an evangelical who is mad about something.

Holiness churches—churches that broke away from Methodism in the mid-nineteenth century and characterized by strict behavioral standards and strict adherence to the Bible. Such churches believe in sanctification, or a second rebirth in Christ, whereby the believer can become sinless, or someone who will chose not to sin.

Mainline Protestants—Episcopalians, Presbyterians, Methodists and others who belong to churches that resisted fundamentalism and who are more or less theologically liberal. Some are politically liberal as well.

Pentecostals—an outgrowth of the Holiness tradition characterized by the belief that God can work miracles today as He did in the age of the apostles. Pentecostals expect believers not only to have a conversion experience but also to experience a dramatic outpouring of the Holy Spirit in which they might speak in tongues. For some glossolalia, or speaking in tongues, identifies a believer who can work other miracles, such as prophesying and healing the sick. Pentecostals adopted premillenialism and other fundamentalist doctrines, and for them all these doctrines are essential to the "full gospel." Some believe in the "prosperity gospel," or the ability to gain wealth through prayer and contributing to the church.

Postmillennialism—the belief that Christians are preparing the way for the Second Coming in a thousand years by making civilization more just and more righteous.

Premillennialism—The contrary belief that civilization is becoming more wicked so that God will intervene and subject civilization to a thousand years of tribulations before He comes again with his army of saints and destroys Satan and the earth.

Reconstructionism—the belief originated by Rousas Rushdoony in the mid-twentieth century that Christians should create a society based directly on strictures of the Old Testament—except when they are contradicted by the New Testament. Reconstructionism calls for a theonomy in which all people on earth abide by biblical laws, no matter how archaic they are, including the death penalty for adultery or witchcraft.

Social Gospel—the view that Christians can create a more just and righteous society by changing not just individual hearts but social and economic institutions and bring in the Kingdom of God on earth.

NOTES

Introduction

1. *Newsweek*, Oct. 25, 1976. Since then pollsters have changed their definition of what constitutes an evangelical. Some still have different theological requirements, and while some count the denominational and church figures, others count those who self-identify as evangelicals. I have used the Pew polls and the figures given by John C. Green and his political science colleagues, unless otherwise stated.

   It must be remembered that no poll can ever be perfectly correct and that the denominations often inflate their numbers, mainly by failing to subtract those who have died or moved away from their home churches.

2. Stephen P. Miller, *The Age of Evangelicalism*, p. 95 (for Conason quote); Rick Warren interview, "Myths of the Modern Megachurch," Pew Forum on Religion and Public Life, May 23, 2005.

3. George Marsden, *Understanding Fundamentalism and Evangelicalism*, 1991, pp. 4–5.

1: The Great Awakenings and the Evangelical Empire

1. McLoughlin, *Revivals, Awakenings, and Reform*, 1978, p. xiii.

2. Ibid., pp. 35–44.

3. Ibid., p. 50; Gaustad, *The Great Awakening in New England*, pp. 14–15; Bushman, *From Puritan to Yankee*, pp. 1–21, 147–63.

4. Heimert, *Religion and the American Mind*, pp. 2–5, 59–60; Gaustad, pp. 14–16; Bushman, p. 143.

5. Ahlstrom, *A Religious History of the American People*, 1:368; Heimert, *Religion and the American Mind*, p. 4; Kidd, *The Great Awakening*, pp. 13–23.

6. Ibid., p. 105; McLoughlin, 1978, p. 46.

7. Ibid., pp. 29–35; Goen, *Revivalism and Separatism in New England*, p. 16.

8. Kidd, p. 66.

9. McLoughlin, 1978, pp. 81–83; Kidd, pp. 35–39. Not long afterward, the Synod revoked the license of a Log College revivalist whom the New Brunswick Presbytery had ordained.

10. McLoughlin, 1978, pp. 84–85; Kidd, p. 60.

11. McLoughlin, 1978, pp. 85–87.

12. Kidd, pp. 158–59.

13. McLoughlin, 1978, p. 77.

14. Heimert, pp. 61–65.

15. Kidd, pp. 138–55, 174.

16. Bushman, *From Puritan to Yankee*, pp. 197–200.

17. Edwards himself seems not to have understood the revolutionary implications of the evangelical message, for he, no less than his forebears, believed in the social order. "There is," he wrote, "a beauty of order in society . . . as when the different members of society have all their appointed office, place and station, according to their several capacities and talents, and every one keeps his place, and continues in his proper business." Bushman, p. 1.

18. Gaustad, pp. 80–101, esp. p. 99; Dorrien, *The Making of American Liberal Theology*, 2001–2006, 1:1–3.

19. Gaustad, pp. 62–67, 74, 110; Bushman, pp. 200–20.

20. Kidd, pp. 174–84; Goen, pp. 159–61; McLoughlin, 1978, pp. 67–68.

21. Kidd, pp. 180–87; Gaustad, pp. 114–16; Goen, pp. 195, 267–72.

22. Donald Mathews, *Religion in the Old South*, pp. 3–10; Marty, *Righteous Empire*, p. 42.

23. Donald Mathews, pp. 15–29; Kidd, pp. 236–48; Goen, p. 296.

24. Donald Mathews, pp. 20–46; McLoughlin, 1978, pp. 92–93; Finke and Stark, *The Churching of America*, p. 33.

25. Hatch, *The Democratization of American Christianity.*

26. Marty, *Righteous Empire*, p. 61; Ahlstrom, 1:526–28. The Methodists, who kept the best statistics, reported that their white southern membership went from 38,000 to 46,000 in the nine years before Cane Ridge, but in the six years afterward it jumped to 80,000. Donald Mathews, p. 50. By then the New and Old Side Presbyterians had reunited and the Separate Baptists merged with other Baptist groups in the South.

27. Hatch, pp. 81–91; Finke and Stark, p. 73; Donald Mathews, p. 52; Ahlstrom, 1:398, 529–31.

28. Donald Mathews, p. 55; Hatch, pp. 95–96; Finke and Starke, pp. 76–82.

29. Hill, *Southern Churches in Crisis*, 1967, p. 26; Ahlstrom, 1:538–44.

30. Hatch, p. 40.

31. Ibid., pp. 18, 32–34, 95–101, esp. p. 98.

32. Ibid., pp. 163–79.

33. Ibid., p. 164.

34. Ibid., p. 171; Ahlstrom, 1:399; Donald Mathews, p. 60.

35. Hill, 1967, pp. 22–26.

36. Donald Mathews, p. 50; Hill, 1967, pp. 22, 25, 51; Finke and Stark, pp. 292–93.

37. Finke and Stark, p. 56. Historians differ on the numbers, but all make the same point. According to Ahlstrom, the Methodists had by 1844 become the largest denomination in the country with over a million members and four thousand itinerant preachers. Ahlstrom, 1:530. In this period, all denominations grew, but as a percentage of religious adherents, the Congregationalists dropped from 20.4 percent in 1776 to 4 percent in 1858; the Presbyterians dropped from 19 percent to 11.6 percent but their numbers kept pace with the population growth. Finke and Stark, p. 56. According to Timothy Smith, by 1855 Methodists and Baptists made up 70 percent of all Protestants and the Methodists 38 percent of the total. Timothy Smith, *Revivalism and Social Reform*, p. 22.

38. Dorrien, 2001–2006, 1:35.

39. Ibid., 1:1–4, 23–25, esp. pp. 35, 33.

40. McLoughlin, 1978, pp. 108–10.

41. Ibid., pp. 115–20; Dorrien, 2001–2006, 1:115–19; Ahlstrom, 1:509.

42. Dorrien, 2001–2006, 1:117; McLoughlin, 1978, p. 119.

43. McLoughlin, 1978, pp. 110–14; but see also Hardman, *Charles Grandison Finney, 1792–1875*; Hambrick-Stowe, *Charles G. Finney and the Spirit of American Evangelism*; Cole, *The Social Ideas of the Northern Evangelists.*

44. Hardman, p. 272; *The Autobiography.*

45. Hardman, pp. 201–2; Hambrick-Stowe, pp. 34–40.

46. McLoughlin, 1978, pp. 125–26; Hatch, pp. 196–200; Hambrick-Stowe; Hardman.

47. Hardman, pp. 135–49, esp. pp. 126–27.

48. Perry Miller, *The Life of the Mind in America*, pp. 23–24; Hardman, p. 151; McLoughlin, 1978, pp. 129–30; Paul Johnson, *A Shopkeeper's Millennium*, pp. 109–11.

49. Cross, *The Burned-over District*, p. 156; Hardman, pp. 192–209; Paul Johnson; Ryan, *Cradle of the Middle Class.*

50. Paul Johnson, pp. 15–94; Hambrick-Stowe, p. 103; Finney, *Memoirs*, "The Revival in Rochester, New York, 1832."

51. Cross, p. 155; Hardman, pp. 192–209; Paul Johnson, pp. 102–8, 113–15; Ryan, pp. 104–246.

52. Paul Johnson, pp. 95–102; Hambrick-Stowe, p. 83.

53. Hambrick-Stowe, p. 80; McLoughlin, 1978, p. 129.

54. Finney, "Sermons on Important Subjects," No. 9, "Stewardship"; Hambrick-Stowe, p. 99.

55. Barnes, *The Antislavery Impulse*, p. 21; Hardman, pp. 157–85, 254–58.

56. Hambrick-Stowe, p. 143; Hardman, pp. 249, 273; Barnes, pp. 29, 59.

57. See Barnes, *The Antislavery Impulse*.

58. Thomas, *Theodore Weld*, pp. 97–100; Barnes, pp. 69–77; Hardman, pp. 268–71.

59. Barnes, pp. 79–82, 135–55; Thomas, pp. 100–7.

60. Hambrick-Stowe, p. 143; Hardman, p. 273, esp. p. 320 for letter to Weld.

61. Hardman, p. 336; Finney, *Memoirs*, "Labors and Revivals in New York City 1832 and Onward."

62. Fletcher, *A History of Oberlin College*, "God's College"; Finney, "Labors and Revivals in New York City 1832 and Onward."

63. Fletcher, *A History of Oberlin College*, "The Guarantee of Academic Freedom"; Hardman, pp. 357–58; Hambrick-Stowe, pp. 194–97.

64. Fletcher, *A History of Oberlin College*, "God's College"; Hardman, pp. 324–33, 344–45; Finney, "Early Labors at Oberlin."

65. Timothy Smith, p. 154; McLoughlin, 1978, p. 128.

66. Timothy Smith, pp. 167–70.

67. Fletcher, *A History of Oberlin College*, "Physiological Reform."

68. Ibid., "The Campaign Against War."

69. Ibid., "Female Reformers."

70. Finney Lectures on Systematic Theology, vol. 2, no. 34, 1846, "Moral Governance."

2: Evangelicals North and South

1. Methodist black membership grew at the same rate as white membership, going from 11,682 in 1790 to 166,885 in 1850. Finke and Stark, pp. 100–1.

2. Donald Mathews, p. 68.

3. Ibid., pp. 68–69.

4. Finke and Stark, p. 105. Initially the Methodists had taken a firm line because, unlike the Baptist ministers, their circuit riders remained independent of the local communities. Donald Mathews, p. 76.

5. Donald Mathews, p. 75.

6. Ibid., p. 77.

7. Ibid., pp. 153–58.

8. Ibid., pp. 159–63; Hill, *The South and the North in American Religion*, 1980, pp. 62–63. The Presbyterians had already split apart. In 1837, the Calvinists, known as the Old School, evicted the New School Presbyterians—and with them all the abolitionists in their denomination. The denomination divided on regional lines in 1861.

9. Hill, 1980, p. 65.

10. Ibid., p. 83.

11. McLoughlin, 1978, pp. 128–30, 137.

12. Hill, 1980, pp. 37–38, 72–74; Donald Mathews, p. 41.

13. Donald Mathews, pp. 20, 44, 58–61, 65; Hill, 1980, pp. 37, 52, 71.

14. Hill, 1980, pp. 52, 73; Donald Mathews, pp. 81–88.

15. Donald Mathews, pp. 175–76; Hill, 1980, pp. 22, 53, 83–86.

16. Donald Mathews, p. 175.

3: Liberals and Conservatives in the Post–Civil War North

1. Morison, Commager, and Leuchtenberg, *The Growth of the American Republic*, 2:35, 50, 63, 108; Weber, *Living in the Shadow of the Second Coming*, p. 84.

2. Morison, Commager, and Leuchtenberg, pp. 70, 93–94.
3. Adams, *Education of Henry Adams*, p. 53.
4. Finke and Stark, p. 23; George Marsden, 1991, p. 14.
5. James Davison Hunter, *American Evangelicalism*, 1983, p. 12; George Marsden, 1991, pp. 14–15.
6. Dorrien, 2001–2006, 1:280, 284.
7. Ibid., 1:112–78.
8. Ibid., 1:143–48.
9. Ibid., 1:147–48; Wikipedia on Bushnell, Munger quote on Bushnell.
10. Dorrien, 2001–2006, 1:406.
11. Dorrien, 2001–2006, 1:288–89, 294–95. Newton Smyth, the only one of the three to study in Germany, did write that modern criticism showed that the Old Testament contained three great currents of Hebrew life: prophetic teaching, priestly lore, and wisdom literature.
12. Ibid., 1:295, 300–1.
13. Ibid., 1:299, 315–18.
14. Morison, *The Oxford History of the American People*, p. 764.
15. Dorrien, 2001–2006, 1:304–11.
16. Ibid., 1:312.
17. Ibid.
18. Ibid., 1:269
19. Ibid., 1:312.
20. Ibid., 2:99–100.
21. Ibid., 2:293, 370–71, 391, 404.
22. Cited in Sandeen, *The Roots of Fundamentalism*, pp. 267–76.
23. Dayton, *Theological Roots of Pentecostalism*, pp. 90–100; Ahlstrom, 2:275, 287–91; George Marsden, *Fundamentalism and American Culture*, 1980, p. 75.
24. Dayton, pp 87–108; Ahlstrom, 2:291–4.
25. George Marsden, 1980, p. 159.
26. Noll, *The Princeton Theology*, 1983, p. 38.
27. Ibid., p. 39.
28. Dorrien, *The Remaking of Evangelical Theology*, 1998, pp. 21–24; Dorrien, 2001–2006, 1:346; George Marsden, 1980, pp. 110–11.
29. Dorrien, 1998, pp. 24–25; George Marsden, 1980, p. 110; Sandeen, pp. 114–18; Noll, 1983, pp. 30–32.
30. Dorrien, 2001–2006, 1:12–14; George Marsden, 1980, pp. 14–16.
31. Dorrien, 1998, pp. 24–25; George Marsden, 1980, pp. 110–11.
32. Sandeen, p. 117.
33. George Marsden, 1980, p. 112.
34. Ibid., pp. 112–13; Dorrien, 1998, p. 17.
35. Dorrien, 1998, pp. 19–23.
36. Ibid., p. 19; Sandeen, pp. 124–25; George Marsden, 1980, p. 113.
37. Sandeen, p. 126.
38. Ibid., pp. 126–29. The casuistry of their position is most evident in their jointly written essay of 1881 titled "Inspiration." In the last paragraph A. A. Hodge and B. B. Warfield wrote that for critics to prove an error in the Bible, they must prove that "each alleged discrepant statement certainly occurred in the original autograph of the sacred book in which it is said to be found" and that "the interpretation . . . is the one which the passage was evidently intended to bear." A clearly impossible task (essay in Noll, 1983, pp. 220–32).
39. Dorrien, 2001–2006, 1:365.
40. George Marsden, 1980, p. 117; Dorrien, 2001–2006, 1:347–67.
41. Dorrien, 1998, p. 31.
42. Weber, pp. 14–15; Sandeen, pp. 36–40, 90–98.
43. Sandeen, pp. 71, 139–41.
44. Ibid., pp. 62–64; George Marsden, 1980, p. 52; Weber, pp. 17–23.

45. George Marsden, 1980, p. 52; Weber, pp. 22–23.
46. Sandeen, pp. 273–77.
47. George Marsden, 1980, pp. 57–58; Dorrien, 1998, pp. 29–30.
48. McLoughlin, *Modern Revivalism*, 1959, p. 259.
49. George Marsden, 1980, p. 33.
50. Pollock, *Moody*, pp. 27–48; McLoughlin, 1959, pp. 170–77; Findlay, *Dwight L. Moody*, pp. 34–124.
51. McLoughlin, 1959, pp. 179–220.
52. Ibid., pp. 179–80.
53. Ibid., pp. 220, 266–67; Pollock, pp. 82, 184.
54. McLoughlin, 1959, pp. 199–205, 221–25, 262–70; Findlay, p. 173.
55. McLoughlin, 1959, pp. 233–45.
56. Ibid., esp. pp. 262, 246–48; George Marsden, 1980, pp. 35–36.
57. McLoughlin, 1959, p. 247; Ahlstrom, 2:202.
58. McLoughlin, 1959, p. 250.
59. George Marsden, 1980, p. 35; McLoughlin, 1959, pp. 25–52.
60. McLoughlin, 1959, p. 213.
61. Ibid., 2004, esp. pp. 258–59, 274–76; George Marsden, 1980, esp. p. 38; Sandeen, pp. 173–74.
62. McLoughlin, 1959, p. 256; Findlay, p. 278. Moody said, "Act the good Samaritan and take them out for a drive in your carriage."
63. George Marsden, 1980, p. 37.
64. McLoughlin, 1959, pp. 276–77, esp. pp. 254–55.
65. Ibid., pp. 252–54.
66. Ibid., pp. 272–73; Szasz, *The Divided Mind of American Protestantism*, p. 76.
67. Ahlstrom, 2:202; Sandeen, pp. 174–79; George Marsden, 1980, pp. 37, 77–80, 100–1.
68. George Marsden, 1980, p. 37.
69. Ibid., pp. 43–44.
70. McLoughlin, 1959, pp. 366–67.
71. Ibid., pp. 366–74.
72. George Marsden, 1980, pp. 47, 60.
73. McLoughlin, 1959, pp. 272–74; Sandeen, pp. 181–83; George Marsden, 1980, pp. 128–29; Carpenter, *Revive Us Again*, pp. 16–17.

4: The Fundamentalist-Modernist Conflict

1. Dorrien, 2001–2006, 2:107; Hopkins, *The Rise of the Social Gospel in American Protestantism*, pp. 302–4.
2. George Marsden, 1980, esp. p. 131; Szasz, *The Divided Mind of American Protestantism*, pp. 59–60.
3. George Marsden, 1980, p. 117.
4. Charles Erdman, "The Church and Socialism," in *The Fundamentals*, ntslibrary.com.
5. McLoughlin, 1959, esp. p. 399; Gorrell, *The Age of Social Responsibility*, pp. 229–30; George Marsden, 1980, pp. 91–93.
6. Sandeen, pp 188–95; George Marsden, 1980, p. 119; Szasz, p. 79; Torrey's foreword to the twelve volumes of *The Fundamentals*, ntslibrary.com.
7. Sandeen, pp. 188, 194, 196, 198–99; Szasz, p. 79.
8. Sandeen, pp. 202–4; George Marsden, 1980, pp. 119–23.
9. In the meantime Stewart and other premillennialists across the country were moving to promote their own distinctive doctrines.
10. Boyer, *When Time Shall Be No More*, pp. 99–100; Sandeen, pp. 208–19; George Marsden, 1980, p. 93.
11. Boyer, pp. 99–100; Sandeen, p. 221; Szasz, pp. 76–77.
12. Blackstone sent a similar memorial to President Woodrow Wilson in 1916. He advocated the conversion of the Jews, but in a 1918 Zionist conference in Philadelphia he was acclaimed a "Father of Zionism." Szasz, p. 81; Weber, pp. 137–40.

13. Weber, pp. 137–40; Szasz, p. 81; Sandeen, p. 191. Blackstone's book became very popular, and by the time of his death in 1936, hundreds of thousands of copies were in print.

14. Beale, *In Pursuit of Purity*, p. 37.

15. Boyer, p. 97; Hankins, *Francis Schaeffer and the Shaping of Evangelical America*, 2008b, pp. 89–90; Beale, p. 37; Sandeen, p. 223.

16. Scofield Reference Bible. See 1917 version at http://classic.studylight.org/; George Marsden, 1980, p. 52; and see Scofield's introduction to the Gospels. Boyer, p. 98; Sandeen, p. 224.

17. Boyer, pp. 97–98. According to Boyer, the Oxford University Press in 1990 estimated that the original version sold over five million or perhaps even over ten million copies between 1909 and 1967. A new version published in 1967 had sold 2.5 million copies by 1990, and it is still in print. Sandeen, p. 222; Stephen Sizer, "Christian Zionism: Dispensationalism and the Roots of Sectarian Theology," www.informationclearinghouse.info/article4531.htm.

18. Sizer, "Christian Zionism." The Assemblies of God and Aimee Semple McPherson's International Church of the Four Square Gospel also adopted Keswick Holiness teachings. Dayton, pp. 164–67; George Marsden, 1980, p. 94.

19. Morison, p. 841.

20. Dorrien, 2001–2006, 1:329, 2:200; Szasz, p. 84.

21. Weber, p. 117; Dorrien, 2001–2006, 2:200; esp. Shailer Mathews, *New Faith for Old*.

22. Morison, p. 848; Boyer, esp. pp. 104, 100–1.

23. Weber, pp. 195–212; George Marsden, 1980, p. 144; Boyer, esp. pp. 101–2.

24. Morison, p. 849; Dorrien, 2001–2006, 1:329–30, 2:200; Weber, esp. pp. 123–24; George Marsden, 1980, p. 145.

25. Dorrien, 2001–2006, 2:200. Gaebelein initially wrote that Christians should not "set to 'improve the world,'" but should obey their government, pray for it, and do their war service without engaging in combat. George Marsden, 1980, p. 144.

26. Ahlstrom, 2:367; Dorrien, 2001–2006, 2:372, Szasz, pp. 84–5. Charles Stelze was one of them. Newell Dwight Hillis, who had taken over Henry Ward Beecher's church in Brooklyn, even spoke favorably of a plan for "exterminating the German people." Ahlstrom, 2:368.

27. McLoughlin, 1959, esp. p. 444; Marsden, 1980, pp. 144, 142.

28. For Gladden, Dorrien, 2001–2006, 1:333–34. For Mathews, Dorrien, 2001–2006, 2:200–201; Ahlstrom, 2:369.

29. Morison, Commager, and Leuchtenburg, p. 384. Debs's sentence was commuted by President Warren Harding in 1921.

30. George Marsden, 1980, pp. 145–47; Weber, pp. 120–21.

31. George Marsden, 1980, pp. 148–51; Weber, pp. 124–25.

32. Weber, pp. 93–94, 121–22.

33. Sandeen, pp. 233–35; Weber, pp. 125–26.

34. Ahlstrom, 2:378–84; George Marsden, 1980, p. 166; Beale, p. 186.

35. Dorrien, 2001–2006, 2:202, 373–74.

36. Weber, p. 126; George Marsden, 1980, pp. 154–55.

37. George Marsden, 1980, p. 149.

38. Gorrell, pp. 314–17.

39. McLoughlin, 1959, pp. 443–44.

40. George Marsden, 1980, p. 156.

41. Szasz, p. 61; Trollinger, *God's Empire*, pp. 1–24.

42. Trollinger, pp. 31–33; Szasz, pp. 81–83.

43. Trollinger, pp. 34–36.

44. Ibid., p. 37.

45. Ibid.; George Marsden, 1980, p. 158; Sandeen, p. 243.

46. Trollinger, pp. 33, 40; Szasz, pp. 90–91; George Marsden, 1980, p. 158; Sandeen, pp. 243–47.

47. Trollinger, p. 41.

48. Ibid., p. 42.

49. Dorrien, 2001–2006, 2:191. The Northern Baptist Convention's leading organizers included

Mathews; Rauschenbusch; Augustus Strong, another Social Gospler; and John D. Rockefeller, a founder of the University of Chicago. Beale, *In Pursuit of Purity*, p. 185. Its first president was the future Supreme Court justice Charles Evans Hughes.

50. Beale, p. 195; George Marsden, 1980, p. 159.
51. Weber, p. 164; George Marsden, 1980, pp. 160–61; Trollinger, pp. 53–54; Beale, pp. 192–95. Massee, who had held many pulpits, was then the pastor of the Baptist Temple in Brooklyn, New York.
52. Weber, p. 164; George Marsden, 1980, p. 167; Trollinger, p. 54.
53. George Marsden, 1980, p. 167; Beale, p. 204.
54. Trollinger, p. 56; George Marsden, 1980, p. 172; Beale, p. 206.
55. Trollinger, pp. 56–57.
56. George Marsden, 1980, p. 162; Trollinger, pp. 56–57; Szasz, p. 96; Weber, p. 166; Sandeen, p. 262.
57. George Marsden, 1980, p. 182.
58. Sandeen, p. 263; Trollinger, pp. 58–59; Szasz, p. 97; George Marsden, 1980, p. 182.
59. Sandeen, p. 251; George Marsden, 1980, p. 172.
60. George Marsden, 1980, p. 171; text of sermon, http://baptiststudiesonline.com/wp-content/uploads/2007/01/shall-the-fundamentalists-win.pdf.
61. Longfield, *The Presbyterian Controversy*, p. 11.
62. George Marsden, 1980, p. 173.
63. Longfield, p. 46.
64. Ibid., pp. 50–51; George Marsden, 1991, pp. 194–97.
65. Text of *Christianity and Liberalism*, www.reformed.org/books/chr_and_lib/.
66. George Marsden, 1980, pp. 175–76, 191; Hankins, *American Evangelicals*, 2008a, esp. p. 32.
67. Longfield, p. 54.
68. George Marsden, 1980, pp. 132–34.
69. Longfield, esp. pp. 66, 56.
70. Ibid., p. 67; Levine, *Defender of the Faith*, pp. 251–52.
71. Levine, p. 262. The books were Vernon Kellogg's *Headquarters Nights* and Benjamin Kidd's *The Science of Power*.
72. Trollinger, pp. 45–6.
73. Levine, pp. 264–65; Longfield, p. 55.
74. Levine, p. 289, esp. p. 278.
75. Longfield, p. 57.
76. Levine, p. 69.
77. Longfield, pp. 282–84.
78. Ibid., pp. 74–76.
79. Ibid., pp. 76–78; George Marsden, 1980, p. 180.
80. Longfield, pp. 78–79; George Marsden, 1980, p. 180.
81. Longfield, pp. 101–2.
82. Sandeen, p. 253; Longfield, esp. p. 128. Fosdick became a celebrated radio preacher, and the Baptist John D. Rockefeller built the magnificent Riverside Church on the Upper West Side of Manhattan for him to preach in.
83. Longfield, p. 148.
84. Ibid., p. 131.
85. George Marsden, 1980, p. 181.
86. Ibid., p. 183; Longfield, esp. p. 149.
87. George Marsden, 1980, pp. 183–84; Longfield, pp. 150–52; Sandeen, p. 253.
88. Longfield, p. 159.
89. Sandeen, p. 254.
90. Ibid., p. 256; Longfield, pp. 162–73.
91. Levine, pp. 277–78.
92. Ibid., p. 325; Szasz, pp. 116–17; Harding, *The Book of Jerry Falwell*, p. 66.

93. George Marsden, 1980, p. 188.
94. Harding, pp. 59–75.
95. Ibid., p. 67; Longfield, p. 155; Levine, esp. pp. 338–39.
96. Levine, pp. 339–41; Harding, pp. 68–69.
97. Harding, p. 70. According to Larson, *Summer for the Gods*, p. 187, there were three thousand people on the lawn.
98. Levine, pp. 347–51; Harding, pp. 70–71.
99. Levine, p. 351; Harding, p. 71.
100. The cause of his death has never been determined, but he suffered from diabetes.
101. Levine, p. 355. During the trial Bryan had privately spoken about taking the anti-evolution fight to seven more state legislatures. Larson, p. 183. Afterward, he spoke to a cheering crowd of six thousand in Winchester, Tennessee. Lienesch, *In the Beginning*, p. 167.
102. Szasz, p. 119; Longfield, p. 154; Harding, p. 67.
103. Harding, pp. 71–72; Levine, p. 347.
104. Trollinger, p. 50.
105. Ibid.; Harding, esp. p. 72. According to Larson, p. 207, several liberal ministers complained to the ACLU about Darrow's treatment of Bryan.
106. Harding, p. 73.
107. Ibid., p. 74.
108. Ibid., p. 73.
109. George Marsden, 1980, pp. 191–92, esp. p. 188.
110. Hankins, *God's Rascal*, 1996, pp. 118–20; Trollinger, p. 60.
111. Larson, pp. 183, 204; Lienesch, pp. 171, 176; Trollinger, p. 50; Levine, p. 276.
112. Carpenter, esp. p. 102; Szasz, p. 123; Trollinger, p. 51. Such conservatives included the Lutherans in Michigan.
113. Carpenter, p. 14.

5: The Separatists

1. Frady, *Billy Graham*, p. 204; McLoughlin, 1959, p. 491; Carpenter, pp. 226–30.
2. Frady, pp. 191–92, 198, 214, 219.
3. Blumhofer, *Aimee Semple McPherson*, pp. 328–30; McLoughlin, 1959, pp. 445–64.
4. Hankins, 1996, pp. 51–53.
5. Carpenter, pp. 101, 103–4; Kemp, *Norris Extravaganza!*, pp. 29, 46–47; Trollinger, pp. 72–73.
6. Trollinger, pp. 73–74; Kemp, pp. 29–30, 33; Ribuffo, *The Old Christian Right*, pp. 117, 127, 193.
7. McLoughlin, 1959, p. 495.
8. See adherents.com for survey; Ahlstrom, 2:448, for estimate and church construction. As Ahlstrom notes, church membership figures are notoriously unreliable, and indeed different estimates were given, but all showed the same trends. According to Will Herberg, church membership stood at 36 percent in 1900, 57 percent in 1950, and nearly 60 percent in 1953. Herberg, *Protestant—Catholic—Jew*, p. 60.
9. In his famous 1955 book *Protestant—Catholic—Jew* the sociologist Will Herberg maintained that American religiosity in this period was permeated by secularism. He also cited surveys showing that 54 percent of Americans said that their religious beliefs had no influence on their ideas of business or politics and that, while 73 percent said they believed in an afterlife, only 5 percent said they had any fear of going to hell. His theory was that Americans in the 1950s were looking for a sense of identity that transcended the ethnic identities of an earlier period.
10. McLoughlin, 1959, pp. 464–65; George Marsden, 1980, pp. 194–95.
11. George Marsden, 1991, pp. 66–67.
12. Carpenter, pp. 16–17; Ahlstrom, 2:402; George Marsden, 1980, p. 194.
13. Bob Jones College was founded in 1927 in Florida; it relocated to Tennessee in 1933; from there it moved to Greenville, South Carolina, in 1947, where, still unaccredited, it became Bob Jones University. Carpenter, pp. 19–23.

14. Ibid., pp. 17–28, 125–40.
15. Trollinger, pp. 89, 95, 99–104.
16. Ibid., pp. 109, 114–17.
17. Ibid., pp. 117–23.
18. Ibid., pp. 133–36. A 1944 Northern Baptist Convention study showed that nearly 40 percent of all NBC pastors in the upper Midwest were Bible school graduates, most of them presumed to be from Northwestern. Trollinger, p. 112.
19. Trollinger, pp. 134–39; Carpenter, pp. 44, 47. In Arizona and Oregon the state conventions were also overwhelmingly conservative because of two strong local leaders.
20. Trollinger, p. 148; Carpenter, p. 48.
21. Falwell, *The Fundamentalist Phenomenon*, 1981, pp. 115, 125. According to Harding, these separatist Baptist networks in the 1970s comprised nearly nine thousand churches with 1.5 million members. Harding, p. 76.
22. Hankins, 1996, pp. 9–13; Kemp, esp. p. 86.
23. Kemp, p. 71; Hankins, 1996, pp. 16–17, 118. The man, D. C. Chipps, had objected to Norris's vilification of the mayor. When he entered the church office, Norris pulled a revolver from his desk drawer. Chipps was unarmed, but Norris put four shots into him.
24. Hankins, 1996, pp. 27–34.
25. Ibid., pp. 29–30; R. Laurence Moore, *Religious Outsiders and the Making of Americans*, esp. pp. 164–65.
26. Hankins, 1996, pp. 48, 52, 87–88, 94–99, 111–14, 147–55.
27. Falwell, 1981, p. 93; Kemp, p. 113; Hankins, 1996, pp. 90–91, 113, 121.
28. Hankins, 1996, pp. 153–57.
29. Ibid., p. 124. On one occasion Norris asked Roy Kemp, the dean of his seminary, to come to his house and into his bathroom to watch him undress and take a cold shower. Norris had told his seminary students he always took cold showers in the morning, and he wanted a witness—so that all his students would have to take cold showers, too. Kemp, who did understand his humor, suspected a practical joke on the students. Kemp, p. 109.
30. Kemp, p. 99.
31. Hankins, 1996, pp. 121–29. Norris rewrote the bylaws for the seminary without consulting Vick, its current president, or its board of directors. Vick resigned, and Norris later forged a letter to make it appear as if the schism had not occurred.
32. Falwell, 1981, pp. 120, 131. The World Baptist Fellowship claimed one thousand churches in 1980, mostly in Texas, Florida, and the Midwest. Ibid., p. 116.
33. Ibid., pp. 126–28; Harding, p. 76. A graduate of the Baptist Bible College, Jerry Falwell was by then a prominent member of the Fellowship, and he served on the board of John R. Rice's Sword of the Lord.
34. Longfield, pp. 176–78, 202–12; George Marsden, *Reforming Fundamentalism*, 1987, p. 42; Kemp, pp. 188–89.
35. Longfield, pp. 180, 210–21; George Marsden, 1987, pp. 43–44; Carpenter, p. 60. McIntire and his allies formed the Bible Presbyterian Church and the Faith Seminary. The strict Calvinist group later renamed itself the Orthodox Presbyterian Church.
36. McLoughlin, 1959, p. 467.
37. Ammerman, *Bible Believers*, 1987, p. 8; George Marsden, 1980, pp. 202–5; Hunter, 1983, pp. 11–14.
38. Carpenter, pp. 58–59, 75; Shirley Nelson interview, May 23, 2011.
39. Carpenter, p. 66; Rudolph Nelson, *The Making and Unmaking of an Evangelical Mind*, p. 27.
40. George Marsden, 1987, p. 48.
41. Dorrien, 1998, pp. 54–55; Carpenter, pp. 142–44. Wright had been brought up a Pentecostal, but he realized that fundamentalism had a broader appeal than his own still marginal tradition and that he could create an umbrella organization only by becoming a fundamentalist. Ockenga may have sympathized with his project because he had been brought up as a Holiness Methodist. Carpenter, pp. 142–43, 189; Dorrien, 1998, p. 54.

42. George Marsden, 1987, p. 48; Carpenter, pp. 145, 148.

43. Carpenter, pp. 146–49.

44. Ibid., pp. 148–53; Cizik, "A History of the Public Policy Resolutions of the National Association of Evangelicals."

45. Carpenter, pp. 150, 153; Cizik, "A History of the Public Policy Resolutions of the National Association of Evangelicals."

46. Carpenter, p. 152.

47. Ibid., pp. 24, 135, 139; George Marsden, 1987, pp. 14–15. CBS and NBC did not sell airtime to religious broadcasters. They allotted free time to Catholics, Protestants, and Jews, but the Federal Council of Churches controlled the selection of Protestants. When in 1943 Mutual followed the example of the other networks, Fuller put together his own network of independent stations, and during the war years he maintained an audience estimated at twenty million.

48. Carpenter, pp. 135–36; George Marsden, 1987, pp. 20, 38–39.

49. Carpenter, pp. 135–36; Dorrien, 1998, p. 50; George Marsden, 1987, pp. 15–16, 38–40. A 1952 study showed that almost two thirds of the Fuller audience was over forty-five and a fourth was sixty-five and above. Two thirds of the heads of households were semiskilled or unskilled laborers. George Marsden, 1987, p. 16.

50. Carpenter, pp. 164, 172–73; William Martin, *A Prophet with Honor*, p. 89; *Time* magazine, Feb. 4, 1946.

51. *Time*, Feb. 4, 1946; Carpenter, pp. 164–66; George Marsden, 1991, p. 91. William Randolph Hearst liked the YFC's emphasis on patriotism and high moral standards, and shortly after this rally all twenty-two Hearst papers carried full-page stories on the movement, giving it national visibility. George Marsden, 1991, p. 27.

6: Billy Graham and Modern Evangelicalism

1. Frady, pp. 199–200.

2. McLoughlin, 1959, p. 484; Frady, pp. 28–54; George Marsden, 1991, pp. 57–62.

3. Frady, pp. 80–87.

4. Graham, *Just As I Am*, pp. 29, 49; Frady, pp. 60–114.

5. Frady, pp. 126–34.

6. McLoughlin, *Billy Graham*, 1960, pp. 40–41; Carpenter, p. 217; Frady, pp. 146–48, 162, 167; George Marsden, 1991, pp. 85, 90–92.

7. George Marsden, 1991, pp. 101–2; Trollinger, p. 152.

8. Frady, p. 175. The quote comes from the authorized biography of Graham by John Pollock, pp. 42–43. Riley was quite capable of delivering such a speech, but young fundamentalist preachers have a propensity to compare themselves to Elisha as they claim succession to a respected elder. Conceivably Graham was calling up these conventional tropes to justify his decision to accept the job.

9. Frady, pp. 175–76; Trollinger, pp. 152–55.

10. George Marsden, 1991, pp. 108, 126–27, 161–62; McLoughlin, 1960, pp. 43–44; Frady, pp. 163, 177, 191.

11. George Marsden, 1991, p. 29.

12. Frady, p. 193.

13. Ibid., pp. 201–3; McLoughlin, 1960, pp. 48–51; Silk, *Spiritual Politics*, p. 54.

14. Carpenter, pp. 173, 217; McLoughlin, 2004, p. 487.

15. Carpenter, pp. 226–29.

16. McLoughlin, 1959, p. 483.

17. Frady, p. 220; McLoughlin, 1960, pp. 156–73. In 1951 Graham made arrangements with the BGEA to take a fixed salary of $15,000 a year. He also got a fee from his newspaper column and royalties from his books. McLoughlin, 1960, p. 67.

18. Frady, pp. 218, 225; McLoughlin, 1960, p. 134; McLoughlin, 2004, pp. 493, 499–500.

19. Frady, p. 232.

20. Ibid., pp. 240–42, 251; McLoughlin, 1960, p. 118.

21. George Marsden, 1991, p. 132.

22. McLoughlin, 1960, pp. 110–15; Long, *Billy Graham and the Beloved Community*, p. 170.

23. Long, pp. 180–81; McLoughlin, 1960, pp. 109, 116.

24. McLoughlin, 1960, pp. 111–12, 116, 118; Long, pp. 57–58.

25. McLoughlin, 1960, p. 139.

26. Frady, p. 237; McLoughlin, 1960, p. 141.

27. Long, p. 26; McLoughlin, 1960, pp. 140–44.

28. FitzGerald, *Way Out There in the Blue*, 2000, pp. 90–93.

29. Acheson, *Present at the Creation*, p. 375.

30. Chernus, *Apocalypse Management*, p. 54, for Adams quote; Chernus, "Eisenhower: Faith and Fear in the Fifties," for Eisenhower quote.

31. Chernus, "Eisenhower: Faith and Fear in the Fifties."

32. Ibid.

33. Inboden, *Religion and American Foreign Policy*, p. 260; Chernus, "Eisenhower: Faith and Fear in the Fifties"; Public Papers of the Presidents, April 23, 1954, for Eisenhower quote.

34. Wuthnow, *The Restructuring of American Religion*, 1988, pp. 58–62.

35. Inboden, esp. pp. 280, 284; Herberg, esp. p. 281. The second conference included representatives of the Muslim, Buddhist, and Hindu faiths.

36. Inboden, p. 60. Eisenhower's family had belonged to the River Brethren, a pacifist Mennonite group, and his mother had become a Jehovah's Witness. Eisenhower was neither, and in the army he had attended nondenominational Protestant services.

37. Gary Scott Smith, *Faith and the Presidency*, 2006, pp. 230–32; Silk, p. 98; Herberg, esp. p. 274. See Chernus, "Eisenhower: Faith and Fear in the Fifties," and Eisenhower's speech, April 23, 1954, Public Papers of the Presidents.

38. McLoughlin, 1959, pp. 510–11; McLoughlin, 1960, pp. 142–45.

39. George Marsden, 1991, pp. 180–81; George Marsden, 1987, p. 159.

40. George Marsden, 1987, pp. 146–52.

41. George Marsden, 1991, pp. 211–12; "In the Beginning . . . Billy Graham Recounts the Origins of CT," *Christianity Today*, Aug. 17, 1981. Interview reprinted Oct. 24, 2006.

42. George Marsden, 1991, pp. 213–14; Inboden, esp. pp. 82–83; George Marsden, 1987, pp. 157–58.

43. "In the Beginning," *Christianity Today*.

44. George Marsden, 1987, pp. 158, 160.

45. Ibid., pp. 158–59.

46. Ibid., p. 160. When in his inaugural address in the spring of 1955 new Fuller president E. J. Carnell called for tolerance toward those who held somewhat different views on the grounds that only God could judge the hearts of others and His commandment was to "Love your neighbor as yourself," Henry joined several other faculty members in condemning his stance as appeasement. Ibid., pp. 147–49.

47. Henry, *The Uneasy Conscience of Modern Fundamentalism*, 1947, p. 3; George Marsden, 1987, p. 160.

48. George Marsden, 1991, p. 216; McLoughlin, 1960, p. 198.

49. George Marsden, 1991, pp. 218–22; Silk, pp. 61–62; George Marsden, 1987, p. 162; McLoughlin, 1960, p. 163.

50. McLoughlin, 1959, pp. 500–1.

51. George Marsden, 1991, p. 220; McLoughlin, 1960, pp. 226–28; George Marsden, 1987, p. 162.

52. George Marsden, 1991, pp. 221–22; George Marsden, 1987, pp. 163–65; Butler, "Billy Graham and the End of Evangelical Unity," pp. 203–4, 218. Graham never attacked his critics by name. As Butler, a fundamentalist historian, writes, this tactic allowed him to appear to stand above the fray and relieved him of the need to answer their criticisms. Butler, p. 197.

53. George Marsden, 1991, pp. 73, 224.

54. McLoughlin, 1969, pp. 59, 162–63; Silk, p. 61. Speaking at a liberal seminary, Graham at-

tempted to bridge the difference between his theology and that of Reinhold Niebuhr. He spoke of the need for "a personal experience of Christ" and added, "or what Niebuhr would call an encounter with the living God," as if the two concepts were the same. George Marsden, 1991, p. 220.

55. Butler, pp. 176–77, 181, 196.
56. Dorrien, 2001–2006, 2:547; Wuthnow, 1988, p. 141.
57. Silk, pp. 62–63, 88; Wuthnow, 1988, esp. pp. 60, 140.
58. Wuthnow, 1988, pp. 140–41.
59. McLoughlin, 1960, p. 162.
60. Frady, p. 292; George Marsden, 1991, p. 226; Silk, p. 62; McLoughlin, 2004, p. 514.
61. George Marsden, 1991, p. 659.
62. Frady, pp. 302–3.
63. George Marsden, 1991, pp. 225, esp. pp. 230–33, 236.
64. George Marsden, 1991, p. 236; McLoughlin, 1959, p. 515; Frady, pp. 310–11.
65. Frady, p. 311; McLoughlin, 1960, pp. 184, 193; George Marsden, 1991, p. 238.
66. McLoughlin, 1960, p. 183. McLoughlin, who was then writing his book *Modern Revivalism*, recorded the results of Graham's crusades in Seattle (1951), Toronto (1955), and San Francisco (1958) as well those of London and Glasgow in 1956–57. McLoughlin, 1960, pp. 187–19. He also tells us that 22,000 of the 55,000-plus decisions in the New York crusade were made by persons under twenty-one. McLoughlin, 1959, p. 516.
67. George Marsden, 1991, p. 239; Butler, p. 243.
68. In his otherwise masterful book, *The Restructuring of American Religion*, the sociologist Robert Wuthnow concluded from contemporary accounts that the 1950s was a period of convergence and that the division that opened in the 1960s owed to the civil rights movement and the Vietnam War. Wuthnow, 1988, p. 138. See also Silk.
69. Dorrien, 2001–2006, 2:468.
70. Ibid., 2:449–50, 454, 457, 468, 537–38.
71. Ibid., 2:455–56, 462.
72. Ibid., 2:460–61.
73. Ibid., 2:454, 457, 469–74; Inboden, pp. 47, 92.
74. George Marsden, 1980, pp. 113–15, pp. 170–71; Dorrien, 1998, p. 94.
75. McLoughlin, 1959, esp. pp. 504, 509.
76. Henry, *Confessions of a Theologian*, 1986, pp. 182–83, 264–71; Dorrien, 1998, p. 105; George Marsden, 1987, p. 169.
77. George Marsden, 1991, p. 168.
78. Ibid., pp. 168–72; McLoughlin, 1960, p. 149. Graham never did hold another segregated crusade, but for reasons perhaps unrelated, he didn't hold another crusade in the South until 1958.
79. Martin, *With God on Our Side*, 1996, pp. 202–3, esp. p. 202; Long, pp. 112–13, 118; McLoughlin, 1960, p. 92; McLoughlin, 1959, esp. p. 505.
80. George Marsden, 1991, p. 295; Long, pp. 113–17; McLoughlin, 1960, p. 149.
81. Silk, esp. pp. 101, 105.
82. McLoughlin, 1959, esp. pp. 503–4; George Marsden, 1991, p. 202.
83. Frady, p. 412; George Marsden, 1991, esp. p. 295.
84. Cizik, "Public Policy Resolutions," Long, pp. 112–13, 118–121, 123–24; George Marsden, 1991, pp. 295–96, 313; Frady, pp. 410–11.
85. Wuthnow, 1988, pp. 144–49.
86. Ibid., pp. 146–47.
87. It did not split the northern denominations, though some conservative Baptists, Methodists, and Presbyterians manifested their dissent by forming special-purpose groups or small schismatic movements, as the fundamentalists had been doing all along. Ibid., p. 150.

7: Pentecostals and Southern Baptists

1. Harrell, *Oral Roberts*, 1985, pp. 16–28; Synan, *The Holiness-Pentecostal Movement in the United States*, 1971, p. 190; Cox, *Fire from Heaven*, pp. 76–77; Robins, *Pentecostalism in America*, p. 15.

2. Donna M. Johnson, *Holy Ghost Girl*, p. 22.

3. Harrell, 1985, p. 26.

4. Synan, 1971, pp. 187, 203, 205–7; Synan, *In the Latter Days*, 1984, pp. 75–80; Cox, p. 75.

5. Poloma, *The Assemblies of God at the Crossroads*, 1989, p. xv; Synan, 1984, p. 84; Dochuk, pp. 36–38; Robins, pp. 74–78.

6. Synan, 1971, p. 173.

7. Robins, pp. 79–80.

8. Ibid., p. 81.

9. Ibid., 83–84. In a sense there has been a resurrection, for today his organization, the Voice of God, publishes his sermons in print, audio, and video and sends them out to countries across the world. Possibly the publications don't include his prediction that the world would end in 1977 and Los Angeles would sink beneath the ocean. Additional sources: "The Teachings of the Prophet William Branham," letusreason.org; branham.org; Gordon Lindsey, "William Branham, a Man Sent from God"; "William Branham / Branhamism," *The Watchman Expositor.*

10. Robins, pp. 84–85. On YouTube there is a film of Allen preaching over a man said to be starving to death because of stomach cancer. At his command, the man gets up from his stretcher, drinks a carton of milk, and eats a ham salad sandwich. "Stomach Cancer Miraculously Healed by Rev. A.A. Allen."

11. Robins, p. 86.

12. Ibid.

13. Harrell, 1985, pp. 64–65, 88–89, 91–92, 110, 256.

14. Ibid., pp. 92–94.

15. Ibid., pp. 13, 91, 119–20, 129, 141–45. His team never counted the number of healings, but they estimated the number of conversions. Four million were reported by 1959.

16. Ibid., pp. 143, 153.

17. Ibid., pp. 138–40, 207, 253–61, esp. p. 258.

18. Roberts had wanted his son Robert to go to a Bible school, but Robert went to Stanford University because he wanted to study foreign languages. While he was there, Oral and his wife worried about his soul, but Robert came back to them, and with his wife, Pattie, served as the lead singers on Roberts's TV shows for many years.

19. Harrell, 1985, pp. 207–9, 211, 221, 223–25.

20. Ibid., pp. 266–72; Poloma, *The Charismatic Movement*, 1982, p. 174.

21. By 1981 five of the ten nationally syndicated television ministries were Pentecostal or charismatic—and their combined weekly audiences exceeded six million. Poloma, 1982, p. 175.

22. The NAE was largely made up of Pentecostals, but the neo-evangelical leadership had paid little attention to them for a decade. In 1960 Thomas Zimmerman, the head of the Assemblies of God, became the president, but Zimmerman was a seasoned administrator and a conservative who could be trusted not to intrude his distinctive beliefs into NAE meetings. He was one of the principal speakers at the Berlin Congress.

23. Harrell, 1985, pp. 204–6.

24. Synan, 1984, pp. 90–92; Poloma, 1982, p. 14.

25. Synan, 1984, pp. 96, 115. These estimates may be too high, but there were no precise counts in the mainline churches. According to Wuthnow, 1988, p. 151, the Catholic charismatic renewal, founded at Notre Dame in 1967, counted more than 350,000 members by the early 1970s.

26. Only David du Plessis, a South African Pentecostal, unaware of American social and ecclesiastical distinctions, did any direct proselytizing. In the 1950s and '60s he took his case for Pentecostalism to the World Council of Churches and the Vatican and from there to the

mainline and Catholic clergy in the United States. In 1958, Henry Pitney Van Dusen, the president of Union Theological Seminary, wrote an article for *Life* magazine inspired by du Plessis calling Pentecostalism "the third force" in the Protestant world. For his efforts, du Plessis was expelled from his American church, the Assemblies of God, in 1962 and reinstated only in 1980. Poloma, 1982, pp. 11–13.

27. For example, most charismatics thought of the experience of the gifts of the Holy Spirit not as a second baptism but as an "actualization" of the grace received at the first water baptism. Then, too, while Pentecostals regarded tongue-speaking as the evidence of Holy Spirit in-filling, charismatics saw it as just one of the gifts mentioned in 1 Corinthians 12 and tended to use it as private prayer language. In addition, Catholics and Episcopalians put emphasis on the liturgy and the sacraments in relation to the workings of the Holy Spirit in the way that Pentecostals did not. Synan, 1984, pp. 120–21; Poloma, 1982, p. 48; Edmund J. Rybarczyk, "Introduction: American Pentecostalism, Challenges and Temptations," in Patterson and Rybarczyk, eds., *The Future of Pentecostalism in the United States*, p. 5.

28. Synan, 1984, p. 119; Robins, pp. 94–95.

29. Wilkerson told his story in *The Cross and the Switchblade*, a 1963 best-seller read widely by Jesus people and charismatics. Robins, p. 98.

30. Enroth, Ericson, and Peters, *The Jesus People*; Robins, pp. 96–99.

31. Assemblies of God website, http://ag.org/top/; Poloma, 1982, p. 10.

32. Synan, 1984, pp. 18–19. As a sign of the times, 44 percent of Fuller Seminary students said they considered themselves "a Pentecostal or a charismatic Christian" in 1982. George Marsden, 1987, p. 269.

33. Leonard, *God's Last and Only Hope*, p. 3.

34. Wilson, *Baptized in Blood*, p. 1; Leonard, pp. 11–13, 19–20.

35. Ammerman, *Baptist Battles*, 1990, p. 42; Hill, 1967, pp. 34–46; Finke and Stark, pp. 157–58; Leonard, p. 13. The Baptist share of all southern adherents went from 30 percent to 43 percent in that period while the Methodist share declined from 42 percent to 28 percent.

36. Leonard, pp. 32–53.

37. Ibid., pp. 39, 53–55; Ammerman, 1990, pp. 44–45.

38. Leonard, pp. 69–71; Eighmy, *Churches in Cultural Captivity*, pp. 129–30.

39. Eighmy, pp. 77–78.

40. Hill, 1967, p. 29; Leonard, p. 2.

41. A small faction broke away from the Southern Episcopal Methodist Church, South, and formed the Southern Methodist Church. Glass, *Strangers in Zion*, pp. 260–70.

42. Ibid., pp. 154–82.

43. Eighmy, pp. 57–141.

44. Ibid., pp. 142–52.

45. Ibid., pp. 153, 180–81, 189–92.

46. Ammerman, 1990, pp. 51–53, 57; Phillips, *American Theocracy*, pp. 165–66. According to Peter Applebome in *Dixie Rising*, some 4.6 million white southerners left the South between 1910 and 1960, principally for the West and the Midwest.

47. Ammerman, 1990, pp. 53–54; U.S. Census. By 1980, 10 percent of the South's population was born outside the region.

48. Hill, 1967, pp. 5–17, 80, 176–77, 183; Ammerman, 1990, p. 55. In 1980 fully three quarters of Southern Baptists worshipped in urban churches. Ammerman, 1990, p. 53.

8: Evangelicals in the 1960s

1. Wuthnow, 1988, pp. 154–55, 167.

2. Ibid.

3. Ibid., pp. 156–57.

4. Williams, *God's Own Party*, pp. 51–52; Martin, 1996, p. 51; Eighmy, pp. 163, 170, 172; SBC website.

5. Martin, 1996, pp. 49–50; Williams, p. 50.
6. Cizik, "Public Policy Resolutions"; Williams, p. 51. Concerns were also voiced by Eugene Carson Blake, president of the National Council of Churches. Both he and Oxnam declared themselves reassured by Kennedy's remarks in Houston. George Marsden, 1991, pp. 49–50. Americans United stemmed from Protestant and Other Americans United for the Separation of Church and State founded in 1947, an anti-Catholic organization.
7. Williams, p. 52.
8. George Marsden, 1991, p. 50.
9. Martin, 1991, pp. 48–54; Williams, esp. pp. 54–55.
10. Williams, p. 55; George Marsden, 1991, pp. 281–82, 301, 309.
11. Williams, pp. 62–64; Eighmy, p. 161.
12. Williams, esp. p. 65; Frady, esp. pp. 437–38; Cizik, "Public Policy Resolutions," p. 11.
13. SBC website: Resolutions; Ammerman, 1990, p. 100; Williams, pp. 66–67.
14. In 1972 Americans United for the Separation of Church and State estimated that 25 percent of the public schools were not complying with *Engel* or *Schempp*. According to one 1970 study, 43 percent of Tennessee teachers continued to read the Bible to their classes. The percentages were probably the same or greater in the Deep South. Williams, p. 67.

      The Southern Baptist Convention as a body stood just as firmly against the use of federal funds for religious institutions, but a 1963 survey showed that aid to Southern Baptist hospitals under the Hill-Burton Act of 1946 amounted to almost $12.8 million. Federal loans for Southern Baptist institutions of higher education through 1962 added up to $36.6 million for dormitories and $4.7 million for students. The state conventions often objected to subsidies for higher education on the grounds that the colleges might pull away from the SBC, but college administrators wanted the proffered funds for buildings, research, and student loans. Eighmy, pp. 160–66; Schäffer, *Piety and Public Funding*, pp. 12–13.
15. McIntire had a southern as well as a northern audience, and he maintained that segregation was not unchristian or contrary to the Scriptures. George Marsden, 1991, p. 79. Interestingly, John R. Rice, immediately after the *Brown* decision, wrote that he could find no biblical basis for enforced segregation and that Christians should obey the law. Still, he added that Communists and other left-wingers were the real threat to peace and to the authority of local governments in the South. Williams, pp. 47–48.
16. Williams, pp. 48, 71; George Marsden, 1991, pp. 78–79.
17. Eighmy, pp. 193–96; text of "Statement" on SBC website.
18. Leonard, p. 22.
19. Ammerman, 1990, pp. 65–66; Eighmy, pp. 194–98; Hill, 1967, p. 209.
20. Williams, pp. 74–78; George Marsden, 1991, p. 80.
21. George Marsden, 1991, pp. 299–300, 302–3, 312, 343; Williams, p. 77; Frady, pp. 260, 264, 266, 395.
22. Cizik, "Public Policy Resolutions," esp. p. 12; Settje, *Faith and War*, esp. p. 70; Williams, esp. pp. 78–80.
23. Wuthnow, 1988, p. 191; Williams, pp. 78–79; SBC resolution on website; Frady, esp. pp. 424–30; George Marsden, 1991, p. 423. The SBC statements were titled "Resolution on Peace" (1967) and "Resolution on Peace and Justice for All Men" (1969), but the SBC had a tradition of calling for peace in the midst of wars, as in World War II. According to Settje, the Christian Life Commission under Foy Valentine constituted the only sustained and adamant voice for ending the Vietnam War. SBC leaders supported the government, and a survey of five hundred ministers in Florida and Louisiana taken by the official newspaper, the *Baptist Post*, in 1968 found 69 percent favored an escalation of the war, and 47 percent favored it even if it might lead to World War III. Settje, pp. 68–69. A sample of all SBC ministers after Nixon's bombing of Cambodia in 1970 found 80 percent of the ministers supported Nixon's policies. Williams, p. 95.
24. Williams, pp. 81, 87; Frady, p. 426; George Marsden, 1991, p. 347; Cizik, "Public Policy Resolutions," pp. 12–13; SBC website for resolutions. In 1967 Graham claimed that the protesters

were "giving comfort to the enemy" and "could make Hanoi confident that it will eventually win." Like other conservatives, many evangelicals blamed the protesters for U.S. inability to win the war. Frady, p. 426.

25. George Marsden, 1991, p. 362.

26. SBC 1967 "Resolution on Peace"; Frady, esp. p. 412.

27. Williams, pp. 89–93; George Marsden, 1991, p. 97.

28. Frady, p. 447; Martin, 1996, pp. 96–97.

29. Williams, pp. 96, 99; George Marsden, 1991, pp. 389–98; Martin, 1996, pp. 145–46; Frady, p. 425.

30. Wuthnow, 1988, p. 194; Swartz, "Left Behind," p. 29.

31. Swartz, "Left Behind," and Quebedeaux, *The Young Evangelicals*, are the main sources for the evangelical left in the 1970s.

32. Swartz, pp. 62–69, 96, 98, 195, 198–211. Students at other evangelical colleges, such as Seattle-Pacific in Washington, Messiah and Goshen in Pennsylvania, Gordon in Massachusetts, Asbury in rural Kentucky, and Trinity in the Chicago suburbs, registered some of the same concerns.

33. Swartz, pp. 70–76, 100, 102, 171; Quebedeaux, pp. 90–94. The InterVarsity's magazine, *HIS*, reached ninety thousand students by the late 1970s. The Coalition for Christian Outreach in Pittsburgh was another progressive student ministry.

34. Quebedeaux, p. 120; Swartz, pp. 58, 85–92.

35. Swartz, pp. 93–94; Ammerman, 1990, pp. 65–67; Eighmy, pp. 194–96; Hill, 1967, p. 209.

36. Swartz, pp. 163, 388–93; Stafford, "Ron Sider's Unsettling Crusade."

37. Swartz, pp. 401–10, text in Appendix A.

38. Ibid., pp. 415–68.

39. Donald W. Dayton's *Discovering an Evangelical Heritage* also concerned the nineteenth-century reformers. John Yoder's *The Politics of Jesus* and Arthur Gish's *The New Left and Christian Radicalism* explored the progressive Anabaptist vision. Richard Mouw's *Political Evangelicalism* gave the progressive Dutch Reformed perspective. *All We're Meant to Be* by Letha Dawson Scanzoni and Nancy A. Hardesty reinterpreted the New Testament from a feminist point of view. And *Twilight of the Saints* by Robert Linder and Richard Pierard criticized the evangelical version of the civil religion.

40. Williams, p. 101; Swartz, p. 486.

41. In 1974–76 Bill Bright was involved with a group trying to mobilize Christian voters for conservative candidates. Its agenda included right-to-work laws, heavier punishments for criminals, a reversion to the gold standard, higher military spending, and a U.S. withdrawal from the U.N.—but none of the "moral" issues. Turner, *Bill Bright and Campus Crusade for Christ*, p. 164; Carlson, "Paving the Way for Title X," p. 391.

42. Williams, p. 114; Harding, p. 190; Carlson, pp. 400–6; R. Laurence Moore, p. 41. Specifically they accepted the guidelines of the American Association of Obstetricians and Gynecologists on abortion in cases of rape, incest, genetic deformity, and the health of the mother— with "health" broadly defined to include social circumstances.

43. See Cizik, "Public Policy Resolutions," for NAE resolution; Harding, p. 191.

44. SBC resolutions on abortion on SBC website; Williams, pp. 115–17; *Baptist Bible Tribune*, Feb. 16, 1973.

45. Henry tells us that by the early 1970s Graham's American crusades were fewer and shorter and in some places with decreasing attendance. Henry, 1986, p. 35.

46. George Marsden, 1991, pp. 427–32; Frady, pp. 473–77.

47. George Marsden, 1991, pp. 432, 472.

48. Henry, 1986, pp. 264–300; George Marsden, 1987, pp. 74–75, 223, 227.

49. George Marsden, 1987, pp. 211–13, 216, 218, 227–30, 251, 254–55, 264–66, 269–76. Throughout the 1950s three quarters of Fuller students would have said that evangelism was more important than social, economic, and political justice; by the end of the 1960s just over a half had the same opinion. In 1970 Senator Mark Hatfield gave the commencement address. A

third of the graduating class cheered him and wore black armbands on their gowns to signify their opposition to the Vietnam War. Swartz, pp. 205–7. In 1975 one former inerrantist at Fuller, Paul Jewett, published *Man as Male and Female,* arguing that the Bible supported gender equality and that the Apostle Paul was simply mistaken when he said that the creation of Adam before Eve implied the necessary subordination of women.

50. George Marsden, 1987, p. 288; Lindsell, *The Battle for the Bible,* 1976.
51. Lindsell, 1976, p. 18. Ockenga was by then the president of Gordon-Conwell, a Reformed seminary in a Boston suburb, but he remained on the board of Fuller until his death in 1985. Carl Henry believed in inerrancy, but he refused to let it define the evangelical coalition he envisioned; in his time at *Christianity Today* some of the contributing editors did not hold to the doctrine. George Marsden, 1987, pp. 279, 287, 290.
52. Henry, 1986, p. 344; George Marsden, 1991, pp. 74–76.
53. Lindsell, 1976, pp. 259–69; Leonard, p. 135; Hankins, *Uneasy in Babylon,* 2002, p. 32.

9: The Fundamentalist Uprising in the South

1. McGirr, *Suburban Warriors,* p. 365; Harding, p. 76.
2. James L. Guth, "The Southern Baptist Clergy, the Christian Right, and Political Activity in the South," in Feldman, *Politics and Religion in the White South,* p. 189; Leonard, pp. 70–72; Ammerman, 1990, pp. 64–65.
3. Ammerman, 1990, pp. 67–68; Leonard, pp. 72–73.
4. Eighmy, p. 196; Ammerman, 1990, p. 68; Leonard, p. 133.
5. Ammerman, 1990, pp. 67–70.
6. I use the term "fundamentalists" here because the dissidents were not just conservatives or inerrantists, and in this phase of their insurgency they fit Marsden's definition of fundamentalists as "Protestants who were willing to wage ecclesiastical and theological war against modernism in theology and the cultural changes that modernists celebrated." George Marsden, 1991, p. 57. The difference was that they never became separatists.
7. Ammerman, 1990, pp. 69–71, 170, 173; Leonard, pp. 135–36; Hankins, 2002, pp. 6–7.
8. Leonard, pp. 118–19, 136–38; Hankins, 2002, pp. 6–7.
9. Leonard, p. 138; Ammerman, 1990, pp. 170, 174; Hankins, 2000, pp. 6–7.
10. FitzGerald, "Liberty Baptist—1981," in FitzGerald, *Cities on a Hill,* 1986, pp. 103–21.
11. FitzGerald, 1986, p. 164.
12. Ruth Tomczak was the managing editor of Falwell's magazine, *Faith Aflame,* and the "creative coordinator" for the Jerry Falwell ministries. She collaborated with Falwell on *Listen, America!*
13. Falwell, *Falwell: An Autobiography,* 1997, pp. 27–39, 50–51, 62–64.
14. Falwell and Towns, *Church Aflame,* p. 26; Strober and Tomczak, *Jerry Falwell,* pp. 17, 19; Falwell, 1997, pp. 105–6; FitzGerald, 1986, p. 146.
15. Falwell, 1997, pp. 107–9, 112–14; FitzGerald, 1986, p. 146.
16. Martin, 1996, p. 211.
17. Even as an adult, Falwell often played practical jokes, but of a less destructive kind. Falwell, 1997, pp. 270–71. See Harding, pp. 85–104.
18. Falwell and Towns, p. 26.
19. Winters, *God's Right Hand,* pp. 15–16; Strober and Tomczak, pp. 21–22.
20. Falwell, 1997, p. 149; FitzGerald, 1986, p. 147.
21. Falwell, 1997, pp. 156–57; Falwell and Towns, p. 77.
22. Ammerman, 1990, pp. 128–42, 146–49.
23. Ibid., pp. 150–55.
24. Harding, p. 13.
25. FitzGerald, 1986, p. 138.
26. Hindson, *The Total Family,* pp. 11–12.
27. Ibid., pp. 71–78.

28. FitzGerald, 1986, p. 140; Hindson, p. 17.
29. Falwell, 1997, p. 192.
30. Ammerman, 1987, p. 46.
31. FitzGerald, 1986, pp. 164–65; Falwell and Towns, pp. 49, 52, 79; Falwell, *America Can Be Saved*, 1979, p. 29.
32. Williams, p. 33; Max Blumenthal, "Agent of Intolerance," *Nation*, May 16, 2007.
33. Williams, p. 46; Falwell, 1997, p. 290; Martin, 1996, p. 68; FitzGerald, 1986, p. 170.
34. FitzGerald, 1986, pp. 129, 170.
35. Harding, p. 112. "Segregation or Integration—Which?" turned up only later. It had been reprinted in the fundamentalist publication *Word of Life* in 1958. Harding found a copy in the Jefferson Memorial Library in Lynchburg in the mid-1980s. Harding, p. 286n19.
36. There were two exceptions. He spoke out against a proposed liberalization of the city liquor laws in 1970 and against the introduction of parimutuel betting in Virginia in 1978. But he was hardly alone. Most of the Protestant clergy opposed these initiatives, and neither had a chance of passing. FitzGerald, 1986, pp. 175–76.
37. Ibid., pp. 152–54.
38. Falwell, 1997, pp. 341–42; Falwell and Towns, pp. 24, 30–31; Strober and Tomczak, p. 132.
39. Harding, pp. 76, 125.
40. See "A Day of Many Solomons," in Falwell, 1979, pp. 116–17, for the call to unity. In Strober and Tomczak, pp. 169–73, there is another sermon with the same message. See Harding, pp. 126–27.
41. FitzGerald, 1986, p. 178.
42. Strober and Tomczak, pp. 64–65; FitzGerald, 1986, p. 178.
43. Strober and Tomczak, pp. 67–69.
44. Harding, pp. 22, 286n25.

10: Jerry Falwell and the Moral Majority

1. Turner, pp. 191–96.
2. FitzGerald 1986; Williams, p. 159.
3. Martin, 1996, p. 203; James L. Guth, "The Politics of the Christian Right," in Green, Guth, Smidt, and Kellstedt, *Religion and the Culture Wars*, pp. 16–17. "Do you approve of the Moral Majority?" became a standard question for pollsters. See also Ammerman, 1990, p. 103; also Liebman and Wuthnow, *The New Christian Right*, p. 104.
4. Ammerman, 1990, pp. 105–6. His Southern Baptist friends included Jerry Vines and Charles Stanley, who joined the Moral Majority board.
5. Martin, 1996, pp. 101–16; McGirr, pp. 227–31, 181.
6. FitzGerald, 1986, pp. 129–30; Lichtman, *White Protestant Nation*, p. 313.
7. FitzGerald, "The Triumphs of the New Right," *New York Review of Books*, Nov. 19, 1981.
8. Williams, p. 109.
9. Welch counted Schlafly as a member of the John Birch Society, but she later denied it. Ehrenreich, *The Hearts of Men*, p. 154.
10. Martin, 1996, p. 162; Lichtman, p. 320.
11. Williams, pp. 105, 110; Martin, 1996, p. 165. A study of ERA voting by state legislatures showed a powerful association between opposition and membership in Mormon and evangelical churches. Lichtman, pp. 320–21.
12. Martin, 1996, pp. 163–67.
13. Ibid., p. 156; Williams, pp. 129–31.
14. Harrell, *Pat Robertson*, 2010, p. 81.
15. Harding, p. 303; Williams, p. 116.
16. Falwell, 1997, pp. 375–68, esp. pp. 358–59.
17. Harding, p. 303.
18. FitzGerald, 1986, p. 178. Ed Dobson, a former close associate of Falwell's, said, "I sat in

the non-smoke-filled back room with the Moral Majority, and I frankly do not remember abortion ever being mentioned as a reason why we ought to do something." Balmer, *Thy Kingdom Come*, pp. 13–16.

19. Williams, p. 147; 1976 SBC resolution on website.
20. Williams, pp. 147–50.
21. Ibid., pp. 151–53; McGirr, p. 258.
22. Strober and Tomczak, pp. 183–85; FitzGerald, 1986, p. 178; Williams, p. 172.
23. FitzGerald, "The Triumphs of the New Right"; Williams, pp. 169–70.
24. Martin, 1996, pp. 152–53, 191; Williams, p. 174; Winters, p. 116; Lichtman, p. 342; Harding, pp. 128, 298n9.
25. Martin, 1996, pp. 168–69; Williams, pp. 163–64; Winters, pp. 109–10. According to Guth in "The Politics of the Christian Right," p. 14, there were sixteen thousand Christian elementary schools by 1980, and many were building high schools. The proposed decision had been preceded by an IRS attempt to revoke the tax-exempt status of Bob Jones University in 1975 because its rules forbade interracial dating.
26. Martin, 1996, p. 173; Williams, p. 164; Balmer, pp. 13–16.
27. Strober and Tomczak, pp. 174–75.
28. Williams, p. 174; Martin, 1996, p. 200; Winters, p. 120; FitzGerald, 1986, p. 180; Lichtman, p. 343.
29. Lichtman, p. 343.
30. Falwell, *Listen, America!*, 1980, pp. 12, 13, 97–98, 104, 132.
31. Ibid., esp. p. 117.
32. Ibid., pp. 19–23, 81, 97–98, 120–22, 252.
33. Ibid., pp. 261–62.
34. Ibid., pp. 255–56.
35. Harding, esp. p. 244.
36. The Joneses did not object to Falwell's entry into politics. During the 1976 election Bob Jones University faculty members and students had put on registration drives and turned out for Ronald Reagan at the Greenville County Republican Convention. Williams, p. 124.
37. Ibid., pp. 82, 152–53.
38. Ibid., p. 166.
39. Ibid., p. 164–66; Guth, "The Politics of the Christian Right," pp. 16–18; Winters, p. 130.
40. Martin, 1996, pp. 198–99, 206–7; Williams, pp. 182–84.
41. Williams, pp. 125, 132, 147; Martin, 1996, pp. 173–90.
42. Williams, p. 188; Martin, 1996, p. 209.
43. John W. York, "Romancing the Right: Romney and Reagan's Similar Struggles Winning Over the GOP Base," Miller Center, University of Virginia, April 12, 2012.
44. Martin, 1996, p. 217.
45. Ibid., p. 214.
46. Text, www.presidency.ucsb.edu/index; Williams, p. 190; Dudley Clendinen, "The Christian New Right's Rush to Power," *New York Times*, Aug. 18, 1980.
47. Kenneth A. Briggs, "Evangelical Preachers Gather to Polish Their Politics," *New York Times*, Aug. 21, 1980; Williams, pp. 187, 190; Martin, 1996, pp. 214–18.
48. Martin, 1996, p. 215; Brian Kaylor, "Anniversary of Harmful Moment in Baptist-Jewish Relations," EthicsDaily.com, Aug. 23, 2010.
49. FitzGerald, 1986, pp. 186–87; Marjorie Hyer, "Evangelist Revises Position on God's Hearing Jews," *Washington Post*, Oct. 11, 1980.
50. FitzGerald, 1986, pp. 187–88.
51. Dudley Clendinen, "Rev. Falwell Inspires Evangelical Vote," *New York Times*, Aug. 20, 1980.
52. FitzGerald, 1986; Winters, p. 133.
53. FitzGerald, 1986, p. 189.
54. Ibid.
55. Guth, "The Politics of the Christian Right," pp. 17, 20–21; James L. Guth and John C. Green,

"The Moralizing Minority: Christian Right Support Among Political Contributors," in Green, Guth, Smidt, and Kellstedt, p. 35; Martin, 1996, pp. 219–20; Williams, pp. 178, 193; Winters, pp. 128–29.

11: The Political Realignment of the South

1. Winters, p. 160; Dobson and Hindson, *The Seduction of Power*, esp. p. 51; Martin, 1996, pp. 225–26, esp. p. 232; Williams, p. 196.
2. FitzGerald, 2000, pp. 149–50.
3. Martin, 1996, pp. 226–27; Lichtman, p. 375; Williams, pp. 197, 202; Guth, "The Politics of the Christian Right," p. 22.
4. Williams, p. 197; Martin, 1996, p. 228.
5. Winters, pp. 188–90; Martin, 1996, pp. 228–29; Williams, esp. p. 196.
6. Martin, 1996, pp. 222, 230; Williams, pp. 199–200.
7. According to a *New York Times*/CBS poll, 72 percent of the public favored the Freeze. Lichtman, p. 372. The Freeze proposal passed the House on May 4, 1983.
8. FitzGerald, 2000, p. 191; George Marsden, 1991, p. 500.
9. Winters, pp. 201–2; Williams, p. 204.
10. Cizik on Dugan, "A History of the Public Policy Resolutions of the National Association of Evangelicals," text of speech, http://voicesofdemocracy.umd.edu/reagan-evil-empire-speech-text/.
11. Martin, 1996, p. 233.
12. Williams, p. 202; Winters, p. 327; Martin, 1996, p. 234.
13. Guth, "The Politics of the Christian Right," pp. 20–21; Williams, p. 203.
14. Dobson and Hindson, p. 41.
15. Lichtman, p. 402; James L. Guth, John C. Green, Lyman A. Kellstedt, and Corwin E. Smidt, "Onward Christian Soldiers: Religious Activist Groups in American Politics," in Green, Guth, Smidt, and Kellstedt, p. 66; Martin, 1996, p. 164; Diamond, *Roads to Dominion*, 1995, p. 243. In 1992 Concerned Women for America claimed a membership of 573,0000 and a budget of $10 million, overwhelming the eighty thousand members of the Schlafly's Eagle Forum. It was less noticed because Beverly LaHaye avoided talk shows and op-eds. Lichtman, p. 402. In 1996 it was one of the three largest Christian right organizations. John C. Green, "The Christian Right and the 1996 Elections: An Overview," in Rozell and Wilcox, *God at the Grass Roots*, p. 5.
16. Lichtman, pp. 357–60.
17. Williams, p. 206; Diamond, 1995, p. 242.
18. FitzGerald, 2000, pp. 233–35; Lichtman, p. 377.
19. Martin, 1996, p. 270; Guth, Green, Kellstedt, and Smidt, "Onward Christian Soldiers," p. 21; Rozell and Wilcox, p. 5; John C. Green, "The Christian Right and the 1998 Elections: An Overview," in Green, Rozell, and Wilcox, *Prayers in the Precincts*, 2000, p. 289.
20. Mark J. Rozell and Clyde Wilcox, "Virginia: When the Music Stops, Choose Your Freedom," in Rozell and Wilcox, pp. 102–3; Williams, pp. 199, 205–6; Winters, pp. 165–66; Clyde Wilcox and Mark J. Rozell, "Conclusion: The Christian Right in Campaign '98," in Green, Rozell, and Wilcox, 2000, p. 289.
21. Wilcox and Robinson, *Onward Christian Soldiers?*, p. 44; Green, Rozell, and Wilcox, 2000, p. 289; Martin, 1996, pp. 242–43; Wilcox and Rozell, "Conclusion," p. 289; Williams, p. 222.
22. Martin, 1996, pp. 270–71; Diamond, 1995, p. 242; Winters, pp. 291–95; FitzGerald, 1986, pp. 195–97. For predictions, see Bruce, *The Rise and Fall of the New Christian Right*, and D'Antonio, *Fall from Grace*.
23. Wuthnow, *After the Baby Boomers*, 2007, pp. 7, 18; Lyman A. Kellstedt, John C. Green, James L. Guth, and Corwin E. Smidt, "Religious Voting Blocs in the 1992 Election: The Year of the Evangelical?," in Green, Guth, Smidt, and Kellstedt, pp. 270–72; Pew Forum on Religion and Public Life, "The American Religious Landscape and Politics, 2004."

24. Dean Kelley, a National Council of Churches official, wrote a highly influential book, *Why Conservative Churches Are Growing*, in 1972.

25. Wuthnow, 2007, p. 18; Putnam and Campbell, *American Grace*, p. 110; Roof and McKinney, *American Mainline Religion*, p. 161.

26. Wuthnow, 2007, pp. 81–83. According to Wuthnow, in the early 1970s only 11 percent of evangelicals, age twenty-one to forty-five, had graduated from college, compared to 20 percent of mainline Protestants in the same age group. The proportion rose to 21 percent by the late 1990s, but by then 36 percent of mainline Protestant young adults had graduated from college. Evangelicals thus remained a generation behind.

27. Roof and McKinney, pp. 170, 176. The evangelical churches did recruit considerably more young adults than the mainline churches, but because a number of their own dropped out or moved to other churches, their conversions did not add much to their numerical growth. Wuthnow, 2007, p. 78.

28. Shibley, *Resurgent Evangelicalism in the United States*, p. 28; SBC and Assemblies of God statistics on websites.

29. Black and Black, *Divided America*, 2007, p. 55.

30. Ibid., pp. 35–38, 211–12; Lichtman, p. 218; Phillips, 2006, p. 178.

31. Black and Black, *The Rise of Southern Republicanism*, 2002, pp. 211–15, 218–19, 26.

32. Rozell and Wilcox, "Conclusion: The Christian Right in Campaign '96," in Rozell and Wilcox, p. 255.

33. James L. Guth, "Southern Baptist Clergy," in Feldman, p. 192; James L. Guth, "The Bully Pulpit: Southern Baptist Clergy and Political Activism, 1980–92," in Green, Guth, Smidt, and Kellstedt, pp. 146–73.

34. Guth, "Southern Baptist Clergy," pp. 199–200.

35. Guth, "The Bully Pulpit," pp. 148, 166; Lichtman, p. 402. In 1988, 81 percent of the SBC clergy voted for George H. W. Bush compared with 69 percent of all church members.

36. Ammerman, 1990, p. 179; Leonard, p. 145.

37. Leonard, pp. 149, 164; Ammerman, 1990, pp. 215–36.

38. Ammerman, 1990, pp. 99–101, 236–43; Leonard, pp. 160–63; Guth, "Southern Baptist Clergy," p. 190.

39. Guth, "The Bully Pulpit," p. 168; Guth, "Southern Baptist Clergy," p. 209.

40. Margaret Paloma, "Pulpits and Politics: The Protestant Clergy in the 1988 Election," in Guth and Green, *The Bible and the Ballot Box*, pp. 86–90.

41. Lyman A. Kellstedt, John C. Green, James L. Guth, and Corwin E. Smidt, "Has Godot Finally Arrived? Religion and Realignment," in Green, Guth, Smidt, and Kellstedt, pp. 291–93, 297.

42. John C. Green, James L. Guth, Corwin E. Smidt, and Lyman A. Kellstedt, "Murphy Brown Revisited: The Social Issues in the 1992 Election," in Cromartie, pp. 51–52, 75.

43. The Pew Forum on Religion and Public Life, "A Faith-Based Partisan Divide," Jan. 2005.

12: The Thinkers of the Christian Right

1. Hankins, 2008, p. xi.

2. Watson, *The Christian Coalition*, p. 110.

3. Edgar, "The Passing of R. J. Rushdoony"; Chris Smith, "His Truth Is Marching On"; Mark Rushdoony, "The Vision of R. J. Rushdoony."

4. Edgar, "The Passing of R. J. Rushdoony"; Chris Smith, "His Truth Is Marching On"; North, "Rushdoony RIP."

5. Edgar, "The Passing of R. J. Rushdoony"; R. J. Rushdoony, "On Earth as It Is in Heaven"; Clarkson, "Theocratic Dominionism Gains Influence"; Tabachnick, "Rushdoony and Theocratic Libertarians on Slavery"; Sebesta and Hague, "The US Civil War as a Theological War."

6. In the 1970s Singer left the Presbyterian Church USA and established the Presbyterian

Church in America to perpetuate the legacy of the Presbyterian Church of the Confederate States of America, and beyond that of "Old School" Presbyterianism. Singer's book, *A Theological Interpretation of American History*, was published in 1964.

The nineteenth-century literature Rushdoony and his colleagues used was later republished, and the thesis of "theological war" taken up by neo-Confederate groups, such as the League of the South, a group best known for its fight in 1996 to keep the Confederate flag flying over the South Carolina state capitol.

7. Tabachnick.
8. North, 2001; Chris Smith; McVicar, "The Libertarian Theocrats." Rushdoony later taught at the Ludwig von Mises Institute in Auburn, Alabama. See the Mises website, https://mises.org.
9. Mark Rushdoony. One of the Chalcedon Foundation's biggest contributors was Howard Ahmanson, who helped found the Institute for Creation Research and contributed to the Discovery Institute, the leading institutional proponent of Intelligent Design.
10. Watson, esp. p. 111; Neuhaus, "Why Wait for the Kingdom?"; Clarkson, esp. p. 31.
11. Clarkson; British Center for Science Education, "In Extremis"; Neuhaus; Sugg, "A Nation Under God"; Edgar.
12. Neuhaus; R. J. Rushdoony, "On Earth as It Is in Heaven"; Clarkson; Watson, p. 111.
13. McVicar.
14. North, "It Usually Begins with Ayn Rand," 2002; Clarkson; McVicar.
15. Neuhaus. Rushdoony was also a contributing editor to *Conservative Digest*.
16. Smith, 2012; McVicar; Mark Rushdoony; Clarkson; Neuhaus; Watson, p. 113.
17. Neuhaus; Moyers; Smith, 2012; Sugg; McVicar; Clarkson, for last Rushdoony quote. On his blog website, garynorth.com, North in 2013 recommended a book on the French Revolution by Nesta Webster, the British Fascist conspiracy theorist of the interwar period.
18. Neuhaus; North, "The Three Legs of Christian Reconstruction's Stool," 1984.
19. North, "The Three Legs of Christian Reconstruction's Stool."
20. Neuhaus; Diamond, 1995, p. 248; McVicar.
21. Williams, pp. 225–26; garynorth.com; Martin, 1996, p. 354; Neuhaus.
22. Neuhaus.
23. Mark Hamilton, "The Dissatisfaction of Francis Schaeffer," *Christianity Today*, March 3, 1997; Frank Schaeffer, *Crazy for God*, p. 399, for condolence note.
24. Hankins, 2008b, p. 78. The review appeared in Calvin College's underground paper.
25. Ibid., pp. 75–76, 78.
26. Ibid., p. 63.
27. Frank Schaeffer, pp. 77–78, 113, 117, 207–11, 253, 256.
28. Hankins, 2008b, pp. 1–15, 28–42, 48–50.
29. Ibid., p. 167.
30. In this section all quotes, direct and indirect, come from Francis Schaeffer, *The Complete Works of Francis Schaeffer*, vol. 5.
31. Ibid., pp. 98, 122; Hankins, 2008b, pp. 42, 165–67. Schaeffer had a friend who introduced him to European art, but he never learned French or any other European language, and he mispronounced many three-syllable words in his mother tongue. (Possibly he was dyslexic.) A startling moment occurs in one of the films: Schaeffer is telling us that Sartre, despite his amoral philosophy, came out bravely against the French war in Algeria—over a film clip of Sartre denouncing American imperialism in Vietnam.
32. Francis Schaeffer, pp. 116, 132; Frank Schaeffer, pp. 204–5.
33. Francis Schaeffer, pp. 196, 179.
34. Frank Schaeffer, pp. 254, 261, 268–69; Ryan Lizza, "The Transformation of Michele Bachmann," *New Yorker*, Aug. 15, 2011.
35. Francis Schaeffer, pp. 226, 233–46. Schaeffer proposed yet another economic threat: the transfer of resources from the rich to the poor countries.
36. Frank Schaeffer, p. 308; Hankins, 2008b, pp. 143–49. Schaeffer went so far as to bar his favor-

ite son-in-law, John Sandri, a Bible scholar with less rigid views, from teaching at L'Abri. Frank Schaeffer, pp. 309–11. Francis Schaeffer's last book, *The Great Evangelical Disaster*, was another defense of inerrancy.

37. Frank Schaeffer, pp. 265–67; Martin, 1996, p. 156. Under the auspices of Billy Graham, Harold O. J. Brown, Koop, Schaeffer, and others had formed the Christian Action Council in 1975 to lobby against *Roe*.

38. Francis Schaeffer, pp. 281–410; Hankins, 2008b, pp. 181–87; Harding, 2000, pp. 192–93.

39. Frank Schaeffer, p. 291; Hankins, 2008b, pp. 190–91; Williams, p. 155; Frank Schaeffer, p. 454; Harding, pp. 192–93.

40. Edgar; Hankins, 2008b, p. 193. Frank later helped Whitehead form the Rutherford Institute, a ministry designed as the "Christian answer to the ACLU." Pat Robertson helped raise the funds, and Gary North was a founding member. Frank Schaeffer, pp. 315–16, 333–34. Whitehead later left Rushdoony's circle and made the institute a legally respectable religious and civil liberties organization, sometimes siding with the ACLU on issues such as those of search and seizure.

41. Francis Schaeffer, pp. 430–32; Noll, Hatch, and Marsden, *The Search for Christian America*, pp. 89–93, 142.

42. Francis Schaeffer, pp. 434, 437.

43. Ibid., pp. 425, 440, 442, 450, 495.

44. Ibid., pp. 457, 470, 489, 490.

45. Ibid., p. 485.

46. Ibid., p. 430; Rutherford, "A Free Disputation Against Pretended Liberty of Conscience."

47. Francis Schaeffer, p. 496; George Marsden, 1991, p. 145.

48. Francis Schaeffer, p. 479; Nelkin, *The Creation Controversy*, p. 201; Hankins, 2008b, p. 209. The law required public schools to give "balanced treatment to creation-science and to evolution-science." The case was important because it was the first time that creationists argued that creationism was a science and had nothing to do with religion. Nelkin, esp. pp. 137–46, and Appendix One.

49. "God in America Interviews Frank Schaeffer," PBS, Oct. 23, 2009. The remark was apropos of Barack Obama's Chicago pastor, and Frank Schaeffer was saying that his father was far more radical.

50. Francis Schaeffer, p. 477; Joe Carter, "A Journalism Lesson for the New Yorker," *First Things*, Aug. 10, 2010. Carter is quoting from a 2008 blog entry for the *Huffington Post* in which Frank Schaeffer did use the phrase "violent overthrow."

51. Francis Schaeffer, pp. 469–73, 482–83, 489.

52. Diamond, 1995, p. 246; Williams, pp. 208–9; Hankins, 2008b, pp. 202–4, 258n81; Frank Schaeffer, pp. 295–300.

53. Francis Schaeffer, p. 423; Martin, 1996, p. 195. See also Cromartie for "Christian worldview."

54. Harding, p. 191.

55. Ibid., pp. 191–93; Swartz, pp. 591–98; Martin, 1996, p. 194; Williams, pp. 207–10.

56. In two polls taken by John Green and his colleagues in 1992 over 40 percent of white evangelicals called themselves pro-choice, Green, Guth, Smidt, and Kellstedt, pp. 276, 283.

57. Martin, 1996, pp. 321–33, 355–56; Williams, pp. 223–25. Martin, 1996, pp. 239–50.

13: Pat Robertson: Politics and Miracles

1. FitzGerald, 1986, p. 195; Ammerman, 1990, p. 105; Guth, "Southern Baptist Clergy."

2. FitzGerald, 1986, pp. 195–96.

3. Green, "The Christian Right in the 1996 Elections," pp. 5–7, 26; John C. Green, James L. Guth, and Kevin Hill, "Faith and Elections: The Christian Right in Congressional Campaigns, 1978–1988," in Green, Guth, Smidt, and Kellstedt, pp. 104, 112; Guth, "The Politics of the Christian Right," in Green, Guth, Smidt, and Kellstedt, pp. 8–9, 11.

4. "God in America Interviews Frank Schaeffer."

5. Harrell, 2010, p. 313.

6. Ibid., p. 88; Williams, p. 214; Watson, p. 35; Boston, *The Most Dangerous Man in America?*, p. 29; Martin, 1996, pp. 265–67.

7. Alen D. Hertzke, "Harvest of Discontent: Religion and Population in the 1988 Presidential Election," in Guth and Green, p. 17; Harrell, 2010, p. 112.

8. CBN website; Harrell, 2010, pp. 1–10; Watson, p. 34; Eskelin, *Pat Robertson*, pp. 43–59.

9. CBN website; Harrell, 2010, pp. 10–13; Eskelin, pp. 60–67.

10. Harrell, 2010, pp. 15–19.

11. Ibid., pp. 20–30; Eskelin, pp. 29–30, 105.

12. Boston, p. 27; Harrell, 2010, pp. 30–31; Eskelin, p. 111.

13. FitzGerald, "Reflections: Jim and Tammy," 1990; Harrell, 2010, p. 31; Eskelin, pp. 124–25.

14. Harrell, 2010, pp. 32–33; Eskelin, pp. 123–28.

15. Martin, 1996, p. 258; Harrell, 2010, pp. 33–34.

16. FitzGerald, 1990; Harrell, 2010, p. 34.

17. Eskelin, pp. 129–30, 136–40, 155; Harrell, 2010, pp. 36–38, 42–43, 52–53, 56–57.

18. Eskelin, pp. 132, 137, 140–49, 153; Harrell, 2010, pp. 39, 40–45, 49, 192. *The Jim and Tammy Show* had been sponsored by Sunbeam Bread.

19. Eskelin, pp. 149–52; Harrell, 2010, pp. 45–48.

20. Harrell, 2010, pp. 88, 323; Watson, pp. 33–34; Boston, pp. 142–44.

21. Harrell, 2010, p. 288; Robertson, *The Secret Kingdom*, 1982.

22. Robertson, 1982, pp. 43–44.

23. Watson, p. 32.

24. Robertson, 1982, pp. 63–65, 69.

25. Ibid., p. 75.

26. Robertson did not just give his own interpretation of biblical passages. After quoting what the Bible tells us that Christ or one of the prophets said, he often wrote, "In effect what he was saying was . . ." and then put his own words within quotation marks—as though they came from the original source. Ibid., pp. 45, 69.

27. Robertson, 1982, pp. 61, 58, 109.

28. Ibid., pp. 150–51.

29. Ibid., pp. 74, 117–18.

30. Ibid., pp. 211–18.

31. Boston, p. 39.

32. Williams, p. 214; Harrell, 2010, pp. 90–93; Watson, p. 35; Martin, 1996, p. 261; Boston, p. 36.

33. Martin, 1996, pp. 259, 265; Boston, p. 38; Williams, p. 213.

34. Boston, pp. 38–39.

35. Martin, 1996, pp. 273, 276; FitzGerald, 1990.

36. Martin, 1996, pp. 278–80.

37. Williams, p. 217.

38. Harrell, 2010, p. 109.

39. Martin, 1996, p. 268; Boston, pp. 54–56.

40. Boston, pp. 39–42; Harrell, 2010, pp. 112–14.

41. Boston, p. 36; Alan D. Hertzke, "Harvest of Discontent: Religion and Populism in the 1988 Election," in Guth and Green, p. 18; Williams, p. 215.

42. Watson, p. 37.

43. Williams, pp. 214–17; Harrell, 2010, p. 100; Martin, 1996, p. 298; Eskelin, pp. 176, 182. Once during the campaign Pat Robertson made the unusual suggestion—based on the biblical Year of the Jubilee—that all private debts be canceled every fifty years. A *Wall Street Journal* editorial called him a "crack pot populist." Williams, pp. 215, 219; Watson, p. 41.

44. Williams, p. 219; Harrell, 2010, pp. 100–1.

45. Sara Diamond, "Candidate Robertson's Central America Policy," 1986, skepticfiles.org

/weird/patrhtm; Diamond, 1995, p. 219, reports that Robertson raised $3 million for the contras as early as 1984.

46. Diamond, 1995, p. 221; Harrell, 2010, esp. p. 103. Aryeh Neier, "Guatemala: Will Justice Be Done?," *New York Review of Books*, June 20, 2013.

47. Diamond, 1986.

48. Watson, pp. 38–39; Harrell, 2010, p. 100; Eskelin, pp. 178–79; Boston, pp. 40, 49–50, 70–71.

49. Boston, p. 50.

50. Harrell, 2010, p. 100; Eskelin, p. 179; Boston, esp. pp. 48–49; Williams, p. 218.

51. Harrell, 2010, p. 97.

52. Barton, *The Myth of Separation*.

53. Eskelin, pp. 179–81.

54. Epps quoted ibid., pp. 178–79. Garret Epps, "Pat Robertson's a Pastor, but His Father Was a Pol," *Washington Post*, Oct. 19, 1989. Willis Robertson opposed *Brown* and signed the 1956 "Southern Manifesto" denouncing the decision. He refused to join Byrd's "Massive Resistance" and came out twice for Adlai Stevenson, as Byrd did not. However, he opposed all the civil rights acts of the 1960s. In retaliation President Lyndon Johnson put up a pro–civil rights Democrat to challenge him in the 1966 Virginia primaries. The challenger, who came from Portsmouth, won by a few hundred votes, ending Willis's Senate career. Pat did not intervene.

55. According to Lawrence Wright, Swaggart before his fall had a viewing audience of 500 million people worldwide. His programs were broadcast on 320 stations in 145 countries, and they brought in a half a million dollars a day. Wright, pp. 50–52. They appeared on PTL as well as CBN.

56. Harrell, 2010, pp. 117–18; Boston, pp. 45–46. Later the CBN bureau chief in Beirut denied ever having any information about the location of the hostages.

57. Martin, 1996, p. 285; Watson, pp. 39–40.

58. Martin, 1996, pp. 288–90; Harrell, 2010, pp. 117–19.

59. Alan D. Hertzke, "Harvest of Discontent: Religion and Populism in the 1988 Election," in Guth and Green, pp. 17–18.

60. Harrell, 2010, pp. 105–8, 119; Martin, 1996, p. 295; Williams, p. 219; Green, "A Look at the Invisible Army," in Guth and Green, p. 32. Guth and Green's survey of Southern Baptist and Assemblies of God ministers who voted in the Republican primaries showed that only one tenth of the SBC ministers and a quarter of the Assemblies of God ministers voted for Robertson (p. 20). A survey of donors to the Robertson campaign showed that 69 percent were Pentecostals or charismatics. John C. Green, "A look at the 'Invisible Army': Pat Robertson's 1988 Activist Corps," in Green, Guth, Smidt, and Kellstedt, p. 48.

61. Martin, 1996, pp. 262–65, 293; Harrell, 2010, pp. 121–22; Lyman A. Kellstedt, John C. Green, James L. Guth, and Corwin E. Smidt, "Grasping the Essentials: The Social Embodiment of Religion and Political Behavior," in Green, Guth, Smidt, and Kellstedt, p. 182.

62. Alan D. Hertzke, "Harvest of Discontent: Religion and Populism in the 1988 Election" in Guth and Green, pp. 18–19; Martin, 1996, pp. 291–2, 226–27; Feldman, p. 260.

63. Harrell, 2010, p. 110.

64. Corwin E. Smidt, John C. Green, Lyman A. Kellstedt, and James L. Guth, "The Spirit-Filled Movements and American Politics," in Green, Guth, Smidt, and Kellstedt, pp. 228–29; Harrell, 2010, p. 71.

65. Harrell, 2010, p. 70; *New International Dictionary of the Pentecostal and Charismatic Movements*, pp. 1060–61; Poloma, 1982, p. 235.

66. Harrell, 2010, pp. 72–73. The Maranatha Campus Ministries (1971–90) gathered up young people high on charismatic experience. Its "shepherds" took control of the personal lives of the students, forbidding dating and often dictating whom they should marry and whom they should not. Robertson spoke to their Dallas Convention in 1984. Apologetics Index on Kingdom Now Theology, 1986.

67. FitzGerald, 1990, is the source except when others are mentioned.

68. "Son of Jim and Tammy Faye Finds His Own 'Grace,'" NPR, Jan. 15, 2011.

69. Shepard, *Forgiven*. According to Shepard, the FCC and the IRS had investigated PTL for years, and though they found evidence of fraud and tax violations, they failed to act, and the Reagan Justice Department declined to prosecute. In 1988, when PTL was in the hands of the courts, the IRS sued the now bankrupt ministry for $56 million in back taxes. Its estimate was that Bakker had taken more than $9 million in "excess compensation" since 1980.

70. Anita Gates, "Tammy Faye Bakker, 65, Emotive TV Evangelist Dies," *New York Times*, July 22, 2007.

71. Harding, "The Born-Again Telescandals."

72. Bakker was sentenced to forty-five years in prison—an unusually harsh sentence for a white-collar crime. On giving his verdict Judge Robert Potter said, "Those of us who do have a religion are sick of being saps for money-grubbing preachers and priests." FitzGerald, 1990. In 1992 the sentence was reduced to eight years, and Bakker was paroled in 1994, after having served not quite five years.

73. Ron French, "Jay Bakker, Son of Televangelists Jim and Tammy Faye, to Start Church in Minneapolis," *Minneapolis Star Tribune*, April 7, 2013; "Son of Jim and Tammy Faye Finds His Own 'Grace.'"

74. Harrell, 2010, p. 71.

75. Andrew Walker, "Thoroughly Modern Sociological Reflections on the Charismatic Movement from the End of the 20th Century," in Hunt, Hamilton, and Walter, *Charismatic Christianity*, pp. 33–35; Stephen Hunt, "Doing the Stuff: The Vineyard Connection," ibid., pp. 89, 93; Cox, pp. 281–85, 291–94; Neuhaus; mikebickle.org; Poloma, *Main Street Mystics*, 2003, p. 266.

76. Clarkson, p. 33; Harrell, 2010, pp. 105, 115, 311–16. In the early 1980s Robertson and North helped John Whitehead start the Rutherford Institute. Frank Schaeffer, pp. 315–16.

77. Ryan Lizza, "Leap of Faith," *New Yorker*, Aug. 15, 2011; Watson, p. 113. The name Regent was significant. According to the university catalogue, "A regent is one who represents the king in his absence." In other words until Christ's return, God's people should rule as his representatives. This is not a premillennial idea.

78. Titus published *God, Man, and Law: The Biblical Principles* in 1994, just after he left Regent, www.jcmatthews.org/uploads/5/3/7/7/5377341/biblical_principles_of_law.pdf. He used Rushdoony's work in the classroom. Robertson used Titus's interpretation of "the laws of nature and nature's God" in *America's Dates with Destiny*. Watson, p. 116.

79. Titus.

80. Harrell, 2010, pp. 246–48.

14: The Christian Coalition and the Republican Party

1. Boston, p. 58; Harrell, 2010, pp. 179–80; Winters, pp. 314–16; Diamond, 1995, pp. 245, 390n65.

2. Harrell, 2010, pp. 189–91.

3. Watson, pp. 42, 77; Williams, p. 228; Diamond, *Not by Politics Alone*, 1998, p. 76; Harrell, pp. 129, 134.

4. Boston, p. 87; Harrell, 2010, pp. 126–28; Frederick Clarkson, "The Christian Coalition," *Church & State*, Americans United, Jan. 1992.

5. Boston, pp. 66–67; Watson, pp. 54–55; Harrell, 2010, p. 134; Frederick Clarkson, "Profile: Christian Coalition," Freedom Writer, Institute for First Amendment Studies, March 1995.

6. Williams, p. 230; Clarkson, 1992; Boston, p. 91.

7. Watson, p. 76.

8. Ibid., p. 53.

9. *Denver Post*, Oct. 26, 1992, in "Christian Coalition of America," updated 2006, *Right Wing Watch*, People for the American Way (hereafter PFAW).

10. Boston, pp. 102–4; "The 1992 Campaign: Robertson Group Is Accused of Illegal Political Activity," *New York Times*, Oct. 22, 1992.

11. Clarkson, 1992; Williams, p. 230; Boston, pp. 105–6.

12. Harrell, 2010, p. 135.

13. Robertson, *The New World Order*, 1991, pp. 37, 92.

14. Ibid., pp. 95–97. Much of the material on the Eastern Establishment can be found in *None Dare Call It Conspiracy* (1971) by Gary Allen with Larry Abraham, two John Birch Society stalwarts. The prologue and the epilogue for the 1985 revised edition were written by Gary North. The idea that demonic forces are working for a new world order appears in Frank Peretti's 1986 novel, *The Present Darkness*. Cox, p. 283.

15. Robertson, 1991, pp. 8–9, 97, 109, 133–34.

16. Ibid., pp. 61, 64, 67–71, 73, 123–26, 177–78, 180–83, esp. pp. 71, 181–82. In Robertson's bibliography Webster's book is cited as *"Secret Societies.* New York: E. P. Dutton 1924, republished in a book club edition by the Christian Book Club of America." The original 1924 title of Webster's book was *Secret Societies and Subversive Movements: The Need for Fascism in Great Britain.* See also Eustace Mullins, *Secrets of the Federal Reserve* (Staunton, VA: Bankers Research Institute, 1983).

17. Robertson, 1991, pp. 261, 264, 256–57.

18. Boston, 125; Michael Lind, "Rev. Robertson's Grand International Conspiracy," *New York Review of Books*, Feb. 2, 1995; Jacob Heilbrunn, "On Pat Robertson: His Anti-Semitic Sources," *New York Review of Books*, June 20, 1995; Michael Lind, "On Pat Robertson: His Defenders," *New York Review of Books*, June 20, 1995; Robertson letter to *New York Times*, March, 4, 1995; Boston, pp. 126–32; Harrell, 2010, pp. 290–93. Lind, a former neoconservative, was mainly outraged that men like William F. Buckley Jr. and a number of neoconservative New York intellectuals had defended Robertson because of the vote-getting power of the Coalition and Robertson's support for the right wing in Israel.

19. Harrell, 2010, pp. 292–93.

20. Ibid., pp. 293, 406n51. The letter is dated 2007.

21. A poll showed that 70 percent of Robertson's television audience preferred Buchanan. Williams, p. 231.

22. Ibid.; Diamond, 1995, p. 290; Diamond, 1998, p. 94; Martin, 1996, p. 235.

23. Williams, p. 232; Diamond, 1995, p. 404n118; Martin, 1996, pp. 235, 238. White evangelicals provided 38 percent of Bush's vote. Rozell and Wilcox, "Conclusion: The Christian Right in Campaign '96," p. 260. Clinton received 28 percent of the white evangelical vote, Perot 17 percent. Martin, 1996, p. 328.

24. Joe Conason, "God Is Their Co-Pilot," *Playboy*, March 1993; Diamond, 1995, p. 296.

25. Watson, p. 54; Boston, p. 60.

26. Diamond, 1998, pp. 100, 254 notes 50 and 51. Green, Guth, Smidt, and Kellstedt, 1996, reported that in the 1994 elections 25 percent of voters were white evangelicals, and of those, 70 percent voted GOP. "The Past As Prologue: The Christian Right in the 1996 Election," Rozell and Wilcox, p. 255.

27. Martin, 1996, p. 340; Harrell, 2010, p. 141; Lind, "Rev. Robertson's Grand International Conspiracy"; Rozell and Wilcox, p. 255. According to John C. Green, moderate Republicans were fighting to regain control in the West and the Midwest, but in the South Christian right dominance was uncontested. Martin, 1996, p. 403n; Williams, p. 232. In the mid-1990s, 74 percent of southern Republican candidates in the gubernatorial and Senate races were social conservatives. Williams, p. 233. "The Past As Prologue," Rozell and Wilcox, p. 255.

28. Harrell, 2010, pp. 141, 145; *Time*, May 15, 1995; Watson, p. 81.

29. Watson, pp. 72, 77–78.

30. Ralph Reed, "Casting a Wider Net," *Policy Review*, June 1993, pp. 31–35. Interestingly, Reed wrote that it was not abortion, as most people thought, but rather government regulation of church schools that had given rise to the Christian right.

31. "A Right-Wing Star Is Born," PFAW.org; Diamond, 1998, p. 98. Falwell and Randall Terry circulated two video films, *The Clinton Chronicles* and *Clinton's Circle of Power*, in which a

former Arkansas state employee accused Clinton of womanizing, drug smuggling, money laundering, and even murder.

32. Martin, 1996, p. 340; Harrell, 2010, p. 138.

33. Thomas W. Waldron, "Christian Coalition Unveils Social Contract with the American Family," *Baltimore Sun*, May 18, 1995; Rozell and Wilcox, "Conclusion: The Christian Right in Campaign '96, p. 260; Martin, 1996, pp. 340–41; Watson, p. 78.

34. Watson, p. 73.

35. Ibid., pp. 67–69, 78. In a 1994 survey of *Christian American*'s readership the Coalition found that Catholics composed only 5 percent. In a follow-up survey in 1995 the Coalition listed Catholics at 16 percent, Jews at 2 percent, and African Americans at 3 percent.

36. Gilgoff, *The Jesus Machine*, p. 98; Watson, p. 74; Williams, p. 234. Reed had supported the senatorial campaigns of Paul Coverdell (R-GA) and Kay Bailey Hutchison (R-TX), who supported abortion rights in certain circumstances.

37. Gilgoff, p. 102.

38. Watson, pp. 73–75; Harrell, 2010, p. 147.

39. Harrell, 2010, p. 142; Watson, pp. 109, 120; Williams, p. 230, for Robertson quote.

40. Watson, esp. p. 72; Boston, pp. 156–57, 160–61; Harrell, 2010, pp. 142–45.

41. Harrell, 2010, pp. 146–50; Wilcox and Robinson, p. 52. Reed dedicated *Active Faith* to Robertson.

42. Rozell and Wilcox, eds., "The Past As Prologue: The Christian Right in the 1996 Election," p. 255; Harrell, 2010, esp. p. 149.

43. Williams, p. 241; Rozell and Wilcox, p. 261; White evangelicals made up 28 percent of the electorate and had given two thirds of their vote to Republican congressional candidates, making them a critical constituency for the GOP. Green, "The Christian Right and the 1996 Election: An Overview," p. 12; Kellstedt, Green, Smidt, and Guth, "The Puzzle of Evangelical Protestantism: Core, Periphery, and Political Behavior," in Green, Guth, Smidt, and Kellstedt, eds., pp. 256, 263.

44. Rozell and Wilcox, "Conclusion: The Christian Right in Campaign '96," p. 8; The Past As Prologue: the Christian Right and the 1996 Election," in Rozell and Wilcox, p. 255; Kellstedt, Green, Smidt, and Guth, "The Puzzle of Evangelical Protestantism," in Green, Guth, Smidt, and Kellstedt, eds., pp. 256, 263.

45. Ibid., p. 261. DOMA was passed in September 1996 with a veto-proof majority. At the time there were very few congressmen ready come out for gay marriage, and Clinton wanted the vote over before the election season began.

46. Watson, p. 85; Harrell, 2010, pp. 150–51. Reed became a member of the Coalition's board of directors and remained friendly with Robertson.

47. Harrell, 2010, p. 153; Williams, pp. 243, esp. p. 245; Watson, pp. 6–7, 87. Hodel had appeared on *The 700 Club* speaking of his born-again experience after his son committed suicide. He was on the board of Focus on the Family; Harrell, p. 152. As secretary of energy, Hodel had recommended against signing an agreement to reduce chlorofluorocarbons (CFCs) to protect the ozone layer, proposing the use of hats and sunglasses to guard against the lethal rays penetrating the ozone-less atmosphere. "Environment: Don Hodel's Ray Ban Plan," *Time*, June 8, 1987.

48. Watson, p. 59; Harrell, 2010, pp. 153–54; Bill Miller and Susan B. Glasser, "A Victory for the Christian Coalition," *Washington Post*, Aug. 3, 1999. The judge ruled that in mailing a flyer supporting Newt Gingrich and in turning over a political list to Colonel Oliver North when he ran for governor of Virginia in 1994, the Coalition had crossed the line into illegal partisan activities.

49. Thomas B. Edsall and Hanna Rosin, "IRS Denies Christian Coalition Tax-Exempt Status," *Washington Post*, June 11, 1999.

50. Miller and Glasser, "A Victory for the Christian Coalition"; Harrell, 2010, pp. 154–55. See adlercolvin.com for 2005 settlement on rules for voter guides. Sekulow, a successful litigator for religious rights, had been the chief counsel for Robertson's American Center for Law and Justice since 1992.

51. Williams, pp. 243–44.

52. Harrell, 2010, p. 156. In July 1997 Robertson said offhandedly on *The 700 Club* that the philandering president might "slip out the back alley by himself" where "some gunman will assassinate him."

53. Harrell, 2010, p. 156.

54. Blumenthal, *Republican Gomorrah*, p. 91; Years later Dennis Hastert, the Speaker of the House from 1999–2007, pleaded guilty to federal charges of paying off a man whom he had sexually abused years before when he worked as a wrestling coach. Federal prosecutors alleged that he had molested four boys.

55. Harrell, 2010, esp. pp. 156–57; "How Clinton's Impeachment Led to the Collapse of the Christian Coalition," interview with Joel Vaughan, rightwingwatch.org, Sept. 15, 2009, www.rightwingwatch.org/content/how-clintons-impeachment-led-collapse-christian-coalition.

56. Harrell, 2010, pp. 159–60. Harrell's example was that Robertson came out for granting the People's Republic of China most-favored-nation status, though the Coalition had strongly opposed it in the past.

57. Harrell, 2010, pp. 159–60, 162, 165; Frank Winter, "The Christian Coalition in Disarray," Institute for First Amendment Studies, March/April 1999; Green, Rozell, and Wilcox, p. 7; Edsall and Rosin, "IRS Denies Christian Coalition Tax-Exempt Status"; interview with Joel Vaughan; Laurie Goodstein, "Debt, Distortion Saps the Christian Coalition's Clout," *New York Times*, Aug. 2, 1999.

58. Harrell, 2010, pp. 166–67; Interview with Joel Vaughan; Goldberg, *Kingdom Coming*, p. 15. Combs hired her relatives, and in 2001 the Coalition was successfully sued for discrimination by ten African American employees, who charged that they had been forced to enter through the back door and to eat in a segregated lunchroom. She moved the national headquarters to Charleston, where it continued to exist as a shell of itself. "The Christian Coalition Once-Formidable Now in Retreat," Americans United, Nov. 2005; "Ralph Reed: The Crash of the Choir-Boy Wonder," PFAW.

59. According to Harrell, Robertson believed he had a God-given entrepreneurial talent. With the thought of building a major endowment for Regent University he embarked on a series of business ventures. He bought a rusting oil refinery in Santa Fe Springs, California, and tried to get permits to restart it, but the refinery had been a major polluter and producer of hazardous waste. The permits were not forthcoming, and he lost $60 million. Then, thanks to an old friend, John Gimenez, he started a company to mine gold in Liberia in 1998, signing an agreement with the Liberian president, Charles Taylor, a U.S. prison escapee, a major human rights violator, and a pillager of his own country as well as of neighboring Sierra Leone. Robertson insisted that Taylor had been converted to Christianity in a Gimenez "Liberia for Jesus" rally, and objected strenuously when in 2003 the George W. Bush administration pressured Taylor to step down to end the civil war he had started. The venture went nowhere. In addition he secured a timber and a diamond concession in Zaire from another rapacious dictator, President Mobutu Sese Seko. U.S. newspapers investigated his company for illegal business dealings, including the use of airplanes owned by Operation Blessing, but couldn't prove it. He lost his shirt, and there were other disastrous investments in American companies. Harrell, 2010, pp. 273–86.

15: The Christian Right and George W. Bush

1. Williams, p. 244.

2. Fred Clarkson, "The Aftermath and Future Shock," www.publiceye.org/conspire/clinton/Clintonculwar8-22.html#P426_119799.

3. "A Letter to Conservatives," Feb. 16, 1999, NationalCenter.org.

4. Clyde Wilcox and Mark J. Rozell. "Conclusion: The Christian Right in Campaign '98," in Green, Rozell, and Wilcox, p. 291; John C. Green, Mark J. Rozell, and Clyde Wilcox, "The

Christian Right's Long Political March," in Green, Rozell, and Wilcox, *The Christian Right in American Politics*, 2003, p. 4. For example, in 1998 only 13 percent of the public agreed that abortion should be banned and another 30 percent agreed it should be limited to cases of rape or incest or when the woman's life was in danger. John C. Green, Mark J. Rozell, and Clyde Wilcox, "The March Goes On: The Christian Right and the 2004 Values Campaign," in Green, Rozell, and Wilcox, 2006, p. 11.

5. "A Letter to Conservatives," Feb. 16, 1999, NationalCenter.org; Clarkson, "The Aftermath and Future Shock."

6. Layman, *The Great Divide*, p. 337; Wilcox and Robinson, p. 52.

7. James Dobson, "Spins, Polls and Courage," *Weekly Standard*, Feb. 21, 1999; "Debate: Should Evangelicals Refocus Their Energies Away from Politics?," *Insight*, March 29, 1999, link in Clarkson, "The Aftermath and Future Shock." The directors of Concerned Women for America and the Federal Research Council also took issue with Weyrich.

8. Mark Rozell, "Bush and the Christian Right: The Triumph of Pragmatism," in Rozell and Whitney, *Religion and the Bush Presidency*, p. 12; Wilcox and Robinson, pp. 53, 111; Williams, p. 246; "Interview: Richard Land," *Frontline*, PBS, 2004.

9. Williams, p. 248; Rozell, "Bush and the Christian Right," pp. 13–18; Buss, *Family Man*, p. 171.

10. Rozell, "Bush and the Christian Right," p. 14; Williams, p. 248. Voters who identified with the Christian right made up a third of the South Carolina electorate, and two thirds of them voted for Bush.

11. Rozell, "Bush and the Christian Right," p. 16; "John McCain Attacks Pat Robertson, Jerry Falwell, Republican Establishment as Harming GOP Ideals," cnn.com transcripts, Feb. 28, 2000; Brian Knowlton, "Republican Says Bush Panders to the 'Agents of Intolerance,'" *New York Times*, Feb. 29, 2000. McCain praised the achievements of Charles Colson and Dobson, but because they were less known, even *The New York Times* failed to report it.

12. C. Danielle Vinson and James L. Guth, "Advance and Retreat in the Palmetto State: Assessing the Christian Right in South Carolina," in Green, Rozell, and Wilcox, 2003, p. 29; Rozell, "Bush and the Christian Right," pp. 12–18; Williams, pp. 246–49.

13. Rozell, "Bush and the Christian Right," pp. 19–20; Wilcox and Robinson, p. 97; Mark Rozell and Debasree Das Gupta, "The Values Vote?," in Green, Rozell, and Wilcox, 2006, p. 13; "Religion and the Presidential Vote," June 21, 2004, Pew Research Center for People and the Press; Ted Olson, "Bush's Chief Advisor Warns That Evangelicals May Be Withdrawing," *Christianity Today*, Dec. 1, 2001.

14. Rozell and Wilcox, pp. 11–19.

15. Hankins, 2002, pp. 103, 220; Gustav Niebuhr, "Southern Baptists Declare Wife Should Submit," *New York Times*, June 16, 1998.

16. Text, SBC website. There were two women on the committee that drafted the amendment: Mrs. Paige Patterson and Mrs. Albert Mohler. Religious scholars pointed out that Ephesians 5:23–31, the passage the statement relied on, also calls for the submission of slaves to their masters, while Ephesians 5:21 calls for husbands and wives to submit to each other. Hankins, 2002, pp. 218–21.

17. Mary Worthen, "How Al Mohler Transformed a Seminary and Helped Change a Denomination and Challenges a Secular Culture," *Christianity Today*, Oct. 1, 2010, sections 1 and 5.

18. Hankins, 2002, pp. 25–27; Worthen, "How Al Mohler Transformed a Seminary," sections 1 and 3.

19. Hankins, 2002, pp. 46, 80–83. Marshall found out that she was accused of "egalitarianism," believing in the equality of the two sexes, and "universalism," the idea that those who do not believe in Jesus might go to heaven. She might have defended herself in a hearing, but she was sure Mohler wanted her out, so she left. Others, including Timothy Weber, Glen Stassen, and David Gushee, resigned. Ibid., p. 94.

20. Worthen, "How Al Mohler Transformed a Seminary," section 8.

21. Hankins, 2002, pp. 46–49.

22. Ibid., p. 50. In his 2008 book, *Culture Shift*, Mohler wrote that action to save the culture must involve political action. Ibid, pp. 4–5. But then in 2011 he told an interviewer, "I don't invest a lot of hope in the political sphere."

23. Hankins, 2002, pp. 23–24; "The Arena: Richard Land Bio," *Politico*, 2011; Louis Jacobson, "Evangelical Christian Lobbyist," *Princeton Alumni Weekly*, Dec. 15, 2008; Nina J. Easton, "Baptist Lobbyist Walks a Fine Line," *Boston Globe*, Oct. 10, 2005.

24. Hankins, 2002, pp. 45, 53.

25. Martin, 1996, pp. 341–42; Buss, pp. 106–9; Gilgoff, pp. 7, 27–29, 45–46. Dobson first came to public attention in 1989 when the notorious serial killer Ted Bundy gave him an interview just before his execution. Bundy, who was also a notorious liar and a publicity addict, told Dobson that he was born again and that an addiction to pornography made him kill. Dobson sold the tapes of his interview for $1 million in the course of a year. Blumenthal, p. 77.

26. Williams, pp. 236–37; Alexander-Moegerle, *James Dobson's War on America*, pp. 40, 80; Buss, pp. 154–55; Gilgoff, pp. 11, 31–32; Green, "The Christian Right and the 1998 Election: An Overview," p. 7. By 2003 Focus had Family Policy Councils in forty states.

27. Alexander-Moegerle, p. 115; Gilgoff, pp. 31–35; Martin, 1996, pp. 347–49; Buss, pp. 156–57; Williams, pp. 236–39. According to sociologists, Focus on the Family members in 1990 were almost entirely evangelicals. Fifty-one percent identified as fundamentalists and 27 percent as charismatics. Guth, Green, Kellstedt, and Smidt, "Onward Christian Soldiers: Religious Activists in American Politics," in Green, Guth, Smidt, and Kellstedt, p. 69.

28. Buss, pp. 159–63; Martin, 1996, p. 343.

29. Buss, esp. pp. 181, 333, 364; Alexander-Moegerle, p. 164. The Kennedy amendment failed by one vote, but it passed in a later session of Congress.

30. Buss, p. 347.

31. Ibid., pp. 11–20, 123.

32. Ibid., pp. 347, 11–20, 17, 24–25, 123; Ahlstrom, 2:289–91.

33. Alexander-Moegerle, p. 98.

34. Buss, pp. 30–36, 43; Dobson, *Dare to Discipline*, p. 27.

35. Buss, pp. 145–46; Alexander-Moegerle, pp. 106–11, 115–16, 128–31.

36. Alexander-Moergerle, pp. 202–8; Martin, 1996, p. 343.

37. Diamond, 1998, pp. 128–29; Buss, p. 335; "Family Talk: Solid Answers: Roots of Homosexuality," *Focus on the Family*; Wikipedia from *The Strong-Willed Child*.

38. Alexander-Moegerle, p. 211. See Tanya Erzen, *Straight to Jesus: Sexual and Christian Conversions in the Ex-Gay Movement* (Berkeley: University of California Press, 2006). In *Dare to Discipline*, written when he was still at USC, Dobson reflected the views of many psychiatrists of the time that homosexuality had its roots in the experiences of early childhood and was not simply a choice. In the 1990s he continued to say it was not a choice, but he insisted that it was preventable and changeable. "Family Talk."

39. Michael Gerson, "A Righteous Indignation," *U.S. News & World Report*, May 4, 1998; Buss, pp. 181–82; Alexander-Moegerle, p. 30.

40. Dobson and Bauer, *Children at Risk*, pp. 22, 37–38.

41. Ibid., pp. 294–95.

42. Dobson's address to the Council for National Policy, Feb. 7, 1998, www.publiceye.org/ifas /cnp/dobson.html; Buss, p. 165. The meeting was not quite as confidential as some of the participants may have thought, for it was reported in *The New York Times* a few days later, and Focus gave the *Times* the text of his speech. Laurie Goodstein, "Conservative Christian Leader Accuses Republicans of Betrayal," *New York Times*, Feb. 12, 1998.

43. Gilgoff, p. 111.

44. Ibid., p. 107; Buss, 168–69; Gerson, "A Righteous Indignation."

45. Jacob Weisberg, "Dobson's Choice," *Slate*, May 9, 1998.

46. Gerson, "A Righteous Indignation."

47. Laurie Goodstein, "Religious Right Frustrated, Trying New Tactic on GOP," *New York Times*, May 23, 1998.

48. Gilgoff, pp. 112–15; Gerson, "A Righteous Indignation"; Blumenthal, p. 99, on DeLay; James Carney, "The GOP Mantra—Keep Dobson Happy," *Time*, May 11, 1998; Williams, p. 243.

49. "Election 1998 Analysis: A Story of Two Republican Parties," Log Cabin Republicans, Nov. 4, 1998; www.pfaw.org/press-releases/1998,2011/religious-right-called-the-tune-voters-wouldnt-dance; Weisberg, "Dobson's Choice."

50. http://heartland.org/policy-documents/debate-should-conservatives-refocus-their-energies-away-politics.

51. "Dobson's Choice: Religious Right Leader Becomes Power Broker," PFAW, Dec. 2005; Kuo, *Tempting Faith*, p. 124; Buss, p. 171.

52. Buss, pp. 172–73; Williams, pp. 251–52; Nina Easton, "The Power and the Glory," *American Prospect*, March 2002.

53. John C. Green, "Bush's Religious Right Challenge," *Christian Science Monitor*, Jan. 23, 2001.

54. Olson, "Bush's Chief Advisor Warns That Evangelicals May Be Withdrawing."

55. James Lamare, J. L. Polinard, and Robert D. Wrinkle, "The Christian Right in God's Country: Texas Politics," in Green, Rozell, and Wilcox, 2000, pp. 41–42.

56. Carin Robinson and Clyde Wilcox, "The Faith of George W. Bush: The Personal, Practical, and Political," in Rozell and Whitney, p. 231. An itinerant evangelist, Arthur Blessitt, carrying a twelve-foot cross around the country, had an extended conversation with Bush in Midland in 1984, but it was politic for Bush to give Graham the credit. Stephen Miller, p. 119.

57. Bruce Lincoln, "Bush's God Talk," Religion Online, first published in *The Christian Century*, Oct. 5, 2004, pp. 22–29.

58. Bruce Lincoln, "Bush's God Talk," *Christian Century*, Oct. 5, 2004; Mansfield, *The Faith of George W. Bush*, pp. 107–11; Richard Land, "The Jesus Factor," *Frontline*, PBS, April 29, 2004.

59. Kuo, pp. 122–25.

60. John C. Green, "Bush's Religious Right Challenge," *Christian Science Monitor*, Jan. 23, 2001.

61. Kaplan, *With God on Their Side*, pp. 84, 149, 161; Jim Whittle, "All in the Family," *Church & State*, Americans United, May 2002; Smidt, Green, Kellstedt, and Guth, "'What Does the Lord Require?' Evangelicals and the 2004 Presidential Vote," in Rozell and Whitney, p. 21.

62. Kuo, pp. 140, 142–44; Amy E. Black and Douglas L. Koopman, "The Politics of Faith-Based Initiatives," in Rozell and Whitney, p. 167.

63. Kaplan, p. 110; David Grann, "Where George Bush Got Compassion," *New York Times Magazine*, Sept. 12, 1999.

64. Kuo, pp. 80–89; Grann, "Where George Bush Got Compassion"; Kaplan, p. 39.

65. Kuo, p. 127.

66. Kaplan, p. 50; Grann, "Where George Bush Got Compassion"; Alison Mitchell, "Bush Draws Campaign Theme from More than the 'Heart,'" *New York Times*, June 12, 2000.

67. Kaplan, p. 50; Kuo, p. 145; "The Jesus Factor," *Frontline*; Axel Schäffer, "Religious Nonprofit Organizations," in Laville and Wilford, *The US Government, Citizen Groups, and the Cold War*, pp. 173–91.

68. Kuo, pp. 160, 163–65; Amy E. Black and Douglas L. Koopman, "The Politics of Faith-Based Initiatives," in Rozell and Whitney, p. 164.

69. Kuo, pp. 165, 177, 195–96.

70. Williams, p. 251; Jim Vanderhei and Elizabeth Crowley, "Bush Keeps Faith with Religious Right," *Wall Street Journal*, June 13, 2001. Concerned Women for America released a report titled "The Bush Administration's Homosexual Agenda: The First 100 Days." But the report made no waves. Tim Goeglein, a White House aide, sold the tax bill as a reduction in family taxes on Christian radio, and it became a major topic in Christian right magazines, Internet sites, and radio and TV talk shows.

71. Kuo, pp. 170–73; Vanderhei and Crowley, "Bush Keeps Faith with Religious Right"; Robin Toner, "Conservatives Savor Their Role as Insiders in the White House," *New York Times*, March 18, 2001.

72. Lee Marsden, *For God's Sake*, p. 121; "The Jesus Factor," *Frontline*. Rove and Goeglein consulted Land before the stem cell decision and gave a heads-up to Dobson. Kaplan, p. 125.

73. Toner, "Conservatives Savor Their Role as Insiders at the White House," *New York Times*, March 18, 2001.

74. Dana Milbank, "Religious Right Finds Its Center in the Oval Office," *Washington Post*, Dec. 24, 2001; Williams, p. 252. By 2007 eight Patrick Henry students had had internships in the White House, and dozens of others had worked in federal agencies. Several had landed in the FBI and CIA, and one in the Coalition Provisional Authority in Iraq.

75. Williams, p. 252; Kaplan, pp. 83–85; Easton, "The Power and the Glory"; Charles Savage, "Scandal Puts Spotlight on Christian Law School," *Boston Globe*, April 8, 2007; Paul Krugman, "For God's Sake," *New York Times*, April 11, 2007.

76. Kaplan, p. 83; Whittle, "All in the Family"; Milbank, "Religious Right Finds Its Center in the Oval Office."

77. Kaplan, p. 124; John W. Wells and David B. Cohen, "Keeping the Charge: George W. Bush, the Christian Right, and the New Vital Center of American Politics," in Rozell and Whitney, p. 137.

78. Wells and Cohen, "Keeping the Charge," pp. 138, 202.

79. Kaplan, p. 125; Wells and Cohen, "Keeping the Charge."

80. www.pewresearch.org/2006/05/02/will-white-evangelicals-desert-the-gop/.

81. Dana Milbank, "Religious Right Finds Its Center in the Oval Office."

82. Williams, p. 254.

83. Lincoln, "Bush's God Talk"; Williams, p. 255; White House text of September 16 address on the South Lawn, http://georgewbush-whitehouse.archives.gov/news/releases/2001, 2009/20010916-2.html.

84. Quotes cited in Lincoln, "Bush's God Talk."

85. Lincoln, "Bush's God Talk." See SBC resolution of June 2002: "We applaud the moral clarity of the President of the United States in his denunciation of terrorist groups as 'evildoers' who must be resisted." See also Dobson on *Larry King Live*, Sept. 18, 2002, CNN.com transcripts: "The very word evil implies that there's a standard . . . that somebody decides what's right and wrong."

86. Steven Waldman, "The Real Reason Evangelicals Love Bush," Sept. 2, 2004, www.beliefnet .com/story/152/story_15216.html.

87. Ibid., for Parshall; Milbank, "Religious Right Finds Its Center in the Oval Office." A senior Bush aide said that the president "does not believe he was chosen for this moment. He just views himself as governing on his beliefs and promises," but Goegelin encouraged such speculation. "I think President Bush is God's man at this hour," he said.

88. Milbank, "Religious Right Finds Its Center in the Oval Office"; Dobson and Hindson, p. 41.

89. Kaplan, pp. 129–30; Robin Toner, "For GOP It's a Moment," *New York Times*, Nov. 6, 2003; Richard W. Stevenson, "Bush Signs Ban on Abortion Procedure," *New York Times*, Nov. 6, 2003; "Our Pro-Life President: Jerry Falwell Recounts Oval Office Prayer After Partial Birth Abortion Ban Signing," *WorldNetDaily*, Nov. 8, 2003; Chuck Colson, "Never Give Up: Banning (Finally) Partial Birth Abortion," *Townhall*, Nov. 6, 2003.

90. Kaplan, pp. 129–30.

91. Richard W. Stevenson, "Bush Signs a Ban on Abortion Procedure, *New York Times*, Nov. 6, 2003; Williams, p. 241; Toner, "For GOP It's a Moment." In July Richard Land had called the procedure "an act of child sacrifice to the pagan gods of convenience, social convention and career well-being." Dwayne Hastings, "Land: Partial-Birth Abortion Another Form of Child Sacrifice," *Baptist Press*, July 16, 2002.

92. The Born-Alive Infants Protection Act of 2002 gave legal protection to infants born alive after a failed attempt at induced abortion. The bill was legally meaningless because infants already had the protection of law, and it passed unanimously in the Senate and by voice vote in the House. The Bush administration made no attempt to enforce it.

    The Unborn Victims of Violence Act of 2004 was the only other right-to-life bill passed in Bush's first term. It provided that anyone who caused injury to a pregnant woman's fetus would be subject to penalties in addition to those exacted for injuring the woman. It made a specific exception for abortion, and it was passed by large majorities in both houses of Congress. Pro-choice advocates maintained that the purpose of the two bills was to build a legal background for a claim that the fetus had the rights of a person. Michelle Goldberg, "How George Bush Will Ban Abortion," *Salon*, Nov. 12, 2003.

93. Colson, "Never Give Up; "Our Pro-Life President"; Toner "For GOP It's a Moment."
94. Goldberg, p. 122; Kaplan, pp. 52–54; Corwin Smidt and James Penning, "Religion and the Bush Presidency," in Rozell and Whitney, p. 157; Kuo, p. 212. According to Kuo, the only appropriation for Faith-Based and Community Initiatives was $30 million for the Compassion Capital Fund.
95. Kaplan, p. 52; Harrell, 2010, pp. 281–82. Operation Blessing was then under investigation by the state of Virginia for hauling equipment to Robertson's diamond-mining operation in Africa. Schäffer, p. 178.
96. Black and Koopman, "The Politics of Faith-Based Initiatives," p. 157; Rozell and Whitney, p. 165; Kuo, p. 240; Kaplan, p. 121; Peter Wallsten, Tom Hamburger, and Nicholas Riccardi, "Bush Rewarded by Black Pastors' Faith," *Los Angeles Times*, Jan. 18, 2005.
97. Kaplan, pp. 59–60; Schäffer, pp. 44, 52–53, Schäffer, "Religious Nonprofit Organizations, the Cold War State and Resurgent Evangelism,"2006, pp. 6, 19. For the history of public funding of religious institutions, Schäffer, pp. 146–47. According to one study, religiously based institutions were by the 1990s receiving more public funds than their secular counterparts, and the more religious were receiving more than the less religious among them.
98. Black and Koopman, "The Politics of Faith-Based Initiatives," p. 156; Schäffer, p. 211; Walker, *Church-State Matters*, pp. 72–77. The language was added to three other Clinton-era bills with only cursory attention from the Congress.

Title VII of the 1964 Civil Rights Act granted houses of worship and certain other religious organizations the right to discriminate in the hiring and firing of clergy and support staff not only on the basis of religious affiliation but also on the basis of religious beliefs and practices.
99. Kaplan, p. 39; Grann, "Where George Bush Got Compassion"; Walker, pp. 79–80. Two of the five cases involving government funding of pervasively religious organizations were brought in Texas and were still pending in 2001.
100. Kuo, p. 223.
101. Schäffer, p. 211; Kuo, p. 223; Black and Koopman, "The Politics of Faith-Based Initiatives," pp. 156–57, 170. According to Kuo, the order also reversed an obscure federal rule prohibiting government contractors—as opposed to grantees—who received more than $10,000 to hire or fire based on faith.

In his first presidential campaign Barack Obama promised to come out against preferential hiring, but found that imposing hiring restrictions would create an upheaval in the existing welfare delivery systems because too many religious groups providing these services had been exempt for a decade or more. Mathew Brown, "US Government's Faith-Based Initiative Moves Ahead While Dodging Controversy," *Deseret News*, May 13, 2013.
102. Kuo, pp. 214–16; Kaplan, p. 52; Goldberg, p. 115. For example, the outside experts asked to review the abstinence-only grants from the Department of Health and Human Services included two representatives from Focus on the Family, three from the Family Research Council, and three from Concerned Women for America.
103. Black and Koopman, "The Politics of Faith-Based Initiatives," pp. 170–71, 141; Kaplan, pp. 49–50; Kuo, pp. 200–1, 205–9, 212.
104. Kaplan, p. 121; text of DiIulio letter to Suskind of Oct. 24, 2002, www.esquire.com/news-politics/a2880/dilulio/.
105. As late as September 2007, more than three years after a majority of Americans had expressed their disapproval of the Iraq War, a majority of evangelicals continued to say that Bush had made the right decision. Williams, p. 256.
106. Richard Cizik, "Silent Evangelical Support for Bush's War Against Iraq," NPR, Feb. 26, 2003.

107. Richard Land, "The Jesus Factor," PBS, April 29, 2004.

108. Kaplan, p. 13; Lee Marsden, p. 238; Spector, *Evangelicals and Israel*, pp. 77–78. Forty-five percent of all white evangelicals had a negative view of Islam—compared to 33 percent of the public as a whole—and negative views were greater among political conservatives, and in rural areas and in the South. "Religion and Politics: Contention and Consensus," Pew Forum on Religion and Public Life, July 24, 2003.

109. On *Larry King Live* on Sept. 29, 2002, Dobson said, "Many factions within Islam are very, very violent." He explained, "The war against the West and against Israel didn't start with 9/11. For us it really began in 1979 when the Iranians, you know, invaded the embassy there. And from that point on they've been doing things like this, so there's a lot of violence within the Islamic faith."

110. Laurie Goodstein, "Seeing Islam as 'Evil' Faith, Evangelicals Seek Converts," *New York Times*, May 27, 2003; Kevin R. den Dulk, "Evangelical 'Internationalists and U.S. Foreign Policy During the Bush Administration," in Rozell and Whitney, p. 224. Just after September 11 *Christianity Today* pronounced, "Religious terrorism is the Communism of the 21st century" and insisted that "Christians have a unique and vital role to play in the historical drama that is unfolding." Williams, pp. 233–54.

111. www.rightweb.irc-online.org/profile/project_for_the_new_american_century.

112. *Larry King Live*, Sept. 29, 2002, http://edition.cnn.com/TRANSCRIPTS/0209/29/lklw.00.html.

113. "Land letter," https://erlc.com/article/the-so-called-land-letter/.

114. Robinson, "The Faith of George W. Bush," p. 224; Lee Marsden, pp. 227–28; NPR Profile: "Silent Evangelical Support for Bush's Proposed War on Iraq," Feb. 26, 2003, www.ncccusa .org/iraq/iraqstatements.html.

115. "Land letter."

116. After the oil crisis of 1973 John F. Walvoord's *Armageddon, Oil and the Middle East Crisis* sold 750,000 copies. After Saddam Hussein invaded Kuwait in 1990, sales of *The Late Great Planet Earth*, published in 1973, had spiked by 83 percent. The *Left Behind* series of novels, by Tim LaHaye and Jerry B. Jenkins, completed in 2000, had sold 55 million copies by 2003. According to one study, readers tended to treat the novels as action fantasies. See Amy Johnson Frykholm, *Rapture Culture: Left Behind in Evangelical America* (New York: Oxford University Press, 2004.) LaHaye, however, had started a Left Behind Prophecy Club with weekly email postings. In one posting LaHaye listed his two top "Signs of the End Times" in 2003 as: (1) Israel reclaims her land, and (2) Saddam's removal clears the way for rebuilding Babylon (Kaplan, p. 35). In his book *The Divided States of America* Land wrote, "I have little if any disagreement with Dr. LaHaye and Mr. Jenkins about the sequence of the eschatological events they portray." However, he wrote, no one knows when the events will occur, and "I would argue that the special role America has to play in the world is not to hasten the second coming of Jesus Christ. That's in the Lord's timetable." Spector, pp. 90, 57, 202.

117. After the Six-Day War, the Israeli government, sensing an erosion of liberal Protestant support, brought hundreds of evangelical pastors to Israel, and a number of them started their own Holy Land tours. In the 1970s and '80s evangelical tourism grew to play a role in the Israeli economy, and many pastors raised funds for Jewish agencies and for projects in Israel. Spector, pp. 145–46; Jim Lobe, "Conservative Christians Biggest Backers of Iraq War," InterPress Service, Nov. 10, 2002.

118. Spector, p. 148; Paul S. Boyer, "When U.S. Foreign Policy Meets Biblical Prophecy," Feb. 25, 2003, www.alternet.org/story/15221.

119. Boyer, "When U.S. Foreign Policy Meets Biblical Prophecy."

120. Carin Robinson and Clyde Wilcox, "The Faith of George W. Bush," p. 227; Lee Marsden, p. 185; Kaplan, p. 28; www.rightweb.irc-online.org/profile/project_for_the_new_american _century.

121. *Larry King Live*, Sept. 29, 2002. Dobson told Land that his Nazarene father had greeted the news of the U.N. vote creating a Jewish state with the words, "that's the fulfillment of biblical prophecy." Land, *The Divided States of America*, p. 208; Lee Marsden, p. 185.

122. Kaplan, p. 25. A poll taken by Echekain's organization found that 28 percent of evangelicals cited the end-time prophecy as the key theological reason for their support of Israel, and 59 percent the Hebrew Bible's promise of blessings on Israel and the Jewish people. A Pew poll of 2003 reported in (Anne Katz p. 136); a survey overseen by John C. Green found that 46 percent of evangelicals believed that Jews remained God's chosen people (John C. Green in "Evangelical Protestants and Jews: A View from the Polls," in Mittleman, Johnson, and Isserman, *Uneasy Allies?*, p. 19).

123. Lobe, "Conservative Christians Biggest Backers of Iraq War"; Lee Marsden, p. 193; Kaplan, p. 26. Stand for Israel's major event was an annual Day of Prayer and Solidarity with Israel celebrated in 25,000 churches in the United States and the rest of the world.

124. www.rightweb.irc-online.org/profile/project_for_the_new_american_century.

125. Franklin Graham and other evangelicals had lobbied for the Sudan Peace Act of 2003 that brought a temporary peace between the two regions and that ended years later with the division of the country along religious lines.

126. Deborah Caldwell, "Should Christian Missionaries Heed the Call in Iraq?," *New York Times*, April 6, 2003; Kaplan, p. 14; Goodstein, "Seeing Islam as an 'Evil' Faith."

127. David Rennie, "Bible Belt Missionaries Set Out on 'War for Souls' in Iraq," *Telegraph*, Dec. 28, 2003.

128. Caldwell, "Should Christian Missionaries Heed the Call in Iraq?"; Laurie Goodstein, "A Nation at War: Missionary Groups Critical of Islam Are Now Waiting to Take Aid to Iraq," *New York Times*, April 4, 2003; Steve Waldman, "Franklin Graham's Foolish Mercy Mission," *Slate*, April 11, 2003.

129. Caldwell, "Should Christian Missionaries Heed the Call in Iraq?"; Waldman, "Franklin Graham's Foolish Mercy Mission"; Rennie, "Bible Belt Missionaries Set Out on 'War for Souls' in Iraq"; Brian Kaylor, "SBC's Evangelistic Claims for Iraq War Fell Apart," Ethics Daily.com, March 19, 2013.

130. Kaplan, p. 15; Rennie, "Franklin Graham's Foolish Mercy Mission"; Rennie, "Bible Belt Missionaries Set Out on 'War for Souls' in Iraq." In March a reporter found eight new evangelical churches in Baghdad, thirty missionaries working there, and 150 others who had come on visits. Charles Duhigg, "Evangelicals Flock into Iraq on Mission of Faith," *Los Angeles Times*, March 18, 2004.

131. Caldwell, "Should Christian Missionaries Heed the Call in Iraq?"; Laurie Goodstein, "Top Evangelicals Critical of Colleagues over Islam," *New York Times*, May 8, 2003. World Relief makes a distinction between proselytizing and evangelism, the first being more or less coercive and the second not. Its advice to volunteers is: "We do not want to force a discussion or make someone feel that services are contingent on conversion. Any sort of physical coercion, moral constraint, or psychological pressure on the client is considered proselytizing and not evangelism," http://worldreliefdurham.org/defining-evangelism-v-proselytism/. World Vision, the largest of the evangelical aid agencies, says on its website it does not evangelize, www.worldvision.org/. Interviewed by *Time* magazine, Al Mohler, president of the SBC's Southern Seminary, seemed not to know that there were any indigenous Christians in Iraq, for he said, "The secular world tends to look at Iraq and say, well, it's Muslim, and that's just a fact, and any Christian influence would be a form of Western imperialism." He then called for religious liberty in Iraq. Broward Liston, "Interview: Missionary Work in Iraq," *Time*, April 15, 2003.

132. Kaylor, "SBC's Evangelistic Claims for Iraq War Fell Apart"; Duhigg, "Evangelicals Flock into Iraq on Mission of Faith."

133. nrb.org.

134. John C. Green, "The Faith Factor: How Religion Influences American Elections," Google e-book, chap. 4; Mark J. Rozell, "Bush and the Christian Right: The Triumph of Pragmatism," in Rozell and Whitney, p. 22.

135. Paul Weyrich, "The Arlington Group," renew.com, Dec. 3, 2004; Mary Leonard, "Gay Marriage Stirs Conservatives Again," *Boston Globe*, Sept. 28, 2003; David D. Kirkpatrick,

"Conservatives Use Issue of Gay Unions as Rallying Tool," *New York Times*, Feb. 8, 2004.

136. Brian S., "Religious Right Frustrated Despite Having Friends in High Places," *Newhouse News*, July 14, 2003.

137. Kirkpatrick, "Conservatives Use Issue of Gay Unions as Rallying Tool."

138. SBC 1996 resolution on website; Klarman, *From the Closet to the Altar*, pp. 55–59.

139. Gilgoff, pp. 141–44.

140. Klarman, pp. 71–2.; Brian S., "Religious Right Frustrated Despite Having Friends in High Places."

141. Gilgoff, pp. 144–45; SBC 2003 resolution on website; Kirkpatrick, "Conservatives Use Issue of Gay Unions as Rallying Tool," for Farris quote.

142. Gilgoff, pp. 144–46; Sheryl Gay Stolberg, "White House Avoids a Stand on Gay Marriage," *New York Times*, July 2, 2003.

143. Gilgoff, p. 146; Williams, p. 257.

144. Gilgoff, p. 154.

145. Perkins denied knowing the list came from Duke, though his signature was on the check. He also denied knowing that the Council of Concerned Citizens, where he spoke on May 17, 2001, was a white supremacist group. Blumenthal, pp. 130–33.

146. Gilgoff, pp. 149–54; Mary Leonard, "Gay Marriage Stirs Conservatives Again."

147. Mary Leonard, "Gay Marriage Stirs Conservatives Again"; Kirkpatrick "Conservatives Use Issue of Gay Unions as Rallying Tool"; Gilgoff, pp. 160–61.

148. Vice President Dick Cheney had an openly gay daughter with a partner, and in one of the debates in 2000 Cheney had said that people should be free to enter into any kind of relationship they wanted, but the decision should be left to the states. Kaplan, p. 150.

149. Wells and Cohen, "Keeping the Charge," in Rozell and Whitney, pp. 140–41.

150. Richard W. Stevenson, "Bush Expected to Endorse Amendment Defining Marriage," *New York Times*, Feb. 4, 2004; Katherine Q. Seeley, "Conservatives Mobilize Against Ruling on Gay Marriage," *New York Times*, Nov. 20, 2003.

151. Williams, p. 259.

152. Ibid., p. 29; Kirkpatrick, "Conservatives Use Issue of Gay Unions as Rallying Tool"; Kaplan, p. 161.

153. Kirkpatrick, "Conservatives Use Issue of Gay Unions as Rallying Tool"; Gilgoff, p. 162; Williams, p. 259; Frank Langfitt, "Many Evangelicals Oppose US Ban on Gay Marriage," *Baltimore Sun*, April 14, 2004; Klarman, pp. 99–100; Wells and Cohen, "Keeping the Charge," p. 141.

154. Kirkpatrick, "Conservatives Use Issue of Gay Unions as Rallying Tool"; Sheryl Henderston Blunt, "A Man and a Woman," *Christianity Today*, Dec. 1, 2003; Williams, p. 258.

155. Kaplan, p. 156; Weyrich, "The Arlington Group"; Gilgoff, pp. 158–59. A couple of organizations, such as Michael Farris's organization and Concerned Women for America, had dropped out of the Arlington Group because the amendment left civil unions and other legal benefits to the states.

156. Wilcox, Merolla, and Beer, "Saving Marriage by Banning Marriage," in Green, Rozell, and Wilcox, 2006, p. 58; Weyrich, "The Arlington Group."

157. Klarman, pp. 31, 70–73. According to a poll taken in the late 1970s, 72 percent of Americans believed that "homosexual relations were always wrong," but by the end of the 1990s the percentage had declined to 60 percent, and among those between the ages of eighteen and twenty-nine only 42 percent thought them "always wrong." In 1985 only 25 percent of Americans knew someone who was gay; in 2000, 74 percent did.

158. Kaplan, p. 164; Klarman, pp. 97–98. Four Pew polls taken between November 2003 and the end of 2004 gave roughly the same percentages.

159. Kirkpatrick, "Conservatives Use Issue of Gay Unions as Rallying Tool."

160. David R. Kirkpatrick, "Backers of Gay Marriage Find Tepid Response in the Pews," *New York Times*, May 16, 2004; Gilgoff, p. 163. According to a poll sponsored by PBS and *U.S. News & World Report*, more than half of evangelicals preferred to rely on the states to stop

gay marriage than to amend the Constitution. Langfitt, "Many Evangelicals Oppose US Ban on Gay Marriage."

161. Alan Cooperman and Thomas Edsell, "Evangelicals Say They Led the Charge," *Washington Post,* Nov. 8, 2004; Wells and Cohen, "Keeping the Charge," p. 142.

162. Williams, p. 261. The bishop of Colorado Springs, Michael Sheridan, said Catholics who support such candidates are jeopardizing their salvation, and Denver bishop Charles Chaput described Catholic voters for Kerry as "cooperating in evil." John Kenneth White and William D'Antonio, "Catholics and the Politics of Change: The Presidential Campaigns of the Two JFKs" in Rozell and Whitney, p. 61.

163. White and D'Antonio, "Catholics and the Politics of Change," p. 60.

164. "Who Is Richard Land?," *Media Matters,* Oct. 4, 2005, quotes the *Baptist Press* of Oct. 11, 2004. Land also remembered Kennedy's speech in Houston and called it "a terrible price to pay." "The Jesus Factor," *Frontline,* PBS.

165. "Interview, Fox News' *Hannity and Colmes,*" July 16, 2004.

166. "The Jesus Factor," *Frontline,* PBS. From interviews with Land conducted on Nov. 18, 2003, and Feb. 4, 2004.

167. "Focus Signs on to ERLC's iVoteValues Initiative," *Baptist Press,* April 12, 2004.

168. "Dobson's Choice," PFAW.

169. Williams, p. 260; Cooperman and Edsall, "Evangelicals Say They Led the Charge."

170. Williams, p. 260; David D. Kirkpatrick, "Bush Allies Till Fertile Soil Among Baptists, for Votes," *New York Times,* June 18, 2004; "Focus Signs on to ERLC's iVoteValues on Initiative."

171. Kirkpatrick, "Bush Allies Till Fertile Soil"; "President's Remarks Via Satellite to the SBC," June 15, 2004, Office of the Press Secretary, Whitehouse.gov.; Michael Foust, "Messengers Stick with SBC Name and Hear from President Bush," SBTS News Wrap-Up, June 25, 2004. The SBC passed a resolution supporting the Federal Marriage Amendment, its language about homosexuals restrained, and resolution urging "all Christians to vote in accordance with biblical values." SBC resolutions, 2004.

172. David D. Kirkpatrick, "Warily a Religious Leader Lifts His Voice in Politics," *New York Times,* May 13, 2004.

173. Gilgoff, pp. 183–84; "Focus Signs on to ERLC's iVoteValues on Initiative"; "Dobson's Choice," PFAW.

174. Gilgoff, p. 168; Klarman, p. 108; "Dobson's Choice," PFAW; Wilcox, Merolla, and Beer, "Saving Marriage by Banning Marriage," pp. 61–62, 65–66.

175. Kirkpatrick, "Warily a Religious Leader Lifts His Voice in Politics"; Gilgoff, p. 167; "Dobson's Choice," PFAW; Blumenthal, p. 167; Wilcox, Merolla, and Beer, "Saving Marriage by Banning Marriage," pp. 62, 65.

176. "Dobson's Choice," PFAW; David D. Kirkpatrick, "National Rally Against Gay Marriage Draws Thousands to Capital," *New York Times,* Oct. 16, 2004, for Dobson quote.

177. Kirkpatrick, "Warily a Religious Leader Lifts His Voice in Politics"; Jeremy Leaming, "The Religious Right's 800-Pound Gorilla," Americans United, February, 2005; Brian MacQuarrie, "Dobson's Spiritual Empire Wields Political Clout," *Boston Globe,* Oct. 9, 2005.

178. Asked if he supported state GOP platform planks that would prohibit gays from teaching in public schools, DeMint replied that he did and added that unmarried pregnant women should also be banned. He later backed off from both statements. Dobson sent out a public letter praising DeMint. James L. Guth, "South Carolina: Integration and Success?," in Green, Rozell, and Wilcox, 2006, pp. 249–50.

179. "Dobson's Choice," PFAW; Blumenthal, pp. 168–78. In 2007 Vitter admitted to patronizing Deborah Palfrey, "the DC Madam," who operated a high-end prostitution ring in Washington.

180. Lois Romano, "GOP Senate Race Heats Up in Oklahoma," *Washington Post,* July 17, 2004.

181. Shad B. Satterthwaite, "Oklahoma: A Battle of Good Versus Evil," in Green, Rozell, and Wilcox, 2006, pp. 202–6; Rob Boston, "The Religious Right and Election 2004," Americans United, December 2004.

182. Green, Rozell, and Wilcox, "The March Goes On," in Green, Rozell, and Wilcox, pp. 4, 13; Wilcox, Merolla, and Beer, "Saving Marriage by Banning Marriage," p. 58; Cooperman and Edsall, "Evangelicals Say They Led the Charge."

183. Gilgoff, pp. 188–89; David D. Kirkpatrick, "Bush Seeks Help from Congregations," *New York Times*, June 3, 2004.

184. Kirkpatrick, "Bush Seeks Help from Congregations"; Gilgoff, p. 189; Alan Cooperman, "Churchgoers Get Direction from Bush Campaign," *Washington Post*, July 1, 2004; Rachel Zoll, "Republican Request for Church Directories Angers Some Religious Leaders," AP, July 23, 2004.

185. Gilgoff, p. 190.

186. Campbell, *A Matter of Faith*, p. 107; Gilgoff, esp. p. 190; John C. Green, "Ohio: The Bible and the Buckeye State," in Green, Rozell, and Wilcox, 2006, p. 87; David D. Kirkpatrick, "Republicans Admit Mailing Campaign Literature Saying Liberals Will Ban the Bible," *New York Times*, Sept. 24, 2004.

187. Wallsten, Hamburger, and Riccardi, "Bush Rewarded by Black Pastors' Faith"; Kuo, p. 212. *Los Angeles Times*, Jan. 18, 2005.

188. Campbell, p. 96; Rozell and Das Gupta, "The Values Vote?," p. 18.

189. Gilgoff, p. 189; Campbell, pp. 6–7, 96; David D. Kirkpatrick, "Churches See Election Role and Spread the Word on Bush," *New York Times*, Aug. 9, 2004; Cooperman and Edsall, "Evangelicals Say They Led the Charge." An employee of D. James Kennedy's Coral Ridge Ministries in charge of registration and get-out-the-vote activities worked for the Bush-Cheney campaign on nights and weekends.

190. Virtually a Christian right tract, the Texas Republican platform of 2004 denounced sodomy, "special rights for homosexuals," and advocated voluntary school prayer. Echoing Barton, it called the United States a "Christian nation" and the separation of church and state "a myth." Text in www.yuricareport.com/GOPorganizations/TexasRPTPlatform2004.pdf.

191. Gilgoff, p. 193.

192. Green, "Ohio: The Bible and the Buckeye State," pp. 79–81.

193. James Dao, "Flush with Victory, Grass Roots Crusader Thinks Big," *New York Times*, Nov. 26, 2004; Gilgoff, pp. 175–78. At one point in his career Burress joined the board of the ex-gay ministry, Exodus International.

194. Green, "Ohio: The Bible and the Buckeye State," p. 82; FitzGerald, "Holy Toledo," 2006; Klarman, p. 107. Companies with state contracts would have been affected, and politicians worried it would deter companies wishing to relocate to Ohio.

195. Gilgoff, pp. 180–81; Green, "Ohio: The Bible and the Buckeye State," pp. 82–84.

196. Green, "Ohio: The Bible and the Buckeye State," pp. 85–86.

197. Gilgoff, pp. 179–80; FitzGerald, 2006.

198. Gilgoff, p. 182; Green, "Ohio: The Bible and the Buckeye State," pp. 84–85.

199. Gilgoff, p. 181; FitzGerald, 2006; Green, "Ohio: The Bible and the Buckeye State," pp. 86–88; Wikipedia, "US Presidential Election in Ohio 2004," for visits and expense.

200. Green, Kellestedt, Smidt, and Guth, "How the Faithful Voted: Religious Communities and the Presidential Vote," in Campbell, pp. 22–25; Rozell and Das Gupta, "The Values Vote?," pp. 14–17; Gilgoff, pp. 194–95; "A Faith-Based Partisan Divide," PEW Forum on Religion and Public Life, Jan. 2005; Boston, "The Religious Right and Election 2004." Evangelicals turned out at a higher rate than in all previous elections. Almost two thirds voted, and in the contested states the total was higher, exceeding the percentage of Catholics who voted.

201. Wilcox, Merolla, and Beer, "Saving Marriage by Banning Marriage," pp. 59–60; David E. Campbell and J. Quinn Monson, "The Case of Bush's Reelection: Did Gay Marriage Do It?," in Campbell, pp. 120–41; Mark J. Rozell "Bush and the Christian Right: The Triumph," in Rozell and Whitney, p. 23; Klarman, p. 112; Gilgoff, pp. 182–83; Paul Taylor, "Wedge Issues on the Ballot," Pew Research Center, July 26, 2006; Wilcox, Merolla, and Beer, "Saving Marriage by Banning Marriage," pp. 68–69; Green, "Ohio: The Bible and the Buckeye State," pp. 88–92.

202. Klarman, p. 112; Gilgoff, p. 182; Green, "Ohio: The Bible and the Buckeye State," pp. 88–90. Nationally African American voters gave Bush 11 percent of their vote in 2004. In Ohio weekly attending black Protestants gave 70 percent of their votes to Issue One and 23 percent to President Bush.

203. David D. Kirkpatrick, "Some Bush Supporters Say They Anticipate a Revolution," *New York Times*, Nov. 4, 2004.

204. Rob Boston, "The Religious Right and Election 2004," *Church & State*, Americans United, Dec. 2004.

205. Kirkpatrick, "Some Bush Supporters Say They Anticipate a Revolution."

206. Adelle M. Banks, "Evangelicals' Political Power: From Question Mark to Exclamation Point," Religion News Service, *Christianity Today*, Nov. 1, 2004.

207. Boston, "The Religious Right and Election 2004."

208. Ibid.

209. Kirkpatrick, "Some Bush Supporters Say They Anticipate a Revolution."

210. Boston, "The Religious Right and the Election 2004."

211. Ibid. Also see "Dobson's Choice," PFAW; Gilgoff, pp. 223–24. According to Gilgoff, the Arlington Group decided it would be better to neuter Specter than to derail him.

212. Boston, "The Religious Right and the Election 2004," for quote; Gilgoff, p. 225.

213. David D. Kirkpatrick, "Backers of Gay Marriage Ban Use Social Security as Cudgel," *New York Times*, Jan. 25, 2005.

214. Ibid.; Karen Tumulty and Mathew Cooper, "Does Bush Owe the Religious Right?," *Time*, Feb. 7, 2005.

215. Kirkpatrick, "Backers of Gay Marriage Ban Use Social Security as Cudgel."

216. David D. Kirkpatrick, "Evangelical Leader Threatens to Use Political Muscle Against Some Democrats," *New York Times*, Jan. 1, 2005; Tumlty and Cooper, "Does Bush Owe the Religious Right?"

217. Tumulty and Cooper, "Does Bush Owe the Religious Right?"

218. Kirkpatrick, "Evangelical Leader Threatens to Use Political Muscle."

219. Jay Grelen, "Alabama Governor Fob James: Leader of the Resistance," *World*, Feb. 27, 2003.

220. Ibid.; Moore and Perry, *So Help Me God*, p. 101.

221. Moore and Perry, pp. 102–3.

222. Ibid., pp. 96, 103–5; Goldberg, p. 26.

223. Moore and Perry, pp. 96, 108–9, 266.

224. Ibid., p. 111. The Alabama Supreme Court clearly wanted to duck the issue. "The State," it wrote, "was seeking to use the tribunal for an advisory ruling on a politically volatile issue" when there was no "actual controversy between the Governor, Attorney General and Judge."

225. Ibid., p. 129. As chief justice, Moore also gained publicity for an opinion in a child custody case in which the Alabama Supreme Court gave custody of a child to its father instead of to its openly gay mother. Alone among the judges, he brought up the subject of homosexuality, calling homosexual conduct "abhorrent, immoral, detestable, a crime against nature." Ibid., p. 154.

226. Ibid., p. 133.

227. Goldberg, p. 26; "Roy Moore," Wikipedia.

228. Moore and Perry, pp. 110, 198. As J. Brent Walker, the executive director of the Baptist Joint Committee, testified to a committee of the U.S. Congress, there are many different translations of the Ten Commandments, and by choosing one version of the Bible over another, Moore was making a theological judgment not just between Catholic and Protestant but between Protestant denominations. Walker, p. 210.

229. Moore and Perry, pp. 136, 200, 205, 221.

230. Ibid., pp. 209, 223–27, 230; Gilgoff, pp. 1–2. According to Kaplan, Focus on the Family members ranked Moore's case as second in importance only to the partial birth abortion bill. Focus created a Stop Judicial Tyranny project and held rallies across the country to complement the efforts of the Alliance Defense Fund. Kaplan, p. 247.

231. Moore and Perry, pp. 209–10.

232. Goldberg, pp. 46–47, 167. Moore went on speaking tours to restore the Ten Commandments to courts and schools. He had some success, but there were two U.S. Supreme Court decisions in 2005 affirming that the courts could depict the Ten Commandments as an integral part of a historical-educational exhibit but not as a government expression of support for a particular religion.

233. Constitution Restoration Act of 2004, 108th Congress, H.R. 3799 IH, Feb. 11, 2004.

234. Text of the Republican platform at www.presidency.ucsb.edu/papers_pdf/25850.pdf.

235. Goldberg, p. 155.

236. Boston, "Religious Right Rabble-Rousers Are Preaching Impeachment"; Goldberg, p. 158.

237. Carl Hulse and David D. Kirkpatrick, "Dobson Says Federal Judiciary Has 'Run Amok,'" *New York Times*, April 7, 2005.

238. Boston, "Religious Right Rabble-Rousers Are Preaching Impeachment"; Michelle Goldberg, "In Theocracy They Trust," *Salon*, April 11, 2005.

239. Dana Milbank, "And the Verdict on Justice Kennedy Is: Guilty."

240. Boston, "Religious Right Rabble-Rousers Are Preaching Impeachment." Schlafly also called for the passage of bills that would remove the court's power over religious displays, the Pledge of Allegiance, same-sex marriage, and the Boy Scouts. Milbank, "And the Verdict on Justice Kennedy, Is: Guilty."

241. Goldberg, "In Theocracy They Trust."

242. Milbank, "And the Verdict on Justice Kennedy Is: Guilty."

243. Boston, "Religious Right Rabble-Rousers Are Preaching Impeachment."

244. Milbank, "And the Verdict on Justice Kennedy Is: Guilty."

245. Ibid.; Goldberg, "In Theocracy They Trust."

246. Blumenthal, p. 114; David D. Kirkpatrick and Sheryl Gay Stolberg, "How a Family's Cause Reached the Halls of Congress," *New York Times*, May 22, 2005; Bob Ditmer, "Dobson Speaks Out About Terri Schiavo," Family News in Focus, Free Republic, Oct. 22, 2003; Gilgoff, p. 126. In Florida "Terri's Law" was seen as a way to stimulate the evangelical vote in 2004, though by December 2003 two thirds of Floridians opposed the law and three quarters believed spouses should have the right to make such decisions. Kenneth D. Wald and Richard K. Scher, "'A Necessary Annoyance'? The Christian Right and the Development of Republican Party Politics in Florida," in Green, Rozell, and Wilcox, 2003, p. 170.

247. "Interview: Dr. James Dobson," *Hannity and Colmes*, Feb. 24, 2005.

248. Ibid.; "Terri Schiavo's Death Brings Stern Warning from SBC's Richard Land," *Christian Music*, May 31, 2005. Land and others used the fact that Michael Schiavo was living with another woman and had two children with her to discredit him.

249. Dwayne Hastings, "SBC's Land on Meet the Press," BP News, May 28, 2005.

250. Kirkpatrick and Stolberg, "How a Family's Cause Reached the Halls of Congress."

251. *Raw Story*, May 21, 2005, and May 30, 2005.

252. Kirkpatrick and Stolberg, "How a Family's Cause Reached the Halls of Congress"; Gilgoff, pp. 127–28.

253. Kirkpatrick and Stolberg, "How a Family's Cause Reached the Halls of Congress."

254. Gilgoff, p. 128; Kirkpatrick and Stolberg, "How a Family's Cause Reached the Halls of Congress." Frist also called the House leaders and warned he would not agree to adjourn Congress until the Schiavo matter was resolved.

255. Frank Rich, "The God Racket, from DeMille to DeLay," *New York Times*, May 27, 2005.

256. Gilgoff, p. 129.

257. Kirkpatrick and Stolberg, "How a Family's Cause Reached the Halls of Congress."

258. Carl Hulse and David D. Kirkpatrick, "House Members Hold Sunday Night Session on Schiavo Bill," *New York Times*, May 20, 2005.

259. Rich, "The God Racket"; Walter R. Roche Jr. and Sam Howe Verhovek, "DeLay's Own Tragic Crossroads," *Los Angeles Times*, May 27, 2005; Kelly Shannon, "Bush Laws in Schiavo Case, Texas at Odds," AP, May 21, 2005.

260. *Nashua Advocate*, May 21, 2005; "A Blow to the Rule of Law," *New York Times*, May 22, 2005.
261. "Most Think Congress Wrong on Schiavo Case," Reuters, May 21, 2005; Charles Babington and Michael A. Fletcher, "Analysis: GOP May Be Out of Step with Public," *Washington Post*, May 22, 2005; Carl Hulse and Adam Nagourney, "DeLay Quickly Steps out of Schiavo Spotlight," *New York Times*, May 26, 2005; Blumenthal, p. 116.
262. Blumenthal, p. 117.
263. Ibid.; Babington and Fletcher, "Analysis: GOP May Be Out of Step with Public," for quote.
264. Milbank, "And the Verdict on Justice Kennedy Is: Guilty."
265. Goldberg, "In Theocracy They Trust"; Blumenthal, p. 118.
266. Boston, "Religious Right Rabble-Rousers Are Preaching Impeachment to Try to Force Courts to Rule Their Way."
267. Milbank, "And the Verdict on Justice Kennedy Is: Guilty"; Vickie Chachen, "Schiavo Judge Attains New Fame, Infamy," AP, May 26, 2005.
268. Gilgoff, p. 131; Goldberg, "In Theocracy They Trust"; Blumenthal, pp. 121–22.
269. Janet Zink and Bill Adair, "Terri Schiavo Derails Social Agenda of the Christian Right," *St. Petersburg Times*, Dec. 20, 2005.
270. Jeremy Leaming, "Full-Court Press: Despite Public Opposition, Religious Right Vows to Continue Backing Judges," Americans United, April 25, 2005.
271. Gilgoff, p. 225.
272. David D. Kirkpatrick, "Frist Set to Use Religious Stage on Judicial Issue," *New York Times*, April 15, 2005.
273. Tom Hamburger and Peter Wallsten, "Frist Initiative Creates Rift in GOP Base," *Los Angeles Times*, April 24, 2005; Carl Hulse and David D. Kirkpatrick, "Judicial Appointments: Casting an Angry Eye on the Courts, Conservatives Prime for Bench-Clearing Brawl in Congress," *New York Times*, March 23, 2005.
274. Goldberg, p. 169.
275. Gilgoff, p. 226.
276. Kirkpatrick, "Frist Set to Use Religious Stage on Judicial Issue"; Leaming, "Full-Court Press."
277. Carl Hulse and David D. Kirkpatrick, "Frist Accused of Exploiting Religious Issues," *New York Times*, April 16, 2005.
278. Goldberg, p. 169.
279. Max Blumenthal, "Justice Sunday Preachers," *Nation*, May 9, 2005.
280. Leaming, "Full-Court Press."
281. Blumenthal, p. 141.
282. Al Mohler, "For the Record: My Address at Justice Sunday," AlMohler.com, April 26, 2005.
283. Ibid.
284. Kirkpatrick, "Frist Set to Use Religious Stage on Judicial Issue," *New York Times*, April 15, 2005; Blumenthal, p. 140; Leaming, "Full-Court Press."
285. "Senators Compromise on Filibuster," CNN.com, May 24, 2005; Gilgoff, p. 227; Blumenthal, p. 142.
286. Jim Abrams, "Senators Avoid Battle over Filibusters," AP, May 24, 2005.
287. Blumenthal, p. 142.
288. Gilgoff, p. 227.
289. David D. Kirkpatrick, "A Year of Work to Sell Roberts to Conservatives," *New York Times*, July 22, 2005.
290. Max Blumenthal, "Preaching Justice, Slaying Demons," *Nation*, Aug. 29, 2005.
291. David D. Kirkpatrick, "Conservative Gathering Is Mostly Quiet on Nominee," *New York Times*, Aug. 15, 2005.
292. Jeannine F. Hunter, "'Justice Sunday' Message: People Hold the Power," *Tennessean*, Aug. 15, 2005.
293. Ibid.; Blumenthal, "Preaching Justice, Slaying Demons."

294. Kirkpatrick, "Conservative Gathering Is Mostly Quiet on Nominee"; Hunter, " 'Justice Sunday' Message."

295. Ibid.

296. Kirkpatrick, "Conservative Gathering Is Mostly Quiet on Nominee."

297. Blumenthal, "Preaching Justice, Slaying Demons"; Hunter, " 'Justice Sunday' Message."

298. Rob Garver, "Megachurch Madness: The Persecution of Christians and Other Themes of Justice Sunday II," *American Prospect* online, Aug. 16, 2005.

299. Hunter, " 'Justice Sunday' Message."

300. H. Allen Orr, "Intelligent Design Isn't," *New Yorker*, May 30, 2005; Chris Mooney, "Inferior Design," *American Prospect*, Aug. 10, 2005; Jodi Wilgorn, "Politicized Scholars Put Evolution on the Defensive," *New York Times*, Aug. 21, 2005. Among the major funders for the Discovery Institute's Center for Science and Culture were foundations headed by Howard Ahmanson, Richard Mellon Scaife, and Phillip F. Anschutz.

301. Jodi Wilgorn, "Politicized Scholars Put Evolution on the Defensive"; Richard Cizik, paper for Yale Conference on Climate Change: Science to Action.

302. Peter Slevin, "In Kansas a Sharp Debate on Evolution," *Washington Post*, May 6, 2005; John Funk, "Kansas School Board Concludes Hearings on Teaching Evolution," Knight Ridder News Service, May 7, 2005.

303. David D. Kirkpatrick, "Conservatives Are Wary over President's Selection," *New York Times*, Oct. 4, 2005; Gilgoff, p. 232.

304. Kirkpatrick, "Conservatives Are Wary over President's Selection"; Gilgoff, p. 232; Jeremy Leaming, "Who Did In Harriet Miers?," Americans United, *Church & State*, November 2005.

305. Kirkpatrick, "Conservatives Are Wary over President's Selection."

306. Leaming, "Who Did In Harriet Miers?"

307. Kirkpatrick, "Conservatives Are Wary over President's Selection."

308. Ibid.; Gilgoff, p. 229.

309. Kirkpatrick, "Conservatives Are Wary over President's Selection"; Gilgoff, p. 237.

310. David D. Kirkpatrick, "New Questions from the Right on Court Pick," *New York Times*, Oct. 6, 2005; Leaming, "Who Did In Harriet Miers?"

311. Charles Krauthammer, "Withdraw the Nominee," *Washington Post*, Oct. 7, 2005.

312. Kirkpatrick, "Conservatives Are Wary over President's Selection"; Leaming, "Who Did In Harriet Miers?"; Maura Reynolds, "Nominee 'Best Person I Could Find,' Bush Says," *Los Angeles Times*, Oct. 5, 2005.

313. Kirkpatrick, "Conservatives Are Wary over President's Selection"; David D. Kirkpatrick, "Endorsement of Nominee Draws Committee's Interest," *New York Times*, Oct. 10, 2005; Leaming, "Who Did In Harriet Miers?"

314. Leaming, "Who Did In Harriet Miers?"; Gilgoff, pp. 235–36.

315. Kirkpatrick, "Endorsement of Nominee Draws Committee's Interest."

316. Gilgoff, p. 236.

317. Ibid.; Leaming, "Who Did In Harriet Miers?"

318. Gilgoff, pp. 236–38.

319. Michael A. Fletcher and Charles Babington, "Senators Assail Miers' Reply, Ask for Details," *Washington Post*, Oct. 20, 2005.

320. Ibid.; Leaming, "Who Did In Harriet Miers?"

321. Fletcher and Babington, "Senators Assail Miers' Reply."

322. Greenburg, *Supreme Conflict*, p. 282.

323. Leaming, "Who Did In Harriet Miers?"

324. Ibid.

325. Ibid.

326. Blumenthal, p. 149.

327. Leaming, "Who Did In Harriet Miers?"

328. Gilgoff, p. 235.

329. Ibid., p. 132; Zink and Adair, "Terri Schaivo Derails Social Agenda of the Christian Right."
330. Ibid.

16: The New Evangelicals

1. Miller, pp. 95, 140–41; Michelle Goldberg, "Michele Bachmann and Rick Perry's Dangerous Religious Bond," *Daily Beast*, Aug. 14, 2011.
2. Chip Berlet, "What Is Dominionism? Palin, the Christian Right and Theocracy," in "The Rise of the Religious Right in the Republican Party," Political Research Associates, on theocracywatch.com, Sept. 5, 2008.
3. Phillips, pp. xii–xiv.
4. Jeff Sharlet, "Inside the Nation's Most Powerful Megachurch," *Harper's*, May 2005, and his book *The Family: The Secret Fundamentalism at the Heart of American Power* (2008). Also Dan Wakefield's *The Hijacking of Jesus: How the Religious Right Distorts Christianity and Promotes Prejudice and Hate* (2006).
5. Chip Berlet and Pam Chamberlain, "Running Against Sodom and Osama," Political Research Associates, October 2006.
6. Sherry Eros and Stephen Eros, "Values Voters Summit Takes on Liberals," *Human Events*, Oct. 2, 2006.
7. Frank James, "Evangelical Turnout in Doubt," *Chicago Tribune*, Oct. 2, 2006.
8. "Activists Find It Tougher to Energize Jaded Evangelical Voters Ahead of Election," AP, Sept. 22, 2006; Eric Gorski, "Dobson Warns of Fallout if Democrats Take Congress," *Denver Post*, Nov. 1, 2006.
9. FitzGerald, 2006.
10. *Florida Baptist Witness*, Aug. 24, 2006.
11. John C. Green and Mark Silk, "The Religion Gap Abides," *Religion in the News*, Spring 2011, vol. 13, no. 2; Tim Jones, "Evangelicals No Longer a Lock for the GOP," *Chicago Tribune*, Nov. 6, 2006; Pew Research Center, "Understanding Religion's Role in the 2006 Election," Dec. 5, 2006.
12. "Exit Polls: Scandals Hurt the GOP More than War," AP, NBC News, Nov. 7, 2006; David R. Jones, "Why the Democrats Won," CBS News, Nov. 8, 2006; Will Lester, "Exit Polls: Scandals and Iraq Hurt the GOP," *Washington Post*, Nov. 8, 2006.
13. "Religion and the 2006 Election," Pew Research Center's Religion and Public Life Project, www.pewforum.org/2006/12/01/religion-and-the-2006-elections/.
14. Boyd, *The Myth of a Christian Nation*, p. 9.
15. Ibid., p. 79.
16. Boyd filled in the history that Francis Schaeffer left out. In the Reformation, he wrote, Protestants of every group, except the Anabaptists, fought each other and fought the Catholics until they exhausted themselves and made the Peace of Westphalia. Also Laurie Goodstein, "Disavowing Conservative Politics, Evangelical Pastor Rattles His Flock," *New York Times*, July 30, 2006.
17. John Cochran, "New Heaven, New Earth," *Congressional Quarterly*, Oct. 17, 2005.
18. Tony Carnes, "Jesus at the G8," *Christianity Today*, July 6, 2005.
19. Rick Warren letter, June 2005, from the ministry's weekly e-newsletter; Marc Gunther, "Will Success Spoil Rick Warren?," *Fortune*, Oct. 31, 2005.
20. Trennis Henderson, "Rick Warren Calls for a New Reformation," Associated Baptist Press, Aug. 1, 2005.
21. Pally, *The New Evangelicals*, p. 166.
22. Elisabeth Bumiller, "Preaching to the Choir? Not This Time," *New York Times*, May 23, 2005; "An Open Letter to the President of the United States, George W. Bush," *Grand Rapids Press*, May 20, 2005. One of Calvin College's benefactors, Richard DeVos of Amway, was a strong supporter of the Christian right. His son Dick DeVos was running for governor of Michigan on the Republican ticket in 2006 against a popular Democrat, Jennifer Granholm.

23. Michael A. Fletcher, "Bush Issues Call to Service," *Washington Post*, May 22, 2005.
24. Laurie Goodstein, "Evangelicals Open Debate on Widening Policy Questions," *New York Times*, March 11, 2005.
25. Ibid.
26. Bill Tammeus, "Evangelicals Focusing on World Issues, Poor," Knight Ridder News Service, Aug. 20, 2005.
27. Goodstein, "Evangelicals Open Debate on Widening Policy Questions."
28. Interview by FitzGerald in spring 2006 in "The Evangelical Surprise," *New York Review of Books*, April 26, 2007.
29. Jones, "Evangelicals No Longer a Lock for the GOP"; and see Nathan, *Who Is My Enemy?*
30. Sheler, *Prophet of Purpose*, pp. 1–91.
31. Ibid., pp. 94–95.
32. According to Sheler, Warren also found a former Pentagon systems analyst to help him organize the project by analyzing and scheduling the various tasks involved. Ibid., p. 104.
33. Ibid., pp. 129–40; Warren, *The Purpose Driven Church*, pp. 157–60.
34. Sheler, pp. 94–140; Warren, p. 142.
35. Sheler, p. 106; Gilley, *This Little Church Went to Market*, p. 93.
36. Gilley, p. 46.
37. Sheler, p. 165.
38. Ibid., p. 177–82.
39. Ibid., pp. 187–89.
40. Ibid., p. 189; Rick Warren, "Myths of the Modern Megachurch," Pew Forum on Religion and Public Life, May 23, 2005, www.pewforum.org/2005/05/23/myths-of-the-modern -megachurch/.
41. Sheler, pp. 198–202. The work was to be done by local people and coordinated via a decentralized Internet-based communications network. In Warren's June letter asking his network to press Bush for debt relief, he wrote that he had 4,500 people testing a prototype. Later he said he would include the Muslim clergy.
42. Normally the idea was to introduce congregants to mission work with the hope that they would contribute money, get engaged, and wouldn't harm the local effort.
43. Sheler, pp. 228–38.
44. Trennis Henderson, "Rick Warren Calls for a New Reformation," Associated Baptist Press, Aug. 1, 2005.
45. Paul Nussbaum, "New Purpose Drives Rick Warren," Knight Ridder News Service, Jan. 26, 2006; Warren, "Myths of the Modern Megachurch."
46. Warren, "Myths of the Modern Megachurch."
47. Ibid.
48. Two months before, Warren had told Larry King that Terri Schiavo was not brain-dead and the removal of her feeding tube was "an atrocity worthy of Nazism." *Larry King Live*, May 22, 2005, CNN transcripts.
49. Warren was not entirely consistent. At the Pew meeting he said, "I agree with a lot of the goals that liberals have for justice and poverty. I just happen to believe that the answer is the church, not the government. I think that throwing away money after it in the government fashion has proven ineffective." Yet at the same time he was helping the singer-activist Bono increase government aid to Africa by billions of dollars, and collaborating with the Kagame government in Rwanda.
50. Those were the figures the NAE gave at the time. The NAE website in 2015 reported the organization had 45,000 local churches from nearly forty denominations with "a constituency of millions." The new history section on the website reported that the height of its membership came after rapid growth in the 1980s, when the total membership was 4.5 million. The thirty-million figure seems to have been someone's estimate of how many people the NAE affected. The new history reported that the organization went into a decline in the 1990s but gives no exact figures.

51. Cizik, "Public Policy Resolutions."

52. Ibid.

53. Amanda Griscom Little, "An Interview with Green Evangelical Leader, Richard Cizik," *Grist Magazine*, Oct. 5, 2005.

54. *Creation Care* magazine, Evangelical Environmental Network, Fall 2004, no. 26.

55. Evangelical Environmental Network, paper; e-mail from Paul Gorman, director of the National Religious Partnership for the Environment; "What Would Jesus Drive?," a campaign discussion paper by Rev. Ron Sider and Rev. Jim Ball.

56. Little, "An Interview with Green Evangelical Leader, Richard Cizik."

57. John Cochran, "New Heaven, New Earth."

58. Ibid., cites Pew poll of 2004.

59. Little, "An Interview with Green Evangelical Leader, Richard Cizik."

60. "Cornwall Declaration," Interfaith Stewardship Alliance, www.cornwallalliance.org.

The Cornwall Declaration was largely a distillation of Beisner's *Where the Garden Meets the Wilderness*. Its authors included a few evangelical economists from places such as Liberty University, but no scientists. Beisner and his allies had their own reading of Genesis 2:15 that highlighted the "dominion" God gave Adam over the other creatures of his creation.

Conceived and established by the Action Institute for Religion and Liberty, in response to the creation of the EEN, the Interfaith Stewardship Alliance had an advisory council that included D. James Kennedy, Father Richard John Neuhaus, Rabbi Daniel Lapin, Father Robert Sirico of the Acton Institute, and Marvin Olasky. The Christian right leaders supporting it included Bill Bright, Charles Colson, James Dobson, Beverly LaHaye, and Donald Wildmon. EEN document; "The Interfaith Stewardship Alliance," www.interfaithstewardship .org; Paul Weyrich, "Environmental Degradation and Evangelicals," Enter Stage Right, Nov. 21, 2005, http://enterstageright.com/archive/articles, 201105, 201105nae.htm.

61. "Focus on the Family Concerned by Global Warming Theory," Family.com, press release, May 10, 2005.

62. Michael Janofsky, "Where Cleaner Air Is a Biblical Obligation," *New York Times*, Nov. 7, 2005; "Heat Stroke," *Christianity Today*, editorial, October 2004; Laurie Goodstein, "Evangelical Leaders Swing Influence," *New York Times*, March 10, 2005; Cizik interview in *Grist*, Oct. 5, 2005; Laurie Goodstein, "Eighty-six Evangelical Leaders Join the Fight over Global Warming," *New York Times*, Feb. 8, 2006.

63. "A Letter to the National Association of Evangelicals on the Issue of Global Warming," Jan. 2006, Interfaith Stewardship Alliance, www.interfaithstewardship.org.

64. Alan Cooperman, "Evangelicals Will Not Take a Stand on Global Warming," *Washington Post*, Feb. 2, 2006.

65. Evangelical Climate Initiative press releases, www.ChristiansandClimate.org. The denominational leaders included Jack Hayford (International Church of the Four Square Gospel), Berten Waggoner (Vineyard Association), Peter Borgdorff (Christian Reformed Church), Bishop James D. Leggett (International Pentecostal Holiness Church). The group also included Ron Sider, David Neff, and several influential African American and Hispanic evangelicals, among them Leggett and Floyd Flake of the Greater Allen AME Cathedral in New York.

66. Evangelical Climate Initiative press releases; Goodstein, "Eighty-six Evangelical Leaders Join the Fight over Global Warming."

67. SBC resolution 2006.

68. Bradford Plummer, "Greener Pastors," *New Republic*, March 12, 2007. It was only later discovered that the Cornwall Alliance was funded by a number of fronts for ExxonMobil and other energy interests. ("The Oily Operators Behind the Religious Disinformation Front, the Cornwall Alliance," ThinkProgress, June 23, 2010.) The Evangelical Climate Initiative and National Religious Partnership for the Environment openly disclosed that they re-

ceived funding from the Pew Charitable Trusts, the Rockefeller Brothers Fund, and the Hewlett Foundation.

69. "Evangelical, Scientific Leaders Launch Effort to Protect Creation," NAE press release, Jan. 17, 2007.

70. Gregory Tomlin, "Letter Asks NAE to Rethink 'Green' Activism," *Baptist Press*, March 9, 2007; Stephanie Simon, "Evangelicals Battle over Agenda, Environment," *Los Angeles Times*, May 10, 2007. The letter also claimed that Cizik in a speech to the World Bank had called for population control and suggested that meant promoting abortion, distributing condoms to the young, and even infanticide, as in China.

71. Gregory Tomlin, "Cizik Gets No Rebuke from the NAE," *Baptist Press*, March 22, 2007. Robert Marcus, "NAE Rebuffs Bush Administration in Joining Anti-Torture Statement," Associated Baptist Press, March 15, 2007. Drafted by the Evangelicals for Human Rights, a group of seventeen theologians and ethicists, principally Glen Stassen of Fuller and David Gushee of Union University, the document, "An Evangelical Declaration Against Torture: Protecting Human Rights in an Age of Terror," specifically attacked the Military Commissions Act Bush had pushed through the Congress that prevented intelligence officials from being held to the same standard as the U.S. military in handling detainees, prevented congressional and judicial oversight over CIA actions, and allowed terrorist suspects to be held indefinitely and tried without the same rules of evidence used in U.S. criminal courts. One who did not sign the torture statement was Mark Tooley of the Institute on Religion and Democracy, where Beisner served as a member of the board. The IRD, according to a fellow board member, Tooley, was founded in 1981 to challenge the mainline Protestant support for Marxist revolutions, particularly those in Central America. Mark D. Tooley, "Evangelicals Must Resist Mainline Trajectory," *Christian Post*, Feb. 23, 2015.

72. Tomlin, "Cizik Gets No Rebuke from the NAE."

73. Barbara Bradley Haggerty, "Evangelical Voters May Be Up for Grabs in '08," NPR, May 18, 2007.

74. Ken Connor, "Conscience, Calling and the Christian Conservative Agenda." *Christian Post*, May 24, 2007.

75. Rachel Zoll, "Christian Right at the Crossroads," boston_com, May 19, 2007.

76. Ekklesia Think Tank, "Spero News: Evangelicals Urged to Drop the E-Word," June 26, 2006.

77. The Barna Group, "Young Have Negative View of Christianity: A New Generation Expresses Its Skepticism and Frustration with Christianity," Sept. 24, 2007. See also *unChristian* (2007) by David Kinnaman, president of the Barna Group.

78. Gunther, "Will Success Spoil Rick Warren?"

79. Nina Easton, "With Anti-Poverty Call Evangelicals Seek New Tone," *Boston Globe*, July 5, 2005.

80. Robert Marus, "Evangelicals Caught in the Middle of Debate over Identity, Direction," Associated Baptist Press, June 25, 2007.

81. E. J. Dionne, "Evangelical Evolution," *Washington Post Writer's Group*, June 19, 2006; Hotline on Call: "Four Reasons Why the Southern Baptist Convention Election Matters to You (If You're Not a Southern Baptist)," June 16, 2000; Mark I. Pinksy, "Who Speaks for American Evangelicals?," *USA Today*, Aug. 6, 2007.

82. Lilian Kwon, "Hybels-Carter Interview Featured Amid Criticism," *Christian Post*, Aug. 14, 2007; David D. Kirkpatrick, "The Evangelical Crack-up," *New York Times Magazine*, Oct. 28, 2007; FitzGerald, "The New Evangelicals," 2008. Bill Hybels's wife, Lynne, wrote for *Sojourners* magazine and often took more of a political role than he did, as on peace in the Middle East.

83. FitzGerald, 2008." Hunter also signed a statement urging the U.N. to stop the atrocities in Darfur, along with Richard Land and others.

84. Alexander Zaitchick, "Alternet Rights and Liberties: Who Would Jesus Deport?," Jan. 29,

2007; Neela Banerjee, "New Coalition of Christians Seeks Changes at Borders," *New York Times*, May 8, 2007.

85. Joel C. Hunter, *A New Kind of Conservative*, 2008.
86. Mark I. Pinsky, "New Evangelicals Are Moving Religious Right to Center," *San Jose Mercury News*, Sept. 22, 2006.
87. Jenny Jarvie, "Christian Coalition Is Splintering," *Los Angeles Times*, Sept. 5, 2006; Alan Cooperman, "Evangelicals Broaden Their Agenda," *Washington Post*, Oct. 19, 2006.
88. Neela Banerjee, "Pastor Chosen to Lead Christian Coalition Steps Down," *New York Times*, Nov. 28, 2006.
89. FitzGerald interview, Feb. 14, 2008; Laurie Goodstein, "Coalition of American Evangelicals Issues a Letter in Support of Palestinian State," *New York Times*, July 28, 2007. The signers included the heads of World Vision and World Relief as well David Neff and Berten Waggoner, head of the Vineyard Association.
90. "Letter to Bush from Evangelical Leaders," *New York Times*, July 29, 2007.
91. FitzGerald, 2008.
92. FitzGerald interview, June 19, 2006.
93. FitzGerald, 2008.
94. Ibid.
95. Ibid.
96. Ibid.
97. Bill Maxell, "Signs That Falwell's Divisiveness Is Fading," *Ocala Star Banner*, May 24, 2007.
98. Beth Reinhard and Alexandra Alter, "The Religious Left Lifts Its Voice in the '08 Campaign," *Miami Herald*, April 6, 2007; FitzGerald, 2008.
99. FitzGerald, 2008, and interview with Hunter, Feb. 14, 2008.
100. Lilian Kuson, "Evangelical Giants Passing: Who Will Defend the Biblical Truth?," *Christian Post*, Sept. 16, 2007.
101. Michael Luo and Laurie Goodstein, "Emphasis Shifts for a New Breed of Evangelicals," *New York Times*, May 21, 2007.
102. Ibid.
103. Alan Cooperman, "Evangelicals at a Crossroads as Falwell's Generation Fades," *Washington Post*, May 22, 2007.
104. Kirkpatrick, "The Evangelical Crack-up."
105. Alexander Alter, "Religious Right at Political Crossroads," *Miami Herald*, May 8, 2007.
106. "Inside the Battle at Coral Ridge," interview by Drew Dyck, *Christianity Today*, Nov. 2014, www.christianitytoday.com/parse/2011/november/inside-battle-at-coral-ridge.html. Around four hundred people, including Kennedy's daughter, broke away and formed another church. The Coral Ridge Ministries, Kennedy's broadcasting arm, continued to engage in politics, but Tullian Tchividjian with a congregation of 2,400 would have nothing to do with it. He later became an ardent critic of the Christian right.
107. Kirkpatrick, "The Evangelical Crack-up."
108. FitzGerald, 2008.
109. Smidt, *American Evangelicals Today*, pp. 79, 86.
110. Cathy Lynn Grossman, "Can the E-Word Be Saved?," *USA Today*, Jan. 23, 2007.
111. FitzGerald, 2008. See Pinsky, *A Jew Among Evangelicals*. See also Amy Sullivan, "When Would Jesus Bolt?," *Washington Monthly*, April 2006.
112. Pew Forum on Religion and Public Life, Feb. 2007: 57 percent of those under thirty said the country was losing ground on pollution, compared to 10 percent of their elders. According to the American Values Survey of October 8, 2008, two thirds of young evangelicals thought abortion should be illegal in all or most cases; 24 percent favored gay marriage and another 28 percent favored civil unions.
113. Pew Forum, "White Evangelicals: Less Republican, Still Conservative," Feb. 2007.
114. Shawn Zeller, "A Crisis of Political Faith for Evangelicals," *CQ Politics*, Sept. 17, 2007.
115. Nancy Gibbs, "The Evangelicals' New Clothes," *Time*, Feb. 10, 2008.

116. Zeller, "A Crisis of Political Faith for Evangelicals."

117. Ibid.; Gibbs, "The Evangelicals' New Clothes."

118. Stephen Thomma, "The Religious Right's Power Ebbs," McClatchy Newspapers, Sept. 30, 2007.

119. Perry Bacon Jr., "Huckabee's Faith Cuts Both Ways," *Washington Post*, Dec. 21, 2007. Huckabee as governor had also accepted thousands of dollars in gifts without reporting them. Robert Novak, "Baptist Brethren Split on Huckabee," *Chicago Sun Times*, Dec. 20, 2007.

120. Bert Grainger, "Will Huckabee's Campaign Encourage Evangelicals to Vote for a Democrat?," *Christian Science Monitor*, Feb. 4, 2008; Ed Stoddard, "Huckabee Moves Beyond Religious Right," Reuters, Jan. 9, 2008; David D. Kirkpatrick, "In Split with Old Guard, Young Evangelicals Warm Up to Huckabee," *New York Times*, Jan. 13, 2008; "DMN Editorial Board Recommends Huckabee for the Republican Nomination," *Dallas Morning News*, Dec. 23, 2007; Thomas Schaller, "Born of GOP's 'Southern Strategy,'" *Baltimore Sun*, Dec. 19, 2007.

121. Kirkpatrick, "In Split with Old Guard, Young Evangelicals Warm Up to Huckabee"; "Mike Huckabee and Barack Obama," *Meet the Press*, Dec. 30, 2007.

122. "A Stealth Mitt Romney Endorsement from the Religious Right's Powerbrokers?," *Time* in partnership with CNN, Jan. 24, 2008; Michelle A. Vu, "Christian Right Still in Search of Ideal Candidate," *Christian Post*, Jan. 21, 2008; Charles C. Haynes, "Presidential Candidates Scramble to Get God Right," *Decatur Daily*, Oct. 14, 2007.

123. Text of Romney's Speech on Religion, *International Herald Tribune*, Dec. 17, 2007; "A Stealth Mitt Romney Endorsement," *Time*.

124. Smidt et al., *The Disappearing God Gap?*, pp. 84–94; Sarah Pulliam, "Super Tuesday Results Show Split Between Evangelicals and Their Spokesmen," *Christianity Today*, Feb. 6, 2008.

125. Pulliam, "Super Tuesday Results Show Split Between Evangelicals and Their Spokesmen."

126. Gibbs, "The Evangelicals' New Clothes."

127. Rheinhard and Alter, "Religious Left Lifts Its Voice in the '08 Campaign."

128. Michelle Vu, "Evangelicals and Progressives Seek to End Culture Wars," *Christian Post*, Oct. 11, 2007; Hannah Elliott, "Democrats, Evangelicals Work Together on Abortion Reduction," *Bloomberg News*, Nov. 13, 2007.

129. Reinhard and Alter, "Religious Left Lifts Its Voice in the '08 Campaign"; Mark I. Pinksy, "The Reverend Joel Hunter Is a Part of a New Generation of Religious Leaders," *Orlando Sentinel*, July 2, 2007. Bill Clinton had used the same formulation as president.

130. Barbara Bradley Haggerty, "Evangelical Voters May Be up for Grabs in '08," NPR, May 16, 2007.

131. Dan Gilgoff, "Beliefnet Poll: Evangelicals Still Conservative, but Defy Issue Stereotypes," Beliefnet.com, 2007.

132. "Young White Evangelicals: Less Republican, Still Conservative," Pew Forum, Feb. 27, 2007.

133. Robert Marus, "Polls, Authors, Say White Evangelicals Embracing Political Independence," Associated Baptist Press, Feb. 12, 2008.

134. "White Evangelical Vote for Democrats Is Up," *U.S. News & World Report*, Feb. 11, 2008.

135. "Seminary Student's Climate Change Project Is Not SBC's," Associated Baptist Press, May 11, 2008. The SBC took the line of Beisner and the Cornwall Alliance.

136. Ibid.

137. Neela Banerjee, "Southern Baptists Back a Shift on Climate Change," *New York Times*, May 10, 2008.

138. Rick Scarborough, "Why I'm Supporting Mike Huckabee for President," *WorldNetDaily*, Jan. 13, 2008.

139. Michelle A. Vu, "Christian Right Leaders Respond to Dobson's Concern," *Christian Post*, March 24, 2008.

140. Ted Olson, "Survey: Evangelical Democrats Favor Hilary," *Christianity Today*, blog, Feb. 11, 2009; Jennifer Riley, "Survey: Young Christian Voters Break from Traditional Right," *Christian Post*, Feb. 27, 2007.

141. Steve Waldman, "Political Perceptions: How Obama Lured Millions of Religious Voters,"

Wall Street Journal, Nov. 5, 2008; Rebecca Sinderbrand. "Analysis: Democrats Woo Disaffected Evangelicals," CNN, Jan. 11, 2008.

142. Dan Gilgoff, "Why the Christian Right Fears Obama," *USA Today*, June 16, 2008.

143. Smidt et al., p. 96.

144. "Beck Failed to Ask Hagee About Controversial Remarks," *Media Matters*, March 5, 2008. In addition to defaming the pope, Hagee preached that God used the Holocaust to force Jews out of Europe and to Israel. "How McCain Shed Pariah Status Among Evangelicals," *All Things Considered*, NPR, Oct. 23, 2008; Zachary Roth, "Rod Parsley's Free Pass," *Columbia Journalism Review*, May 14, 2008.

145. Smidt et al., pp. 100–1. Land said of the two pastors, "Both of these guys hold positions which anyone who knows evangelical life well would know would be problematic for someone running for national office." "How McCain Shed Pariah Status Among Evangelicals."

146. Peter Wallenstein, "John McCain's Ohio Disconnect," *Los Angeles Times*, June 9, 2008.

147. Smidt et al., p. 154.

148. "How McCain Shed Pariah Status."

149. David Brody, "The Brody File: A Turning Point for McCain," *Christian Broadcasting Network News*, September 3, 2008.

150. Wayne Slater, "Evangelical Right Slow to Support McCain," *Dallas Morning News*, Oct. 5, 2008.

151. David Brody, "The Brody File: Franklin Graham, Obama Shake Hands at Private Pastor's Meeting," *CBN News*, June 11, 2008.

152. Max Blumenthal, "Inside Obama's Christian Crusade," *Nation*, July 2, 2008.

153. "McCain and Obama Seek to Reach Out to Evangelical Voters," *PBS NewsHour Online*, Aug. 18, 2008; "How McCain Shed Pariah Status Among Evangelicals."

154. Smidt et al., p. 123.

155. Sinderbrand, "Analysis: Democrats Woo Disaffected Evangelicals." In July 2008 a *Newsweek* poll showed that 12 percent of the electorate thought Obama was a practicing Muslim and 26 percent that he had been raised a Muslim. Smidt et al., p. 115.

156. Smidt et al., pp. 136–37.

157. Collen Lack, "Democrats Open Faith-Filled Convention with Prayer," 9News.com, Aug. 24, 2008.

158. Ibid.; Dana Goldstein, "Women's Issues and the Democratic Platform," *American Prospect*, Aug. 12, 2008.

159. "Can We Come to the Party?," *Christianity Today*, Oct. 27, 2008, editorial.

160. Terry Eastland, "Clinging to Her Religion," *Weekly Standard*, Sept. 29, 2008.

161. "How McCain Shed Pariah Status Among Evangelicals."

162. Jill Zuckerman, "McCain Faces Resistance from the Right," *Chicago Tribune*, Feb. 21, 2008; "How McCain Shed Pariah Status Among Evangelicals."

163. Smidt et al., pp. 157–58, 161, 198.

164. Slater, "Evangelical Right Slow to Support McCain."

165. Eric Gorsky and Rachel Zoll, "Christian Right Intensifies Attacks on Obama," AP, Oct. 14, 2008.

166. www.wnd.com/files/Focusletter.pdf.

167. Ibid.

168. Gorsky and Zoll, "Christian Right Intensifies Attacks on Obama."

169. Amy Sullivan, "Obama's Religious Appeal Bringing (Some) Evangelicals In," *Time*, Nov. 5, 2008.

170. Some publications differed in the percentages of white evangelicals they reported for McCain and Obama: Pew, 73–26 percent; *USA Today*, 74–24 percent; *New York Times*, 74–24 percent; Smidt et al., pp. 74–76.

171. Laurie Goodstein, "Obama Made Gains Among Younger Evangelicals," *New York Times*, Nov. 5, 2008.

172. Sullivan, "Obama's Religious Appeal Bringing (Some) Evangelicals In."

173. Laurie Goodstein, "Obama Made Gains Among Younger Evangelicals"; Christine Page, "The Obamavangelical Reformation," *Huffington Post*, Nov. 15, 2008.

174. Sullivan, "Obama's Religious Appeal Bringing (Some) Evangelicals In."

175. Ibid.

176. "Young White Evangelicals Less Republican, Still Conservative," Pew Research Center; *Relevant*, Jan./Feb. 2008, no. 31.

17: The Transformation of the Christian Right

1. Jim Wallis and three prominent black preachers were his other spiritual advisors.

2. Bob Allen, "Liberals, Evangelicals Call for Common Agenda," Associated Baptist Press, Jan. 15, 2009; "Come Let Us Reason Together: A Governing Agenda," Faith in Public Life, Jan. 15, 2009.

3. Dan Gilgoff, "On Abortion and Gay Rights, Evangelicals and Liberals Join to Advise Obama," *U.S. News & World Report*, Jan. 15, 2009.

4. Robert Stein, "Analysis: Both Sides Wary of Obama's Search for Common Ground on Abortion," *Washington Post*, Feb. 9, 2009. Three days after the inauguration Obama rescinded the Mexico City policy, the gag rule on abortion for international aid agencies, and at the same time persuaded House Democrats to drop from a stimulus bill a plan to allow Medicaid to expand contraceptive services. Democrats pressured him to reverse Bush's executive order allowing religious groups receiving federal funding to discriminate in employment, but after studying the matter, he left the order in place.

5. Gilgoff, p. 25.

6. Jennifer Riley, "Churches, Groups Look to Obama for Promised Change," *Christian Post*, Jan. 12, 2009.

7. Bob Allen, "Christian and Other Faith Leaders Urge Congress to Close Guantánamo," Associated Baptist Press, Nov. 18, 2009.

8. Allen, "Liberals, Evangelicals, Call for Common Agenda."

9. Jennifer Riley, "Dobson Admits to Struggling After the Election," *Christian Post*, Nov. 7, 2008.

10. Ibid.

11. Erik Gorski, "Evangelical Group Faces Serious Shortfall," AP, Aug. 11, 2009; Laurie Goodstein, "Radio Show for Focus on the Family Founder," *New York Times*, Jan. 16, 2010; Steve Rabey, "For Giant Evangelical Ministry, Midlife Crisis at 25," *New York Times*, July 27, 2002.

12. Cara Degette, "More Layoffs at Focus," *Colorado Independent*, Nov. 7, 2008. According to the *Independent*, Focus had 1,500 workers in 1991; in 2008 just before a round of layoffs it pumped more than $500,000 to the passage of California's Proposition 8.

13. Rita Healy, "Is Dobson's Political Clout Fading?," *Time*, Jan. 28, 2009.

14. Dan Gilgoff, "What James Dobson's Resignation Means for Focus," *U.S. News & World Report*, Feb. 27, 2009.

15. Ibid.

16. Healy, "Is Dobson's Political Clout Fading?" Dobson's monthly newsletter had a circulation of 2.4 million copies in 1994 and 1.1 million in 2008.

17. Stephanie Simon, "Evangelical Group Seeks Broader Tent," *Wall Street Journal*, Feb. 6, 2010; Sarah Pulliam Bailey, "Refocusing on the Family," *Christianity Today*, July 1, 2011. According to an internal survey, only 7 percent of the 121 new radio programs begun by mid-2011 addressed public policy. Laurie Goodstein, "Radio Show to Focus on the Family Founder," *New York Times*, Jan. 16, 2010. Daly even promised to have Focus sit down with pro-choice organizations to discuss how to decrease the number of abortions, though Focus officials seem to have used the conversations to press for the use of ultrasound photos of the fetus.

18. Bailey, "Refocusing on the Family"; Goodstein, "Radio Show to Focus on the Family

Founder"; "James Dobson Was Pushed Out of Focus, Says Influential Evangelical," *Huffington Post*, May 11, 2010.

19. Goodstein, "Radio Show to Focus on the Family Founder"; Rob Boston, "Dobson Unretires," Americans United, *Wall of Separation*, Jan. 7, 2010.

20. Goodstein "Radio Show to Focus on the Family Founder"; Buss, pp. 257–60. Focus also gave Ryan the rights to Focus's three teen magazines with a combined circulation of 200,000, which Ryan said he would publish online, but did not. It was in many ways a tribute to Dobson that he had resigned at the behest of his board and had not changed the Focus rules where his son was concerned.

21. Simon, "Evangelical Group Seeks Broader Tent."

22. Bailey, "Refocusing on the Family"; Sarah Posner, "Children of God," *American Prospect*, Feb. 19, 2010. Oddly, Daly launched Rising Voice at the Conservative Political Action Committee convention, where it seemed wildly out place amid the Tea Party mania.

23. Bailey, "Refocusing on the Family"; and an observer, a student from Colorado College. Focus hired Tim Goeglein, who had resigned from the Bush White House in 2008 after admitting to writing columns with plagiarized passages, to connect the organization to conservatives in Washington.

24. Pat Robertson's two sons were also successful in carrying on their father's business, one as the administrator of CBN and the other complementing his father as a host of *The 700 Club*, but neither spoke out politically, and Pat, more eccentric all the time, had lost all political influence. He came out for legalizing marijuana, and for assassinating President Hugo Chávez of Venezuela. He blamed the Haiti earthquake of 2010 on the pact its founders had made with the devil to liberate themselves from the French.

25. Sarah Posner, "Former Employer: Racism and Abuse in Religious Right Organization," *Religion Dispatches*, Oct. 13, 2010.

26. Janet I. Tu, "Local News: Religious Right Is a 'Leaderless Army,'" *Seattle Times*, July 21, 2009; Joe Hallet and Meredeth Heagney, "Can Faith Have a Prayer in Politics?," *Columbus Dispatch*, May 8, 2011. Weyrich died in 2009; Howard Phillips in 2013.

27. "The Future of Evangelicals, a Conversation with Pastor Rick Warren," Pew Research Center, Forum on Religion and Public Life, Nov. 13, 2009.

28. Colson and Father Richard John Neuhaus, who had subsequently died, had made the case for a rapprochement with a document titled "Evangelicals and Catholics Together" in 1994. Robert George and Timothy George had assisted in the writing of the constitutional amendment banning gay marriage in 2003.

29. Robert P. Jones, "Pope Francis's Challenge to the Evangelical-Catholic Coalition," *Atlantic*, April 21, 2014.

30. The Manhattan Declaration website; Kyle Mantyla, "The Right's New Manhattan Project," *Right Wing Watch*, Nov. 20, 2009; "The Manhattan Declaration: A Call of Christian Conscience," *First Things*, Nov. 20, 2009.

31. Mantyla, "The Right's New Manhattan Project"; Laurie Goodstein, "Christian Leaders Unite on Political Issues," *New York Times*, Nov. 20, 2009.

32. USCCB website on the health care reform, May 20, 2009. Bishop Murray statement to congressional committee.

33. "David M. Herszenhorn and Jackie Calmes, "Abortion Was at the Heart of Wrangling," *New York Times*, Nov. 7, 2009. In 2008 the Democrats had gained a large and diverse majority, and some of them came from conservative districts where antiabortion groups were strong.

34. John Gehring, "Catholic Bishops as Culture Warriors," Catholic Alliance for the Common Good, www.faithstreet.com; USCCB website: health care reform: timetable. See bulletin insert, May 11, 2010.

35. Vanessa Williams, Theda Skocpol, and John Coggins, "The Tea Party and the Remaking of Republican Conservatism," scholar.harvard.edu, vol. 9, no. 1, March 2011.

36. According to the CBS/*New York Times* poll of April 2010 Sarah Palin was the most popular

personality. Sixty-six percent of those who identified with the Tea Party had a favorable impression of her, though only 40 percent said she would make a good president; 59 percent had a favorable impression of Glenn Beck; and 57 percent approved of George W. Bush, while 57 percent of all Americans did not approve of him.

37. Ben Smith, "Libertarian Streak in Tea Party Worries Some Evangelicals," *Politico*, March 12, 2010.

38. Adele M. Stan, "Overshadowed by the Tea Party Movement, the Christian Right Scrambles to Claim It Isn't Racist," *Alternet*, Sept. 22, 2009.

39. Jake Sherman, "Protesters March on Washington," *Wall Street Journal*, Sept. 12, 2009.

40. Smith, "Libertarian Streak in Tea Party Worries Some Evangelicals."

41. Kate Zernike and Megan Thee-Brenan, "Poll Finds Tea Party Backers Wealthier and More Educated," *New York Times*, June 14, 2010; Brian Montopoli, "Tea Party Supporters: Who They Are and What They Believe," *CBS News*, Dec. 14, 2012.

42. "The Tea Party and Religion," Pew Research Center, Forum on Religion and Public Life, Feb. 23, 2011.

43. Zernike and Thee-Brenan, "Poll Finds Tea Party Backers Wealthier and More Educated," *New York Times*, June 14, 2010; "Fact Sheet: 'Teavangelicals': Alignments and Tensions Between the Tea Party and White Evangelicals," Public Religion Research Institute, Nov. 7, 2011. According to the Institute, 40 percent of those who identified with the Tea Party also identified as white evangelicals. Less than one third of both Tea Party sympathizers and white evangelicals said abortion should be legal in all or most cases, and smaller percentages of both favored same-sex marriage. Jones, *The End of White Christian America*, pp. 95–96.

44. Montopoli, "Tea Party Supporters: Who They Are and What They Believe."

45. "The Tea Party and Religion," Pew Research Center.

46. Kate Zernike, "Tea Party Set to Win Enough Races for Wide Influence," *New York Times*, Oct. 14, 2010; Stan, "Overshadowed by the Tea Party Movement."

47. Tobin Grant, "Evangelicals and Tea Party Overlap in Congress," *Christianity Today*, Feb. 2011.

48. Posner, "Former Employer: Racism and Abuse in Religious Right Organization."

49. Hallet and Heageny, "Can Faith Have a Prayer in Politics?"

50. Ibid.

51. Bill Berkowitz, "Gerson and Colson Urge Religious Right Activists to Stay Involved in Politics," *Buzzflash*, Nov. 4, 2010; Stan, "Overshadowed by the Tea Party Movement."

52. Mark Silk, "The End of the Christian Right," *Religion in the News*, Winter 2012, vol. 12, no. 3.

53. Williams, Skocpol, and Coggins, "The Tea Party and the Remaking of Republican Conservatism."

54. Lisa Miller, "Obama and Big Government vs. 'God's America,'" *Newsweek*, Dec. 9, 2010.

55. Williams, Skocpol, and Coggins, "The Tea Party and the Remaking of Republican Conservatism"; Montopoli, "Tea Party Supporters: Who They Are and What They Believe." According to the CBS/*New York Times* poll, 88 percent of Tea Party supporters disapproved of Obama's performance, but when asked what they didn't like about Obama, a plurality of 19 percent said they just didn't like him. Sixty-four percent said Obama had increased taxes for most Americans, when in fact the vast majority of Americans had gotten a tax cut under the Obama administration. See also John Blake, "Evangelical Leaders Take on Beck for Assailing Social Justice Churches," CNN.com, May 12, 2010. Jerry Falwell Jr. said that the pastors who preach social justice are "trying to twist the gospel to say the gospel supported socialism."

56. Adelle M. Banks, "Glenn Beck Leads but Will Evangelicals Follow?," Religion News Service, *Salt Lake City Tribune*, Aug. 31, 2010; Robert Marus, "Conservatives, Moderate Baptist Thinkers Criticize Glenn Beck's Rally," Associated Baptist Press, September 1, 2010.

57. Robert Parnham, "Glenn Beck's Generic God," *On Faith* blog, Aug. 31, 2010.

58. Marus, "Conservatives, Moderate Baptist Thinkers Criticize Glenn Beck's Rally."

59. Ibid.

60. Williams, Skocpol, and Coggins, "The Tea Party and the Remaking of Republican Conservatism."

61. Pally, pp. 192–94.

62. Michelle Goldberg, "Dodging Bombs for Peace," *Salon*, April 24, 2003.

63. Tom Strobe, "Land: Quality of Life Would Suffer Under Bill," *Baptist Press*, Aug. 7, 2009.

64. Pew Forum, "Religious Groups Weigh In on Health Care," Oct. 1, 2009; Northland press release, Aug. 19, 2009.

65. Pew Forum, "Religious Groups Weigh In on Health Care."

66. Robert Marus, "Healing the Sick: Religious Groups Fighting to Prevent Reform Debacle," Associated Baptist Press, Sept. 21, 2009.

67. Jeff Bromley, "Health Care Debate Splits Religious Audience," Jacksonville.com, Aug. 31, 2009; Bob Allen, "Evangelical Leaders Support Abortion Compromise," Associated Baptist Press, Dec. 18, 2009. The Hyde amendment of 1976 had banned the federal government from paying for abortions except for those caused by rape or incest and those that affected the health of the mother. Both sides wanted to see the Hyde amendment respected, and the argument was about "elective" abortions. However, because of competing economic interests, Obama's health care plan was something of a Rube Goldberg machine in which states and insurance companies played various roles, and federal government funds could be used to subsidize individual health care plans.

68. Mark Tooley, "An Unholy Compromise: Evangelical Leaders and Catholics Who Backed Abortion Funding in Obamacare," Juicy Ecumenism, Institute on Religion and Democracy blog.

69. Julia Duin, "Faithful Find Divine Debate on Health Care Bill," *Washington Times*, Dec. 24, 2009; "NAE Opposes Federal Funding of Abortion," letter/statement, NAE, Dec. 22, 2009.

70. Alicia Cohen, "Obama Administration Pulls Faith Leaders on Health Care Bill," *Christianity Today*, Jan. 28, 2011.

71. Joel Hunter, "Uninsured Deserve Lawmakers' Compassion," *Orlando Sentinel*, June 12, 2015.

72. Michelle A. Vu, "Evangelicals Disagree on Climate Change Bill," *Christian Post*, May 14, 2009.

73. "Interview: NAE President Leith Anderson on Richard Cizik's Resignation," *Christianity Today*, Dec. 11, 2008.

74. Ibid.

75. Sarah Pulliam, "What Cizik's Resignation Means for Creation Care," *Christianity Today*, 2008.

76. It was one of the NAE's three priorities in 2009, nae.net/lovingtheleastofthese/.

77. Lauren Kearns, "Green Evangelicals," in Steensland and Goff, *The New Evangelical Social Engagement*, pp. 167–69.

78. Strode, "Land: Quality of Life Would Suffer." In the fall of 2010 the Cornwall Alliance released "Resisting the Green Dragon," a set of twelve thirty-minute DVDs, aimed at younger evangelicals with introductions and commentary by Tony Perkins, Janet Parshall, and others. In a quasi-conspiratorial fashion, it linked environmentalism—the Green Dragon—to socialism, to global governance, and to population control. Kearns, "Green Evangelicals," p. 168; Green Dragon website.

79. Alexander Bolton, "Democrats Put Faith in Religious Right to Help Boost Party Agenda," *The Hill*, May 17, 2010.

80. Carl Hulse and Adam Nagourney, "McConnell Shuns Bipartisanship," *New York Times*, March 16, 2010.

81. Jennifer Riley, "Survey: Evangelicals Greener but Still Skeptical," *Christian Post*, Sept. 23, 2008; David Roach, "Poll: Pastors Skeptical of Global Warming," *Baptist Press*, April 18, 2011.

82. Molly Redden, "Whatever Happened to the Evangelical-Environmental Alliance?," *New Republic*, Nov. 3, 2011.

83. Adelle M. Banks, "Evangelicals Find New Unity on Immigration," Religion News Service, *Christianity Today*, May 13, 2010.

84. Ibid.; Laurie Goodstein, "Evangelicals Are Joining Obama on Immigration Overhaul," *New York Times*, July 18, 2010.

85. Goodstein, "Evangelicals Are Joining Obama on Immigration Overhaul."

86. Alexander Zaitchik, "Who Would Jesus Deport?," *SPLC Intelligence Report*, Jan. 28, 2007.

87. Tobin Grant, "Strange Bedfellows on Immigration, Cocaine and Campaign Finance," *Christianity Today*, July 2010.

88. Ibid.

89. Goodstein, "Evangelicals Are Joining Obama on Immigration Overhaul."

90. Grant, "Strange Bedfellows on Immigration, Cocaine and Campaign Finance."

91. Zaitchik, "Who Would Jesus Deport?"

92. Ibid.

93. Banks, "Evangelicals Find New Unity on Immigration." In 2015 a Pew study showed that 25 percent of Assemblies of God members were Latinos. Joel Osteen, who rarely took a policy position, came out for immigration reform. His Houston congregation included numerous Hispanics. Neela Banerjee, "New Coalition of Christians Seeks Changes at the Borders," *New York Times*, May 8, 2007.

94. Jeannine Hunter, "Why Evangelicals Are Supporting Immigration Reform," *Washington Post*, June 25, 2012.

95. Michael Lipka, "The Most and Least Racially Diverse US Religious Groups," Pew Research Center, July 27, 2015. An analysis based on the 2014 Pew Religious Landscape Survey found that 6 percent of SBC members were African American and 3 percent Latino. The SBC's own study suggested there were many more. The LifeWay study of 2011 showed that 20 percent of SBC congregations, or 10,000 of 46,000 congregations, were non-Anglo. Most were African American, but there had been a 63 percent increase in Hispanic congregations and a 55 percent increase in Asian congregations from 1998 to 2011. Tobin Perry, "Ethnic Congregations Up 66% Since '98," *Baptist Press*, Jan. 23, 2013.

96. Goodstein, "Evangelicals Are Joining Obama on Immigration Overhaul."

97. "Few Say Religion Shapes Immigration, Environmental Views," Pew Forum on Religion and Public Life, Sept. 17, 2010. Only 10 percent of the Tea Party favored a path to citizenship for the undocumented. Pew survey, Feb. 23, 2011.

98. Mark Tooley, "Evangelicals and Immigration," *American Spectator*, Oct. 21, 2009.

99. Sarah Pulliam, "Solution Stalemate on Immigration," *Christianity Today*, June 4, 2007.

100. Sarah Kramer, "What Happened in 2010? Immigration," WNYC, Dec. 20, 2010.

101. Tobin Grant, "Polling: Evangelicals Cut Aid to the World's Poor, Unemployed," *Christianity Today*, Feb. 22, 2011; Tobin Grant, "Polling: Evangelicals Fix Deficits with Spending Cuts, Tax Increases," *Christianity Today*, Feb. 21, 2011.

102. "Circle of Protection," *Insight Magazine*, NAE, Spring 2011; NAE, "Lowering the Debt, Raising the Poor," resolution, May 21, 2011.

103. "Circle of Protection," *Insight Magazine*.

104. Grant, "Polling: Evangelicals Cut Aid to the World's Poor, Unemployed."

105. Peter Wallerstein, "Ads by Christian Groups Pressure Lawmakers to Protect the Poor in Debt Talks," *Washington Post*, July 26, 2011; Circle of Protection website.

106. Circle of Protection website.

107. Evangelical Immigration Table website, 2015.

108. Ibid.; Trip Gabriel, "Evangelical Groups Call for New Stance on Illegal Immigration," *New York Times*, June 12, 2012.

109. Napp Nazworth, "Evangelical Ads Changed Attitudes on Immigration, Study Finds," *Christian Post*, Sept. 5, 2014.

110. James A. Smith, "Mormonism's 'False Gospel' Does Not Bar Evangelical Votes for Mormon Candidates, Mohler Says," *Florida Baptist Witness*, Oct. 9, 2012.

111. Steve Holland, "Evangelical Leader Billy Graham Offers to Help Romney," *Chicago Tribune*, Oct. 11, 2012; Mary Wisniewski, "Election Blurring of Church-State Separation Draws Complaints," *Chicago Tribune*, Nov. 12, 2012.

112. Wisniewski, "Election Blurring of Church-State Separation Draws Complaints."

113. "Religious Right's Ralph Reed Field-Tests Plans for Beating Obama," *Alternet*, July 10, 2012.

114. Phyllis Schlafly, "Republican Platform Best Yet," *Washington Times*, Aug. 27, 2012.

115. Peter Montgomery, "Six Right-Wing Zealots and the Crazy Ideas Behind the Most Outrageous Republican Platform Ever," *Alternet*, Aug. 28, 2012. Text of platform: www.gop.com/2012-republican-platform_home.

116. "2012 Exit Polls: How the Faithful Voted," Pew Research Center, Forum on Religion and Public life, Nov. 8, 2012.

117. Bob Semintana, "Christian Right Falls from Mainstream," *Tennessean*, Nov. 28, 2012; "After Obama's Election, Religious Right Demands Repentance and Resistance," *Right Wing Watch*, PFAW, Nov. 8, 2012; Cheryl Wetzstein, "Values Activists Concede 'Bruising,'" *Washington Times*, Nov. 8, 2012.

118. "Don Wildmon Says America Chose Chaos by Electing Obama," *Right Wing Watch*, PFAW, Nov. 13, 2012; Kyle Mantyla, "Hagee: God Will Hold America Responsible for Reelecting Obama," *Right Wing Watch*, PFAW, Nov. 14, 2012; D. Becksma, "Religious Right Activists Urge Civil Disobedience in Wake of the Election," *God Discussion*, Nov. 9, 2012.

119. Rick Holmes, "Rejecting the Religious Right," Nov. 11, 2012, blogs.wickedlocal.com/holmesandco/2012/11/rejecting-the-religious-right/#axzz4LxPfgl5v.

120. "Growing Support for Same-Sex Marriage," Pew Research Center, Forum on Religion and Public Life, Feb. 7, 2012.

121. "Survey: A Shifting Landscape: A Decade of Change in American Attitudes About Same-Sex Marriage and LGBT Issues," Public Religion Research Institute, Feb. 26, 2014.

122. Fred Clark, "Religious Right Splits: Hucksters Say Double-Down: True Believers Want to Try Something New," *Patheos*, Nov. 24, 2012.

123. Michelangelo Signorile, "Commentary: 5 Reasons Why the Religious Right Is Warning of a Revolution," *San Diego Gay and Lesbian News*, Nov. 14, 2012.

124. "Nones on the Rise," Pew Research Center, Forum on Religion and Public Life, Oct. 9, 2012; "Social and Political Views of the Unaffiliated," Pew Research Center, Oct. 9, 2012.

125. Semintana, "Christian Right Falls from the Mainstream."

126. "Exit Poll Analysis on the 2012 Election," Pew Research Center, Nov. 7, 2012.

127. Clark, "Religious Right Splits"; "How the Faithful Voted: Preliminary Analysis," Pew Research Center, Nov. 7 2012.

128. Signorile, "Commentary: 5 Reasons Why the Religious Right Is Warning of a Revolution." Even Tony Perkins saw the need to connect with a larger demographic group and called "values issues" a bridge to Hispanics, Asians, and other nonwhite groups. Wetzstein, "Values Activists Concede 'Bruising.'"

129. Sara Gates, "Latino Evangelical Voters Join Forces with Catholics, Finding Common Ground on Health Care," *Huffington Post*, Aug. 24, 2012; "Latino Voters in the 2012 Election," Pew Hispanic Center, Nov. 7, 2012. Hispanics mirrored the rest of the population on marriage equality and abortion rights. Signorile, "Commentary: 5 Reasons Why the Religious Right Is Warning of a Revolution." Catholics made up 59 percent of the Latino electorate in 2012, but some Latinos had left the Catholic Church, and many became evangelicals, but unlike in Latin America, many become unaffiliated. "Former Hispanic Catholics in US Make Different Religious Choices than Latin American Counterparts," Pew Research Center, Nov. 24, 2014. By 2014, 55 percent of Latinos in the U.S. were Catholics, 18 percent were unaffiliated, 16 percent were evangelicals, and 5 percent mainline Protestants. "The Shifting Religious Identity of Latinos in the US," Pew Research Center, Fact Tank, May 7, 2014. Still, some of the historically white U.S. Pentecostal denominations thrived because of them. In 2015 the Assemblies of God was 25 percent Latino, and the Church of God (Cleveland,

Tennessee) 28 percent Latino. Michael Lipka, "The Country's Most and Least Religiously Diverse Groups," Pew Research Center, Fact Tank, July 27, 2015.

130. "Latino Voters in the 2012 Election," Pew Hispanic Center, Nov. 7, 2012; "Survey: 2012 Post-Election American Values Survey and 2012 Ohio Values Survey," Public Religion Research Institute, Nov. 15, 2012.

131. Barbara Bradley Haggerty, "For Religious Conservatives Election Was a Disaster," NPR, Nov. 8, 2012.

132. Ibid.

133. Robert Jeffress, "A GOP Compromise Needed Between Evangelicals and Moderates," *Dallas Morning News*, Nov. 21, 2012.

134. Pew Research Center, "Religion Among the Millennials," Feb. 18, 2010, p. 93.

135. Ibid.

136. Will Hall, "What Do the Numbers Mean? Is the Southern Baptist Convention in Decline?," *Baptist Press*, July 5, 2009.

137. Ed Stoddard, "Southern Baptists (and Republicans) Old, White and in Decline," FaithWorld (blog archive), Reuters, June 25, 2009.

138. Hall, "What Do the Numbers Mean?"

139. Text of resolution, SBC website.

140. Hall, "What Do the Numbers Mean?" The Catholic Church was 34 percent Latino. "Here Are the Country's Most and Least Racially Diverse Religious Groups," Michael Lipka of the PEW Research Center, July 27, 2015.

141. Rob Phillips, "Southern Baptist Convention Faces Further Decline Without Renewed Evangelism Emphasis," LifeWay Research, 2009.

142. Emma Green, "Baptists, Just Without Baptisms," *Atlantic*, May 14, 2014.

143. Libby Lovelace, "LifeWay Research Finds the New Church View of Young Adults." LifeWay Research, Dec. 5, 2006.

144. Bob Allen, "SBC Leader Cites Calvinism as Top Challenge," Associated Baptist Press, Oct. 19, 2011; Adelle M. Banks, "Southern Baptists Meet as Membership Decline Continues," Religion News Service, June 4, 2014. Twenty-nine percent of SBC seminary graduates were Calvinists in large part because of the influence of Al Mohler.

145. See Bill Leonard's *God's Last and Only Hope*.

146. Amy Sullivan, "Richard Land Goes Out on the Bottom," *New Republic*, Aug. 7, 2012.

147. Ibid.

148. Alex Koppleman, "Christian Right Leader Sorry for Comparing Emmanuel to Mengele," *Salon*, Oct. 18, 2009.

149. Ibid.

150. Art Toalson, "SBC's Richard Land Endorses Romney," *Baptist Press*, Oct. 26, 2012.

151. Rev. Mark Woods, "Is Southern Baptist Convention in Terminal Decline?," *Christianity Today*, June 11, 2015.

152. Adelle M. Banks, "Why Is the Southern Baptist Convention Cutting Hundreds of Jobs?," *Huffington Post*, Aug. 27, 2015. From 2009 on the International Missions Board had a shortfall every year that amounted to $210 million by 2015.

153. "Evangelicals' New Chief Says Days of Moral Majority Are Over," WUNC/NPR, "Tell Me More," Aug. 30, 2013.

154. Ed Kilgore, "Russell Moore Has Prophetic Moment," *Washington Monthly*, Dec. 4, 2014.

155. Nicola Menzie, "Often White Christians Assume That Normal Christianity Is White, Southern Baptist Leader Russell Moore Says," *Christian Post*, May 24, 2015.

156. Sarah Pulliam Bailey, "How a Southern Baptist Leader Became Surprising Voice on Confederate Flag," *Washington Post*, June 24, 2015.

157. Emma Green, "Russell Moore and the ERLC Push for Racial Reconciliation in the Southern Baptist Convention," *Atlantic*, April 7, 2015; Tom Stode, "Prison Reform Bill Draws ERLC Support," *Baptist Press*, June 5, 2015.

158. "Evangelicals' New Chief Says Days of Moral Majority Are Over"; WUNC/NPR; Russell Moore, "Young Evangelicals Reject Christian Right but Not Moving Left, Prefer to Be Freakish," *Christian Post*, May 29, 2014.

159. "Is Christianity Dying?," *Moore to the Point* blog, June 12, 2013; Bob Allen, "2013 in Baptist News," *Baptist News*, Dec. 30, 2013. Interview with Dr. Joel Hunter, March 17, 2016.

160. "A Shifting Landscape and a Decade of Change in American Attitudes About Same-Sex Marriage and LGBT Issues."

161. Sarah Pulliam Bailey, "Evangelical Leader, Russell Moore, Denounces 'Ex-Gay Therapy,'" *Huffington Post*, Oct. 29, 2014.

162. Brian Tashman, "Tony Perkins: Stop Saying 'God Bless America' After Gay Marriage Ruling," *Right Wing Watch*, July 10, 2015.

163. Michael F. Haverluck, "Franklin Graham Blasts Obama for 'Gay Marriage' Ruling," *OneNewsNow*, June 29, 2015.

164. Brian Tashman, "James Dobson: Gay Marriage Signals the Fall of Western Civilization," *Right Wing Watch*, May 4, 2015.

165. Laren Markoe, "Righteous or Repugnant: Religious Responses to the Same-Sex Marriage Decision," Religion News Service, June 26, 2015.

166. Sarah Eekhoff Zylstra and Morgan Lee, "'Outrage and Panic' Are Off-Limits, Say Evangelical Leaders on Same-Sex Marriage," *Christianity Today*, June 26, 2015.

167. Ibid.; ERLC, "Here We Stand: An Evangelical Declaration on Marriage," *Christianity Today*, June 26, 2015.

168. "Supreme Court Redefines Marriage," NAE press release, June 26, 2015.

169. ERLC, "Here We Stand."

170. Sarah Pulliam Bailey. "From Franklin Graham to Tony Campolo, Some Evangelicals Are Splitting over Gay Marriage," *Washington Post*, June 9, 2015; Mark A. Kellner, "Evangelical Leaders Debate over Gay Marriage as Supreme Court Decision Nears," *Deseret News*, June 12, 2015. Neff had by then stepped down as editor of *Christianity Today*, and his successor did not endorse gay marriage.

171. Evangelicals for Marriage Equality website, June 26, 2015.

172. "A Statement from Dr. Joel C. Hunter on Today's Supreme Court Decision Regarding Gay Marriage," Northland press release, June 26, 2015.

173. Carol Kuruvilla, "Meet the Evangelicals Who Cheered the SCOTUS Ruling," *Huffington Post*, July 1, 2015.

174. Candace Chellew-Hoge, "Nobody Is Innocent: David Gushee on Sexual Ethics, Suffering and Full Inclusion for LGBT Christians," *Religion Dispatches*, Nov. 17, 2015.

175. Garrett Epps, "What Makes Indiana's Religious-Freedom Law Different?," *Atlantic*, March 30, 2015; David Cole, "The Angry New Frontier: Gay Rights vs. Religious Liberties," *New York Review of Books*, May 7, 2015; Alan Blinder and Campbell Robertson, "Proposed Bills Would Protect Opponents of Gay Rights," *New York Times*, March 3, 2016; Richard Fausett and Alan Blinder, "Bias Laws Deepen Rifts in North Carolina," *New York Times*, April 12, 2016; Jones, *The End of White Christian America*, p. 144.

Epilogue

1. Pew Research Center, "Public's View on Human Evolution," Dec. 30, 2012.

2. Jonathan Merritt, "Trump Reveals the End of the Religious Right's Preeminence," *Atlantic*, Feb. 27, 2016, E. J. Dionne, "Is the GOP Losing Its Religion?," *Washington Post*, June 1, 2016.

3. Russell Moore, "Have Evangelicals Who Supported Trump Lost Their Values?," *New York Times*, Sept. 17, 2015; Steve Benen, "Republican Presidential Race Spells Trouble for Religious Right," MSNBC, May 4, 2016.

4. Jenna Johnson, "Donald Trump on Waterboarding: Torture Works," *Washington Post*, Feb. 17, 2016.

5. Sarah Pulliam Bailey, "Evangelical Leaders Are Frantically Looking for Ways to Defeat

Donald Trump," *Washington Post*, Dec. 10, 2016; YouTube, Aug. 8, 2015; Mark Galli, "Why Donald Trump Threatens to Trump the Gospels," *Christianity Today*, Jan. 27, 2016; "New Southern Baptist Leader on the Issues and the State of the Church," WBUR, Aug. 21, 2013; Russell Moore, "Is Donald Trump Right About Closing the Border to Muslims?," Dec. 7, 2015, www.russellmoore.com/2015/12/07/is-donald-trump-right-about-closing-the-border -to-muslims/; Ruth Graham, "Can America's Largest Denomination Do Anything to Stop Trump?," *Slate*, April 28, 2016; Tom Strode, "Despite Wins Trump Faces Difficult Path," *Baptist Press*, March 16, 2016.

6. Graham, "Can America's Largest Denomination Do Anything to Stop Trump?"; Peter Montgomery, "Donald Trump Is Disrupting Religious Right's Christian-America Dreams," *Huffington Post*, Feb. 25, 2016; Russell Moore, "Have Evangelicals Who Supported Trump Lost Their Values?," *New York Times*, Sept. 17, 2015; Russell Moore, "Trump Is Not the Moral Leader We Need," *National Review*, Jan. 22, 2016; Leah Marieann Klett, "Russell Moore Criticizes 'Evangelical' Leaders Who Endorse Donald Trump," *Gospel Herald*, March 2, 2016.

7. Mugambi Joet, "Why Evangelicals Like Trump," *New Republic*, June 13, 2016; Geoffrey Layman, "Where Is Trump's Evangelical Base? Not in Church," *Washington Post*, March 29, 2016.

8. Pew Religious Landscape Survey 2014; Layman, "Where Is Trump's Evangelical Base? Not in Church."

9. Jeremy W. Peter, "Evangelicals Are Warming to the Idea of Trump," MSNBC, May 15, 2016; Albert Mohler briefing, Feb. 29, 2016; David Lane, "This Would Guarantee a Hillary Clinton Presidency," *Charisma*, March 29, 2016; Samuel Smith, "Christians Should Vote Third Party Rather than the Lesser of Two Evils," *Christian Post*, March 4, 2016.

10. Jonathan Merritt, "Why Do Evangelicals Support Donald Trump?," *Atlantic*, Sept. 3, 2015; Steve Benen, "Trump Victory Spells Trouble for the Christian Right," MSNBC, March 4, 2016.

11. Esme E. Deprez, "Abortion Clinics Are Closing at Record Pace, *Bloomberg News*, Feb. 24, 2016; Erik Eckholm, "Abortion Providers in Texas Sue over Restrictive Rule That Could Close Clinics," *New York Times*, April 2, 2014; Erik Eckholm, "Texas Ruling on Abortion Leads to Call for Clarity," *New York Times*, June 11, 2015; Adam Lipka, "Supreme Court Strikes Down Texas Abortion Restrictions," *New York Times*, June 27, 2016; "A Major Victory for Abortion Rights," editorial, *New York Times*, June 27, 2016; Erik Eckholm, "Anti-Abortion Group Presses Ahead Despite Supreme Court Ruling," *New York Times*, July 10, 2016.

12. Richard Flory, "America Is Changing Fast: 5 Stories to Watch in 2016," *Religion Dispatches*, Dec. 29, 2015.

13. Pew Research Center, "Major New Survey Explores the Shifting Religious Identification of Latinos in America," May 7, 2014. Seventy percent of Latino evangelicals identified as or leaned Democratic despite their social conservatism; Eileen Patten, "The Nation's Latino Population Is Defined by Its Youth," Pew Research Center, April 20, 2016; Russell Moore, "A White Church No More," *New York Times*, May 6, 2016; "America's Changing Religious Landscape," Pew Research Center, May 12, 2015.

14. Jonathan Merritt, "The Rise of the Christian Left in America," *Atlantic*, July 25, 2013; Guy Molyneux and Ray Teixeira, "The Generation Gap on Government," Center for American Progress, July 27, 2010; "America's Changing Religious Landscape," Pew Research Center; Patten, "The Nation's Latino Population Is Defined by Its Youth"; Michael Lipka, "Millennials Are Increasing Growth of 'Nones,'" Pew Research Center, May 12, 2015; Robert P. Jones, "Southern Evangelicals Are Dwindling, Taking GOP Edge with Them," *Atlantic*, Oct. 7, 2014.

15. NAE newsletter, May 24, 2016; Jonathan Merritt, "Does Russell Moore Really Represent Southern Baptists?," On Faith and Culture, Religion News Service, Feb. 3, 2016; Julie Zauzmer, "The Southern Baptist Convention Votes to Condemn Confederate Battle Flag," *Washington Post*, June 15, 2016; Sarah McCammon, "Southern Baptists Split with Donald Trump on Refugee Resettlement," NPR, June 16, 2016.

16. NAE, "Reduce the Threat of Nuclear Catastrophe." Leith Anderson signed a statement with the Union of Concerned Scientists calling on Obama to scale back the deployed U.S. strategic weapons by a third, to take the land-based missiles off hair-trigger alert, and to persuade Russia to do the same. The statement was also signed by the National Latino Evangelical Coalition and the U.S. Conference of Catholic Bishops. NAE newsletter, Oct. 20, 2016; Evangelical Environmental Network, "NAE Issues Strong Statement on Creation Care and Climate."

17. Robert P. Jones, "Evangelicals Discover Moral Ambiguity in the Death Penalty," *Atlantic*, Oct. 25, 2015; text of resolution in NAE press release, "NAE Recognizes Different Views on Death Penalty," Oct. 19, 2015.

BIBLIOGRAPHY

Books and Dissertations

Acheson, Dean. *Present at the Creation: My Years in the State Department*. New York: W. W. Norton, 1969.

Adams, Henry. *The Education of Henry Adams: An Autobiography*. Boston: Houghton Mifflin, 1918.

Ahlstrom, Sydney E. *A Religious History of the American People*. 2 vols. Garden City, NY: Doubleday, 1975.

Alexander-Moegerle, Gil. *James Dobson's War on America*. Amherst, NY: Prometheus Books, 1977.

Ammerman, Nancy Tatom. *Baptist Battles: Social Change and Religious Conflict in the Southern Baptist Convention*. New Brunswick, NJ: Rutgers University Press, 1990.

———. *Bible Believers: Fundamentalists in the Modern World*. New Brunswick, NJ: Rutgers University Press, 1987.

Amstutz, Mark. *Evangelicals and Foreign Policy*. New York: Oxford University Press, 2013.

Applebome, Peter. *Dixie Rising: How the South Is Shaping American Values, Politics, and Culture*. New York: Harcourt, 1996.

Balmer, Randall. *Thy Kingdom Come: How the Religious Right Distorts the Faith and Threatens America: An Evangelical's Lament*. New York: Basic Books, 2006.

Barnes, Gilbert Hobbs. *The Antislavery Impulse, 1830–1844*. New York: Harcourt, 1964.

Barton, David. *The Myth of Separation*. Aledo, TX: Wallbuilders Press, 1989.

Beale, David O. *In Pursuit of Purity: American Fundamentalism Since 1850*. Greenville, SC: Unusual Publications, 1986.

Beardsley, Frank Grenville. *A Mighty Winner of Souls*. New York: American Tract Society, 1937.

Black, Earle, and Merle Black. *Divided America: The Ferocious Power Struggle in American Politics*. New York: Simon & Schuster, 2007.

———. *The Rise of Southern Republicanism*. Cambridge: Harvard University Press, 2002.

Blumenthal, Max. *Republican Gomorrah: Inside the Movement That Shattered the Party*. New York: Nation Books, 2009.

Blumhofer, Edith L. *Aimee Semple McPherson: Everybody's Sister*. Grand Rapids, MI: William B. Eerdmans, 1993.

Boston, Robert. *The Most Dangerous Man in America? Pat Robertson and the Rise of the Christian Coalition*. Amherst, NY: Prometheus Books, 1996.

Boyd, Gregory A. *The Myth of a Christian Nation: How the Quest for Political Power Is Destroying the Church*. Grand Rapids, MI: Zondervan, 2005.

Boyer, Paul S. *When Time Shall Be No More: Prophecy Belief in Modern American Culture*. Cambridge: Harvard University Press, 1992.

Bromley, David G., and Anson Shupe, eds. *New Christian Politics*. Macon, GA: Mercer University Press, 1984.

Bruce, Steve. *The Rise and Fall of the New Christian Right*. New York: Oxford Press, 1988.

Bushman, Richard. *From Puritan to Yankee: Character and the Social Order in Connecticut, 1690–1765*. Cambridge: Harvard University Press, 1967.

Buss, Dale. *Family Man: The Biography of Dr. James Dobson.* Carol Stream, IL: Tyndale House Publishers, 2005.

Butler, Farley Porter Jr. "Billy Graham and the End of Evangelical Unity." PhD diss., University of Florida, 1976, https://archive.org/details/billygrahamendofoobutl.

Campbell, David E., ed. *A Matter of Faith: Religion in the 2004 Presidential Election.* Washington, DC: Brookings Institution Press, 2007.

Carpenter, Joel A. *Revive Us Again: The Reawakening of American Fundamentalism.* New York: Oxford University Press, 1997.

Chernus, Ira. *Apocalypse Management: Eisenhower and the Discourse of National Insecurity.* Stanford, CA: Stanford University Press, 2008.

Cole, Charles C. *The Social Ideas of the Northern Evangelists, 1826–1860.* New York: Columbia University Press, 1954.

Cox, Harvey. *Fire from Heaven: The Rise of Pentecostal Spirituality and the Reshaping of Religion in the Twenty-first Century.* Cambridge, MA: Da Capo, 1995.

Cromartie, Michael, ed. *Disciples and Democracy: Religious Conservatives and the Future of American Politics.* Grand Rapids, MI: William B. Eerdmans, 1994.

Cross, Whitney R. *The Burned-over District: The Social and Intellectual History of Enthusiastic Religion in Western New York, 1800–1850.* New York: Harper & Row, 1950.

D'Antonio, Michael. *Fall from Grace: The Failed Crusade of the Christian Right.* New York: Farrar, Straus & Giroux, 1989.

Davis, David Brion. *Antebellum Reform.* New York: Harper & Row, 1967.

Dayton, Donald W. *Theological Roots of Pentecostalism.* Grand Rapids, MI: Francis Asbury Press, 1987.

Diamond, Sara. *Not by Politics Alone.* New York: Guilford Press, 1998.

———. *Roads to Dominion: Right-Wing Movements and Political Power in the United States.* New York: Guilford Press, 1995.

Dobson, Ed, and Edward Hindson. *The Seduction of Power: Preachers, Politics and the Media.* Old Tappan, NJ: Fleming H. Revell, 1988.

Dobson, James. *Dare to Discipline.* Wheaton, IL: Tyndale House Publishers, 1970.

Dobson, James, and Gary L. Bauer. *Children at Risk: What You Need to Know to Protect Your Family.* Dallas: Word Publishing, 1990.

Dochuk, Darren. *From Bible Belt to Sunbelt: Plain Folks Religion, Grassroots Politics, and the Rise of Evangelical Conservatism.* New York: W. W. Norton, 2010.

Dorrien, Gary. *The Making of American Liberal Theology: Imagining Progressive Religion, 1805–1990.* 3 vols. Louisville, KY: Westminster John Knox Press, 2001–2006.

———. *The Remaking of Evangelical Theology.* Louisville, KY: Westminster John Knox Press, 1998.

Ehrenreich, Barbara. *The Hearts of Men: American Dreams and the Flight from Commitment.* New York: Anchor, 1983.

Eighmy, John Lee. *Churches in Cultural Captivity: A History of Social Attitudes of Southern Baptists.* With revised introduction, conclusion, and bibliography by Samuel S. Hill. Knoxville: University of Tennessee Press, 1987.

Enroth, Ronald M., Edward W. Ericson Jr., and C. Breckinridge Peters. *The Jesus People: Oldtime Religion in the Age of Aquarius.* Grand Rapids, MI: William B. Eerdmans, 1972.

Eskelin, Neil. *Pat Robertson: A Biography.* Shreveport: Huntington House, 1987.

Falwell, Jerry. *America Can Be Saved.* Murfreesboro, TN: Sword of the Lord Publishers, 1979.

———. *Capturing a Town for Christ.* Old Tappan, NJ: Fleming H. Revell, 1973.

———. *Falwell: An Autobiography.* Lynchburg, VA: Liberty House Publishers, 1997.

———. *Listen, America!* Garden City, NY: Doubleday, 1980.

———. *Strength for the Journey.* New York: Simon & Schuster, 1987.

Falwell, Jerry, ed., with Ed Dobson and Edward Hindson. *The Fundamentalist Phenomenon: The Resurgence of Conservative Christianity.* Garden City, NY: Doubleday, 1981.

Falwell, Jerry, and Elmer Towns. *Church Aflame.* Nashville: Impact Books, 1971.

Feldman, Glenn, ed. *Politics and Religion in the White South*. Lexington: University Press of Kentucky, 2005.

Findlay, James M. Jr. *Dwight L. Moody: American Evangelist, 1837–1899*. Chicago: University of Chicago Press, 1969.

Finke, Roger, and Rodney Stark. *The Churching of America, 1776–2005: Winners and Losers in Our Religious Economy*. New Brunswick, NJ: Rutgers University Press, 2005.

Finney, Charles G. His collected works, including his *Memoirs* and all of his written sermons, can be found at the Gospel Truth Ministries website (www.gospeltruth) in their original forms with his letters and other materials. The site also contains Fletcher's late-nineteenth-century history of Oberlin College in its original form.

FitzGerald, Frances. *Cities on a Hill: A Journey Through Contemporary American Cultures*. New York: Simon & Schuster, 1986.

———. *Way Out There in the Blue: Reagan, Star Wars and the End of the Cold War*. New York: Simon & Schuster, 2000.

Fletcher, Robert Samuel. *A History of Oberlin College: From Its Foundation Through the Civil War*. New York: Arno Press, 1971. www.gospeltruth.

Frady, Marshall. *Billy Graham: A Parable of American Righteousness*. Boston: Little, Brown, 1979.

Frykholm, Amy Johnson. *Rapture Culture: Left Behind in Evangelical America*. New York: Oxford University Press, 2004.

Gaustad, Edwin Scott. *The Great Awakening in New England*. New York: Harper, 1957.

Gibbs, Nancy, and Michael Duffy. *The Preacher and the Presidents: Billy Graham in the White House*. New York: Center Street, 2007.

Gilgoff, Dan. *The Jesus Machine: How James Dobson, Focus on the Family, and Evangelical America Are Winning the Culture War*. New York: St. Martin's Press, 2007.

Gilley, Gary E. *This Little Church Went to Market: The Church in the Age of Entertainment*. Xulon Press, 2002.

Glass, William R. *Strangers in Zion: Fundamentalists in the South, 1900–1950*. Macon, GA: Mercer University Press, 2001.

Goen, C. C. *Revivalism and Separatism in New England, 1740–1800*. New Haven: Yale University Press, 1962.

Goldberg, Michelle. *Kingdom Coming: The Rise of Christian Nationalism*. New York: W. W. Norton, 2006.

Gorrell, Donald K. *The Age of Social Responsibility: The Social Gospel in the Progressive Era, 1900–1920*. Macon, GA: Mercer University Press, 1988.

Graham, Billy. *Just As I Am: The Autobiography of Billy Graham*. New York: Harper, 1997.

Green, John C., James L. Guth, Corwin E. Smidt, and Lyman A. Kellstedt. *Religion and the Culture Wars: Dispatches from the Front*. Lanham, MD: Rowman & Littlefield, 1996.

Green, John C., Mark J. Rozell, and Clyde Wilcox, eds. *The Christian Right in American Politics: Marching to the Millennium*. Washington, DC: Georgetown University Press, 2003.

———. *Prayers in the Precincts: The Christian Right and the 1998 Election*. Washington, DC: Georgetown University Press, 2000.

———. *The Values Campaign? The Christian Right in the 2004 Elections*. Washington, DC: Georgetown University Press, 2006.

Greenburg, Jan Crawford. *Supreme Conflict: The Inside Story of the Struggle for Control of the United States Supreme Court*. New York: Penguin, 2007.

Guinness, Os. *Dining with the Devil: The Megachurch Movement Flirts with Modernity*. Grand Rapids, MI: Baker Books, 1993.

Guth, James L., and John C. Green, eds. *The Bible and the Ballot Box: Religion and Politics in the 1988 Election*. Boulder, CO: Westview Press, 1991.

Hadden, Jeffrey K. *The Gathering Storm in the Churches*. Garden City, NY: Doubleday, 1969.

Hadden, Jeffrey K., with Anson Shupe. *Televangelism: Power and Politics on God's Frontier*. New York: Henry Holt, 1988.

Hambrick-Stowe, Charles E. *Charles G. Finney and the Spirit of American Evangelism.* Grand Rapids, MI: William B. Eerdmans, 1996.

Hankins, Barry. *American Evangelicals: A Contemporary History of a Mainstream Religious Movement.* Lanham, MD: Rowman & Littlefield, 2008a.

———. *Francis Schaeffer and the Shaping of Evangelical America.* Grand Rapids, MI: William B. Eerdmans, 2008b.

———. *God's Rascal: J. Frank Norris and the Beginnings of Southern Fundamentalism.* Lexington: University Press of Kentucky, 1996.

———. *Uneasy in Babylon: Southern Baptist Conservatives and American Culture.* Tuscaloosa: University of Alabama Press, 2002.

Harding, Susan F. *The Book of Jerry Falwell: Fundamentalist Language and Politics.* Princeton: Princeton University Press, 2000.

Hardman, Keith. *Charles Grandison Finney, 1792–1875: Revivalist and Reformer.* Syracuse: Syracuse University Press, 1988.

Harrell, David Edwin Jr. *Oral Roberts: An American Life.* Bloomington: Indiana University Press, 1985.

———. *Pat Robertson: A Life and Legacy.* Grand Rapids, MI: William B. Eerdmans, 2010.

Hart, D. G. *From Billy Graham to Sarah Palin: Evangelicals and the Betrayal of American Conservatism.* Grand Rapids, MI: William B. Eerdmans, 2011.

Hatch, Nathan O. *The Democratization of American Christianity.* New Haven: Yale University Press, 1989.

Heimert, Alan. *Religion and the American Mind: From the Great Awakening to the Revolution.* Cambridge: Harvard University Press, 1966.

Henry, Carl F. H. *Confessions of a Theologian: An Autobiography.* Waco, TX: Word Books, 1986.

———. *Evangelicals in Search of Identity.* Waco, TX: Word Books, 1976.

———. *The Uneasy Conscience of Modern Fundamentalism.* Grand Rapids, MI: William B. Eerdmans, 1947.

Herberg, Will. *Protestant—Catholic—Jew: An Essay in American Religious Sociology.* Garden City, NY: Doubleday, 1955.

Hill, Samuel S. Jr. *The South and the North in American Religion.* Athens: University of Georgia Press, 1980.

———. *Southern Churches in Crisis.* New York: Holt, Rinehart & Winston, 1967.

Hill, Samuel S. Jr., and Dennis E. Owen. *The New Religious-Political Right in America.* Nashville: Abingdon Press, 1982.

Hindson, Edward E. *The Total Family.* Wheaton, IL: Tyndale House Publishers, 1980.

Hofstadter, Richard. *Anti-Intellectualism in American Life.* New York: Vintage, 1963.

Hopkins, Charles Howard. *The Rise of the Social Gospel in American Protestantism, 1865–1915.* New Haven: Yale University Press, 1940.

Hunt, Stephen, Malcolm Hamilton, and Tony Walter, eds. *Charismatic Christianity: Sociological Perspectives.* New York: St. Martin's Press, 1997.

Hunter, James Davison. *American Evangelicalism: Conservative Religion and the Quandary of Modernity.* New Brunswick, NJ: Rutgers University Press, 1983.

———. *Culture Wars: The Struggle to Define America.* New York: Basic Books, 1991.

———. *Evangelicalism: The Coming Generation.* Chicago: University of Chicago Press, 1987.

———. *To Change the World: The Irony, Tragedy, and Possibility of Christianity in the Late Modern World.* New York: Oxford University Press, 2010.

Hunter, Joel C. *A New Kind of Conservative.* Ventura, CA: Regal, 2008.

———. *Prayer, Politics & Power: What Really Happens When Religion and Politics Mix?* Wheaton, IL: Tyndale House Publishers, 1988.

———. *Right Wing, Wrong Bird: Why the Tactics of the Religious Right Won't Fly with Most Conservative Christians.* Longwood, FL: Church Press, 2006.

Inboden, William. *Religion and American Foreign Policy, 1945–1960.* New York: Cambridge University Press, 2008.

Johnson, Donna M. *Holy Ghost Girl: A Memoir.* New York: Gotham, 2011.

Johnson, Paul E. *A Shopkeeper's Millennium: Society and Revivals in Rochester, New York, 1815–1837.* New York: Hill & Wang, 1978.

Jones, Robert P. *The End of White Christian America.* New York: Simon & Schuster, 2016.

Kaplan, Esther. *With God on Their Side: George W. Bush and the Christian Right.* New York: New Press, 2004.

Kemp, Roy A. *Norris Extravaganza! A Biography of Dr. J. Frank Norris, My Reminisce.* Fort Worth: Calvary Publications, 1975.

Kidd, Thomas S. *The Great Awakening.* New Haven: Yale University Press, 2007.

Kinnaman, David, with Gabe Lyons. *Unchristian: What a New Generation Really Thinks About Christianity.* Grand Rapids, MI: Baker Books, 2007.

Klarman, Michael J. *From the Closet to the Altar: Courts, Backlash, and the Struggle for Same-Sex Marriage.* New York: Oxford University Press, 2013.

Kuo, David. *Tempting Faith: An Inside Story of Political Seduction.* New York: Free Press, 2006.

LaHaye, Tim. *The Battle for the Mind.* Old Tappan, NJ: Fleming H. Revell, 1980.

Land, Richard. *The Divided States of America.* Nashville: Thomas Nelson, 2007.

Larson, Edward L. *Summer for the Gods: The Scopes Trial and America's Debate Over Science and Religion.* New York: Basic Books: 1997.

Laville, Helen, and Hugh Wilford, eds. *The US Government, Citizen Groups, and the Cold War: The State-Private Network.* New York: Routledge, 2006.

Layman, Geoffrey. *The Great Divide: Religious and Cultural Conflict in American Party Politics.* New York: Columbia University Press, 2001.

Leonard, Bill J. *God's Last and Only Hope: The Fragmentation of the Southern Baptist Convention.* East Lansing: University of Michigan Press, 1990.

Levine, Lawrence W. *Defender of the Faith: William Jennings Bryan: The Last Decade, 1915–25.* New York: Oxford University Press, 1965.

Lichtman, Allan J. *White Protestant Nation: The Rise of the American Conservative Movement.* New York: Atlantic Monthly Press, 2007.

Liebman, Robert C., and Robert Wuthnow, eds. *The New Christian Right: Mobilization and Legitimation.* New York: Aldine, 1983.

Lienesch, Michael. *In the Beginning: Fundamentalism, the Scopes Trial, and the Making of the Antievolution Movement.* Chapel Hill: University of North Carolina Press, 2007.

Lindsell, Harold. *The Battle for the Bible.* Grand Rapids, MI: Zondervan, 1976.

———. *The Bible in the Balance.* Grand Rapids, MI: Zondervan, 1979.

Linsey, Hal. *The Late Great Planet Earth.* Grand Rapids, MI: Zondervan, 1970.

Long, Michael G. *Billy Graham and the Beloved Community.* New York: Palgrave Macmillan, 2006.

Longfield, Bradley J. *The Presbyterian Controversy: Fundamentalists, Modernists, and Moderates.* New York: Oxford University Press, 1991.

Mansfield, Stephen. *The Faith of George W. Bush.* New York: Penguin, 2003.

Marsden, George M. *Fundamentalism and American Culture: The Shaping of Twentieth-Century Evangelicalism, 1870–1925.* New York: Oxford University Press, 1980.

———. *Reforming Fundamentalism: Fuller Seminary and the New Evangelicalism.* Grand Rapids, MI: William B. Eerdmans, 1987.

———. *Understanding Fundamentalism and Evangelicalism.* Grand Rapids MI: William B. Eerdmans, 1991.

Marsden, Lee. *For God's Sake: The Christian Right and US Foreign Policy.* London: Zed Books, 2008.

Martin, William. *A Prophet with Honor: The Billy Graham Story.* New York: William Morrow, 1991.

———. *With God on Our Side: The Rise of the Religious Right in America.* New York: Broadway Books, 1996.

Marty, Martin E. *Righteous Empire: The Protestant Experience in America.* New York: Dial, 1970.

Mathews, Donald G. *Religion in the Old South.* Chicago: University of Chicago Press, 1977.

Mathews, Shailer. *New Faith for Old: An Autobiography.* New York: Macmillan, 1936.

McGavran, Donald A. *Understanding Church Growth*. 3rd ed. Grand Rapids, MI: William B. Eerdmans, 1980.

McGirr, Lisa. *Suburban Warriors: The Origins of the New American Right*. Princeton: Princeton University Press, 2001.

McLaren, Brian D. *A Generous Orthodoxy*. Grand Rapids, MI: Zondervan, 2004.

McLoughlin, William G. Jr. *Billy Graham: Revivalist in a Secular Age*. New York: Ronald Press, 1960.

———. *Modern Revivalism: Charles Grandison Finney to Billy Graham*. New York: Ronald Press, 1959.

———. *Revivals, Awakenings, and Reform: An Essay on Religion and Social Change in America*. Chicago: University of Chicago Press, 1978.

Miller, Perry. *The Life of the Mind in America: From the Revolution to the Civil War*. New York: Harcourt, Brace & World, 1965.

Miller, Stephen P. *The Age of Evangelicalism: America's Born-Again Years*. New York: Oxford University Press, 2014.

Millerman, Alan, Byron J. Johnson, and Nancy Issman, eds. *Uneasy Allies? Evangelical and Jewish Relations*. Lanham, MD: Lexington Books, 2007.

Mohler, R. Albert Jr. *Culture Shift: Engaging Current Issues with Timeless Truth*. Colorado Springs: Multnomah Books, 2008.

Moore, R. Laurence. *Religious Outsiders and the Making of Americans*. New York: Oxford University Press, 1986.

Moore, Roy, with John Perry. *So Help Me God: The Ten Commandments, Judicial Tyranny, and the Battle for Religious Freedom*. Los Angeles: WND Books, 2005.

Morison, Samuel Eliot. *The Oxford History of the American People*. New York: Oxford University Press, 1965.

Morison, Samuel Eliot, Henry Steele Commager, and William E. Leuchtenburg. *The Growth of the American Republic*. Vol. 2, 6th ed. New York: Oxford University Press, 1969.

Nathan, Rich. *Who Is My Enemy? Welcoming People the Church Rejects*. Grand Rapids, MI: Zondervan, 2002.

Nelkin, Dorothy. *The Creation Controversy: Science or Scripture in the Schools*. New York: W. W. Norton: 1982.

Nelson, Rudolph. *The Making and Unmaking of an Evangelical Mind: The Case of Edward Carnell*. New York: Cambridge University Press, 1987.

Nelson, Shirley. *The Last Year of the War*. New York: Harper & Row, 1978.

Noll, Mark A. *The Rise of Evangelicalism: The Age of Edwards, Whitefield and the Wesleys*. Downer's Grove, IL: InterVarsity Press, 2003.

———. *The Scandal of the Evangelical Mind*. Grand Rapids, MI: William B. Eerdmans, 1994.

———, ed. *The Princeton Theology, 1812–1921*. Grand Rapids, MI: Baker Book House, 1983.

Noll, Mark A., Nathan O. Hatch, and George M. Marsden. *The Search for Christian America*. Westchester, IL: Crossway Books, 1983.

Pagels, Elaine. *Adam and Eve and the Serpent*. New York: Random House, 1988, 1989.

Pally, Marcia. *The New Evangelicals: Expanding the Vision of the Common Good*. Grand Rapids, MI: William B. Eerdmans, 2011.

Patterson, Eric, and Edmund Rybarczyk, eds. *The Future of Pentecostalism in the United States*. Lanham, MD: Rowman & Littlefield, 2007.

Phillips, Kevin. *American Theocracy: The Peril and Politics of Radical Religion, Oil, and Borrowed Money in the 21st Century*. New York: Viking, 2006.

Pinsky, Mark I. *A Jew Among Evangelicals: A Guide for the Perplexed*. Louisville, KY: Westminster John Knox Press, 2006.

Pollock, J. C. *Moody: A Biographical Portrait of a Pacesetter in Modern Mass Evangelism*. Grand Rapids, MI: Zondervan, 1972.

Pollock, John. *Billy Graham: The Authorized Biography*. New York: McGraw-Hill, 1966.

Poloma, Margaret M. *The Assemblies of God at the Crossroads: Charisma and Institutional Dilemmas*. Knoxville: University of Tennessee Press, 1989.

———. *The Charismatic Movement: Is There a New Pentecost?* Boston: G. K. Hall, 1982.

———. *Main Street Mystics: The Toronto Blessing and Reviving Pentecostalism.* Walnut Creek, CA: Altamira Press, 2003.

Pritchard, G. A. *Willow Creek Seeker Services: Evaluating a New Way of Doing Church.* Grand Rapids, MI: Baker Books, 1996.

Putnam, Robert D., and David E. Campbell. *American Grace: How Religion Unites and Divides.* New York: Simon & Schuster, 2010.

Quebedeaux, Richard. *The Young Evangelicals: Revolution in Orthodoxy.* New York: Harper & Row, 1974.

Ribuffo, Leo. *The Old Christian Right: The Protestant Far Right from the Great Depression to the Cold War.* Philadelphia: Temple University Press, 1983.

Robertson, Pat. *The New World Order.* Dallas: Word Publishing, 1991.

Robertson, Pat, with Bob Slosser. *The Secret Kingdom: A Promise of Hope and Freedom in a World of Turmoil.* Nashville: Thomas Nelson, 1982.

Robins, R. G. *Pentecostalism in America.* Santa Barbara, CA: Praeger, 2010.

Roof, Wade Clark, and William McKinney. *American Mainline Religion: Its Changing Shape and Its Future.* New Brunswick, NJ: Rutgers University Press, 1987.

Roose, Kevin. *The Unlikely Disciple: A Sinner's Semester at America's Holiest University.* New York: Grand Central Publishing, 2009.

Rosin, Hanna. *God's Harvard: A Christian College on a Mission to Save America.* Orlando, FL: Harcourt, 2007.

Rozell, Mark J., and Gleaves Whitney, eds. *Religion and the Bush Presidency.* New York: Palgrave Macmillan, 2007.

Rozell, Mark J., and Clyde Wilcox, eds. *God at the Grass Roots, 1996: The Christian Right in the 1996 Elections.* Lanham, MD: Rowman & Littlefield, 1997.

Ryan, Mary P. *Cradle of the Middle Class: The Family in Oneida County, 1790–1865.* New York: Cambridge University Press, 1981.

Sandeen, Ernest R. *The Roots of Fundamentalism: British and American Millenarianism, 1800–1930.* Chicago: University of Chicago Press, 1970.

Schaeffer, Francis A. *The Complete Works of Francis Schaeffer: A Christian World View. Volume 5: A Christian View of the West.* Wheaton, IL: Crossway Books, 1982.

Schaeffer, Frank. *Crazy for God.* New York: Carroll & Graf, 2007.

Schäffer, Axel R. *Piety and Public Funding: Evangelicals and the State in Modern America.* Philadelphia: University of Pennsylvania Press, 2012.

Schaller, Thomas F. *Whistling Past Dixie: How Democrats Can Win Without the South.* New York: Simon & Schuster, 2006.

Sehat, David. *The Myth of American Religious Freedom.* New York: Oxford University Press, 2011.

Settje, David. E. *Faith and War: How Christians Debated the Cold and Vietnam Wars.* Google books online.

Sheler, Jeffrey L. *Prophet of Purpose: The Life of Rick Warren.* New York: Doubleday, 2009.

Shepard, Charles E. *Forgiven: The Rise and Fall of Jim Bakker and the PTL Ministry.* New York: Atlantic Monthly Press, 1989.

Shibley, Mark A. *Resurgent Evangelicalism in the United States: Mapping Cultural Change Since 1970.* Columbia: University of South Carolina Press, 1996.

Sider, Ronald J. *Rich Christians in an Age of Hunger.* 4th ed. Dallas: Word Publishing, 1997.

Sider, Ronald J., and Diane Knippers, eds. *Toward an Evangelical Public Policy: Political Strategies for the Health of a Nation.* Grand Rapids, MI: Baker Books, 2005.

Silk, Mark. *Spiritual Politics: Religion and America Since World War II.* New York: Simon & Schuster, 1988.

Smidt, Corwin E. *American Evangelicals Today.* Lanham, MD: Rowman & Littlefield, 2013.

Smidt, Corwin E., Kevin R. den Dulk, Bryan T. Froehle, James M. Penning, Stephen V. Mosma, and Douglas L. Koopman. *The Disappearing God Gap? Religion in the 2008 Presidential Election.* New York: Oxford University Press, 2010.

Smith, Gary Scott. *Faith and the Presidency: From George Washington to George Bush.* New York: Oxford University Press, 2006.

Smith, Timothy L. *Revivalism and Social Reform: American Protestantism on the Eve of the Civil War.* Baltimore: Johns Hopkins University Press, 1980.

Spector, Stephen. *Evangelicals and Israel: The Story of American Christian Zionism.* New York: Oxford University Press, 2009.

Steensland, Brian, and Philip Goff, eds. *The New Evangelical Social Engagement.* New York: Oxford University Press, 2014.

Strober, Gerald, and Ruth Tomczak. *Jerry Falwell: Aflame for God.* New York: Thomas Nelson, 1979.

Swartz, David R. "Left Behind: The Evangelical Left and the Limits of Evangelical Politics, 1965–1988." PhD diss., Department of Philosophy, Notre Dame University, 2008.

Synan, Vinson. *The Holiness-Pentecostal Movement in the United States.* Grand Rapids, MI: William B. Eerdmans, 1971.

———. *In the Latter Days: The Outpouring of the Holy Spirit in the Twentieth Century.* Ann Arbor, MI: Servant Books, 1984.

———. *The Twentieth-Century Pentecostal Explosion: The Exciting Growth of Pentecostal Churches and Charismatic Renewal Movements.* Altamonte Springs, FL: Creation House, 1987.

Szasz, Frederick Morton. *The Divided Mind of American Protestantism, 1880–1930.* Tuscaloosa: University of Alabama Press, 1982.

Thomas, Benjamin Platt. *Theodore Weld: Crusader for Freedom.* New Brunswick, NJ: Rutgers University Press, 1950.

Tilton, Robert. *God's Laws of Success.* Tulsa: Harrison House, 1983.

Titus, Herbert W. *God, Man, and Law: The Biblical Principles.* Oak Brook, IL: Institute in Basic Life Principles, 1994, www.lonang.com.

Trollinger, William Vance Jr. *God's Empire: William Bell Riley and Midwestern Fundamentalism.* Madison: University of Wisconsin Press, 1990.

Turner, John G. *Bill Bright and Campus Crusade for Christ: The Renewal of Evangelicalism in Postwar America.* Chapel Hill: University of North Carolina Press, 2008.

Walker, J. Brent. *Church-State Matters: Fighting for Religious Liberty in Our Nation's Capital.* Macon, GA: Mercer University Press, 2008.

Wallis, Jim. *God's Politics: Why the Right Gets It Wrong and the Left Doesn't Get It.* New York: Harper Collins, 2005.

Warren, Rick. *The Purpose Driven Church: Growth Without Compromising Your Message or Your Mission.* Grand Rapids, MI: Zondervan, 1995.

Warren, Rick, *The Purpose Driven Life.* Grand Rapids, MI: Zondervan, 2002.

Watson, Justin. *The Christian Coalition: Dreams of Restoration, Demands for Recognition.* New York: St. Martin's Press, 1977.

Weber, Timothy P. *Living in the Shadow of the Second Coming: American Premillennialism, 1875–1982.* Grand Rapids, MI: Zondervan, 1983.

Wilcox, Clyde, and Carin Robinson. *Onward Christian Soldiers? The Religious Right in American Politics.* Boulder, CO: Westview Press, 2010.

Williams, Daniel K. *God's Own Party: The Making of the Christian Right.* New York: Oxford University Press, 2010.

Wills, Garry. *Under God: Religion and American Politics.* New York: Simon & Schuster, 1990.

Wilson, Charles Reagan. *Baptized in Blood: The Religion of the Lost Cause, 1865–1920.* Athens: University of Georgia Press, 1980.

Winters, Michael Sean. *God's Right Hand: How Jerry Falwell Made God a Republican and Baptized the American Right.* New York: HarperCollins, 2012.

Wright, Lawrence. *Saints and Sinners.* New York: Alfred A. Knopf, 1993.

Wuthnow, Robert. *After the Baby Boomers: How Twenty- and Thirty-Somethings Are Shaping the Future of American Religion.* Princeton: Princeton University Press, 2007.

———. *The Restructuring of American Religion: Society and Faith Since World War II.* Princeton: Princeton University Press, 1988.

Articles, Papers, Websites, Government Documents

Boyer, Paul S. "When US Foreign Policy Meets Biblical Prophecy," *Alternet*, Feb. 19, 2003. www .alternet.org/story/15221/when_u.s._foreign_policy_meets_biblical_prophecy.

British Center for Science Education (BCSE). "In Extremis—Rousas Rushdoony and His Connections." www.bcseweb.org.uk/index.php/Main/RousasRushdoony.

Carlson, Allan C. "Paving the Way for Title X: How Protestants Swallowed the Pill and Evangelicals 'Out-Libertined' the Mainline." In *The Family in America: A Journal of Public Policy*. www .familyinamerica.org/files/FIA_fall10.Carlson.pdf.

Chernus, Ira. "Eisenhower: Faith and Fear in the Fifties." http://spot.colorado.edu/~chernus/ Research/EFaithAndFear.htm.

Cizik, Richard. "A History of the Public Policy Resolutions of the National Association of Evangelicals." www.ibrarian.net.

———. Paper for Yale Conference on Climate Change: Science to Action, Aspen, CO, Oct. 6–8, 2005.

Clarkson, Frederick. "Theocratic Dominionism Gains Influence." Four-part series, PublicEye.org archives, Political Research Associates.

Durant, Gregg Loren. "Judicial Warfare: The Christian Reconstruction Movement and Its Blueprint for Dominion." Yuricareport.com/Dominionism/HistoryofReconstructionmovement.html.

Edgar, William. "The Passing of R. J. Rushdoony." *First Things*, Aug./Sept. 2001.

FitzGerald, Frances. "Come One, Come All." *New Yorker*, Dec. 3, 2007.

———. "Holy Toledo." *New Yorker*, July 31, 2006.

———. "The New Evangelicals." *New Yorker*, June 30, 2008.

———. "Reflections: Jim and Tammy." *New Yorker*, April 23, 1990.

Griffith, Bobby G. Jr. "Protesting the Struggle: Carl McIntire and the Civil Rights Movement 1954–1964." https://wonderboystudios.com/download-protesting-the-struggle-carl-mcintyre -and-the-civil-rights.pdf.

Harding, Susan. "The Born-Again Telescandals." Institute for Advanced Study, University of Michigan, April 1989 (draft).

McVicar, Michael. "The Libertarian Theocrats: The Long and Strange History of R. J. Rushdoony and Christian Reconstructionism." Part of PhD diss., Department of Comparative Studies, Ohio State University, PublicEye.org archives, Political Research Association website.

Moore, Russell D. "The Gospel According to Jane Roe: Abortion Rights and the Reshaping of Evangelical Theology." *Southern Baptist Journal of Theology*, Summer 2003.

Neuhaus, Richard John. "Why Wait for the Kingdom? The Theonomist Temptation." *First Things*, May 1990.

North, Gary. "The Bible Mandates Free Capitalism." *Specific Answers*, blog, Jan. 5, 2005.

———. Blog. Garynorth.com.

———. "The Eschatalogical Crisis of the Moral Majority." *Christian Reconstructionism*, vol. 4, no. 3 (Jan./Feb. 1981).

———. "It Usually Begins with Ayn Rand." Dec. 16, 2002, LewRockwell.com.

———. "A Letter to Charismatics." *Christian Reconstructionism*, vol. 9, no. 4 (July/Aug. 1985).

———. *Political Polytheism: The Myth of Pluralism.* garynorth.com/freebooks/docs/pdf /political_polytheism.pdf.

———. "Rushdoony RIP." Feb. 10, 2001, LewRockwell.com.

———. "The Three Legs of Christian Reconstruction's Stool." *Christian Reconstructionism*, vol. 8, no. 1 (Jan./Feb. 1984), Free Books from the Christian Institute of Economics.

Olson, Walter. "Invitation to a Stoning." Reason.com, Nov. 1998.

Public Papers of the Presidents. www.archives.gov/federal-register/publications/presidential -papers.html.

Rushdoony, Mark R. "The Vision of R. J. Rushdoony." Sept. 16, 2007, Chalcedon Foundation. chalcedon.edu.

Rushdoony, R. J. "On Earth as It Is in Heaven," interview with Bill Moyers, Dec. 23, 1987.

Rutherford, Samuel. "A Free Disputation Against Pretended Liberty of Conscience." *Reformed Perspectives*, vol. 9, no. 10 (March 4–10, 2007), thirdmill.org.

Schäffer, Axel R. "Religious Nonprofit Organizations, the Cold War State and Resurgent Evangelicalism, 1945–1990." In Helen Laville and Hugh Wilford, eds., *The US Government, Citizen Groups and the Cold War: The State Private Network*. London: Routledge, 2006, pp. 173–91.

Sebesta, Edward H., and Euan Hague. "'The US Civil War as a Theological War: Confederate Christian Nationalism and the League of the South." *Canadian Review of American Studies*, vol. 32, no. 3 (2002). theocracywatch.org.

Smith, Chris. "His Truth Is Marching On." *California Magazine*, California Berkeley Alumni Association, Fall 2012.

Stafford, Tim. "Ron Sider's Unsettling Crusade." *Christianity Today*, April 27, 1992.

Sugg, John. "A Nation Under God." *Mother Jones*, December 2005. Quote from Gary North's *Political Polytheism*.

Tabachnick, Rachel. "Rushdoony and Theocratic Libertarians on Slavery." Talk to Action, July 13, 2010.

ACKNOWLEDGMENTS

I NEVER WOULD have had the courage—or the foolhardiness—to write this book without the encouragement and help of my friend Susan Harding. We met in the early 1980s, when we were both involved in writing about Jerry Falwell. Her book, *The Book of Jerry Falwell* (2000), is a model of modern anthropology. I was writing for *The New Yorker* about Falwell's community, and we began a discussion about evangelicals that has gone on ever since. We went on a trip together to see the empires of the other televangelists, W.A. Criswell, Jimmy Swaggart, Oral Roberts, and Jim and Tammy Faye Bakker. More recently we went to the Fuller Theological Seminary. With Susan I learned more from the interviews than I ever would have by myself.

I am grateful to *The New Yorker* for publishing four articles that contain some of the material in this book: Reporter at Large: "A Disciplined, Charging Army," (1981); Reflections: "The Bakkers" (1990); The Political Scene: "Holy Toledo" (2006); and The Annals of Religion: "The New Evangelicals" (2008.) I am also grateful to the *New York Review of Books* for publishing "The Surprising Evangelicals" in 2007.

I am most grateful for the fellowship from the John Simon Guggenheim Memorial Foundation that gave me precious time and the opportunity to take other trips to see evangelical pastors and Christian right leaders.

Material from this book was presented at the Joanna Jackson Goldman Memorial Lectures on American Civilization and Government at the New

York Public Library's Humanities and Social Sciences Library in March 2009. Made possible by a gift from the estate of Eric F.Goldman, the lectures are intended to stimulate discussion of contemporary issues that have long-term significance for American democracy. I am grateful for the selection of my unfinished work.

The Bobst Library at New York University was an invaluable resource in writing the history of evangelicals, and I thank the New York Institute for the Humanities for giving me access to its collection.

I thank Professor Susan Harding of University of California, Santa Cruz, Professor Gary Dorrien of Union Theological Seminary, Professor Nancy Ammerman of Boston University, and Professor William Martin of the Baker Institute for Public Policy at Rice University for reading the galleys and helping me avoid many mistakes and omissions.

Alice Mayhew was, as ever, an encouraging and skillful editor. She rarely puts her foot down, but when she does, she is always right. Her assistant, Stuart Roberts, could not have been more helpful in guiding me through the editorial process. The copy editors at Simon & Schuster are properly exacting and have corrected many mistakes in the text and in the end notes.

Above all, I thank my husband, Jim Sterba, for putting up with me for all these years.

INDEX

Page numbers beginning with 641 refer to endnotes.